Program The Internet of Things with Swift for iOS

Ahmed Bakir
Gheorghe Chesler
Manny de la Torriente

Apress®

Program the Internet of Things with Swift for iOS

ISBN-13 (pbk): 978-1-4842-1195-3

ISBN-13 (electronic): 978-1-4842-1194-6

Managing Director: Welmoed Spahr
Lead Editor: Michelle Lowman
Technical Reviewer: Charles Cruz
Editorial Board: Steve Anglin, Louise Corrigan, Jonathan Gennick, Robert Hutchinson, Michelle Lowman, James Markham, Susan McDermott, Matthew Moodie, Jeffrey Pepper, Douglas Pundick, Ben Renow-Clarke, Gwenan Spearing
Coordinating Editor: Mark Powers
Copy Editor: Lori Jacobs
Compositor: SPi Global
Indexer: SPi Global
Artist: SPi Global
Cover Designer: Anna Ishchenko

Distributed to the book trade worldwide by Springer Science+Business Media New York, 233 Spring Street, 6th Floor, New York, NY 10013. Phone 1-800-SPRINGER, fax (201) 348-4505, e-mail `orders-ny@springer-sbm.com`, or visit `www.springeronline.com`. Apress Media, LLC is a California LLC and the sole member (owner) is Springer Science + Business Media Finance Inc (SSBM Finance Inc). SSBM Finance Inc is a Delaware corporation.

For information on translations, please e-mail `rights@apress.com`, or visit `www.apress.com`.

Apress and friends of ED books may be purchased in bulk for academic, corporate, or promotional use. eBook versions and licenses are also available for most titles. For more information, reference our Special Bulk Sales–eBook Licensing web page at `www.apress.com/bulk-sales`.

Any source code or other supplementary materials referenced by the author in this text is available to readers at `www.apress.com/9781484211953`. For detailed information about how to locate your book's source code, go to `www.apress.com/source-code/`. Readers can also access source code at SpringerLink in the Supplementary Material section for each chapter.

Contents at a Glance

About the Authors xv

About the Technical Reviewer xvii

Introduction ix

Chapter 1: Building Your First Internet of Things App 1

Chapter 2: Getting Started with Swift 33

Chapter 3: Accessing Health Information Using HealthKit 59

Chapter 4: Using Core Motion to Save Motion Data 99

Chapter 5: Integrating Third-Party Fitness Trackers and Data Using the Fitbit API 119

Chapter 6: Building Your First watchOS App 169

Chapter 7: Building an Interactive watchOS App 201

Chapter 8: Building a Stand-Alone watchOS App 225

Chapter 9: Connecting to a Bluetooth LE Device 247

Chapter 10: Building Location Awareness with iBeacons 295

Chapter 11: Home Automation Using HomeKit 343

■ Chapter 12: Building an App That Interacts with a Raspberry Pi 397

■ Chapter 13: Using Keychain Services to Secure Data 427

■ Chapter 14: Using Touch ID for Local Authentication 443

■ Chapter 15: Using Apple Pay to Accept Payments 457

Index 485

Contents

About the Authors xv

About the Technical Reviewer xvii

Introduction ix

Chapter 1: Building Your First Internet of Things App 1

Ahmed Bakir 1

Setting up the Project 2

Building the User Interface 7

Creating the Table View Controller 8

Creating the Map View Controller 18

Requesting Location Permission 22

Accessing the User's Location 26

Displaying the User's Location 28

Populating the Table View 28

Populating the Map 30

Summary 32

■ **Chapter 2: Getting Started with Swift** 33
Ahmed Bakir 33
Why Use Swift? 34
Basic Swift Syntax 35
Calling Methods (Hello World) 35
Defining Variables 36
Compound Data Types 37
Conditional Logic 38
Enumerated Types 39
Loops 40
Object-Oriented Programming in Swift 41
Building a Class 41
Protocols 42
Method Signatures 43
Accessing Properties and Methods 44
Instantiating Objects 45
Strings 46
Formatting Strings 46
Collections 47
Casting 50
Swift-Specific Language Features 50
Optionals 50
Try-Catch Blocks 52
Mixing Objective-C and Swift in Projects 54
Calling Swift from Objective-C 56
Summary 57
■ **Chapter 3: Accessing Health Information Using HealthKit** 59
Ahmed Bakir 59
Introduction 59

Getting Started 61
Setting Up the User Interface 61
Setting Up the Project for HealthKit 79
Prompting the User for HealthKit Permission 83
Retrieving Data from HealthKit 88
Displaying Results in a Table View 92
Fetching Background Updates 95
Summary 97
■Chapter 4: Using Core Motion to Save Motion Data 99
Ahmed Bakir 99
Introduction 99
Using Core Motion to Access Motion Hardware 100
Requesting User Permission for Motion Activity 100
Querying for Step Count 103
Detecting Live Updates to Step Count 106
Detecting Activity Type 108
Saving Data to HealthKit 110
Summary 117
■Chapter 5: Integrating Third-Party Fitness Trackers and Data Using the Fitbit API 119
Gheorghe Chesler 119
Introduction to the Fitbit API 119
The RESTful API 120
Fitbit RESTful API Implementation Details 122
Setting Up a Local Playground with Apache 123
The OAuth1.0a Authentication Model 125
The Fitbit OAuth Implementation 126
Fitbit API Call Rate Limits 127
Making async Calls 128
Using callbacks as Parameters 128

Setting up a Fitbit-compatible iOS Project 130
The View Controller 130
The Logger Library 133
Setting up a Basic Set of Crypto Functions 133
The API Client Library 137
The OAuth Library 151
Testing What We Have so Far 157
Making requests to the Fitbit API 159
Retrieving the User Profile 161
Retrieving and Setting Data in the API 163
OAuth versions: Working in both worlds 167
Summary 168
Chapter 6: Building Your First watchOS App 169
Ahmed Bakir 169
Introduction 169
watchOS Apps vs. iOS Apps 170
Setting Up Your Project 172
Debugging your watchOS App 176
Adding a Table to your watchOS App 176
Defining the Table 181
Fetching Data from your iOS App 187
Building a Detail Page with a Custom Layout 190
Presenting the Detail Interface Controller 196
Summary 199
Chapter 7: Building an Interactive watchOS App 201
Ahmed Bakir 201
Introduction 201
Using Force Touch to Present Menus 202
Resetting the Location List 206
Presenting a Detail View Controller 207
Simulating Force Touch 209

Adding Buttons to an Interface Controller 210
Passing Information Between Interface Controllers 213
Using a Delegate to Pass Information on Dismissal 215
How to Add Notes Using Text Input 217
Sending Data Back to the Parent iOS App 219
Summary 223
Chapter 8: Building a Stand-Alone watchOS App 225
Ahmed Bakir 225
Using Core Location to Request Current Location 226
Reverse Geocoding an Address 229
Using NSTimer to Create Reminders 233
Making Network Calls from Your watchOS App 238
Handling a JSON Response 243
Summary 245
Chapter 9: Connecting to a Bluetooth LE Device 247
Manny de la Torriente 247
Introduction to the Apple Bluetooth stack 247
Key Terms and Concepts 248
Core Bluetooth Objects 249
Building Your First Bluetooth LE Application 250
Backlog 251
Base Application and Home Scene 251
Central Role Scene 252
Peripheral Role Scene 253
Editable Text 255
Setting Up the Project 256
Building the Interface 256
Using a Central Manager 264

Connecting to a Bluetooth LE Device in Your App 268
Building the Interface 268
Keeping Things Clean with Delegation 272
Scanning for Peripherals 276
Discover and Connect 280
Explore Services and Characteristics 281
Subscribe and Receive Data 281
Peripheral Role 284
Building the Interface 284
Delegate Setup 285
Setting up a Service 288
Advertising Services 289
Sending Data 291
Enabling Your App for Background Communication 292
Bluetooth Best Practices 293
Central Role Devices 293
Peripheral Role Devices 293
Summary 294
Chapter 10: Building Location Awareness with iBeacons 295
Manny de la Torriente 295
Introduction to iBeacons 295
iBeacon Advertisement 295
iBeacon Accuracy 295
Privacy 296
Region Monitoring 296
Ranging 296
Building the iBeaconApp Application 297
Creating the Project 298
Setting Background Capabilities 298

Building the Home Scene 299
Setting Up UI Elements 300
Creating an Outlet Connection 301
Setting up Constraints 302
Creating a Custom Button 303
Detecting Bluetooth State 307
Building the Region Monitor Scene 310
The RegionMonitor Class 315
Using the Delegation Pattern 315
Creating the RegionMonitor Class 316
Delegate Methods 317
RegionMonitor Methods 321
Authorization and Requesting Permission 322
CLLocationManagerDelegate Methods 324
Building the iBeacon Scene 333
The BeaconTransmitter Class 336
Defining the BeaconTransmitterDelegate Protocol 336
Summary 341
Chapter 11: Home Automation Using HomeKit 343
Manny de la Torriente 343
Introduction to HomeKit Concepts 343
HomeKit Delegation Methods 344
Building a HomeKit Application 345
Requirements 345
HomeKit Accessory Simulator 346
Creating the Project 346
Enabling HomeKit 348
Building the Homes Interface 348
Implementing the Home Manager Delegate Methods 351
Adding a New Home to the Home Manager 357
Removing an Accessory from a Home 367

Transitioning to the Services Scene 393
Running the Application 394
Adding Accessories 394
Summary 395
■Chapter 12: Building an App That Interacts with a Raspberry Pi 397
Gheorghe Chesler 397
About Your Raspberry Pi 397
Control Interfaces on your Raspberry Pi 399
Setting up your Raspberry Pi 400
Choosing the Scripting Language 401
Configuring I2C 401
Configuring GPIO 404
Install PyGlow 405
Providing an API to Control your Device 406
Install Flask 406
Setting up an iOS Project for Our App 409
Allowing Outgoing HTTP Calls 409
The View Controller 410
The Logger Library 413
Summary 426
■Chapter 13: Using Keychain Services to Secure Data 427
Gheorghe Chesler 427
Hardware Security on iOS Devices 429
Securing the File Data 430
The Apple Keychain 431
The Apple Keychain Services 432
Components of a Keychain Item 432
Implementing Keychain Services for Storing Passwords 432
Retrieving Data from Keychain Services 434

Invalidating Keychain Service Records....435
Setting Up an Application to Test Keychain Services....436
The View Controller....436
Summary....442
Chapter 14: Using Touch ID for Local Authentication....443
Manny de la Torriente....443
Introduction to Touch ID....443
LocalAuthentication Use Cases....444
Building a Touch ID Application....444
Creating the Project....447
Building the Interface....447
Implementing the UITableView Methods....451
Integrating Touch ID for Fingerprint Authentication....452
Evaluating Authentication Policies....452
Touch ID Authentication without Keychain....452
User-Defined Fallback for Authentication....454
Run the Application....455
Things to Remember....455
Summary....455
Chapter 15: Using Apple Pay to Accept Payments....457
Gheorghe Chesler....457
Apple Pay vs. Alternative Payment Systems....457
Apple Pay Prerequisites....459
Using Apple Pay to accept payments....460
Configuring your Environment for Apple Pay....466
Implementing Apple Pay payments with Stripe....476
The View Controller code....482
Summary....484
Index....485

About the Authors

Ahmed Bakir is the founder and lead developer at devAtelier LLC (`www.devatelier.com`), a San Diego-based mobile development firm. After spending several years writing software for embedded systems, he started developing apps out of coffee shops for fun. Once the word got out, he began taking on clients and quit his day job to work on apps full time. Since then, he has been involved in the development of over 20 mobile projects, and has seen several enter the top 25 of the App Store, including one that reached number one in its category (Video Scheduler). His clients have ranged from scrappy startups to large corporations, such as Citrix. In his downtime, Ahmed can be found on the road, exploring new places, speaking about mobile development, and still working out of coffee shops.

Gheorghe Chesler is a senior software engineer with expertise in Quality Assurance, System Automation, Performance Engineering, and e-Publishing. He works at ServiceNow as a Senior Performance Engineer, and is a principal technical consultant for Plural Publishing, a medical-field publishing company. His preferred programming language is Perl (so much so that he identifies with the Perl mascot, hence the camel picture), but also worked on many Java and Objective-C projects.

Manny de la Torriente has over 30 years of software development experience, having worked on every level from engineering to management. Manny started out in software by doing programming for sound engineering and then moved into game engine development and low-level video playback systems. Manny is known to switch between iOS and Android depending on how exciting the project is.

About the Technical Reviewer

Charles Cruz is a mobile application developer for the iOS, Windows Phone, and Android platforms. He graduated from Stanford University with B.S. and M.S. degrees in engineering. He lives in Southern California and runs a photography business with his wife (www.bellalentestudios.com). When not doing technical things, he plays lead guitar in an original metal band (www.taintedsociety.com). Charles can be reached at codingandpicking@gmail.com and @CodingNPicking on Twitter.

Introduction

Ahmed Bakir

What Is the Internet of Things?

The Internet of Things refers to the push to make applications and hardware devices, or "things," "smart" by receiving or logging data from the Internet and other things. The goal of the Internet of Things is to use these additional data sources to make common tasks in your life richer and easier to perform.

One of the earliest drivers of the Internet of Things was the Quantified Self movement, a trend that suggested people could lose weight and exercise at more sustainable levels by constantly logging and monitoring their diet and workout information. Although this started out with data gleaned from calorie-counting journals and pedometers, the creation of apps like MyFitnessPal, which would help you find caloric information for your afternoon snack, and devices like the FitBit, which automatically logged your pedometer data to the Internet, pushed Quantified Self into the mainstream.

Another example of the Internet of Things in action would be a smart TV. Several years ago, your TV was a "dumb" screen, only displaying the output from the input devices you connected to it, such as a cable box, game console, or VCR (do you remember those?). Fast forwarding to the future, today's TVs commonly include WiFi cards and "smart" application platforms that allow you to perform some of your most common tasks, such as streaming videos from Netflix or browsing photos from Instagram directly from the TV, without having to connect a computer. While many TVs are not yet at the point where they have "intelligent" features, such as suggesting cooking shows because you watch a lot of them, the hope is that having Internet connectivity and an application platform will inspire developers to program these applications for TVs.

A significant distinction between today's Internet of Things and previous attempts to connect devices to the Internet is that the barrier of entry has dropped significantly. Whereas previously, the only way to build an Internet-connected device was to have a staff of highly trained hardware and software engineers building a proprietary platform for years, today you can go to any electronics store or web site and buy an Arduino or Raspberry Pi, which puts the motherboard of a computer from a few years ago in the palm of your hand for about $30. These devices were designed to give hobbyists and students an easy way to enter electronics (previously, it was a very expensive hobby—the voice of experience), but also include all the core features you need to build a connected device: a CPU, the ability to run high-level programming languages (such as Python), a WiFi card, a display port (generally HDMI), and a series of GPIO (general purpose input/ouptut) pins, which allow you to connect electronic components, such as timer chips and LED lights.

Consumers and companies have noticed the demand of connected devices, and the ease of entry into the market, making this the perfect time to learn how to program for the Internet of Things! Who knows, maybe your app will be the one that drives personalized toast into the mainstream (the best way of making sure people don't steal your lunch)!

What Is the Purpose of This Book?

The purpose of this book is to teach you how to build iOS applications, in Swift, that use Apple's native application programming interfaces (APIs), which connect to popular Internet of Things (IoT) devices and services. We have framed our narrative around the following four classes of devices:

- Fitness and health trackers
- Apple Watch
- Generic hardware accessories
- Authentication and payment systems

These device families represent some of the most popular classes of IoT accessories, while allowing us to teach you several different ways of connecting to IoT devices, including native iOS libraries (e.g., HealthKit and WatchKit), generic hardware interfaces (e.g., Bluetooth), third-party data logging services (e.g., FitBit), and local networking (over WiFi). The beauty of today's IoT is that that there are so many ways of connecting your devices, based on widely adopted open standards, reducing your need to learn proprietary protocols. Our goal is that by exposing you to different ways of connecting to IoT devices, you will have a handy toolbox of skills that will cover most of the use cases you will be asked to implement.

This book is presented in a tutorial style, which takes cues from modern software engineering practices, such as code reviews and Agile programming. Each chapter in this book is framed around a project you will be learning how to implement, which will be described via requirements and "stories" indicating why they are important. In a similar manner, our explanations will go deep into the code, pulling in best practices from Apple's specifications and other applications. Whenever necessary, we will pull in brief explanations of underlying topics, such as delegate programming and OAUTH authentication, so you do not need to keep flipping back and forth between different books. Our goal for this book is to give you a deep understanding of the projects you will be implementing, rather than copy-and-paste snippets. As anyone who has survived a major iOS upgrade (e.g., iOS6 to iOS7) can attest, knowing the core concepts helps you fix your code way faster than memorizing single-use snippets.

What Do I Need to Know to Use This Book?

This book is intended to serve as a guide to implementing specific topics in iOS. It is structured in a way that guides beginners and intermediate-level programmers through the information they need to understand the topic, while also allowing advanced readers to skip to exactly what they are looking for. That being said, this text is written with a few assumptions in mind.

- The reader has a solid understanding of core programming concepts (object-oriented programming, pointers, functions)
- The reader has a working knowledge of the basics of iOS development (using XCode, Interface Builder, and Cocoa Touch libraries)
- The reader has programmed in Swift or Objective-C before

As Swift and XCode are ever evolving tools, the first two chapters of this book cover IDE and syntax basics. Our goal with these chapters is to help developers who are still transitioning to Swift from Objective-C and those who have not yet had a chance to review Apple's dense API update documents.

For expanded coverage of the Swift programming language, iOS programming, and XCode, we recommend the texts listed in Table 1, also available from Apress.

Table 1. Recommended References

Topic	Title and Author
Introductory iOS Development	Beginning iPhone Development with Swift by David Mark, Jack Nutting, Kim Topley, Fredrik Olsson, and Jeff LaMarche (Apress, 2014)
Using XCode and the Debugger	Beginning XCode: Swift Edition by Matthew Knott (Apress, 2014)
Intermediate iOS Development	Learn iOS8 App Development by James Bucanek (Apress, 2014)
Swift Syntax	Swift for Absolute Beginners by Gary Bennett and Brad Lees (Apress, 2014)

The most up-to-date reference for iOS programming is Apple's official iOS Developer Library, which you can access from the "Documentation and API Reference" option in Xcode's "Window" menu (shown in Figure 1) or online at `https://developer.apple.com/library/ios/navigation/`).

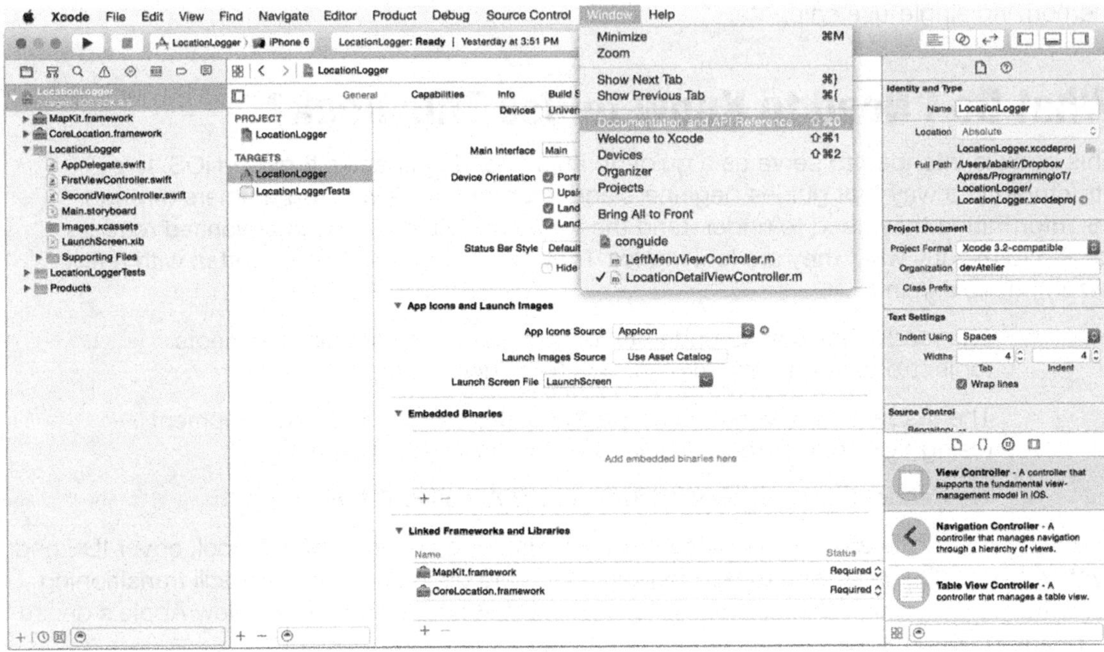

***Figure 1.** Accessing the iOS Developer Library from XCode*

> **Caution** Always use the latest version of the iOS Developer Library as your API reference. Apple often makes major deprecations and parameter changes, even in minor point version updates. The best way to stay up-to-date is by staying on the latest XCode version or accessing the iOS Developer Library web site.

What Do I Need to Get Started?

This book is designed around the workflow of developing an application on your computer and testing it on a physical device, which is potentially paired with a hardware accessory. The projects in this book depend on APIs which are not available in the iOS simulator. Apple's requirements for developing and testing iOS applications with a physical device are the same as those required to submit an application to the App Store:

- An Intel-based Mac running OS X Yosemite (10.10) or later
- XCode 7 or later

- An iPhone or iPad capable of running iOS9.1 or greater (iPhone 5 or greater, iPad2/iPad mini or greater)
- A valid Apple ID to register for free, device-based testing of your apps

Starting in summer 2015, Apple removed the requirement of having a paid iOS Developer Program membership to test your apps on an iOS device. A paid membership is still required to submit your apps to the App Store, use TestFlight for beta testing, and debug Apple server-based APIs, such as Apple Pay. You can sign up for an Apple Developer Program membership by going to the Apple Developer Programs web site (`https://developer.apple.com/programs/`) and selecting the Enroll button, as shown in Figure 2. Upon receipt of your fees in the Apple Store, the Apple ID you selected will be available for use in the Apple Developer Program.

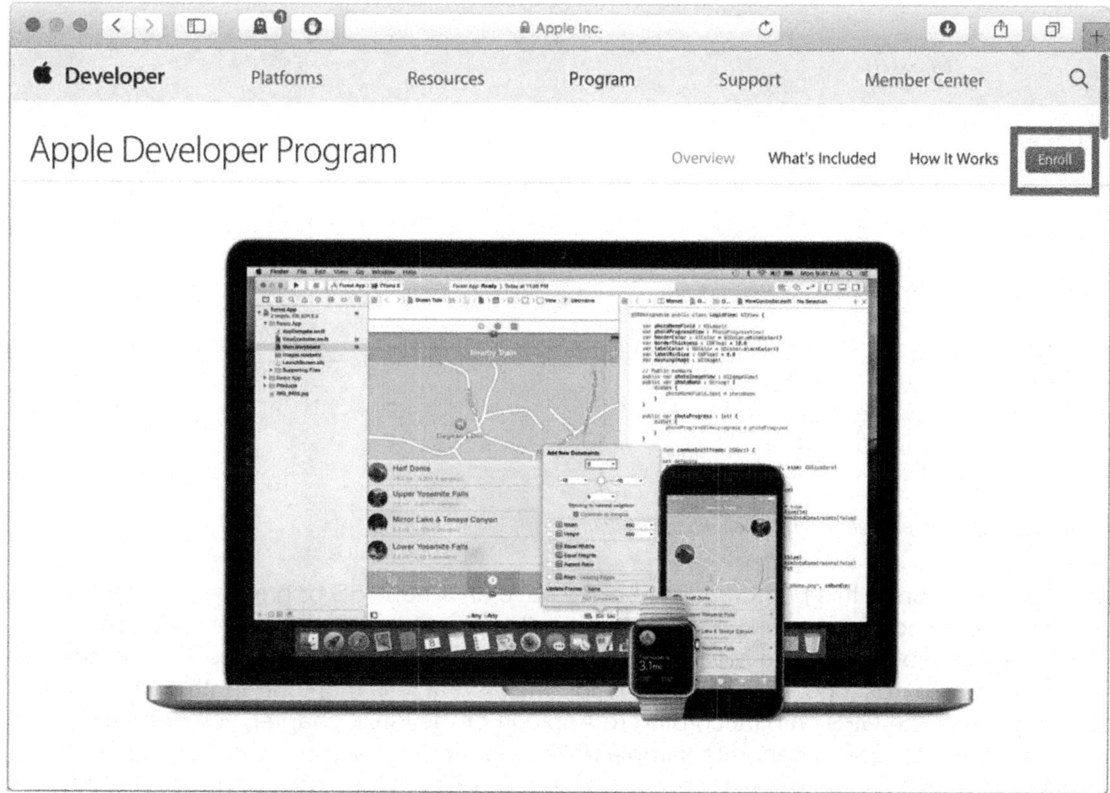

Figure 2. *Signing up for a paid Apple Developer Program account*

> **Note** If you are signing up for a corporate developer account, you will need to provide Apple with additional information to identify your entity, such as a Dunn & Bradstreet number. It will take extra time to process your account.

The projects in this book are designed to be “universal,” meaning they can run on iPhone or iPad. The user interfaces are designed primarily for the iPhone, but they will be scaled up and work the same way on the iPad, as shown in Figure 3 for this chapter’s example.

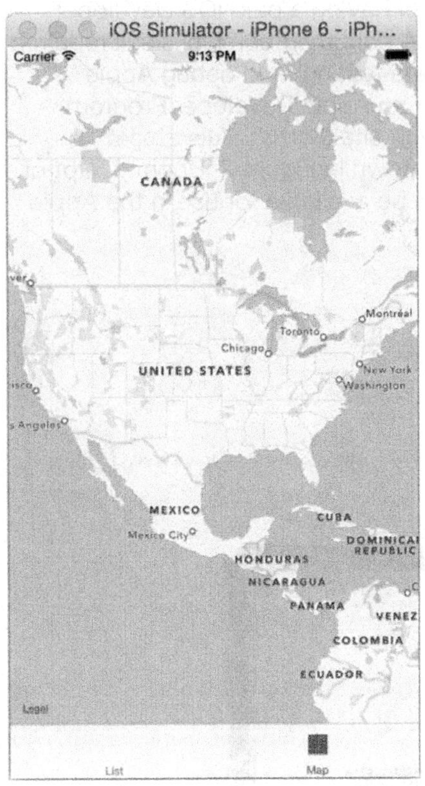

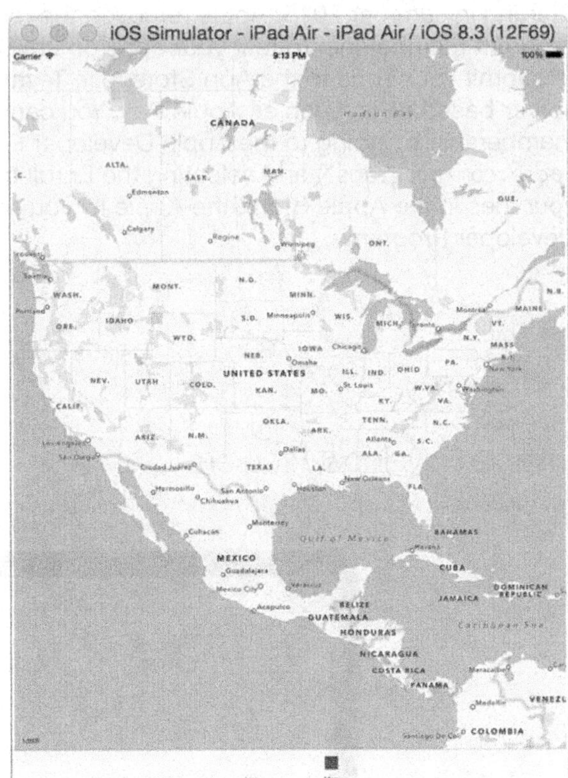

***Figure 3.** Sample project user interface on iPhone vs iPad*

The Health section of this book requires you to have an iPhone 5S or greater, in order to use the Core Motion framework. iPads and older iPhones do not have the M-series motion co-processor chip which Core Motion provides access to. This chip includes an advanced pedometer and gyroscope, which allow motion tracking at less than one-tenth of the power consumption of the GPS chip (according to Apple.) For the FitBit chapter, you need a free account on `Fitbit.com` to generate sample data to test with, but you do not need a FitBit hardware device. You can manually enter in steps, caloric intake, and weight from the FitBit web site.

The first two chapters of the Apple Watch section can be implemented using the Apple Watch simulator; however, the last chapter takes advantage of Core Location features that are not supported by the simulator. The Apple Watch is still a hardware platform that is being optimized, so it is a good idea to use an Apple Watch to test your applications for realistic performance data.

The Bluetooth section requires you to have at least two iOS devices. The first chapter teaches you how to set up a direct link between two devices over Bluetooth. To keep the narrative focused, you will learn how to configure an iOS device for the two core roles of Bluetooth: central manager and peripheral. Having two devices allows you to test quickly and reliably. For the iBeacon chapter, you will learn how to configure an iPhone as an iBeacon, but you can also use a hardware beacon for testing (they are available as USB dongles at most electronics web sites for about $20-$30).

The "Internet of Secure Things" chapter (authentication and payment systems) requires you to have an iPhone 5S or later for the Touch ID chapter and an iPhone 6 or later for the Apple Pay chapter. The Touch ID sensor (identified by a metallic ring around the home button) is available on every iPhone since the 5S and every iPad since the iPad Mini3 and iPad Air. It cannot be emulated in software. Similarly, Apple Pay requires an NFC sensor and additional authentication chip that are only available in the iPhone 6/6 Plus or later, and iPad Mini 3/iPad Air 2 or later.

Chapter 1

Building Your First Internet of Things App

Ahmed Bakir

To help introduce you to the style of this book, your first project will be a very simple application that demonstrates several of the steps you will take when building an Internet of Things application: creating a project, including hardware-specific frameworks, retrieving data, and displaying it. For your first project, you will create an application that logs the user's location using his phone's GPS chip and displays it on a map. This app could be used to help him find his car if he has the tendency to forget where it is (like a certain author). Figure 1-1 shows the mock-up, indicating the major user interface (UI) components and the flow of the application. The application you will create will follow the guideline set by this mock-up closely.

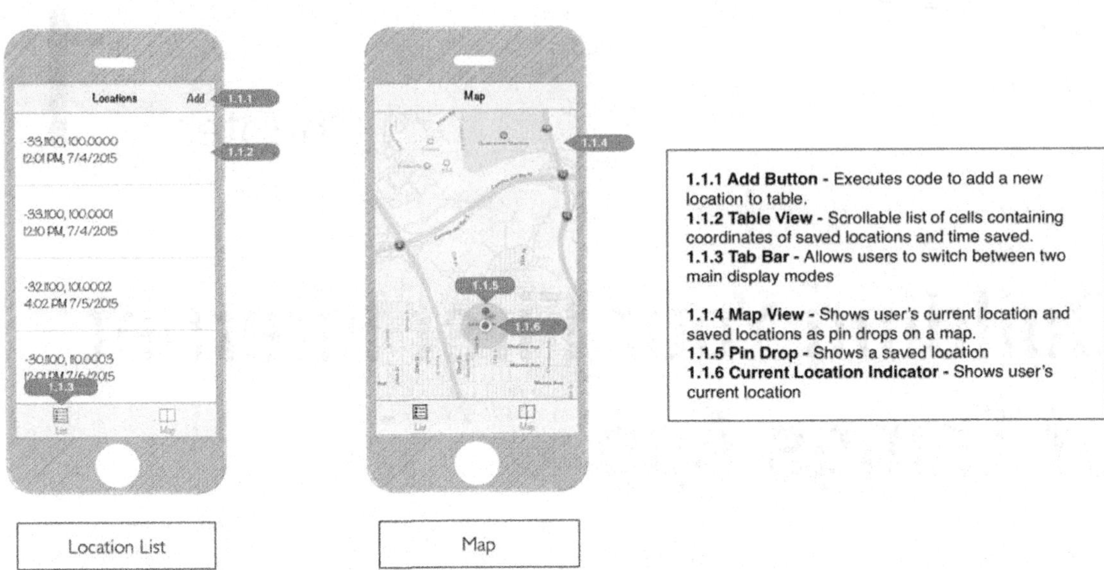

***Figure 1-1.** Mock-up for the CarFinder application*

CarFinder has a tab-driven UI. The first tab displays a list of locations the user has saved, with timestamps, and a button for adding new locations. The second tab displays these saved locations on a map. You will work through the CarFinder project taking the following steps:

1. Set up the project (and its dependencies).
2. Build the UI for the application.
3. Request permission to use the GPS hardware on the user's device.
4. Access the user's location information.
5. Consume and visualize the user's location information.

A working Xcode project for this application, including the complete source code, is available in the Source Code/Download area of the Apress web site at `www.apress.com`. All of the source code for the book is packaged in a single zip file; the CarFinder project is in the `Ch1` folder. Let's get started.

Setting up the Project

The focus of the CarFinder application is to quickly save and retrieve location information. A *tab bar* is a common UI element in iOS that displays a series of buttons at the bottom of the screen. Clicking any of these buttons allows you to quickly switch between screens. An example of a tab bar is in the built-in iOS Music application, which allows you to quickly switch search filters (e.g., Album, Artist, and Title) by clicking buttons in the tab bar, as shown in Figure 1-2.

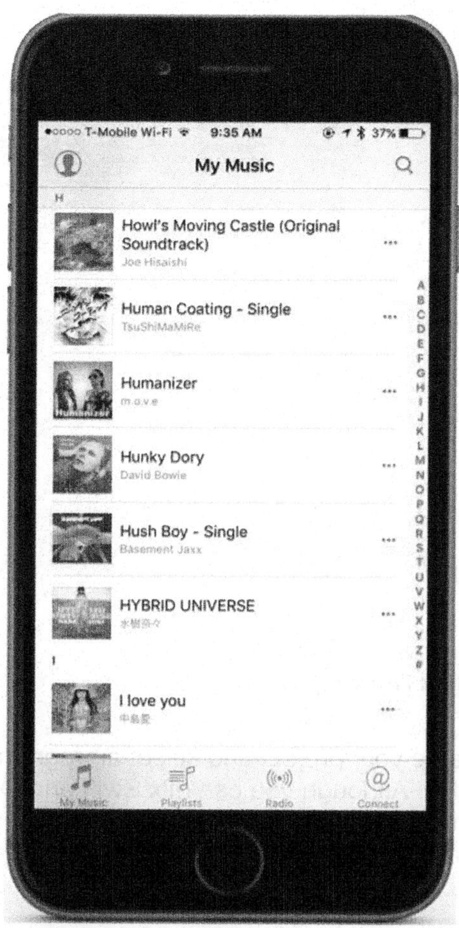

Figure 1-2. Example of a tab bar in the iOS Music application

The tab bar controller is also helpful to developers for two reasons: you do not need to do any programming to connect the tab bar buttons to a screen (you can set up the layout and all connections using Interface Builder's point-and-click tools.)

To implement the CarFinder application, open Xcode and create a new project using the Tabbed Application template, as shown in Figure 1-3.

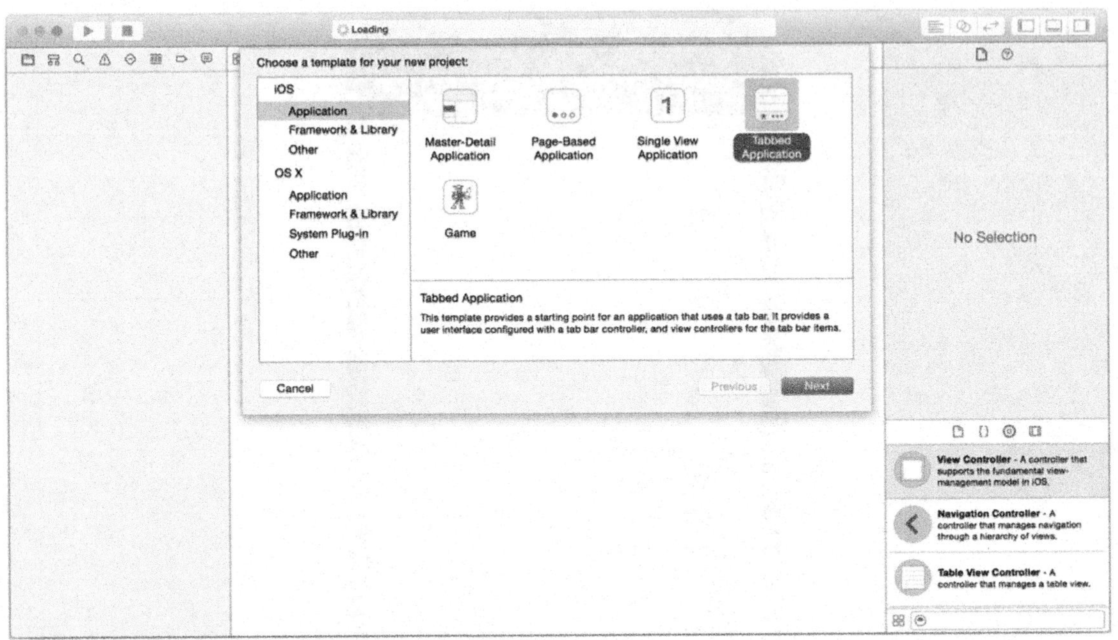

***Figure 1-3.** Selecting the template for a Tabbed Application*

Next, you will be asked to name your project and select a programming language for the project, as shown in Figure 1-4. Although you can mix Swift and Objective-C in modern Xcode projects, the programming language setting pre-populates your project with common build settings for your language (such as modules for Swift and pre-compiled headers for Objective-C). All the projects in this book are written in Swift, so use the Swift setting.

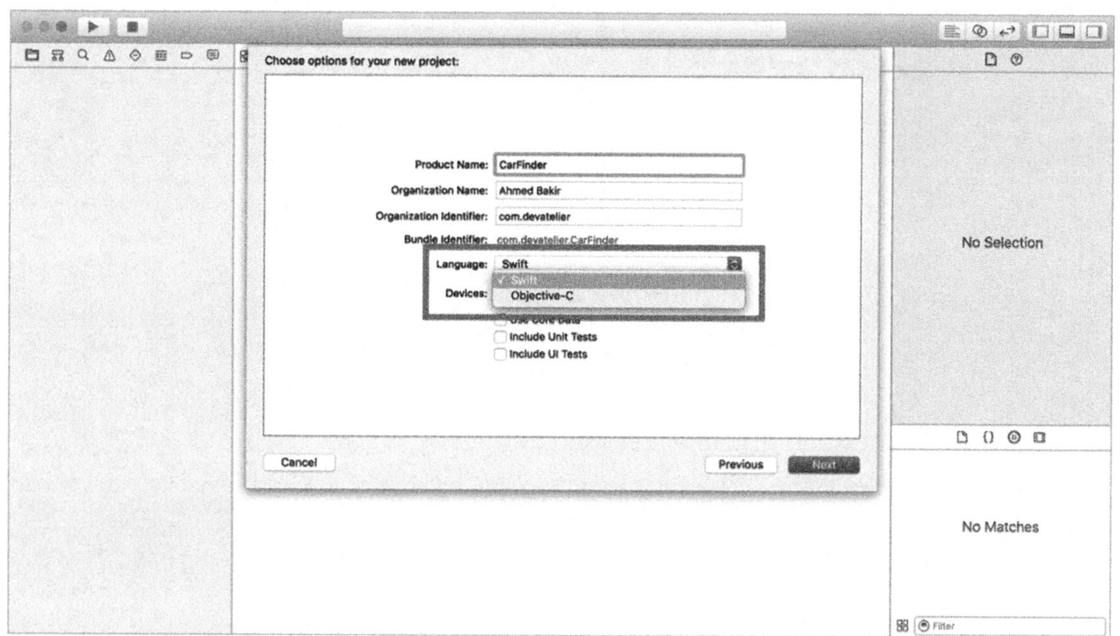

Figure 1-4. *Selecting a programming language for your project*

You will also find a Devices setting on this screen, which allows you to specify whether you want your app to run on iPhone only, iPad only, or both (Universal). This project focuses on accessing GPS hardware which is available on both devices, so you can leave the template set to Universal.

> **Note** You can change the `Devices` setting at any time by clicking on your app's Project file (the top file in the Project Hierarchy.) The `Devices` drop-down will be available there too.

The `CoreLocation` and `MapKit` frameworks in Cocoa Touch enable the core features of this application—retrieving location information and displaying it on a map. A framework is a pre-compiled library that allows you to add a group of related functions to your application without being at risk of breaking the code or its dependencies. Practically, it does not make sense to include every available framework in a sample project, so you need to manually add the ones you want. As shown in Figure 1-5, to add frameworks to your project, select your project file in the Project Navigator (the left-most pane of Xcode) and scroll to the bottom of the General Project Settings page, where you will find a section entitled Linked Frameworks and Libraries. Clicking the `Plus` button will bring up a pop-up window with a scrollable list of all the frameworks installed on your Mac.

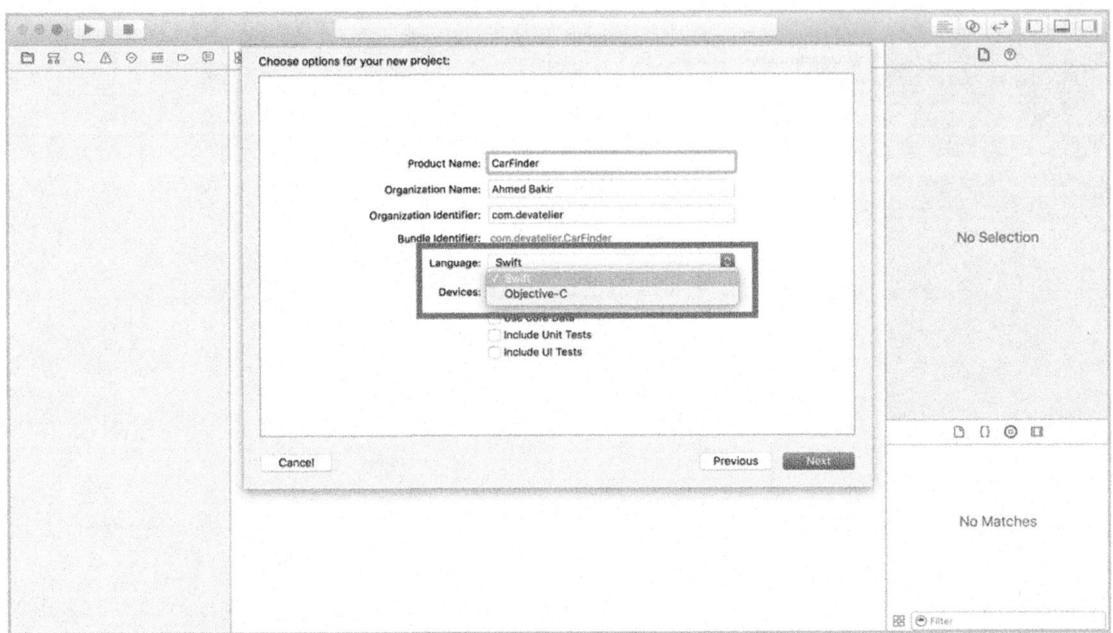

Figure 1-5. Adding frameworks to a project

To complete the operation, select the `CoreLocation` and `MapKit` frameworks and press the Add button. Frameworks will appear in the Linked Frameworks and Libraries section once you have successfully included them in your project, as shown in Figure 1-6.

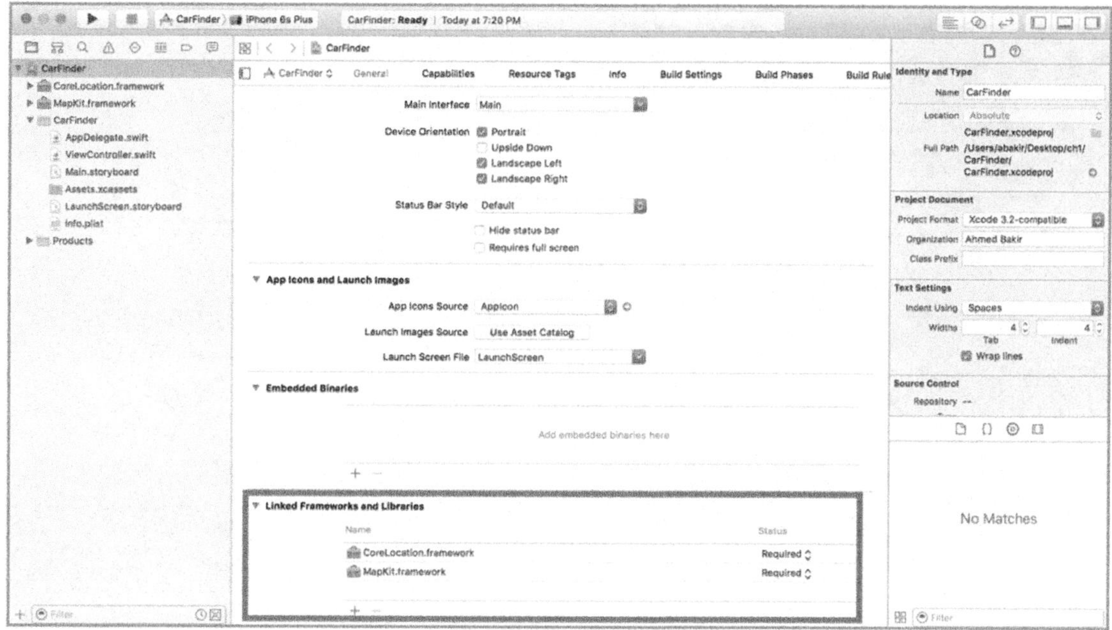

Figure 1-6. Project with the CoreLocation and MapKit frameworks included

> **Note** Every iOS project includes `UIKit` and `Foundation` by default. `UIKit` powers the core user interface controls and `Foundation` implements core high-level programming features like strings and arrays.

Building the User Interface

Now that you know the project is all set to compile correctly, you need to lay out the UI in Interface Builder and create source code to define its properties and behavior in your project. The default storyboard for a Tabbed Application is a container view controller that connects to two blank view controllers, as shown in Figure 1-7. You can access your storyboard from the `Main.storyboard` file. For the CarFinder application, you will want to replace the first view controller with a table view controller and add a map view to the second view controller (`MapKit` maps are provided as views intended to be embedded in view controllers).

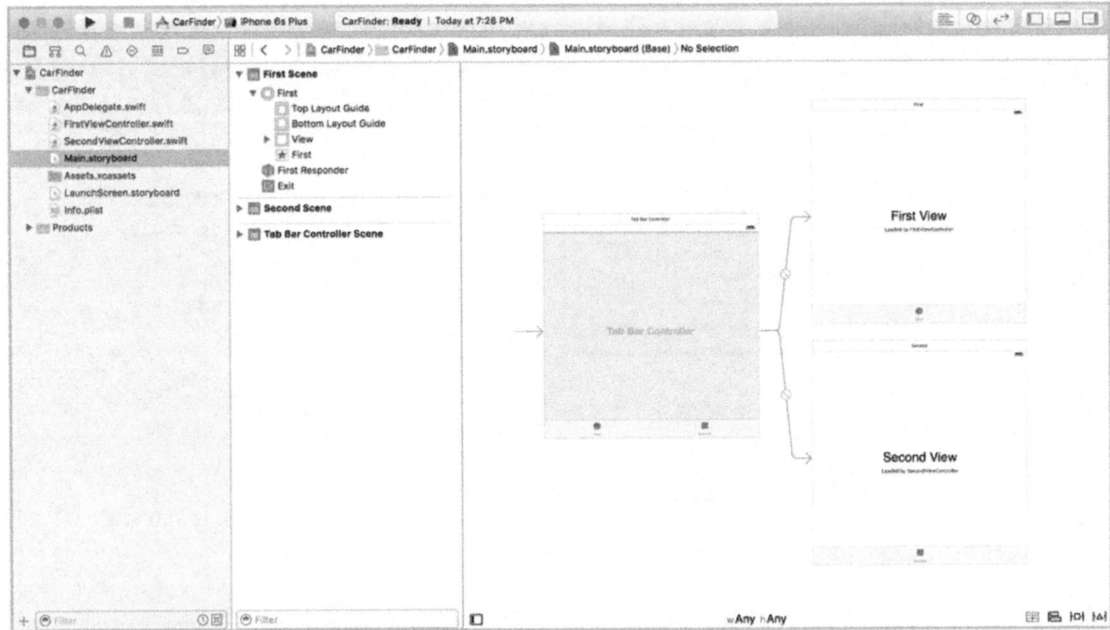

Figure 1-7. Default storyboard for a Tabbed Application

Creating the Table View Controller

To replace the first view controller with a table view controller, click it in Interface Builder. Your selection will be confirmed by a blue border around the view controller, as well as highlighting in the view hierarchy pane, as shown in Figure 1-8.

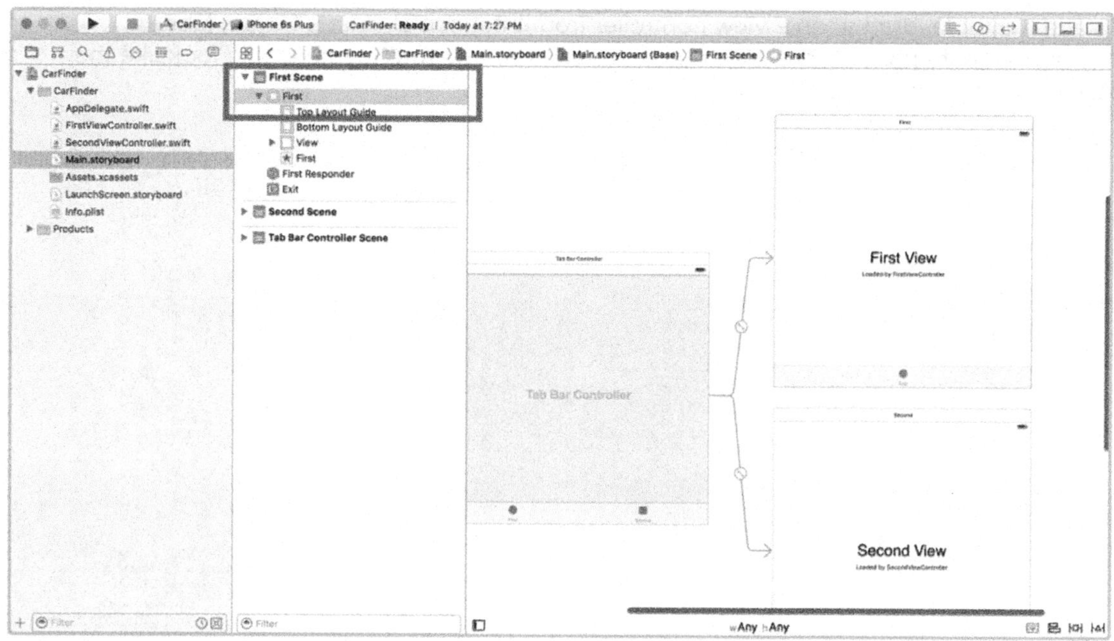

Figure 1-8. Selecting a view controller

Next, press the Delete key to delete it. Your storyboard should now look like the example in Figure 1-9.

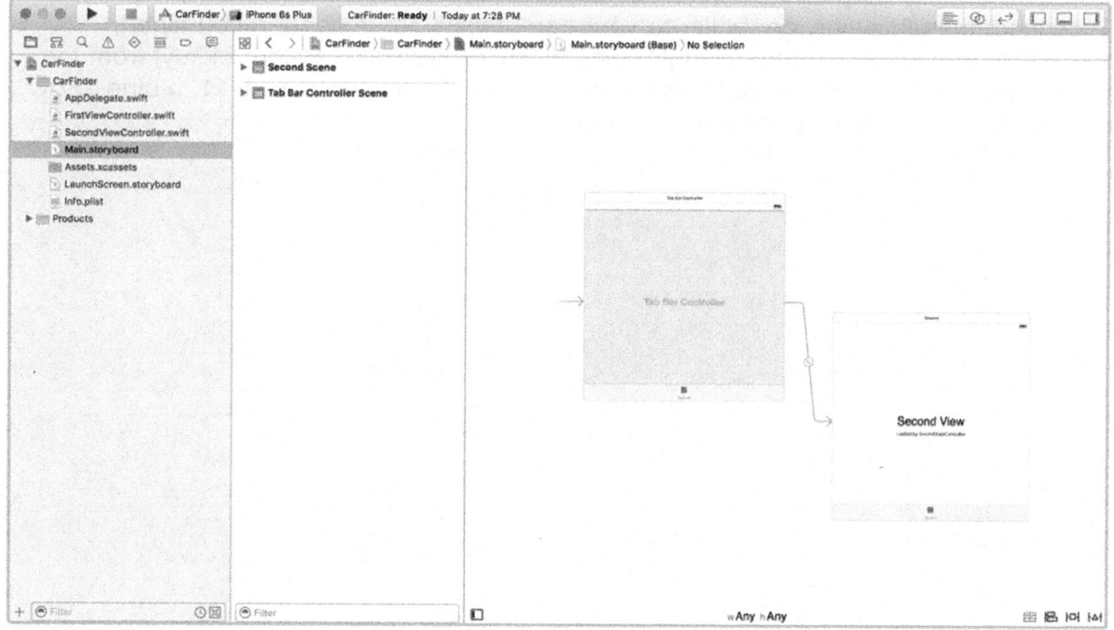

Figure 1-9. Storyboard, minus first view

To add the table, drag a table view controller from Interface Builder's Object Library (the bottom right pane) and drop it onto your storyboard. Your result should look like the storyboard in Figure 1-10.

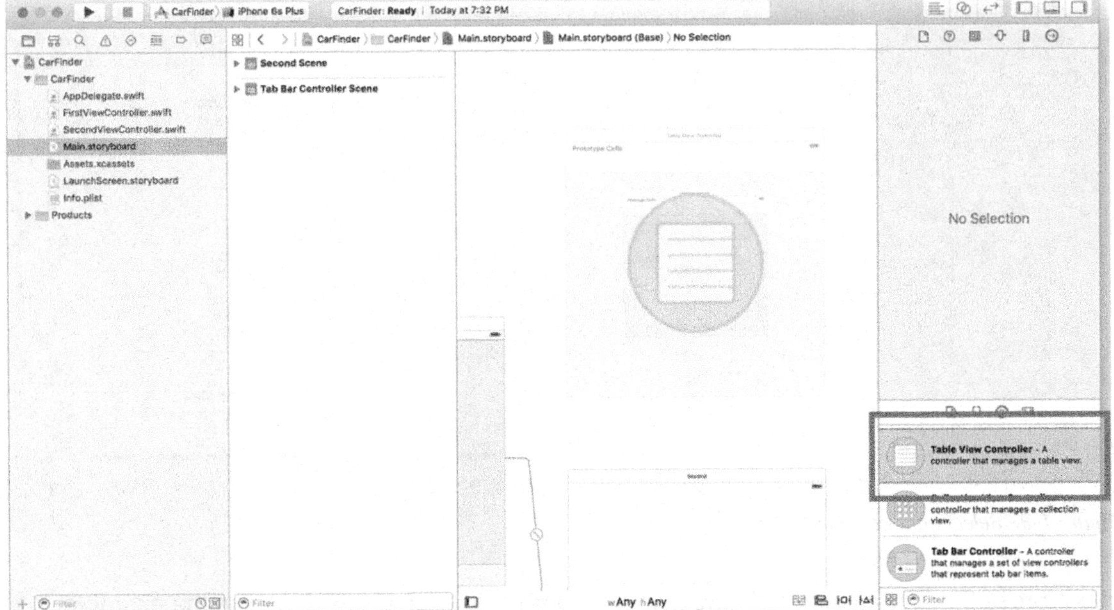

Figure 1-10. Adding a table view controller to your storyboard

To connect the table view controller to your parent view controller (the container), perform a `control-drag` (hold down the mouse while pressing the Control key) from the parent view controller to the table view controller. As shown in Figure 1-11, a blue arrow will appear indicating the connection.

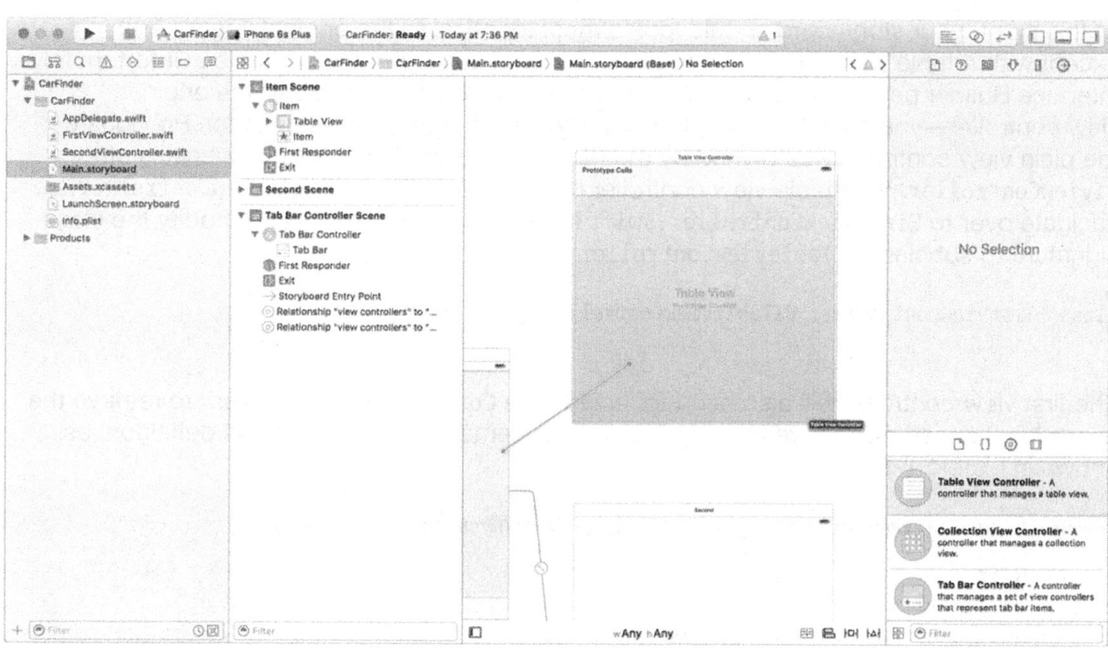

Figure 1-11. Connecting storyboard elements

Releasing your `Control-Click` will bring up a pop-up menu, shown in Figure 1-12, allowing you to specify the relationship between the two view controllers. Select the "view controllers" relationship; this is the relationship type required for a tab bar.

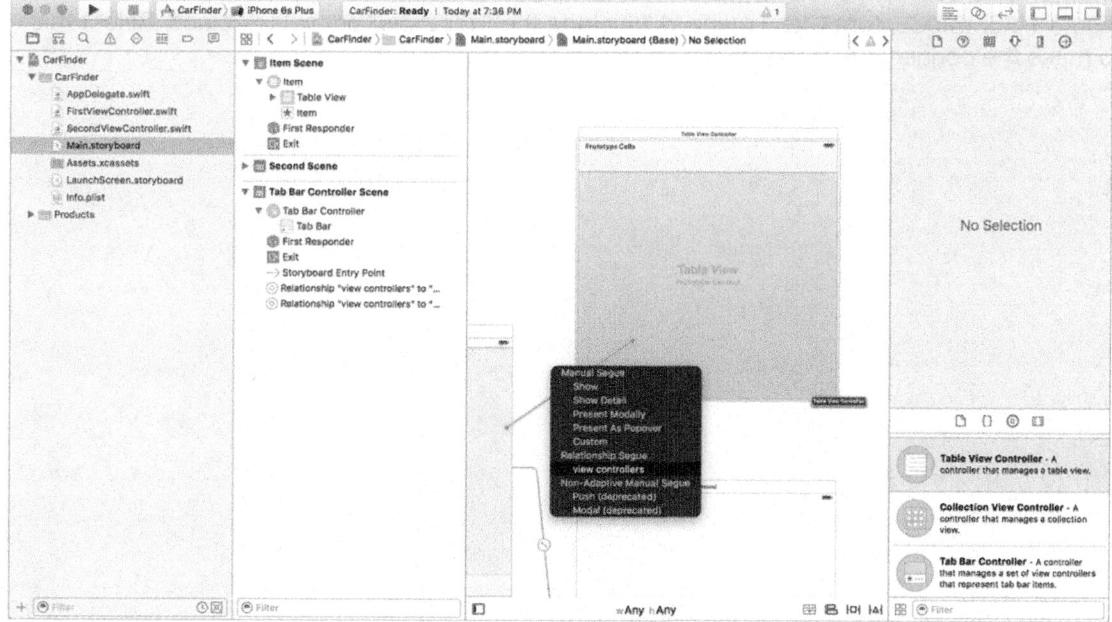

Figure 1-12. View controller segue pop-up menu

At this point, your storyboard should look almost identical to the original (Figure 1-8), except with a table view controller replacing the original, plain view controller. Unfortunately, Interface Builder needs a little bit of help to learn that you have replaced the original view controller—you need to tell it what class "owns" the new view controller. Previously, the plain view controller was owned by the `FirstViewController` class, a subclass of `UIViewController`. Your table view controller needs to subclass `UITableViewController`, so navigate over to `FirstViewController.swift` in the Project Navigator and modify the class signature to subclass `UITableViewController`.

```
class FirstViewController: UITableViewController {
}
```

The first view controller will also need to include the `CoreLocation` framework to retrieve the user's location, so make sure to add an `import` statement before your class definition, as shown in Listing 1-1.

Listing 1-1. Adding CoreLocation to the FirstViewController Class (FirstViewcontroller.swift)

```
import UIKit
import CoreLocation
class FirstViewController: UITableViewController {
        ...
}
```

Connecting to a Table View Controller

Now that the class is correctly defined, you can connect it to a table view controller in the storyboard. To make this connection, select the table view controller in your storyboard file and navigate over to the Identity Inspector (the third tab in Xcode's right pane). As shown in Figure 1-13, the Custom Class menu will include the `FirstViewController` class. Select this to make the connection.

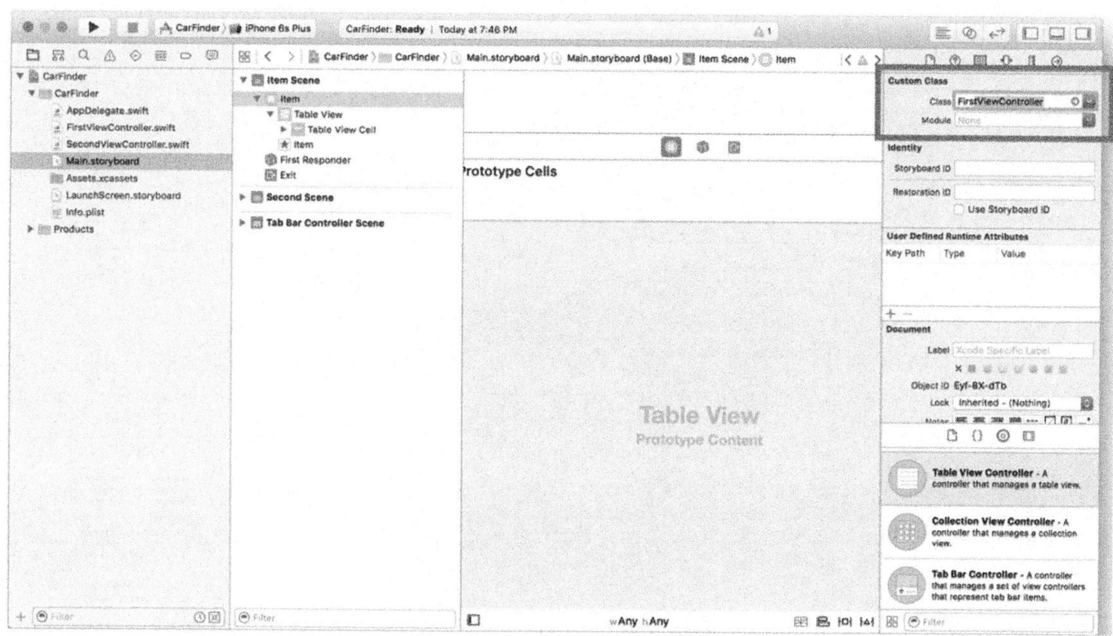

Figure 1-13. Connecting a table view controller to a class in your project

> **Note** Make sure to also select your project name under the Module menu; Swift uses modules to group code in projects, similar to a namespace in C++ or C#. Manually selecting this option prevents the risk of future compilation issues when your project becomes more complex.

To complete this screen, you need to perform two more steps: create an Add button to the screen and select a template for each cell in the table view.

Table-driven iOS apps prefer to put an action button (such as Add) in a navigation bar at the top of the table. This makes for a consistent experience across multiple levels of detail (the left button is used for navigation while the right is used for actions). By default, a table view controller, does not come with a navigation bar; to add one, you will need to embed the view controller in a navigation view controller. Fortunately, Xcode makes this effortless. To embed any view controller in a navigation view controller, select the target view controller and then navigate to Xcode's Editor menu. From there, select Embed In > Navigation Controller, as shown in Figure 1-14.

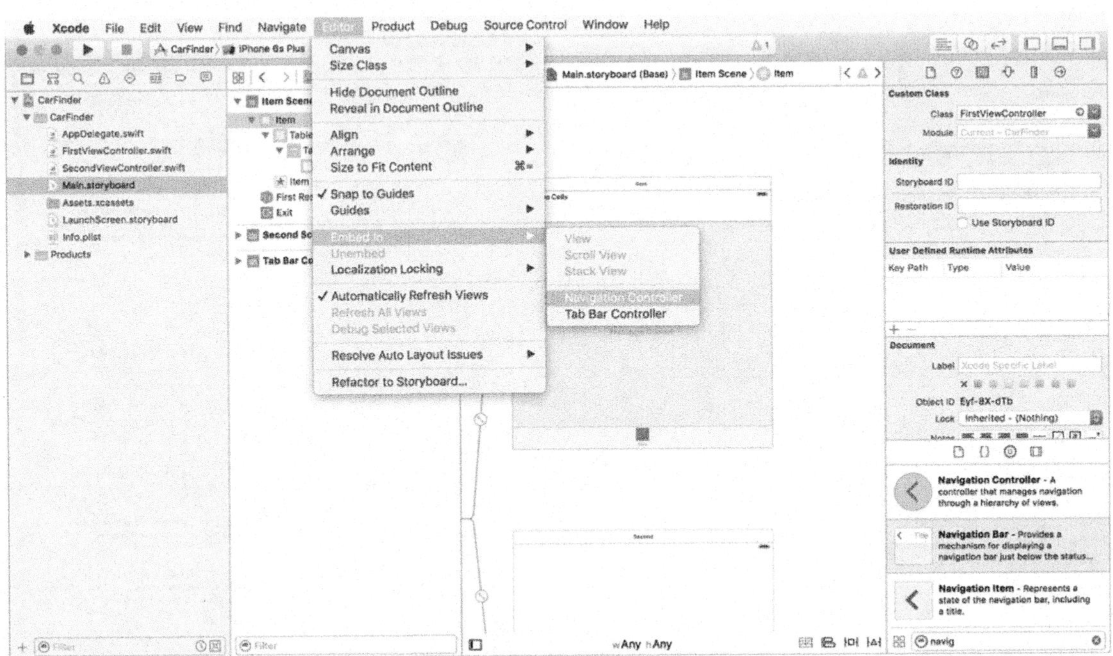

Figure 1-14. Xcode menu for adding a navigation view controller

Your storyboard should now look like the one in Figure 1-15; your tab bar controller connects to a navigation view controller, which contains your table view controller.

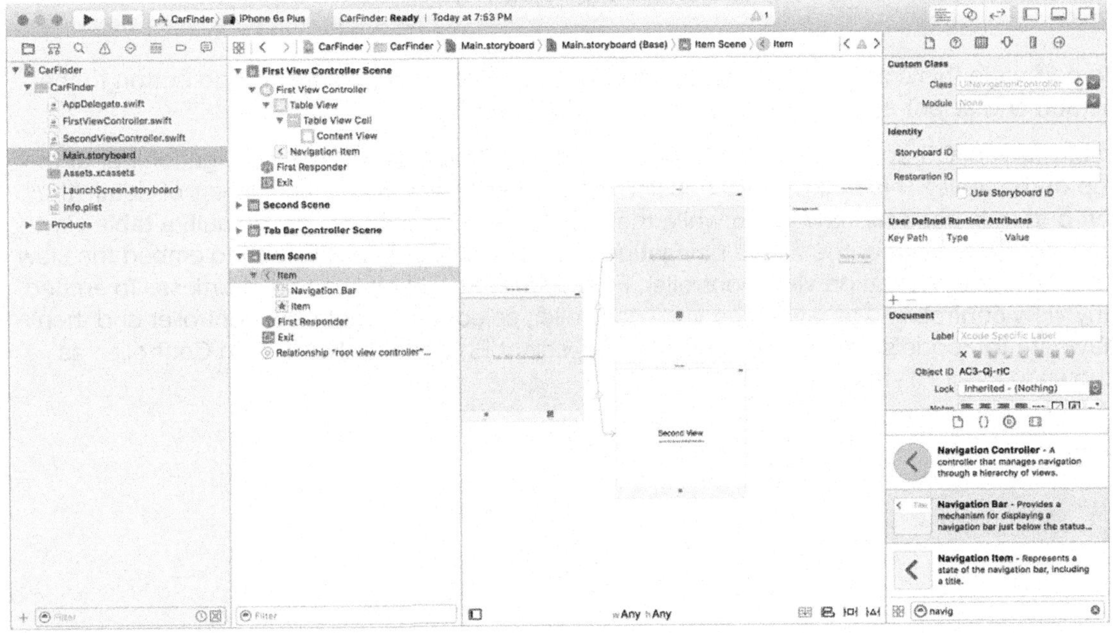

Figure 1-15. Storyboard with a table view controller embedded in a navigation controller

Creating an Add Button

To create an Add button, select a Bar Button Item from the Object Library and drag it onto your table view controller's navigation bar, as shown in Figure 1-16. Rename this button Add Location by double-clicking its title (the default title is "Item").

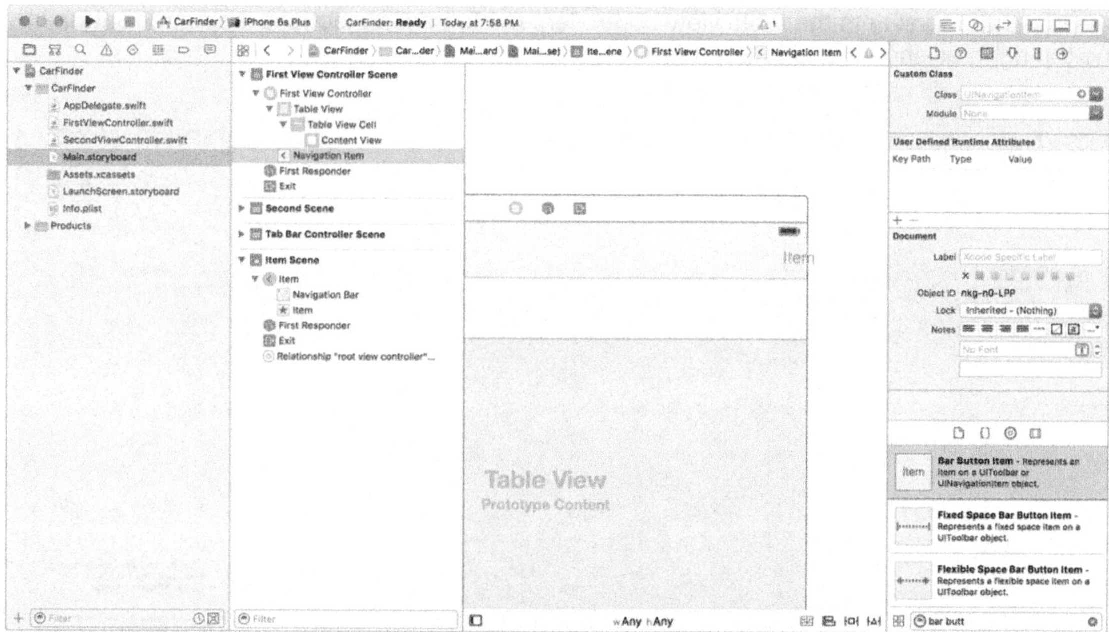

***Figure 1-16.** Adding a button to your table view controller's navigation bar*

To make the button do something, you need to connect it to a "selector," or handler method. Interface Builder will scan your view controller's owner class for a list of methods that are marked as "actions"; these are indicated by adding the `@IBAction` compiler directive to the front of the method signature.

First, you need to make a *stub* or placeholder function that you can use to connect the code to Interface Builder. Modify the definition for the `FirstViewController` class (in `FirstViewController.swift`) to add an Interface Builder-compatible `addLocation()` function as shown in Listing 1-2.

***Listing 1-2.** Adding a Stub for the addLocation Function*

```
class FirstViewController: UITableViewController {

    @IBAction func addLocation() {
        //Replace this comment with your actual implementation
    }
```

```
    override func viewDidLoad() {
        ...
    }

}
```

Next, switch back to Interface Builder and select the `FirstViewController` scene again (the one that represents the table view controller). Click the Connections Inspector button in the top right, as shown in Figure 1-17.

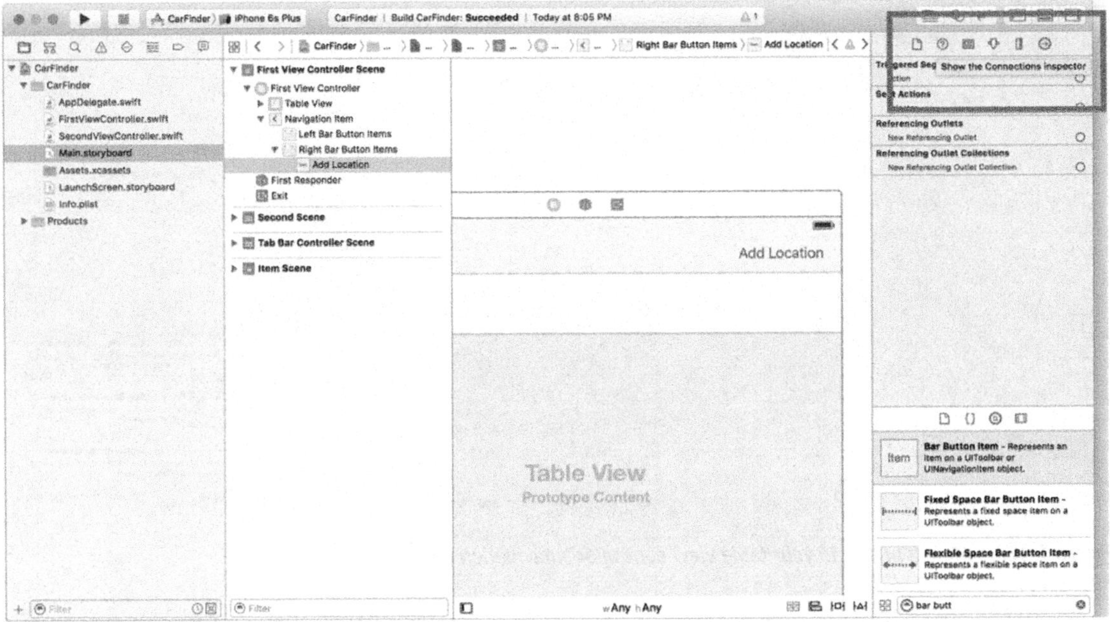

***Figure 1-17.** Selecting the Connection Inspector*

To connect the Add button to your selector, make sure `Main.storyboard` is your current document and click the Assistant Editor button in the upper right section of Xcode, as shown in Figure 1-17.

The Connection Inspector is indicated by an arrow in a circle. When you click it, the right pane of Interface Builder shows a list of *connections*, representing actions for a UI element (such as the function that should be called when it is pressed) and its corresponding object in the code. These connections are what tie your code to Interface Builder. For this example, you need to connect the function that should be called when you press the Add button.

To connect the Add button to the `addLocation()` function, click the radio button next to selector in the Connections Inspector pane. A *selector* in Swift is a reference to a function. As shown in Figure 1-18, drag a line from the radio button onto the table view controller. As happens when you select a segue, a pop-up will appear allowing you to choose the function you want to connect as the `selector` action.

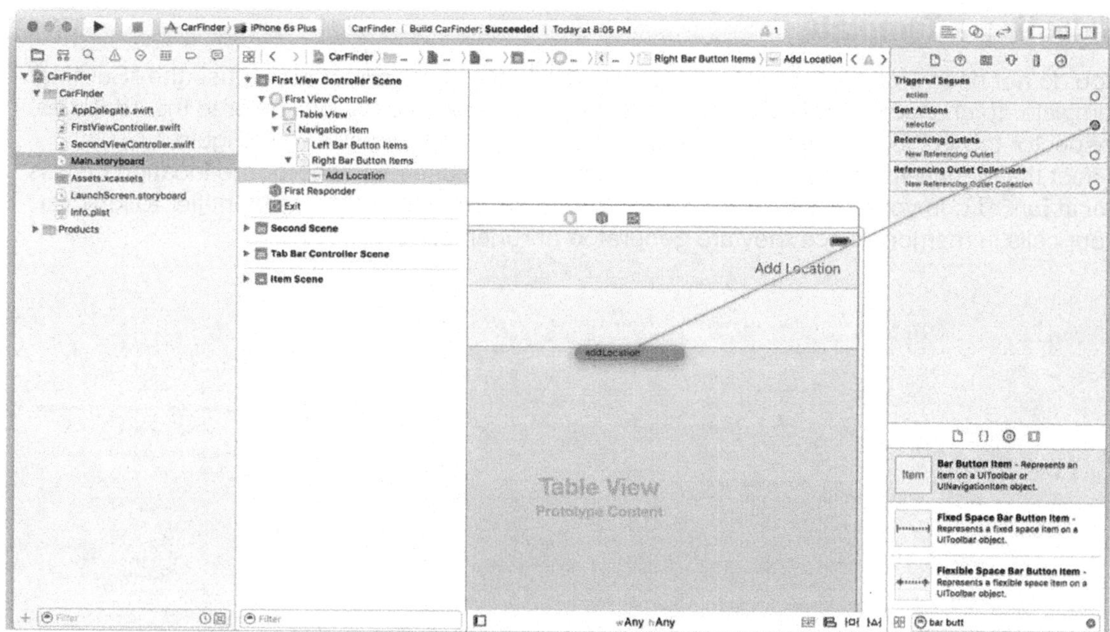

Figure 1-18. Connecting a button to an action in Interface Builder

To verify that the connection was made successfully, check the Connection Inspector after choosing the `addLocation()` method. Add Location should now appear in a bubble next to selector, as shown in Figure 1-19.

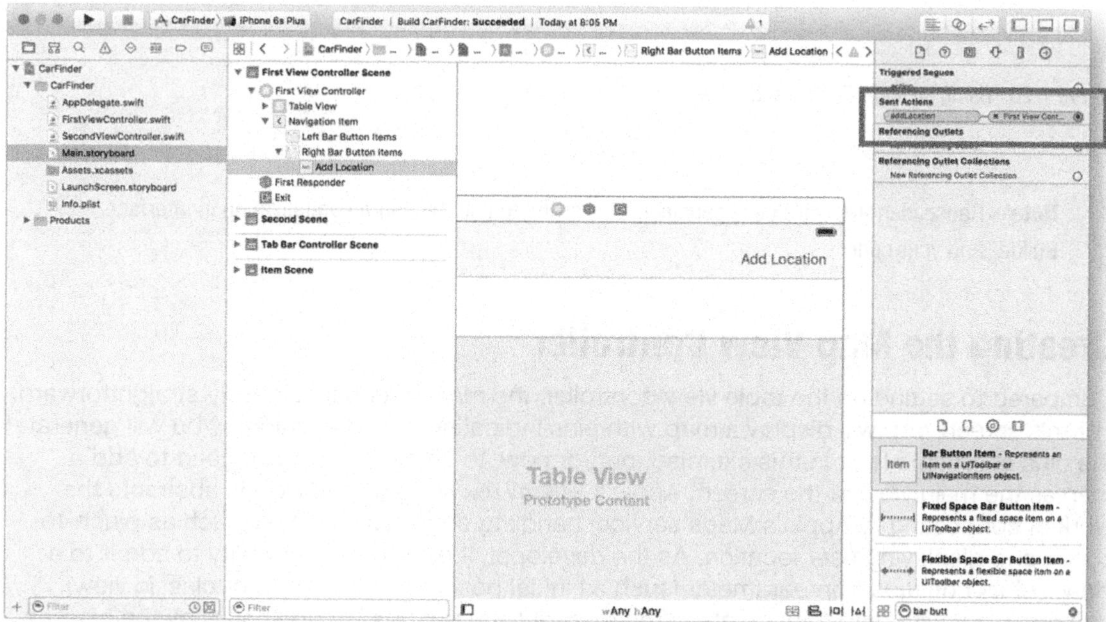

Figure 1-19. Verifying a selector connection

Selecting a Template

You do not need to define a custom class for the table view cells; you can use the "Subtitle" template. To change the cell type, click it in Interface Builder and navigate over to the Attributes Inspector tab in the right pane (the fourth icon from the left). As shown in Figure 1-20, select the identifier text view to enable text entry. The reuse identifier for the location cells is `LocationCell`. In your initialization code for the table, you will need this identifier to look up your cells in memory, since they are generated at runtime.

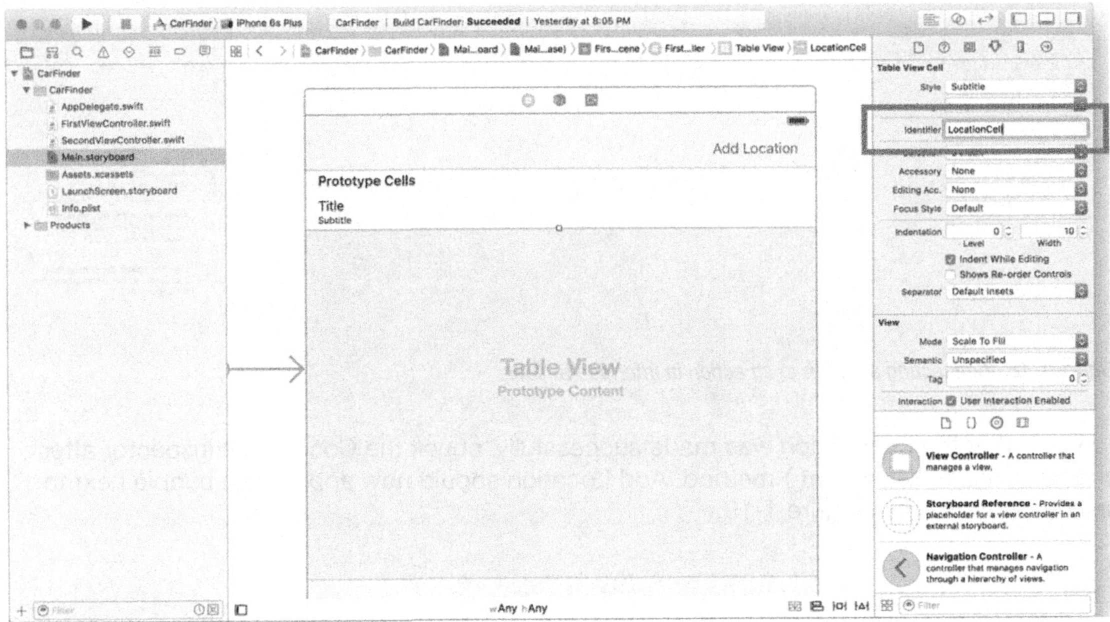

***Figure 1-20.** Using an identifier to name a cell*

> **Note** Reuse identifiers are case sensitive. Be careful to use the same capitalization in Interface Builder and your code.

Creating the Map View Controller

Compared to setting up the table view controller, the map screen is relatively straightforward. For this screen, you will display a map with pins indicating saved locations. You will generate the pins at runtime later in this exercise, but for now, to set up the UI, you need to add a map as the main view of the screen. Apple's `MKMapView` class (MapKit view) abstracts the work of connecting to Apple's Maps service, handling common gestures (such as pinch-to-zoom) and displaying user location. As the developer, it is your responsibility to add it to a view, set its configuration parameter (such as initial position and satellite or classic view), and provide it with data (pin) points in the form of "annotations," represented by the classes that implement the `MKAnnotation` protocol.

To add a map view to the second tab's view controller, begin by switching back to Interface Builder. Click each of the existing labels on the second view controller and hit the Delete key to delete them. Next, find the "MapKit View" object in the Object Library and drag it onto the second view controller. At this point, the layout for the second view controller should look like the one in Figure 1-21.

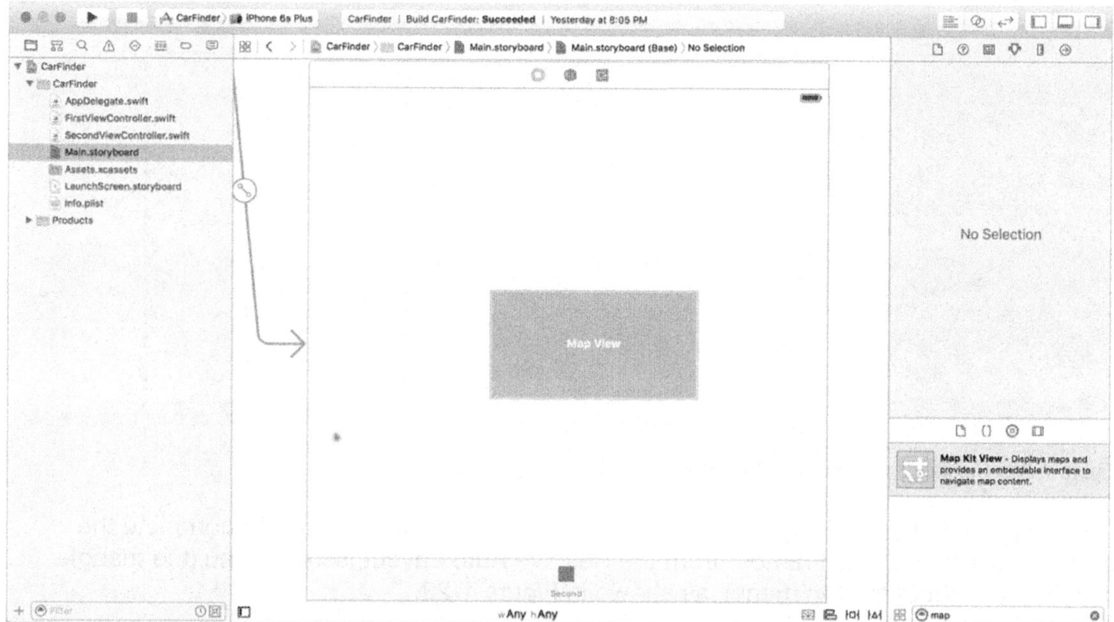

Figure 1-21. Second view controller with misplaced Map View

The wireframes indicate that the map should fill the entire screen. Unless you have perfect luck, the map will not be positioned dead center in the view or fit the edges perfectly. To fix this, use Interface Builder's Pin tool to set the auto-layout constraints for the map (the icon at the bottom right of the main screen, to the left of the triangle icon). Auto-layout is a convenient feature of storyboards that allows you to set rules for how an element should scale across different screen sizes, reducing your burden of implementing this logic in your code. As shown in Figure 1-22, in the pop-up that appears after clicking the Pin tool while the Map View is selected, uncheck the Constrain to margins check box and set all of the neighbor constraints (the ones around the box) to 0.

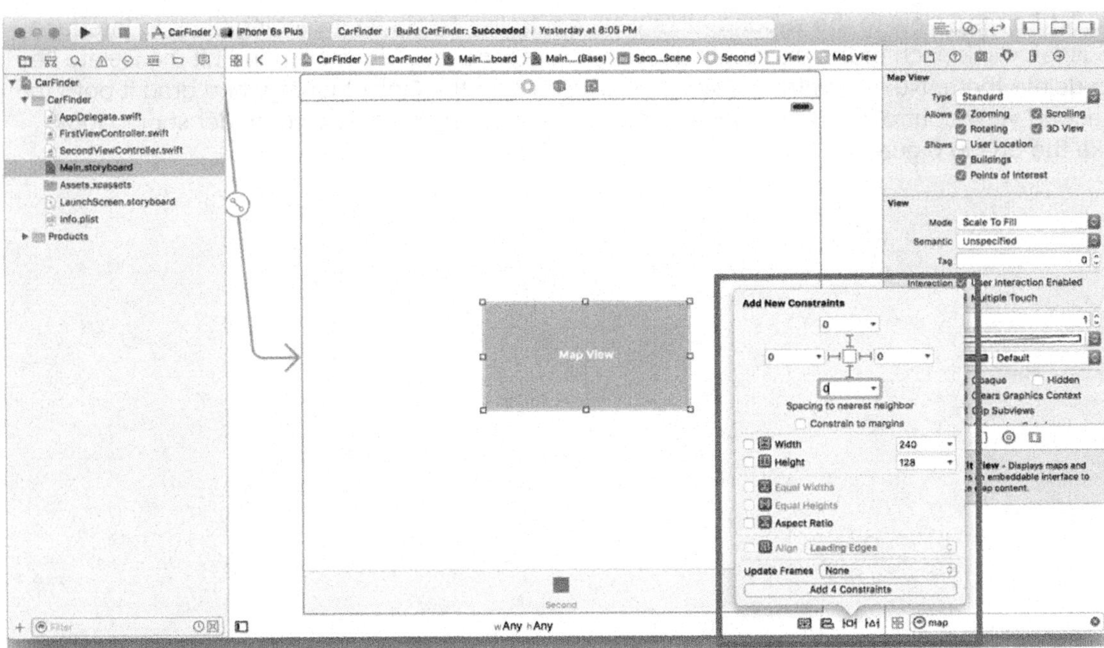

Figure 1-22. Pinning constraints for a UI element

The storyboard still needs a little help to fully configure the constraints. To complete the process, select "Update Frames" from the Resolve Auto Layout Issues menu (the triangle icon, to the right of the Pin menu), as shown in Figure 1-23.

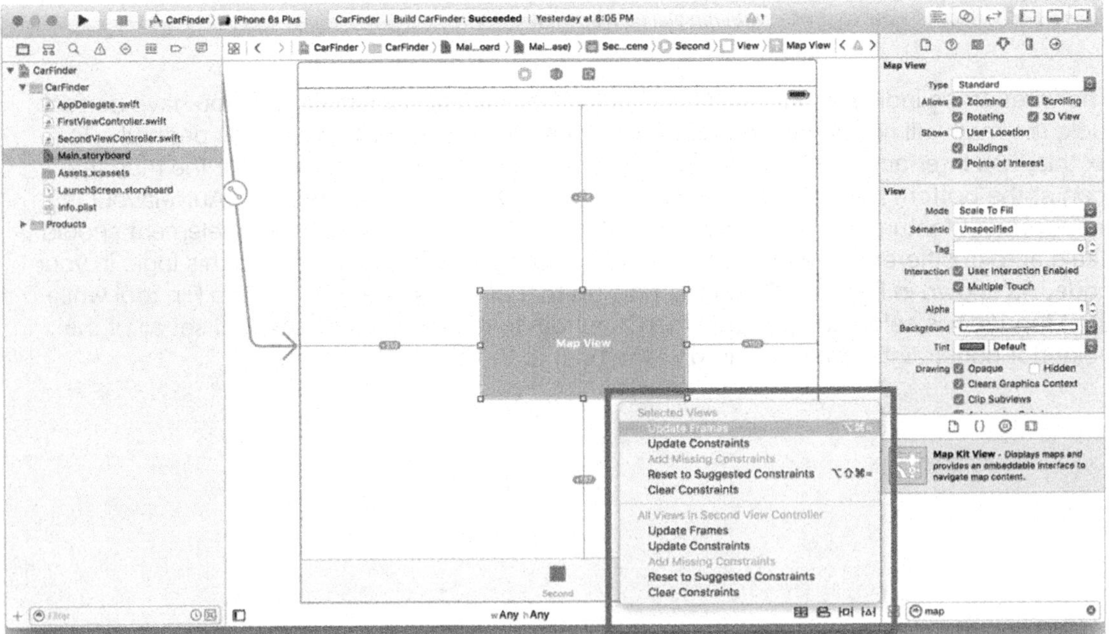

Figure 1-23. Resolving auto-layout conflicts

Having added the element to the storyboard, you need to add it to your class. As shown in Listing 1-3, include the `MapKit` framework in the `Second View Controller` class (`SecondViewController.swift`) and add the Map View as a property.

Listing 1-3. Adding a Map View to the SecondViewController Class (SecondViewController.swift)

```
import UIKit
import MapKit

class SecondViewController: UIViewController {
        @IBOutlet var mapView : MKMapView?
}
```

We will cover the semantics of this declaration more in Chapter 2, but for now, it is important to note the following:

- The `@IBOutlet` compiler directive makes the property available to Interface Builder.
- The property is defined as an inherently *strong* pointer (`var`) because you will need to modify its values later.
- All properties that are tied to a storyboard element need to be defined as optional. The design pattern for user interface elements in Swift is to treat them as nonexistent rather than being a "nil" value if they are not tied to a storyboard element.

Next, you need to revisit Connections Inspector in Interface Builder to make the connection between the storyboard and the code. Follow the same steps you used for the Add button to select the button and navigate over to Connections Inspector (the last tab in Interface Builder's right pane). To connect a property of a class to a storyboard, you need to set the Referencing Outlet connection. As shown in Figure 1-24, to complete the connection, drag a line from the New Referencing Outlet radio button to the Map View (the origin point of the line). Select the `mapView` property from the pop-up that appears.

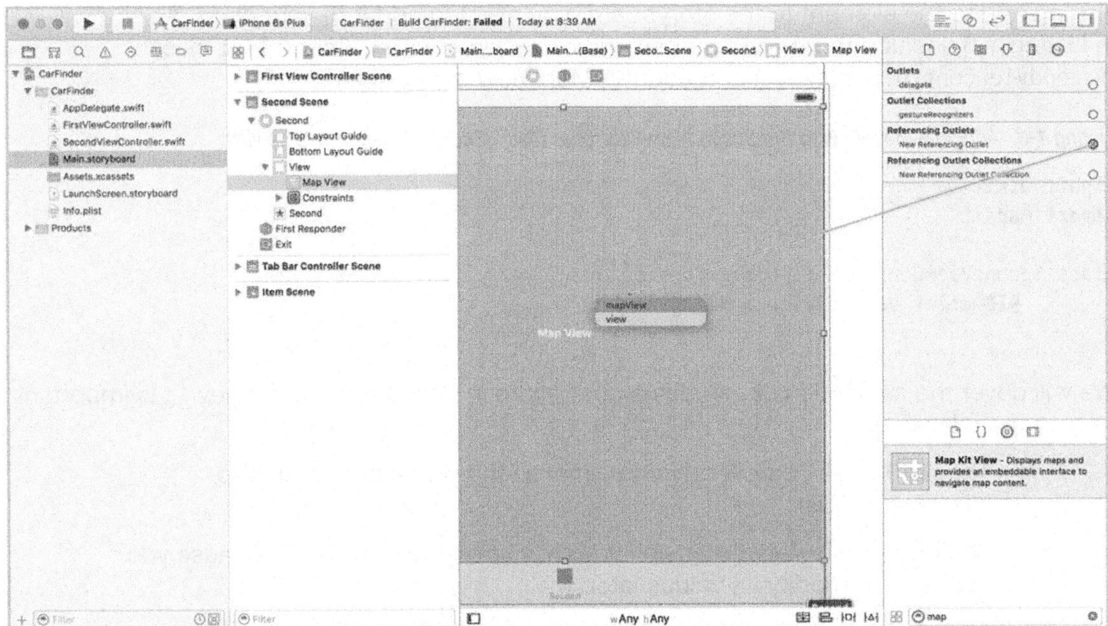

Figure 1-24. Connecting the Map View to the storyboard

As with the Add button, verify that the connection was successful by making sure the bubble next to Referencing Outlet is filled in with `mapView`.

If you build and run the app on your device or the simulator, you'll see that your UI is now nearly complete with a working map in the second view and an empty list in the first view (which now says Item).

Requesting Location Permission

Before moving into how to access the user's location, we need to address a theme that comes up commonly in developing any hardware-connected iOS app: device permissions. You may remember, a few years back, that Apple received bad press for secretly logging users' locations. Apple's argument was that this data was intended to help improve the accuracy of its mapping service; however, the backlash was so great over privacy concerns and the risks of that data being abused by hackers that Apple responded by disabling the feature and implementing a system-wide API for requesting permission to access sensitive user information and hardware (such as health data, location, and the camera).

Apple, and the authors, suggest an "adaptive" strategy for requesting device permissions. Namely, prompt the user the first time you need to use a sensitive resource (in order to unlock access to it within your app) and have mechanisms in place to "adapt" to the loss of that resource. For instance, if a user does not allow your app to access his location, display a prompt that allows him to manually specify an address or place for the app, or to disable the location-dependent feature altogether.

The first step you need to follow to enable this property is to add the `Maps` capability to your application. This is what informs the user that you need to access his location—when he or she downloads and first installs your application. To enable this capability, select your project file from the Project Navigator (Xcode's left pane) and click the Capabilities tab, as shown in Figure 1-25. To enable maps, click the switch to set it to on.

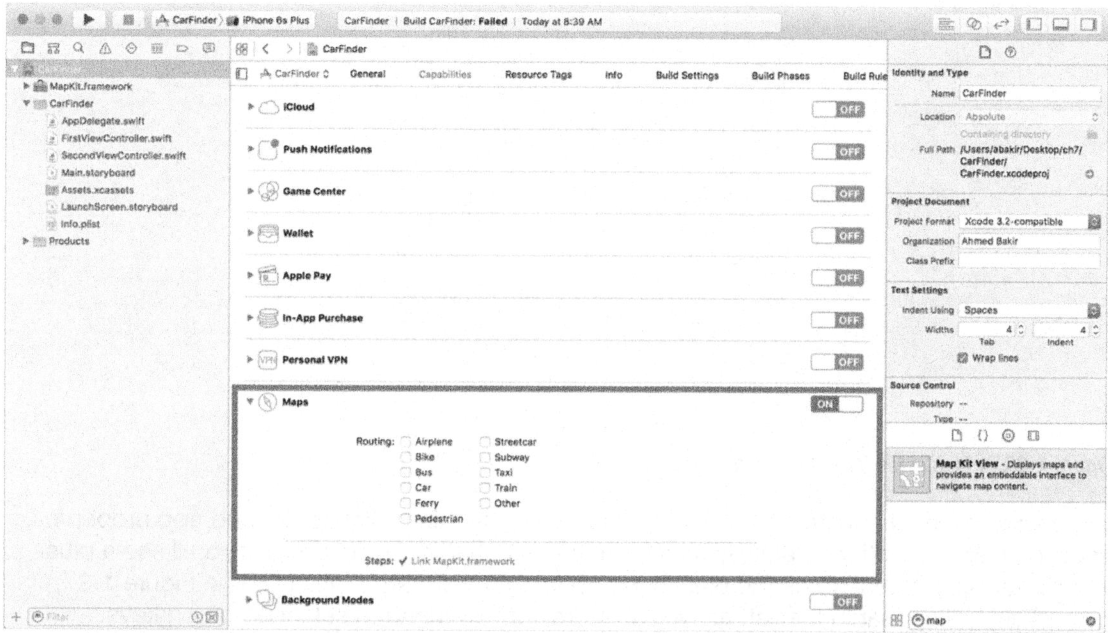

***Figure 1-25.** Setting Maps capability*

Next, you need to set the message that will appear when the user is asked for location permission. To create this string, you need to add a key to your app's `Info.plist` file. While your project is still selected in the Project Navigator, click the Info tab. This will bring up your app's settings as a list of key-value pairs, as shown in Figure 1-26.

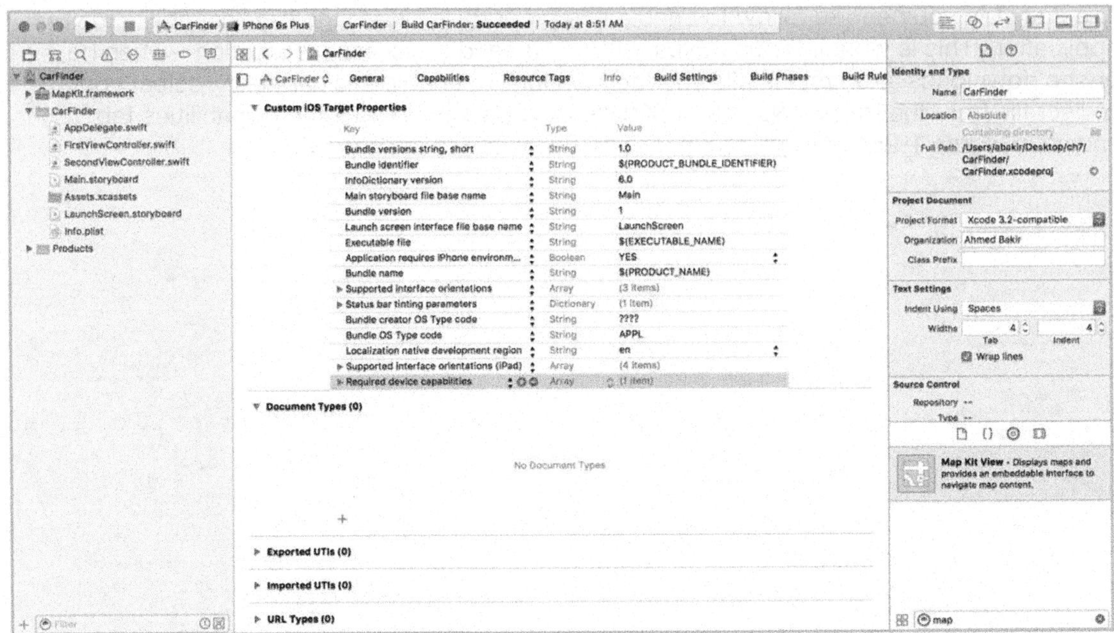

Figure 1-26. Info.plist file for the CarFinder project

The section labeled "Custom iOS Target Properties" contains a list of required app properties, many of them added by default by Xcode. Hover over the last property and you'll see a plus and minus sign appear. Click the plus sign to add a new property. As shown in Figure 1-27, a new field will appear in the list, as well as a drop-down menu to select common keys.

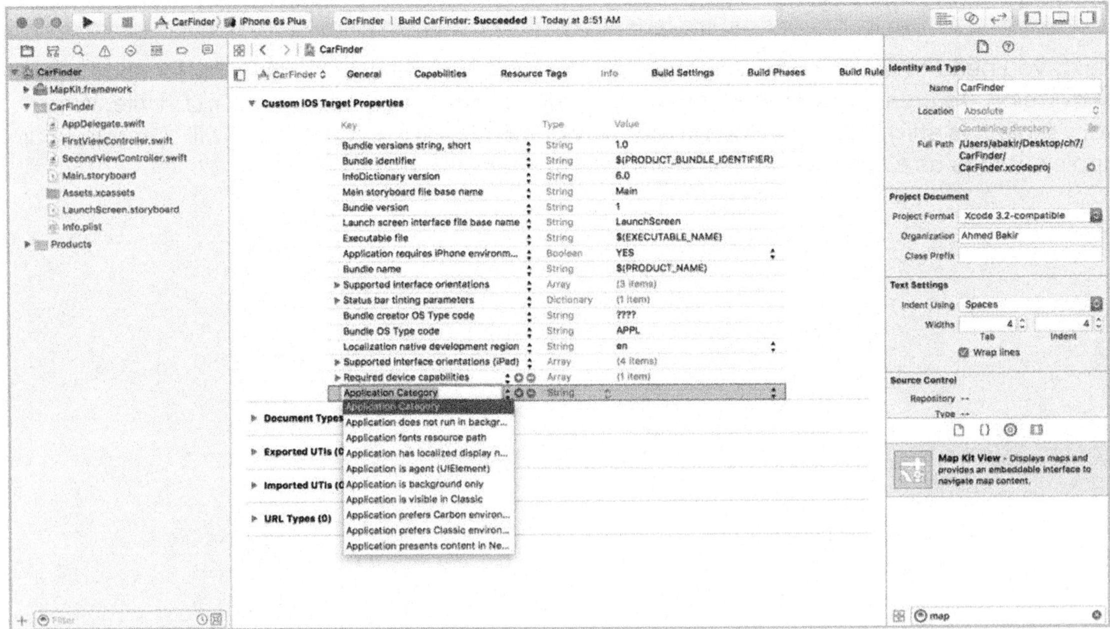

Figure 1-27. Interface for adding a new key-value pair

In the key text field, type in NSLocationWhenInUseUsageDescription for the key name. The type should be string. In the value text field, type in "This app uses location information."

Next, you need to make more code changes, so switch back to the FirstViewController.swift file.

Add CLLocationManagerDelegate to your class declaration so we can enable location updates. Then add locationManager and current location as class variables, as shown in Listing 1-4.

Listing 1-4. Adding Location Manager Delegate to the FirstViewController class

```
class FirstViewController: UITableViewController, CLLocationManagerDelegate {
    var locationManager = CLLocationManager()
    var currentLocation = CLLocation()
}
```

Conveniently, Apple provides a class called CLLocationManager, which can poll the operating system for your device's authorization status, bring up an authorization prompt, and enable/disable location polling. The CLLocationManager class has a method called authorizationStatus(), which will return an enum value representing the authorization status of your application. It is best to check this value when any location-dependent screen in your application appears. iOS suppresses repeated requests; the prompt will not appear again until the user uninstalls your app. For the CarFinder application, this is the First View Controller table view. Trigger the authorization check in the viewDidAppear() method of the FirstViewController.swift file, which fires every time the view controller is active.

Listing 1-5. Polling for Location Permission (FirstViewController.swift)

```
override func viewDidAppear(animated: Bool) {
    super.viewDidAppear(animated)

    //locationManager.delegate = self
    locationManager.desiredAccuracy = kCLLocationAccuracyNearestTenMeters

    switch (CLLocationManager.authorizationStatus()) {

    case .AuthorizedWhenInUse, .AuthorizedAlways:
        locationManager.startUpdatingLocation()
    case .Denied:
        let alert = UIAlertController(title: "Permissions error", message: "This app needs
        location permission to work accurately", preferredStyle: UIAlertControllerStyle.Alert)
        let okAction = UIAlertAction(title: "OK", style: UIAlertActionStyle.Default, handler: nil)
        alert.addAction(okAction)
        presentViewController(alert, animated: true, completion: nil)

    case .NotDetermined:
        fallthrough
    default:
        locationManager.requestWhenInUseAuthorization()

    }
```

You always want to check for at least three status levels in your code: Authorized, Not Determined, and Denied. As shown in Listing 1-5, use the Authorized state to begin polling for location. For the Denied state, we show an alert view, indicating that the application needs location permission. Finally, we use the Not Determined state and default case of the `switch` statement to prompt the user to authorize the app.

In our example, you will notice that the call to check status, `authorizationStatus()`, takes place on the `CLLocationManager` class, while the call to perform operations such as `startUpdatingLocation()` takes place on an instance. `authorizationStatus()` does not depend on an object; it simply queries the system, so it is defined as a class (public) method, whereas operations are defined as private methods since they can only be performed if an object is instantiated. If the authorization state has been determined to be denied, show an alert message via the `UIAlertController` class.

> **Note** We request the "in-use" permission for the CarFinder app because we only need to request the user's location while the app is active.

Having set ourselves as the delegate, we also need to add its required methods which include the `locationManager` call with `didUpdateLocations` so our location data is fresh when we are ready to store it.

Accessing the User's Location

Having prompted the user for the location permission, you are now ready to begin retrieving and logging his location data. For the CarFinder application, you will initiate this action when the user presses the Add button in the first view controller's toolbar. When you take this action, you will save the user's latitude and longitude, as well as a timestamp indicating when the action happened. The table view in the first view controller should refresh at this time to indicate that a new record has been added. If the user disabled location permission, you should provide some dummy data, such as the latitude and longitude of your favorite coffee shop.

It can take some time to find the precise coordinates of a phone once you start using location services. That's why we start location services when the app starts and update a class variable each time it changes. This variable is used only when we need it (i.e., when we want to save our location).

Now that you have the location and timestamp data for the user's location, you need to save it somewhere that can be shared between the first and second view controllers. It needs to be a generic object that can be accessed or modified by either. To solve this problem, we suggest creating a singleton object, which our sample calls `DataManager`. A singleton is an instance of a class that is lazy-loaded (initialized the first time it is accessed). Singletons are commonly used in hardware "manager" classes, where you want to control all operations through a single object and have abstracted these operations to be independent of any class that is using them.

Create a new class by choosing File ➤ New ➤ File from the Xcode menu bar. It's a Swift file and we'll name it `DataManager.swift`.

Listing 1-6 provides the class definition for the `DataManager` class. When other classes access the `sharedInstance` property, the class will be lazy-loaded. The static keyword ensures that if it has already been initialized, the existing object will be returned; the `_let_` keyword ensures that the instance will be thread-safe. Remember to include the `CoreLocation` framework to ensure symbols resolve properly.

***Listing 1-6.** Definition for DataManager Class*

```
import Foundation
import CoreLocation

class DataManager {
    static let sharedInstance = DataManager()
    var locations : [CLLocation]

    private init() {
        locations = [CLLocation]()
    }

}
```

The `DataManager`'s main role is to manage a list of `CLLocation` objects. To accomplish this, we use an array of `CLLocation` objects as a `strong` property of the class (the default allocation the using the `var` keyword is `strong`). You do not need to define getter or setter methods, as arrays in Swift are mutable by default.

Having defined the `DataManager` class, you can now use it in the `FirstViewController` class. As shown in Listing 1-7, after retrieving the user's current location, expand the `addLocation()` function to append the value in the locations array that is managed by the `DataManager` singleton. If the user did not authorize the app to use GPS permissions, create a new record using a hard-coded set of coordinates.

***Listing 1-7.** Saving Locations*

```
@IBAction func addLocation(sender: UIBarButtonItem) {

    var location : CLLocation

    if (CLLocationManager.authorizationStatus() != .AuthorizedWhenInUse) {
        location = CLLocation(latitude: 32.830579, longitude: -117.153839)
    } else {
        location = locationManager.location!
    }

    DataManager.sharedInstance.locations.insert(location, atIndex: 0)

}
```

> **Note** This example saves locations in memory; they will not persist between multiple sessions. To persist data, we suggest using Core Data or saving your data to a plaintext file.

Displaying the User's Location

Having defined a method for retrieving the user's location and managing saved responses, you are ready to display the data. It is best to start with the table view in the first view controller.

Populating the Table View

To populate a table view controller, you need to specify a data source and implement the methods specified the `UITableViewDelegate` protocol, which is included by default with the `UITableViewController` class. For the data source, you will use the locations array from the `DataManager` singleton.

The methods you will need to implement for the `UITableViewDelegate` protocol are as follows:

- `numberOfSectionsInTableView(_:)`
- `tableView(_:numberOfRowsInSection:)`
- `tableView(_:cellForRowAtIndexPath:)`

All these functions need to be implemented in in the `FirstViewController` class (`FirstViewController.swift`).

The `UITableView` class uses a two-dimensional grid represented by the `indexPath` to represent the positions of elements in the table. For a one-dimensional array, the number of sections is defined as 1. Implement the `numberOfSectionsInTableView(_:)` method as shown in Listing 1-8

Listing 1-8. Implementing numberOfSectionsInTableView(_:)

```
override func numberOfSectionsInTableView(tableView: UITableView) -> Int {
    return 1
}
```

Similarly, the number of rows in a one-dimensional array is the number of elements. As shown in Listing 1-9, return the `count` property of the entries array.

Listing 1-9. Implementing tableView(_:numberOfRowsInSection:)

```
override func tableView(tableView: UITableView, numberOfRowsInSection section: Int) -> Int {
    return DataManager.sharedInstance.locations.count
}
```

Now you need to use the data from the entries array to populate your table view cells. In the `tableView(_:cellForRowAtIndexPath:)` method, retrieve the location entry that corresponds with the row that is being operated upon, and then tie it to a cell by looking it up in memory via its *reuse identifier*, the label we defined on the storyboard earlier. Listing 1-10 describes this process. Since we are using the Subtitle cell style, we can directly access the `textLabel` and `detailLabel` properties on the table view cell.

***Listing 1-10.** Implementing tableView(_:cellForRowAtIndexPath:)*

```
override func tableView(tableView: UITableView, cellForRowAtIndexPath indexPath:
NSIndexPath) -> UITableViewCell {
    let cell = tableView.dequeueReusableCellWithIdentifier("LocationCell", forIndexPath: indexPath)
    cell.tag = indexPath.row
    // Configure the cell...

    let entry : CLLocation = DataManager.sharedInstance.locations[indexPath.row]
    let dateFormatter = NSDateFormatter()
    dateFormatter.dateFormat = "hh:mm:ss, MM-dd-yyyy"

    cell.textLabel?.text = "\(entry.coordinate.latitude), \(entry.coordinate.longitude) "

    cell.detailTextLabel?.text = dateFormatter.stringFromDate(entry.timestamp)

    return cell
}
```

As a final step to tie up the table view, you should refresh the table once a new item has been added. To refresh a table view at any time, call the `reloadData()` method after updating your data source, as shown in Listing 1-11.

***Listing 1-11.** Refreshing the Table*

```
@IBAction func addLocation(sender: UIBarButtonItem) {

        var location : CLLocation

        if (CLLocationManager.authorizationStatus() != .AuthorizedWhenInUse) {
            location = CLLocation(latitude: 32.830579, longitude: -117.153839)
        } else {
            location = locationManager.location!
        }

        DataManager.sharedInstance.locations.insert(location, atIndex: 0)

    tableView.reloadData()

}
```

> **Note** Core Data has a delegate method that reduces your need to manually refresh a database-based table view. For simple arrays and data structures, it is easiest to refresh the table manually.

Populating the Map

Once again, compared to the table view, the map is relatively straightforward to populate with data. Following the example of the table view, we need to retrieve saved locations from the DataManager singleton when the view appears. To plot data on the map, we need to create pin drops, represented by the MKPointAnnotation class, which implements the MKAnnotation protocol. In your SecondViewController class (SecondViewController.swift), implement the viewDidAppear(_:) method as shown in Listing 1-12.

Listing 1-12. Setting the Data Source for the Map View

```
override func viewDidAppear(animated: Bool) {
    super.viewDidAppear(animated)

    let locations = DataManager.sharedInstance.locations
    var annotations = [MKPointAnnotation]()

    for location in locations {
        let annotation = MKPointAnnotation()
        annotation.coordinate = location.coordinate
        annotations.insert(annotation, atIndex: annotations.count)
    }

    let oldAnnotations = mapView!.annotations
    mapView?.removeAnnotations(oldAnnotations)

    mapView?.addAnnotations(annotations)

}
```

While map views are extremely customizable and meant to handle a lot of user interactions, the MKMapView class is designed to be loaded once from an array of annotations. As shown previously, remember to clear the existing annotation array before loading your new one. This also helps the user interface, as the viewDidAppear(_:) is called every time the user switches tabs.

Finally, to make the map fit to the area surrounding the user's pin drops, you need to call the regionThatFits(_:) method. As shown in Listing 1-13, modify the viewDidAppear() method to include this logic. Use the first valid annotation as the basis for your calculation.

Listing 1-13. Resizing the Map View

```
override func viewDidAppear(animated: Bool) {
    super.viewDidAppear(animated)

    let locations = DataManager.sharedInstance.locations
    var annotations = [MKPointAnnotation]()
```

```
    for location in locations {
        let annotation = MKPointAnnotation()
        annotation.coordinate = location.coordinate
        annotations.insert(annotation, atIndex: annotations.count)
    }

    let oldAnnotations = mapView!.annotations
    mapView?.removeAnnotations(oldAnnotations)

    mapView?.addAnnotations(annotations)

    if (annotations.count > 0) {
        let region = MKCoordinateRegionMake(annotations[0].coordinate,
        MKCoordinateSpanMake(0.1, 0.1))
        mapView?.regionThatFits(region)
    }
    mapView?.showsUserLocation = true
}
```

Now that you have fully implemented the CarFinder project, the result should look as shown Figure 1-28, complete with a fully functional location table, Add button, and location map.

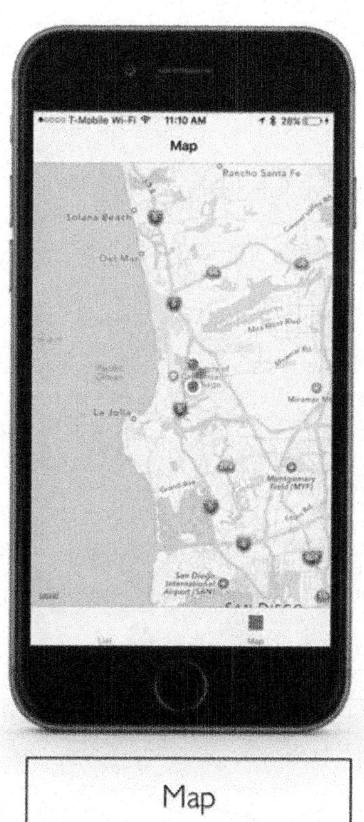

Figure 1-28. Completed CarFinder application

Summary

To help introduce you to the style of the projects in this book, we described a simple app to access a user's location based on his phone's GPS reading and to display it on a table and map view. This exercise reviewed the basics of setting up a project, creating a user interface, requesting device permissions, and digesting location data. Several of the projects in this book will require you to implement "adaptive" strategies around device permissions, due to their sensitive nature. You will also revisit maps later, when you learn about how to use iBeacons, which are Bluetooth-based proximity sensors that allow iOS devices to do cool things like send you notifications when you walk by the Apple Store.

Chapter 2

Getting Started with Swift

Ahmed Bakir

As it is one of the newest programming languages on the market, one would be remiss to start a Swift book without offering the reader a brief introduction to the language. Readers who already feel comfortable with Swift can skip this chapter entirely or just reference the sections they are curious about.

Immediately upon its announcement at the 2014 Apple Worldwide Developers Conference (WWDC), Swift became one of the fastest adopted programming languages in recent history. To help aid this rapid acceptance, Apple designed the language to be fully compatible with existing Objective-C code and all of Cocoa/Cocoa Touch (the frameworks you use to build OS X and iOS apps).

In the past year, however, the sudden appearance of Swift has presented two problems: it has been hard to find good information on how the language works and it has been a grueling process to keep up with Apple's updates to the language. In addition to being one of the fastest adopted languages, Swift has also been one of the most rapidly changing. Since June 2014, the Apple developer community has seen four major revisions of the language, Swift 1.0, 1.1, 1.2, and 2.0. With each of the language updates comes a revision to Cocoa Touch, meaning you need to modify your code to resolve compilation errors. Imagine waking up one day and seeing that your once functional program no longer compiles.

To help you hit the ground running with this book, I will briefly review Swift syntax, how the language implements core programming concepts like object-oriented programming, and workflow tasks like integrating Objective-C into your projects. In this chapter, I will pull in knowledge from Swift projects I have consulted on, focusing on language features that have proved particularly troublesome for my clients, including optionals and try-catch blocks.

For a more complete description of the language, I highly recommend *Beginning iPhone Development with Swift: Exploring the iOS SDK* by Mark,Topley, Nutting, Olsson and LeMarche (Apress, 2016). The authors intend their book to be a complete guide to programming Swift via Cocoa Touch tutorials. This book assumes you have mastered those concepts and are ready to dive headfirst into Internet of Things concepts using Cocoa Touch. You can also download Apple's own guide to the language, *The Swift Programming Language* from the iBooks Store.

> **Note** This book is written for and tested against Swift 2.1 on XCode 7.1/OS X 10.11 "El Capitan."

Why Use Swift?

Following "Should I learn to program in iOS or Android?," the most common question I receive these days is "Should I program in Objective-C or Swift?" The short answer to both is to pick the platform or language you are more comfortable with and stick with that.

Created with the goal of being "Objective-C without the C," Swift was designed to allow a wider audience of developers, eschewing the message-passing syntax of Objective-C (those annoying square brackets) and the heavy dependence on understanding advanced concepts from C, such as pointers. If you are coming from Java and Python, many features of Swift will seem very familiar to you, such as dot-syntax for calling methods and try-catch blocks. This was an intentional design decision. I am currently teaching an Objective-C course and the number one complaint from my students is Objective-C's square brackets; they are a derivative of Smalltalk, a ground-breaking language that never received wide adoption outside advanced programming courses but remains in use today. I tell people it takes a couple of weeks to "get over them," but they remain daunting. For many people, the dot-syntax alone is a compelling reason to use Swift.

Since OS X and iOS are the only modern platforms that use Objective-C, it is often hard for people to differentiate concepts that come from Objective-C and concepts that come from Cocoa [Touch]. To help with that, at the 2015 WWDC, Apple announced that it is open-sourcing Swift, in hopes of encouraging its wider adoption in education and non-Apple platforms, such as Linux. The extra data points should prove extremely valuable when trying to understand core programming concepts.

One of the most compelling reasons to develop for an Apple platform is the extremely prolific developer community, which has produced a wealth of open source libraries and a massive history of solutions to common bugs. For this reason, Apple was eager to announce that Swift was fully compatible with all of Cocoa Touch and existing Objective-C code when Swift first came. As mentioned in the introduction, I can validate that this claim is true, but you may end up updating your code to keep up with changes in Swift. This may seem discouraging, but remember, you are programming for a closed platform; this is always the case for major updates. Before anyone knew about Swift, many of us were shuffling to make our old apps work in the drastically updated iOS7.

What I have noticed is that for most people, neither Swift nor Objective-C is the major hurdle to learning iOS development. Nine times out of ten, it is learning Cocoa Touch. Apple's APIs (application programming interfaces) have a very "descriptive" nature, where they generally describe every parameter in the method name. For many beginners, this makes it hard to guess where/how to get started. The good news is, Apple has backported its documentation and provides complete API documentation for every method in Cocoa Touch in both Swift and Objective-C. Most of the problems you will run into will not be about the syntax of a "for" loop; instead they will be about what set of Cocoa Touch methods you call to perform the behaviors you need, and how you need to configure them. Swift and Objective-C are just tools for accomplishing that; pick the one you like using more.

Basic Swift Syntax

In this section, I briefly introduce several basic Swift syntax concepts to help you become familiar with the language and the following examples. As many of you are coming from Objective-C, I will prefix each Swift example with the corresponding Objective-C code. These examples are not meant to be part of any project, so take them as short, working examples. As mentioned in the introduction, all of these examples are written against the standard for Swift 2.0.

Calling Methods (Hello World)

In Objective-C, to print "Hello World" on the console, you would use the `NSLog()` method:
`NSLog(@"Hello World");`

In Swift, the equivalent is as follows:

```
print("Hello World")
```

You should notice a couple of big differences:

No semicolons: Swift uses the newline character to separate lines.

No @ symbol: Swift has its own `String` class, which is implemented as a simple character array. In Objective-C, the @ symbol served as a literal, a shortcut for creating NSString objects without calling its constructor.

`print`: Swift uses this familiar method name from C and Java to allow you to print a line directly to the console.

Calling a method with multiple parameters in Objective-C looks as follows:

```
NSInteger finalSum = [self calculateSumOf:5 andValue:6];
```

Self represents the receiver (the object that is "receiving" the message")

`CalculateSumOf:` represents the method name

5 represents the first parameter that is being passed

`andValue` represents the second parameter's label

6 represents the second parameter that is being passed.

In Swift, you call methods with multiple parameters by adding them to a comma-delimited list within the parentheses (as you would in C or Java):

```
var finalSum = calculateSum(5, 6)
```

If the method defines labels for its parameters, add the labels in front of the values:

```
var finalSum = calculateSum(firstValue: 5, secondValue: 6)
```

> **Note** Unless specifically required by a method, you can omit the first parameter's label.

Defining Variables

After "Hello World," every programming lesson must continue with a discussion of variables. In Objective-C, you created variables by declaring the type, variable, and value:

```
NSInteger count = 5;
```

In Swift, you declare variables by specifying their name and mutability (var or let), and optionally:

the data type and initialization value:

```
var count : Int = 5
```

All variables defined with var in Swift are mutable, meaning you can change their values at runtime without re-initializing the variable—for example, NSMutableString or NSMutableArray.

The let keyword is similar to const in Objective-C and C; this is a constant value that is not meant to change.

Swift infers data types, so if you prefer, you can omit the type from your declaration:

```
var count = 5
```

Swift also allows you to store float (decimal) and Boolean values in variables directly.

To store a float in Objective-C:

```
float average = 2.4;
```

To store a float in Swift:

```
var average : float = 2.4
```

You can use Double or Long to specify the size of the variable, just as in Objective-C

To store a Boolean in Objective-C:

```
BOOL isInitialized = YES;  // or NO
```

To store a Boolean in Swift:

```
var  isInitialized : Bool = true  // or false
```

Custom types follow the same rules in Objective-C and Swift as other types: insert the type's name before the variable name:

In Objective-C:

```
MyType myVariable;
myVariable.name = @"Bob"; //name is a property of the type
```

In Swift:

```
var myVariable : MyType
MyVariable.name = "Bob"
```

Objects require a slightly different process for initialization, which I will cover in the section "Object-Oriented Programming in Swift."

Compound Data Types

In most programming languages, like Java and Objective-C, the only data types provided out of the box are primitives for storing values like integers, Booleans, and decimal values directly in memory. For more complicated data, you need to define your own types using structs or classes. While Swift provides this functionality, it does differentiate types that are provided by the language or the program.

Instead, it separates types into named types, which are named by the language or program, and compound types, which allow you to return multiple, distinct values under the guise of "one variable." These are commonly called tuples in Swift and other languages.

You define a tuple in Swift by replacing the type with a series of types in parentheses:

```
var myStatistics : (Int, Int, Float)
```

To set values, embed those in parentheses as well:

```
var myStatistics : (Int, Int, Float) = (2, 2, 5.2)
```

Tuples operate similarly to structs in Objective-C, which are custom data types you define (unlike an object, they do not have methods). For reference, remember that a struct in Objective-C is defined thus:

```
typedef struct {
        NSString *name;
        NSString *description;
        NSInteger displayOrder;
} MyType;
```

In this example, `name`, `description`, and `displayOrder` are the properties of the struct, and `MyType` is the name.

To replicate this behavior in Swift, by treating a tuple like a named type, use the _typealias_ keyword:

```
typealias MyType = (String, String, Int)
```

You can then instantiate a tuple using your type name as you would any other type:

```
var myVariable: MyType = ("Bob", "Bob is cool", 1)
```

Conditional Logic

In Objective-C, you implemented the most basic kind of conditional logic by placing a comparison in parentheses, as part of an `if` statement:

```
if (currentValue < maximumValue) {
}
```

In Swift, this syntax is largely unchanged, except the requirement for parentheses is gone:

```
if currentValue < maximumValue
```

An if-else statement retains this rule as well:

```
if currentValue < maximumValue {
        //Do something
} else if currentValue == 3 {
        //Do something else
}
```

> **Note** All the comparison operators you are familiar with from Objective-C are still valid in Swift.

In Objective-C, you could use a ternary operator to combine an if-else and an assignment

```
NSInteger value = (currentValue < maximumValue) ? currentValue : maximumValue  ;
```

In this block of statement, you check if the `currentValue` is less than the `maximumValue`. If the statement is true, set value to `currentValue`; else set value to `maximumValue`.

This syntax is still available in Swift, and mostly unchanged:

```
var value = currentValue < maximumValue ? currentValue : maximumValue
```

When you wanted to check against multiple values in Objective, you used a `switch` statement, with a `case` block for each value:

```
switch(currentValue) {
        case 1: NSLog("value 1");
                break;
```

```
        case 2: NSLog("value 2");
                break;
        case 3: NSLog("value 3");
                break;
}
```

The good news is the `switch` statement is also available in Swift, with a couple of changes:

1. `switch` statements in Swift allow you to compare objects. The Objective-C requirement for comparing values has been eliminated in Swift.
2. `switch` statements in Swift no longer fall through by default. This means you do not have to add a `break;` statement at the end of each `case`.
3. `switch` statements in Swift need to be exhaustive (meaning they cover all values, or include a `default` case). This requirement is a best practice for code security and prevents unexpected comparisons.

In Swift, the `switch` statement described previously would look as follows:

```
switch currentValue {
        case 1: println("value 1")
        case 2: NSLog("value 2")
        case 3: NSLog("value 3")
        default: NSLog("other value)
}
```

Enumerated Types

In Objective-C, you use an enumerated type to group related values and to reduce errors from "magic numbers," values that are hard-coded into your code.

In Objective-C, enumerated types (`enums`) are defined as such:

```
typedef enum {
        Failed = -1,
        Loading,
        Success
} PlaybackStates;
```

Where `PlaybackStates` is the name of the `enum`, `Failed`, `Loading`, and `Success` are the three possible values, and -1 is the initial value of the first item in the `enum`. In Objective-C, if not explicitly defined, `enums` start at 0 and increment by 1. Objective-C `enums` can only store discrete, increasing values, such as integers or characters.

In Swift, the syntax for defining an enumerated type is similar, except you indicate the value type and use the case keyword to indicate each named value:

```
enum PlaybackStates : Int {
        case Failed = -1,
        case Loading,
        case Success
}
```

Swift does not try to automatically increment values like in Objective-C, so you can store any type of value in an enum, including String.

To use a value from an enum in Objective-C, you replace your magic number with the value's name. You can store the value in an integer or a variable with the enum's name as its type:

```
NSInteger myPlaybackState = Failed;
PlaybackState myPlaybackState = Failed;
```

For conditional statements:

```
if (myPlaybackState == Failed)
```

In Swift, the easiest way to use an enum is by appending the value name to the type:

```
var myPlaybackState = PlaybackStates.Failed
```

This applies for conditionals as well:

```
if myPlaybackState == PlaybackState.Failed
```

If you are trying to retrieve the value that is stored in an enum member, use the rawValue property. For instance, if you are trying to translate PlaybackState to an Int value:

```
let playbackStateValue : Int = PlaybackState.Failed.rawValue
```

Loops

The syntax for all of the major types of loops (for, for-each, do, do-while) are largely unchanged in Swift. Two major changes are that you do not need to declare your type and parentheses are once again optional:

```
for name in nameArray {
        print ("name = \(name)")
}
```

Also, there is a major addition in Swift that can improve your loops: *ranges*. Ranges in Swift allow you to specify a set of values that you can use to iterate a loop or as part of comparison.

There are two major types of ranges in Swift:

- Closed Ranges, expressed as `x...y`, create a range that starts at x and includes all values including y
- Half-Open Ranges, expressed as `x..y`, create a range that starts at x and includes all values up to y

You could use a range in a `for-each` loop as follows:

```
for i in 1..5  {
        print (i)
}
```

(This would print the numbers 1-4.)

Object-Oriented Programming in Swift

Now that you have a little bit of understanding of the basic syntax of Swift, I will start to cover Swift syntax as it applies to object-oriented programming.

Building a Class

Unlike Objective-C, Swift does not have a concept of interface files (`.h`) and implementation files (`.m`). In Swift, your entire class is declared within a `.swift` file.

In Objective-C, a class declaration consisted of:

- Class name
- Parent class
- Property declarations (in interface file)
- Method definitions (in implementation file)

In Objective-C, you declared a class in your header file:

```
@interface LocationViewController: UIViewController {
        @property NSString *locationName;
        @property Double latitude;
        @property Double longitude;
        -(NSString)generatePrettyLocationString;
}
@end
```

`@Interface` specified that you were declaring a class. `UIViewController` was the name of the parent class you were subclassing. `@property` indicated a variable as an instance variable, or property of the class. Finally, you also included method signatures in this block, so that they could be accessible by other classes.

In your .m file, you would define (or implement) the methods of your class, in the @implementation block:

```
@implementation LocationViewController {
        -(NSString)generatePrettyLocationString {
                //Do something here
        }
}
```

Swift does not split classes into .h and .m files; instead, all declarations and definitions take place in your .swift file.

You define classes in Swift with the class keyword:

```
class LocationViewController: UIViewController {

        var locationName : String?
        var latitude: Double = 1.0
        var longitude: Double = -1.0

        func generatePrettyLocationString -> String {
                //Do something
        }
}
```

Properties are included in a class by placing them inside the class block. Swift enforces property initialization. There are three ways to resolve compilation errors that occur as a result of not including an initial value for a property:

- Specify a value when you declare the variable
- Specify that the variable is an optional (explained further in this section)
- Create a constructor (init) method that sets initial values for every property in the class.

Method implementations are also included directly inside the class block. There is no need to forward-declare signatures as in C or Objective-C.

Protocols

Protocols are a concept from Objective-C that allows you to define a limited interface between two classes, via a delegate property. For instance, when you use the iPhone's camera, the class that presents the camera declares itself as implementing the UIImagePickerControllerDelegate protocol and defines the two methods that the protocol specifies for passing back information from the camera (without creating and managing a camera object in your code).

In Objective-C, to indicate that you will be implementing a protocol, you add the protocol's name to your class declaration, after your parent class, in carrots:

```
@interface LocationViewController: UIViewController
<UIImagePickerControllerDelegate>
```

In Swift, you simply add the protocol's name after the parent class, separated by a comma:

```
class LocationViewController : UIViewController, UIImagePickerControllerDelegate {
        ...
}
```

You can do this for an infinite number of protocols by appending the protocol names, separated by commas:

```
class LocationViewController : UIViewController, UIImagePickerControllerDelegate,
UITextFieldDelegate {
        ...
}
```

Method Signatures

Before defining a method in Swift, let's investigate a method signature in Objective-C:

```
-(BOOL)compareValue1:(NSInteger)value1 toValue2:(NSInteger)value2;
```

In this line of code, you can see that the return type comes before the method name and that each of the parameters is provided after a colon. You add labels to every parameter after the first one, to increase readability.

In Swift, you declare a method by placing the func keyword in front of the method name and then including the input parameters and output parameters in parentheses:

```
func compareValues(value1: Int, value2: Int) -> (result: Bool)
```

Swift uses -> to separate the input parameters and return parameters.

As with variables in Swift, you indicate the type of each parameter by appending the type name with a colon.

If your method does not return anything, you can omit the return parameters and ->:

```
func isValidName(name: String) {
}
```

Since tuples are everywhere in Swift, you can also return a tuple from a method:

```
func compareValues(value1: Int, value2: Int) -> (result: Bool, average: Int) {
}
```

Accessing Properties and Methods

The concept of accessing a method or property on an object is referred to as message-passing. In Objective-C, the primary way of passing messages was through Smalltalk syntax:

```
[receiver message];
```

where receiver represents the object that is being acted upon, and message represents the property or method you are trying to access.

In Swift, you can access a property or method of an object by using dot-syntax, as you would in C or Java. This includes classes that were defined in Objective-C.

```
receiver.message()
```

In Objective-C, you always have to use Smalltalk syntax to access a method. To call the `reloadSubviews` method on a `UIView` object in Objective-C, you would make a call like the following:

```
[myView reloadSubviews];
```

In Swift, the same line of code would look like this:

```
myView.reloadSubviews()
```

If you were passing multiple parameters to a method in Objective-C, you would append the labels and values:

```
[myNumberManager calculateSumOfValueA:-1 andValueB:2];
```

In Swift, simply include the extra parameters in the parentheses:

```
myNumberManager.calculateSum(-1, valueB:2)
```

In Objective-C you had two ways of reading the value of a property. Through Smalltalk syntax:

```
CGSize viewSize = [myView size];
```

or through dot-syntax:

```
CGSize viewSize = myView.size;
```

In Swift, you always use dot-syntax to access properties.

```
var viewSize: CGSize = myView.size
```

To set a value for a property in Objective-C, you could use dot-syntax to set the value of a property:

```
myView.size = CGSizeMake(0,0, viewWidth, viewHeight);
```

But, you could also use an autogenerated setter method:

```
[myView setSize:CGSizeMake(0,0, viewWidth, viewHeight)];
```

In Swift, you always use dot syntax to set the value of a property:

```
myView.size = CGSizeMake(0,0, viewWidth, viewHeight)
```

Instantiating Objects

In Objective-C, you would instantiate an object by allocating it in memory and then calling its constructor method:

```
NSMutableArray *fileArray = [[NSMutableArray alloc] init];
```

Some classes have constructors that allow you to pass in parameters.

```
NSMutableArray *fileArray = [[NSMutableArray alloc] initWithArray:otherArray];
```

Some classes also have convenience constructors, which serve as shortcuts for the process of allocating and initializing an object.

```
NSMutableArray *fileArray = [NSMutableArray arrayWithArray:otherArray];
```

Things are a bit easier in Swift. Swift automatically allocates memory, removing the `alloc` step. Additionally, the default constructor for a class in Swift is the class name with an empty set of parentheses appended to the end:

```
var fileArray = Array()
```

If the class you are initializing takes parameters in its constructor, call the constructor as you would any other method:

```
var myView = UIView(frame: myFrame)
```

If you are instantiating an object from an Objective-C class, you need to call its constructor as a method:

```
var mutableArray = NSMutableArray()
```

> **Note** Swift has its own classes to represent Strings, Arrays, Dictionaries, and Sets, but you are free to use the Objective-C classes to maintain compatibility with older APIs or libraries.

Strings

In Objective-C, to represent a string, you would use the NSString class. To initialize a string, you could use a constructor method:

```
NSString *myString = [[NSString alloc] initWithString: @"Hello World"];
```

You could also use the @ symbol to load the value directly, using Objective-C's *literal* syntax:

```
NSString *myString = @"Hello World";
```

In Swift, the class for representing strings is String. You load values directly:

```
Let myString = "Hello"
```

In Objective-C, NSString objects are immutable, meaning you cannot append or remove characters at runtime, unless you assigned a new value to the string. To resolve this issue, you could use the NSMutableString class in Objective-C, which allows you to mutate its objects at runtime:

```
NSMutableString *myString = [NSMutableString stringWIthString@"Hello"];
[myString appendString:@" world"]; //result is "Hello world"
```

In Swift, String objects defined with var are mutable. You can append values using the append function:

```
var myString = "Hello"
myString.append(" world") //result is "Hello world"
```

> **Note** You can continue to use the NSString and NSMutableString classes in Swift, but it is only recommended for interfacing with Objective-C classes.

Formatting Strings

In Objective-C, when you wanted to insert a value from an object into a string, you had to use a string formatter to build a custom string:

```
NSString *summaryString = [NSString
    stringWithFormat:@"int value 1: %d,  float value 2: %f, string value 3: %@", -1, 2.015,
@"Hello"];
```

For each value you wanted to insert into the string, you needed to use a combination of characters, referred to as a format specifier, to substitute the variable you wanted to insert into the string. Format specifiersgenerally consist of the % character and a letter indicating the value type (e.g., @ for string, d for integer value, and f for float value).

Swift makes it easier for you to insert a value into a string by placing the variable's name in parentheses, prepended by a forward slash:

```
let value1 = -1
let value2 = 2.015
let value3 = "Hello"
var summaryString = "int value 1: \(value1), float value 2: \(value2), string value 3: \
(value3)"
```

In Objective-C, to limit the number of decimal places that appeared in a float value, you would add a period and the number of spaces in front of the format specifier for the float:

```
NSString *summaryString = [NSString
    stringWithFormat:@"float value: %0.2f", 2.015];
```

To replicate this in Swift, use the String constructor method which specifies format as its input.

```
var summaryString = String(format:  "float value: %0.2f", 2.015)
```

The syntax is the same as that for Objective-C, where you pass in the format string and then a comma-separated list of values to replace the format specifiers.

Collections

In both Objective-C and Swift, the following are three classes referred to as collections, which "collect" similar objects together into one object:

Arrays: An ordered collection of objects. These preserve the order you use to load items. You retrieve items by indicating their position in the collection.

Set: An unordered collection of objects. These are used to test "membership" of objects–for instance, if an object exists in a set. You retrieve objects by specifying a subset.

Dictionary: An unordered collection of objects, which is identified by "keys." These are also called key-value pairs. You retrieve objects by specifying their keys.

In Objective-C, you used the `NSArray` class to represent arrays. Arrays in Objective-C contain objects only, and can be initialized with several convenience constructor methods, including `[NSArray arrayWithObjects:]`.

```
NSArray *stringArray = [NSArray arrayWithObjects:@"string 1",
    @"string 2", @"string 3"]
```

In Swift, you can declare an array by providing its values in square brackets when you define the variable.

```
var stringArray = ["string 1", "string 2", "string 3"]
```

Swift does not place the same restriction on the contents of an array, so you can initialize it with scalar values (such as Ints).

```
var intArray = [1, 3, 5]
```

If you do not want to initialize your array with values, declare a variable type for the input by placing the type name in square brackets:

```
var intArray : [Int]
```

You can also use subscript notation to read or change values in a Swift array.

```
var sampleString = stringArray[3]
```

In Objective-C, NSArray objects are immutable. To make an array mutable, you defined it using the NSMutableArray class:

```
NSMutableArray *stringArray = [NSMutableArray arrayWithObjects:@"string 1",
  @"string 2", @"string 3"]
```

Remember, by defining your array with the var keyword, you make it a mutable variable, allowing you to "mutate" existing values or add new ones at runtime. For instance, you can use the plus (+) operator to append values to the array.

```
stringArray += "string4"
```

You can also change a value by specifying a value at an index

```
stringArray[2] = "This is now the coolest string".
```

In Objective-C, you create a set by initializing it with a comma-separated list of objects:

```
NSSet *mySet = [NSSet setWithObjects: @"string 1", @"string 2", @"string 3"];
```

You could also create a set with an array.

```
NSSet *mySet = [NSSet setWithArray: stringArray];
```

To membership, you use the containsObject method:

```
if ([mySet containsObject:"string 1"]) {
        print("success!")
}
```

In Swift, you create a set by using the Set class and specifying the type of its members:

```
var stringSet: Set<String>
```

You can initialize a set with an array:

```
var stringSet: Set<String> = ["string 1", "string 2", "string 3"]
```

Similarly, you can mutate the set if it is defined as a mutable variable (with the `var` keyword).

```
StringSet += "hello world"
```

To create a dictionary in Objective-C, you pass in arrays of keys and values. The two are matched according to the order you pass them in.

```
NSDictionary *myDict = [NSDictionary dictionaryWithObjects:@"string 1", @"string 2",
@"string 3", nil forKeys:@"key1", @"key2", @"key3"];
```

You could also use literal shortcut to initialize a dictionary in Objective-C.

```
NSDictionary *myDict = @{@"key1" : @"string 1", @"key2" : @"string 2", @"key3" : @"string 3" };
```

To access a value from a dictionary in Objective-C, you specified its key.

```
NSString *string = [myDict objectForKey:@"key1"];
```

In Swift, you define a dictionary by specifying the types of its keys and values.

```
var myDict = [String, String]()
```

The empty brackets specify that you are creating an empty dictionary.

To initialize a dictionary with key-value pairs, pass them in using literal syntax. For Swift dictionaries, this is a comma-separated list of key-value pairs (connected with colons).

```
var myDict  : [String, String] = ["key1" : "string 1", "key2": "string 2", "key3" : "string 3"]
```

To retrieve an object from a dictionary, use the following key:

```
let myString = myDict["key1"]
```

If the dictionary is a mutable variable, you can mutate values or append new key-value pairs at runtime.

```
myDict["key3"] = "this is the coolest string"
```

Casting

In Objective-C, to cast an object from one class to another, you would prepend the class name and optionally an asterisk, identifying your pointer.

```
UINavigationController *navigatonController = (UINavigationController *)segue.
destinationController;
```

In Swift, casting is as easy as using the as keyword.

```
let navigationController = segue.destinationController as UINavigatonController
```

Simply add the as keyword and the class name to the result, and the compiler will do the rest for you. You can even insert this keyword inline, wherever you would normally use your object:

```
for (file as String in fileArray) {}
```

Swift-Specific Language Features

In this section, I will review that which my clients found particularly difficult when adopting Swift—particularly, optionals and try-catch blocks. These do not translate directly to language features in Objective-C and need extra care to use correctly.

Optionals

In Objective-C, the nil keyword is used to represent an object that is null. Null is the "initial" state of values, before they are initialized or after they have been "reset." For an object, a pointer points to an empty area in memory. For scalar variables, it is the value 0. The idea is, an object that has been initialized correctly will have a non-null value; a non-null value is considered "valid." It is also common for methods to return nil values in error conditions.

In Objective-C, a common way to check if an object is valid is by checking for nil. For instance, to check if a value exists for a key in a dictionary

```
if ( myDict["coolestKey"} != nil) {
        //success
}
```

If the value for that key does not exist in the dictionary, it will return nil.

In Objective-C, this applies for properties of a class as well. If a property has not been initialized, attempting to retrieve it will return nil.

```
if (myLocationManager.locationString != nil) {
        //success
}
```

In Objective-C, if you try to perform an operation on a nil pointer, you will crash your application.

Swift attempts to resolve this issue through the concept of optionals. An optional is a type that can represent a nil, or an uninitialized value. To define a variable as an optional, append the ? operator to the type name:

```
var myString : String?
```

You will commonly see this syntax in class properties. In Swift, all properties need to be valid when they are initialized. There are three ways to resolve this issue.

1. Specify a value for the property when declaring it.

```
class LocationManager: NSObject {
        var locationString : String = "Empty string"
}
```

2. Create a constructor which initializes the property.

```
class LocationManager: NSObject {
        var locationString : String

        init(locationString: String) {
                self.locationString = locationString
        }

}
```

3. Define the property as an optional.

```
class LocationManager: NSObject {
        var locationString  : String?
}
```

When trying to access the property, check if it is nil before trying to use it.

```
if myLocationManager.locationString != nil {
        //success
}
```

If the property you are trying to access has properties you want to access (for instance, a `UIView` object), you need to "unwrap" your class's property before using it. This operation is referred to as "optional-chaining." The general idea is, tell the compiler that your property is an optional and then try to check if the derived property is non-nil; if it is, create a variable to contain the property. In the case of checking if a subview exists on a `UIViewController`:

```
if  let mapViewSize = self.mapView?.size {
        //success
        print("size = \(mapViewSize)")
}
```

The ? operator lets the compiler know that the property is an optional. If the optional returns nil, it will not attempt to access the derived property and will not execute the success block.

If you have confirmed that an optional property is non-nil, you can access its derived properties by force-unwrapping it. Force-unwrapping is indicated by the ! operator.

```
if (self.mapView != nil) {

        let mapViewSize = self.mapView!.size
        print("size = \(mapViewSize)")
}
```

If you do not check that the property is non-nil before force-unwrapping, your application will crash.

Try-Catch Blocks

The major difficulty of error passing in Swift is that it does not directly translate over from Objective-C. In Objective-C, you would catch an error by passing an `NSError` object by reference. This object would be mutated by the method you called; an error would be represented by a non-nil value.

In Swift, methods throw errors using exceptions. You can catch these using a try-catch block.

In Objective-C, to return an error, you define a method that takes a pointer to an `NSError` object.

```
-(void)translateString:(NSString *)inputString error:(NSError **)error {
}
```

To modify the object, "dereference" it using the * operator. This allows you to perform operations on the object that is represented by the pointer.

```
-(void)translateString:(NSString *)inputString error:(NSError **)error {

        *error = [NSError errorWithDomain:NSCocoaErrorDomain code:400
userInfo:userInfoDict];
}
```

In this example, we create a new `NSError` object using a domain (an `enum` representing the general "kind" of error), an error code represented by an integer value, and a dictionary containing any other information we want to pass back about the error.

To call the method from Objective-C, create an error object and pass a "reference" to it using the & operator.

```
-(void)myMethod {
        NSError *error;
        [self translateString:@"hello" error:&error];
}
```

To define a method that returns an error in Swift, add the "throws" keyword after the parameter list, and before the return values list:

```
func translateString(inputString: String) throws -> Void {

}
```

Swift defines a protocol called ErrorType, which allows you to create exceptions that translate to NSError properties when called from Objective-C. To define your error, create an enum that uses this protocol. Specify any codes and domains for your error types.

```
enum TranslationError : Int, ErrorType {
        case EmptyString = -100
        case UnrecognizedLanguage = 1000
        case InvalidString = 1001
}
```

To throw an exception, use the throw keyword, specifying the enum and error type.

```
func translateString(inputString: String) throws -> Void {
        if (inputString  == nil) {
                throw TranslationError.EmptyString
        }
}
```

To catch an error, use a try-catch block. Place the error-prone code in a do block; prepared the try keyword to the line that is going to throw the exception. Catch the exception in the catch block.

```
do {
        let myString : String = nil
        try translateString(myString)
} catch TranslationError.InvalidString  {
        print("this is an invalid string")
}
```

If you want to try to catch multiple exceptions of the same type, add additional catch blocks.

```
do {
        let myString : String = nil
        try translateString(myString)
} catch TranslationError.InvalidString  {
        print("this is an invalid string")
} catch TranslationError.EmptyString  {
        print("this is an empty string")
}
```

> **Note** You need a try-catch block for each method you try to call that returns an exception. Methods should only return one type of exception.

Mixing Objective-C and Swift in Projects

Swift lets you import classes written in Objective-C and call Objective-C methods. This import capability is extremely valuable, because you can import any of the existing Cocoa Touch APIs or your existing Objective-C code.

If your project is going to be primarily in Swift, make sure that you specify Swift as the primary language when creating it from `Xcode > New > Project`, as shown in Figure 2-1.

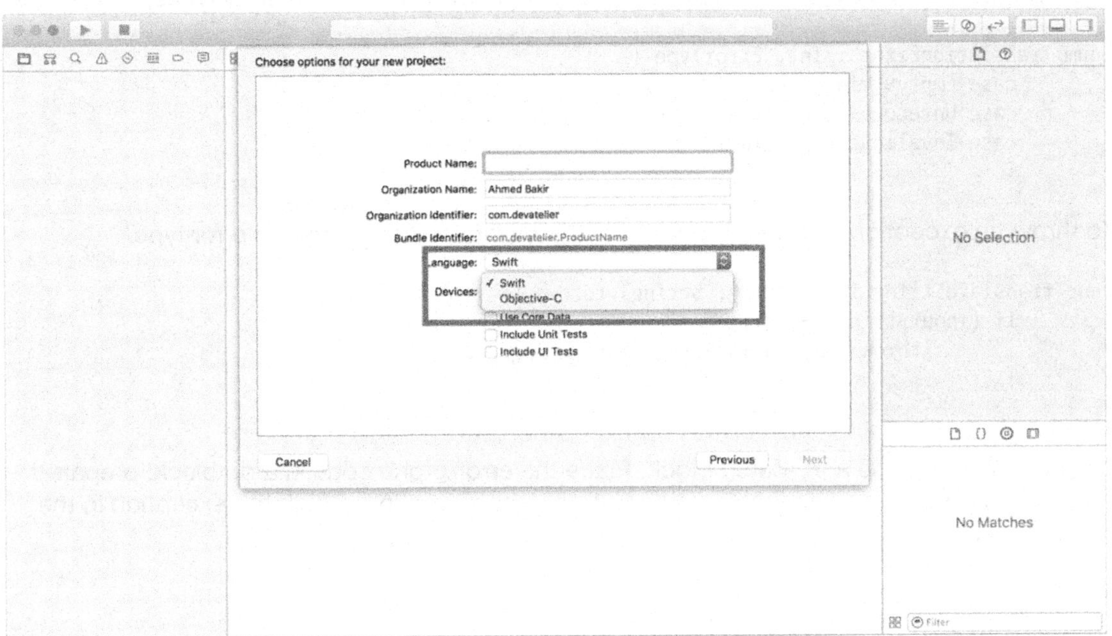

Figure 2-1. Creating a Swift project

To add an Objective-C class to your Swift project, follow the same process you would use for an Objective-C project: drag and drop the files onto the Project Navigator, or select Add Files to `<Project Name>` from the File menu, as shown in Figure 2-2.

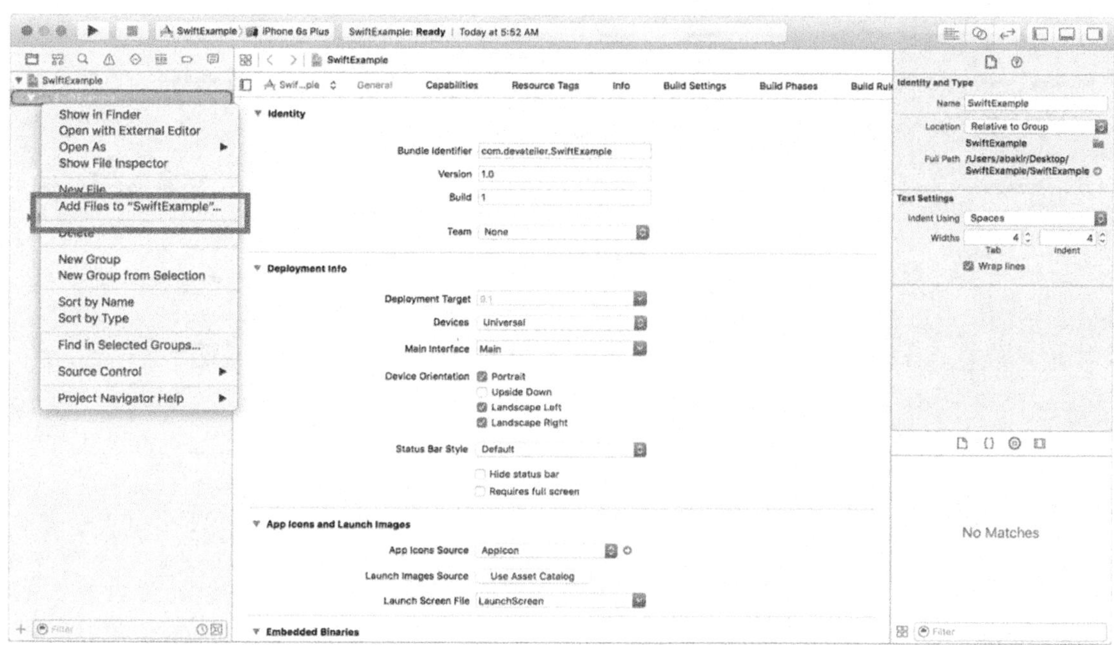

***Figure 2-2.** Importing files into your project*

To access an Objective-C class from a Swift file, simply create an object using the type and constructor specified by the class, and call methods via dot-syntax.

```
var myObjcString : NSMutableString = NSMutableString(string: "Hello")
myObjcString.appendString(" world")
```

The compiler takes care of converting constructors and other methods to Swift-style syntax for you, take advantage of autocompletion to help you, as shown in Figure 2-3.

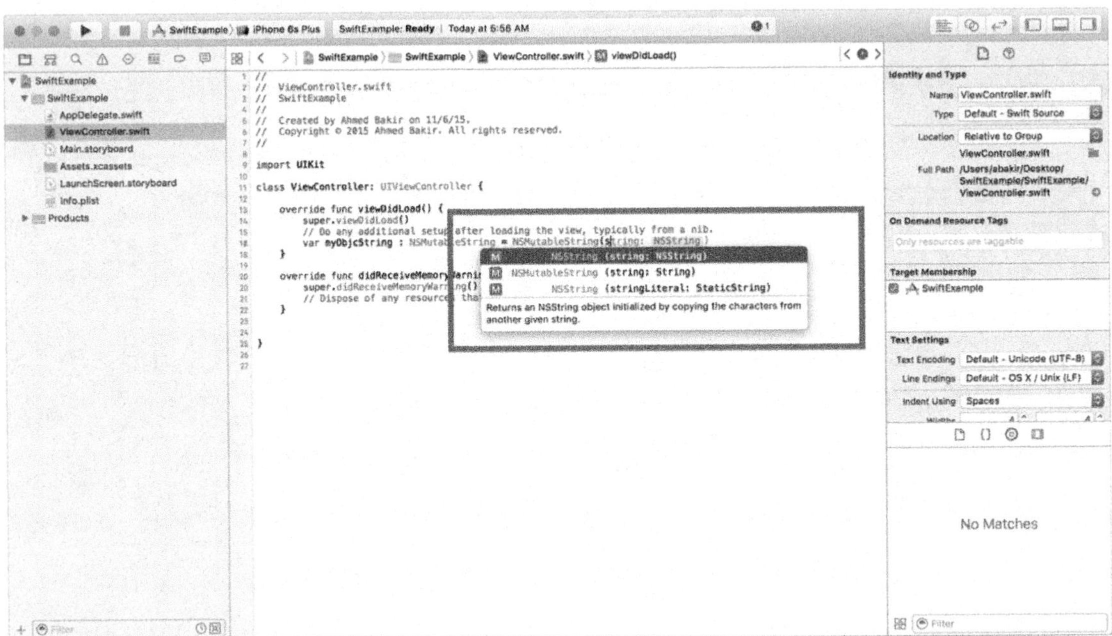

***Figure 2-3.** Autocompletion results for NSMutableString*

Calling Swift from Objective-C

You can also call Swift classes and methods from Objective-C, as long as you are aware of a few rules.

- If you are subclassing a Foundation class (e.g., `NSString`) or a Cocoa Touch class (e.g., `UIViewController`), it will be available when importing your Swift file into an Objective-C class.
- Within a Swift-compatible class, if a method uses a language feature not available in Objective-C, such as an optional or tuple, it will not be available to Objective-C. Attempt to resolve these issues by writing methods that can translate directly to Objective-C.
- Objective-C mutates `NSError` objects for passing back errors, while Swift 2.0 uses exceptions. To make a method that is compatible between the two languages, remember take advantage of the `ErrorType` protocol, as described in the section "Try-Catch Block."
- You can make an `enum` available to Objective-C by prepending the `@objc` keyword. Similarly, make sure the types in your `enum` are compatible with Objective-C (increasing, discrete values like integers or characters)

```
@Objc enum PlaybackStates : Int {
        case Failed = -1,
        case Loading,
        case Success
}
```

> **Note** The @objc keyword is used globally throughout Swift as a way of explicitly defining a type, method, or class as Objective-C compatible.

Summary

In this chapter, I introduced Swift by comparing how Objective-C and Swift implement basic syntax and object-oriented programming concepts. You noticed that while Swift brings significant syntax changes to iOS development, its methods are designed to work like Objective-C. For the most part, by using Swift method syntax, you can call any Objective-C Cocoa Touch method from Swift. In instances where this is not possible, there are ways to use protocols like `ErrorType` to produce output that is compatible with Objective-C. To make the chapter particularly useful, I paid special attention to optionals and try-catch blocks, two language features that are not implemented in Objective-C.

Chapter 3

Accessing Health Information Using HealthKit

Ahmed Bakir

Introduction

For the last few years, Apple has provided two core frameworks that have sped up the time to develop iOS health apps considerably: HealthKit and Core Motion. HealthKit provides a central repository for all apps to sync health data and Core Motion provides access to the iPhone's accelerometer and pedometer, allowing you to retrieve limited health information about a user without external accessories.

HealthKit was a baffling surprise to everyone when it was announced; no one could figure out why Apple would "compete" with its partners by building a framework to do the same thing they had all been doing for years, tracking information. As time progressed, HealthKit's role became very clear—it eliminated the need for a different app for every health accessory on the market and every discrete kind of data. Before HealthKit, there was no way for your heart rate monitor to share data with your running app, unless the two companies had collaborated. After HealthKit, any accessory maker or developer could opt into the service, allowing users to have a clearer snapshot of their overall health. Since HealthKit is a public application programming interface (API); anyone (including you) is able to build apps that can publish information to it or retrieve information from it. Keeping in line with Apple's philosophy that a user's sensitive data should stay on his or her device, HealthKit is not synced with any cloud services and requires its own set of permissions to access it.

In a similar manner, Apple started baking a hardware chip into all iPhones and iPod Touches, starting with the iPhone 5S, called the Motion Co-Processor. This chip builds a pedometer, accelerator, gyroscope, and other sensors into the devices with advantages in power and accuracy that were not available via the old methods of calculating a user's distance traveled via GPS. Core Motion provides a useful subset of health information that could help you build a health application without any external logging accessories.

In this chapter, you will start building the RunTracker app, pictured in Figure 3-1, which lists a user's previous workouts and allows the user to log new ones. This chapter will focus on setting up the project's user interface and HealthKit permissions. In Chapter 4, you will learn how to use CoreMotion to convert live data to HealthKit objects.

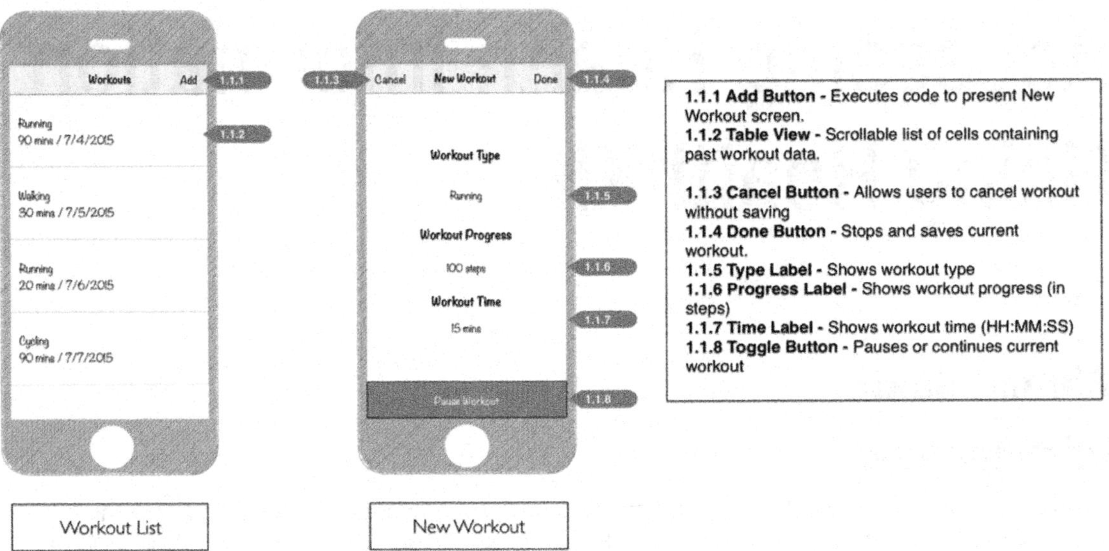

***Figure 3-1.** Wireframe for the RunTracker app*

Users enter the app at a table view, which lists running and walking workouts that have been saved to HealthKit by all apps, including your own. After pressing the Add button, users are taken to a detail screen, which allows them to log a new workout. The detail screen consists of a Start button, which toggles tracking, and a set of labels which show live data from Core Motion, including the user's distance traveled, workout length, and current activity type.

In building the RunTracker app, you will learn about the following concepts in HealthKit and Core Motion:

- How HealthKit and Core Motion protect data and hardware with permissions
- How HealthKit represents data, including units
- How to retrieve information from HealthKit
- How to receive real-time activity updates from HealthKit

As with the other projects in this book, the source code for the RunTracker project is available in the Source Code/Download tab on the book's page at `www.apress.com`.

Getting Started

Before getting too far into the implementation details of HealthKit, you need to set up the project. In this section, I will walk you through the process of setting up the user interface and the extra steps you need to take to allow your application to use HealthKit.

> **Note** As HealthKit is only available on iPhones, the user interface for this project is designed for iPhone layouts.

Setting Up the User Interface

The RunTracker application consists of two primary view controllers: the activity table, which lists all workouts the user has logged on his device, and the create screen, which allows the user to log a new workout.

As has been the case for the other applications you have built so far, start by navigating to the File menu and selecting New ➤ Project. In the template picker that appears, select the Single View Application template, as shown in Figure 3-2.

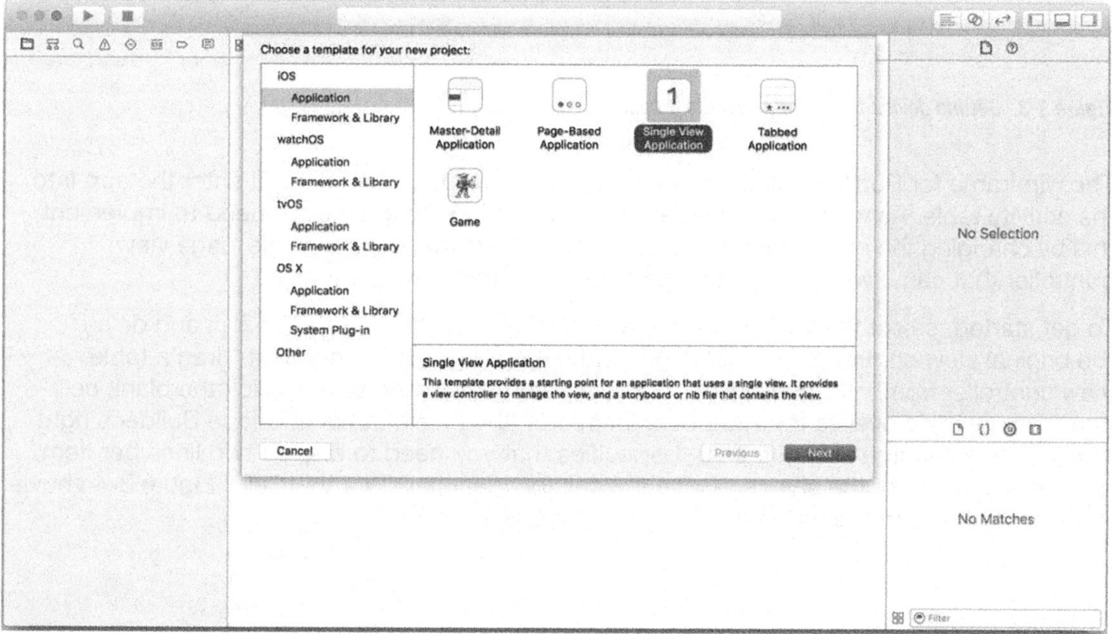

***Figure 3-2.** Creating a single-view application*

When asked to select a device target, change the setting from Universal to iPhone, as shown in Figure 3-3.

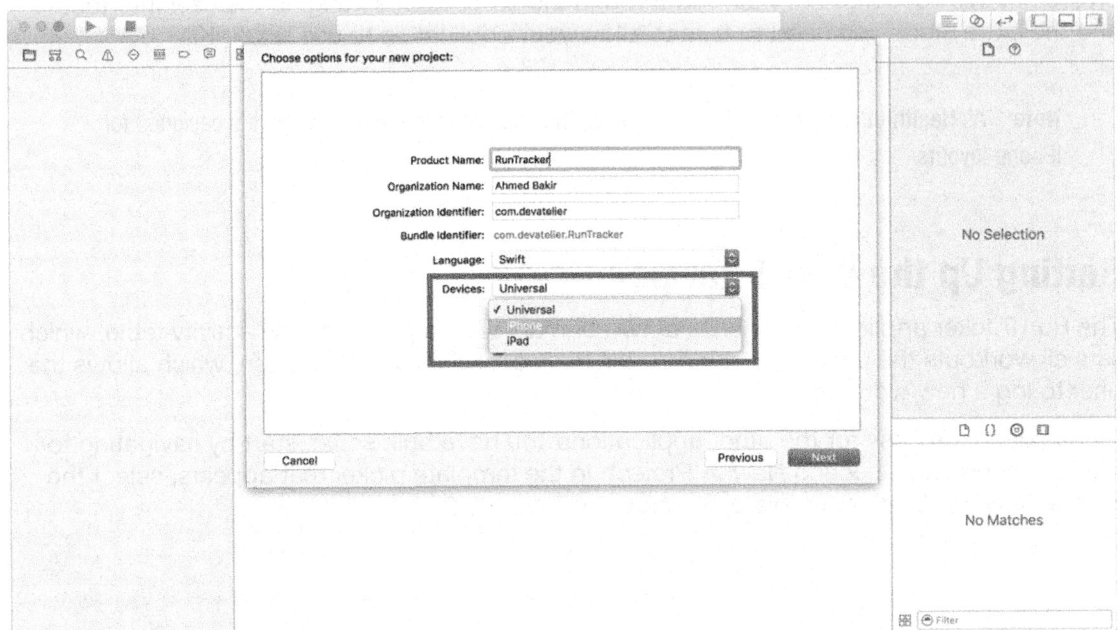

Figure 3-3. Setting device target for project to iPhone

The wireframe for RunTracker, from Figure 3-1 indicates that the user will enter the app into the activity table. As with the CarFinder application from Chapter 1, we need to implement this by changing the entry point of the application from the original single-page view controller that came with the project template to a table view controller.

To get started, select the Main storyboard for your project (`Main.storyboard`) and delete the original view controller by selecting it and hitting the `Delete` key. Next, drag a table view controller from Interface Builder's object library onto storyboard. Click the blank cell and then navigate over to the Attributes Inspector (the fourth tab in Interface Builder's right panel). The wireframe from Figure 3-1 specifies that you need to display two lines per item, so select Subtitle for the style and give the cell the identifier "WorkoutCell." Figure 3-4 shows the storyboard, with the cell identifier settings highlighted.

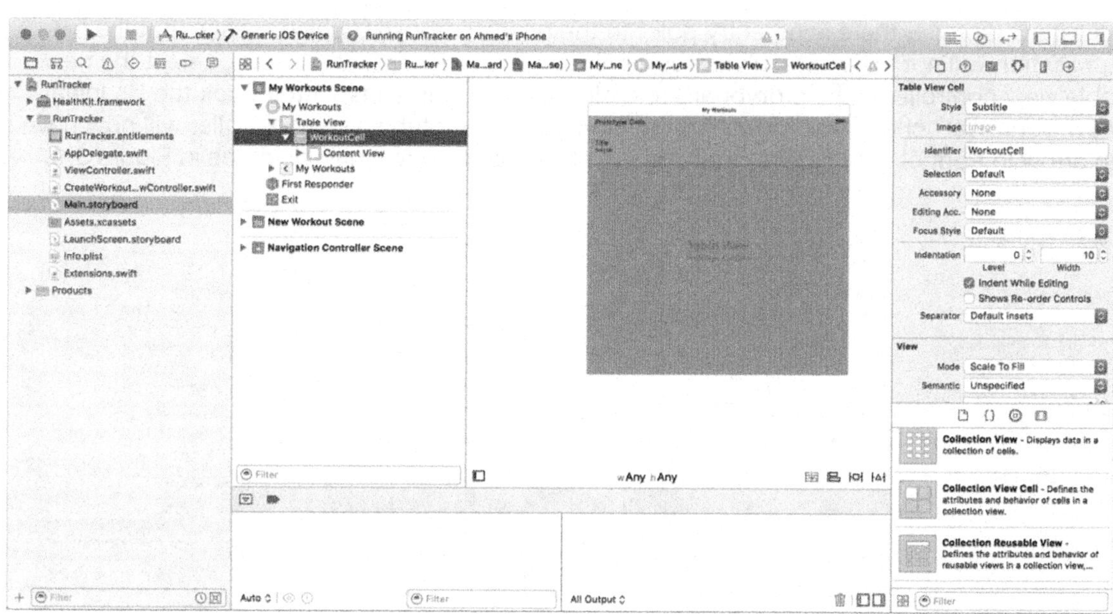

Figure 3-4. Storyboard with table view

To change the name of the view controller, double-click the area in the middle of the navigation bar. As shown in Figure 3-5, an editable text area will appear, in which you can type in a name for the workout table.

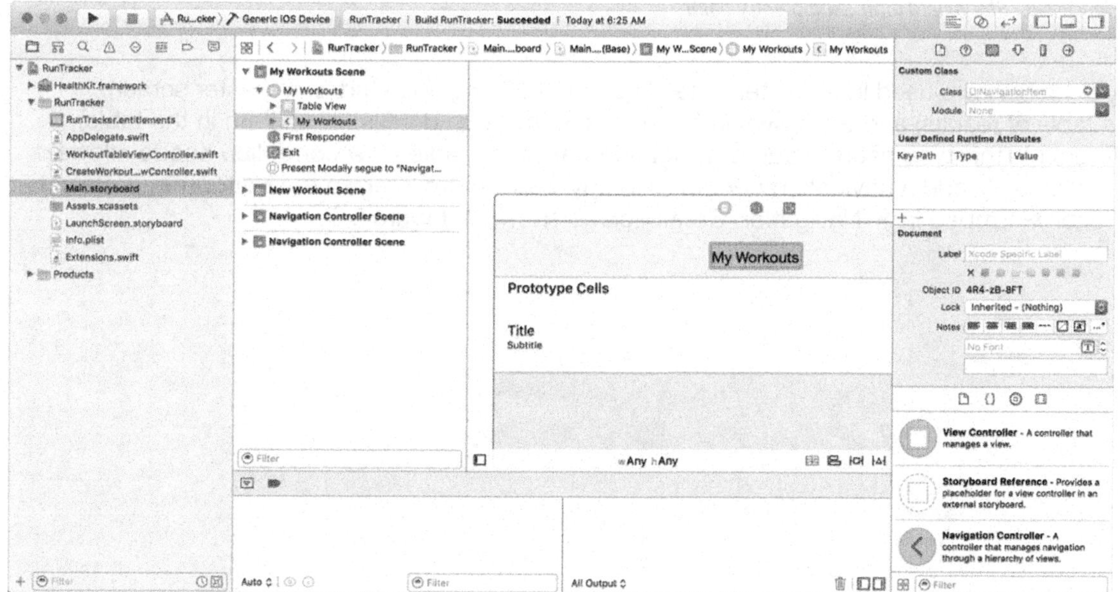

Figure 3-5. Editing a navigation item's title

As with Chapter 1, there is no entry point to the new storyboard, which means that the application will not know which view controller to load first. To fix this issue, select the new table view controller in the storyboard and click the Attributes Inspector. Click the "Is Initial View Controller" check box to the right in Figure 3-6. Your table view controller will now have an arrow in front of it, indicating that it is the storyboard's new entry point, as in Figure 3-6.

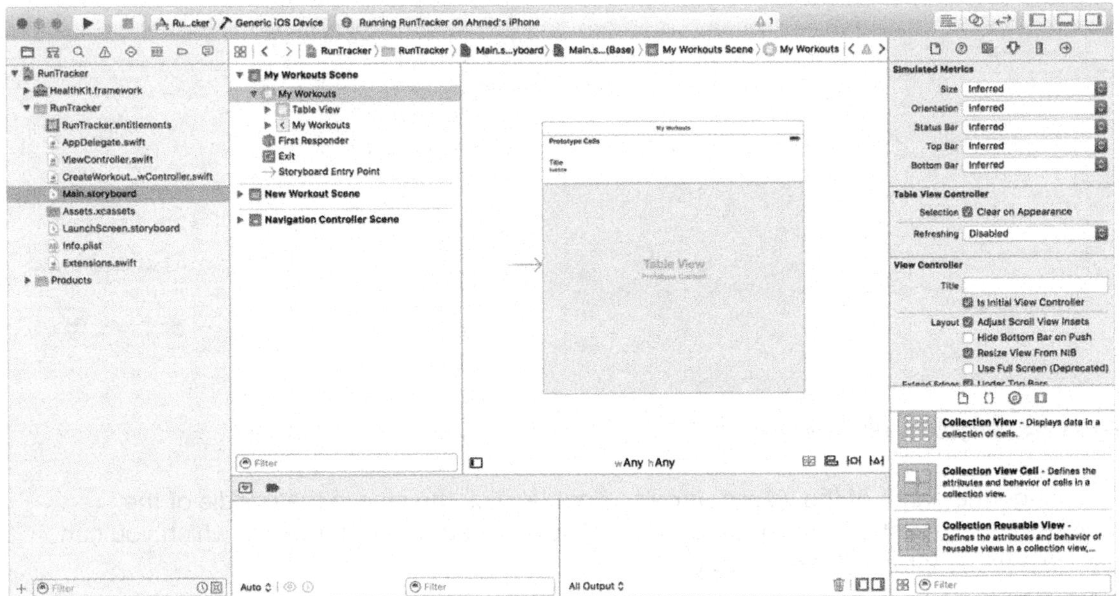

Figure 3-6. Storyboard after setting entry point

Most tables are used in a master-detail fashion, meaning you start at a master screen (a table of results) and drill down into detail screens (e.g., details for an item in the table). To enable this, you need to add a navigation bar to the table view controller. Xcode allows you to easily add a navigation controller to any view controller from the Editor menu. Select Editor ➤ Embed In ➤ Navigation Controller, as shown in Figure 3-7.

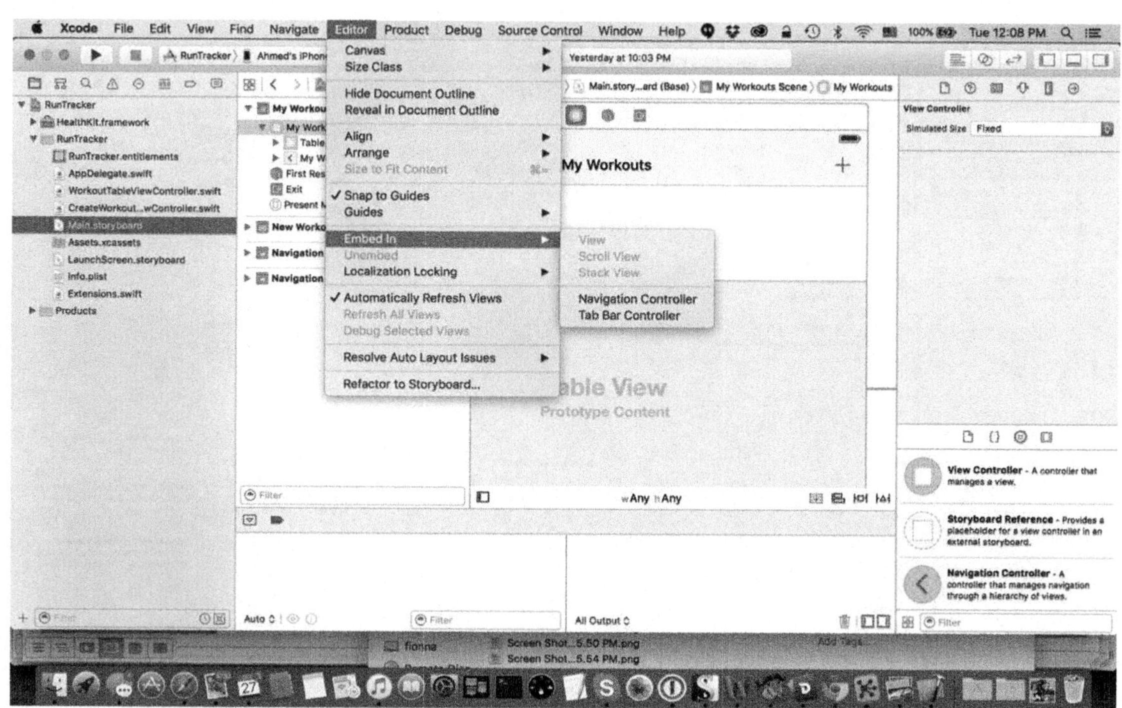

Figure 3-7. Xcode menu path to embed a selection in a navigation controller

After applying the change, you will notice that your table view controller is linked to a navigation controller, as shown in Figure 3-8. You will also notice that entry point has shifted to the navigation controller. The "Embed In" feature is particularly convenient because it preserves your existing hierarchy of segues (connections between storyboard items).

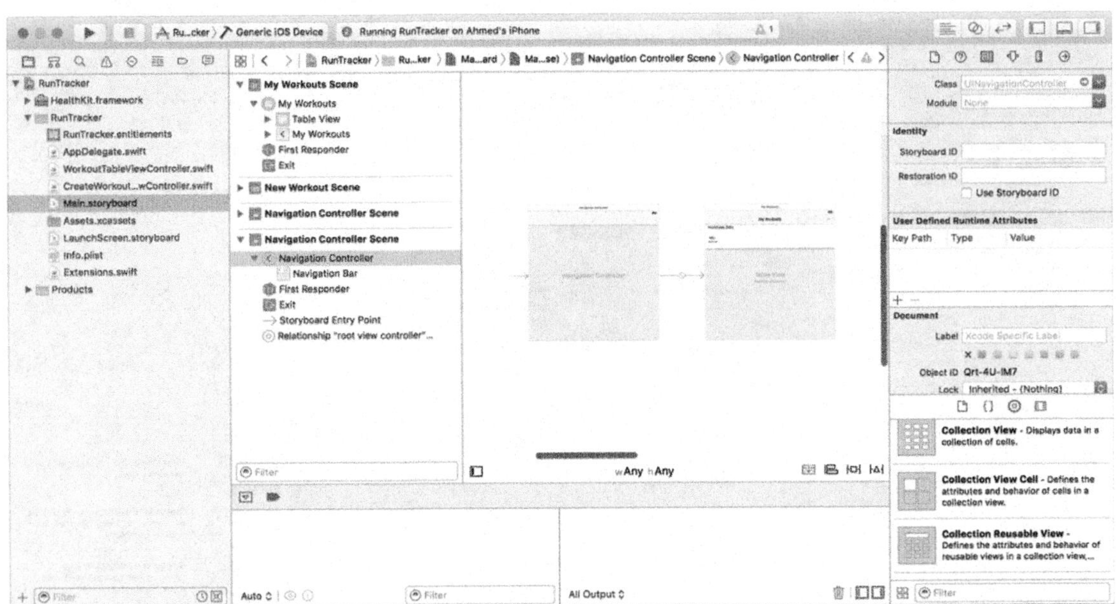

***Figure 3-8.** Storyboard after embedding a selection in a navigation controller*

To connect the new table view controller to your custom functionality, you need to create a class for it. In the File menu, select New ➤ File. When prompted for a file type, choose Cocoa Touch class and create a subclass of `UITableViewController` named `WorkoutTableViewController`, as shown in Figure 3-9.

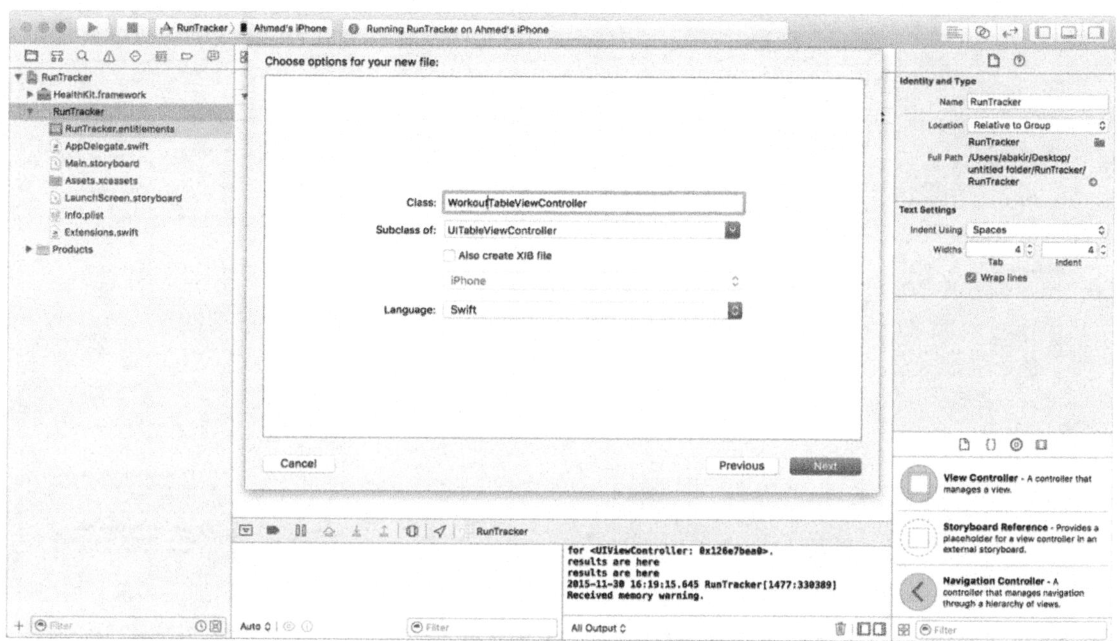

***Figure 3-9.** Adding a UITableViewController subclass to the project*

Connect the new class to your storyboard by selecting the table view controller and selecting the Identity Inspector (third tab of the right pane). As shown in Figure 3-10, change the name to WorkoutTableViewController. You can verify that the operation was successful by making sure the "Module" field displays "Current - RunTracker," indicating the namespace for the RunTracker project.

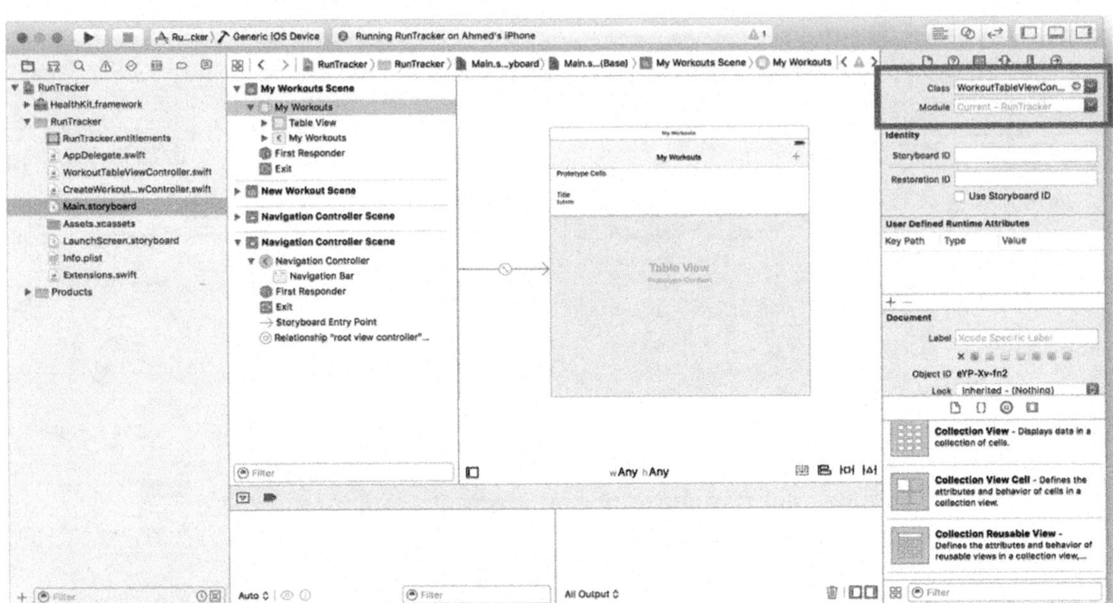

Figure 3-10. *Changing a view controller's parent class and verifying its module*

To allow users to log new workouts, you need to add the "view screen" to your storyboard. This view controller allows the user to start or stop his or her workout, view his current progress, and return to the workout table, either by saving or by canceling his current workout. Following the same processes you used to add a table view to the storyboard, drag a view controller onto the storyboard, create a new file that is a subclass of `UIViewController` called `CreateWorkoutViewController`, and link the two together using the Identity Inspector.

The user interface for the create screen consists of labels to indicate workout type, progress, and time; a large button at the bottom of the screen to start or pause the workout; and a navigation bar with Done and Cancel buttons, to allow the user to exit and return to the workout table. I have included the definition for the `CreateWorkoutViewController` class in Listing 3-1, including the properties for the labels and buttons and stubbed functions for the button event handlers.

Listing 3-1. *Class Definition for CreateWorkoutViewController*

```
import UIKit
import HealthKit
import CoreMotion

class CreateWorkoutViewController: UIViewController {

    @IBOutlet weak var typeLabel: UILabel!
    @IBOutlet weak var progressLabel: UILabel!
    @IBOutlet weak var timeLabel: UILabel!

    @IBOutlet weak var toggleButton: UIButton!
}
```

To start implementing the user interface, drag several labels onto the view controller, as shown in Figure 3-11.

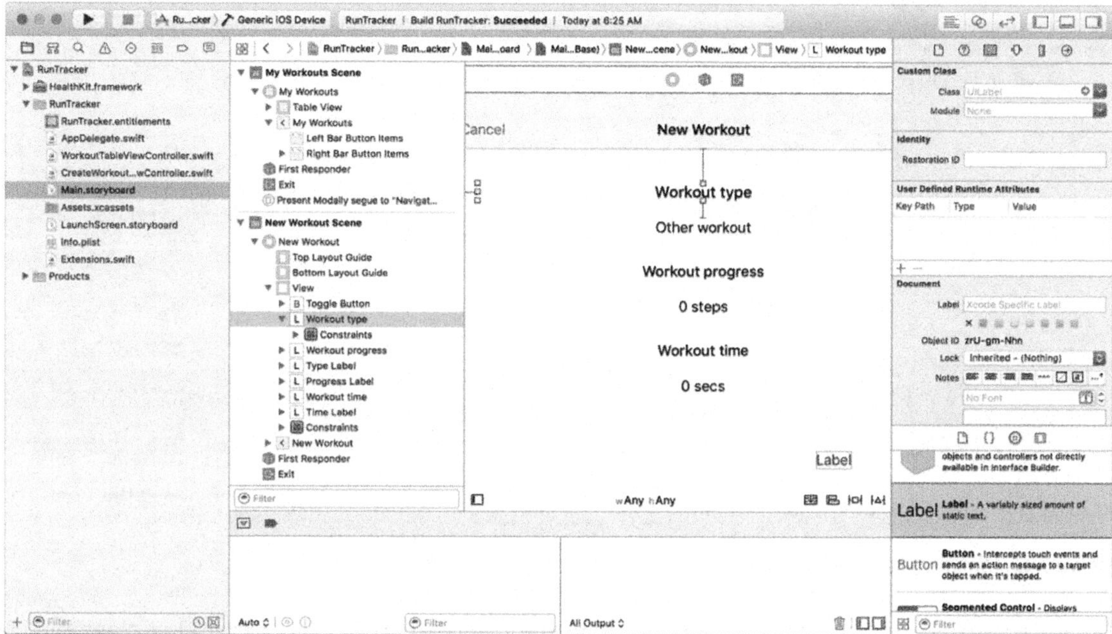

***Figure 3-11.** Adding labels to View Controller*

Change the text weight of the static text labels (for example, Workout Type) to bold by selecting a label and navigating over to the Attributes Inspector. Use the Font drop-down, as shown in Figure 3-12 to change the font family or weight.

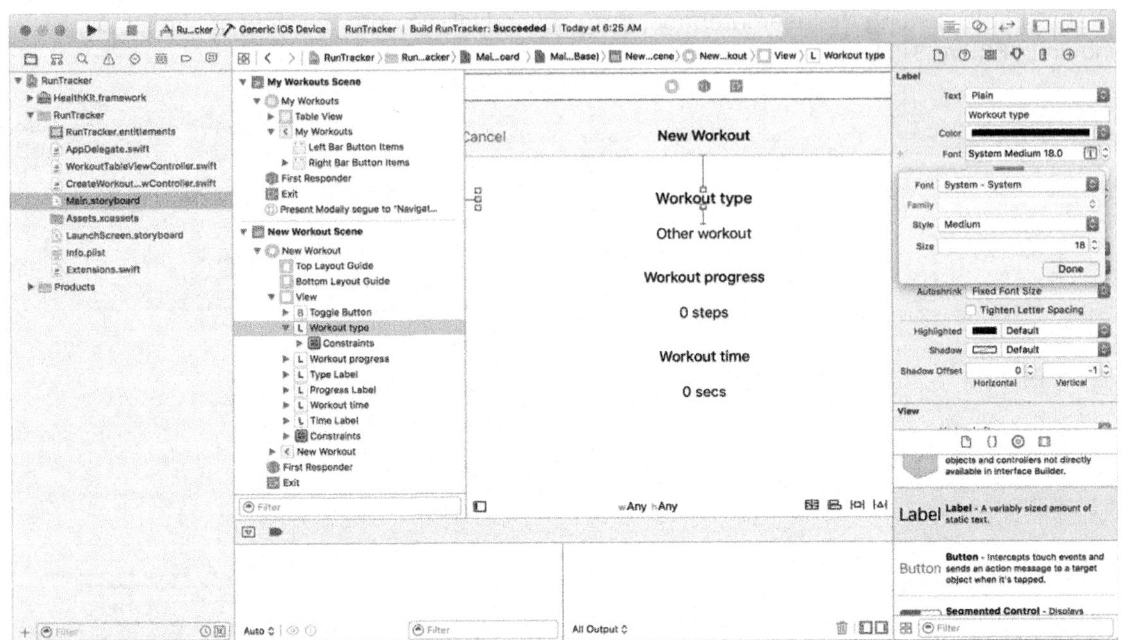

***Figure 3-12.** Changing label attributes*

For the status labels, remember to link them to the `CreateWorkoutViewController` class by selecting them, navigating over to the Connections Inspector (the last tab in the right pane), and dragging a line from the New Referencing Outlet radio box to the view controller. As shown in Figure 3-13, a pop-up will appear indicating the property name.

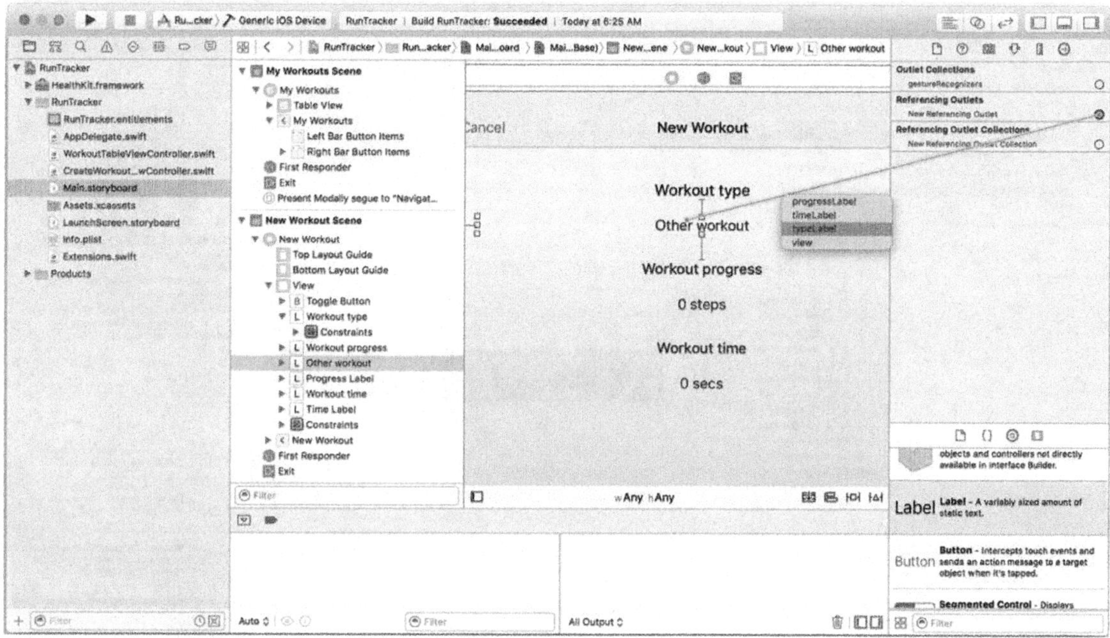

***Figure 3-13.** Connecting labels to their referencing outlets*

Drag a button onto the view controller to represent the Toggle Workout button. To create the "big blue button" appearance of the button, resize its edges to touch the sides of the screen and change the text color to white by selecting the Text Color drop-down in the Attributes Inspector, as shown in Figure 3-14.

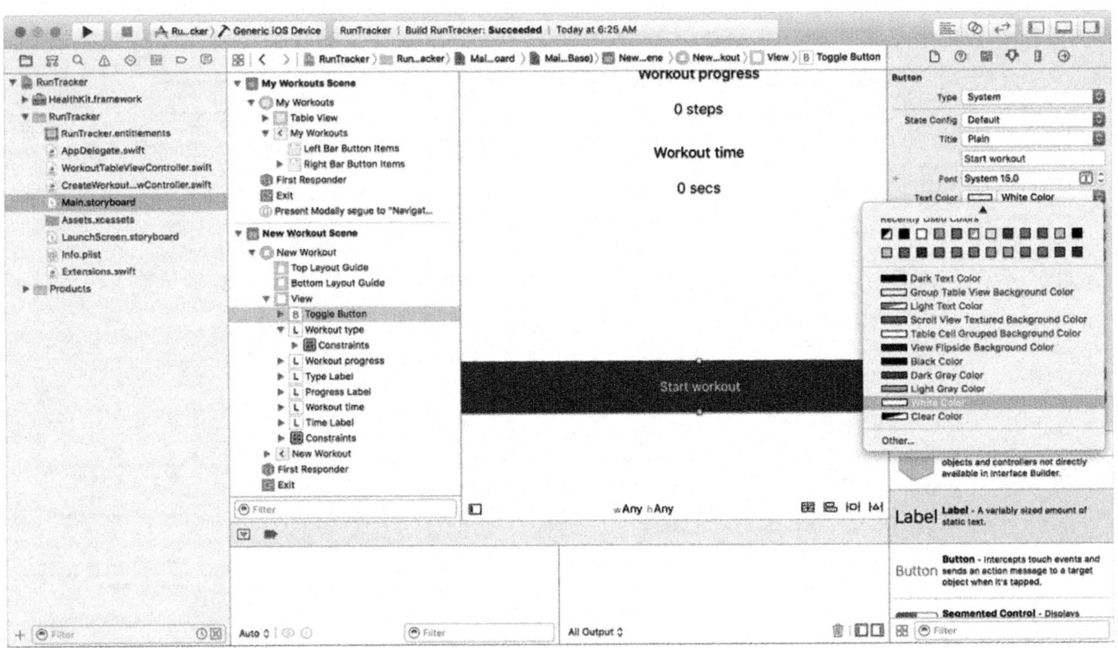

***Figure 3-14.** Changing the text color for a button*

To change the background color of the button, scroll down to the View section of the Attributes Inspector and select the Background color drop-down, as shown in Figure 3-15. Pick your favorite shade of blue.

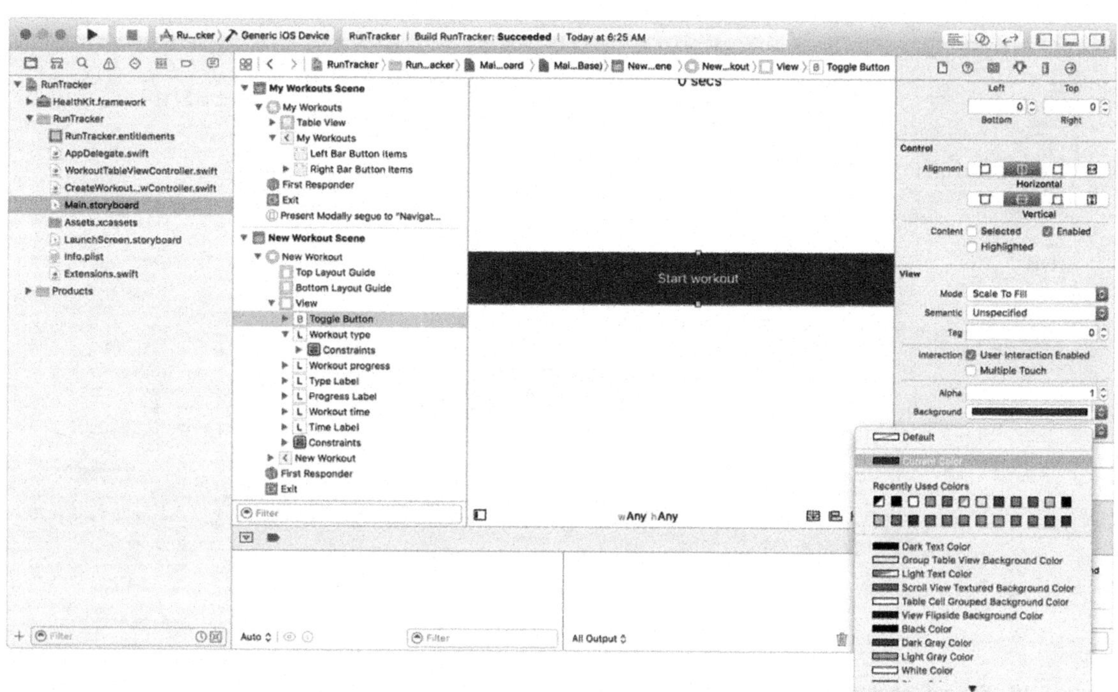

***Figure 3-15.** Changing the button's background color*

To preserve the appearance of the button on different screen sizes, set autolayout constraints using the Pin menu, as shown in Figure 3-16. To force the button to stay at the bottom of the screen on all devices, select the dotted lines on the left, right, and bottom edges of the square. To fix the height at 60 pixels on all screens, select the check box next to height. You can follow the same process to pin the positions and sizes of the labels, except you will pin them to the top of the screen.

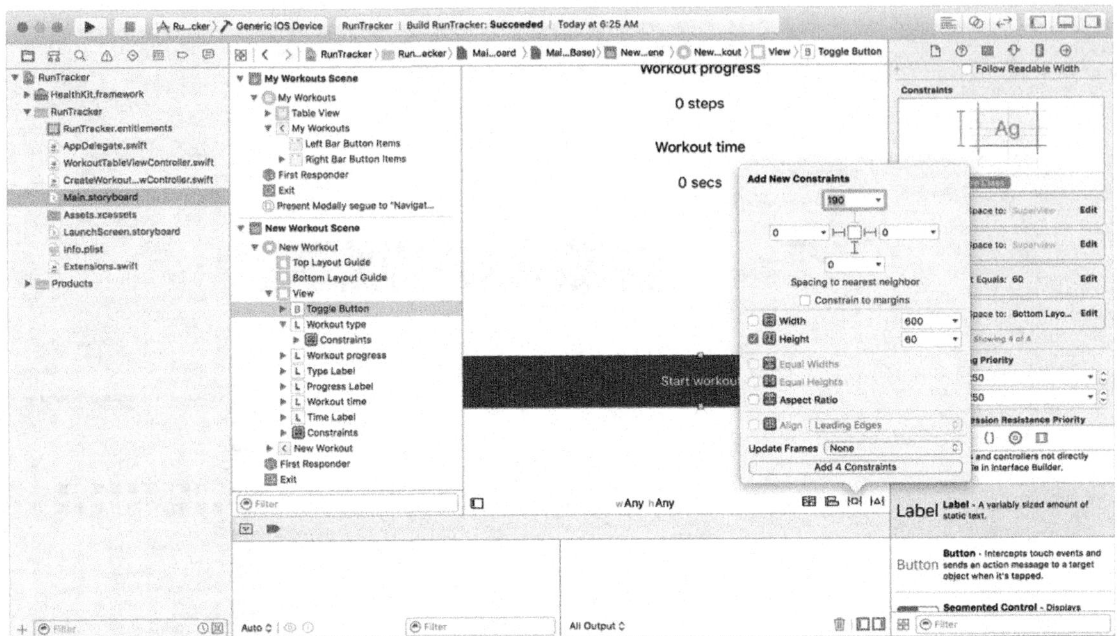

Figure 3-16. Setting constraints for the button

To make the button functional, use the Connections Inspector to connect the Referencing Outlet, following the same steps you used to connect the labels. To connect the function that will be called when the user presses the button, `toggleWorkout()`, you need to connect it to a user interface event. As shown in Figure 3-17, click the radio button representing "Touch Up Inside" and drag a line over to the view controller. Select the method signature for the `toggleWorkout()` function. If it does not appear, make sure you define the method with the `@IBAction` macro in front of the func keyword.

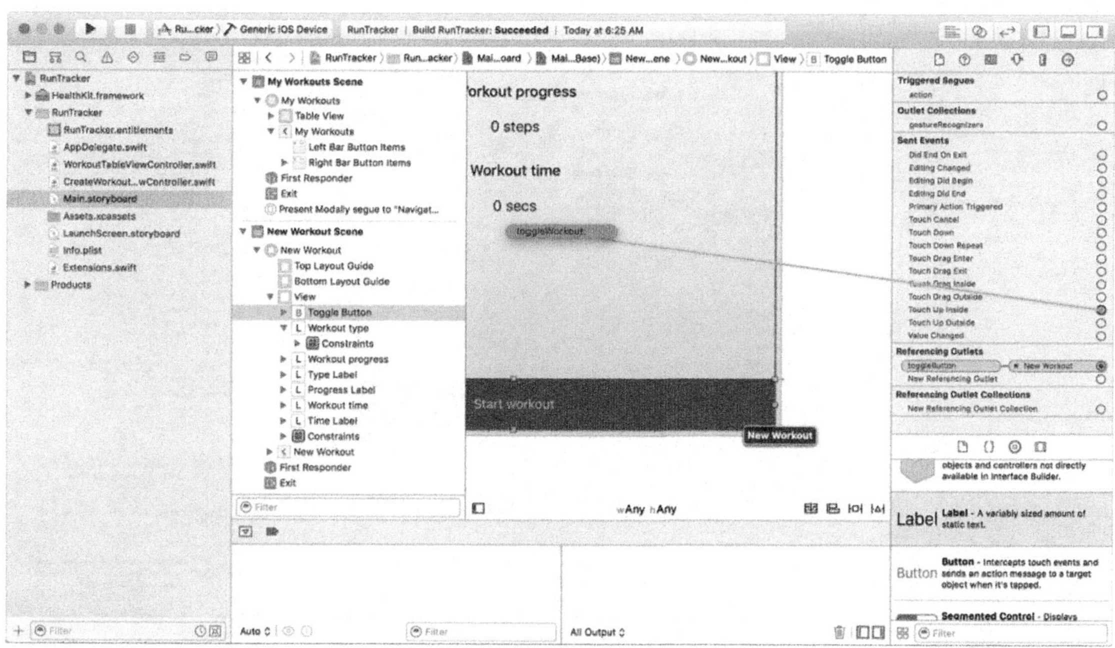

Figure 3-17. Click Touch Up Inside and drag a line to the view controller

For the final steps of setting up the user interface, you need to connect the Done and Cancel buttons in the navigation bar and present the create screen from the workout table. To create the Done and Cancel buttons, start by embedding the create screen in a navigation controller, using the Embed In option from Editor menu, as you did for workout table. Drag bar buttons from the Object library onto the navigation bar, as shown in Figure 3-18. Bar buttons differ from buttons in the Object library, in that they are subclasses of `UIBarButtonItem`. They respond to a smaller set of user interface events than a `UIButton` and include special identifiers to style them for common navigation events, such as canceling a view or selecting a done state.

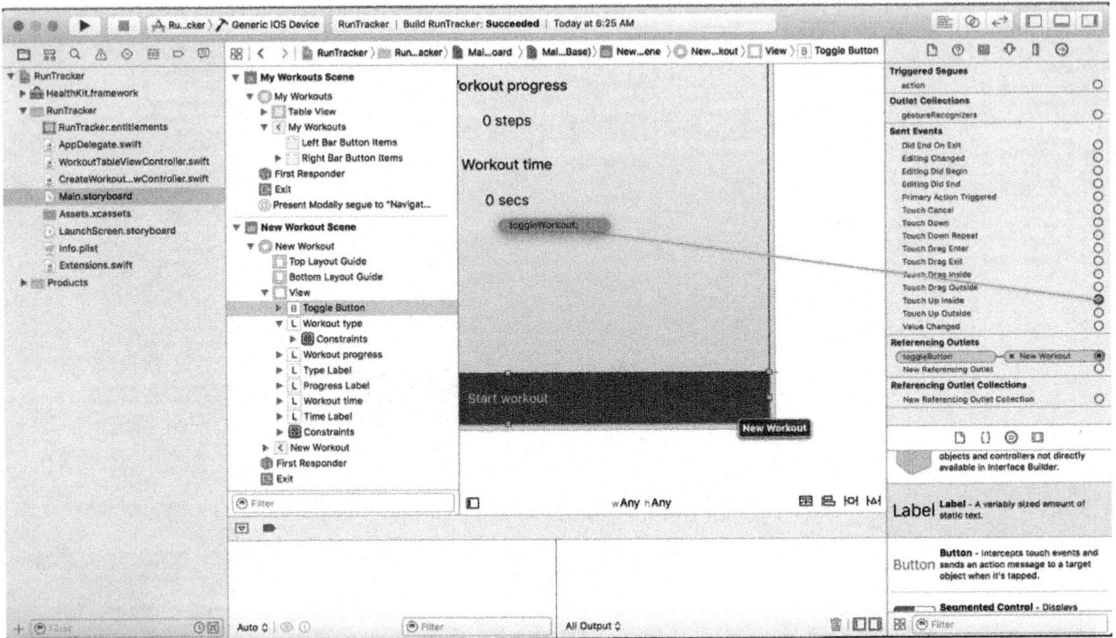

Figure 3-18. *Dragging bar buttons onto the navigation bar*

To change the appearance of a bar button item, click it and navigate over to the Attributes Inspector. As shown in Figure 3-19, you can use a preconfigured display by selecting a system item type from the System Item drop-down. For the Done and Cancel buttons, choose Done and Cancel, respectively.

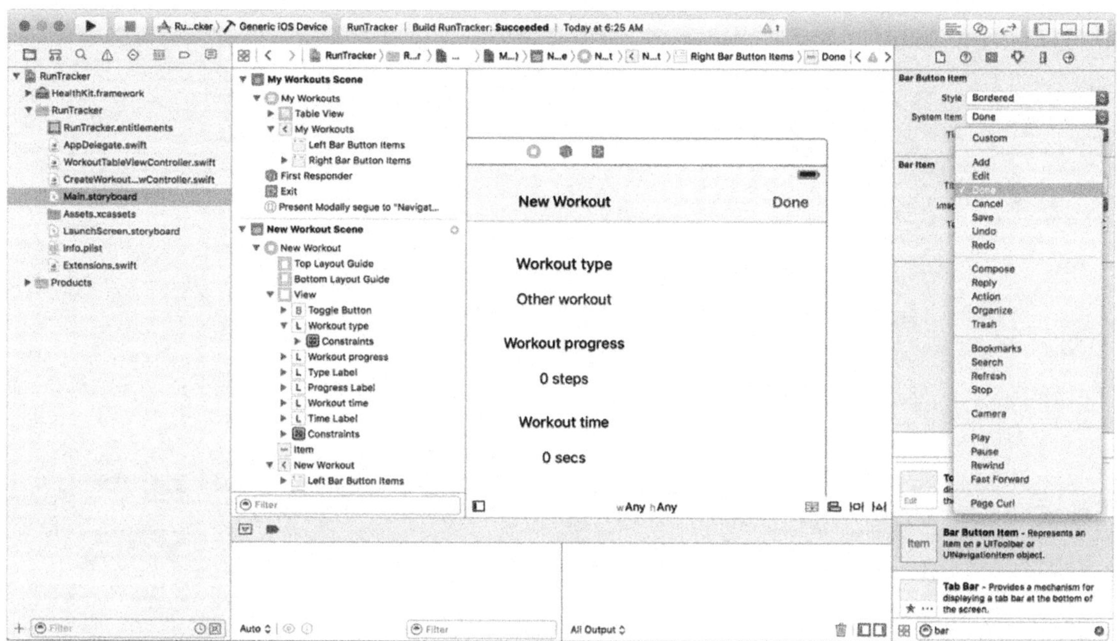

***Figure 3-19.** Selecting a system item type for a UIBarButtonItem*

To connect a bar button item to an action, navigate over to the Connections Inspector. The "Sent Actions" section for a bar button item only has one entry, selector, indicating that you can only connect one handler method to a bar button item. As with connecting a `UIButton`, click on the radio box next to "selector" and drag a line over to the view controller, as shown in Figure 3-20. For the Done button, select the `done()` method. For the Cancel button, select `cancel()`.

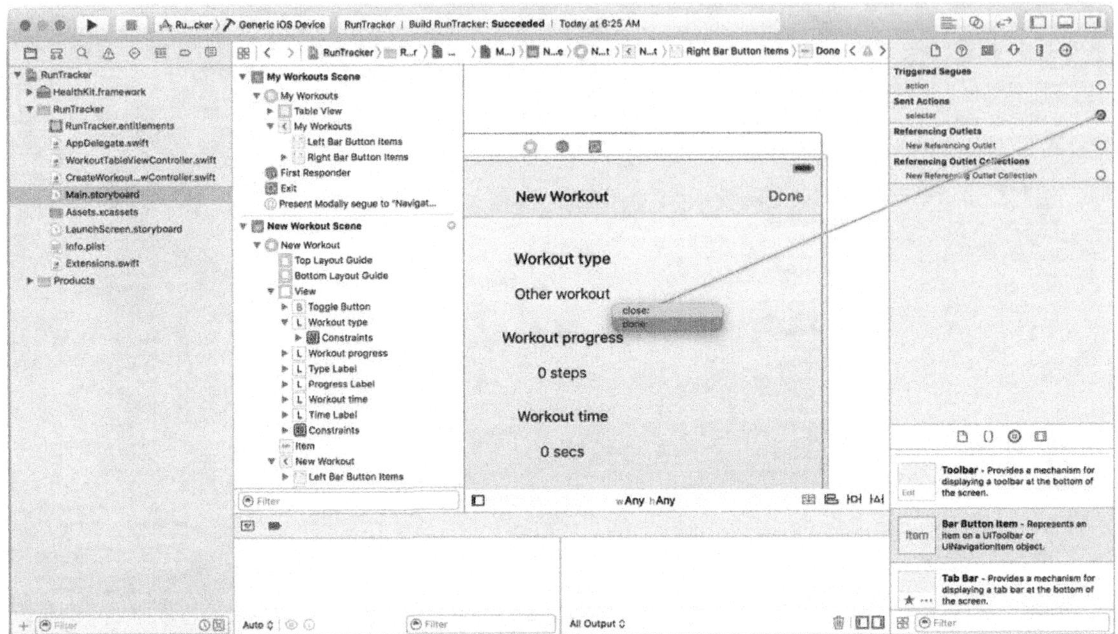

***Figure 3-20.** Selecting a handler method for a UIBarButtonItem*

You will use an Add button to present the create screen from the workout table. Add a bar button to the navigation controller for the workout table and set its style to Add. Rather than using a method to present the create screen, you will use a segue. Segues are a convenient feature of Interface Builder which allow you to visually connect two view controllers via a button or other touchable user interface element and specify properties of the connection, such as how the new screen should be presented, without having to write any code. By overriding the `prepareForSegue()` method, you can implement custom logic to pass data between view controllers that are connected with a segue.

To make the segue between the Add button and create screen, select the Add button and navigate over to the Connections Inspector in Interface Builder. Hold down the radio box next to "action," under the Triggered Segue section, and drag a line to the destination view controller. As shown in Figure 3-21, this will be the navigation controller that contains the create screen.

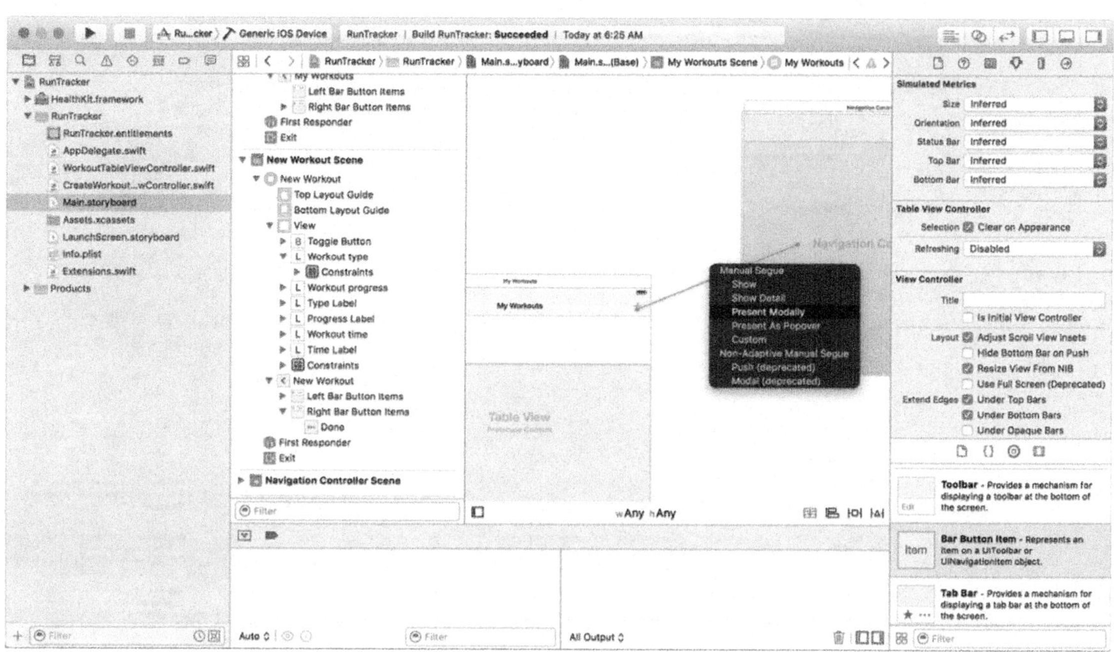

***Figure 3-21.** Creating a segue between a cell and a detail view controller*

Setting Up the Project for HealthKit

Every Xcode project has a feature called "device capabilities." Device capabilities are a set of flags you need to set in your project before you can access sensitive APIs that the user may want to opt out of, such as the Apple Pay wallet or health information from HealthKit. As with the GPS feature in the CarFinder app, users will be prompted to enable the feature once they have installed the app. Apple goes a step further with HealthKit and will prevent your application from compiling if you try to include HealthKit in your project without enabling the device capabilities.

To enable HealthKit for your application, click your project in the Project Navigator. Select the Capabilities tab. As shown in Figure 3-22, you will be presented with a list of switches indicating capabilities you have enabled for your application.

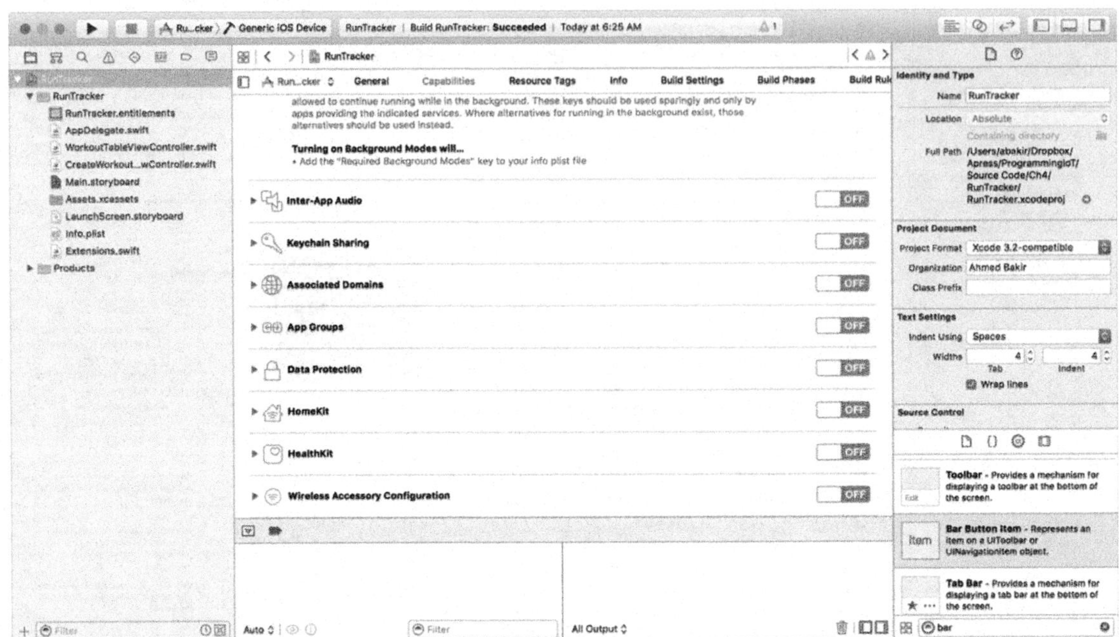

***Figure 3-22.** Default capabilities*

Scroll down to Health and select the ON position for the switch control. Xcode will prompt you to select a Development Team for your project, as shown in Figure 3-23. To use HealthKit, not only do you need to specify the capability for your project but you also need an app ID registered with the Apple Developer Connection. Selecting your Developer Account and logging in will automatically create this record for you.

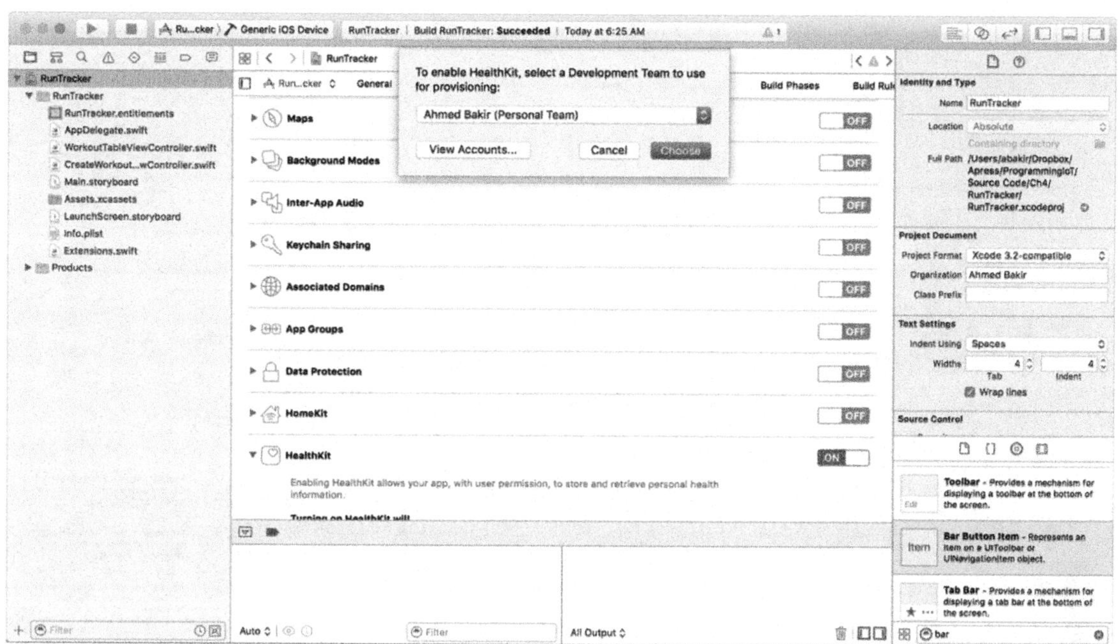

***Figure 3-23.** App registration*

> **Note** If you are on a free developer account for device testing, you can register an application name for testing. However, to distribute your app on the App Store, you will need to upgrade to a paid Apple Developer Program account.

After registering your app ID, you will notice a series of check marks under the Health section, indicating that your application has met all of the requirements for HealthKit, as shown in Figure 3-24.

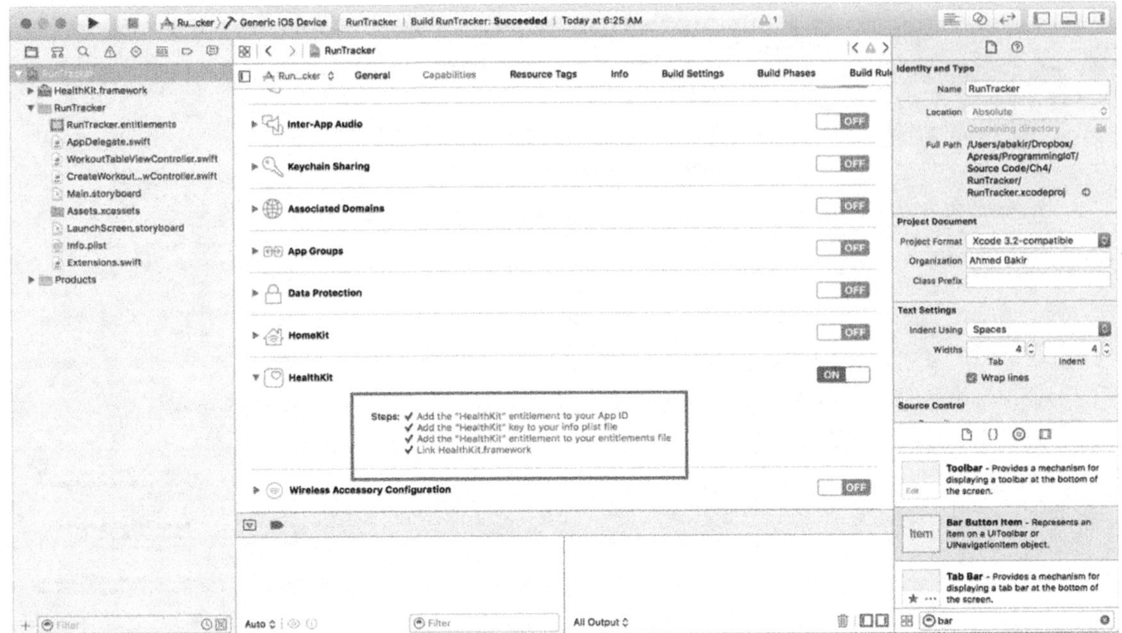

Figure 3-24. Capabilities after enabling HealthKit

> **Note** For the RunTracker project, you will not need to enable any other device capabilities. If you are looking to add location tracking, you should enable Maps. If you want to add the ability to play audio while your app is backgrounded, enable Background Modes.

One of the check boxes indicates that the HealthKit framework has been added to your project. To use the HealthKit API, modify your `WorkoutTableViewController` and `CreateWorkoutViewController` classes to include the framework, as shown in Listings 3-2 and 3-3.

Listing 3-2. Initial Class Definition for WorkoutTableViewController

```
import UIKit
import HealthKit

class WorkoutTableViewController: UITableViewController {
}
```

Listing 3-3. Initial Class Definition for CreateWorkoutViewController

```
import UIKit
import HealthKit

class CreateWorkoutViewController: UIViewController {
}
```

Prompting the User for HealthKit Permission

To enable the project to work with HealthKit, you had to set it as a "capability." Referring to the CarFinder application from Chapter 1, you will remember that when you access sensitive hardware or information, you need to perform two steps:

- Verify that the hardware or API is available on a device
- Ask the user for permission to use the resource

Apple enforces this design pattern by providing you with APIs to prompt for permission and hardware status. To enforce the design pattern, your application will crash at runtime if you try to access a resource that does not exist or which your application does not have permission to use.

To query if a device is HealthKit compatible, use the `isHealthDataAvailable()` public method on the `HKHealthStore()` class. As shown in Listing 3-4, you should call this method at the entry point for the first view controller that needs to use HealthKit. For the RunTracker application, this is the `viewDidLoad()` method of the `WorkoutTableViewController` class.

Listing 3-4. Querying for HealthKit availability When Starting the App (WorkoutTableViewController.swift)

```
override func viewDidLoad() {
        super.viewDidLoad()

        tableView.dataSource = self
        tableView.delegate = self

        // Do any additional setup after loading the view, typically from a nib.

        if (HKHealthStore.isHealthDataAvailable()) {

                //success!

        } else {
                //HealthKit unavailable
                presentErrorMessage("HealthKit not available on this device")
        }
}
```

If the device does not support HealthKit (e.g., an iPad), you should handle the error. In this case, I have created a method called `presentErrorMessage()`, which takes a string as input and displays a `UIAlertController`, as shown in Figure 3-25.

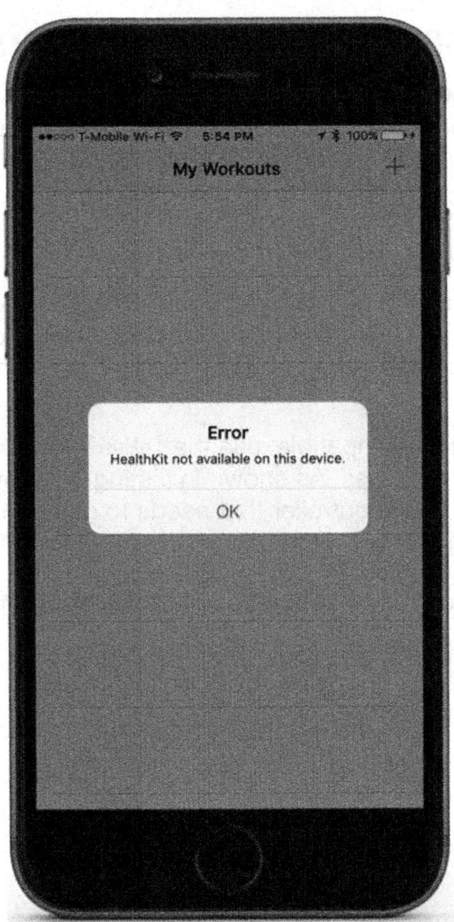

Figure 3-25. *UIAlertController presenting an error*

Listing 3-5 provides the definition for the `presentErrorMessage()` method.

Listing 3-5. ***Method to Generate Error Alerts (WorkoutTableViewController.swift)***

```
func presentErrorMessage(errorString : String) {
    let alert = UIAlertController(title: "Error", message: errorString, preferredStyle:
    UIAlertControllerStyle.Alert)
    let okAction = UIAlertAction(title: "OK", style: UIAlertActionStyle.Default, handler: nil)
    alert.addAction(okAction)
    presentViewController(alert, animated: true, completion: nil)
}
```

Having established that the device is capable of using HealthKit, you need to prompt the user to enable your application to read and write to HealthKit. The primary class you will use for your data operations against HealthKit is `HKHealthStore`. To get started, add a `HKHealthStore` object to the `Workout Table View Controller` class, and instantiate it once your application has established that HealthKit is available on a user's device, as shown in Listing 3-6.

Listing 3-6. Initializing a HKHealthStore When Opening the App (WorkoutTableViewController.swift)

```
override func viewDidLoad() {
        super.viewDidLoad()


        // Do any additional setup after loading the view, typically from a nib.

        if (HKHealthStore.isHealthDataAvailable()) {

            healthStore = HKHealthStore()


        } else {
            //no health kit data available
            presentErrorMessage("HealthKit not available on this device")

        }
    }
```

One of the key advantages of HealthKit is that it provides granular tracking of numerous health data metrics, including heart rate, step count, a user's weight, and calories consumed. You can find the latest, complete set of data types HealthKit in Apple's HealthKit Constant Reference (`https://developer.apple.com/library/ios/documentation/HealthKit/Reference/HealthKit_Constants/`).

HealthKit also provides grouping types, such as workouts, which let you abstract units of data into activities, such as a morning jog. When prompting a user for HealthKit permission, you need to specify the types of data you want to read and write using the `requestAuthorizationToShareTypes()` method of the `HKHealthStore` class. The user will be presented with a view controller provided by iOS reflecting the permissions you have requested, as shown in Figure 3-26. You will be notified of the user's selections via the completion block that executes when the user closes the permission view.

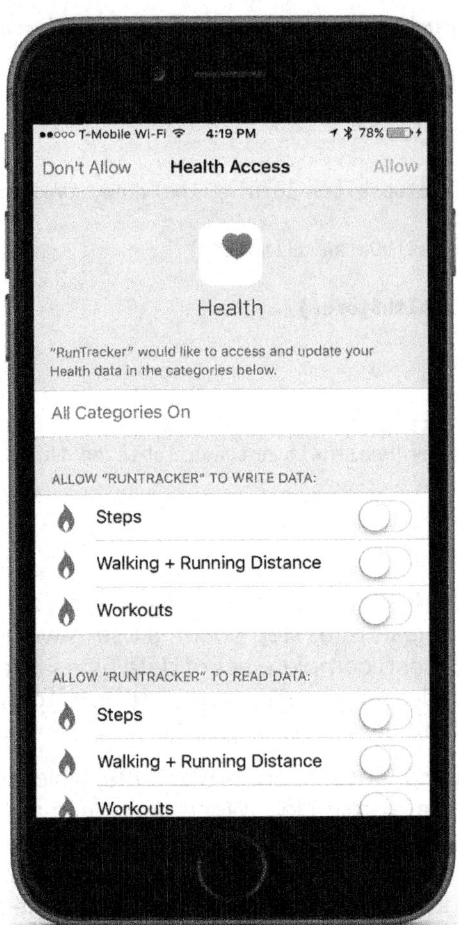

***Figure 3-26.** HealthKit permission view*

For the RunTracker application, you are going to request a limited set of information related to a run—specifically the number of steps the user took and the distance the user traveled. To make the data into something more abstract, you should group it into workouts, rather than just displaying straight step counts. This also allows you to handle the user stopping to catch his breath during a workout.

To use the `requestAuthorizationToShareTypes()` method, you need to specify the data types that you will read or write and a completion handler for when the permissions view has dismissed.

HealthKit uses the `HKSampleType` abstract class to represent "samples" of data, such as a user's heart rate at a given time, or the distance the user traveled between two times. `HKSampleType` is an abstract class, so in order to use it, you need to specify a type for the sample, such as a quantity (an amount of data) or a category (for data that is more qualitative, such as workout type). In Listing 3-7, I have requested permission for step count, distance traveled, and workouts. I have also implemented a simple completion handler, which checked whether permission was granted or rejected.

Listing 3-7. Requesting HealthKit Permission When Opening the App (WorkoutTableViewController.swift)

```
override func viewDidLoad() {
        super.viewDidLoad()

        tableView.dataSource = self
        tableView.delegate = self

        // Do any additional setup after loading the view, typically from a nib.

        if (HKHealthStore.isHealthDataAvailable()) {

            healthStore = HKHealthStore()

            let stepType : HKQuantityType? = HKQuantityType.quantityTypeForIdentifier(
            HKQuantityTypeIdentifierStepCount)
            let distanceType : HKQuantityType? = HKQuantityType.
            quantityTypeForIdentifier(HKQuantityTypeIdentifierDistanceWalkingRunning)
            let workoutType : HKWorkoutType = HKObjectType.workoutType()

            let readTypes : Set =  [stepType!, distanceType!, workoutType]
            let writeTypes : Set = [stepType!, distanceType!,  workoutType]


            healthStore?.requestAuthorizationToShareTypes(writeTypes, readTypes: readTypes,
            completion: { (success: Bool, error: NSError?) -> Void in
                //set

                if success {
                    //success

                    //get workouts


                } else {
                    //Denied
                    self.presentErrorMessage("HealthKit permissions denied")

                }

            })


        } else {
            //no health kit data available
        }
    }
```

There are a few unique bits of syntax here to point out. You will notice that the `HKQuantityType` objects are optional. Apple adds this limitation to handle these types not existing as a device. You can safely unwrap them using the ! operator here, because you verified that HealthKit is available on the device. Similarly, you may be wondering why

HKWorkoutType is not an HKQuantityType object; workout type is quantitative, so it is not represented by a quantity of data, but rather a descriptor (e.g., running workout). Finally, the requestAuthorizationToShareTypes() method takes Sets as input. Unlike an array, a Set is not sorted; it is just a group of related values. You initialize a Set exactly as you would an array, except you need to provide the Set type, so the compiler does not try to infer that you are creating an array when it sees square brackets.

Retrieving Data from HealthKit

In order to populate the workout table, you need to retrieve workout data from HealthKit. HealthKit's primary class for retrieving data is HKQuery, which, as its name implies, performs a query for a sample type that you specify. Users expect a data table to be up to date, so for the workout table, you should query HealthKit for new data as soon as the app launches, and whenever you add a new workout. This is a two-step process in HealthKit: you need to create a query that fetches a given sample type and you need a query that observes when there are new results for a given sample type. These are represented by the HKQuery subclasses, HKSampleQuery and HKObserverQuery.

To begin, start by implementing the query to fetch workouts when the user opens the app. In Listing 3-8, I perform this step by making a call to a function called getWorkouts() after verifying that the app has access to HealthKit.

Listing 3-8. Performing a Workout Query When Opening the App (WorkoutTableViewController.swift)

```
override func viewDidLoad() {
        super.viewDidLoad()

        ...

        // Do any additional setup after loading the view, typically from a nib.

        if (HKHealthStore.isHealthDataAvailable()) {

            healthStore = HKHealthStore()

            let stepType : HKQuantityType? = HKQuantityType.quantityTypeForIdentifier(HKQuan
            tityTypeIdentifierStepCount)
            let distanceType : HKQuantityType? = HKQuantityType.
            quantityTypeForIdentifier(HKQuantityTypeIdentifierDistanceWalkingRunning)
            let workoutType : HKWorkoutType = HKObjectType.workoutType()

            let readTypes : Set =  [stepType!, distanceType!, workoutType]
            let writeTypes : Set = [stepType!, distanceType!,  workoutType]


            healthStore?.requestAuthorizationToShareTypes(writeTypes, readTypes: readTypes,
            completion: { (success: Bool, error: NSError?) -> Void in
                //set
```

```
                if success {
                    //success

                    //get workouts

                    self.getWorkouts()

                } else {
                    //Denied
                    self.presentErrorMessage("HealthKit permissions denied")

                }

            })


        } else {
            //no health kit data available
        }
    }
```

In the `getWorkouts()` function, you will want to create a `HKSampleQuery`, perform a command to run it, and then save the results into an object the table view can use as a data source. The constructor you will use to create an `HKSampleQuery` is `init(sampleType: predicate: limit: sortDescriptors: resultsHandler: HKSampleQuery)`. The constructor requires you to provide a sample type, a limit on the number of results, and a block of code to perform when the query has completed executing. Optionally, you can provide a predicate to further filter the results and a sort descriptor to sort the results.

Start by tackling the parameters you already know. For the data type, you know you want to fetch workouts.

```
let workoutType = HKObjectType.workoutType()
```

For the sort descriptor, users expect to see workouts in the order "most recent first," so sort by start date, in descending order.

```
let sortDescriptor = NSSortDescriptor(key: HKSampleSortIdentifierStartDate, ascending: false)
```

To make the app load faster, it is a good idea to set a limit on the number of items. For my implementation of the application, I want to show only the workouts for the last month, with a maximum of 30 items. The easiest way to build an HKQuery predicate is by using the public method, `predicateForSamplesWithStartDate(NSDate?, endDate: NSDate?, options: HKQueryOptions)`, which specifies a start date, end date, and additional options.

The end date should be "now," which you can retrieve by creating a new `NSDate()` object with the default constructor.

```
let now =  NSDate()
```

For the start date, you need to perform a little extra logic to calculate the date "a month ago." Fortunately, the `NSCalendar` class provides a method that allows you to calculate an offset date, `dateByAddingUnit(NSCalendarUnit, value: Int, toDate: NSDate, options: NSCalendarOptions)`. To calculate the date a month ago, specify Month for the unit and an offset of -1, based on the current date.

```
let oneMonthAgo = calendar.dateByAddingUnit(NSCalendarUnit.Month, value: -1, toDate: now,
options: NSCalendarOptions(rawValue: 0))
```

You can now create your workout predicate with the two date objects.

```
let workoutPredicate = HKQuery.predicateForSamplesWithStartDate(oneMonthAgo, endDate: now,
options: HKQueryOptions.None)
```

The final parameter is a block that will execute when the query is complete. When the query completes, you will want to check that the operation was successful, store the results somewhere the table view can access them, and tell the table to reload with the new results.

First, you need to create an instance variable for the `WorkoutTableViewController` class to store the results from the query. In Listing 3-9, I have modified the class definition to include this array, called workouts. Since the results are `HKWorkout` objects, initialize the array as an empty array containing this type.

***Listing 3-9.** Adding workoutArray to the Table View Controller*

```
class WorkoutTableViewController: UITableViewController {
        var healthStore:  HKHealthStore?

    var workouts = [HKWorkout]()

    override func viewDidLoad() {
        ...
    }
}
```

To save the results, verify that the array contains `HKWorkout` objects and then save a copy, as shown in Listing 3-10.

***Listing 3-10.** Appending Results to workoutArray*

```
if let workouts = results as? [HKWorkout] {
    self.workouts = workouts
}
```

Finally, to refresh the table view, call the `reloadData()` method and modify the previous code to include this change, as shown in Listing 3-11.

Listing 3-11. Updating the User Interface After Adding a Workout

```
if let workouts = results as? [HKWorkout] {
    self.workouts = workouts

    dispatch_async(dispatch_get_main_queue(), { () -> Void in
        self.tableView.reloadData()
    })
}
```

You need to perform this operation in a `dispatch_aync()` block because iOS only performs user interface updates from the main thread of execution. Completion handlers execute on background threads.

With all the parameters in place, you can now create your `HKSampleQuery` object, as shown in Listing 3-12.

Listing 3-12. Creating an HKSampleQuery Object to Query for Workouts

```
let workoutQuery = HKSampleQuery(sampleType: workoutType, predicate: workoutPredicate,
limit: 30, sortDescriptors: [sortDescriptor]) { (query: HKSampleQuery, results: [HKSample]?,
error: NSError? ) -> Void in
    print("results are here")
    if error == nil {
        if let workouts = results as? [HKWorkout] {
            self.workouts = workouts

            dispatch_async(dispatch_get_main_queue(), { () -> Void in
                self.tableView.reloadData()
            })
        }
    } else {
        self.presentErrorMessage("Error fetching workouts")
    }
}
```

Listing 3-13 provides the completed `getWorkouts()` method. You will notice that after creating the query, you need to call `executeQuery` on the `healthStore` object to execute it. All `HKQueries` need to be executed to run; think of them like blueprints to a house. The blueprint tells you how to build the house, but you need to give the blueprint to a contractor to actually build the house.

Listing 3-13. Completed getWorkouts() Function (WorkoutTableViewController.swift)

```
func getWorkouts() {

    let workoutType = HKObjectType.workoutType()

    let sortDescriptor = NSSortDescriptor(key: HKSampleSortIdentifierStartDate,
    ascending: false)

    let now = NSDate()
```

```
    let calendar = NSCalendar.currentCalendar()

    let oneMonthAgo = calendar.dateByAddingUnit(NSCalendarUnit.Month, value: -1,
    toDate: now, options: NSCalendarOptions(rawValue: 0))

    let workoutPredicate = HKQuery.predicateForSamplesWithStartDate(oneMonthAgo,
    endDate: now, options: HKQueryOptions.None)

    let workoutQuery = HKSampleQuery(sampleType: workoutType, predicate: workoutPredicate,
    limit: 30, sortDescriptors: [sortDescriptor]) { (query: HKSampleQuery,
    results: [HKSample]?, error: NSError? ) -> Void in
        print("results are here")
        if error == nil {
            if let workouts = results as? [HKWorkout] {
                self.workouts = workouts

                dispatch_async(dispatch_get_main_queue(), { () -> Void in
                    self.tableView.reloadData()
                })
            }
        } else {
            self.presentErrorMessage("Error fetching workouts")
        }
    }

    healthStore?.executeQuery(workoutQuery)

}
```

Displaying Results in a Table View

Now that you have valid data to initialize the workouts table, you need to modify the `WorkoutTableViewController` to use the workouts array as its data source. Start by specifying that your class is the table view delegate and data source, as shown in Listing 3-14.

Listing 3-14. Setting a View Controller as a Table View Delegate and Data Source

```
override func viewDidLoad() {
    super.viewDidLoad()

    tableView.dataSource = self
    tableView.delegate = self
}
```

Table views in iOS can display information from a two-dimensional array, consisting of sections and rows. Your data source for this application is a one-dimensional array, containing a list of workouts, in order. Specify 1 for the number of sections in the table view, by overriding the `numberOfSectionsInTableView()` method, as shown in Listing 3-15.

Listing 3-15. Specifying Number of Sections in a Table View

```
override func numberOfSectionsInTableView(tableView: UITableView) -> Int {
    return 1
}
```

For the number of rows, return the number of items in the array, as shown in Listing 3-16.

Listing 3-16. Specifying Number of Rows in a Table View

```
override func tableView(tableView: UITableView, numberOfRowsInSection section: Int) -> Int {
    return workouts.count
}
```

To display the results, you need to override the `func tableView(tableView: UITableView, cellForRowAtIndexPath indexPath: NSIndexPath) -> UITableViewCell` method. This takes an index path as its input (the section and row number for an item) and returns a `UITableViewCell` object that has been initialized with values from the corresponding data source item. To follow the wireframe for the application, you will want to display the workout type, date, and duration.

Accessing the workout item is straightforward; you simply provide the row. Making the values human-readable is a bit more complicated. Workout type is stored as an enum (enumerated type). To convert this to a string, perform a `switch()` statement, operating on the enum value that receives. Unfortunately, you need to create the strings yourself, as shown in Listing 3-17.

Listing 3-17. Converting Workout Types to Human-Readable Strings

```
switch(workout.workoutActivityType) {
case HKWorkoutActivityType.Running:
    workoutTypeString = "Running"
case HKWorkoutActivityType.Walking:
    workoutTypeString = "Walking"
case HKWorkoutActivityType.Elliptical:
    workoutTypeString = "Elliptical"
default:
    workoutTypeString = "Other workout"
}
```

To display the date, you need to create a date formatter. The `NSDateFormatter` class manages different formats for date and time, based on common patterns or user-defined ones. It also provides a convenient method to output a string based on the format you specify. For my implementation, I chose to display a verbose date string and a short time string, as shown in Listing 3-18.

Listing 3-18. Displaying Time as a Human-Readable String

```
let dateFormatter = NSDateFormatter()
dateFormatter.dateStyle = NSDateFormatterStyle.MediumStyle
dateFormatter.timeStyle = NSDateFormatterStyle.ShortStyle

cell.textLabel?.text = "\(workoutTypeString) / \(timeString)"
cell.detailTextLabel!.text = dateFormatter.stringFromDate(workout.startDate)
```

Similarly, for the workout duration, to display minutes and seconds, you need to convert the output, an `NSTimeInterval` value in seconds, to a human-readable string. To perform this operation, I created an extension method for the `NSTimeInterval` class called `toString(inputTime: NSTimeInterval)`. This method takes an `NSTimeInterval` as an input and returns a string. For instance, you can call the method as follows:

```
let timeString = NSTimeInterval().toString(workout.duration)
```

Extensions allow you to add methods to existing classes without subclassing a parent class. To define an extension, simply create an extension block, specifying the name of the class you want to extend and the name of the method you want to create. To organize your project in a logic fashion, I recommend creating a separate file to contain all of your extensions. For the RunTracker project, I created a file named `Extensions.swift` (see Listing 3-19 for its definition).

Listing 3-19. Using an Extension File to Create Time Strings (Extensions.swift)

```
import Foundation

extension NSTimeInterval {

    func toString(input: NSTimeInterval) -> (String) {
        let integerTime = Int(input)
        let hours = integerTime / 3600
        let mins = (integerTime / 60) % 60
        let secs = integerTime % 60

        var finalString = ""

        if hours > 0 {
            finalString += "\(hours) hrs, "
        }

        if mins > 0 {
            finalString += "\(mins) mins,"
        }

        if secs > 0 {
            finalString += "\(secs) secs"
        }
        return finalString
    }

}
```

With all the data now in a human-readable format, you can create your `UITableViewCell`. Listing 3-20 provides the complete implementation of the `cellForRowAtIndexPath()` method. Note that you need to use the same cell identifier as the one you specified in the storyboard (in this case, WorkoutCell).

Listing 3-20. Initializing Table View Cells (WorkoutTableViewController.swift)

```
override func tableView(tableView: UITableView, cellForRowAtIndexPath
indexPath: NSIndexPath) -> UITableViewCell {
    let cell = tableView.dequeueReusableCellWithIdentifier("WorkoutCell",
    forIndexPath: indexPath)

    let workout = workouts[indexPath.row]

    let workoutTypeString : String
    let timeString = NSTimeInterval().toString(workout.duration)

    switch(workout.workoutActivityType) {
    case HKWorkoutActivityType.Running:
        workoutTypeString = "Running"
    case HKWorkoutActivityType.Walking:
        workoutTypeString = "Walking"
    case HKWorkoutActivityType.Elliptical:
        workoutTypeString = "Elliptical"
    default:
        workoutTypeString = "Other workout"
    }

    let dateFormatter = NSDateFormatter()
    dateFormatter.dateStyle = NSDateFormatterStyle.MediumStyle
    dateFormatter.timeStyle = NSDateFormatterStyle.ShortStyle

    cell.textLabel?.text = "\(workoutTypeString) / \(timeString)"
    cell.detailTextLabel!.text = dateFormatter.stringFromDate(workout.startDate)

    return cell
}
```

Fetching Background Updates

Now that the `WorkoutTableViewController` class can fetch workout samples on demand, you should complete the implementation of the user interface by adding a `HKObserverQuery` to refresh the table whenever you have saved a new workout. The beauty of HealthKit is that observer queries apply to HealthKit as a whole, meaning you will get an update regardless of whether your app posts an update or another app posts the update.

The process for implementing a `HKObserverQuery` is extremely similar to an `HKSampleQuery`: specify the type to query, predicates to filter the query, and a completion handler to execute when the query completes. The constructor you will use to build a HKObserverQuery is `init(sampleType:predicate:updateHandler:)`.

You will notice that this constructor does not provide a results array when the query completes executing. To remedy this, in your completion handler, execute a sample query to get the latest results. Since you already defined one via the `getWorkouts()` method, call it in your completion handler, as shown in Listing 3-21.

Listing 3-21. Performing a HealthKit Background Query (WorkoutTableViewController.swift)

```
let backgroundQuery = HKObserverQuery(sampleType: workoutType, predicate: nil,
updateHandler: { (query: HKObserverQuery, handler: HKObserverQueryCompletionHandler,
error: NSError? ) -> Void in

    if error == nil {
            self.getWorkouts()
    }

})
```

The final question is, "where should I put this query?" You should initialize an observer query in the class that manages your primary data source. For the RunTracker application, that is `WorkoutTableViewController`. Place the observer query and the `executeQuery()` call in your `viewDidLoad()` method, after verifying that the application has HealthKit permission, as shown in Listing 3-22.

Listing 3-22. Completed viewDidLoad method, Including Observer Query (WorkoutTableViewController.swift)

```
override func viewDidLoad() {
    super.viewDidLoad()

    tableView.dataSource = self
    tableView.delegate = self

    // Do any additional setup after loading the view, typically from a nib.

    if (HKHealthStore.isHealthDataAvailable()) {

        healthStore = HKHealthStore()

        let stepType : HKQuantityType? = HKQuantityType.quantityTypeForIdentifier(HKQuantity
        TypeIdentifierStepCount)
        let distanceType : HKQuantityType? = HKQuantityType.
        quantityTypeForIdentifier(HKQuantityTypeIdentifierDistanceWalkingRunning)
        let workoutType : HKWorkoutType = HKObjectType.workoutType()

        let readTypes : Set =  [stepType!, distanceType!, workoutType]
        let writeTypes : Set = [stepType!, distanceType!,  workoutType]

        healthStore?.requestAuthorizationToShareTypes(writeTypes, readTypes: readTypes,
        completion: { (success: Bool, error: NSError?) -> Void in
            //set
```

```
            if success {
                //success

                //get workouts

                let backgroundQuery = HKObserverQuery(sampleType: workoutType,
                predicate: nil, updateHandler: { (query: HKObserverQuery,
                handler: HKObserverQueryCompletionHandler, error: NSError? ) -> Void in

                    if error == nil {
                            self.getWorkouts()
                    }

                })

                self.healthStore?.executeQuery(backgroundQuery)

                self.getWorkouts()

            } else {
                //Denied
                self.presentErrorMessage("HealthKit permissions denied")

            }

        })

    } else {
        //no health kit data available
    }
}
```

You will notice two calls to getWorkout() in Listing 3-22. Both are necessary, as one executes when the view is loaded from memory and the other executes whenever the observer query has detected that you have saved a new workout to HealthKit.

Summary

In this chapter, you learned how to use HealthKit to access health information, display a user's past workouts in the RunTracker app, and lay the foundation to create new ones. During this process, you learned about the special steps necessary to set up HealthKit compatibility in your application, how HealthKit represents data, and how HealthKit uses queries to access data. In the next chapter, we will complete the application by accessing step count form the pedometer using Core Motion, converting it to workout and quantity units that HealthKit can digest, and saving it to HealthKit.

Chapter 4

Using Core Motion to Save Motion Data

Ahmed Bakir

Introduction

In the last chapter, you learned how to set up an application for HealthKit, Apple's shared repository for health data, and query for specific health data types. In this chapter, you will learn how to use Core Motion to access live motion data from a user's device, and how to save it back to HealthKit, where it will be accessible to all applications.

In this chapter, you continue to expand the RunTracker app that you started in Chapter 3. In this chapter, we cover the following concepts:

- How to access hardware using Core Motion
- How to save information collected over time using Core Motion
- How to save information to HealthKit
- How to receive real-time activity updates from Core Motion and HealthKit

As with the other projects in this book, you can find the complete source code for the RunTracker project in the Ch4 folder of the Source Code bundle available on this book's web page at Apress.com/9781484211953.

Using Core Motion to Access Motion Hardware

In Chapter 3, we set up the workout table view and HealthKit permissions for RunTracker; now it is time to move on to collecting data that you can save back to HealthKit. Saving data to HealthKit works much like retrieving it: you specify a data type, a quantity of data collected, and a time range. For the RunTracker application, you will use the Core Motion framework to access the pedometer on the user's device. From the pedometer, you can detect the number of steps the user has traveled and even the type of activity the user is engaged in (walking, running, bicycling). You will take advantage of both of these in creating the interface for the RunTracker application.

Core Motion has been iOS's motion-sensing framework since iOS 4. Developers have been using it for years to access the built-in accelerator and gyroscope (enabling thousands of racing games ever since). However, until the M-series of motion coprocessors, there was never an easy way to access step data. You could use the accelerator to detect when the device experienced a "bump" in movement, but you had to develop your own code to define a "step." Similarly, you could use a GPS to determine how far a user moved, but doing so would drain the battery quickly.

Although iOS 7 added an interface to the M-series motion coprocessor to the Core Motion framework, iOS 8 fully unlocked it, allowing you to retrieve data directly as steps and activity types. Core Motion takes care of all the work to define what a step is, what it corresponds to in terms of distance, and what the user was doing when the step was registered (for example, running or walking).

Swift streamlines the process of including common frameworks into your project, so you do not need to add Core Motion manually to our project to begin using it. However, you will need to include it in the classes that need to access its application programming interfaces (APIs). For the RunTracker application, the `CreateWorkoutViewController` class is responsible for pulling fitness data from Core Motion and displaying statistics during a workout. Begin by modifying the class definition to include the framework as shown in Listing 4-1.

***Listing 4-1.** Adding Core Motion to the CreateWorkoutViewController Class*

```
import UIKit
import CoreMotion

class CreateWorkoutViewController: UIViewController {
..
}
```

Requesting User Permission for Motion Activity

Although not explicitly defined as a device capability in your project settings, you implement Core Motion using the same design pattern. In order to use Core Motion, you need to

- Verify that Core Motion is available on a user's device
- Ask the user for permission to access Core Motion

- Verify that the desired hardware is available on a user's device
- Ask the user for permission to access the hardware

The Core Motion class that manages motion events and the motion activity permission is `CMMotionActivityManager`. Strictly speaking, a motion activity is defined as an event that corresponds to the type of movement the user is currently engaged in, whether that is walking, running, or even driving. You query for motion activity status by calling the public method `isActivityAvailable()`. This method returns a `bool` value, indicating whether the user has given your app permission to access motion activity.

The first time you ask the user for Core Motion permission, he or she will see an alert view managed by iOS, as shown in Figure 4-1. Privacy permissions are keyed by application identifier, meaning subsequent launches (or reinstalls) of your application will not prompt the user to select the permission level again. (Users can change their permission level at any time by selecting the Privacy option in the iOS Settings application.)

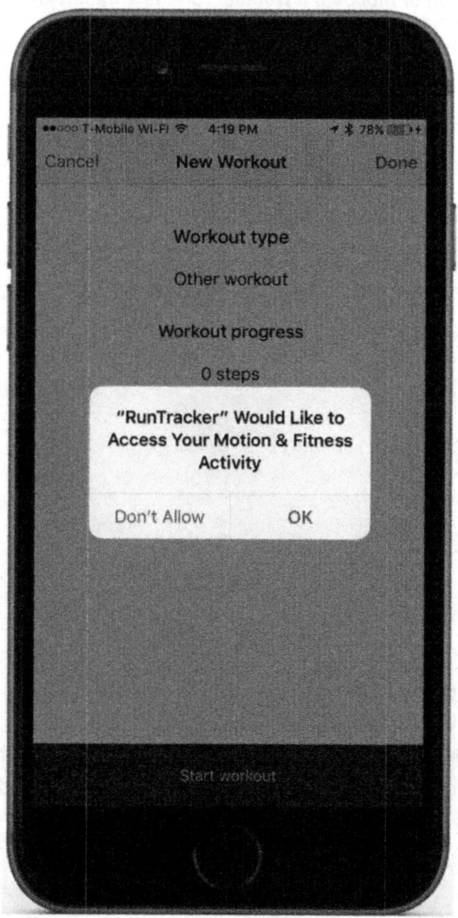

Figure 4-1. Core Motion permission alert

As with HealthKit, you need to make sure the user's device has the hardware you want to access. Additionally, you should check that the device is capable of producing the data you want to log. The `CMPedometer` class provides access to the pedometer on a user's device. To check if step data is available, call the `isStepCountingAvailable()` public method.

In the workout screen, you had to prompt the user for HealthKit permission as soon as the screen loaded, in order to load the table with valid data. In the create screen, you should initiate the request for Core Motion permission when the user attempts to start a workout. This is initiated by pressing the Start Workout button, which calls `toggleWorkout()`. Depending on whether or not a workout is in progress, the method will call `startWorkout()` to begin accessing the pedometer or `stopWorkout()` to save progress. The flag for determining whether a workout is in progress is stored as a Boolean instance variable, called `workoutActive`. Listing 4-2 describes the `toggleWorkout()` method for the create workout view controller (`CreateWorkoutViewController.swift`) and adds the `workoutActive` flag as part of the class definition.

Listing 4-2. Button Handler for Starting or Stopping a Workout (CreateWorkoutViewController.swift)

```
import UIKit
import CoreMotion

class CreateWorkoutViewController: UIViewController {
      var workoutActive = false
      . . .
    @IBAction func toggleWorkout(sender: UIButton) {

        if (workoutActive) {

            self.stopWorkout()

        } else {

            self.startWorkout()

        }
        workoutActive = !workoutActive

    }
}
```

In Listing 4-2 I chose to wrap the logic of starting a workout in the `startWorkout()` method. This is where you will place your permission handling code. When you have established that your application has permission to use Core Motion, change the color and state of the Start Workout button to indicate that you have started the workout. Listing 4-3 provides the `startWorkout()` method.

Listing 4-3. Starting a Workout (CreateWorkoutViewController.swift)

```
func startWorkout() {
    self.timer = NSTimer.scheduledTimerWithTimeInterval(1.0, target: self, selector:
    "updateTime", userInfo: nil, repeats: true)

    if initialStartDate == nil {
        initialStartDate = NSDate()
    }
    startDate = NSDate()

    //start counting steps
    toggleButton.backgroundColor = UIColor.redColor()
    toggleButton.setTitle("Pause workout", forState: UIControlState.Normal)

    if (CMMotionActivityManager.isActivityAvailable() && CMPedometer.
    isStepCountingAvailable()) {
        //success

    }
}
```

Querying for Step Count

By this point, it should be no surprise that HealthKit and Core Motion share many design similarities. Just as you had to instantiate the HKHealthStore object to retrieve HealthKit data, you need to instantiate a `CMPedometer` object to access the pedometer on a user's device. As shown in Listing 4-4, add a `CMPedometer` object to the `CreateWorkoutViewController` class and initialize it when you have established that the device has permission to use Core Motion.

Listing 4-4. Initialize CMPedometer

```
func startWorkout() {

    //start counting steps
    toggleButton.backgroundColor = UIColor.redColor()
    toggleButton.setTitle("Pause workout", forState: UIControlState.Normal)

    if (CMMotionActivityManager.isActivityAvailable() && CMPedometer.
    isStepCountingAvailable()) {
        pedometer = CMPedometer()
    }
}
```

Core Motion also implements concepts of queries to retrieve a set of data between two times and an observer query to retrieve updates to a data set. The CMPedometer method for retrieving steps between two times is `queryPedometerDataFromDate(NSDate, toDate: NSDate, withHandler: CMPedometerHandler)`. This method takes two `NSDate` objects as parameters and executes a block when it has completed executing, which returns a `CMPedometerData` object and error. The `CMPedometer` object contains values including number of steps and distance traveled, calculated based on hardware events and metrics that iOS has observed about a user, including his stride length. As with earlier HealthKit queries, you should use the time the user started his workout as the start time and the time he ended his workout as the "end time." This also specifies that you will need to perform the pedometer query in the `stopWorkout()` method. First, add an `NSDate` object to your class indicating the start time, and initialize it in the `startWorkout()` method, as shown in Listing 4-5.

***Listing 4-5.** Tracking Start Time (CreateWorkoutViewController.swift)*

```
class CreateWorkoutViewController: UIViewController {

    ..
    var startDate : NSDate?

    ...

    func startWorkout() {
        startDate = NSDate()
        ...
    }

}
```

Next, you need to implement your query logic in the `stopWorkout()` method. In this method, change the state of the Workout button back to start and attempt to query for step data after establishing that the pedometer is active (the object should be initialized). You will save the number of steps to HealthKit, but for now, display it in the progress label. Listing 4-6 provides the implementation for the `stopWorkout()` function.

***Listing 4-6.** Querying for Total Steps When Ending a Workout (CreateWorkoutViewController.swift)*

```
func stopWorkout() {
    //stop the workout

    self.timer?.invalidate()

    //pause timer
    toggleButton.backgroundColor = UIColor.blueColor()
    toggleButton.setTitle("Continue workout", forState: UIControlState.Normal)

    //save steps
    if (pedometer != nil && startDate != nil) {
        let now = NSDate()

        pedometer?.stopPedometerUpdates()

    } else {
                self.presentErrorMessage("Could not access pedometer")
            }
        })
```

```
        //increase duration
        duration += now.timeIntervalSinceDate(startDate!)
    }
}
```

To further improve the user experience, you should use an NSTimer to update the time label every second after the workout has started; this gives users the "clock" functionality that they expect from other workout devices, such as a watch. In Listing 4-7, I have added an NSTimer to the `CreateWorkoutViewController` class and initialized it in the `startWorkout()` method. I specify that the timer should repeat every second and call the `updateTime()` method when it fires.

Listing 4-7. Adding an NSTimer to the CreateWorkoutViewController Class

```
class CreateWorkoutViewController: UIViewController {

    ..
    var timer: NSTimer?
      ...

    func startWorkout() {
        self.timer = NSTimer.scheduledTimerWithTimeInterval(1.0, target: self,
        selector: "updateTime", userInfo: nil, repeats: true)
        //start counting steps
        toggleButton.backgroundColor = UIColor.redColor()
        toggleButton.setTitle("Pause workout", forState: UIControlState.Normal)

        if (CMMotionActivityManager.isActivityAvailable() && CMPedometer.
        isStepCountingAvailable()) {
            pedometer = CMPedometer()
                        ...
            }
}
```

The `updateTime()` method creates a string based on the number of seconds that have passed since the timer started and updates the `timeLabel` property. Listing 4-8 provides the `updateTime()` method. Once again, you can use the `toString()` method created earlier to make a human-readable string based on a `NSTimeInterval` value.

Listing 4-8. Enabling Updates to the Workout Time Label (CreateWorkoutViewController.swift)

```
func updateTime() {

    let now = NSDate()

    if (startDate != nil) {
        let totalTime : NSTimeInterval = duration + now.timeIntervalSinceDate(startDate!)

        dispatch_async(dispatch_get_main_queue(), { () -> Void in
                self.timeLabel!.text = NSTimeInterval().toString(totalTime)
        })
    }
}
```

Finally, to stop the timer, call the `invalidate()` method on the timer instance variable, as shown in Listing 4-9. One of the design decisions that drives a repeating `NSTimer` is that in order to stop it, you must maintain a pointer to the object and explicitly call the `invalidate()` method to stop it from firing again. Maintaining pointers is tiresome, but it allows you to control multiple repeating timers.

Listing 4-9. Stopping the Workout Timer (CreateWorkoutViewController.swift)

```
func stopWorkout() {
    //stop the workout

    self.timer?.invalidate()
    //pause timer
    toggleButton.backgroundColor = UIColor.blueColor()
    toggleButton.setTitle("Continue workout", forState: UIControlState.Normal)

    //save steps
    if (pedometer != nil && startDate != nil) {
            ...
    }
}
```

Detecting Live Updates to Step Count

The `startPedometerUpdatesFromDate(NSDate, withHandler: CMPedometerHandler)` method in the `CMPedometer` class allows you to query for real-time updates to the pedometer. This is not ideal for tracking the grand total of steps collected during a workout, as iOS controls the update frequency and it is not guaranteed to be timely. However, it is useful for the create workout screen, as you can use it to update the user interface.

Using `startPedometerUpdatesFromDate()` is much simpler than querying for a set of pedometer data; you simply need to provide a handler method and start date. Since the updates will be continuous while a workout is active, it makes sense to start the query when the user has started the workout. The wireframe for the RunTracker application specifies that a user can pause and resume a workout before saving it, so add another `NSDate` object to the class to specify the initial start time of the workout, as shown in Listing 4-10.

Listing 4-10. Modified CreateWorkoutViewController Class, Including an Initial Start Date Property

```
class CreateWorkoutViewController: UIViewController {

    ...
    @IBOutlet weak var timeLabel: UILabel!

    ...

    var startDate : NSDate?
    var initialStartDate : NSDate?
```

```
    var timer: NSTimer?

    @IBAction func toggleWorkout(sender: UIButton) {
        ...
    }
}
```

Having established this second NSDate object, you can now query for sample data using the initial start time at the end of the workout, as shown in Listing 4-11. Remember to update the total workout time and to check for any errors while performing your query.

Listing 4-11. Querying for HealthKit data When Ending a Workout (CreateWorkoutViewController.swift)

```
func stopWorkout() {
    //stop the workout

    self.timer?.invalidate()

    //pause timer
    toggleButton.backgroundColor = UIColor.blueColor()
    toggleButton.setTitle("Continue workout", forState: UIControlState.Normal)

    //save steps
    if (pedometer != nil && startDate != nil) {
        let now = NSDate()

        pedometer?.stopPedometerUpdates()

        pedometer?.queryPedometerDataFromDate(startDate!, toDate: now, withHandler: { (data:
        CMPedometerData?, error: NSError?) -> Void in
            if (error == nil) {

                if let activityType = HKQuantityType.quantityTypeForIdentifier(
                HKQuantityTypeIdentifierStepCount) {

                    let numberOfSteps = data?.numberOfSteps.doubleValue

                    self.progressLabel?.steps = "\(numberOfSteps)"

                }

            } else {
                self.presentErrorMessage("Could not access pedometer")
            }
        })

        //increase duration
        duration += now.timeIntervalSinceDate(startDate!)
    }
}
```

Finally, you need to do some housekeeping when the workout has stopped. To prevent the pedometer from firing updates while the workout is paused or after you have exited the create screen, call the `stopPedometerUpdates()` method. Listing 4-12 describes the modified `stopWorkout()` method, which includes this call.

Listing 4-12. Stopping Pedometer Updates When Ending a Workout (CreateWorkoutViewController.swift)

```
func stopWorkout() {
    //stop the workout

    self.timer?.invalidate()

    ...

    //save steps
    if (pedometer != nil && startDate != nil) {
        let now = NSDate()

        pedometer?.stopPedometerUpdates()
        ...
        //increase duration
        duration += now.timeIntervalSinceDate(startDate!)
    }
}
```

Detecting Activity Type

Another advantage of Core Motion is that you can detect the type of activity the user is engaged in, such as running, walking, or bicycling. This feature will be extremely useful in the RunTracker application, as you need to tag workouts with a type. The class for accessing activity status in Core Motion is `CMActivityManager`. To receive activity updates, call the `startActivityUpdatesToQueue(NSOperationQueue, withHandler: CMMotionActivityHandler)` method, specifying an operation queue (the main queue) and a completion handler that should execute when an update is received. In Listing 4-13, I have added an activity manager to the `startWorkout()` method.

Listing 4-13. Beginning Polling for Motion Activities When Starting a Workout (CreateWorkoutViewController.swift)

```
func startWorkout() {
    self.timer = NSTimer.scheduledTimerWithTimeInterval(1.0, target: self,
    selector: "updateTime", userInfo: nil, repeats: true)

    if initialStartDate == nil {
        initialStartDate = NSDate()
    }
    startDate = NSDate()

    //start counting steps
    toggleButton.backgroundColor = UIColor.redColor()
    toggleButton.setTitle("Pause workout", forState: UIControlState.Normal)
```

```
    if (CMMotionActivityManager.isActivityAvailable() && CMPedometer.
    isStepCountingAvailable()) {
        pedometer = CMPedometer()

        //show total steps

        ...
        let activityManager = CMMotionActivityManager()

        activityManager.startActivityUpdatesToQueue(NSOperationQueue.mainQueue(),
        withHandler: { (activity: CMMotionActivity?) -> Void in

            if activity?.stationary == false {
                self.lastActivity = activity
            }

            var activityString = "Other activity type"

            if (activity?.stationary == true) {
                activityString = "Stationary"
            }

            if (activity?.walking == true) {
                activityString = "Walking"
            }

            if (activity?.running == true) {
                activityString = "Running"
            }

            if (activity?.cycling == true) {
                activityString = "Cycling"
            }

            dispatch_async(dispatch_get_main_queue(), { () -> Void in
                self.typeLabel.text = activityString
            })

        })

    } else {
        presentErrorMessage("Pedometer not available")
    }

}
```

Core Motion does not reveal activity types as human-readable strings, just like HealthKit. As a further complication, Core Motion does not provide an enum for storing the activity type. To check activity type, you must iterate through properties representing common values.

To create a workout in HealthKit, you must specify a workout type. Earlier, I saved the last known workout type to an instance variable named `lastActivity`, excluding stationary activities (users expect to see active workout types like running or walking). In Listing 4-14, I have modified the class definition once again to include the `lastActivity` property.

Listing 4-14. Adding a Property to Save the User's Last Motion Activity (CreateWorkoutViewController.swift)

```
class CreateWorkoutViewController: UIViewController {

    ...

    var timer: NSTimer?

    var lastActivity : CMMotionActivity?

    var pedometer : CMPedometer?
    ...

    @IBAction func toggleWorkout(sender: UIButton) {
        ...
    }

}
```

Saving Data to HealthKit

To complete the round-trip process for the fitness data you collected, you need to save it back into HealthKit. In the RunTracker application, you will save the steps you collected to HealthKit and you will compile these segments together as a single workout in HealthKit. To begin, you need to give the create workout screen access to HealthKit. As with the workout table, add an `HKHealthStore` property to the `CreateWorkoutViewController` class and include the HealthKit framework, as shown in Listing 4-15.

Listing 4-15. Adding an HKHealthStore to the CreateWorkoutViewController Class (CreateWorkoutViewController.swift)

```
import UIKit
import CoreMotion
import HealthKit

class CreateWorkoutViewController: UIViewController {

    ...
    var healthStore:  HKHealthStore?
    var startDate : NSDate?
    var initialStartDate : NSDate?
    ...

    @IBAction func toggleWorkout(sender: UIButton) {
        ...
    }

}
```

While it would be easy to create another HKHealthStore, it is wiser to share the one you created for the workout table. You can take advantage of segues to share the health store from the workout table with the create workout view. In the WorkoutTableViewController class, implement the prepareForSegue() method to detect when a segue has fired. As shown in Listing 4-16, after determining that it is a "CreateWorkoutSegue," extract the destination view controller of the segue. You can set the healthManager property on this view controller to the health store from the workout table.

Listing 4-16. Sharing a Health Store Between Classes (WorkoutTableViewController.swift)

```
override func prepareForSegue(segue: UIStoryboardSegue, sender: AnyObject?) {

    if (segue.identifier == "CreateWorkoutSegue") {

        if let navVC = segue.destinationViewController as? UINavigationController {

            if let createVC = navVC.viewControllers[0] as? CreateWorkoutViewController {
                createVC.healthStore = self.healthStore
            }

        }

    }
}
```

Now that you have initialized your healthStore property, you can perform save operations to save data. Remember that in the stopWorkout() method, after executing the step query, you displayed it in a label. To make the RunTracker application fully functional, you need to save it to HealthKit. The method for saving a piece of data in a health store is:

saveObject(HKObject, withCompletion: { (Bool, NSError?) -> Void in }). This method takes an HKObject as input and executes a completion handler when it has finished attempting to save the object.

For the input parameter, you need to convert step count to an HKQuantitySample. As shown in Listing 4-17, follow the same process you used earlier to look up the unit and type object for steps. Once you have these two parameters, you can create a new HKQuantitySample. For the quantity value, convert your step count from the pedometer to a double value.

Listing 4-17. Creating an HKQuantitySample Object When Ending a Workout (CreateWorkoutViewController.swift)

```
func stopWorkout() {
    //stop the workout

    self.timer?.invalidate()

    //pause timer
    toggleButton.backgroundColor = UIColor.blueColor()
    toggleButton.setTitle("Continue workout", forState: UIControlState.Normal)
```

```
    //save steps
    if (pedometer != nil && startDate != nil) {
        let now = NSDate()

        pedometer?.stopPedometerUpdates()

        pedometer?.queryPedometerDataFromDate(startDate!, toDate: now,
        withHandler: { (data: CMPedometerData?, error: NSError?) -> Void in
            if (error == nil) {

                if let activityType = HKQuantityType.quantityTypeForIdentifier(HKQuantity
                TypeIdentifierStepCount) {

                    let numberOfSteps = data?.numberOfSteps.doubleValue

                    let countUnit = HKUnit(fromString: "count")

                    let stepQuantity = HKQuantity(unit: countUnit, doubleValue: numberOfSteps!)

                    let activitySample = HKQuantitySample(type: activityType,
                    quantity: stepQuantity, startDate: self.startDate!, endDate: now)

        //increase duration
        duration += now.timeIntervalSinceDate(startDate!)
    }
}
```

For the save operation, you need to define a completion handler. Since the RunTracker application aggregates segments into a single workout, append the newly created HKQuantitySample into an array as shown in Listing 4-18.

***Listing 4-18.** Saving HKQuantitySample Objects When Ending a Workout (CreateWorkoutViewController.swift)*

```
func stopWorkout() {
    //stop the workout

    self.timer?.invalidate()

    //pause timer
    toggleButton.backgroundColor = UIColor.blueColor()
    toggleButton.setTitle("Continue workout", forState: UIControlState.Normal)

    //save steps
    if (pedometer != nil && startDate != nil) {
        let now = NSDate()

        pedometer?.stopPedometerUpdates()
```

```
        pedometer?.queryPedometerDataFromDate(startDate!, toDate: now, withHandler: {
        (data: CMPedometerData?, error: NSError?) -> Void in
            if (error == nil) {

                if let activityType = HKQuantityType.quantityTypeForIdentifier(HKQuantity
                TypeIdentifierStepCount) {

                    let numberOfSteps = data?.numberOfSteps.doubleValue

                    let countUnit = HKUnit(fromString: "count")

                    let stepQuantity = HKQuantity(unit: countUnit, doubleValue: numberOfSteps!)

                    let activitySample = HKQuantitySample(type: activityType, quantity:
                    stepQuantity, startDate: self.startDate!, endDate: now)

                    self.healthStore?.saveObject(activitySample, withCompletion: {
                    (completed : Bool, error : NSError?) -> Void in
                        if (error == nil) {

                            //add to sample array
                            self.sampleArray.append(activitySample)

                        } else {
                            self.presentErrorMessage("Error saving steps")
                        }
                    })

                }

            } else {
                self.presentErrorMessage("Could not access pedometer")
            }
        })

        //increase duration
        duration += now.timeIntervalSinceDate(startDate!)
    }
}
```

In Listing 4-19, I have modified the class definition to include the sample array.

Listing 4-19. Adding an HKSample Sample Array to the CreateWorkoutViewController Class

```
class CreateWorkoutViewController: UIViewController {

    ...

    var sampleArray = [HKSample]()
    ...

    @IBAction func toggleWorkout(sender: UIButton) {
        ...
    }

}
```

Creating a Workout Object in HealthKitAs mentioned in the design for the RunTracker application, the user presses the Done button to complete his workout and saves it to HealthKit. In the handler for the Done button, `done()`, you should create a new `HKWorkout` object and save it to HealthKit, similar to the way you saved `HKQuantitySamples` every time the user paused his workout.

To create a new workout, use the constructor `HKWorkout(activityType: HKWorkoutActivityType, startDate: NSDate, endDate: NSDate)`. For the activity type, convert the last valid `CMMotionActivity`, stored in the `lastActivity` property to an `HKWorkoutType`. As shown in Listing 4-20, I have added this logic to the `done()` method by specifying an `HKWorkoutType` based on the activity's type property.

Listing 4-20. Converting Activity Type to Workout Type

```
@IBAction func done(sender: UIBarButtonItem) {

        //create new workout object
        let now = NSDate()

        if workoutActive {
            self.stopWorkout()
        }

        var workoutType = HKWorkoutActivityType.Walking

        if lastActivity != nil {
            if (lastActivity?.walking == true) {
                workoutType = HKWorkoutActivityType.Walking
            }
            if (lastActivity?.running == true) {
                workoutType = HKWorkoutActivityType.Running
            }

            if (lastActivity?.cycling == true) {
                workoutType = HKWorkoutActivityType.Cycling
            }
        }

}
```

The rest of the logic for saving a workout is relatively straightforward. As shown in Listing 4-21, you can now create an `HKWorkout` and save it using the health store's `saveObject()` method. For the start time, use the initial start time when the user started the first segment of his workout.

Listing 4-21. Saving HKWorkout

```
@IBAction func done(sender: UIBarButtonItem) {

        //create new workout object
        let now = NSDate()
```

```
        if workoutActive {
            self.stopWorkout()
        }

        var workoutType = HKWorkoutActivityType.Walking

      ..

        if initialStartDate != nil {

            let workout = HKWorkout(activityType: workoutType, startDate: initialStartDate!,
            endDate: now)

            self.healthStore?.saveObject(workout, withCompletion: { (completed: Bool,
            error: NSError?) -> Void in
                //workout

..

        }

    }
```

To associate a set of samples to a workout, use the method:

```
addSamples(_:toWorkout:completion:)
```

which requires a set of samples, a workout, and a completion handler. As shown in Listing 4-22, use the sampleArray and newly created workout as your input, and exit the view controller when the operation has completed successfully.

Listing 4-22. Associating Samples to a Workout

```
@IBAction func done(sender: UIBarButtonItem) {

    ..

    if initialStartDate != nil {

        let workout = HKWorkout(activityType: workoutType, startDate: initialStartDate!,
        endDate: now)

        self.healthStore?.saveObject(workout, withCompletion: { (completed: Bool,
        error: NSError?) -> Void in
            //workout

            if error == nil {

                self.healthStore?.addSamples(self.sampleArray, toWorkout: workout,
                completion: { (completed : Bool, error: NSError?) -> Void in
```

```
                    //
                    if error == nil {
                        print("steps saved successfully!")

                        self.dismissViewControllerAnimated(true, completion: nil)

                    } else {
                        self.presentErrorMessage("Error adding steps")
                    }
                })

            } else {
                self.presentErrorMessage("Error saving workout")
            }
        })

        //add samples

         //save

    }

}
```

Having implemented all of the changes in this chapter, the RunTracker app should now be complete and look like the screenshot in Figure 4-2.

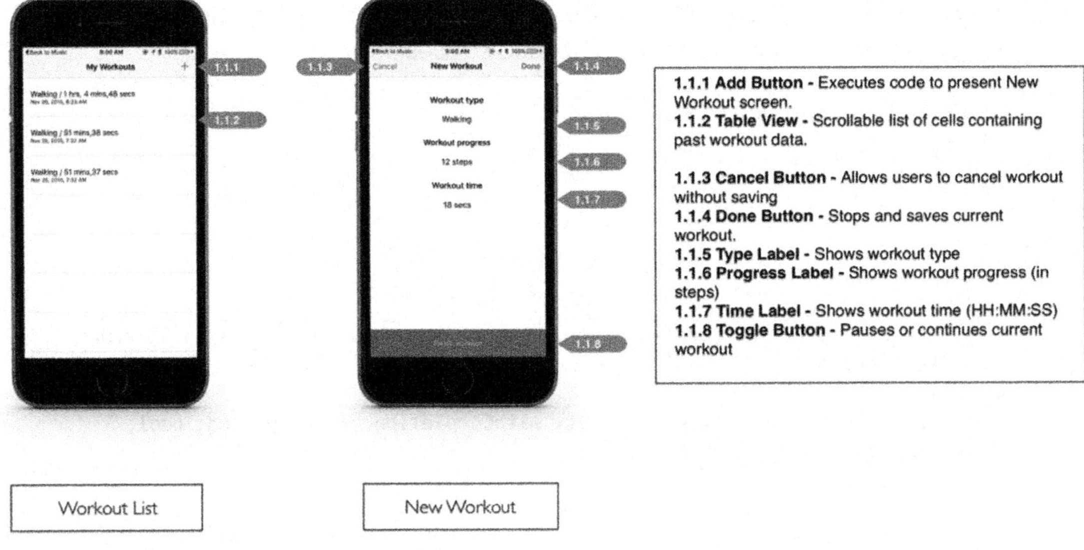

***Figure 4-2.** Completed RunTracker application*

Summary

In this chapter, you learned how to use HealthKit and Core Motion to track a user's fitness activity by building the RunTracker activity, which displayed a user's past workouts, and allowed the user to create new ones. Through the process of building RunTracker, you learned about the similarities between the two frameworks, including how they require user permission and hardware checks before you can start using them. You also learned about queries, which allow you to poll for data on demand and receive updates when a data source has changed. Finally, you converted data from the pedometer into a data type that HealthKit could use and saved it back to HealthKit.

Chapter 5

Integrating Third-Party Fitness Trackers and Data Using the Fitbit API

Gheorghe Chesler

One would be remiss to discuss health sensors without mentioning the most popular connected motion tracker on the market, the Fitbit. Through its web-based API (application programming interface), Fitbit allows developers to access activity logged from its hardware, as well as related health information from Fitbit's ecosystem, including meals and weight. This chapter will teach developers how to connect to the API from within their apps, as well as how to retrieve information from it and log new activities.

Introduction to the Fitbit API

The Fitbit devices are health metrics trackers that record detailed minute-by-minute steps, distance, calorie burn data, and sleep records. The devices are popular because they are very light and cover the basic needs for health tracking.

The step data, calorie counts, sleep records, and heart rate (if measured by your tracker) will be stored for 30 days. This data will all upload to your account as soon as you are able to sync and will then be reflected on your dashboard.

You can sync your tracker through any computer, as long as it has the Fitbit software installed and a base station (for Ultra tracker) or a wireless sync dongle (for all other trackers) plugged into the computer. There is, of course, a free iPhone app available that makes it possible to sync the data when you are on the road. You can only have one tracker paired to one `Fitbit.com` account.

The communication between the Fitbit tracker and the sync device is using a proprietary protocol that syncs the data with your online Fitbit account. Fitbit provides an API that allows you to access your stored health data from the app you develop in Swift.

The Fitbit API is a RESTful API that provides access to Fitbit data such as tracker collections, profile, and statistical data. This API is under continuous development and new features will be made available on an ongoing basis. The Fitbit API uses OAuth for authentication. The documentation for the Fitbit API can be found at `https://dev.fitbit.com/docs`.

The Fitbit API allows you to interact with your account data found on the Fitbit server. It is important to realize that you will not be able to interact with and get the data from your device directly. If you do not have an Internet connection, the Fitbit device will store data in the Fitbit application, but that data will not reach the Fitbit server until you get back online, so you will only be able to get the latest version of your data when you have a stable Internet connection.

Recently Fitbit consolidated the API responses from XML to JSON (JavaScript Object Notation). In this chapter we will use requests that return data in JSON format. The API does not currently enforce SSL (Secure Sockets Layer); it is, however, recommended to use SSL for all communications, or at least for the OAuth handshake.

The RESTful API

A **RESTful API** is built following a **RE**presentational **S**tate **T**ransfer architecture that defines best-practice rules for building scalable web services. Avoiding the complexity of SOAP (Simple Object Access Protocol) and WSDL (Web Services Description Language)-based APIs, a RESTful API usually relies on the HTTP verbs `GET, PUT, POST, and DELETE` to retrieve and send data to the remote servers. This data can be in a variety of formats, where JSON is the most popular.

GET is used to read data from a service, either as a set or as a unique record. Take, for example, the following request:

```
GET https://api.genericapi.com/v1/user
```

This will retrieve the user record with the `id=123`. It is up to the API to decide in what format to deliver the data, but in our case the data will be returned as JSON, something like:

```
{ "id" : "123", "login": "jsmith", "firstName" : "Jim", "lastName" : "Smith"}
```

Usually the `GET` request can be followed by a URL (uniform resource locator)-encoded string of parameters, as key-value pairs, as in the following example:

```
GET https://api.genericapi.com/v1/item?color=green&size=large
```

We see this all the time in URLs, so there is nothing unusual about it. Another method is to encode the params as part of the URL:

```
GET https://api.genericapi.com/v1/item/color/green/size/large
```

The documentation of the API you implement should give full detail on how to compose a GET request such as:

```
GET https://api.genericapi.com/v1/user
```

PUT is used to update a known record. Per the specification, PUT replaces the known record data with a set of different values. Depending on who is implementing the API, PUT can be also used to update just a subset of values instead of changing the entire data record. If it deviates from the specification, we usually find a clear definition of what PUT does in the documentation of the API.

When an id is defined in the request, PUT will replace the addressed entity, and if it does not exist, it will create it. PUT must contain a payload, which is the data record it updates. Look, for example, at the following requests:

```
PUT https://api.genericapi.com/v1/user/123
{ "login": "jsmith", "firstName" : "Jane", "lastName" : "Smith"}

PUT https://api.genericapi.com/v1/user
{ "id" : "123", "login": "jsmith", "firstName" : "Jane", "lastName" : "Smith"}
```

The two requests should have the same effect, updating the user with the id=123. Depending on the implementation, the API will return either the updated record or just a 200 OK response.

The PUT operation is known as idempotent, meaning that no matter how many times you repeat it given the same data, the result will be the same.

POST is used to create a new record. It is uncommon for the POST action to take an element id, as the API usually assigns the id. It is common for the POST action to return the inserted record, populated with the assigned record id. Take, for example, the following request/response:

```
POST https://api.genericapi.com/v1/user
{ "login": "jdoe", "firstName" : "John", "lastName" : "Doe"}

Response(200 OK):
{ "id" : "133", "login": "jdoe", "firstName" : "John", "lastName" : "Doe"}
```

DELETE is used to delete records, given their record id. It usually returns no response other than the regular 200 OK responses. There is not much to it other than the URL containing the id to be deleted.

```
DELETE https://api.genericapi.com/v1/user/123
```

The Return Format

Usually the return format for a request is specified in the header of the request, with the key-value pair.

```
Accept: application/json
```

Some APIs choose instead to use a file extension appended to the URL of the request, to recognize the desired format for the response. In this case there is no requirement for the return format specified in the header. This is the case for the Fitbit API, as we will see further on. Taking examples from above, following is how it would look:

```
GET https://api.genericapi.com/v1/item/color/green/size/large.json

POST https://api.genericapi.com/v1/user.json
```

A RESTful API takes the REST specification as a guideline, and you will rarely see this implemented strictly. It is not uncommon to see POST being used instead of PUT, or the other way around, or even using a POST to delete an item.

Fitbit RESTful API Implementation Details

Taking the general ideas defined in the previous section, here are some things that are particular to the Fitbit API:

- The patterns used in the service URL
- The format of POST data

The URL for a service is segmented in a service and object/subservice, with some magic added to it. Normally, when we GET from a service, the preferred order is the API version, followed by the service name, followed by the id of the entity, then a GET string, URL-encoded, and separated from the base URL by a question mark. In the case of PUT/POST operations, the agreed-upon standard is to send the data in the body of the message.

Fitbit composes the service URL a bit differently, making everything a part of the URL, and avoiding dealing with more complexity and eventually performance impact on its end. Take, for example, the following calls:

```
GET /1/user/228TQ4/profile.json

GET /1/user/-/profile.json
```

The user id is 228TQ4 but is followed by the name of the object/subservice being requested, and the extension shows the preferred response format, so there is no need to set the HTTP header field Accept. To make matters more interesting, if the user id is the id of the current user, we need to specify a dash (this is the magic part). If we consider the fact that the id is the user id, not the profile id, we see here the assumption being made that a user can have only one profile, and there is no need to expose the profile id.

Here is an example where the GET parameters are encoded in the URL path. Following are the resource URLs for getting body weight data:

```
GET /<api-version>/user/-/body/log/weight/date/<date>.<response-format>

GET /<api-version>/user/-/body/log/weight/date/<base-date>/<period>.<response-format>

GET /<api-version>/user/-/body/log/weight/date/<base-date>/<end-date>.<response-format>
```

Here are actual calls following the foregoing patterns:

```
GET /1/user/-/body/log/weight/date/2010-02-21.json

GET /1/user/-/body/log/weight/date/2010-03-27/1w.json

GET /1/user/-/body/log/weight/date/2010-03-27/2010-04-15.json
```

Somebody at Fitbit must have thought that this was a good idea, but there is a free-style assumption made here. Normally, even if you decide to use the URL as a kitchen sink, it would be a good idea to keep things consistent: instead, we look at “body/log/weight/date” to represent something like “these are the keys for the values that follow,” but even that does not hold, since the date can stand for one date (start), begin-end dates, or start date followed by the period.

Composing a URL for a request should not require a degree in creative writing, but that’s the Fitbit API and we need to adapt to it, so great care has to be taken when writing services that make a specific request, given that there is no clear rule of composition for the URLs of Fitbit’s API requests.

For `POST` requests, things are again rather different than the standard usage. The Fitbit API requires us to send the `POST` data as a URL-encoded string, as part of the `POST` URL. One of the advantages of sending `POST` data in the body of the message is that it would not land in the HTTP server activity logs, and it would not be exposed in the actual URL, but then it would be a bit more tedious to sign a request. This is perhaps the reason that Fitbit decided to take this approach, as much as it is not the most secure. Examples of `POST` requests follow:

```
POST /1/user/-/bp.json?date=2015-04-24&weight=73

POST /1/user/-/bp.json?date=2015-04-23&diastolic=80&systolic=120
```

From the current implementation we can see that Fitbit has limited the available verbs to just `GET` and `POST`, not making active use of `PUT` or `DELETE`. This can, of course, change with the ongoing development of the API.

Setting Up a Local Playground with Apache

To be able to test our code way before we are ready to deal with the complexities of the OAuth implementation, we need to set up a local web server. The safe assumption is that you are working on a Mac, so Apache is already installed for you.

For OSX versions before Yosemite, you can use Web Sharing to set up a local web server. OS X 10.10 Yosemite comes with the Apache 2.4 pre-installed, but there is no longer a Web Sharing preference pane in System Preferences.

You can install one of the online available Web Sharing preference panes or simply use the provided `apachectl` command from your terminal.

To start up the web server, simply bring up Terminal (/Applications/Utilities/Terminal) and type the following:

```
$ sudo apachectl start
```

To stop apache you would type:

```
$ sudo apachectl stop
```

If you start Apache now, you can reach your server in a browser by pointing it at the URL: `http://127.0.0.1/` or even `http://localhost/`, and you should see a simple header that says:

"It works!"

The document that contains the "It works!" text is called `index.html.en` and is located in the `/Library/WebServer/Documents` folder. Your current user does not own this folder, so you will not have permissions right away to create files. The easiest way to get permissions there is to change the flags on that folder. For that, you have to execute a command as root, using sudo:

```
$ sudo chmod 777 /Library/WebServer/Documents
```

You will be asked to enter your user password, which is the same password you use to log in to your Mac. By default, the users on a Mac have administrator privileges, so you should be able to use sudo to change flags or ownership of files and folders that are not owned by your user.

Now your user can create new documents in that folder: this is where we will create the two test documents used to verify the requests made by the first version of the APIClient library.

A more elaborate way would be to edit the Apache config file, and point it to a folder in your home folder. There is enough information available online on how to do this: for the time being, all we need is to create two test files in that folder, and start Apache, so we will take the easy route.

Creating the Test Documents

The easiest way is to use the same Terminal screen and vi to create the files. If you are not familiar with using vi, you can use any other popular console text editor (nano, cat, or echo):

```
vi /Library/WebServer/Documents/data.json
```

Paste the following text into vi, then save the file:

```
{"Response":{"key":"value"}}
```

To edit the second file

```
vi /Library/WebServer/Documents/badData.json
```

paste the following text into vi, then save the file.

```
{"Response":{{"key":"value"}}
```

The second file is intentionally populated with malformed JSON: this will allow us to test the handling of bad or incomplete responses that we might get from the API. Remember, just because you are talking to a public API does not mean it will always work perfectly, or return valid responses: your code will have to be able to compensate and handle the errors properly.

If you already started Apache, there is no need to restart it: what we added are two static documents and Apache will properly recognize them when they are present in the document folder.

The OAuth1.0a Authentication Model

The OAuth1.0a authentication model is a rather complex set of interactions between the consumer and the service provider, which is in our case the Fitbit API.

In a simplified way, the following steps are required to access your protected resources:

1. The consumer requests a request token
2. Using the request token, the consumer obtains the user authorization
3. The consumer then requests an access token from the service provider
4. Using the access token, the consumer can now make requests to access the protected resources

To use the Fitbit API we need to sign up for a developer account and register the application. Once we do so, we get the following bits of information that we will use in crafting the requests to the Fitbit API:

- Client (consumer) key
- Client (consumer) secret
- Temporary credentials (request token) URL
- Token credentials (access token) URL
- Authorize URL

The authentication information is usually passed in the header of the request, as key-value pairs. This allows you to build test cases or run tests from the command line, as in the example in Listing 5-1.

Listing 5-1.

```
$ curl -X POST -i -H 'Authorization: OAuth oauth_consumer_key="abcd1234", oauth_nonce="123",
oauth_signature="q4567aacc%3D", oauth_signature_method="HMAC-SHA1", oauth_timestamp="1429137772",
oauth_version="1.0"' https://api.fitbit.com/oauth/request_token
```

One important note here is that the curl example request is in one line. Curl is a command-line tool that allows us to perform a GET/POST request and retrieve the contents of the request.

The Fitbit OAuth Implementation

The Fitbit API is making a transition from OAuth 1.0a to OAuth 2.0 as authentication protocol. In this chapter, we will use the OAuth 1.0a, which is the current production version. When Fitbit will transition to OAuth 2.0, you will have to change your application to use the new version.

The upgrade from one authentication protocol to another is usually staged, so that first the new protocol is made available to developers, then as a beta to the general public. The developers migrate their code to the new protocol at their convenience, and that equates to using a different base URL for each authentication protocol, so both authentication protocols will be available for a reasonable period of time.

When the API operators observe from the amount of API traffic that the old authentication protocol is not being used, or has minimal usage, only then will they declare the old protocol obsolete and announce a date of when the support for it will be discontinued.

As a developer it is good to keep in touch with the latest documentation for the APIs you are implementing, so that you can give yourself ample time to upgrade your application to the new authentication protocol.

For the current OAuth 1.0a implementation, Fitbit follows strictly the specification of the protocol.

Following are the steps to making an OAuth 1.0a request:

1. The client acquires a key and secret from Fitbit by registering an application at `dev.fitbit.com`.
2. The client builds an application that uses content from Fitbit.
3. The user requests to view content in the client application.
4. The client requests and receives temporary credentials from Fitbit.
5. The client redirects the user to Fitbit in order for the user to authorize the client application.
6. The user approves the client application, and Fitbit redirects the user to the client application site, passing a verifier.
7. The client requests and receives token credentials from Fitbit using the verifier it received.
8. Using token credentials, the client makes calls to access Fitbit resources on behalf of the user.

To help with the implementation of the current authentication protocol, the Fitbit developer site has an OAuth tutorial page under "Authentication."

Step 5 involves a bit more work in the UI (user interface), such as displaying the redirect URL in a browser. On that page you will have a form where you will have to agree that the app can have read/write access to your account. Upon confirmation of access, you will get a verifier code, which you will need to use to request the token credentials used in this chapter.

The code in this chapter will work with the token credentials obtained in Step 8: we will not do a complete implementation; we will be focusing instead on creating the basics for signing OAuth requests and making the API requests once the token credentials are obtained.

You need to complete Steps 3 to 7 on your own. The signing mechanism for the requests is the same—just the list of elements to be used in the signature is different, but very well documented on the Fitbit support site, where you can double-check your process by testing every step by hand and comparing the output with the output of your code.

Once we established the signature process for the common-case scenario (Step 8) it will be very easy for you to create functions that sign with a different set of parameters, as we will show later on.

Fitbit API Call Rate Limits

The documentation for API call rate limits can be found on the Fitbit page under "Basics/ Rate Limits"/.

At the time of writing of this book, the Fitbit API set limits to the number of calls that can be made to the API in a given amount of time. When doing the full implementation in your application, your code has to be aware and able to handle the case when it hits one of the rate limits shown in the sections "The client+viewer rate limit" and "The client cate limit."

The Fitbit API has two separate rate limits on the number of calls you can make. Both are hourly limits that reset at the start of the hour.

The Client+Viewer Rate Limit

All Read calls (as well as a couple of sensitive Read & Write) are rate limited with the current quota of 150 calls/hour. You can make 150 API requests per hour for each user who has authorized your application to access his or her data. This rate limit is applied when you make an API request using your application's consumer key and secret with the user's access token and token secret.

The Client Rate Limit

Your application can make 150 API requests per hour without a user access token and token secret. These types of API requests are for retrieving non-user data, such as Fitbit's general resources.

Response Headers

Fitbit API responses include headers that provide you with your rate limit status.

- `Fitbit-Rate-Limit-Limit`: the quota number of calls
- `Fitbit-Rate-Limit-Remaining`: the number of calls remaining before hitting the rate limit
- `Fitbit-Rate-Limit-Reset`: the number of seconds until the rate limit resets

Hitting the Rate Limit

Your application will receive an HTTP 429 response from the Fitbit API when a request is not fulfilled due to reaching the rate limit. A "Retry-After" header is sent with the number of seconds until your rate limit is reset and you can begin making calls again.

Making async Calls

The Fitbit API is an external resource that might or might not be available to your device. This depends on your Internet connection availability, as well as any factors that prevent your device from accessing the Fitbit API. Additionally, sometimes API calls take longer than expected.

For this reason, the calls we make to the API need to be made as async calls. As an application user, this gives you the ability to do other things in your app, while the application is taking its time to communicate with the API and make the data transfers to and from the Fitbit API.

The simplest form of an async call is the following:

Listing 5-2.

```
var url: NSURL = NSURL(string: "http://127.0.0.1/data.json")!
var request = NSMutableURLRequest(URL: url)
request.HTTPMethod = "GET"
NSURLConnection.sendAsynchronousRequest(request, queue: NSOperationQueue.mainQueue()) {
      (urlResponse : NSURLResponse!, data : NSData!, error: NSError!) -> Void in
      // do something here with the response data
}
```

The block of code after the list of parameters of `sendAsynchronousRequest()` is the code being called when the API sends back a response and the connection is closed. The data object is the content of the API response, as an NSData object. This is necessary since it is not a guarantee that the API will always return JSON: the service being called could deliver an image or other binary file, which we will have to handle as necessary. For the purpose of this chapter we will assume that our responses are always JSON strings, and our code will handle the response accordingly.

The other side of async calls is that we do not have direct control over their flow—once launched, we need to provide a handler for the response async call that was triggered as the result of a button click. Your code needs to disable that button action to prevent duplicate calls from happening until a valid response has been received and the data has been successfully processed.

Using callbacks as Parameters

We aggregate most of the API functionality in the `APIClient.swift` library. This makes sense, because we don't want to duplicate this code for every type of call we make, and every service.

Listing 5-3.

```
Our apiRequest function has the following signature:
func apiRequest (
service: APIService,
    method: APIMethod,
    id: String!,
    urlSuffix: NSArray!,
    inputData: [String:String]!,
    callback: (responseJson: NSDictionary!, responseError: NSError!) -> Void ) {
        // Api call code here
}
```

We can see that one of the parameters is the callback parameter, which defines the signature of the callback function being passed to it. The callback function will be called in the block of code passed to the async call, after the API response has been received.

The following is the sample code for a generic GET handler using our APIClient:

Listing 5-4.

```
func getData (service: APIService,
   id: String!=nil, urlSuffix: NSArray!=nil, params: [String:String]!=[:]) {
   var blockSelf = self
   var logger: UILogger = viewController.logger
   self.apiRequest(
     service,
     method: APIMethod.GET,
     id: id,
     urlSuffix: urlSuffix,
     inputData: params,
     callback: { (responseJson: NSDictionary!, responseError: NSError!) -> Void in
         if (responseError != nil) {
            logger.logEvent(responseError!.description)
            // Handle here the error response in some way
         } else {
             blockSelf.processGETData(service, id: id, urlSuffix: urlSuffix, params: params,
             responseJson: responseJson)
         }
    })
}
```

We see here that we make a copy of self in the `blockSelf` variable. This is necessary, since the callback code block is a closure that does not have the context of the caller. If we pass self directly, this will block it from being garbage collected when it goes out of scope or gets destroyed. In this case self is the APIClient instance we use to make API calls, and we will run into memory leaks over time if we create/destroy the APIClient instance.

Setting up a Fitbit-compatible iOS Project

To implement OAuth in Swift, we could use an available library that supports both OAuth 1.0a and OAuth 2.0 to simplify the transition when Fitbit will default to OAuth 2.0. For the purpose of this book, we will implement the OAuth layer ourselves, instead of relying on a third-party library. We will also show how to make use of some Objective-C libraries where needed, to avoid re-inventing the wheel in Swift, and keep the scope of the Swift code small.

We begin by creating an empty, single-page project. This chapter aims to show how to communicate with the Fitbit API, not how to build an UI interface around it, so our application will be minimalistic, exposing just a few UI elements to trigger actions and track the communication with the Fitbit API, and making inline changes to some view controller functions as we go along.

The View Controller

A basic view controller for this chapter will only show a few buttons and a text area that we will use to display the communication with the API.

To initialize and to be able to use these buttons and fields, they have to be assigned macros that make them available/visible in the Interface Builder. We also define the variables used for the API and logger objects. Since these will be initialized at a later time, these variables need to be defined in the view controller as optional:

Listing 5-5.

```
class ViewController: UIViewController {
    @IBOutlet var labelButton : UIButton!
    @IBOutlet var textArea : UITextView!
    var api: APIClient!
    var logger: UILogger!
```

In the `viewDidLoad()` function we initialize the API object, as well as the log library that will output text to our textArea field. The content and functionality of these libraries will be explained as we go.

Listing 5-6.

```
override func viewDidLoad() {
    super.viewDidLoad()
    api = APIClient(parent: self)
    logger = UILogger(out: textArea)
}
```

To assign an action to a button, we create a function that performs the action, and is also annotated with the proper macro to make it available in the Interface Builder. We will add a log statement to show the beginning of the request, and we can also change the title of the button, while it is pressed.

Listing 5-7.

```
@IBAction func clickButton() {
    logger.logEvent("=== Good Request ===")
    api.getData(APIService.GOOD_JSON)
    labelButton.setTitle("Good Request Sent", forState: UIControlState.Normal)
}
@IBAction func unclickButton() {
    labelButton.setTitle("=== Good Request ===", forState: UIControlState.Normal)
}
```

Notice that we used the `APIService.GOOD_JSON` and `APIService.BAD_JSON` service names. This is a first-step implementation that uses mock services from a local server and gets in return a pre-formatted, static content, so that we can test the code. This will be later replaced by actual services like, for example, `APIService.ACCOUNT` or `APIService.PROFILE`. These are distinct values from enums that we define in the `APIClient.swift` library.

We can wire these button actions in the storyboard (Figure 5-1).

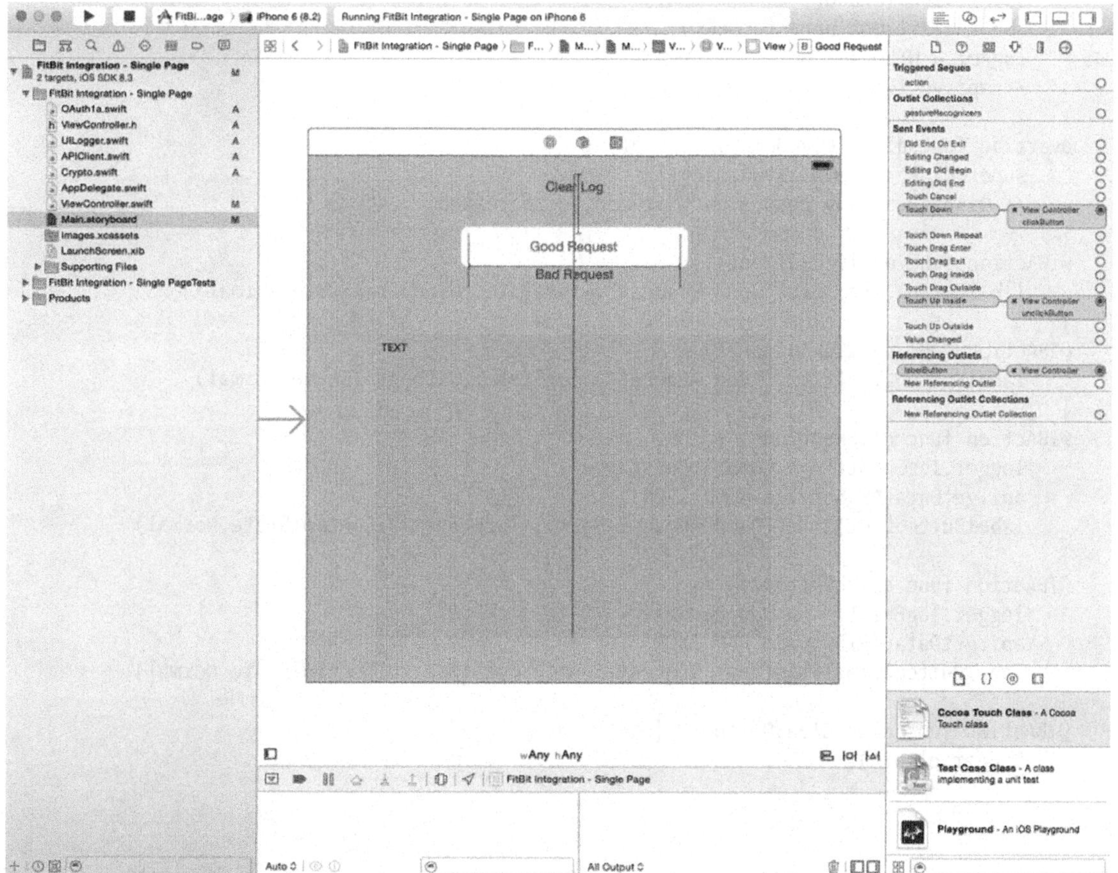

***Figure 5-1.** Wiring actions in the storyboard*

This is the entire `ViewController.swift` code that we will use to test the internal wiring of the APIClient library. You might notice that we commented out the `goLive()` method, that would set the baseURL for the API to the liveBaseURL in the APIClient library(more on this later).

Listing 5-8.

```
import UIKit
class ViewController: UIViewController {
    @IBOutlet var clearButton : UIButton!
    @IBOutlet var labelButton : UIButton!
    @IBOutlet var labelButton2 : UIButton!
    @IBOutlet var textArea : UITextView!
    var api: APIClient!
    var logger: UILogger!

    required init(coder aDecoder: NSCoder) {
        super.init(coder: aDecoder)
    }
    override func viewDidLoad() {
        super.viewDidLoad()
        api = APIClient(parent: self)
        logger = UILogger(out: textArea)
        // api.goLive()
    }
    override func didReceiveMemoryWarning() {
        super.didReceiveMemoryWarning()
        // Dispose of any resources that can be recreated.
    }
    @IBAction func unclickButton() {
        labelButton.setTitle("Good Request", forState: UIControlState.Normal)
    }
    @IBAction func unclickButton2() {
        labelButton2.setTitle("Bad Request", forState: UIControlState.Normal)
    }
    @IBAction func clickButton() {
        logger.logEvent("=== Good Request ===")
        api.getData(APIService.GOOD_JSON)
        labelButton.setTitle("Good Request Sent", forState: UIControlState.Normal)
    }
    @IBAction func clickButton2() {
        logger.logEvent("=== Bad Request ===")
        api.getData(APIService.BAD_JSON)
        labelButton2.setTitle("Bad Request Sent", forState: UIControlState.Normal)
    }
    @IBAction func clickClearButton() {
        logger.clear()
    }
}
```

When you implement your application, you will most likely have a series of requests triggered by either a sync button or a timer, all the time keeping in mind that the API has a call rate limitation.

The Logger Library

The logger library was assigned a variable in the view controller that will keep an instance of the logger around with the proper target assigned—in our case we use a text area field for the activity logging.

To keep things simple, we implement just a couple of functions that will allow us to track the API activity. These functions will interact with the textArea field we set up in the view controller. Just as in the view controller, the textArea field is declared optional, as it will be initialized in the `init()` function. The code in Listing 5-9 goes in the `UILogger.swift` file:

Listing 5-9.

```
import Foundation
import UIKit

class UILogger {
    var textArea : UITextView!
    required init(out: UITextView) {
        dispatch_async(dispatch_get_main_queue()) {
            self.textArea = out
        };
        self.clear()
    }

    func clear() {
       dispatch_async(dispatch_get_main_queue()) {
            self.textArea!.text = ""
      }
    }

    func logEvent(message: String) {
        dispatch_async(dispatch_get_main_queue()) {
           self.textArea!.text = textArea!.text.stringByAppendingString("=> " + message + "\n")
        }
    }
}
```

Setting up a Basic Set of Crypto Functions

Since the data to and from the API is of String type, the easiest way to set up the basic crypto functions is to set up a few extensions on the String object to handle SHA1 and HMAC hashing (the SHA and HMAC are hashing algorithms). We can set this in a separate file in our project, called `Crypto.swift`.

The `sha1()` function is provided as a convenience method that allows you to create fingerprints of results when testing against the API. It is not used in the OAuth signing process, and was implemented just to show how something like this could be done.

The `hmac()` function is used for creating the OAuth signature. You can verify its functionality with the Google OAuth request signature test page at `http://oauth.googlecode.com/svn/code/javascript/example/signature.html`. This is an easier-to-use test resource than the one provided by the Fitbit developer site, and it allows you to provide any combination of keys and tokens.

The `escapeUrl()` function is conveniently placed in the same context, because we will use it for composing the signature base string. It could have been a library function in its own right, but since it is conceivable that other parts of the product might use a good escaping tool, we decided to use it as an overload to the String object. Believe it or not, there is no NSCharacterSet with this set of characters, which is pretty odd, as this is the most useful set when composing an URL string.

There are a couple of enums in this library that are used by the `hmac()` function: we could have just used the values for SHA1 and saved ourselves the extra work with the enums, but with the full list configured, you can reuse this code for any other API that uses another hashing method than SHA1.

The functions are relying on Objective-C code that does the heavy work, so we need to set up a bridging header file. For that, create a new file in the project, give it a name(`Crypto.h`) and a location(Fitbit Integration - Single Page), and associate it with the current folder, as seen in Figure 5-2.

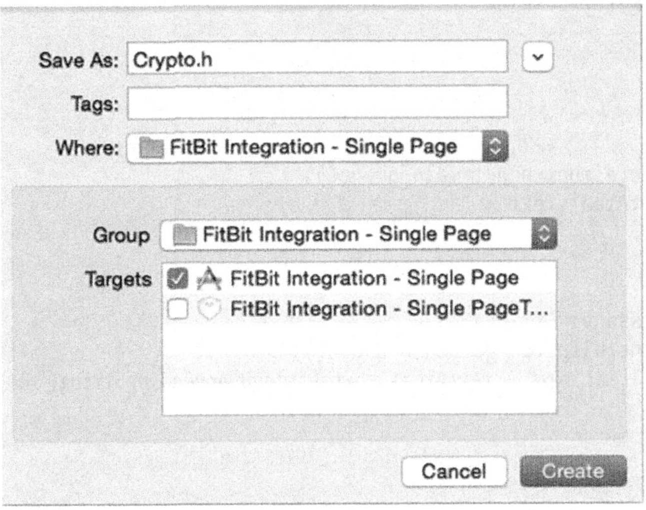

***Figure 5-2.** Saving the new crypto header file*

Listing 5-10 shows the content of the `Crypto.h file`: we added two lines that include the code resources we will use for calculating SHA1 checksums and HMAC-SHA1 signatures. The ifndef section needs to stay as it is.

Listing 5-10.

```
#import <CommonCrypto/CommonCrypto.h>
#import <CommonCrypto/CommonHMAC.h>

#ifndef FitBit_Integration___Single_Page_Crypto_h
#define FitBit_Integration___Single_Page_Crypto_h
#endif
```

Once the header file has been created, we need to move it up in the project file hierarchy, by drag-and-dropping it to the top of the file list. Then we need to set up the path for the bridging header (Fitbit Integration - Single Page/Crypto.h) in our project under **Build Settings / Swift Compiler - Code Generation**, as shown in Figure 5-3.

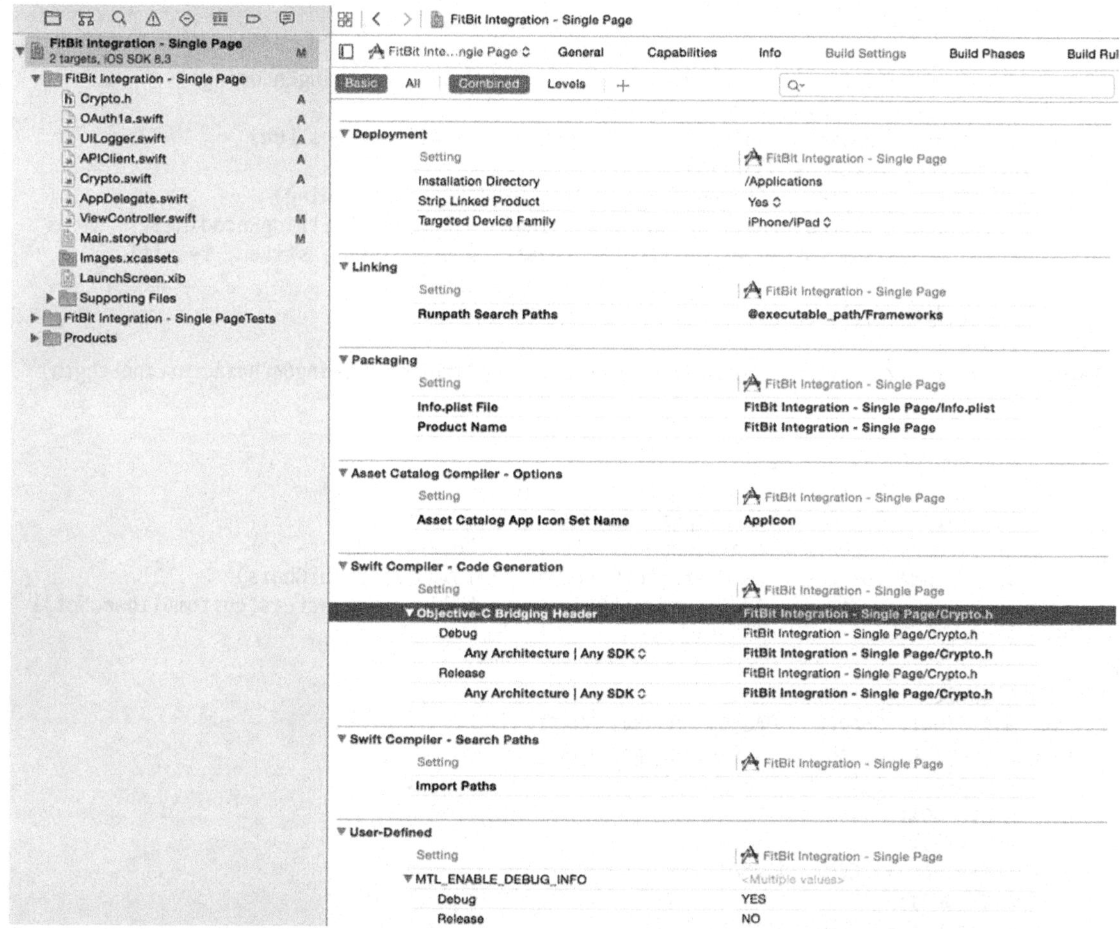

Figure 5-3. *Setting up the path for the bridging header in the project*

Crypto.swift

Listing 5-11.

```
import Foundation
extension String {
    func sha1() -> String {
        let data = self.dataUsingEncoding(NSUTF8StringEncoding)!
        var digest = [UInt8](count:Int(CC_SHA1_DIGEST_LENGTH), repeatedValue: 0)
        CC_SHA1(data.bytes, CC_LONG(data.length), &digest)
        let output = NSMutableString(capacity: Int(CC_SHA1_DIGEST_LENGTH))
```

```
        for byte in digest {
            output.appendFormat("%02x", byte)
        }
        return output
    }

    func hmac(algorithm: HMACAlgorithm, key: String) -> String {
        let str = self.cStringUsingEncoding(NSUTF8StringEncoding)
        let strLen = Int(self.lengthOfBytesUsingEncoding(NSUTF8StringEncoding))
        let digestLen = algorithm.digestLength()
        let result = UnsafeMutablePointer<CUnsignedChar>.alloc(digestLen)
        let objcKey = key as NSString
        let keyStr = objcKey.cStringUsingEncoding(NSUTF8StringEncoding)
        let keyLen = Int(objcKey.lengthOfBytesUsingEncoding(NSUTF8StringEncoding))
        CCHmac(algorithm.toCCHmacAlgorithm(), keyStr, keyLen, str!, strLen, result)
        let data = NSData(bytes: result, length: digestLen)
        result.destroy()
        return
data.base64EncodedStringWithOptions(NSDataBase64EncodingOptions.Encoding64CharacterLineLength)
    }

    func escapeUrl() -> String {
        var source: NSString = NSString(string: self)
        var chars = "abcdefghijklmnopqrstuvwxyz"
        var okChars = chars + chars.uppercaseString + "0123456789.~_-"
        var customAllowedSet = NSCharacterSet(charactersInString: okChars)
        return source.stringByAddingPercentEncodingWithAllowedCharacters(customAllowedSet)!
    }
}
enum HMACAlgorithm {
    case MD5, SHA1, SHA224, SHA256, SHA384, SHA512
    func toCCHmacAlgorithm() -> CCHmacAlgorithm {
        var result: Int = 0
        switch self {
        case .MD5:
            result = kCCHmacAlgMD5
        case .SHA1:
            result = kCCHmacAlgSHA1
        case .SHA224:
            result = kCCHmacAlgSHA224
        case .SHA256:
            result = kCCHmacAlgSHA256
        case .SHA384:
            result = kCCHmacAlgSHA384
        case .SHA512:
            result = kCCHmacAlgSHA512
        }
        return CCHmacAlgorithm(result)
    }
```

```
    func digestLength() -> Int {
        var result: CInt = 0
        switch self {
        case .MD5:
            result = CC_MD5_DIGEST_LENGTH
        case .SHA1:
            result = CC_SHA1_DIGEST_LENGTH
        case .SHA224:
            result = CC_SHA224_DIGEST_LENGTH
        case .SHA256:
            result = CC_SHA256_DIGEST_LENGTH
        case .SHA384:
            result = CC_SHA384_DIGEST_LENGTH
        case .SHA512:
            result = CC_SHA512_DIGEST_LENGTH
        }
        return Int(result)
    }
}
```

The API Client Library

We created this library for the functions that make async requests to the API. You can find the complete code at the end of this section; for now we will discuss parts of the API client library code. The header of the class contains the URLs and other variables needed for the API functionality.

Listing 5-12.

```
class APIClient {
    var apiVersion: String!
    var baseURL: String = "http://127.0.0.1"
    var liveBaseURL: String = "https://api.fitbit.com"
    var liveAPIVersion: String = "1"
    var requestTokenURL: String = "https://api.fitbit.com/oauth/request_token"
    var accessTokenURL: String = "https://api.fitbit.com/oauth/access_token"
    var authorizeURL: String = "https://www.fitbit.com/oauth/authorize"
    var viewController: ViewController!
    var oauthParams: NSDictionary!
    var oauthHandler: OAuth1a!

    required init (parent: ViewController!) {
        viewController = parent
        oauthParams = [
            "oauth_consumer_key" : "6cf4162a72ac4a4382c098caec132782",
            "oauth_consumer_secret" : "c652d5fb28f344679f3b6b12121465af",
            "oauth_token" : "5a3ca2edf91d7175cad30bc3533e3c8a",
            "oauth_token_secret" : "da5bc974d697470a93ec59e9cfaee06d",

        ]
        oauthHandler = OAuth1a(oauthParams: oauthParams)
    }
```

We added the oauthParams in the init function for convenience—your code will have to gather/compose these values when you do a complete implementation of the OAuth/signup process. The requestTokenURL, accessTokenURL, and authorizeURL were also added to show where they would best be located, but they are not used in the code of this chapter.

When you write tests, you might want to change between the liveBaseURL and liveAPIVersion and a local test URL that is the default for the baseURL, as we do in our case to test the good and bad JSON. A simple function will allow you to switch to live mode, as follows:

```
func goLive () {
    baseURL = liveBaseURL discussing
    apiVersion = liveAPIVersion
 }
```

A generic function to perform a GET from a service looks as shown in Listing 5-13.

Listing 5-13.

```
func getData (service: APIService, id: String!=nil, urlSuffix: NSArray!=nil,
params: [String:String]!=[:]) {
    var blockSelf = self
    var logger: UILogger = viewController.logger
    self.apiRequest(
        service,
        method: APIMethod.GET,
        id: id,
        urlSuffix: urlSuffix,
        inputData: params,
        callback: { (responseJson: NSDictionary!, responseError: NSError!) -> Void in
            if (responseError != nil) {
                logger.logEvent(responseError!.description)
                // Handle here the error response in some way
            }
            else {
               blockSelf.processGETData(service, id: id, urlSuffix: urlSuffix, params: params,
               responseJson: responseJson)
            }
        }
    )
}
```

For the urlSuffix we use the NSArray data type that will hold all elements of the URL being accessed. We saw in The Fitbit OAuth implementation that there is no clear rule to composing an API URL; the API service calls have instead service names and values mashed up in a slash-delimited string. Since some of these could be numbers, the NSArray type is ideal because by default it contains AnyObject elements. We also pass the urlSuffix to the processGETData function, so that we can make a decision about what to do with the response, given the service being called, the optional id of the item, and the urlSuffix. We also defined default values for urlSuffix and params to allow our functions to make calls without providing all nil parameters in tow.

The optional input params is a dictionary with strings for keys and values. This is the most convenient format, considering that POST is not any different from GET in the way the parameters are passed to the API.

The block passed to the NSURLConnection.sendAsynchronousRequest is a closure, which is why we need to assign the blockSelf variable that will be used to make calls in the context of the APIClient library.

The function would be the actual handler of that response, which takes the generic form.

```
func processGETData (service: APIService, id: String!, urlSuffix: NSArray!,
params: [String:String]!=[:], responseJson: NSDictionary!) {
    // do something with data here
 }
```

Just like the GET request, the POST request can have the same structure:

Listing 5-14.

```
func postData (service: APIService, id: String!=nil, urlSuffix: NSArray!=nil,
params: [String:String]!=[:]) {
    var blockSelf = self
    var logger: UILogger = viewController.logger
    self.apiRequest(
        service,
        method: APIMethod.POST,
        id: id,
        urlSuffix: urlSuffix,
        inputData: params,
        callback: { (responseJson: NSDictionary!, responseError: NSError!) -> Void in
            if (responseError != nil) {
                logger.logEvent(responseError!.description)
                // Handle here the error response in some way
            }
            else {
                blockSelf.processPOSTData(service, id: id, urlSuffix: urlSuffix,
                params: params, responseJson: responseJson)
            }
    })
}
func processPOSTData (service: APIService, id: String!, urlSuffix: NSArray!,
params: [String:String]!=[:], responseJson: NSDictionary!) {
    // do something with data here
}
```

Of course, we can implement the request process in many different ways, but having a common handler for an API request type allows us to avoid a callback hell.

We notice that the verb is not a string but an enum value: APIMethod.GET. This is an enum that we define in this library, to provide easy access to the verbs as strings, rather than using the strings directly. It also gives us control on which HTTP verbs are supported by the API client. This code goes at the end of APIClient.swift.

Listing 5-15.

```
enum APIMethod {
    case GET, PUT, POST, DELETE
    func toString() -> String {
        var method: String!
        switch self {
        case .GET:
            method = "GET"
        case .PUT:
            method = "PUT"
        case .POST:
            method = "POST"
        case .DELETE:
            method = "DELETE"
        }
        return method
    }
    func hasBody() -> Bool {
        var hasBody: Bool
        switch self {
        case .GET:
            hasBody = false
        case .PUT:
            hasBody = true
        case .POST:
            hasBody = true
        case .DELETE:
            hasBody = false
        }
        return hasBody
    }
}
```

The `hasBody()` function is provided here as an example that could be useful in the `apiRequest` to properly format the request, so that `GET` and `DELETE` use the parameters as key-value pairs, while the `PUT` and `POST` use it as JSON. This is not necessary in our case, since the Fitbit API does not actually use a `POST` body but, rather, does a `POST` to a URL with the data formatted as URL-encoded parameters.

There is another enum we define in the APIClient library that provides shortcuts to actual services via the `toString()` function. We saw this in the view controller used as `APIService.GOOD_JSON`. We will extend this later to add other services and also provide a function to return the suffix we might want to use for some calls, but for now this is the basic format. As in Listing 5-15, the code in Listing 5-16 goes at the end of `APIClient.swift`.

Listing 5-16.

```
enum APIService {
    case USER, ACTIVITIES, FOODS, GOOD_JSON, BAD_JSON
    func toString() -> String {
        var service: String!
        switch self {
        case .USER:
            service = "user"
        case .ACTIVITIES:
            service = "activities"
        case .FOODS:
            service = "foods"
        case .GOOD_JSON:
            service = "data"
        case .BAD_JSON:
            service = "badData"
        }
        return service
    }
}
```

We added the extra bits like GOOD_JSON and BAD_JSON to allow us to do internal testing. These bits point to the test pages we created when we set up the local Apache playground. Since our apiRequest() function will handle adding the .son suffix to each URL, we only use the file base name.

Next to be defined is the apiRequest() function. This function will make the actual API request, and that includes handling the OAuth signing and eventual verification of the response data. The method signature is showing that the only required params are the service, the method, and the callback function.

Listing 5-17.

```
func apiRequest (
        service: APIService,
        method: APIMethod,
        id: String!,
        urlSuffix: NSArray!,
        inputData: [String:String]!,
        callback: (responseJson: NSDictionary!, responseError: NSError!) -> Void ) {
    // Code goes here
}
```

The services currently available are USER, ACTIVITIES, and FOODS— the API overloads them with a variable list of params, so in essence your calls will need to provide the larger APIService, and then provide via the urlSuffix the URL path extension to point to the right resource. This will be explained in more detail later on.

As for the content of the method, following is what we need to do for an API request:

- Compose the base URL of the service
- Add the URL suffix if it was specified
- Add the extension for the return data type
- Create the OAuth signature and populate the request headers
- Serialize and append to the URL the input params
- Make the API request as an async call

In the code block passed to the async call, we also need to do the following:

- Verify the OAuth signature of the response (if provided)
- De-serialize the JSON response
- Call the callback function

To compose the base URL of the service, we use the following code in Listing 5-18:

Listing 5-18.

```
var serviceURL = baseURL + "/"
if apiVersion != nil {
     serviceURL += apiVersion + "/"
}
serviceURL += service.toString()
if id != nil && !id.isEmpty {
     serviceURL += "/" + id
}
var request = NSMutableURLRequest()
request.HTTPMethod = method.toString()
```

If you recall, we saw in the Fitbit API implementation details that when an id is not provided, it is replaced by a dash in some requests. This kind of magic is not something we want to handle here: instead we rely on the caller to provide an id if one is needed, or the dash otherwise.

In the same segment, we create the request object and assign it the request method. The `serviceURL` is still being composed, so it would be premature to assign it to the request at this point.

If this API would support a JSON request body for `POST` requests, we could use something like the code in Listing 5-19 to serialize the input data.

Listing 5-19.

```
var error: NSError?
request.HTTPBody = NSJSONSerialization.dataWithJSONObject(inputData, options: nil,
error: &error)
if error != nil {
    callback(responseJson: nil, responseError: error)
    return
}
request.addValue("application/json", forHTTPHeaderField: "Content-Type")
```

Unfortunately the Fitbit API is not that fancy, and it takes instead a simple URL-encoded set of params appended to the POST URL.

To handle the composition of the URL, we create the asURLString() function. This takes a dictionary of input params and creates a URL-encoded string, with the parameters sorted alphabetically. Sorting the parameters is not a requirement in the URL request, but we will use the same code in the OAuth library.

Listing 5-20.

```
func asURLString (inputData: [String:String]!=[:]) -> String {
    var params: [String] = []
    for (key, value) in inputData {
        params.append( "=".join([ key.escapeUrl(), value.escapeUrl()] ))
    }
    params = params.sorted{ $0 < $1 }
    return "&".join(params)
}
```

The URL suffix needs to be made part of the URL—we got in the input an NSArray of strings or numbers that will be used to compose the suffix—they will be all reduced to a simple string, appended to the base URL.

```
// The urlSuffix contains an array of strings that we use to compose the final URL
if urlSuffix?.count > 0 {
    serviceURL += "/" + urlSuffix.componentsJoinedByString("/")
}
```

Adding the extension for the return data type is a rather simple matter. We also set the HTTP header for Accept, even if the Fitbit API does not require it. This is good practice, and it is possible that they will end up using it at some point.

```
// All URLs need to have have at least the .json suffix, if not already defined
if !serviceURL.hasSuffix(".json") && !serviceURL.hasSuffix(".xml") {
    serviceURL += ".json"
}
request.addValue("application/json", forHTTPHeaderField: "Accept")
```

To create the OAuth signature and populate the request headers, we will make use of the crypto library for the hmac encoding. The OAuth1a library instance prepared as the oauthHandler is used to sign the request, given an optional list of parameters in urlParameters. The extra argument signUrl is not used here and is not shown because the method signature defines a default value (nil) for it, but it could be used when signing with a partial URL like in the case of getting the temporary token (not shown in this chapter).

Before we create the OAuth signature, we need to assign the following serviceURL to the request:

```
request.URL = NSURL(string: serviceURL)
oauthHandler.signRequest(request, urlParameters: urlParameters)
```

Now we are ready to make the API request as an async call. Note how we created a local variable logger that points to the logging handler of the view controller—this is necessary because inside the closure we don't have visibility to variables and functions from the current library or from ViewController. The callback block for the async calls contains the basic code needed to handle the result data and call the callback function that we got when apiRequest() was invoked. Once again, when interpreting the response, an error can occur parsing the JSON data, which will be handled by the callback function.

To parse an API response into a JSON object, we use an NSDictionary object that will hold any combination of key-values. This is necessary since the API responses can contain any combination of numbers, strings, arrays, dictionaries, and NSDictionary supports by default AnyObject types. The NSJSONReadingOptions.MutableContainers specifies that arrays and dictionaries be created as mutable objects.

```
var jsonResult: NSDictionary?
var rData: String = NSString(data: data, encoding: NSUTF8StringEncoding)! as String
if data != nil {
    jsonResult = NSJSONSerialization.JSONObjectWithData(data, options: NSJSONReadingOptions.
    MutableContainers, error: &error) as? NSDictionary
 }
```

When encountering an error case that we need to report, we can create our own error object. To do this in Swift, we use the following approach:

```
error = NSError(domain: "response", code: -1, userInfo: ["reason":"blank response"])
```

We added some logging for the response data, with an example on how to pretty-print JSON to the text area used for logging. We do want to format the response in such a way that is easy to read, and pretty-printed JSON appears as one key-value per line, nicely indented.

Listing 5-21.

```
var blockSelf = self
var logger: UILogger = viewController.logger
NSURLConnection.sendAsynchronousRequest(request, queue: NSOperationQueue.mainQueue()) {
    (urlResponse : NSURLResponse!, data : NSData!, error: NSError!) -> Void in
    //the request returned with a response or possibly an error
    logger.logEvent("URL: " + serviceURL)
    var error: NSError?
    var jsonResult: NSDictionary?
```

```
    if urlResponse != nil {
        blockSelf.extractRateLimits(urlResponse)
        var rData: String = NSString(data: data, encoding: NSUTF8StringEncoding)! as String
        if data != nil {
            jsonResult = NSJSONSerialization.JSONObjectWithData(data, options:
            NSJSONReadingOptions.MutableContainers, error: &error) as? NSDictionary
        }
        var logResponse: String! = blockSelf.prettyJSON(jsonResult)
        logResponse == nil
            ? logger.logEvent("RESPONSE RAW: " + (rData.isEmpty ? "No Data" : rData) )
            : logger.logEvent("RESPONSE JSON: \(logResponse)" )
        print("RESPONSE RAW: \(rData)\nRESPONSE SHA1: \(rData.sha1())")
    }
    else {
        error = NSError(domain: "response", code: -1, userInfo: ["reason":"blank response"])
    }
    callback(responseJson: jsonResult, responseError: error)
}
```

Displaying pretty-formatted JSON can be useful in other places too, so we extracted the following code in the `prettyJSON()` function:

```
func prettyJSON (json: NSDictionary!) -> String! {
        var pretty: String!
        if json != nil && NSJSONSerialization.isValidJSONObject(json!) {
            if let data = NSJSONSerialization.dataWithJSONObject(json!, options:
            NSJSONWritingOptions.PrettyPrinted, error: nil) {
                pretty = NSString(data: data, encoding: NSUTF8StringEncoding) as? String
            }        }          return pretty
    }
```

To parse the response and extract the API rate limits, we need to extract from the response header the following key-value pairs:

```
Fitbit-Rate-Limit-Limit: 150
Fitbit-Rate-Limit-Remaining: 149
Fitbit-Rate-Limit-Reset: 1478
```

The function `extractRateLimits()` will take care of that, and it will also throw some statements in the console log that will help with the debugging. We already defined the variables in the APIClient header, and we update these with every API call we make. Since we have the `rateLimitTimeStamp` value, we can use this to compare with the current timestamp and see whether the `rateLimitTimeStamp + rateLimitReset` is smaller than the current timestamp; then we can make the next API call with confidence and otherwise handle the issue inside the application, returning an error early, instead of making a call that we know is going to fail. This can be easily implemented in the `apiRequest()` so we leave this as an exercise for the reader.

Listing 5-22.

```
func extractRateLimits (response: NSURLResponse) {
    if let urlResponse = response as? NSHTTPURLResponse {
        if let rl = urlResponse.allHeaderFields["Fitbit-Rate-Limit-Limit"] as? NSString as?
        String {
            rateLimit = rl.toInt()
            print("RESPONSE HEADER rateLimit: \(rl)")
        }
        if let rlr = urlResponse.allHeaderFields["Fitbit-Rate-Limit-Remaining"] as? NSString
        as? String {
            rateLimitRemaining = rlr.toInt()
            print("RESPONSE HEADER rateLimitRemaining: \(rlr)")
        }
        if let rlx = urlResponse.allHeaderFields["Fitbit-Rate-Limit-Reset"] as? NSString as?
        String {
            rateLimitReset = rlx.toInt()
            rateLimitTimeStamp = String(format:"%d",
            Int(NSDate().timeIntervalSince1970)).toInt()
            print("RESPONSE HEADER rateLimitReset: \(rlx), checked at: \(rateLimitTimeStamp)")
        }
    }
}
```

The Code for APIClient.swift

Listing 5-23 shows the code we have so far for the APIClient library (`APIClient.swift`):

Listing 5-23.

```
import Foundation
class APIClient {
    var apiVersion: String!
    var baseURL: String = "http://127.0.0.1"
    var liveBaseURL: String = "https://api.fitbit.com"
    var liveAPIVersion: String = "1"
    var requestTokenURL: String = "https://api.fitbit.com/oauth/request_token"
    var accessTokenURL: String = "https://api.fitbit.com/oauth/access_token"
    var authorizeURL: String = "https://www.fitbit.com/oauth/authorize"
    var viewController: ViewController!
    var oauthParams: NSDictionary!
    var oauthHandler: OAuth1a!
    var rateLimit: Int!
    var rateLimitRemaining: Int!
    var rateLimitReset: Int!
    var rateLimitTimeStamp: Int!

    required init (parent: ViewController!) {
        viewController = parent
        oauthParams = [
            "oauth_consumer_key" : "6cf4162a72ac4a4382c098caec132782",
            "oauth_consumer_secret" : "c652d5fb28f344679f3b6b12121465af",
```

```
            "oauth_token" : "5a3ca2edf91d7175cad30bc3533e3c8a",
            "oauth_token_secret" : "da5bc974d697470a93ec59e9cfaee06d",
        ]
        oauthHandler = OAuth1a(oauthParams: oauthParams)
    }

    func goLive () {
        baseURL = liveBaseURL
        apiVersion = liveAPIVersion
    }
   func postData (service: APIService, id: String!=nil, urlSuffix: NSArray!=nil,
   params: [String:String]!=[:]) {
        var blockSelf = self
        var logger: UILogger = viewController.logger
        self.apiRequest(
            service,
            method: APIMethod.POST,
            id: id,
            urlSuffix: urlSuffix,
            inputData: params,
            callback: { (responseJson: NSDictionary!, responseError: NSError!) -> Void in
                if (responseError != nil) {
                    logger.logEvent(responseError!.description)
                    // Handle here the error response in some way
                }
                else {
                    blockSelf.processPOSTData(service, id: id, urlSuffix: urlSuffix,
                     params: params, responseJson: responseJson)
                }
        })
    }
    func processPOSTData (service: APIService, id: String!, urlSuffix: NSArray!,
    params: [String:String]!=[:], responseJson: NSDictionary!) {
        // do something with data here
    }
    func getData (service: APIService, id: String!=nil, urlSuffix: NSArray!=nil,
    params: [String:String]!=[:]) {
        var blockSelf = self
        var logger: UILogger = viewController.logger
        self.apiRequest(
            service,
            method: APIMethod.GET,
            id: id,
            urlSuffix: urlSuffix,
            inputData: params,
            callback: { (responseJson: NSDictionary!, responseError: NSError!) -> Void in
           if (responseError != nil) {
               logger.logEvent(responseError!.description)
                   // Handle here the error response in some way
               }
```

```
            else {
                blockSelf.processGETData(service, id: id, urlSuffix: urlSuffix,
                params: params, responseJson: responseJson)
            }
        })
    }

    func processGETData (service: APIService, id: String!, urlSuffix: NSArray!,
    params: [String:String]!=[:], responseJson: NSDictionary!) {
        // do something with data here
    }

    func apiRequest (
        service: APIService,
        method: APIMethod,
        id: String!,
        urlSuffix: NSArray!,
        inputData: [String:String]!,
        callback: (responseJson: NSDictionary!, responseError: NSError!) -> Void ) {
        // Compose the base URL
        var serviceURL = baseURL + "/"
        if apiVersion != nil {
            serviceURL += apiVersion + "/"
        }
        serviceURL += service.toString()

        if id != nil && !id.isEmpty {
            serviceURL += "/" + id
        }
        var request = NSMutableURLRequest()
        request.HTTPMethod = method.toString()
        // The urlSuffix contains an array of strings that we use to compose the final URL
        if urlSuffix?.count > 0 {
            serviceURL += "/" + urlSuffix.componentsJoinedByString("/")
        }
        // All URLs need to have have at least the .json suffix, if not already defined
        if !serviceURL.hasSuffix(".json") && !serviceURL.hasSuffix(".xml") {
            serviceURL += ".json"
        }
        request.addValue("application/json", forHTTPHeaderField: "Accept")

        request.URL = NSURL(string: serviceURL)
        // Sign the OAuth request here
        oauthHandler.signRequest(request, urlParameters: inputData)
        if !inputData.isEmpty {
            serviceURL += "?" + asURLString(inputData: inputData)
            request.URL = NSURL(string: serviceURL)
        }
        //now make the request
```

```
var blockSelf = self
var logger: UILogger = viewController.logger
NSURLConnection.sendAsynchronousRequest(request, queue: NSOperationQueue.mainQueue()) {
    (urlResponse : NSURLResponse!, data : NSData!, error: NSError!) -> Void in
    //the request returned with a response or possibly an error
    logger.logEvent("URL: " + serviceURL)
    var error: NSError?
    var jsonResult: NSDictionary?
    if urlResponse != nil {
        blockSelf.extractRateLimits(urlResponse)
        var rData: String = NSString(data: data, encoding: NSUTF8StringEncoding)! as String
        if data != nil {
            jsonResult = NSJSONSerialization.JSONObjectWithData(data, options:
            NSJSONReadingOptions.MutableContainers, error: &error) as? NSDictionary
        }
        var logResponse: String! = blockSelf.prettyJSON(jsonResult)
        logResponse == nil
            ? logger.logEvent("RESPONSE RAW: " + (rData.isEmpty ? "No Data" : rData) )
            : logger.logEvent("RESPONSE JSON: \(logResponse)" )
        print("RESPONSE RAW: \(rData)\nRESPONSE SHA1: \(rData.sha1())")
    }
    else {
        error = NSError(domain: "response", code: -1, userInfo: ["reason":"blank response"])
    }
    callback(responseJson: jsonResult, responseError: error)
}
    func asURLString (inputData: [String:String]!=[:]) -> String {
        var params: [String] = []
        for (key, value) in inputData {
            params.append( "=".join([ key.escapeUrl(), value.escapeUrl()] ))
        }
        params = params.sorted{ $0 < $1 }
        return "&".join(params)
    }
    func prettyJSON (json: NSDictionary!) -> String! {
        var pretty: String!
        if json != nil && NSJSONSerialization.isValidJSONObject(json!) {
            if let data = NSJSONSerialization.dataWithJSONObject(json!, options:
            NSJSONWritingOptions.PrettyPrinted, error: nil) {
                pretty = NSString(data: data, encoding: NSUTF8StringEncoding) as? String
            }
        }
        return pretty
    }

    func extractRateLimits (response: NSURLResponse) {
        // Fitbit-Rate-Limit-Limit: 150
        // Fitbit-Rate-Limit-Remaining: 149
        // Fitbit-Rate-Limit-Reset: 1478
```

```
        if let urlResponse = response as? NSHTTPURLResponse {
            if let rl = urlResponse.allHeaderFields["Fitbit-Rate-Limit-Limit"] as? NSString
            as? String {
                rateLimit = rl.toInt()
                print("RESPONSE HEADER rateLimit: \(rl)")
            }
            if let rlr = urlResponse.allHeaderFields["Fitbit-Rate-Limit-Remaining"] as?
            NSString as? String {
                rateLimitRemaining = rlr.toInt()
                print("RESPONSE HEADER rateLimitRemaining: \(rlr)")
            }
            if let rlx = urlResponse.allHeaderFields["Fitbit-Rate-Limit-Reset"] as? NSString
            as? String {
                rateLimitReset = rlx.toInt()
                rateLimitTimeStamp = String(format:"%d", Int(NSDate().
                timeIntervalSince1970)).toInt()
                print("RESPONSE HEADER rateLimitReset: \(rlx), checked
                at: \(rateLimitTimeStamp)")
            }
        }
    }
}
enum APIService {
    case USER, ACTIVITIES, FOODS, GOOD_JSON, BAD_JSON
    func toString() -> String {
        var service: String!
        switch self {
        case .USER:
            service = "user"
        case .ACTIVITIES:
            service = "activities"
        case .FOODS:
            service = "foods"
        case .GOOD_JSON:
            service = "data"
        case .BAD_JSON:
            service = "badData"
        }
        return service
    }
}
enum APIMethod {
    case GET, PUT, POST, DELETE
    func toString() -> String {
        var method: String!
        switch self {
        case .GET:
            method = "GET"
        case .PUT:
            method = "PUT"
        case .POST:
            method = "POST"
```

```
        case .DELETE:
            method = "DELETE"
        }
        return method
    }
}
```

The OAuth Library

This library (OAuth1a.swift) handles the signing of the requests, not making the request themselves. There is more work for you to do to integrate all the steps in the OAuth process, and the best choice here is to build a good foundation, get the signing process right, and extend this later as needed.

The header of the library contains the essential variables specific to the signing process like the signatureMethod, oauthVersion and all the keys and tokens involved in any request. The init function assigns values for these, if they were provided. Depending on the request we are signing, we might need just a subset of them.

This code in Listing 5-24 and all other code in this section is saved in the OAuth1a.swift file:

Listing 5-24.

```
import Foundation
class OAuth1a {
    var signatureMethod: String = "HMAC-SHA1"
    var oauthVersion: String = "1.0"
    var oauthConsumerKey: String!
    var oauthConsumerSecret: String!
    var oauthToken: String!
    var oauthTokenSecret: String!

    required init (oauthParams: NSDictionary) {
        oauthConsumerKey = oauthParams.objectForKey("oauth_consumer_key") as! String
        oauthConsumerSecret = oauthParams.objectForKey("oauth_consumer_secret") as! String
        oauthToken = oauthParams.objectForKey("oauth_token") as! String
        oauthTokenSecret = oauthParams.objectForKey("oauth_token_secret") as! String
    }
...
}
```

We saw that the elements that help randomize the signature are the timestamp and the nonce. The timestamp is just the epoch time and can be easily read from NSDate. We are only interested in the Int value of this, which is the epoch time in seconds. This is found in the signRequest() function listed below:

```
let timeStamp = String(format:"%d", Int(NSDate().timeIntervalSince1970))
```

We created a separate function for the nonce, which makes things very easy for the caller. It takes an alphanumeric string that contains all valid characters then runs a random pointer over the string and extracts a character at that index until we get a random string in the desired length:

Listing 5-25.

```
func randomStringWithLength (len : Int) -> String {
    let letters : NSString = "abcdefghijklmnopqrstuvwxyzABCDEFGHIJKLMNOPQRSTUVWXYZ0123456789"
    var randomString : NSMutableString = NSMutableString(capacity: len)

    for (var i=0; i < len; i++){
        var length = UInt32(letters.length)
        var rand = arc4random_uniform(length)
        randomString.appendFormat("%C", letters.characterAtIndex(Int(rand)))
    }
    return randomString as String
}
```

Signing the Request

The main function in this library is `signRequest()`. It takes the request object, the URL parameters, as well as an optional alternative URL to be used for signing the request. The first thing we do is to prepare the `timeStamp`, `nonce`, and the URL to be used for signing. These are the variable parts in our signature. To make debugging easy we added some console logging statements. There is no need to log these to the text area on the screen, since it would crowd the space and provide little value once we get the first request right.

Listing 5-26.

```
func signRequest (request: NSMutableURLRequest, urlParameters: [String:String]!=[:],
signUrl: String!=nil) {
    let timeStamp = String(format:"%d", Int(NSDate().timeIntervalSince1970))
    var nonce = randomStringWithLength(11)
    var baseUrl: String
    if signUrl == nil {
        baseUrl = (request.valueForKey("URL") as! NSURL).absoluteString!
        print("REQUEST URL: " + baseUrl)
    }
    else {
        baseUrl = signUrl
        print("SIGN URL: " + signUrl)
    }
    print("TIMESTAMP: " + timeStamp)
    print("NONCE: " + nonce)
```

To calculate the signature we follow the guidance from the OAuth 1.0a specs, and we will find that the Fitbit API is following them indeed to the letter. In fact, we built this initially using the Google interactive OAuth 1.0a page, and it just worked with Fitbit. The order of the params has to be preserved exactly as shown. We also log in to the console the elements that contribute to the signature, to be able to verify the output with the API support page. It is important to observe that we escape both the `baseUrl` and the `normalizedParameters` strings once more before joining them into the `signatureBaseString`. We also notice that the `urlParameters` are mixed with the OAuth parameters; in fact, the resulting URL string needs to be sorted alphabetically by keys. The sorting is case-sensitive, so Z comes before a.

The signing key for hmac() is the concatenated values (each first encoded per Parameter Encoding) of the Consumer Secret and Token Secret, separated by an '&' character (ASCII code 38) even if empty.

Listing 5-27.

```
var signatureParams: [String:String] = [:]
    for (key, value) in urlParameters {
        signatureParams.updateValue(value, forKey: key)
    }
    signatureParams.updateValue(oauthConsumerKey, forKey: "oauth_consumer_key")
    signatureParams.updateValue(nonce, forKey: "oauth_nonce")
    signatureParams.updateValue(signatureMethod, forKey: "oauth_signature_method")
    signatureParams.updateValue(timeStamp, forKey: "oauth_timestamp")

    if oauthToken != nil {
        signatureParams.updateValue(oauthToken, forKey: "oauth_token")
        request.setValue(oauthToken, forHTTPHeaderField: "oauth_token")
    }
    signatureParams.updateValue(oauthVersion, forKey: "oauth_version")

    var normalizedParameters: String = asURLString(inputData: signatureParams)

    var signatureBaseString: String = "&".join([
        request.HTTPMethod,
        baseUrl.escapeUrl(),
        normalizedParameters.escapeUrl()
        ])
    // the key is the concatenated values (each first encoded per Parameter Encoding)
    // of the Consumer Secret and Token Secret, separated by an '&' character (ASCII code 38)
    even if empty
    var signKey = oauthConsumerSecret.escapeUrl() + "&" + oauthTokenSecret.escapeUrl()
    var signature = signatureBaseString.hmac(HMACAlgorithm.SHA1, key: signKey)

    print("SIGNATURE STRING: " +  signatureBaseString)
    print("SIGNATURE KEY: " +  signKey)
    print("SIGNATURE: " +  signature)
```

Now that we have the signature, we need to populate the request header with the correct string. Here, too, the alphabetic order of the parameters is important.

Listing 5-28.

```
// This exact order has to be preserved
    let header: OAuth1aHeader = OAuth1aHeader(name: "OAuth")
    header.add("oauth_consumer_key", value: oauthConsumerKey)
    header.add("oauth_nonce", value: nonce)
    header.add("oauth_signature", value: signature)
    header.add("oauth_signature_method", value: signatureMethod)
    header.add("oauth_timestamp", value: timeStamp)
    header.add("oauth_token", value: oauthToken)
```

```
    header.add("oauth_version", value: oauthVersion)
    let hParams = header.asString()

    print("HEADER: Authorization: " + hParams)
    request.setValue(hParams, forHTTPHeaderField: "Authorization")
```

Creating the OAuth H

The code that puts together correctly the header entry and escapes the values is tucked away in an inner class, at the end of the `OAuth1a.swift` file:

Listing 5-29.

```
class OAuth1aHeader {
    var hName: String!
    var params: Array<String>!
    required init (name: String) {
        params = Array<String>()
        hName = name
    }
    func add (key: String, value: String) {
        params.append(key + "=\"" + value.escapeUrl() + "\"")
    }
    func asString () -> String {
        var hParams: String = ", ".join(params)
        return hName + " " + hParams
    }
}
```

We did not create a common library for the APIClient and this OAuth1a library, so we need to duplicate some code that encodes the URL for signing. Sorting of parameters was not needed in the actual URL but is needed for the correct OAuth signature.

Listing 5-30.

```
func asURLString (inputData: [String:String]!=[:]) -> String {
    var params: [String] = []
    for (key, value) in inputData {
        params.append( "=".join([ key.escapeUrl(), value.escapeUrl()] ))
    }
    params = params.sort { $0 < $1 }
    return "&".join(params)
}
```

This was all the work needed for the OAuth signature. It wasn't that bad, right? As a bonus, we added the `signTempAccessToken()` function that can be used for the signing of the first step in registering the access of your app to a user account. Notice that the `requestUrl` is stripped of the protocol and the host part, so that instead of the full URL `https://api.fitbit.com/oauth/request_token` only the `oauth/request_token` path is used for signing.

Listing 5-31.

```
func signTempAccessToken (request: NSMutableURLRequest) {
    // This request does not use the URL for signing, but rather the path oauth/request_token
    var requestUrl = request.valueForKey("URL") as? NSURL
    var urlPath: String = requestUrl!.path!
    urlPath = String( dropFirst(urlPath) )
    signRequest(request, signUrl: urlPath)
}
```

The code for OAuth1a.swift

Here is the complete code in the OAuth1a.swift library.

Listing 5-32.

```
import Foundation
class OAuth1a {
    var signatureMethod: String = "HMAC-SHA1"
    var oauthVersion: String = "1.0"
    var oauthConsumerKey: String!
    var oauthConsumerSecret: String!
    var oauthToken: String!
    var oauthTokenSecret: String!

    required init (oauthParams: NSDictionary) {
        oauthConsumerKey = oauthParams.objectForKey("oauth_consumer_key") as! String
        oauthConsumerSecret = oauthParams.objectForKey("oauth_consumer_secret") as! String
        oauthToken = oauthParams.objectForKey("oauth_token") as! String
        oauthTokenSecret = oauthParams.objectForKey("oauth_token_secret") as! String
    }

    func randomStringWithLength (len : Int) -> String {
        let letters : NSString = "abcdefghijklmnopqrstuvwxyzABCDEFGHIJKLMNOPQRSTUVWXYZ0123456789"
        var randomString : NSMutableString = NSMutableString(capacity: len)

        for (var i=0; i < len; i++){
            var length = UInt32(letters.length)
            var rand = arc4random_uniform(length)
            randomString.appendFormat("%C", letters.characterAtIndex(Int(rand)))
        }
        return randomString as String
    }

func signRequest (request: NSMutableURLRequest, urlParameters: [String:String]!=[:],
signUrl: String!=nil) {
        let timeStamp = String(format:"%d", Int(NSDate().timeIntervalSince1970))
        var nonce = randomStringWithLength(11)
        var baseUrl: String
```

```
if signUrl == nil {
    baseUrl = (request.valueForKey("URL") as! NSURL).absoluteString!
    print("REQUEST URL: " + baseUrl)
}
else {
    baseUrl = signUrl
    print("SIGN URL: " + signUrl)
}
print("TIMESTAMP: " + timeStamp)
print("NONCE: " + nonce)

// The signing params need to be sorted alphabetically
var signatureParams: [String:String] = [:]
for (key, value) in urlParameters {
    signatureParams.updateValue(value, forKey: key)
}
signatureParams.updateValue(oauthConsumerKey, forKey: "oauth_consumer_key")
signatureParams.updateValue(nonce, forKey: "oauth_nonce")
signatureParams.updateValue(signatureMethod, forKey: "oauth_signature_method")
signatureParams.updateValue(timeStamp, forKey: "oauth_timestamp")

if oauthToken != nil {
    signatureParams.updateValue(oauthToken, forKey: "oauth_token")
    request.setValue(oauthToken, forHTTPHeaderField: "oauth_token")
}
signatureParams.updateValue(oauthVersion, forKey: "oauth_version")

var normalizedParameters: String = asURLString(inputData: signatureParams)

var signatureBaseString: String = "&".join([
    request.HTTPMethod,
    baseUrl.escapeUrl(),
    normalizedParameters.escapeUrl()
    ])
// the key is the concatenated values (each first encoded per Parameter Encoding)
// of the Consumer Secret and Token Secret, separated by an '&' character
(ASCII code 38) even if empty
var signKey = oauthConsumerSecret.escapeUrl() + "&" + oauthTokenSecret.escapeUrl()
var signature = signatureBaseString.hmac(HMACAlgorithm.SHA1, key: signKey)

print("SIGNATURE STRING: " +  signatureBaseString)
print("SIGNATURE KEY: " +  signKey)
print("SIGNATURE: " +  signature)

// This exact order has to be preserved
let header: OAuth1aHeader = OAuth1aHeader(name: "OAuth")
header.add("oauth_consumer_key", value: oauthConsumerKey)
header.add("oauth_nonce", value: nonce)
header.add("oauth_signature", value: signature)
header.add("oauth_signature_method", value: signatureMethod)
header.add("oauth_timestamp", value: timeStamp)
```

```
        header.add("oauth_token", value: oauthToken)
        header.add("oauth_version", value: oauthVersion)
        let hParams = header.asString()

        print("HEADER: Authorization: " + hParams)
        request.setValue(hParams, forHTTPHeaderField: "Authorization")
    }

    func asURLString (inputData: [String:String]!=[:]) -> String {
        var params: [String] = []
        for (key, value) in inputData {
            params.append( "=".join([ key.escapeUrl(), value.escapeUrl()] ))
        }
        params = params.sorted{ $0 < $1 }
        return "&".join(params)
    }

    func signTempAccessToken (request: NSMutableURLRequest) {
       // This request does not use the URL for signing, but rather the path oauth/request_token
        var requestUrl = request.valueForKey("URL") as? NSURL
        var urlPath: String = requestUrl!.path!
        urlPath = String( dropFirst(urlPath) )
        signRequest(request, signUrl: urlPath)
    }

    class OAuth1aHeader {
        var hName: String!
        var params: Array<String>!
        required init (name: String) {
            params = Array<String>()
            hName = name
        }
        func add (key: String, value: String) {
            params.append(key + "=\"" + value.escapeUrl() + "\"")
        }
        func asString () -> String {
            var hParams: String = ", ".join(params)
            return hName + " " + hParams
        }
    }
```

Testing What We Have so Far

With the code we have so far, we can make requests to the local host, provided that we set up the local playground with Apache and we have the two test documents in place. We clicked the Good Request once the Bad Request once, and in Listing 5-33 we can see the Xcode console output of the `println()` statements.

Listing 5-33.

```
REQUEST URL: http://127.0.0.1/data.json
TIMESTAMP: 1429481277
NONCE: OPrkKRdgn8I
SIGNATURE STRING: GET&http%3A%2 F%2 F127.0.0.1%2Fdata.json&oauth_consumer_key%3D6cf4162
a72ac4a4382c098caec132782%26oauth_nonce%3DOPrkKRdgn8I%26oauth_signature_method%3DHMAC-
SHA1%26oauth_timestamp%3D1429481277%26oauth_token%3D5a3ca2edf91d7175cad30bc3533e3c8a%26oau
th_version%3D1.0
SIGNATURE KEY: c652d5fb28f344679f3b6b12121465af&da5bc974d697470a93ec59e9cfaee06d
SIGNATURE: 2Efcl/SN9s+xR9qRTObIsNQwkpI=
HEADER: Authorization: OAuth oauth_consumer_key="6cf4162a72ac4a4382c098caec132782", oauth_
nonce="OPrkKRdgn8I", oauth_signature="2Efcl%2FSN9s%2BxR9qRTObIsNQwkpI%3D", oauth_signature_
method="HMAC-SHA1", oauth_timestamp="1429481277", oauth_token="5a3ca2edf91d7175cad30bc3533e3
c8a", oauth_version="1.0"
RESPONSE RAW: {"Response":{"key":"value"}}

RESPONSE SHA1: 5ae11e3b34fdcd7fba984695e9001511c9e0aa8d

REQUEST URL: http://127.0.0.1/badData.json
TIMESTAMP: 1429481278
NONCE: oOHgLcjefM6
SIGNATURE STRING:
GET&http%3A%2 F%2 F127.0.0.1%2FbadData.json&oauth_consumer_key%3D6cf4162a72ac4a4382c09
8caec132782%26oauth_nonce%3DoOHgLcjefM6%26oauth_signature_method%3DHMAC-SHA1%26oauth_
timestamp%3D1429481278%26oauth_token%3D5a3ca2edf91d7175cad30bc3533e3c8a%26oauth_
version%3D1.0
SIGNATURE KEY: c652d5fb28f344679f3b6b12121465af&da5bc974d697470a93ec59e9cfaee06d
SIGNATURE: DMB81a3oUO16lJa7YvUJpYguunQ=
HEADER: Authorization: OAuth oauth_consumer_key="6cf4162a72ac4a4382c098caec132782", oauth_
nonce="oOHgLcjefM6", oauth_signature="DMB81a3oUO16lJa7YvUJpYguunQ%3D", oauth_signature_
method="HMAC-SHA1", oauth_timestamp="1429481278", oauth_token="5a3ca2edf91d7175cad30bc3533e3
c8a", oauth_version="1.0"
RESPONSE RAW: {"Response":{{"key":"value"}}

RESPONSE SHA1: bd28faef1bc309899ed8540105c86ad23c1f27e7
```

Our simulator screenshot in Figure 5-4 shows the results of our activity. Now we are ready to test against the live API, and see if our OAuth work paid off.

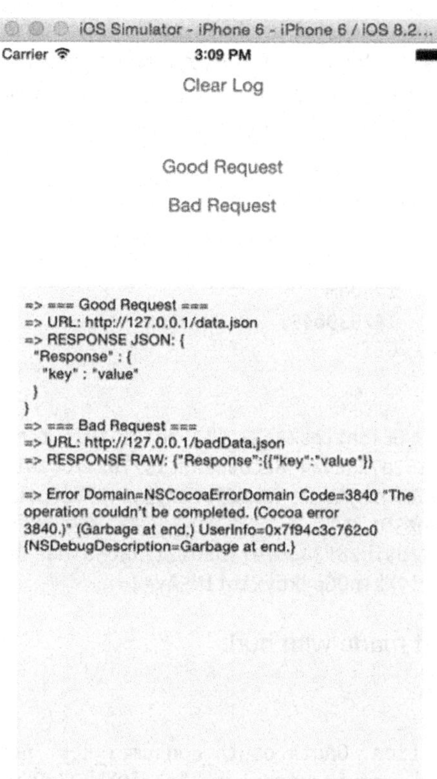

Figure 5-4. The simulator screenshot

Making requests to the Fitbit API

By now we know that there is no magic to the API request process; it is just important to assemble all the parts of the request in the correct order.

- Get the correct tokens and create the OAuth signature with all elements in the correct order.
- Keep track of the rate limiting parameters that could cripple your app if there is too much traffic.
- Build a parser that handles the JSON output.

On the Fitbit developer page, we can use the debug tool to place an API request, now that we know our access token and access token secret. Keep in mind that the request is signed not only with the access token and the access token secret but also with the `oauth_consumer_key`, which will be used by the API to identify the user account being accessed. The `oauth_consumer_key` is present in the Header, while the `oauth_consumer_secret` is used together with `oauth_token_secret` to sign the Base String.

Listing 5-34 shows the dissected request for the user profile, when we make the request using curl. Shown are the defaults for a profile that has not been updated since the creation of the account. The format of the response is well documented on the Fitbit developer site.

Listing 5-34.

```
Access Token:           5a3ca2edf91d7175cad30bc3533e3c8a
Access Token Secret:    da5bc974d697470a93ec59e9cfaee06d
Request URL:                   https://api.fitbit.com/1/user/-/profile.json
Nonce:                         random
Timestamp:                     1429396457
Type:                          GET

API request values:
Base string:                   GET&https%3A%2 F%2Fapi.fitbit.com%2 F1%2Fuser%2 F-%2Fprofile.
json&oauth_consumer_key%3D6cf4162a72ac4a4382c098caec132782%26oauth_nonce%3Drandom%26oauth_
signature_method%3DHMAC-SHA1%26oauth_timestamp%3D1429396457%26oauth_token%3D5a3ca2edf91d7175c
ad30bc3533e3c8a%26oauth_version%3D1.0
Signed with:                c652d5fb28f344679f3b6b12121465af&da5bc974d697470a93ec59e9cfaee06d
Signature:                  c2wi9Xk+nOGpjRoyxtotIM5AyA4=
```

Listing 5-35 shows the request made with curl.

Listing 5-35.

```
$ curl -X GET -i -H 'Authorization: OAuth oauth_consumer_key="6cf4162a72ac4a4382c098ca
ec132782", oauth_nonce="random", oauth_signature="c2wi9Xk%2BnOGpjRoyxtotIM5AyA4%3D", oauth_
signature_method="HMAC-SHA1", oauth_timestamp="1429396457", oauth_token="5a3ca2edf91d7175cad
30bc3533e3c8a", oauth_version="1.0"' https://api.fitbit.com/1/user/-/profile.json
```

Listing 5-36 shows the output of the curl request.

Listing 5-36.

```
HTTP/1.1 200 OK
Server: nginx
X-UA-Compatible: IE=edge,chrome=1
Expires: Thu, 01 Jan 1970 00:00:00 GMT
Cache-control: no-cache, must-revalidate
Pragma: no-cache
Fitbit-Rate-Limit-Limit: 150
Fitbit-Rate-Limit-Remaining: 149
Fitbit-Rate-Limit-Reset: 1478
Set-Cookie: JSESSIONID=5D7EA76F7CB0C45BF1A7A020C9BAC55B.fitbit1; Path=/; HttpOnly
Content-Type: application/json;charset=UTF-8
Content-Language: en
Content-Length: 657
Vary: Accept-Encoding
Date: Sat, 18 Apr 2015 22:35:21 GMT
```

```
{"user":{"avatar":"http://www.fitbit.com/images/profile/defaultProfile_100_male.gif",
"avatar150":"http://www.fitbit.com/images/profile/defaultProfile_150_male.gif","country":
"US","dateOfBirth":"","displayName":"","distanceUnit":"en_US","encodedId":"3BRQLQ",
"foodsLocale":"en_US","gender":"NA","glucoseUnit":"en_US","height":0,"heightUnit":
"en_US","locale":"en_US","memberSince":"2015-04-02","offsetFromUTCMillis":-25200000,
"startDayOfWeek":"SUNDAY","strideLengthRunning":86.60000000000001,"strideLengthWalking":
67.10000000000001,"timezone":"America/Los_Angeles","topBadges":[],"waterUnit":
"en_US","waterUnitName":"fl oz","weight":62.5,"weightUnit":"en_US"}}
```


To make live requests, we need to uncomment the `api.goLive()` in the ViewController library, and our requests will go directly to the Fitbit API. Of course, you need to make sure that the oauthParams in the APIClient are set to the values you generated while going through the registration steps of your application, as shown in section "The Fitbit OAuth Implementation."

Retrieving the User Profile

Not to forget, we have two test buttons in the view controller that test against the local documents. The easiest way to test if the API is working is to repurpose the code and make a user profile request. In the `ViewController.swift` file we have the following:

```
@IBAction func clickButton() {
    logger.logEvent("=== Good Request ===")
    // api.getData(APIService.GOOD_JSON) // TEST CALL
    api.getData(APIService.USER, id: "-", urlSuffix: NSArray(array: ["profile"]))
    labelButton.setTitle("Good Request Sent", forState: UIControlState.Normal)
}
```

We click the button and here is our first API call made through the application works. In the Xcode console we see the full detail of the request/response (see Listing 5-7).

Listing 5-37.

```
REQUEST URL: https://api.fitbit.com/1/user/-/profile.json
TIMESTAMP: 1429482687
NONCE: eTYGnygDYr4
SIGNATURE STRING: GET&https%3A%2 F%2Fapi.fitbit.com%2 F1%2Fuser%2 F-%2Fprofile.json&oauth_
consumer_key%3D6cf4162a72ac4a4382c098caec132782%26oauth_nonce%3DeTYGnygDYr4%26oauth_
signature_method%3DHMAC-SHA1%26oauth_timestamp%3D1429482687%26oauth_token%3D5a3ca2edf91d7175
cad30bc3533e3c8a%26oauth_version%3D1.0
SIGNATURE KEY: c652d5fb28f344679f3b6b12121465af&da5bc974d697470a93ec59e9cfaee06d
SIGNATURE: a+CWGxlsJiiJGc7ezIZVNtw3ASA=
HEADER: Authorization: OAuth oauth_consumer_key="6cf4162a72ac4a4382c098caec132782",
oauth_nonce="eTYGnygDYr4", oauth_signature="a%2BCWGxlsJiiJGc7ezIZVNtw3ASA%3D",
oauth_signature_method="HMAC-SHA1", oauth_timestamp="1429482687", oauth_token=
"5a3ca2edf91d7175cad30bc3533e3c8a", oauth_version="1.0"
```

```
RESPONSE HEADER rateLimit: 150
RESPONSE HEADER rateLimitRemaining: 149
RESPONSE HEADER rateLimitReset: 1713, checked at: 1429482687
RESPONSE RAW: {"user":{"avatar":"http://www.fitbit.com/images/profile/defaultProfile_100_
male.gif","avatar150":"http://www.fitbit.com/images/profile/defaultProfile_150_male.gif",
"country":"US","dateOfBirth":"","displayName":"","distanceUnit":"en_US","encodedId":
"3BRQLQ","foodsLocale":"en_US","gender":"NA","glucoseUnit":"en_US","height":0,"heightUnit":
"en_US","locale":"en_US","memberSince":"2015-04-02","offsetFromUTCMillis":-25200000,"
startDayOfWeek":"SUNDAY","strideLengthRunning":86.60000000000001,"strideLengthWalking"
:67.10000000000001,"timezone":"America/Los_Angeles","topBadges":[],"waterUnit":
"en_US","waterUnitName":"fl oz","weight":62.5,"weightUnit":"en_US"}}
RESPONSE SHA1: caa14550567548b173a0a904f0b3c7bae6d7452a
```

Figure 5-5 shows the screenshot of the user profile as it was read.

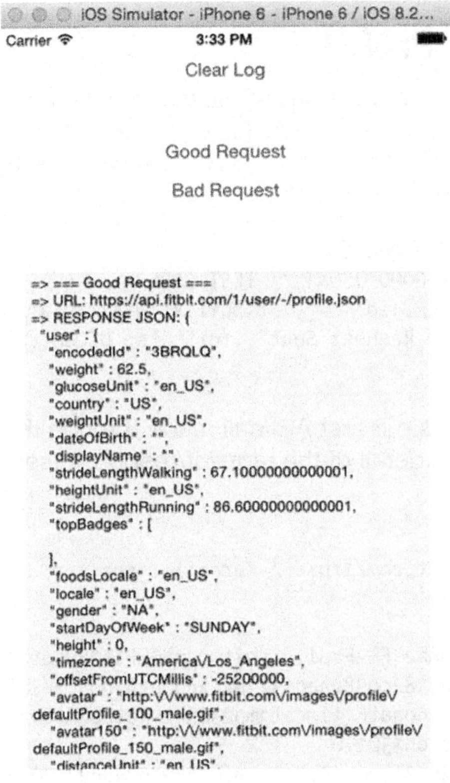

Figure 5-5. Screenshot of the user profile

Retrieving and Setting Data in the API

Like retrieving the user profile, this is a simple GET with a given API target. The following is a nonexhaustive list of targets you can currently query that retrieve and set user data:

- Get/Set body measurements
- Get/Set body weight and body fat
- Get/Set blood pressure and heart rate
- Get/Set glucose

With the exception of body weight and body fat, all the foregoing targets are unfortunately on the list of deprecated API features (as of October 2014). We expect that ultimately all services will be migrated to OAuth 2.0. Deprecated means that the features are still available but are not actively developed and will be later replaced by other features. The deprecated services will still be available for a while, after the new services are in place.

Fitbit announced three new products at the time of writing of this book: Charge, Charge HR, and Surge. The Fitbit API will provide access to the all-day heart rate and GPS data from these devices; however, these data types will be accessible exclusively via OAuth 2.0.

As the transition to OAuth 2.0 will be happening in the coming months, there is little point in detailing here how to use the entire set of deprecated API services. To make things easy we will show how to get and set a few data points: all other services are similar in nature to the request response, and well documented on the Fitbit developer page.

Getting the Blood Pressure

We will repurpose our "Good Request" Button in the ViewController.swift file to make this request:

```
@IBAction func clickButton() {
    logger.logEvent("=== Good Request ===")
    // api.getData(APIService.GOOD_JSON) // TEST CALL
    // api.getData(APIService.USER, id: "-", urlSuffix: NSArray(array: ["profile"]))
    api.getBloodPressure()
    labelButton.setTitle("Good Request Sent", forState: UIControlState.Normal)
}
```

The function we wrote in the APIClient is rather simple, and it makes use of the abstraction we created with getData(). This method is located in the APIClient.swift file.

```
func getBloodPressure (date: NSDate?=NSDate()) {
    let formatter = NSDateFormatter()
    formatter.dateFormat = "yyyy-MM-dd"
    let currentDate = formatter.stringFromDate(date!)
    print("CURRENT DATE: \(currentDate)");
    getData(APIService.USER, id: "-", urlSuffix: NSArray(array: ["bp/date", currentDate ]))
}
```

The function makes the following API call:

```
GET /1/user/-/bp/date/2015-04-23.json
```

Naturally, since we did not send any blood pressure information to the API yet, the default response is blank, as shown below. Your response handler needs to be able to deal with an empty response.

```
{"bp":[]}
```

Keep in mind that this response right now goes nowhere. When you implement your application, you will have decide how to handle it in the `processGETData()` callback function in the API, based on the data you set in the `urlSuffix` param, which we now know can be composed of the service name and its parameters.

When there are records for the blood pressure in the system, our response will be more like the following example shown in Listing 5-38:

Listing 5-38.

```
{
    "average": {
            "condition":"Prehypertension",
            "diastolic":85,
            "systolic":115
    },
    "bp": [
        {
            "diastolic":80,
            "logId":483697,
            "systolic":120
        },
        {
            "diastolic":90,
            "logId":483699,
            "systolic":110,
            "time":"08:00"
        }
    ]
}
```

Setting the Blood Pressure

Continuing to abuse the "Good Request" Button, we change things once again, this time calling the new function. Keep in mind that these are both async methods, and the way we implement them here is not necessarily the best way, as there is no guarantee which one reaches the API first, and they both rely on the `processGETData()` in the APIClient to handle the response. This function is in `ViewController.swift`.

```
@IBAction func clickButton() {
    logger.logEvent("=== Good Request ===")
    // api.getData(APIService.GOOD_JSON) // TEST CALL
    api.getData(APIService.USER, id: "-", urlSuffix: NSArray(array: ["profile"]))
    labelButton.setTitle("Good Request Sent", forState: UIControlState.Normal) }
```

We keep the `getBloodPressure()` function we wrote before, since we will need to read back the data we are setting so we create the `setBloodPressure()` function(located in `APIClient.swift`):

```
func setBloodPressure (date: NSDate?=NSDate()) {
    let formatter = NSDateFormatter()
    formatter.dateFormat = "yyyy-MM-dd"
    let currentDate = formatter.stringFromDate(date!)
    let request: [String:String] = ["diastolic":"80","systolic":"120","date": currentDate]
    postData(APIService.USER, id: "-", urlSuffix: NSArray(array: ["bp" ]), params: request)
}
```

This function makes the following API call:

```
POST /1/user/-/bp.json?date=2015-04-23&diastolic=80&systolic=120
```

The API responds with the data that was just inserted, with a populated logId.


```
{
    "bpLog": {
        "diastolic":80,
        "logId":1298241959,
        "systolic":120
    }
}
```


If we now make a call to get the blood pressure data, we get the full detail, including the friendly health warning. It is important to note that there is no timestamp, because we did not provide one, the field being optional.


```
{
    "average": {
            "condition":"Prehypertension",
            "diastolic":80,
            "systolic":120
    },
    "bp": [
            {
                "diastolic":80,
                "logId":1298241959,
                "systolic":120
            }
      ]
}
```

Logging the Body Weight

Just as we did for blood pressure, the service that lets you set and get body weight data has a similar implementation. To set the body weight, we call the service with the parameters listed in the API docs, very much like we did with the other service. Save this function in the `APIClient.swift`.

```
func setBodyWeight (date: NSDate?=NSDate()) {
    let formatter = NSDateFormatter()
    formatter.dateFormat = "yyyy-MM-dd"
    let currentDate = formatter.stringFromDate(date!)
    let
    postData(APIService.USER, id: "-", urlSuffix: NSArray(array: ["body/log/weight" ]),
    params: request)
}
```

This function makes the following API call:

```
POST /1/user/-/bp.json?date=2015-04-24&weight=73
```

The GET is no different from the blood pressure call, other than the URL path(`APIClient.swift`):

```
func getBodyWeight (date: NSDate?=NSDate()) {
    let formatter = NSDateFormatter()
    formatter.dateFormat = "yyyy-MM-dd"
    let currentDate = formatter.stringFromDate(date!)
    getData(APIService.USER, id: "-", urlSuffix: NSArray(array: ["body/log/weight/date",
    currentDate ]))
}
```

This function makes the following API call:

```
GET /1/user/-/body/log/weight/date/2015-04-24.json
```

The response from API is JSON data in the following format:


```
{
    "weight":  [
            {
                "bmi":0,
                "date":"2015-04-24",
                "logId":1429919999000,
                "time":"23:59:59",
                "weight":73
            }
        ]
}
```

OAuth versions: Working in both worlds

The current version of the API used by Fitbit is OAuth 1.0a. This is a stable, very secure, and reliable protocol but intrinsically complex. Just as is the case with PGP encryption, complex and secure crypto and protocols are being replaced by others that might not be so good, but they are convenient to implement.

OAuth 1.0a is signing every request, and that can be a resource drain on either side of the implementation (client/server). At the same time, there is no clear separation of roles between the authorization server and the resource server since a lot of data needed for signing is common to these roles. Granted, OAuth 1.0a has its place for the security it offers; alone for the sheer advantage of being able to sign and trust every request, it might never completely go away, but ease of implementation is not its forte. Consider, however, that with OAuth 1.0a when correctly implemented, the chance of success for a Man-in-the-Middle type of attack is extremely low, while with token-based protocols like OAuth 2.0, it's a simple matter of breaking SSL, which in the last years is developing holes much like Swiss cheese.

A lot of the recent API implementations favor OAuth 2.0.

OAuth 2.0 also accommodates much easier native applications with specifically suited workflows. It also provides a very clear separation of roles between the authentication server and the server handling the request.

Viewed on an elementary level, OAuth 2.0 defines the following workflow:

- Authenticate with the authorization server, and get an authorization code
- Request from the authorization server a set of access and refresh tokens
- Using the access token, request restricted resources from the resource server
- Periodically use the refresh token to get from the authorization server a new access token

The access token is set to have an expiration date, and the lifetime of one token varies with the implementation.

Given that OAuth 2.0 also gets a bad rap from security experts for the many loose ends in the specification and the potential for abuse and misrepresentation of the caller, it is conceivable that further versions of the standard will come up in the next years. For that matter alone, it would serve you well to follow the development of the standard and how service providers like Fitbit follow up with it.

In the case of Fitbit, the company announced support for OAuth 2.0, but there was no clear detail of implementation available at the time of writing this chapter. If you need to deliver your application right now, you should write services following the current OAuth 1.0a standard, but also be ready to provide upgrades to your app that will use the OAuth 2.0 services when they become public and well documented.

Consider that we went through a rather complex process to implement (in part) the OAuth 1.0a for the Fitbit API in its current version; looking back at the code, it wasn't all that bad. Writing code for OAuth 2.0 is likely to be easier, at least because you won't need to sign every request, and you can reuse much of this code: in fact you will have to, because for a good while you will have to live in both worlds, as Fitbit transitions the API from OAuth 1.0a to OAuth 2.0.

As mentioned at the beginning of this chapter, the transition from old to new is a gradual process for most APIs. Your application will be alive and well for quite a while, and you will have the time to study, implement, test, and deliver an upgraded version of your app that supports OAuth 2.0. What is most likely to happen is that Fitbit will offer specific services only on OAuth 2.0; so, for that reason alone, you will have to upgrade your app to support it as soon as it becomes available.

Summary

We learned in this chapter how to build an API to communicate with the Fitbit API and implement a few calls that get and set health data. Since this API, as most APIs out there, is under constant development, you might need to implement new or different calls to the API to do what we did here, as well as add support for OAuth 2.0 for the new API version, but the basic principles remain the same.

Chapter 6

Building Your First watchOS App

Ahmed Bakir

Introduction

In late 2014, Apple replied to the vocal concerns of many of its critics and consumers by introducing a completely new "product category" — the Apple Watch. This came as a surprise to (almost) everyone, why would the most profitable computer company in history enter the smart watch market, a "fad" that had yet to achieve a killer app? Similarly, how would they address people's bias as to how watches should look and work (they've only been around for a few thousand years)? And what would they do to make it an app platform?

The answer was to apply the lessons they had learned about mobile computing (low energy, low memory, limited screen size) to a device that was even smaller than the original iPhone. Much like the iPhone, the Apple Watch runs an operating system based on another in their family (watchOS, a subset of iOS), it has an open API (Application Programming Interface) that anyone can develop software for, and it has an App Store that users can access through iTunes. Due to the limited screen size and input devices on a watch (a touch screen and digital crown), watchOS apps are not intended to be as fully featured as iOS apps and as distributed as "extensions" of iPhone applications on the App Store. This has the positive side effect of allowing you to share data and pass off tasks to the parent application.

As the name implies, watchOS is a complete operating system, allowing watch applications to run independently when an iPhone is not present, such as when you are at the gym. Many of the frameworks on watchOS are taken directly from iOS, such as Core Data, Core Motion, and Core Location, but with a limited featured set. One of the key concepts in developing a resource-limited computer system, such as a smart watch, is that you should only include the functionality you need to make it fit in the resources you have; e.g., a smart watch does not need the advanced home screen of a phone to launch an app.

In this chapter, you will learn how to get started in Apple Watch development by adding an Apple Watch extension to the CarFinder application from the first chapter. As shown in Figure 6-1, the extension exposes a table view that allows users to view a list of their logged locations and details about each, including a map and the GPS coordinates. This exercise is intended to help you learn the basics of watchOS app architecture and how to use Xcode to develop watchOS apps. In the following chapters, you will learn more advanced features to make the app even more useful, such as logging location from the watch, adding speech-to-text to the app, and accessing data sources from the Internet directly on the watch. The completed version of the project is available in the Ch7 folder of this book's source code bundle on the Apress website.

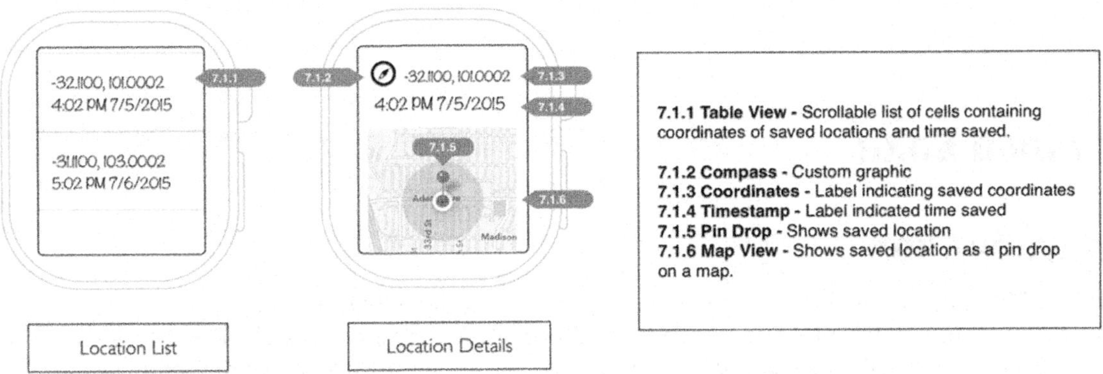

***Figure 6-1.** Mock-up of CarFinder Watch App*

watchOS Apps vs. iOS Apps

Before moving into how you build a watchOS app, it is good to know how watchOS apps differ architecturally from iOS apps (aside from running on a different operating system.) To reduce the learning curve for developers coming from iOS and OS X, Apple aimed to make both platforms functionally similar (even retaining some of the same class names and API calls), but changes had to be made to fit the operating system on the watch's limited resources.

The most significant difference between watchOS and iOS that will help you understand the delta between the platforms is that you cannot create new user interface objects at runtime on watchOS. Although both platforms adopt Model-View-Controller (MVC) as their main design pattern for user interface development, on watchOS, you can only update or present existing element at runtime. More simply put, this means, if an element or view controller is defined on the storyboard for your watchOS app, then you can access it at runtime. Since you cannot instantiate new user interface elements, you will learn new tricks to work around this limitation, such as setting elements to "invisible" during runtime. For better or worse, watchOS implements storyboards in the same manner as iOS and OS X (where you define the layout and tie it to parent classes in Interface Builder.)

The lack of runtime user interface changes in watchOS is also reflected in how watchOS apps are built and distributed on the App Store. When you compile an iOS or OS X app, the source code files are compiled into object code and all of the resources (storyboards, images, and any other files you manually add to your project) are bundled into one `.app` file. When you download an iOS or OS X app, the entire .app file is installed on the device. On the other hand, watchOS apps produce two output files (a "WatchKit app" and a "WatchKit extension"), which are packaged and inside of your iOS app's `.app` file. There is a bit of term overloading here, which I will explain. A WatchKit app refers to the storyboard file and other static resources that you include in your project file. A WatchKit extension contains all of the compiled source code for your watchOS project. When you choose to install a watchOS app on your Apple Watch, iOS grabs these files from the iOS app's bundle and copies them over to your watch. You can take advantage of this bundling to create "shared groups", which allow you to share files between your iOS app and watchOS app.

> **Note** WatchKit refers to the base framework for watchOS app development. watchOS includes another similarly named framework called ClockKit, which is used to build a *complication*, or plug-in, for Apple Watch's built-in watch faces.

In the introduction, I mentioned that watchOS includes many of the frameworks you are familiar with from Cocoa Touch. Some of these frameworks, and their intended uses, are listed in Table 6-1. In watchOS 2.0 and higher, these frameworks are installed on the watch, allowing your watchOS app to execute commands from these frameworks without being connected to the phone. It also has the side effect of allowing you to access the Apple Watch's hardware, such as the heart rate monitor, accelerometer and GPS directly.

Table 6-1. *Cocoa Touch Frameworks Available on watchOS*

Framework	Intended Purpose
Contacts	Access to the user's contacts, including all relevant metadata
Core Data	Database operations
Core Location	Access to the user's current location
CoreGraphics	Lightweight drawing and graphics operations.
EventKit	Access to the user's calendars and reminders

One important omission you will note is `UIKit`. watchOS only supports a limited subset of user interface elements, which are managed by the WatchKit. Since you can not instantiate new elements at runtime or perform more complicated actions on them, such as rotation, animation, or modifying how they are drawn, many of the functions of `UIKit` are extraneous on the Apple Watch. The primary WatchKit class you will use in this book is `WKInterfaceController`, which takes the place of `UIViewController`. The WatchKit user interface class names all start with `WKInterface` (ex, `WKInterfaceLabel`, `WKInterfaceButton`, `WKInterfaceMap`).

A final note to make about watchOS apps is the nature of its interfaces. Unlike an iOS app, a watchOS has three distinct user interfaces: the main interface for the app, a "glance" interface, and a "notification" interface. As the name implies, the main interface is what shows up on the screen when the app is launched. The glance interface is a single-page dashboard for your app that users can install in their "glance" menu, which comes up when the user swipes up from the bottom on their Apple Watch screen. The notification interface is another single-page interface that is initiated when the user receives a notification from your watchOS app's iOS counterpart. As these interfaces are initiated by three separate events, your storyboard will reflect this with three "entry points" and three "scenes", or workflows, as opposed to the single scene you are used to from traditional iOS development.

Setting Up Your Project

To create a new Apple Watch app, you will need to add it as a new build target of an iPhone application. A `build target` in Xcode is a set of configuration instructions that tell it how to build your project, such as which files to compile, what the target OS is, and what constants to apply. On large applications, it's common to have "debug" and "release" targets to build a log-message heavy version of the application that sends data to a test server, and another performance-optimized version that sends it to the "production" server. For this project, the Apple Watch app target tells Xcode to bundle the Apple Watch-specific source files together into an application that can be run on watchOS.

The project for this application extends the CarFinder project from Chapter 1, so duplicate it and open it up in Xcode. To add a new target, go to the File menu in Xcode and select `New` ➤ `Target`, as shown in Figure 6-2.

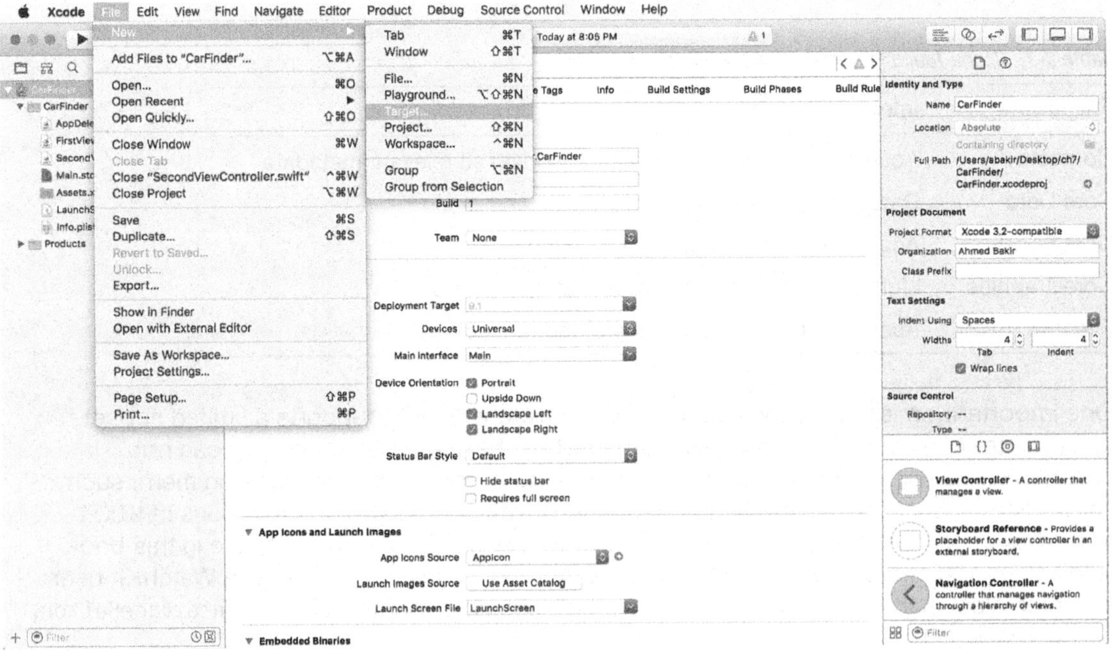

Figure 6-2. Xcode menu for creating a new build target

You will be presented with the modal dialog shown in Figure 6-3, asking you to select a platform and application type. Select watchOS as your platform and WatchKit Application as your target type.

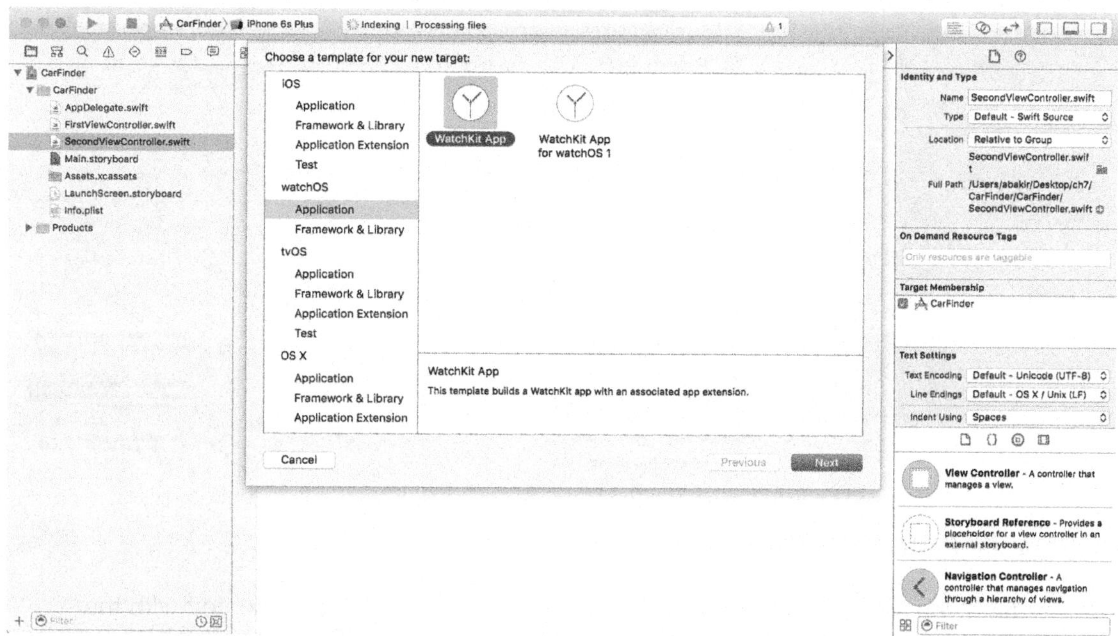

Figure 6-3. *Creating a new build target*

> **Caution** The `Apple Watch` target under the `iOS` hierarchy tree builds an app for watchOS 1. All of the examples in this book are written for watchOS 2 to take advantage of its expanded feature set and more performant application architecture.

In a similar manner to an iOS application, you will be asked to name your WatchKit application and select some template options. As shown in Figure 6-4, I have chosen to give the name the WatchKit app "CarFinder - watchOS." The WatchKit app takes the iOS app's name when it runs on the user's watch, so the actual name of the target is only used internally. A unique target name will make it faster for you to navigate between code in your project.

I have also enabled the checkbox for "Include Notification Scene". Apple recommends selecting "Include Notification Scene" even if you are not implementing a notification for a while, as their template will generate a scheme (an additional run-time configuration that is applied to a target) and local file you can use to test notifications (as opposed to setting up and connecting to an Apple Push Notification Service-enabled server).

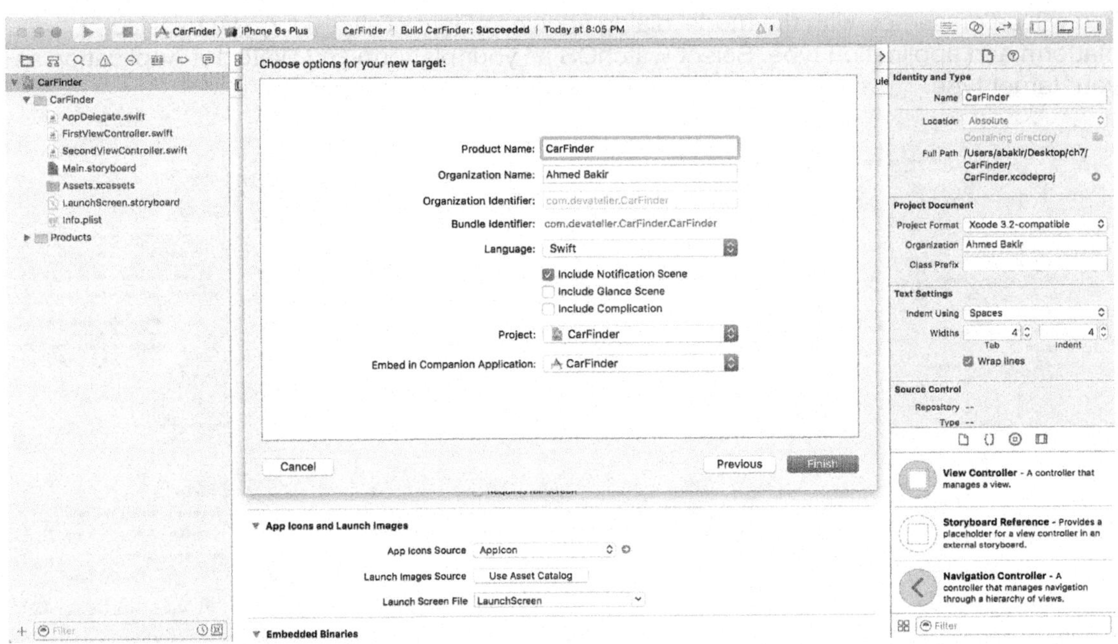

Figure 6-4. Configuring your WatchKit target

The first time you set up a WatchKit target for a project, you may be presented with the dialog box in Figure 6-5, which asks you to activate the scheme. Select `Activate`.

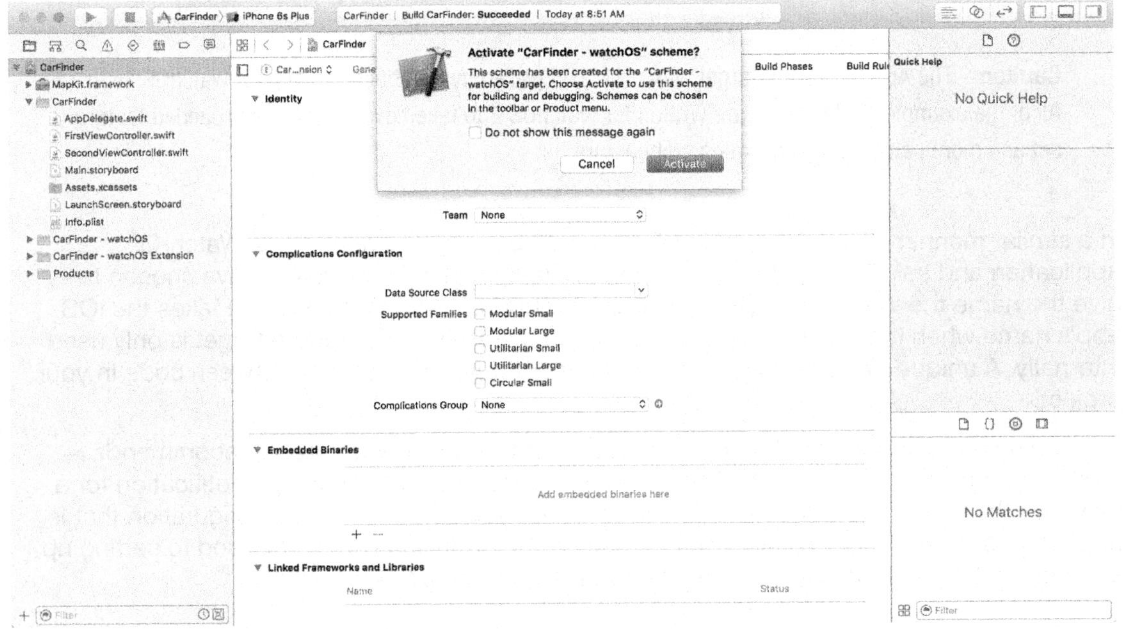

Figure 6-5. Activating the watchOS app build scheme

When working with Xcode projects that target different platforms (like watchOS + iOS), activate the schemes that you are actively developing on. Disable schemes for targets you are not using to speed up your compile time.

After activating the scheme, Xcode will take you back to the default view for your project. As shown in Figure 6-6, you will notice "CarFinder - watchOS" and "CarFinder - watchOS Extension" folders have been added to the project hierarchy, corresponding to WatchKit's definition of the two pieces of an app. The `Interface.storyboard` file contains the scenes (or storyboard entry points) for the app's main interface and its notification interface; you will make all your storyboard changes in this file. In the same manner as a new iOS application, it comes pre-configured with parent classes tied to each view controller.

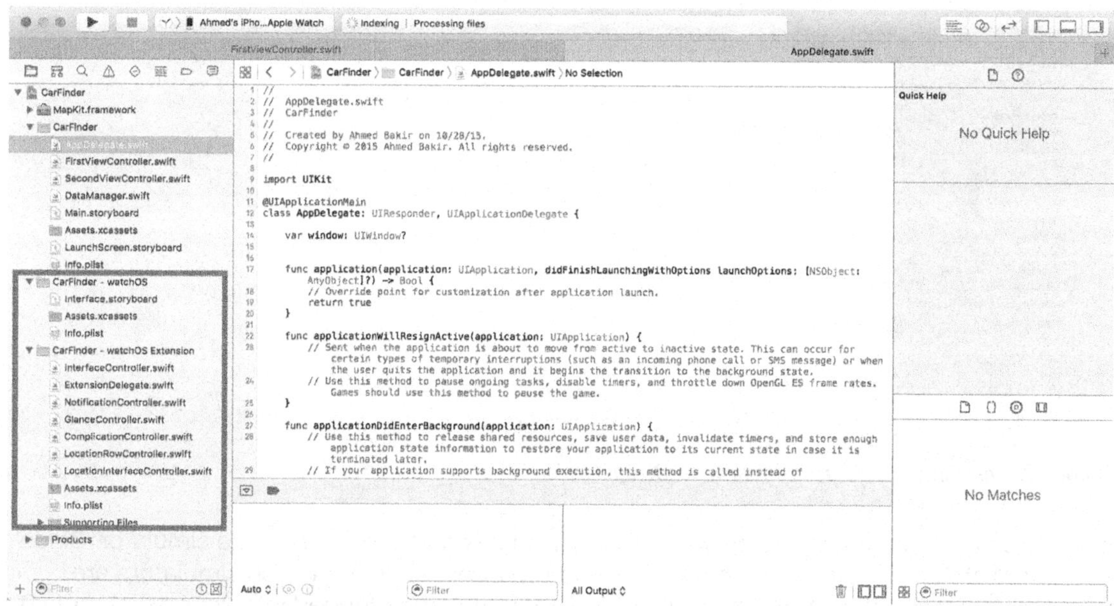

Figure 6-6. Changes to the CarFinder project

Debugging your watchOS App

The process of running a watchOS application is much like that of running an iOS application: after selecting your build scheme, you pick a target device to run it on. As shown in Figure 6-7, you select your run target by clicking on the `Active Scheme` drop-down menu, next to the run/stop buttons in the top left corner of the Xcode main window.

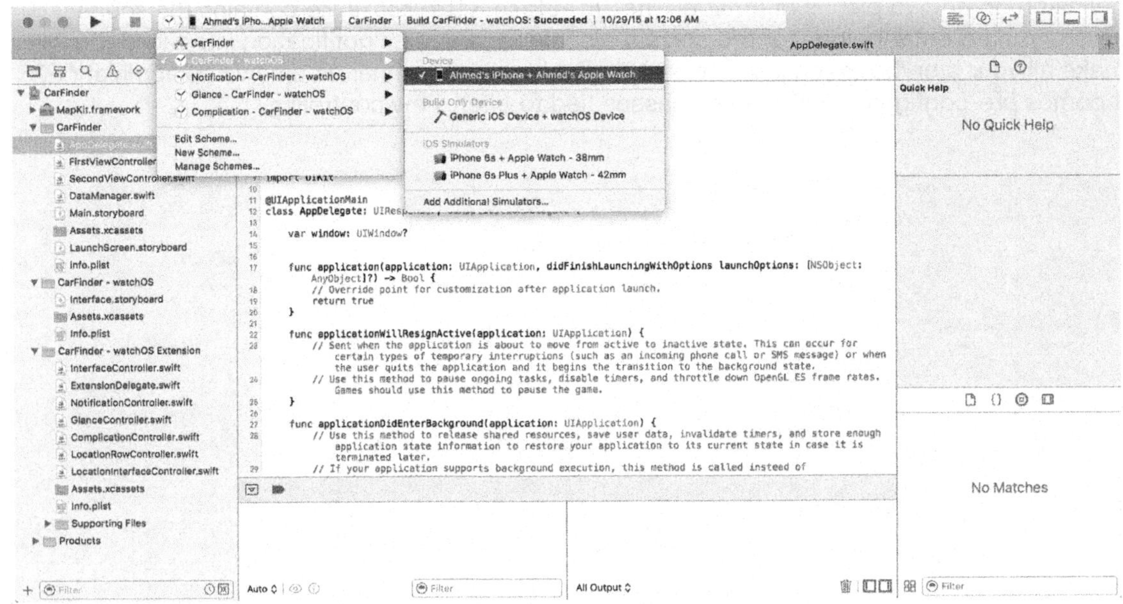

Figure 6-7. Selecting a run target for your watchOS application

Just like on iOS, you can run your watchOS app on a physical device or in a simulator. Since an Apple Watch must be paired to an iPhone to run apps, all of the watch simulators are paired to an iPhone simulator. Similarly, your iPhone must be plugged into your development computer and your Apple Watch must be paired, unlocked, and in range to debug on it. If these requirements are not met, your iPhone will be marked as an "ineligible device (no paired watch)".

Once you have initiated a run session on an Apple Watch, you can perform all of the debugging operations you are used to, including setting breakpoints and viewing live console output.

Adding a Table to your watchOS App

Now that your watchOS app is part of the CarFinder project, you are ready to start development. To begin, you will add a table view controller to the main screen for the app and populate its data with content from the iOS app. This first is intended to introduce you to working with watchOS storyboards, initializing a table view controller on watchOS, and transferring data between an iOS device and the Apple Watch. In the next section, you will learn how to build a detail view for each item in the table view controller, and in the next chapter, you will learn how to pull in data from the Internet.

There are two primary layout types for an Interface Controller (WatchKit's equivalent of a View Controller from iOS): tables and pages. A WatchKit table implements the same concept as a table view controller in iOS: a single-column list of rows (elements) that is populated by a data source and can scroll up and down. A page implements the same concept as a page view controller from iOS: a series of single-page screens that you navigate through by swiping left or right on the touch screen. For this project, you will use a table for the list of locations and a page to represent the details screen. By default, the main interface controller for your app will be blank. To add a table to this interface controller, which will act as the location list, find the Table element from Object library in Interface Builder (the bottom-right scrolling pane) and drag it onto the interface controller, as shown in Figure 6-8. Remember to select `Interface.storyboard` from the Project Navigator to edit the storyboard for your watchOS app.

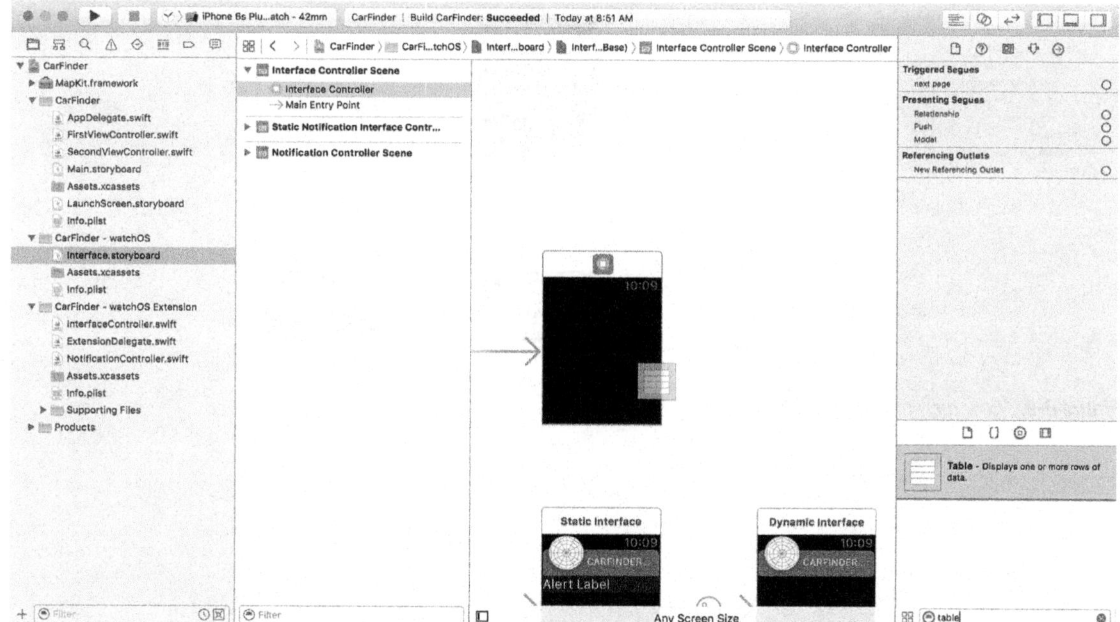

Figure 6-8. Adding a table to your main interface controller

Your result will look like Figure 6-9, where your blank interface controller is replaced with a placeholder for a table row. Your view hierarchy will show a table on top of the interface controller, which contains a table row controller, and a group.

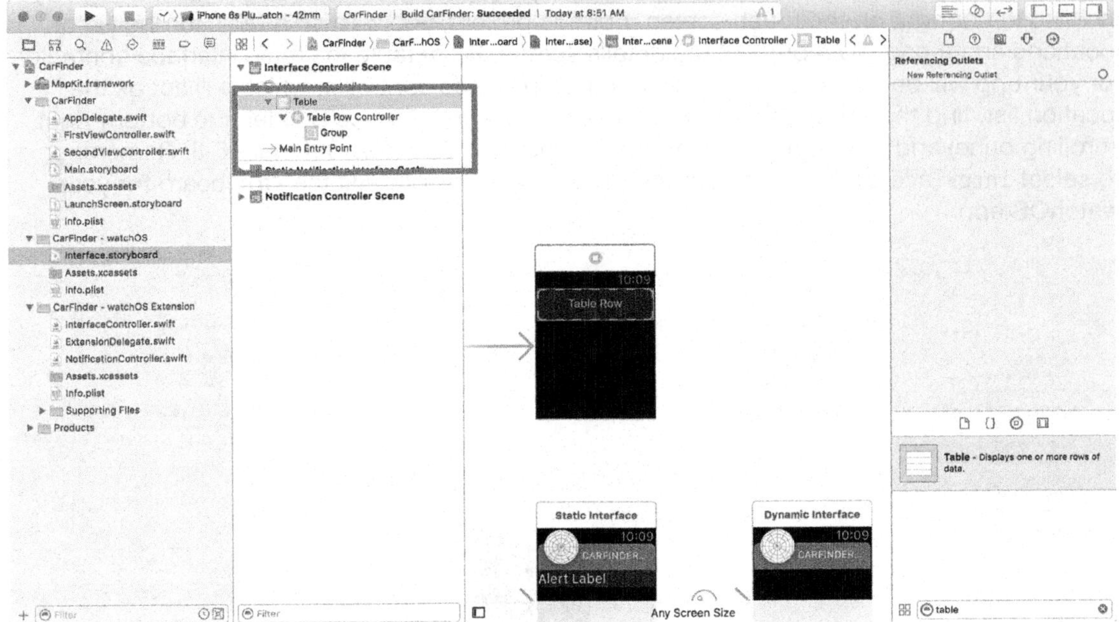

Figure 6-9. View hierarchy after adding a table

Referring back to iOS programming terminology, your interface controller class acts as the "table view delegate" and provides the functions that define how many rows and sections the table will have, as well as how to populate each row with data from the data source. The table row controller is a separate class that allows you to define a custom layout for each row. Unlike iOS, there are no styles (templates) for row types (e.g., default, subtitle), so you must always define a custom table row controller. For the CarFinder WatchKit app, each row should have two labels: one containing the latitude and longitude of each location and another representing the time when the location was saved. To implement this, drag two labels from Interface Builder's Object Library onto the table row placeholder in your interface controller. The result should look like Figure 6-10, where the labels are located adjacent to each other in the row.

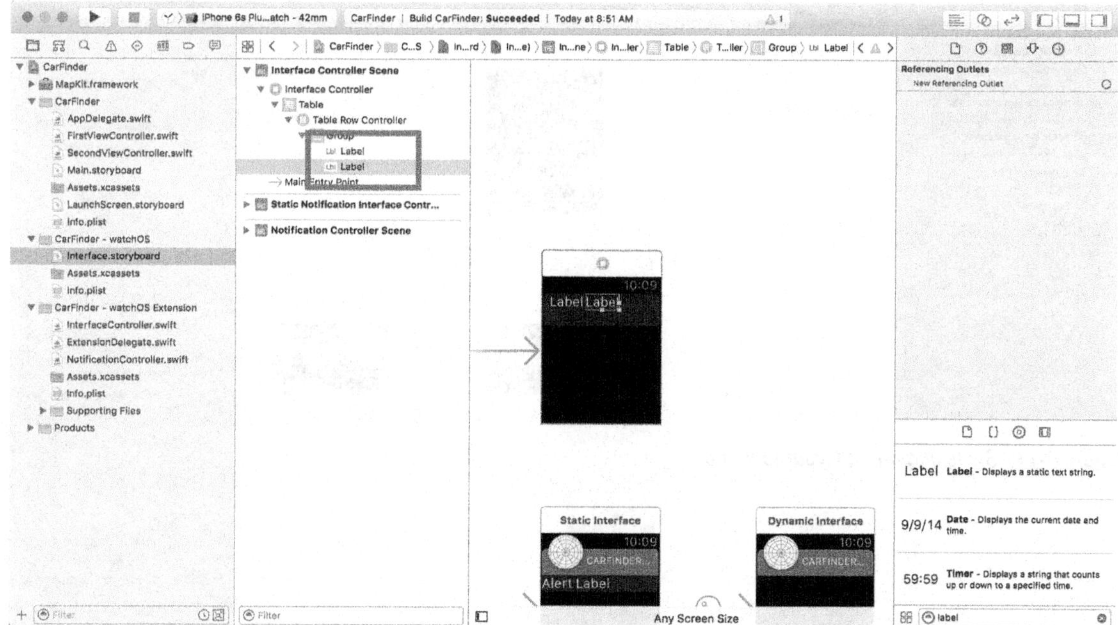

Figure 6-10. ***Result of adding labels to your row***

To make the row match our mockup in Figure 6-1, you need to change the configuration of the row's `group` layout to vertical. Groups in WatchKit implement a concept similar to tables in HTML, they are blank slates you use to position user interface elements relative to each other. To position the labels below each other, select the group in your table's view hierarchy, and switch the `Layout` attribute to "Vertical'" in Interface Builder's Attributes Inspector (the second to last tab in the right pane), as shown in Figure 6-11.

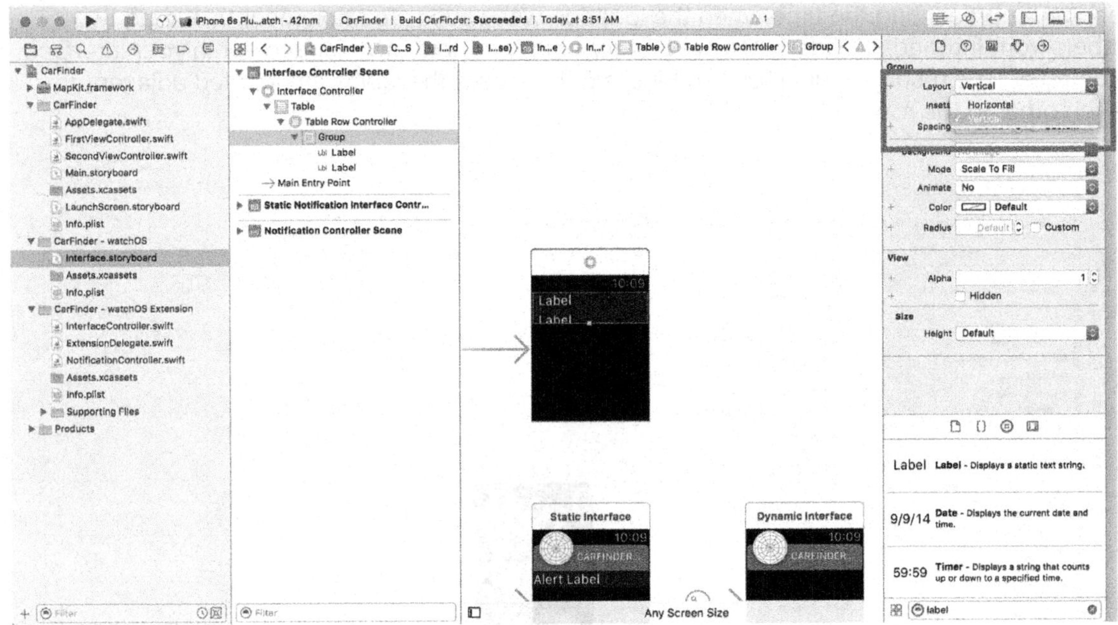

***Figure 6-11.** Switching group layout to vertical*

To finish polishing the row, increase the height of the row by dragging on its bottom edge. Use the Attributes Inspector to change the style of the second label to "Subhead", as shown in Figure 6-12. Using font styles allows your app's text to resize relatively, a useful feature for accessibility, where a user may increase the size of the text on their devices globally, to adjust for vision issues.

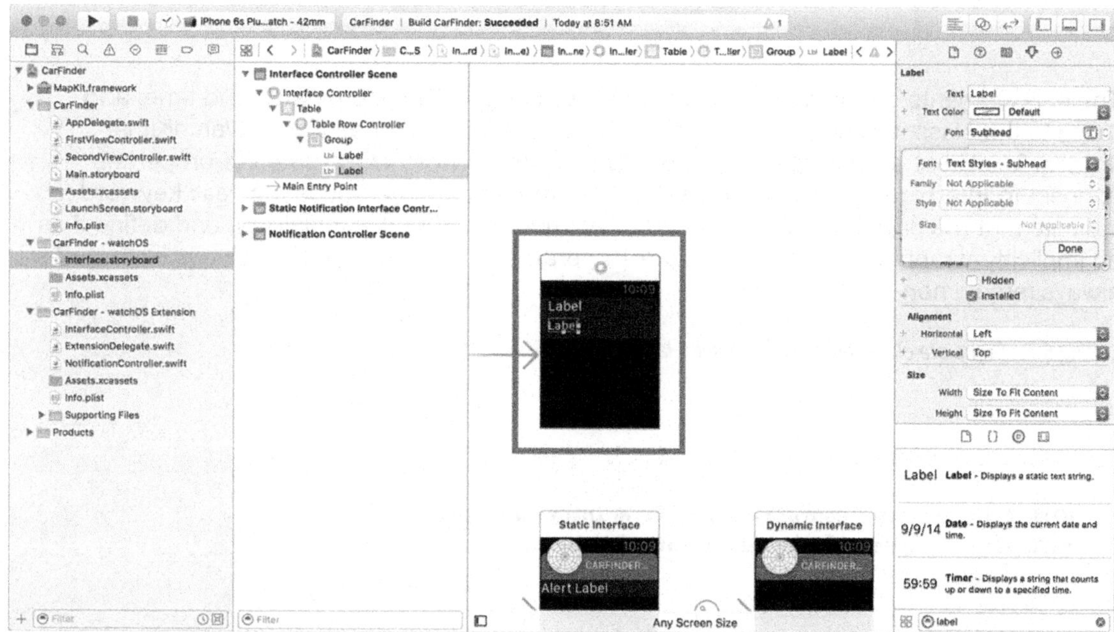

Figure 6-12. Completed table row

> **Note** You do not need to worry about adjusting the width of each label, as the default behavior for a label is to resize it to fill the width of the screen.

Defining the Table

Having visually laid out the table, you can begin defining it in code. To start out, begin by creating a subclass of `NSObject` named `LocationRowController` to represent the table row controller, as shown in Listing 6-1. Save the file as `LocationRowController.swift`. As of this writing, WatchKit does not define a parent class for table row controllers, so you need to use Swift's generic parent class for objects, `NSObject`.

Listing 6-1. Class definition for LocationRowController table row controller

```
import WatchKit

class LocationRowController: NSObject {

}

}
```

The only elements on the row are the labels representing the coordinates and time, add these to the class, as shown in Listing 6-2. The parent class for a label in WatchKit is `WKInterfaceLabel`. Remember to use the `@IBOutlet` keyword to indicate the properties connect to Interface Builder elements. For memory management, use the `weak` keyword to indicate that the property does not need to be modified after it is initialized, and define it as an implicitly-wrapped optional, using the ! operator, to indicate that the value is expected to always remain non-nil.

Listing 6-2. Complete class definition, including labels.

```
import WatchKit

class LocationRowController: NSObject {

    @IBOutlet weak var CoordinatesLabel: WKInterfaceLabel?
    @IBOutlet weak var TimeLabel: WKInterfaceLabel?

}
```

As with any other Interface Builder-backed class, your next step is to connect user interface elements and parent classes. Although the interface controller is already connected to the `InterfaceController` class via Xcode's default project settings, you will need to manually connect the table row controller you added. To perform this operation, select the table row controller in your view hierarchy and then navigate over to the Identity inspector in Xcode (the third middle tab in the right pane.) As shown in Figure 6-13, select the `LocationRowController` class as the parent class.

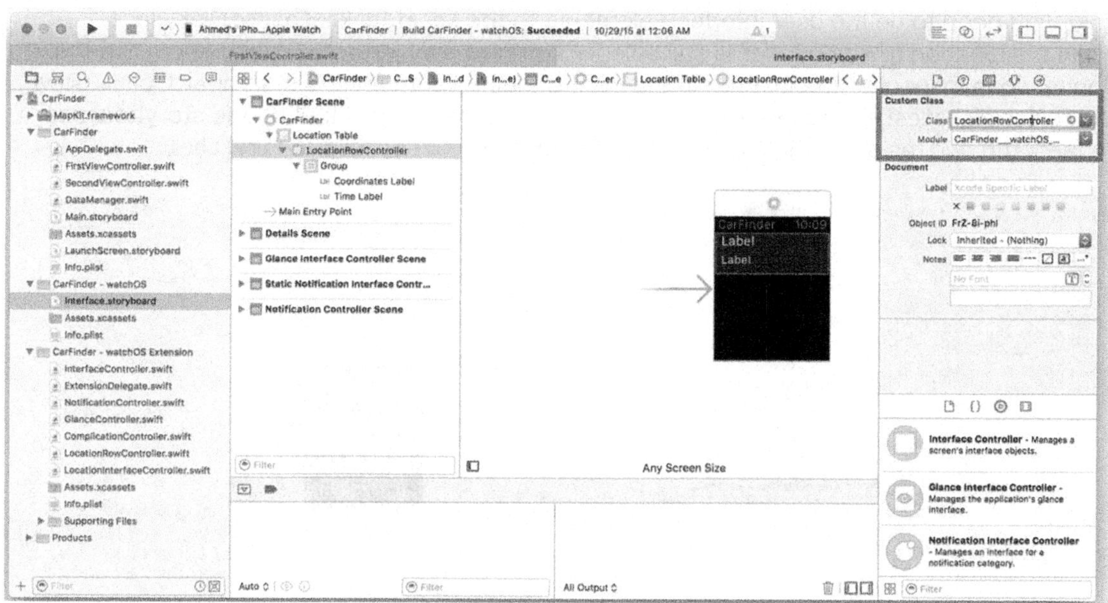

Figure 6-13. *Assigning the parent class for the table row controller*

The delegate methods for populating the table refer to table row controllers as "types", which are represented through their storyboard "Identifiers". As shown in Figure 6-14, navigate over to the Attributes Inspector, and set "LocationRowController" as the identifier for the class.

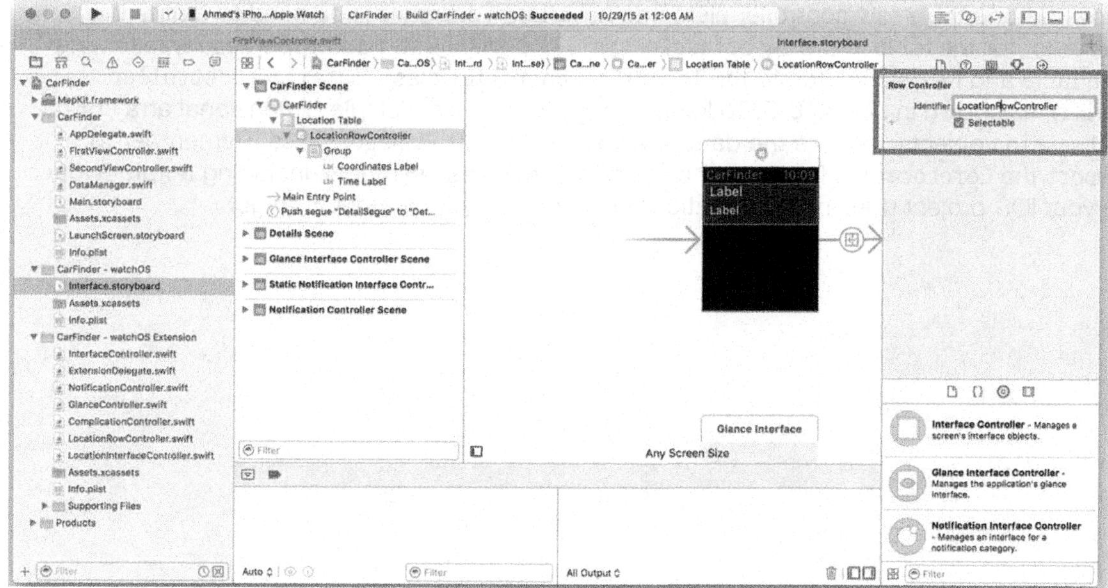

Figure 6-14. *Setting a row type*

Next, you need to tie the user interface elements to the `LocationRowController` class. While the location row controller is still selected in the view hierarchy, navigate over to the Connections Inspector (the last tab in the right pane). As with an iOS storyboard, click down on the `CoordinatesLabel` outlet radio box and release it over the label on the storyboard to connect the two, as shown in Figure 6-15. Repeat the process for the `TimeLabel`.

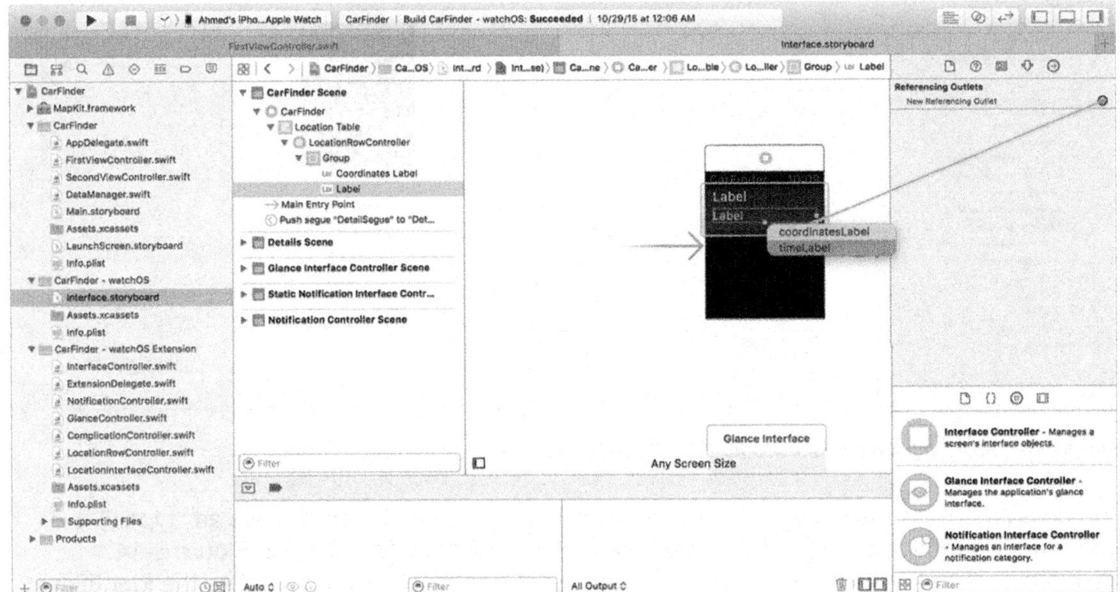

Figure 6-15. Connecting WatchKit user interface elements to a class

Now that the table row controller elements have been assigned, you need to define the behavior for the table in the `InterfaceController` class. First, add properties representing the table and its data source to the `InterfaceController` class (`InterfaceController.swift`), as shown in Listing 6-3. To keep things simple, use a single dimensional array of `CLLocation` objects, just like the data provided by the `DataManager` class. Remember to `import` the `CoreLocation` framework class to resolve these symbols; including a framework in your iOS project does not automatically include it in your watchOS target.

Listing 6-3. Adding properties for the table and data source to the InterfaceController class

```
import WatchKit
import Foundation
import CoreLocation

class InterfaceController: WKInterfaceController {

    @IBOutlet weak var LocationTable: WKInterfaceTable?

    override func awakeWithContext(context: AnyObject?) {
        super.awakeWithContext(context)

        ...
    }

    ...

}
```

As with any other Interface Builder object, connect the `LocationTable` property to the `InterfaceController` class via the Connection Inspector, as shown in Figure 6-16.

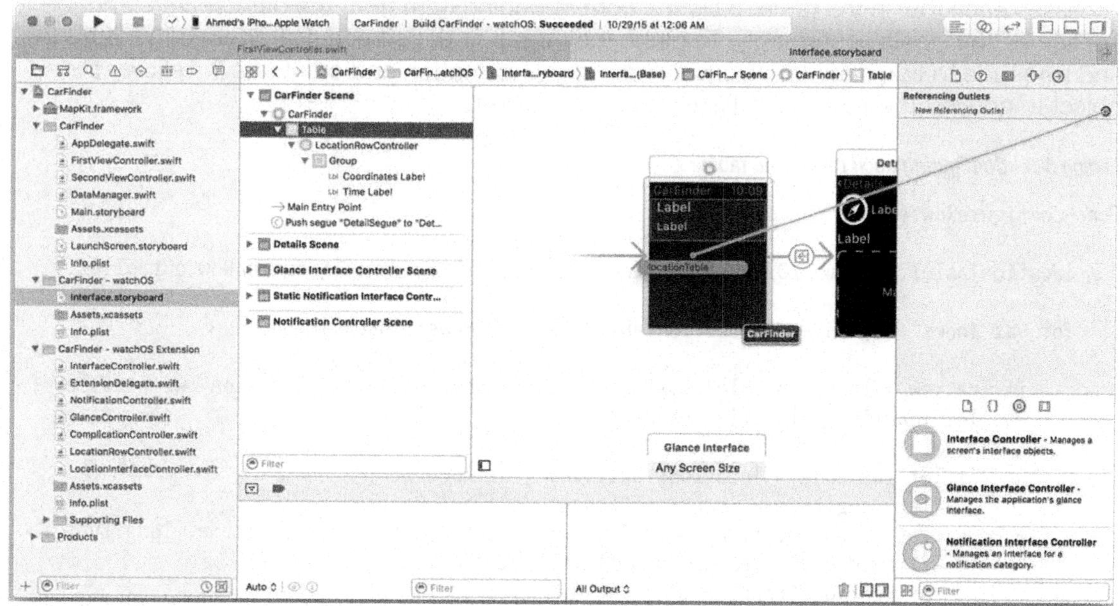

Figure 6-16. Connecting the LocationTable property

Just like with iOS, there are three key behaviors you need to implement to fully define a WatchKit table: the number of rows in the table, how to configure each row, and what action to perform when a row has been selected. You will implement the final behavior (selection) in the next section, for now, the focus is populating the table.

To specify the number of rows in the table, in the `InterfaceController` class's entry method, `awakeWithContext(_:)`, call the method, `setNumberOfRows(_:withRowType:)`, specifying the length of the `locations` array as the row count, and "LocationRowController" as the row type, corresponding to our earlier definition in Figure 6-10. Your `awakeWithContext(_:)` method should look like the example in Listing 6-4.

Listing 6-4. Specifying the number of rows in a table

```
override func awakeWithContext(context: AnyObject?) {
    super.awakeWithContext(context)

    // Configure interface objects here.
    LocationTable.setNumberOfRows(locations.count, withRowType: "LocationRowController")

}
```

You can access each row via the `rowControllerAtIndex(_:)` method. To configure the entire table at once, I have created a convenience method named `configureRows` in the InterfaceController class (InterfaceController.swift), shown in Listing 6-5. This method accesses each row in the table, pulls the corresponding item from the data source, and configures the labels accordingly. To make the output fit the screen, I shortened the latitude and longitude to two decimal places using a string formatter, and created a `DateFormatter` object to convert the `timestamp` `Date` object to a string.

Listing 6-5. Configuring each row in the table

```
func configureRows() {

    locationTable?.setNumberOfRows(locations.count, withRowType: "LocationRowController")

    for var index = 0; index < locationTable?.numberOfRows; index++ {

        if let row = locationTable?.rowControllerAtIndex(index) as? LocationRowController {
            let location = locations[index]

            if let latitude = location["Latitude"] as? Double {
                let longitude = location["Longitude"] as! Double
                let formattedString = String(format: "%0.3f, %0.3f", latitude, longitude)
                //row.coordinatesLabel?.setText("\(latitude),
                \(location["Longitude"]!)")
                row.coordinatesLabel?.setText(formattedString)

            }
            if let timeStamp = location["Timestamp"]  as? NSDate {
                let dateFormatter = NSDateFormatter()
                dateFormatter.dateStyle = NSDateFormatterStyle.ShortStyle
```

```
                dateFormatter.timeStyle = NSDateFormatterStyle.ShortStyle
                row.timeLabel?.setText(dateFormatter.stringFromDate(timeStamp))
            }

        }

    }
}
```

You will need to configure the table when the table view appears on the screen or any time the data source is updated. To intercept the event when the table view appears, add the call to `configureRows` at the bottom of the `willActivate(_:)` method for the `InterfaceController` class, as shown in Listing 6-6. You will handle data source updates in the next chapter.

Listing 6-6. Calling the configureRows method

```
override func willActivate() {
    // This method is called when watch view controller is about to be visible to user
    super.willActivate()

    self.configureRows()
}
```

> **Note** The `awakeWithContext(_:)` method is called when an interface controller is loaded from a storyboard for the first time. This is the first event to fire when an interface controller is loaded and only fires once, whereas `willActivate:` fires every time the interface controller is presented, such as when you are coming back from a detail screen or menu.

Fetching Data from your iOS App

Now that the table view is configured to display data, it's time to populate the `locations` array with data from the CarFinder iOS app. The primary method for sharing data between an iOS app and WatchKit app in watchOS 2 is through the `WatchConnectivity` framework. Following Apple's pattern of "availability", or performing an operation only when a resource is available to your application, `WatchConnectivity` provides a subscription-based service that negotiates the link between your iPhone and Apple Watch and transmits messages when the link is stable. Similar to notifications, you need to establish sending and receiving endpoints in each of your applications, and messages are only received when you declare yourself as a "receiver."

To enable both of your applications as `WatchConnectivity`-compatible, you need to subscribe to `WatchConnectivity`'s "default session", after checking if the feature is available on your device (this is defined as an Apple Watch being paired to your phone, with your watchOS app is installed on it.) In the CarFinder iOS app, place this block of code in the `viewDidLoad` method of `FirstViewController` class, as shown in Listing 6-7. The view controller with the closest access to the main data source should be the one you use to handle `WatchConnectivity` messages.

Listing 6-7. Preparing the iOS App for WatchConnectivity

```
import UIKit
import CoreLocation
import WatchConnectivity

class FirstViewController: UITableViewController, WCSessionDelegate {

    ...

    override func viewDidLoad() {
        super.viewDidLoad()

        let locationManager = CLLocationManager()

        ...

        if (WCSession.isSupported()) {
            let session = WCSession.defaultSession()
            session.delegate = self
            session.activateSession()
        }
    }

}
```

To send and receive `WatchConnectivity` messages, you need to set your class as a delegate of the `WCSessionDelegate` protocol. In Listing 6-7, this is indicated by adding `WCSessionDelegate` to the list of protocols in the class definition and by setting the class as a delegate object in your setup block.

In your WatchKit Extension, you need to follow the same steps. The main difference will be that you will use the `awakeWithContext(_:)` method in the `InterfaceController` class. See Listing 6-8.

Listing 6-8. Preparing the WatchKit Extension for WatchConnectivity

```
import WatchKit
import Foundation
import CoreLocation
import WatchConnectivity

class InterfaceController: WKInterfaceController, WCSessionDelegate {

    @IBOutlet weak var LocationTable: WKInterfaceTable!
    var locations = [CLLocation]()

    override func awakeWithContext(context: AnyObject?) {
        super.awakeWithContext(context)
```

```
        // Configure interface objects here.
        LocationTable.setNumberOfRows(locations.count, withRowType: "LocationRowController")

        if (WCSession.isSupported()) {
            let session = WCSession.defaultSession()
            session.delegate = self
            session.activateSession()
        }

    }

    ...

}
```

In this chapter, to provide a positive experience for your users, you will use WatchConnectivity to fetch the latest list of locations from the CarFinder iOS app as soon as the CarFinder watchOS app is launched on the watch. To provide the best experience, the method you select should be fast (users don't want to wait for data the first time they load the app) and non-blocking (users don't want to wait for a frozen app to resolve itself.) To enable this, you will use WatchConnectivity's updateApplicationContext(_:) method to transfer a Dictionary object from the CarFinder iOS app to the CarFinder WatchKit extension. As shown in Listing 6-9, you should send this event every time the data source is updated, which is after a new location has been added to the list. In this example, I converted the array into a dictionary by storing it as the value for the Locations key.

***Listing 6-9.** Sending a dictionary to a WatchKit extension from an iOS app*

```
@IBAction func addLocation(sender: UIButton) {

    ...

    var sharedLocations = DataManager.sharedInstance.locations
    tableView.reloadData()

    if (WCSession.isSupported()) {
        do {
            let userDict = ["Locations": sharedLocations]
            try WCSession.defaultSession().updateApplicationContext(userDict)
        } catch {
            print("Error transferring data")
        }
    }
}
```

Application contexts in WatchConnectivity are instantaneous transfers as soon as the link is established with the subscribing counterpart application. Additionally, for data sources that update frequently, only the most recent version of the dictionary is sent; old versions are discarded.

To receive the dictionary, you need to implement the session:didReceiveApplicationContext: delegate method in your WatchKit extension. As shown in Listing 6-10, you implement this in the InterfaceController class. After receiving the message, override the existing locations array with the new version from the received dictionary and call the configureRows method to update the user interface.

Listing 6-10. Receiving a dictionary from WatchConnectivity

```
func session(session: WCSession, didReceiveApplicationContext applicationContext:
             [String : AnyObject]) {
    let locationsArray = applicationContext["Locations"] as! [CLLocation]
    locations = locationsArray

    configureRows()
}
```

> **Note** This example saves locations in memory; they will not persist between multiple sessions. To persist data, we suggest using Core Data or saving your data to a plaintext file.

Building a Detail Page with a Custom Layout

To make the CarFinder WatchKit app even more useful, you will implement the detail screen for each item in the location list. In addition to teaching you how to implement the selection action for the WatchKit table element, this section will also focus on building a page-based interface controller with a custom layout.

The first step in building a detail controller is to place it on your storyboard. To add a new interface controller to your watchOS app, drag an Interface Controller object from the Interface Builder's object library onto your storyboard. Similarly, you need to create a new subclass of WKInterfaceController to define its behavior; for the CarFinder WatchKit app, this file is called LocationInterfaceController. As with previous examples, use the Identity Inspector to set the parent class to LocationInterfaceController.

Referring back to the mockup for the app in Figure 6-1, the detail screen for the CarFinder WatchKit app displays the timestamp for the location on the first line, next to a GPS icon. The coordinates for the location are displayed on a line beneath this, and under that is a map with a pinpoint indicating the recorded location. By default, a Group in WatchKit can only display items by positioning them adjacently, horizontally or vertically. To implement your custom interface, you can get around this limitation by placing two groups on your interface. As shown in Figure 6-17, drag two groups on to your interface controller. Your view hierarchy will be updated to reflect these new groups.

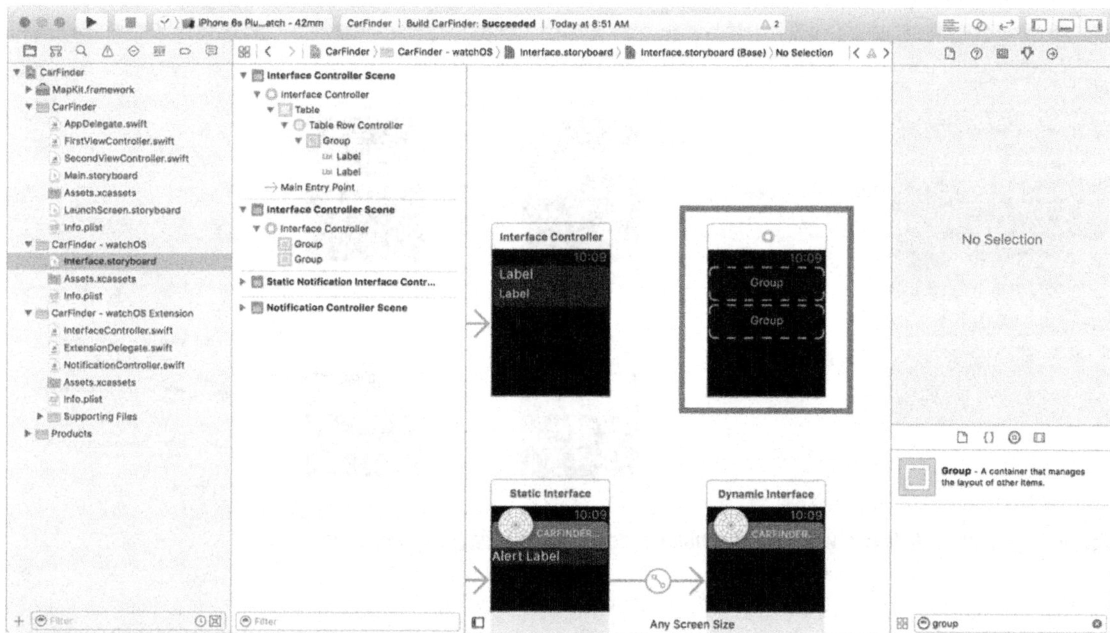

Figure 6-17. Adding multiple groups to your interface controller

Note You can place as many groups as you want on a page-based interface, but only one for a table interface.

Now that the groups are ready, you can start adding user interface elements onto them. Start out by setting the layout of the group at the top to `Horizontal`, using the Attributes Inspector. Next, drag an Image and Label onto the group. Unfortunately, by default, your Label will be hidden, as shown in Figure 6-18.

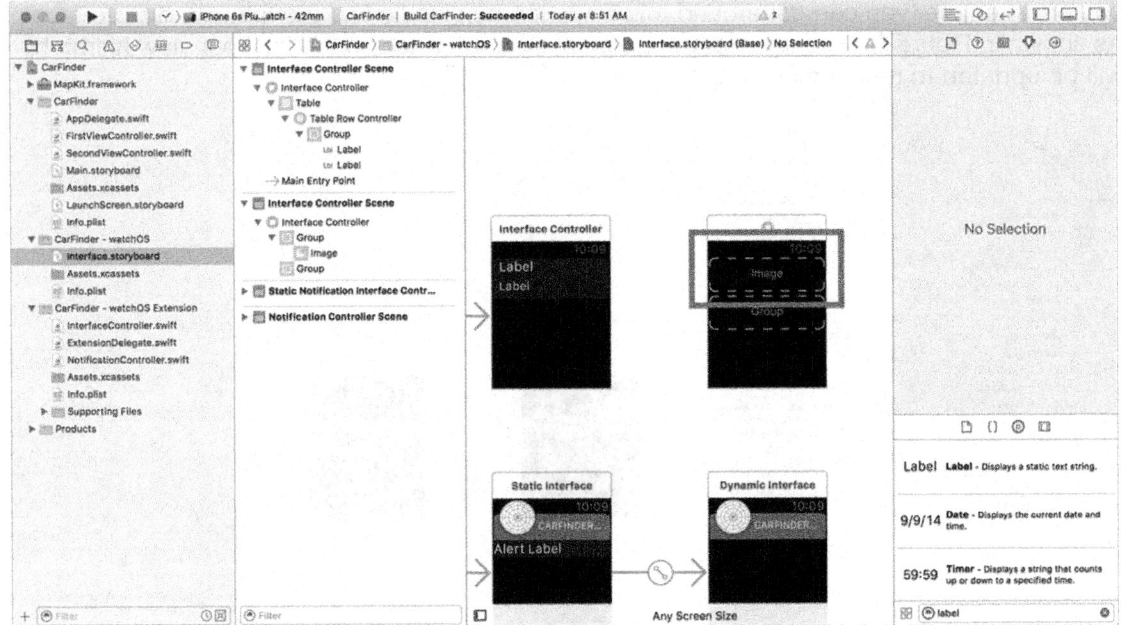

Figure 6-18. Default behavior when adding multiple items to a vertically aligned group

To fix this, grab the right-edge of the image placeholder and drag it to the left, until it becomes square shaped, matching the general shape of the icon from the mockup. After adjusting the image's size, the label reappears in the group, as shown in Figure 6-19.

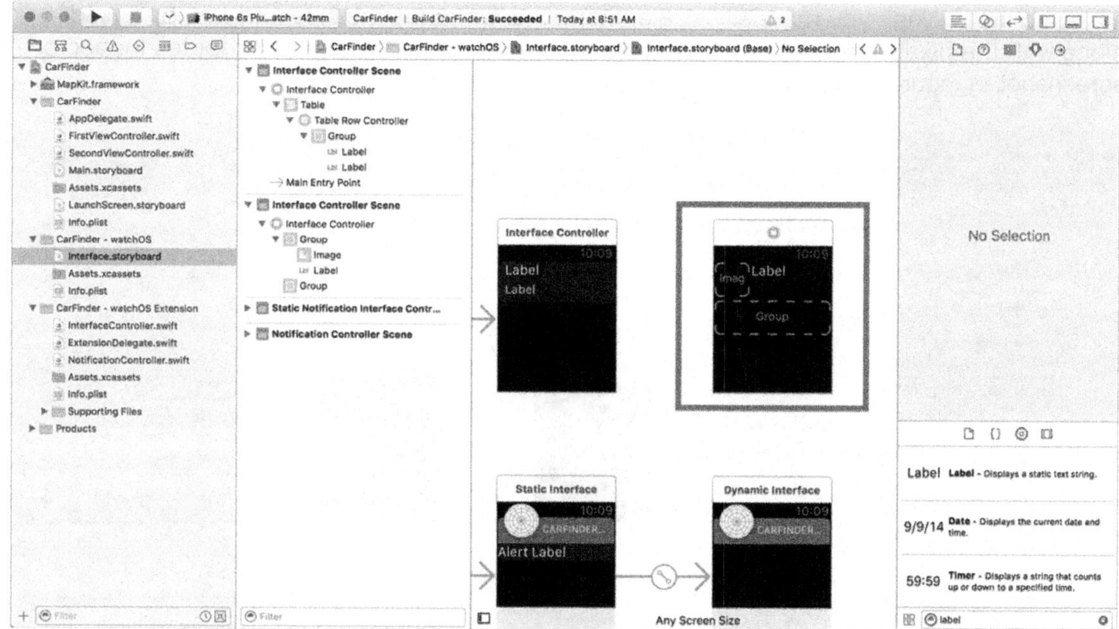

Figure 6-19. Group after adjusting image size

Like an iOS app, watchOS apps can run on multiple screen sizes (the 38mm and 42mm watches). Unfortunately, watchOS storyboards do not yet support auto-layout. To resolve this, the default size settings for user interface elements in WatchKit are set to "Size to Fit Content." This setting works opposite to the `ScaleAspectFill` content mode for `UIView` objects in iOS. Instead of the content resizing to fill the container, the container resizes to fill the content! When you manually size an item, this switches the size attribute to "Fixed" along with the pixel width or height of your adjustment, as shown in the Attributes Inspector screenshot in Figure 6-20.

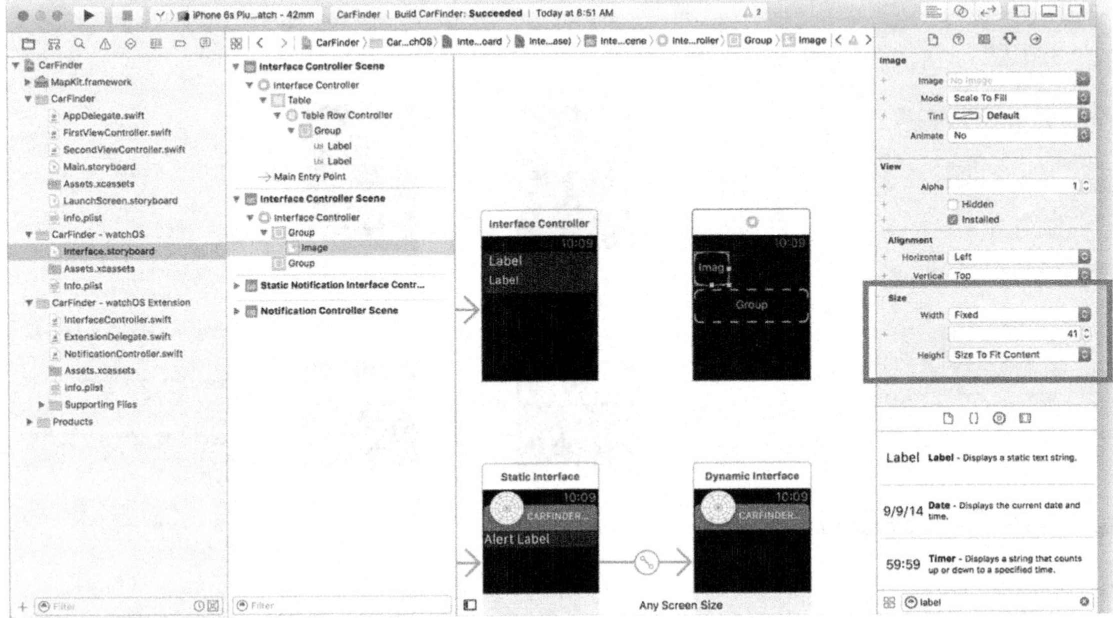

Figure 6-20. Attributes inspector after adjusting image size

When you have multiple elements in a horizontal group, use this limitation to your advantage by fixing the size of certain elements and keeping others flexible. Automatic resizing can be troublesome for images, but users expect to see text sizes and padding decrease with labels.

A side-effect of adjusting the size of the image is that your label will be aligned to the top edge of the group. To fix this, select the label and change the vertical position attribute to `Center`, as shown in Figure 6-21.

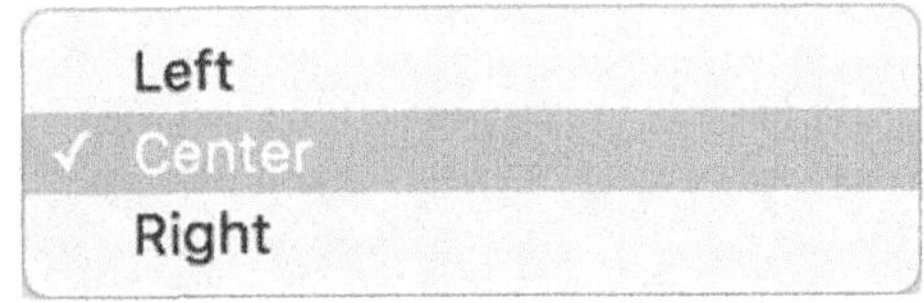

Figure 6-21. Changing the vertical position of an item in a group

Luckily, the group containing the map and time stamp label is a bit easier. Change the layout to vertical and drag Label and Map objects into the group. Your final user interface should look like the screenshot in Figure 6-22. You will notice that the size of the interface controller has increased to reflect that there is more content on the screen than can fit at once. By default, interface controllers work like `UIScrollViews` in iOS, where everything inside of the scroll view scrolls. I have included a graphic in the source code bundle named `compass.png` that you can use in your project for the compass icon.

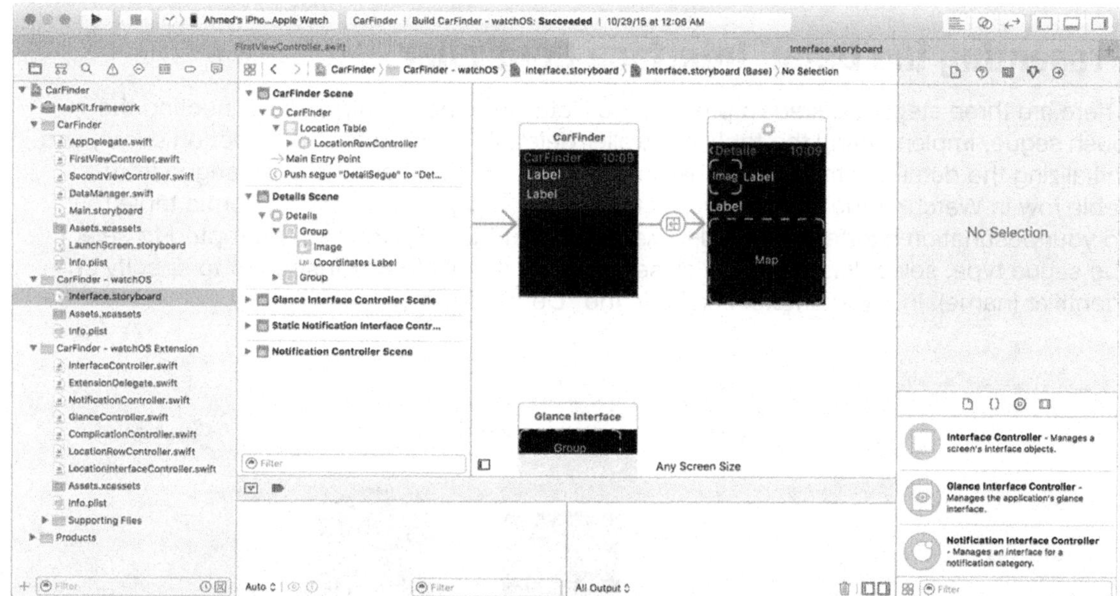

Figure 6-22. Final user interface for detail interface controller

As you would expect, to make this all work, you need to define these elements in your class. You can find the definition for the `LocationInterfaceController` class, including the properties for the user interface elements in Listing 6-11. As always, after adding these items to your class, connect them to your storyboard in Interface Builder.

Listing 6-11. Definition for LocationInterfaceController class

```
import WatchKit
import Foundation
import CoreLocation

class LocationInterfaceController: WKInterfaceController {

    @IBOutlet weak var LocationMap: WKInterfaceMap!
    @IBOutlet weak var CoordinatesLabel: WKInterfaceLabel!
    @IBOutlet weak var TimeLabel: WKInterfaceLabel!
```

```
    override func awakeWithContext(context: AnyObject?) {
        super.awakeWithContext(context)

        // Configure interface objects here.
    }

    ...

}
```

Presenting the Detail Interface Controller

There are three steps required to present the Detail interface controller: connecting the push segue, implementing the table controller delegate method for the selection event, and initializing the detail controller with the correct data. You connect the push segue from a table row in WatchKit the same way you would in iOS: by `CTRL+clicking` from a table row to your destination interface controller. As shown in Figure 6-23, when prompted to select the segue type, select `Push`. As with all segues, use the Attributes Inspector to specify an identifier (name). In my example, I call this the "DetailSegue".

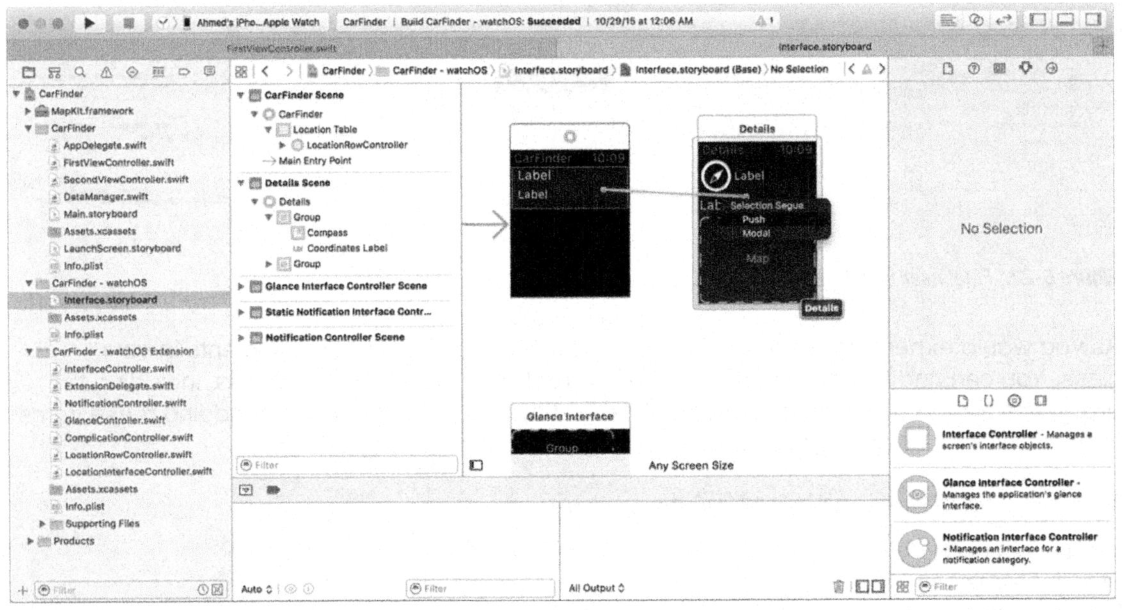

Figure 6-23. Connecting the push segue

The push segue presents the detail interface controller after catching the selection event in the main interface controller. There are two primary ways to handle selection events in WatchKit: the `table(_:didSelectRowAtIndex:)` method, which allows you to perform an action based on a table's selected row, and the `contextForSegueWithIdentifier(_:inTable:rowIndex:)` method, which sends a context (object) to your destination interface controller, based on the selected row of your table. This fits the requirements perfectly. Luckily, the implementation is quite simple too. As shown in Listing 6-12, in your `InterfaceController` class, upon catching a segue named "DetailSegue", return the location specified by the selected row in the table. For all other segue identifiers, return `nil`.

Listing 6-12. Implementing the table selection segue handler

```
override func contextForSegueWithIdentifier(segueIdentifier: String, inTable table:
WKInterfaceTable, rowIndex: Int) -> AnyObject? {

    if (segueIdentifier == "DetailSegue") {
        return locations[rowIndex]
    }

    return nil
}
```

Now that you have successfully created the logic and handler for the selection event, you are ready to use this information to initialize your detail interface controller. In Listing 6-12, the object you passed back from the `contextForSegueWithIdentifier(_:inTable:rowIndex:)` method was called a context. By no coincidence the method that fires when an interface controller is loaded for the first time is called `awakeWithContext:`. As shown in Listing 6-13, to initialize a `LocationInterfaceController` with from a context, check if the input object is a `CLLocation` object like you expect, and then use it to set the values for your user interface elements.

Listing 6-13. Catching the table selection event in the detail interface controller (LocationInterfaceController.swift)

```
override func awakeWithContext(context: AnyObject?) {
    super.awakeWithContext(context)

    // Configure interface objects here.
    if let location = context as? CLLocation {
        //
        let dateFormatter = NSDateFormatter()
        dateFormatter.dateStyle = NSDateFormatterStyle.FullStyle

        let prettyLocation = String(format: "(%.2f, %.2f)", location.coordinate.longitude,
                                    location.coordinate.latitude)
        let prettyTime = dateFormatter.stringFromDate(location.timestamp)

        CoordinatesLabel.setText(prettyLocation)
        TimeLabel.setText(prettyTime)
```

```
        LocationMap.addAnnotation(location.coordinate, withPinColor: WKInterfaceMapPinColor.Red)

        let mapRegion = MKCoordinateRegionMake(location.coordinate,
        MKCoordinateSpanMake(0.1, 0.1))

        LocationMap.setRegion(mapRegion)

    }
}
```

Further emphasizing the similarities of watchOS to iOS, you will notice that the process of initializing a `WKInterfaceMap` was exactly like that of initializing an `MKMapView`: first you define a pin and then you set the region.

At this point, you now have a functional CarFinder app! Your user interface should look like the example in Figure 6-24 when you run it on an Apple Watch. The user can select an item in the location list table to view its details, which include a map of the area, coordinates, and the time saved.

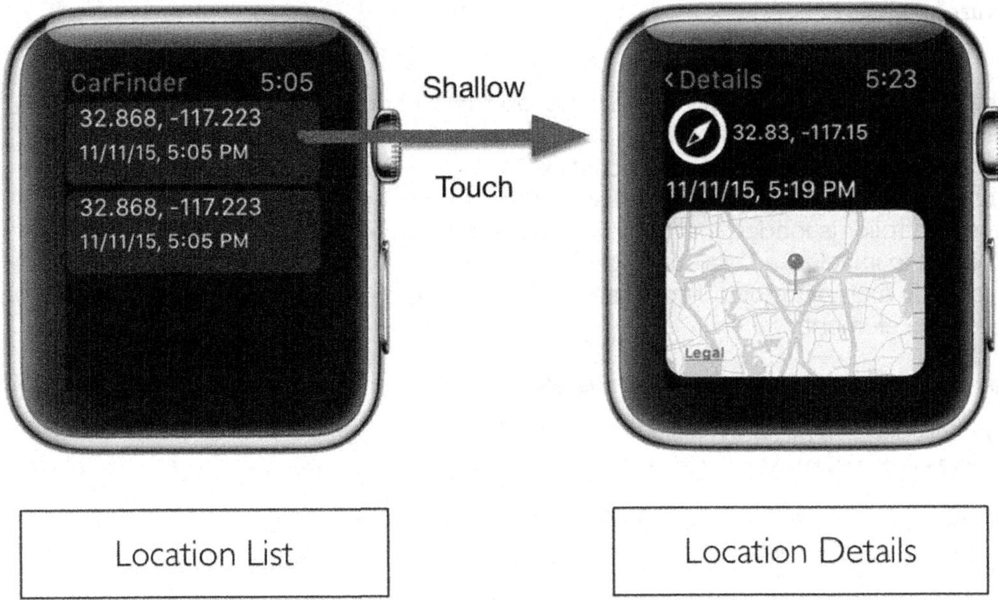

Figure 6-24. User Interface for CarFinder when running on an Apple Watch

Summary

In this chapter, you learned the ins-and-outs of building an Apple Watch app by creating the CarFinder WatchKit app, which pulls the list of saved locations from the CarFinder iOS app on the user's iPhone. After a quick introduction to the Apple Watch and its basic application architecture, you began to explore the similarities between watchOS and iOS development by setting up your watchOS build target. Building the user interface in Interface Builder and tying its outlets to classes you defined in code strengthened the extent of these similarities. To round things out, you explored different user interface elements and layout styles, and learned about key WatchKit event delegate methods, giving you a good foundation for future chapters, where you will explore more advanced elements and behaviors.

Chapter 7

Building an Interactive watchOS App

Ahmed Bakir

Introduction

In this chapter, you will learn how to make the CarFinder watchOS app even more powerful by adding interactive features. While an app that can let you view information from your iPhone is great, there is even more value in an app that allows you to create new data from your watch. The interactive features you will add to the CarFinder app in this chapter will demonstrate the following features of watchOS:

- How to add context menus to an interface controller
- How to add buttons to an interface controller
- How to add text to an item using text input
- How to pass data between interface controllers
- How to pass data back to your iOS companion app

The examples in this chapter expand upon the CarFinder app from Chapter 6. The updated source code for CarFinder is available in the Source Code/Download area on this book's web page www.apress.com).

Using Force Touch to Present Menus

Force Touch is the feature built into the Apple Watch's touchscreen, which allows you to detect how much pressure the user applied to the screen. Users can perform different actions depending on whether they press the screen with a light touch ("shallow press" in Apple's terminology) or a hard touch ("deep press"). The standard User Experience (UX) for Apple Watch apps is to use shallow presses to select an item and Force Touch to bring up a contextual menu, allowing the user to perform related actions. Figure 7-1 provides an example of a contextual menu.

***Figure 7-1.** watchOS contextual menu*

In the CarFinder app, you will implement a contextual menu to allow the user to add a new location and to reset the location list. If the user chooses to add a new location, a modal screen will allow him to confirm or reject his current location. If the user chooses to reset the location list, she will be returned to the initial location list interface controller with an empty data set.

To add a contextual menu to an interface controller, open the storyboard for your watchOS app (`Interface.storyboard`) and drag a Menu from the Object Library onto your desired view controller, as shown in Figure 7-2. For the CarFinder app, the initial interface controller (the `InterfaceController` class) will be your destination.

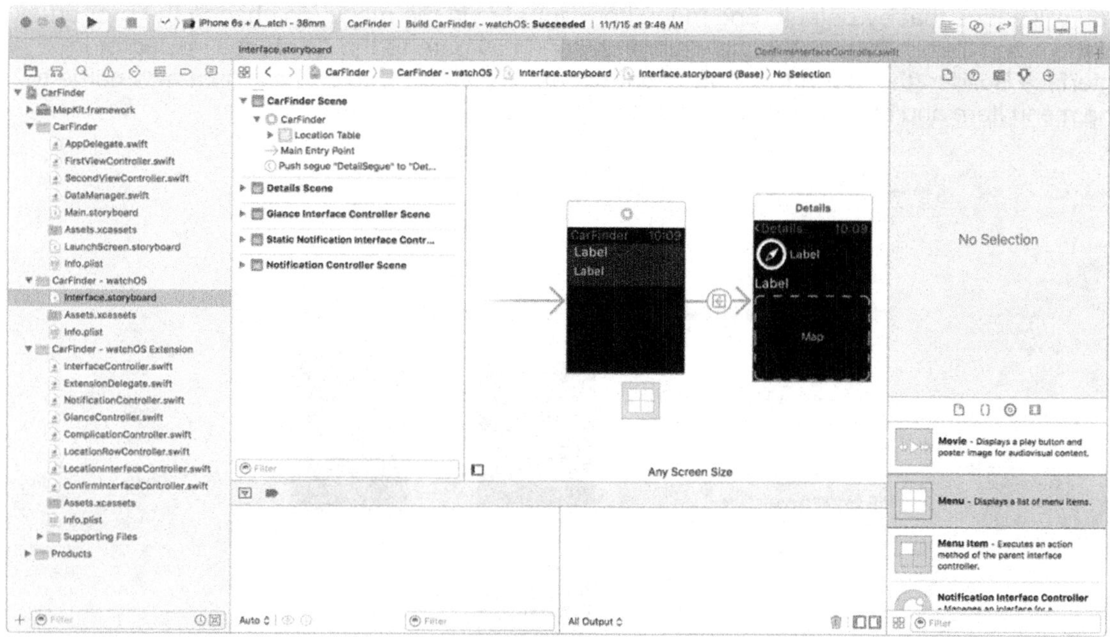

Figure 7-2. Adding a menu to the main interface controller

Unfortunately, Interface Builder does not give you any feedback on the storyboard to indicate that an interface controller has a menu attached to it. To verify that you have successfully added a menu to your interface controller, select its scene on the storyboard and check to make sure a menu item appears in the view hierarchy, as shown in Figure 7-3.

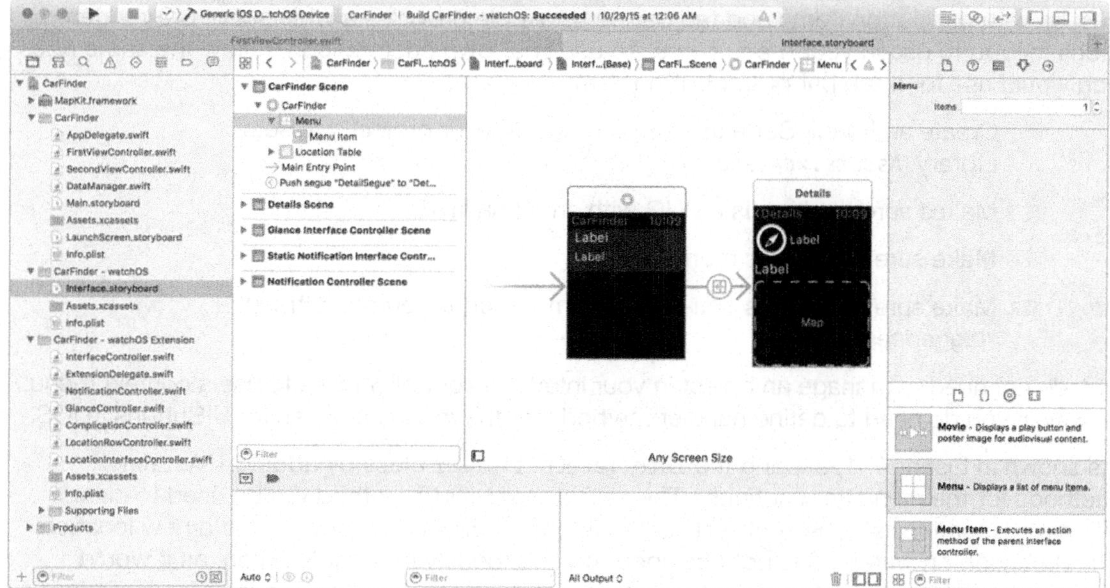

Figure 7-3. Verifying that a menu is in an interface controller's view hierarchy

You will notice that by default, one menu item appears in the menu. To change the properties of the menu item, click it in the view hierarchy and navigate to the Attributes inspector in Interface Builder (the fourth tab in the right pane). From here, you can assign a new name to the menu item and change the icon, as shown in Figure 7-4.

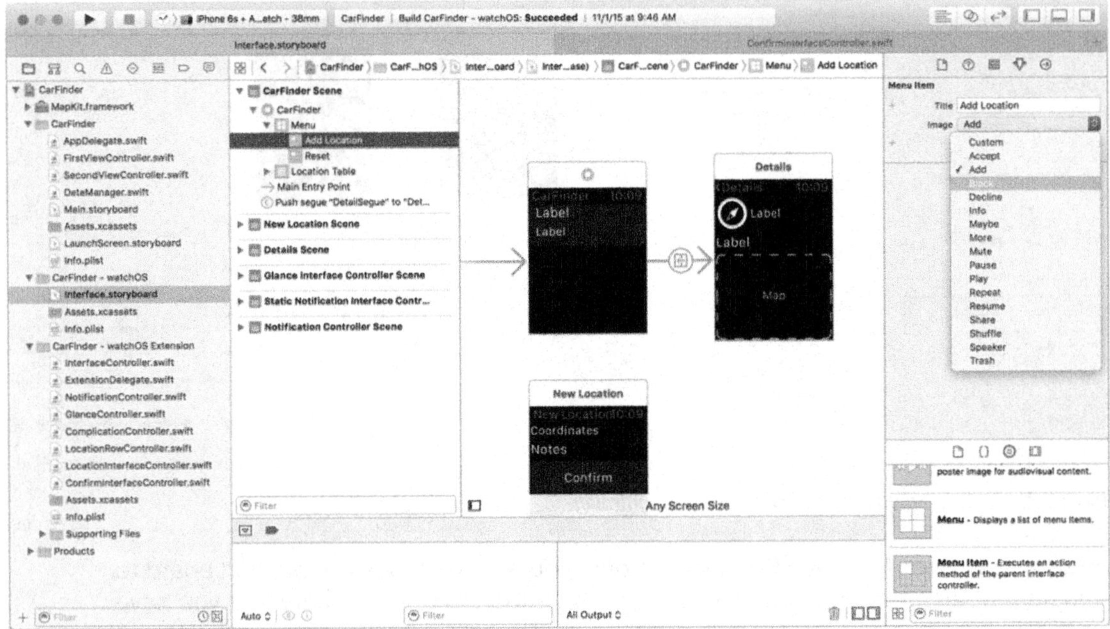

Figure 7-4. Modifying a menu item

Just as with bar button items and tab bar items, Apple provides a wide set of pre-rendered icons for you to use in your menu items. To use your own custom icon, follow the same rules you would use for a tab bar or bar button item:

- Create an Image Set entry for your icon in your project's Assets Library (`Assets.xcasssets`)
- Makes sure the icon is a PNG with an alpha layer
- Make sure the icon is monotone
- Make sure the icon is anti-aliased (smoothed to remove bitmap "jaggedness")

You do not need to manage an object in your interface controller class to use a context menu; however, you do need to define handler methods for the menu items, as for UIButtons in iOS.

As shown in Listing 7-1, expand the `InterfaceController` class by adding `IBAction` methods for the menu item actions. The `resetLocations()` method will be used to clear the saved location list. The `requestLocations()` method will be used to add a new location. CoreLocation on watchOS is not designed to continuously monitor location, as it would drain the watch's battery too quickly, so you need to manually request a location based on a user action.

Listing 7-1. Adding Menu Item Actions to InterfaceController.swift

```
class InterfaceController: WKInterfaceController, WCSessionDelegate {

        @IBAction func requestLocation() {

 }

        @IBAction func resetLocations() {

 }

}
```

As with button actions, in order to tie a menu item to a handler method, you need to use the Connection Inspector (last tab of right panel in Interface builder). As shown in Figure 7-5, drag a line from the `selector` radio box to the CarFinder scene. A pop-up will appear allowing you to choose the `requestLocation()` or `resetLocations()` method.

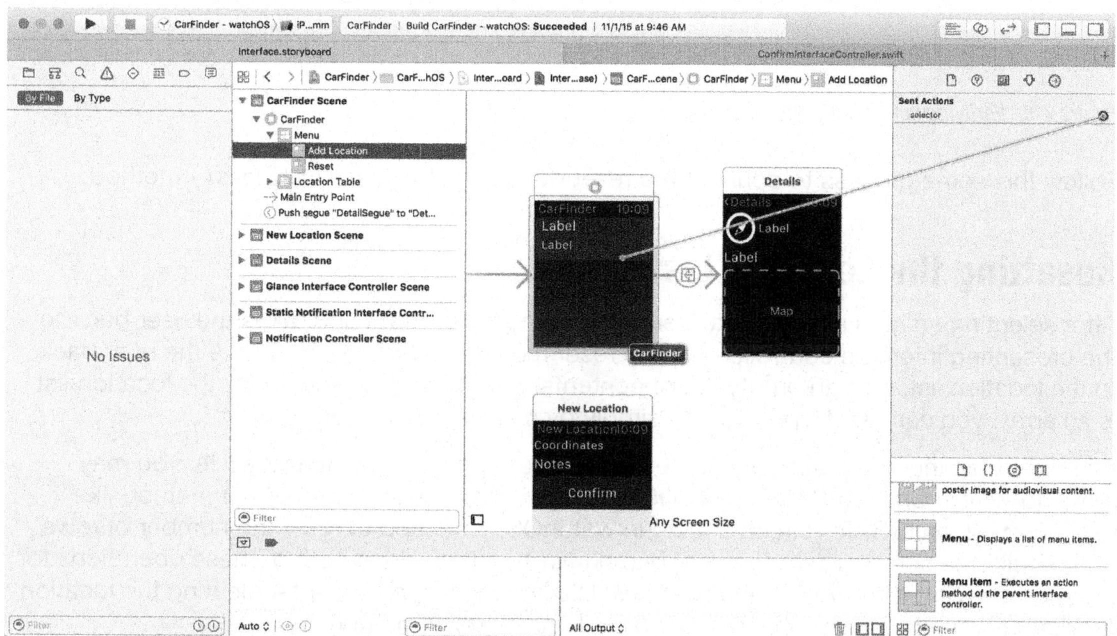

Figure 7-5. Connecting a menu item to a selector

You can verify that the operation was successful by checking that the Connection Inspector has linked the bubbles in the Sent Actions section, as indicated in Figure 7-6.

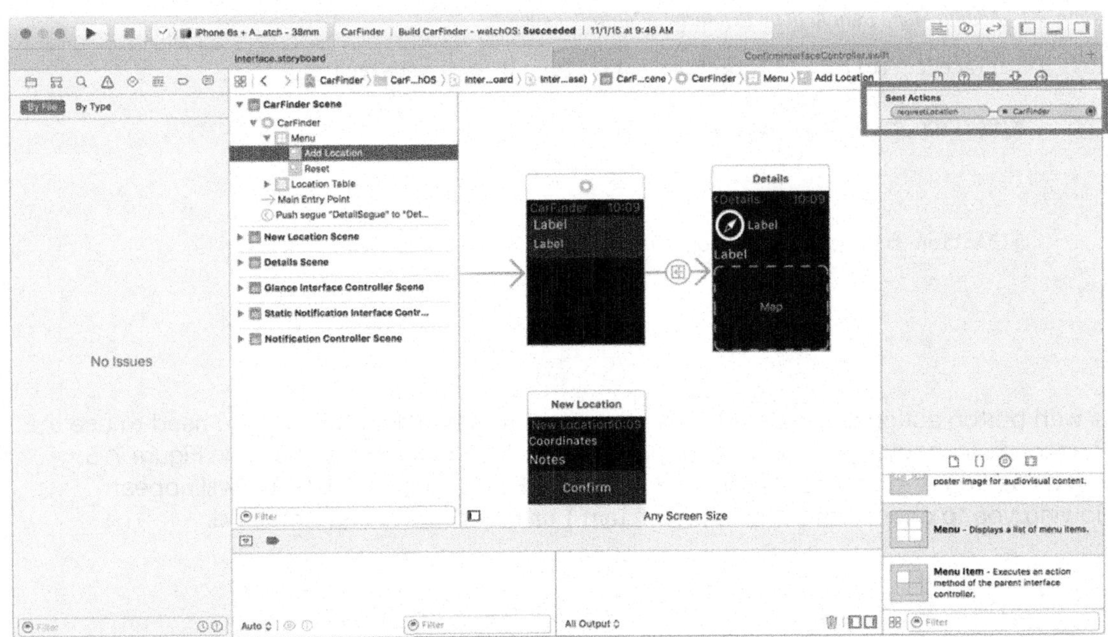

Figure 7-6. Verifying connections have been set

Follow this same process to connect the reset button to the `resetLocations()` method.

Resetting the Location List

After selecting an item in a context menu, the menu disappears and takes the user back to the presenting interface controller. For the reset menu item, you want to take the user back to the location list, with an empty set of contents. Since the data source for the location list is an array, you can reset the contents simply by clearing out the array.

However, clearing out the array is not enough to refresh the user interface (UI). You may remember from Chapter 6 that watchOS tables do not have a `reloadData()` method like `UITableViews` on iOS. To refresh a table in watchOS, you need to reset the number of rows and rebuild the cells. Luckily, the `configureRows()` method does both of these operations for us. As shown in Listing 7-2, using your `resetLocations()` method, after clearing the location array, you can rebuild the table using the `configureRows()` method.

Listing 7-2. Resetting the Location List

```
@IBAction func resetLocations() {
    //data source = empty set
    locations = [Dictionary<String, AnyObject>]()

    configureRows()
}
```

Presenting a Detail View Controller

Although it would be extremely convenient to present interface controllers from menu items via a segue in Interface Builder, as of this writing, that has not yet been implemented in watchOS. To present an interface controller from a menu item, you need to use the method `presentControllerWithName(_:context:)`, specifying a name (storyboard identifier) for the interface controller you want to present and information you want to pass along to this interface controller via a context object.

To begin, you need to add an interface controller to your storyboard that represents the confirm screen. As shown in Figure 7-7, drag a new Interface Controller object to your storyboard.

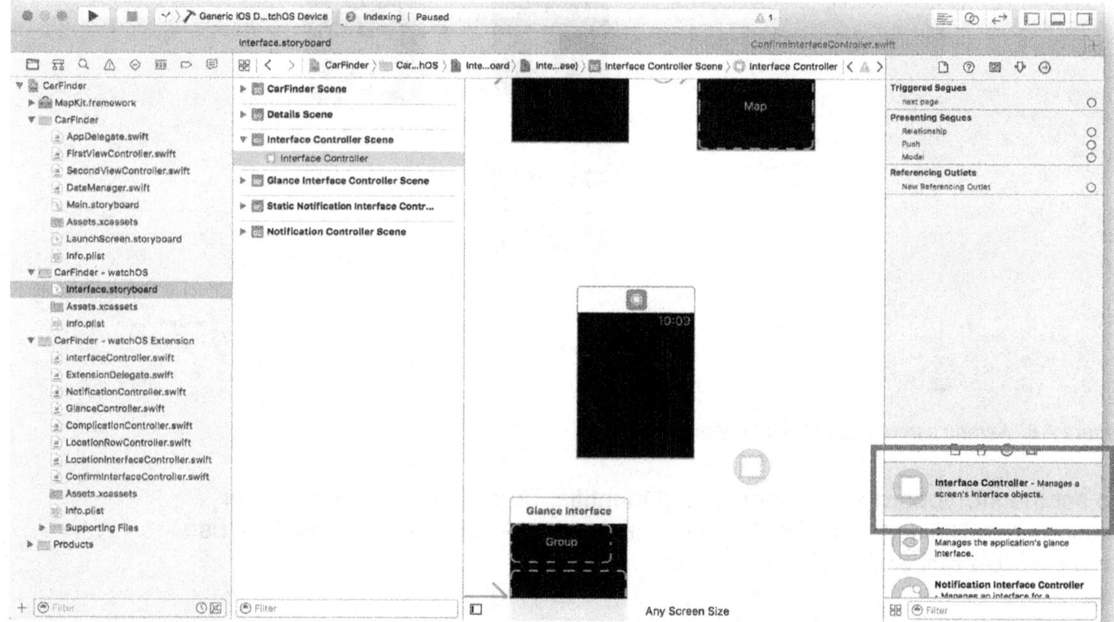

Figure 7-7. Adding a Details interface controller

To represent this interface controller in code, create a subclass of `WKInterfaceController`, named `ConfirmInterfaceController`. Listing 7-3 provides the definition for the `ConfirmInterfaceController` class, including the properties for the UI.

Listing 7-3. Definition for ConfirmInterfaceController Class

```
class ConfirmInterfaceController: WKInterfaceController {

    @IBOutlet weak var coordinatesLabel: WKInterfaceLabel?
    @IBOutlet weak var noteLabel: WKInterfaceLabel?
}
```

To connect the code and storyboard, remember that you need to set a parent class and storyboard identifier. To set the parent class, click the scene for the Interface Controller and click the Identity Inspector in Interface Builder. As shown in Figure 7-8, set the parent class to `ConfirmInterfaceController`.

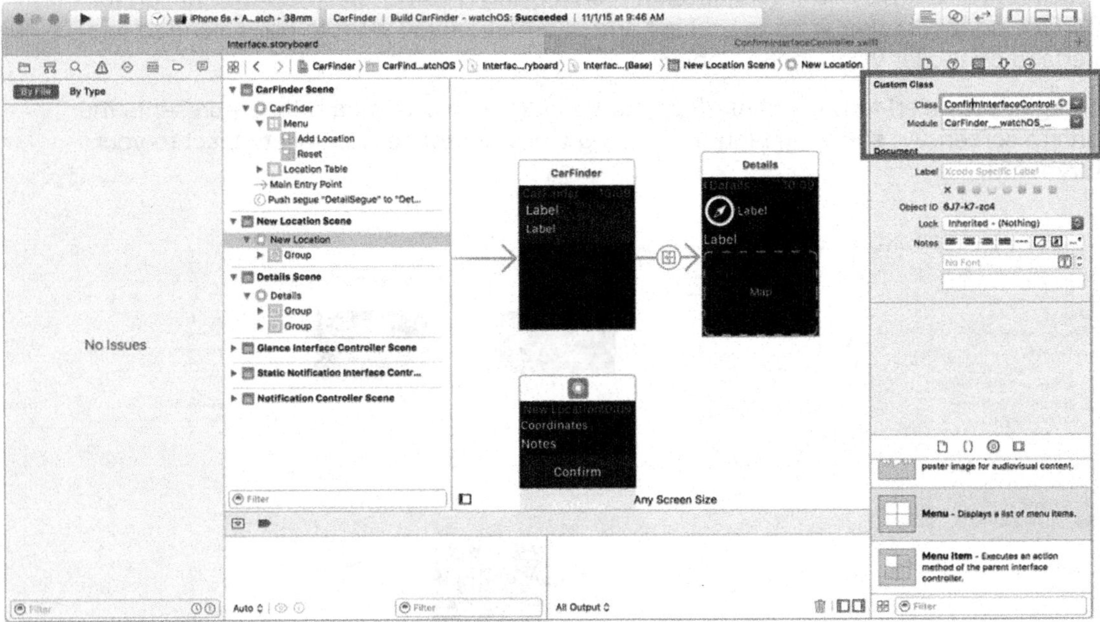

Figure 7-8. Setting parent class for an Interface Controller

To set the storyboard as the storyboard identifier and (optionally) the title for the Interface Builder, click the Attributes Inspector. As shown in Figure 7-9, use `ConfirmInterfaceController` identifier.

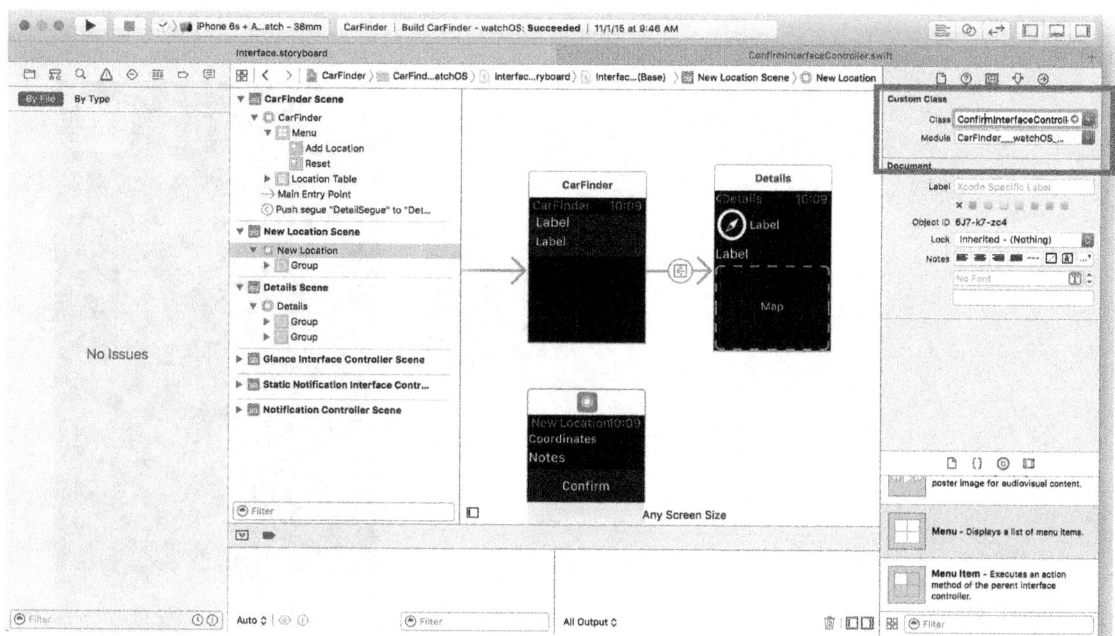

Figure 7-9. Setting the storyboard identifier for an Interface Controller

Having established the Details interface controller, you can now rest assured that calling the `presentControllerWithName()` method will function correctly, given the storyboard identifier `ConfirmInterfaceController`. Listing 7-4 provides the definition for the `requestPermission()` method, which at this point presents the confirm interface controller from the main interface controller. Place this code in your `InterfaceController.swift` file.

Listing 7-4. Presenting the ConfirmInterfaceController

```
func requestLocation() {
    presentControllerWithName("ConfirmInterfaceController", context: nil)

}
```

Simulating Force Touch

While it is possible to debug Force Touch primarily by running it on your watch, it could be a potentially time-consuming effort, due to the time required to install a watchOS app and establish a debugging session. By default, all touches in the watchOS simulator are treated as shallow presses. You can simulate deep press events by changing the Force Touch Pressure in the simulator. To modify this setting, go to the Hardware Menu in the watchOS simulator and select Force Touch Pressure, as shown in Figure 7-10.

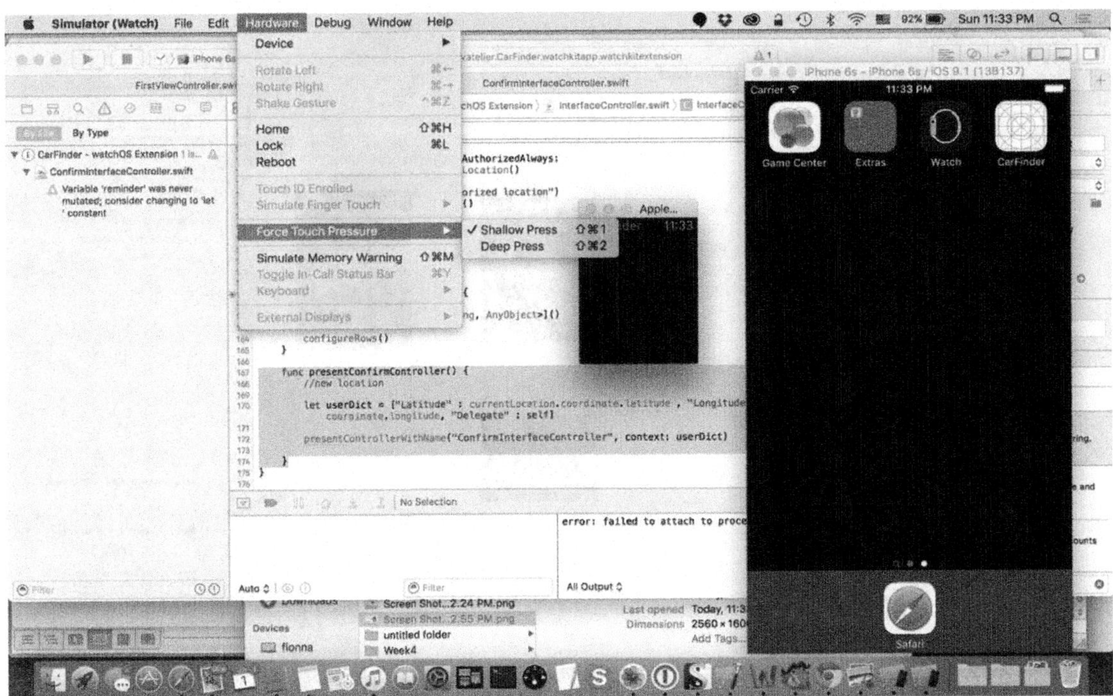

Figure 7-10. Enabling deep press events

Unfortunately, once you toggle the setting, all touches will retain it. This could have some negative side effects, as a deep press on a menu dismisses it. During your debugging session, remember to keep switching the mode between deep press and shallow press to simulate realistic user interaction.

Adding Buttons to an Interface Controller

Now that you are able to present the interface controller for the confirm screen, you need a way of exiting it, either by confirming that the location is correct or by dismissing the view. For the CarFinder application, you will perform these actions using the `WKInterfaceButton` class, which is intended to provide similar functionality to a UIButton in iOS. As watchOS is a subset of iOS, you cannot catch touch events to the same level of granularity as an iOS app, such as "touch down repeat." However, you can trigger a method via a selector or perform a segue when the button is pressed.

Apple suggests that when you plan to use buttons in your watchOS apps, you opt for a purely vertical layout. You can also place buttons into a horizontal layout, but I suggest two at most, since the touch area on the Apple Watch is so small. For the interface of the `ConfirmInterfaceController`, you will use a purely vertical layout to contain all of the UI items. Start by adding a Group object to your Interface Controller. As shown in Figure 7-11, set the layout to Vertical.

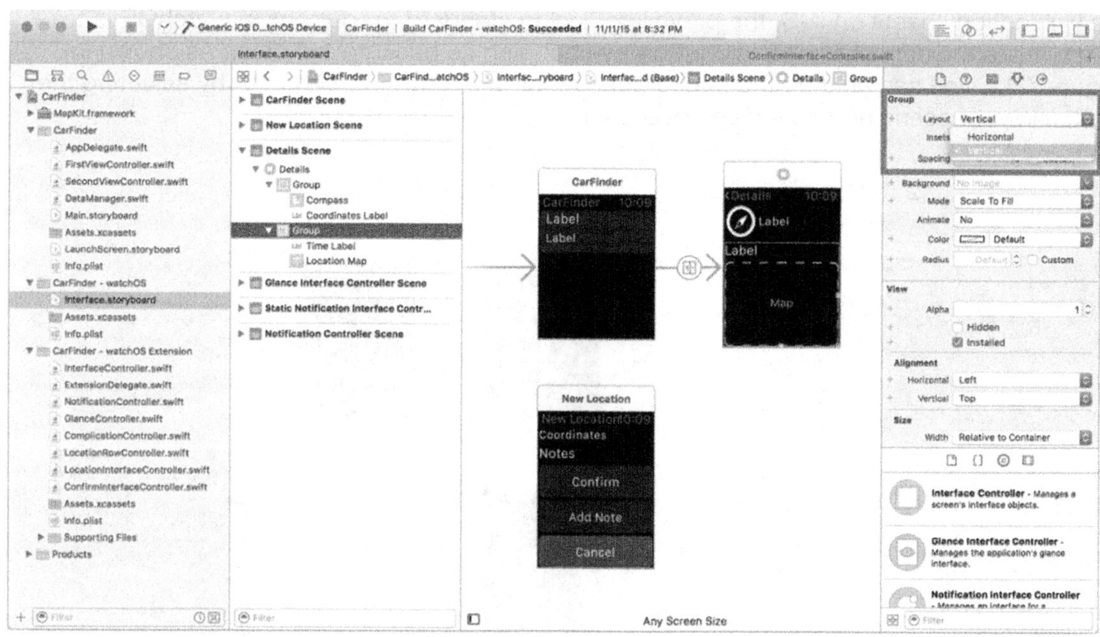

Figure 7-11. Setting vertical layout on a group

Drag three buttons and two labels onto the Group, as shown in Figure 7-12. You do not need to connect the buttons to properties in your class, but make sure you connect the Note and Coordinates label to the `noteLabel` and `coordinatesLabel` properties via the Connection Inspector.

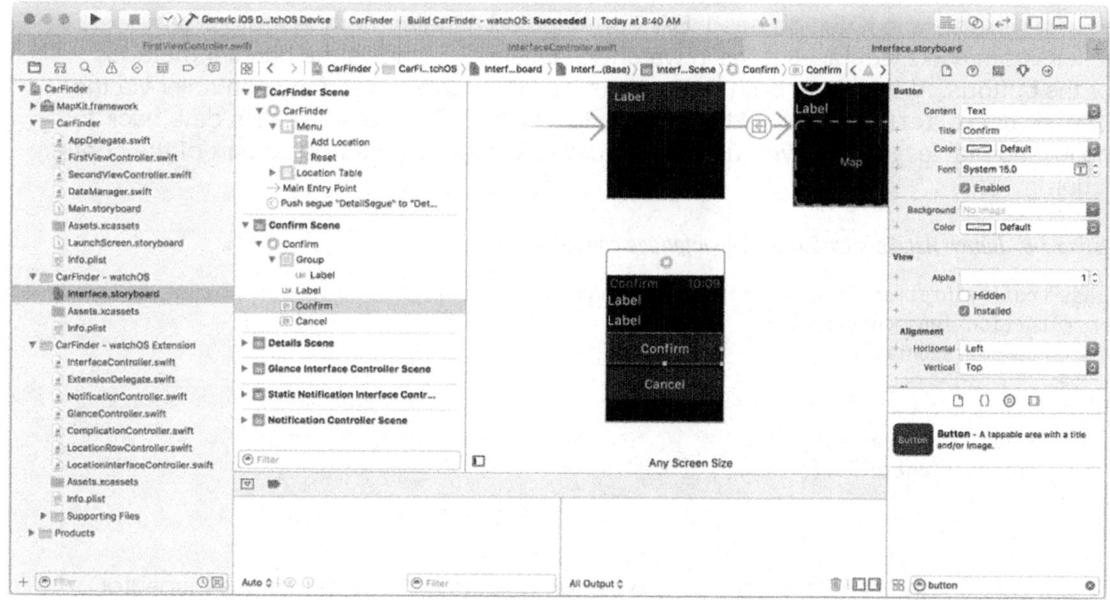

Figure 7-12. Final storyboard layout for ConfirmInterfaceController

As with action sheets on iOS, the prevailing design standard for buttons in watchOS is to differentiate the cancel or dismiss button by changing its background color. As shown in Figure 7-13, you can change the background color of a button in watchOS by selecting the button in your scene and navigating over to the Attributes Inspector.

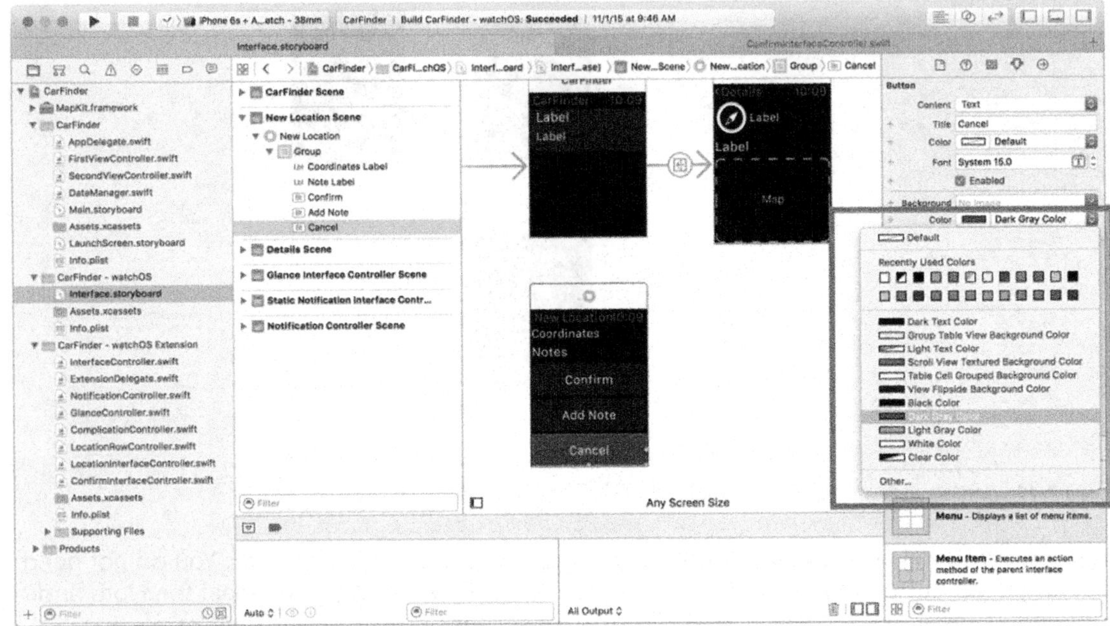

***Figure 7-13.** Changing the background color for a button*

As with UIButtons in iOS, you need IBAction-enabled handler methods to perform actions from a `WKInterfaceButton` in watchOS. Listing 7-5 shows the handler methods for the buttons. At this time, both buttons dismiss the confirm interface controller via the `dismissController()` method of the `WKInterfaceController` class. To pass data back to the location table, you will eventually add a call to a delegate method as part of the confirm action.

***Listing 7-5.** Button Handlers for the confirm interface controller*

```
class ConfirmInterfaceController: WKInterfaceController {
    @IBAction func confirm() {
        dismissController()
    }

    @IBAction func cancel() {
        dismissController()
    }
}
```

Finally, connect the handler methods and button objects using Connections Inspector in Interface Builder. As shown in Figure 7-14, make your connections from the Sent Action selector.

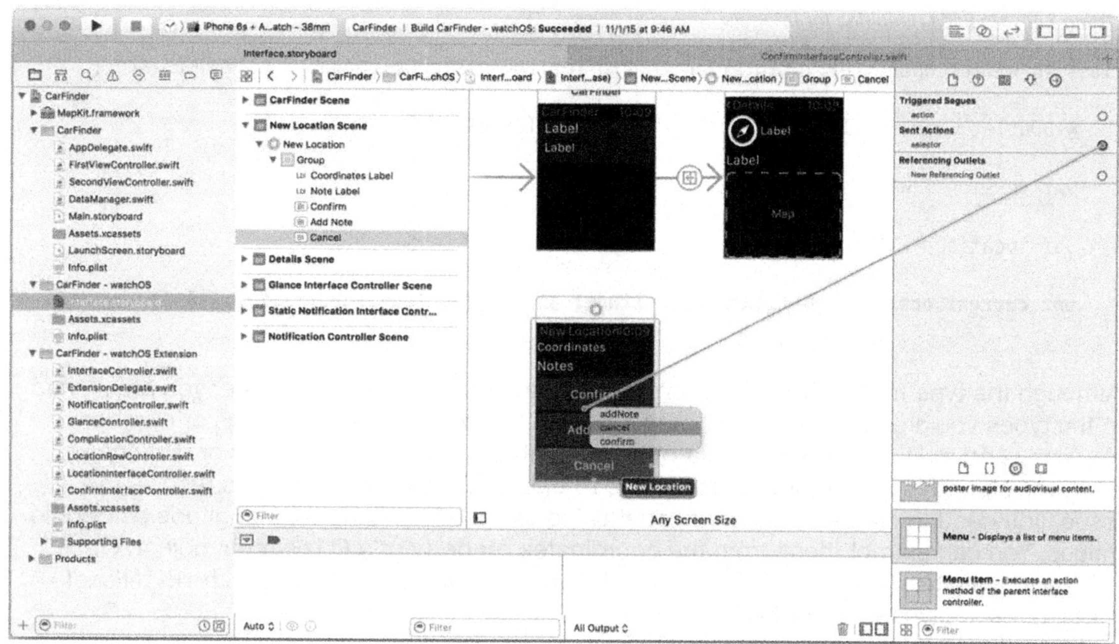

***Figure 7-14.** Connecting button actions*

Passing Information Between Interface Controllers

Having established a way to present the confirm interface controller, you now need a way to initialize it with real data. For the CarFinder application, you will want to show users their current location, so they can save the entry or cancel the prompt. I will cover the specifics of how to use `CoreLocation` natively on the watchOS application in the section "How to Add Notes Using Text Input"; however, for now, you can assume that you will need to pass an object that contains latitude and longitude data.

Remember that earlier in this chapter, you used the method `presentControllerWithName(_:context:)`, to present the confirm interface controller with a storyboard identifier. The other parameter you left blank was context. All subclasses of `WKInterfaceController` implement an `awakeWithContext()` method, which responds to "waking" the view controller with a context, or a data object that you can safely pass between interface controllers. By generating a valid context object from the location list and overriding the `awakeWithContext()` method in the `ConfirmInterfaceController` class, you can initialize the confirm interface controller with location data.

To begin, you need an object that contains the user's location. I have chosen to implement this by adding a `CLLocation` object to the `InterfaceController` class and initializing it with a known location. This adds an extra layer of safety if the user denies the app location permission, or if there is another issue resolving the user's location. Listing 7-6 provides the modified definition for the `InterfaceController` class, adding a `CLLocation` object to the `InterfaceController` class.

Listing 7-6. Modified Definition for InterfaceController class

```
class InterfaceController: WKInterfaceController, WCSessionDelegate, ConfirmDelegate {

    @IBOutlet weak var locationTable: WKInterfaceTable?

    var session : WCSession?

    var locations = [Dictionary<String, AnyObject>]()

    var currentLocation = CLLocation(latitude: 32.830579, longitude: -117.153839)
}
```

Although the type for the context parameter specifies AnyObject, in practice, you are limited in the types you are allowed to use, primarily primitive data types like strings or numbers. You can send multiple pieces of data over by combining them into an array or dictionary; however, as of this writing, it is not possible to pass a CLLocation object. To resolve this issue, you need to create a dictionary containing the user's latitude and longitude as double values. You can extract these from the coordinates property of a CLLocation object. Once you have built the dictionary, you can pass it over using the presentControllerWithName() method, as shown in Listing 7-7.

Listing 7-7. Sending a User's Location While Presenting an Interface Controller

```
func requestLocation() {
    //new location

    let userDict = ["Latitude" : currentLocation.coordinate.latitude , "Longitude" :
    currentLocation.coordinate.longitude, "Delegate" : self]

    presentControllerWithName("ConfirmInterfaceController", context: userDict)

}
```

In the ConfirmInterfaceController class, you complete the process by overriding the awakeFromContext() method. For now, all you need to do when you receive the context data is initialize the coordinatesLabel by extracting the appropriate values out of the dictionary, as shown in Listing 7-8.

Listing 7-8. Overriding awakeWithContext in the Confirm Interface Controller

```
override func awakeWithContext(context: AnyObject?) {
    super.awakeWithContext(context)

    if let inputDict = context as? Dictionary<String, AnyObject>{
        //

        if let inputDelegate = inputDict["Delegate"] as? ConfirmDelegate {
            delegate = inputDelegate
        }
```

```
        if let latitude = inputDict["Latitude"] as? Double {
            let longitude = inputDict["Longitude"] as! Double
            currentLocation = CLLocation(latitude: latitude, longitude: longitude)

            let formattedString = String(format: "%0.3f, %0.3f", latitude, longitude)
            coordinatesLabel?.setText(formattedString)
            }
    }

    // Configure interface objects here.
}
```

Using a Delegate to Pass Information on Dismissal

As you have just learned, it is rather straightforward to pass data to an interface controller while presenting it. Unfortunately, Apple does not provide a method this convenient for passing back data when dismissing an interface controller in watchOS. However, by taking advantage of delegation you can create your bridge between the classes.

The driving concepts behind delegation are that you specify a class to "delegate" a piece work to and define the messages that will be passed back through a protocol. The class that requests the work declares itself as implementing the protocol and sets itself as the delegating object, allowing it to respond to messages from the outsourced class. Delegates are perfect for establishing a message-passing scheme between two classes, without specifying all the details of implementation.

For the CarFinder app, the data we are interested in passing back from the confirm interface controller is whether the user decided to save the location. The location list *delegates* the work of making the determination to the confirm interface controller, so you need to define your protocol there.

Protocols are defined by specifying a **protocol** block with the protocol name and a list of methods that its delegate needs to implement. Listing 7-9 provides the protocol definition for the `ConfirmInterfaceController` class. Protocol blocks are defined before classes, as the corresponding class includes a property placed on the protocol.

Listing 7-9. Protocol Definition for CustomInterfaceController

```
protocol ConfirmDelegate {
    func saveLocation()
}
```

To call methods via a protocol, you need to implement a delegate property on your class. You can then call methods from the protocol on this property, which will be sent to the class that has declared itself as your delegate. In Listing 7-10, I have added the delegate property to the `ConfirmInterfaceController` class; it is an optional variable with the protocol name as its type.

Listing 7-10. Adding a Delegate Property to the ConfirmInterfaceController Class

```
class ConfirmInterfaceController: WKInterfaceController {

    @IBOutlet weak var coordinatesLabel: WKInterfaceLabel?
..
    var delegate: ConfirmDelegate?

}
```

For the final major piece of the implementation in the `ConfirmInterfaceController`, call the `saveLocation()` delegate method. As shown in Listing 7-11, make this call part of the `confirm()` handler method, before dismissing the interface controller.

Listing 7-11. Calling a Delegate Method

```
@IBAction func confirm() {
    delegate?.saveLocation(self.note)
    dismissController()
}
```

The implementation is much easier in the class that is delegating work, `InterfaceController`. In this class, you need to do the following:

- Declare that you are implementing the `ConfirmDelegate` protocol
- Provide an implementation for the methods that the protocol exposes (`saveLocation()`)
- Let the `ConfirmInterfaceController` know that you are the delegate.

To declare that the `InterfaceController` is implementing the `ConfirmDelegate` protocol, add the protocol name to the class signature, with a comma separating it from the parent class name, as shown in Listing 7-12.

Listing 7-12. Declaring That a Class Is Implementing a Protocol

```
class InterfaceController: WKInterfaceController, WCSessionDelegate,
CLLocationManagerDelegate, ConfirmDelegate {
}
```

The compiler will immediately throw an error stating that the `InterfaceController` does not implement all of the methods of the `ConfirmDelegate` protocol. To resolve this issue, implement the `saveLocation()` method. When the user has confirmed that he wants to save his current location, append the current location to the locations array and refresh the table. Listing 7-13 provides the implementation for the `saveLocation()` method.

Listing 7-13. Saving a Location

```
func saveLocation(note :String) {
    //add a new record here
    let locationDict = ["Latitude" : currentLocation.coordinate.latitude , "Longitude" :
    currentLocation.coordinate.longitude, "Timestamp" : currentLocation.timestamp]
    locations.insert(locationDict, atIndex: 0)

}
```

Finally, to receive messages, you need a way of specifying that the `InterfaceController` object associates with the delegate property of the `ConfirmInterfaceController` class. In iOS, you would use the `instantiateViewController()` method on a `UIStoryboard` object to make this connection; however, this method is not available on watchOS. But, you can pass the pointer along by adding it to your context dictionary. In Listing 7-14, I have modified the `requestLocation()` method to include a delegate key.

***Listing 7-14.** Adding a Delegate Object to the Context Dictionary*

```
func requestLocation() {
    //new location

    let userDict = ["Latitude" : currentLocation.coordinate.latitude , "Longitude" :
    currentLocation.coordinate.longitude, "Delegate" : self]

    presentControllerWithName("ConfirmInterfaceController", context: userDict)

}
```

To extract this value from the context dictionary, go back to the `ConfirmInterfaceController`. In the `awakeForContext` method, verify that the value exists and that it has the type `ConfirmDelegate`. As shown in Listing 7-15, once this check has passed, you can set the property.

***Listing 7-15.** Extract the Delegate from Your Context*

```
override func awakeWithContext(context: AnyObject?) {
    super.awakeWithContext(context)

    if let inputDict = context as? Dictionary<String, AnyObject>{
        //

        if let inputDelegate = inputDict["Delegate"] as? ConfirmDelegate {
            delegate = inputDelegate
        }
    }
}
```

You are now able to pass messages upon dismissing the confirm interface controller!

On a closing note, did you like my pun? Driving concepts? CarFinder? Ha, ha, ha!

How to Add Notes Using Text Input

To illustrate another way of accepting user input in your application, you will learn how to add text input. This feature brings up a modal, shown in Figure 7-15, which allows the user to add text in the form of an emoji, a pre-string string, or through Siri text-to-speech recognition.

Figure 7-15. Text input modal

For the CarFinder application, you will want to trigger this modal when the user clicks the "Add Note" button. To help the user, you should pre-populate the picker with strings that relate to location notes, such as "next to light pole" or "across from house."

> **Note** You need to use an Apple Watch to test text input, as the simulator does not support Siri.

To present the text input modal, use the method, `presentTextInputControllerWithSuggestions(_:allowedInputMode:)`, which allows you to specify an array of suggestion strings, limits on the types of input accepted (e.g., no emoji), and a completion handler. Listing 7-16 provides the implementation for the CarFinder app. As a reminder, this goes in the `ConfirmInterfaceController` class.

Listing 7-16. Presenting the Text Input Modal

```
@IBAction func addNote() {
    let suggestionArray = ["On curb", "Next to house", "Next to lightpole"]
    presentTextInputControllerWithSuggestions(suggestionArray, allowedInputMode:
    WKTextInputMode.AllowEmoji) { (inputArray: [AnyObject]?) -> Void in
        if let inputStrings = inputArray as? [String] {
            if inputStrings.count > 0 {
                let savedString = inputStrings[0]

                dispatch_async(dispatch_get_main_queue()) {
                    self.noteLabel?.setText(savedString)
                    self.note = savedString
                }

            }
        }
    }

}
```

The `String` type in Swift allows a wider character set than `NSString` in Objective-C, so you do not need to set any limits on the input type. Emoji will display in-line when provided as input to a string.

As another reminder, remember that you need to set text for the noteLabel on the main thread, as UI updates only execute on the main thread.

To pass the note back to the `InterfaceController`, expand the `ConfirmDelegate` protocol's `saveLocation()` method to include a "Note" parameter. Listing 7-17 provides the modified protocol declaration. Place this code in `ConfirmInterfaceController.swift`.

Listing 7-17. Expanding the ConfirmDelegate Protocol to Allow notes()

```
protocol ConfirmDelegate {
    func saveLocation(note: String)
}
```

Listing 7-18 includes the modified `confirm()` method for the `ConfirmInterfaceController` class, which pulls in the note that was saved earlier.

Listing 7-18. Sending a Note to the Delegate

```
@IBAction func confirm() {
    delegate?.saveLocation(self.note)
    dismissController()
}
```

You will implement the saveLocation() delegate method in the `InterfaceController` class, which will allow you to extract the note as an input parameter.

Sending Data Back to the Parent iOS App

For the final piece of the interactive version of CarFinder, you will send locations that the watch app created back to the parent iOS app. Once again, you can rely on your old friend WatchConnectivity to help communicate between your watchOS app and its parent iOS app.

While the primary method for sending data to the Apple Watch from an iOS app is through the `updateApplicationContext()` method on a WKSession, there are a few more options available for sending information from the Apple Watch to its parent iOS application. Table 7-1 provides an overview of these methods and their intended uses.

Table 7-1. Methods for Transferring Data from the Apple Watch to an iOS Application

Method	Purpose
sendMessage:replyHandler:errorHandler:	*Send a context containing data to the parent app immediately. Queue any old versions of the dictionary that have not yet been processed.*
transferFile:metadata:	*Transfer a file to the parent app.*
transferUserInfo:	*Transfer a dictionary to the parent app. Queue any old versions of the dictionary that have not yet been processed.*
updateApplicationContext:error:	*Transfer a dictionary to the parent app. Discard any old versions of the dictionary that have not yet been processed.*

For the CarFinder application, you want to post location updates as the user creates them. The messages will be infrequent, but they need to be queued and delivered in order. For this reason, you will use the `sendMessage()` method to post location updates back to the companion iOS app.

In the flow of the CarFinder app, the save action happens in the `saveLocation()` method of the `InterfaceController` class. At this point, you have a context dictionary containing the latitude and longitude information for a new location. The `sendMessage()` method takes a dictionary as input; it would make sense to pass the input dictionary directly to the iOS app, which has its own logic for adding a location based on latitude and longitude. Listing 7-19 provides the modified `saveLocation()` method, which includes the `sendMessage()` call.

Listing 7-19. Calling sendMessage() from the InterfaceController Class

```
func saveLocation(note :String) {
    //add a new record here
    let locationDict = ["Latitude" : currentLocation.coordinate.latitude , "Longitude" :
    currentLocation.coordinate.longitude, "Timestamp" : currentLocation.timestamp,
    "Note" : note]
    locations.insert(locationDict, atIndex: 0)

    session?.sendMessage(locationDict, replyHandler: nil, errorHandler: { (error: NSError)
    -> Void in
        print(error.description)
    })

}
```

You will notice the completion handlers for the error and reply states are very light in my example. In general, you should not show an error alert unless the failing action will hinder the user's experience with the app. In this example, I did not implement any custom logic for the reply handler because the watchOS UI does not update based on a successful post to the iOS app.

To receive a message from a watchOS app in an iOS app, you need to expand your AppDelegate class, which handles external events and launching your app, to handle watchKit extension messages. To handle the watchKit extension messages, you need to implement the delegate method func application(application: UIApplication, handleWatchKitExtensionRequest userInfo:reply:), which receives a dictionary containing information from the watchOS app and a reply method signature, which you can use to send a reply back to the watchOS app. This allows you to send a confirmation back to the app or update the UI on the watch.

Receiving the message in the iOS parent app is one thing, but in order to do something with it, you need to send a message to the location list, represented by the FirstViewController class. Best practices in Apple development suggest against creating a singleton or maintaining pointers to view controllers in your app delegate. However, you can use a much more generic message-passing method to get the update to the FirstViewController class: notifications.

With notifications, you specify a name for your message (the notification name) and post a message using that name. Generally, the data is transferred in a dictionary, which is extremely convenient, because your input is also a dictionary. A notification is sent to anyone who wants to listen. A class will declare itself as an "observer" of a notification and specify a selector or completion handler that should execute when the notification is received.

Listing 7-20 provides the handleWatchKitExtensionRequest() method for the AppDelegate, including the call to post a notification. Place this code in AppDelegate.swift.

Listing 7-20. Receiving Messages from the CarFinder watchOS App

```
func application(application: UIApplication, handleWatchKitExtensionRequest userInfo:
[NSObject : AnyObject]?, reply: ([NSObject : AnyObject]?) -> Void) {

    NSNotificationCenter.defaultCenter().postNotificationName("LocationUpdateNotification",
    object: nil, userInfo: userInfo)

}
```

To observe the notification, in the FirstViewController's viewDidLoad() method, implement the addObserver() method. As shown in Listing 7-21, I have chosen to use a completion handler to process the notification.

Listing 7-21. Processing the watchOS Notification

```
NSNotificationCenter.defaultCenter().addObserverForName("LocationUpdateNotification",
object: nil, queue: NSOperationQueue.mainQueue()) { (notif: NSNotification) -> Void in
    //

    if let location = notif.userInfo as? [String : AnyObject] {

        if let latitude = location["Latitude"] as? Double {
            let longitude = location["Longitude"] as! Double

            let location = CLLocation(latitude: latitude, longitude: longitude)
            DataManager.sharedInstance.locations.insert(location, atIndex: 0)
```

```
            self.tableView.reloadData()

        }
    }

}
```

Now that you have added interactive features to CarFinder, your app should look like Figure 7-16. The new app retains the location list from the original CarFinder app, while adding an expanded details page and menu options to add and delete locations.

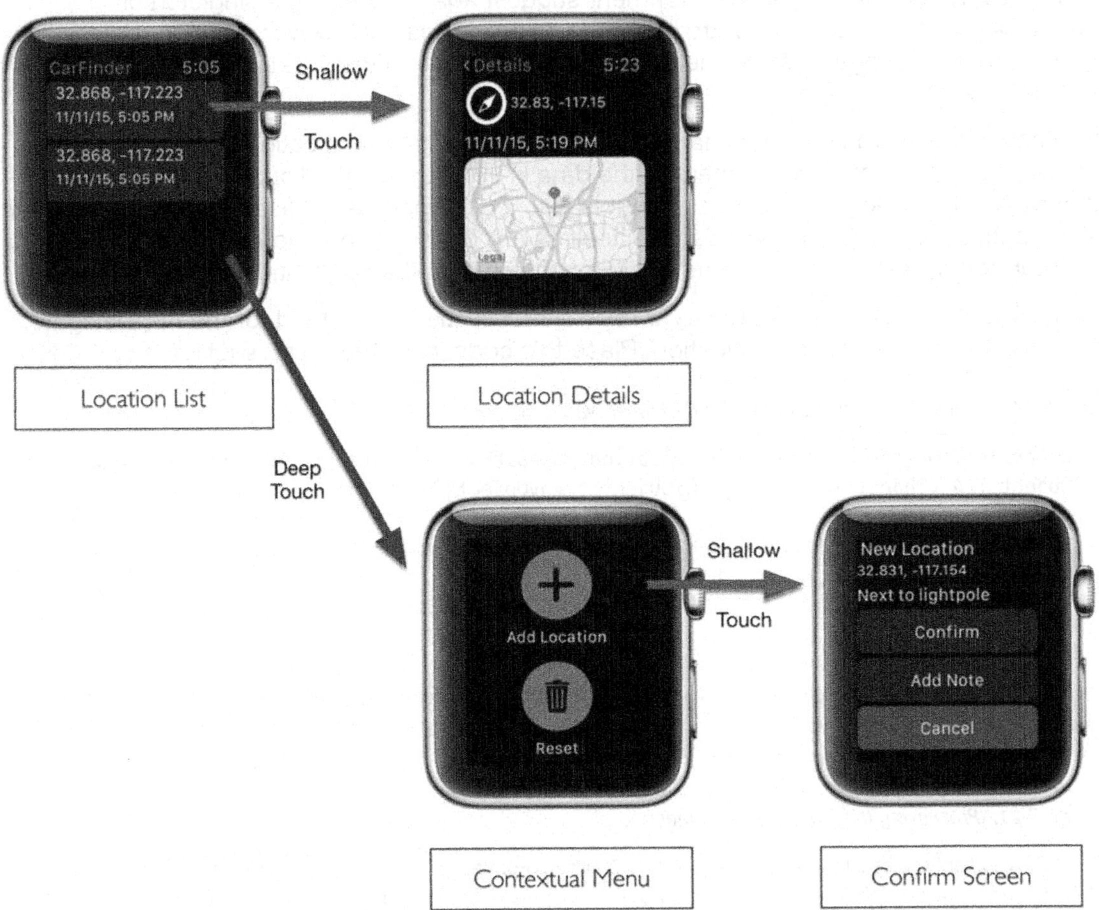

Figure 7-16. Expanded user interface for interactive CarFinder app

Summary

In this chapter, you learned how to make a watchOS app interactive by adding the ability to create a new location from the watch, add notes using text input, and post the new item back to the parent app. Along the way, you learned that much of the battle lies in properly passing data between interface controllers and to the parent app. You saw that you could use an application context to post data to an interface controller while presenting it, delegates to post data after dismissing an interface controller, and the WatchConnectivity class to post information back to your parent iOS app.

Chapter 8

Building a Stand-Alone watchOS App

Ahmed Bakir

In this chapter, you will learn about one of the greatest attributes of watchOS 2: its capabilities that let you build an app that runs natively, even offline, without maintaining an active connection to your parent iOS app. So far, you have noticed that watchOS 2 apps share many design features with iOS apps, including interface controllers (view controllers), notifications, and delegation. With watchOS 1, you were limited to building "listener" apps, designed to respond to data manifests from a parent app; they were not intended to provide anything more than consumption. watchOS 2 bridges a huge gap because it allows you to build apps that not only are designed like iOS apps but also function like iOS apps.

To go even further, watchOS 2 started bundling stripped-down versions of Cocoa Touch frameworks into the operating system (OS) itself. These frameworks bake the logic of accessing hardware, playing back media, and other weighty operations into the watch, allowing your apps to operate completely independently. These frameworks are extremely useful because they abstract the "hard work" away from you, allowing you to focus on the business logic of your applications rather than the technical details (such as how to decode an MP4 video).

There are too many frameworks in watchOS 2 to cover them all exhaustively, but in this chapter, I will focus on Core Location, which allows you to perform more advanced location features like geocoding. I will also cover a very popular Cocoa Touch API (application programming interface) which has made its way over to watchOS, NSTimer, which allows you to present timed events to users. Finally, you will learn how to use the networking features of the Foundation framework (the base for all Apple programming), which now allows you to make HTTP calls to the Internet directly from your watch.

For this chapter, you will revisit your old friend, CarFinder, taking advantage of these features to further improve the application. You can find the updated version of CarFinder in the Ch8 folder for this book in the Source Code/Download area of the Apress web site (www.apress.com).

Using Core Location to Request Current Location

In Chapter 7's implementation of the CarFinder app, you used hard-coded coordinates to initialize the CLLocation object passed along to the confirm interface controller. In this section, you will learn how to use CoreLocation to retrieve the user's current location. Additionally, since user location is a permission, you will also need to use CoreLocation to prompt the user for location permission.

In the new CarFinder application, you will ask the user for location permission the first time he tries to add a location from the contextual menu. Once the user has approved the permission, request his current location and take him to the confirm interface controller.

The process of adding a framework to your watchOS app is exactly like the one for an iOS app: import the desired framework in your classes. Most of your Core Location operations will take place on the InterfaceController and ConfirmInterfaceController classes, so add the import statement to both. To perform location operations in CoreLocation, you will also need an instance of the CLLocationManager class. Listing 8-1 includes the modified definition for the InterfaceController class, including the import statement and CLLocationManager object. Follow the same steps for all classes that use CoreLocation.

***Listing 8-1.** Adding CoreLocation to a watchOS Class*

```
import WatchKit
import Foundation
import CoreLocation
import WatchConnectivity

class InterfaceController: WKInterfaceController, WCSessionDelegate,
CLLocationManagerDelegate, ConfirmDelegate {

    @IBOutlet weak var locationTable: WKInterfaceTable?

    var session : WCSession?

    var locations = [Dictionary<String, AnyObject>]()
    var locationManager:  CLLocationManager?
    var currentLocation = CLLocation(latitude: 32.830579, longitude: -117.153839)

    override func awakeWithContext(context: AnyObject?) {
        super.awakeWithContext(context)
        ...
    }

    ...

}
```

The process of bringing up the location permission screen in watchOS is similar to that of iOS: query for authorization status and call the correct method to request permission if the status is not authorized or denied. Fortunately, in Chapter 7, you defined the `requestPermission()` method to bring up the confirm interface controller. You can take advantage of that here by replacing that with the code to make the permission query in `ConfirmInterfaceController.swift`, as shown in Listing 8-2.

Listing 8-2. Modified requestLocation() Method, Including Permission Query

```
@IBAction func requestLocation() {

    //do not initialize until the user tries to request a location
    locationManager = CLLocationManager()
    locationManager?.delegate = self

    switch (CLLocationManager.authorizationStatus()) {

    case .AuthorizedWhenInUse, .AuthorizedAlways:
        locationManager?.requestLocation()
    case .Denied:
        print("user has not authorized location")
        presentConfirmController()
    case .NotDetermined:
        fallthrough
    default:
        locationManager?.requestWhenInUseAuthorization()
    }
}
```

To make the code easier to read, I have grouped the old code to present the confirm interface controller into a method called `presentConfirmController` (Listing 8-3). This encapsulates the work of building a context dictionary from the `currentLocation` property and presenting the interface controller.

Listing 8-3. Presenting the Confirm Interface Controller

```
func presentConfirmController() {
    //new location

    let userDict = ["Latitude" : currentLocation.coordinate.latitude , "Longitude" :
    currentLocation.coordinate.longitude, "Delegate" : self]

    presentControllerWithName("ConfirmInterfaceController", context: userDict)

}
```

Using the GPS sensor on any connected device is one of the most power-hungry operations you can perform. While the iPhone and iPad have been optimized to reduce this cost, the Apple Watch is not yet at that state, so all location requests need to be on demand. In the example in Listing 8-2, when the status has been determined to already be authorized, the call to `requestLocation()` is made, which performs the on-demand location request.

Unfortunately, neither the permission request nor the location request makes it obvious what you are supposed to do when you have permission or a location. To implement these, you will need to implement the `CLLocationManagerDelegate` protocol and its methods to handle permission and location updates. Begin by updating your class definition to include the `CLLocationManagerDelegate` protocol, as shown in Listing 8-4.

***Listing 8-4.** Updating the Class Definition to Include CLLocationManagerDelegate*

```
class InterfaceController: WKInterfaceController, WCSessionDelegate,
CLLocationManagerDelegate, ConfirmDelegate {
}
```

Next, you need to make sure the `CLLocationManager` object is initialized correctly, including its delegate property. Accomplish that by initializing the object at the top of the `requestLocation()` method, as shown in Listing 8-5.

***Listing 8-5.** Initializing the Location Manager*

```
@IBAction func requestLocation() {

    //do not initialize until the user tries to request a location
    locationManager = CLLocationManager()
    locationManager?.delegate = self

    switch (CLLocationManager.authorizationStatus()) {

    case .AuthorizedWhenInUse, .AuthorizedAlways:
        locationManager?.requestLocation()
    case .Denied:
        print("user has not authorized location")
        presentConfirmController()
    case .NotDetermined:
        fallthrough
    default:
        locationManager?.requestWhenInUseAuthorization()
    }
}
```

For permissions requests in `CoreLocation`, you need to implement the `didFailWithError` and `didChangeAuthorization` delegate methods, both of which trigger compilation errors if they are not included in your project. Listing 8-6 provides the `didFailWithError()` method for the `InterfaceController` class (`InterfaceController.swift`). In my implementation, I print out an error message in this class, since I provided a default current location value when initializing the `currentLocation` property.

***Listing 8-6.** Handling Permissions Failure*

```
func locationManager(manager: CLLocationManager, didFailWithError error: NSError) {
    //do nothing, we have a default value
    print(error.description)
}
```

When the user has granted your app permission to use a location, you can query the `locationManager` for the user's current location. As shown in Listing 8-7, in the `InterfaceController` class (`InterfaceController.swift`), perform this operation by checking that the status has changed to "AuthorizedWhenInUse" in the `didChangeAuthorization` delegate method.

Listing 8-7. Handling Permissions Success

```
func locationManager(manager: CLLocationManager, didChangeAuthorizationStatus status:
CLAuthorizationStatus) {
    if status == CLAuthorizationStatus.AuthorizedWhenInUse {
        manager.requestLocation()
    } else {
        //do nothing, use default location
    }
}
```

Finally, you need to handle the event that triggers when the location manager has fetched the user's current location. The `updateLocations()` delegate method handles this event. As shown in Listing 8-8, when this event is triggered, verify that at least one valid location has been received, and use that to initialize the `currentLocation` property of the class. From there present the confirm interface controller.

Listing 8-8. Handling Location Updates

```
func locationManager(manager: CLLocationManager, didUpdateLocations
locations: [CLLocation]) {
    if locations.count > 0 {
        currentLocation = locations[0]

        presentConfirmController()

    }
}
```

Reverse Geocoding an Address

One of the challenges in the original CarFinder app was that it only displayed a user's location as latitude and longitude. I don't know about you, but I am a bit rusty on converting latitude and longitude to street addresses. `CoreLocation`, however, is not, and by taking advantage of its `CLGeocoder` class, we can use Apple's reverse geocoding servers to retrieve this information. This API has been available for years on iOS. Conveniently, it is also available on watchOS 2.

For the CarFinder app, you should use reverse geocoding to replace the coordinates on the user interface (UI) with a human-readable string containing the user's street address (street number and name). Reverse geocoding is a service-based API, meaning that you have to wait for Apple's servers to respond with a result. As you can guess, this means the reply time is indeterminate, and you will need to handle the response on a view where the user can wait for the result to come in. In the CarFinder app, it makes sense to make this call on the confirm view. From there, you can pass the street address back to the location list in your delegate method, along with saved notes.

You can reverse geocode a set of coordinates with the `CLGecoder` private method `reverseGeocodeLocation(:_, completionHandler:)`, which takes a `CLLocation` object as input and executes a completion handler when it receives a response from Apple's geocoding server. In the response is an array of places that match the given coordinates and an `NSError` object, which is non-nil if an error occurred during the request.

For the confirm screen, you should start the request as soon as the interface controller is presented. When you receive the request, you should extract the street name and number (represented by the `thoroughfare` and `subThoroughfare` properties) and save them to a string, which you will use to update the UI and location list.

Listing 8-9 provides the updated implementation for the `awakeFromContext()` method for the `ConfirmInterfaceController` class. Since you cannot access the text string from a label, save a copy of the generated string in a property named address.

***Listing 8-9.** Updated ConfirmInterfaceController Class*

```
override func awakeWithContext(context: AnyObject?) {
    super.awakeWithContext(context)

    if let inputDict = context as? Dictionary<String, AnyObject>{
        //

        if let inputDelegate = inputDict["Delegate"] as? ConfirmDelegate {
            delegate = inputDelegate
        }
        if let latitude = inputDict["Latitude"] as? Double {
            let longitude = inputDict["Longitude"] as! Double
            currentLocation = CLLocation(latitude: latitude, longitude: longitude)

            let formattedString = String(format: "%0.3f, %0.3f", latitude, longitude)
            coordinatesLabel?.setText(formattedString)

            let geocoder = CLGeocoder()

            geocoder.reverseGeocodeLocation(currentLocation!, completionHandler: {
            (placemarks: [CLPlacemark]?, error: NSError?) -> Void in
                //sd
                if error == nil {
                    if placemarks?.count > 0 {
                        let currentPlace = placemarks![0]
                        let placeString = "\(currentPlace.subThoroughfare!)
                        \(currentPlace.thoroughfare!)"
```

```
                            dispatch_async(dispatch_get_main_queue()) {
                                self.coordinatesLabel?.setText(placeString)
                                self.address = placeString
                            }
                        }
                    }
                })
            }
        }

        // Configure interface objects here.
    }
```

In terms of execution time, reverse geocoding is an expensive operation. It is also certain that the results will not change for a given address. We can save time in the app by passing the address to the location list. To enable this, modify the `ConfirmDelegate` protocol delegate in `ConfirmInterfaceController.swift` to add the address as a return parameter, as shown in Listing 8-10.

Listing 8-10. Adding Address to the ConfirmDelegate Protocol

```
protocol ConfirmDelegate {
    func saveLocation(note: String, address: String)
}
```

Listing 8-11 provides the modified `confirm()` method of the `InterfaceController` class (`InterfaceController.swift`), which includes the address in the call to the delegate.

Listing 8-11. Sending the Address to the Delegate Object

```
@IBAction func confirm() {
    let noteString = self.note!
    let addressString = self.address!

    delegate?.saveLocation(noteString, address: addressString)
    dismissController()
}
```

On the receiving side, you need to modify the `saveLocation()` delegate method to include the address by adding it as a key-value pair. Listing 8-12 provides the modified `saveLocation()` method for the `InterfaceController` class.

Listing 8-12. Adding Address to the saveLocation() Delegate Method

```
func saveLocation(note: String, address: String) {

    //add a new record here
    let locationDict = ["Latitude" : currentLocation.coordinate.latitude , "Longitude" :
    currentLocation.coordinate.longitude, "Timestamp" : currentLocation.timestamp,
    "Note" : note, "Address": address]
    locations.insert(locationDict, atIndex: 0)
```

```
    session?.sendMessage(locationDict, replyHandler: nil, errorHandler: { (error: NSError)
    -> Void in
        print(error.description)
    })

}
```

Finally, to display the address, modify the `configureRows()` method in the location list (`InterfaceController.swift`), which builds each table cell to use the human-readable address, instead of latitude and longitude, as shown in Listing 8-13.

Listing 8-13. Modifying the Table View to Include Address

```
func configureRows() {

    self.locationTable?.setNumberOfRows(locations.count, withRowType:
    "LocationRowController")

    for var index = 0; index < locations.count; index++ {

        if let row = self.locationTable?.rowControllerAtIndex(index) as?
        LocationRowController {
            let location = self.locations[index]

            if let address = location["Address"] as? String {
                row.coordinatesLabel?.setText(address)
            } else if let latitude = location["Latitude"] as? Double {
                let longitude = location["Longitude"] as! Double
                let formattedString = String(format: "%0.3f, %0.3f", latitude, longitude)
                //row.coordinatesLabel?.setText("\(latitude), \(location["Longitude"]!)")
                row.coordinatesLabel?.setText(formattedString)

            }

            if let timeStamp = location["Timestamp"]  as? NSDate {
                let dateFormatter = NSDateFormatter()
                dateFormatter.dateStyle = NSDateFormatterStyle.ShortStyle
                dateFormatter.timeStyle = NSDateFormatterStyle.ShortStyle
                row.timeLabel?.setText(dateFormatter.stringFromDate(timeStamp))
            }

        }

    }

    //self.locationTable?.setNumberOfRows(locations.count, withRowType:
    "LocationRowController")
}
```

> **Note** You should use an if-else to display the latitude and longitude if the human-readable address is not available.

The final version of the CarFinder table UI should now include human-readable addresses, like the example in Figure 8-1. Much better, in my humble opinion!

Figure 8-1. Updated table for CarFinder app

Using NSTimer to Create Reminders

Another convenient feature Apple has ported to watchOS is the `NSTimer` class, which allows you to schedule actions to be executed after a period of time has elapsed. In a parking app, this is useful, as it can remind a user to go back to her car before the meter expires. In the WatchKit app, you will expose this feature by adding an Add Time button to the `ConfirmInterfaceController` class, where the user saves the location. On iOS, `EventKit` provides a modal for entering in time. On watchOS, you need to build it yourself. For this app, every time the user presses the Add Time button, add 15 minutes to the reminder. When the user saves the location, he will be able to use the total time to create a reminder alert, which will appear on his watch. Reflect this by adding a label for meter timer to the confirm interface controller on the storyboard, as well as a button to increment the timer. Listing 8-14 provides the modified class definition for the `ConfirmInterfaceController` class (`ConfirmInterfaceController.swift`), which includes these new properties.

Listing 8-14. Modified Class Definition for ConfirmInterfaceController, Including New Timer Properties

```
class ConfirmInterfaceController: WKInterfaceController {

    @IBOutlet weak var coordinatesLabel: WKInterfaceLabel?
    @IBOutlet weak var noteLabel: WKInterfaceLabel?
    @IBOutlet weak var timeLabel: WKInterfaceLabel?
```

```
    var currentLocation : CLLocation?
    var delegate: ConfirmDelegate?
    var note: String = ""
    var address: String = ""

    var totalTime : NSTimeInterval = 0.0

    override func awakeWithContext(context: AnyObject?) {
        super.awakeWithContext(context)
        ...
        }

}
```

Figure 8-2 shows the modified storyboard.

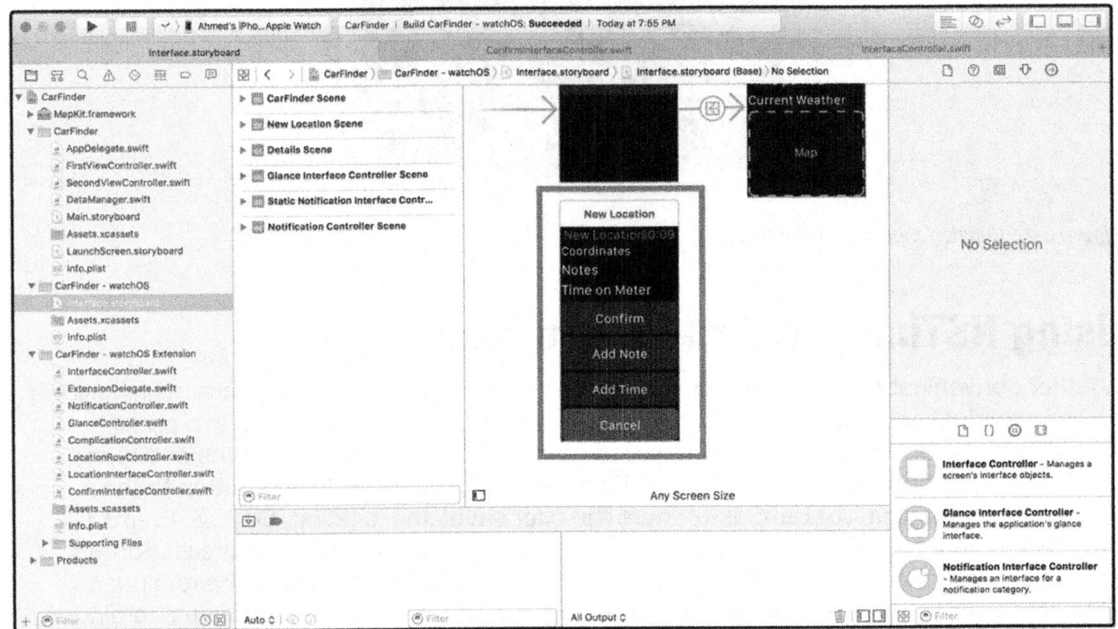

Figure 8-2. Modified storyboard including add reminder button

When the user interacts with the Add Time button, you should increment the total time stored in the class, as well as update the label that mirrors the current setting. As with the other action buttons on the confirm interface controller, you should use the Add Time button to build a configuration and act upon it when the user hits the Confirm button. Listing 8-15 provides the `incrementTime()` method, which performs this logic, for the `ConfirmInterfaceController` class. Remember to hook this function up to the button using Interface Builder's connection inspector after defining it.

Listing 8-15. Saving Total Time Updates (ConfirmInterfaceController.swift)

```
@IBAction func incrementTime() {
    dispatch_async(dispatch_get_main_queue()) {
        self.totalTime += 15

        let timeString = String(format: "%0.0f", self.totalTime)

        self.timeLabel?.setText("\(timeString) mins")
    }

}
```

The NSTimer class allows you to schedule an action to be executed later by specifying the offset (in seconds) and the selector (method signature). For the CarFinder application, you will present an alert view and make the watch vibrate via the taptic sensor. When you specify a selector, you need to provide the signature for the method and a target and the name of the class where it is defined. For the CarFinder app, the function you want to call is the one that presents the alert and generates the haptic feedback (vibration). Since alerts are presented modally (full screen over another interface controller), the logic to present the alert should be in an interface controller that will remain static.

The confirm interface controller disappears after you press the Confirm button, so it is a bad choice. The location list, represented by InterfaceController.swift, is the primary screen on the CarFinder and is also the first screen the user sees when she re-enters the app, so that would be the best place to initialize the timer. However, you need a way of bridging the gap between the ConfirmInterfaceController class and InterfaceController. To solve this problem, you can further expand the ConfirmDelegate protocol to add a third parameter, specifying the time the user selected. As shown in Listing 8-16, expand the protocol definition in ConfirmInterfaceController.swift to include an NSTimeInterval parameter that represents the saved time.

Listing 8-16. Expanding the ConfirmDelegate Protocol to Include Time

```
protocol ConfirmDelegate {
    func saveLocation(note: String, address: String, time: NSTimeInterval)
}
```

Similarly, in the confirm() method, the handler for the Confirm button, send the totalTime property to the delegate object, as shown in Listing 8-17. The NSTimeInterval type represents time in seconds, so multiply the saved value by 60 to convert it to minutes.

Listing 8-17. Sending Time to the ConfirmDelegate Delegate Object (ConfirmInterfaceController.swift)

```
@IBAction func confirm() {
    let noteString = self.note
    let addressString = self.address
    delegate?.saveLocation(noteString, address: addressString, time: self.totalTime * 60)
    dismissController()
}
```

Back in the interface controller class (InterfaceController.swift), you can now initialize the timer when handling the saveLocation(_:address:time) message from the ConfirmDelegate protocol. There are two primary methods for initializing a timer, scheduledTimerWithTimeInterval:target:selector:userInfo:repeats: and timerWithTimeInterval:target:selector:userInfo:repeats:. The main difference between these methods is that the former starts the countdown right away, while the latter is intended to be started later. For the CarFinder app, you should start the timer right away. As shown in Listing 8-18, the time will come from the time parameter, InterfaceController (self) will be the target, and the selector will be the showAlert(_:) method. In this example, I also build a dictionary to use for the userInfo parameter, so I can pass extra data to the showAlert(_:) method.

Listing 8-18. Initializing the Timer (InterfaceController.swift)

```
func saveLocation(note: String, address: String, time: NSTimeInterval) {

    //add a new record here
    let locationDict = ["Latitude" : currentLocation.coordinate.latitude , "Longitude" :
    currentLocation.coordinate.longitude, "Timestamp" : currentLocation.timestamp,
    "Note" : note, "Address": address]
    locations.insert(locationDict, atIndex: 0)

    session?.sendMessage(locationDict, replyHandler: nil, errorHandler: { (error: NSError)
    -> Void in
        print(error.description)
    })

    let userDict = ["address" : address]

    NSTimer.scheduledTimerWithTimeInterval(time, target: self, selector: "showAlert:",
    userInfo: userDict, repeats: false )
}
```

> **Note** A timer can also be configured to be called once or to repeat at an interval. Refer to Chapter 4 (Using Core Motion to Save Motion Data) for an example of a repeating timer.

Now, you can begin implementing the alert that should appear when the timer fires. Conveniently enough, Apple has chosen to port over the main logic of alert view controllers to watchOS, including its modal presentation style and ability to add multiple actions (buttons with completion handlers). Figure 8-3 provides a screenshot of the alert you will create. It displays a reminder message, the address where the user parked his car, and an OK button for the user to dismiss the alert.

Figure 8-3. Screenshot of alert controller on watchOS

To build an alert, you need to specify an alert title and a message and provide a set of actions for the user to act upon. Conveniently, you build your alert and present it on watchOS using one method: `presentAlertControllerWithTitle(_:message:preferredStyle:actions)`. For the CarFinder app, the only action you need is OK to dismiss the alert. For the alert message and title, display a generic warning instructing the user to return to his car. Listing 8-19 provides the implementation for the `showAlert(_:)` method that builds the alert. In this example, I extract the address from the `userInfo` property of the timer.

Listing 8-19. Presenting an Alert (InterfaceController.swift)

```
func showAlert(timer: NSTimer) {

    var reminderMessage = "Please return to your car"

    if let userInfo = timer.userInfo as? [String: String] {
        reminderMessage+="at \(userInfo["address"])"
    }

    print("Meter is out of time.")

    let okAction = WKAlertAction(title: "OK", style: WKAlertActionStyle.Default)
    { () -> Void in
        print("OK button pressed")
    }

    presentAlertControllerWithTitle("Meter expired", message: reminderMessage,
    preferredStyle: WKAlertControllerStyle.Alert, actions: [okAction])

    timer.invalidate()
}
```

To make the watch vibrate, use the playHaptic(_:) method on the Apple-provided singleton which represents your device (WKInterfaceDevice.captureDevice()), as shown in Listing 8-20. Apple provides several pre-configured vibration types that you can specify to indicate different events via the WKHapticType enum. The Notification type is the most powerful one and appropriate for what the CarFinder app needs to do (remind the user to go back to his car).

Listing 8-20. Making the Watch Vibrate

```
func showAlert(timer: NSTimer) {

    var reminderMessage = "Please return to your car"

    if let userInfo = timer.userInfo as? [String: String] {
        reminderMessage+="at \(userInfo["address"])"
    }

    print("Meter is out of time.")

    WKInterfaceDevice.currentDevice().playHaptic(WKHapticType.Notification)

    let okAction = WKAlertAction(title: "OK", style: WKAlertActionStyle.Default)
    { () -> Void in
        print("OK button pressed")
    }

    presentAlertControllerWithTitle("Meter expired", message: reminderMessage,
    preferredStyle: WKAlertControllerStyle.Alert, actions: [okAction])

    timer.invalidate()
}
```

Making Network Calls from Your watchOS App

As you learned with Fitbit, there is a huge wealth of information out there for you to access via third party APIs. The primary means of communication between your app and an API is through HTTP. Previously, this had been limited to the realm of iOS apps only; however, watchOS 2 has an expanded subset of Foundation (the core framework that powers all Apple platforms) which includes networking capabilities. As you will learn in this chapter, this allows you to perform HTTP requests (including GET and POST) directly on an Apple Watch using its Wi-Fi radio, even without a tethered iPhone.

In this section, you will use the Weather Underground API to access the weather conditions for a saved location, based on its zip code. Weather Underground requires you to sign up as a developer to get an API key to use its services. The examples in this section use Weather Underground's free developer account, which you can sign up for at www.wunderground.com/weather/api.

> **Note** Remember that starting with iOS9, Apple adds a firewall for HTTP operations. All network operations must be transmitted over HTTPS, unless specific domains are whitelisted in your `Info.plist` file.

The primary class for performing network operations in watchOS is `NSURLSession`, which manages requests in the form of "tasks" or queueable units of execution. As shown in Table 8-1, Apple provides several pre-configured task types. For the CarFinder app, you want to retrieve data from an external host, asynchronously, via HTTP `GET`. The Data Task type is the most appropriate for this situation.

Table 8-1. NSURLSession Task Types

Task Type	Purpose
Data task	Used to download binary data in the foreground (NSData)
Upload task	Used to upload binary data or files in the foreground or background
Download task	Used to download files in the foreground or background

Local weather is useful as a statistic when viewing the details of an item, so you will implement the look-up in the `LocationInterfaceController` class (`LocationInterfaceController.swift`), which manages the display of an item. To begin, add a label for the temperature to the class, as shown in Listing 8-21.

Listing 8-21. Adding a Label to the Class

```
class LocationInterfaceController: WKInterfaceController {

    @IBOutlet weak var locationMap: WKInterfaceMap?
    @IBOutlet weak var coordinatesLabel: WKInterfaceLabel?
    @IBOutlet weak var timeLabel: WKInterfaceLabel?
    @IBOutlet weak var weatherLabel: WKInterfaceLabel?

    var currentLocation : CLLocation?

    override func awakeWithContext(context: AnyObject?) {
        super.awakeWithContext(context)
        ...
    }
}
```

As shown in Figure 8-4, add a label in your storyboard scene, after the time label. Be sure to connect the property via the Connection Inspector in Interface Builder.

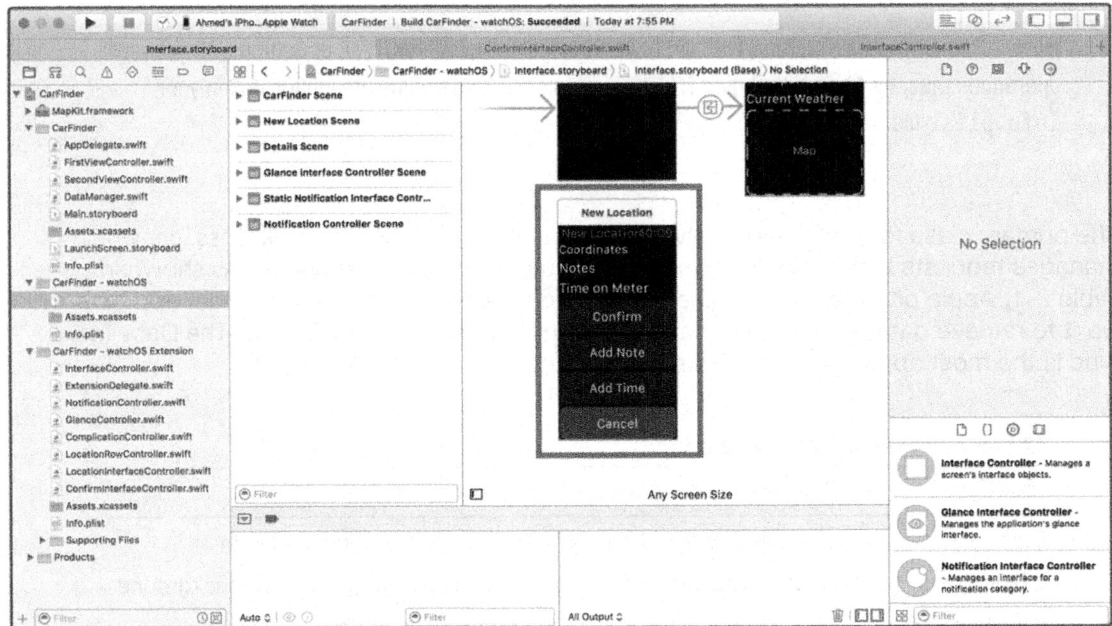

Figure 8-4. Adding a label to the storyboard

To perform the weather look-up, you need to provide Weather Underground with a zip code. In the `awakeWithContext()` method of the class, add a geocoder to convert the location to a place-mark with human-readable attributes (Listing 8-22).

Listing 8-22. Performing a Weather Look-up (LocationInterfaceController.swift)

```
override func awakeWithContext(context: AnyObject?) {
    super.awakeWithContext(context)

    // Configure interface objects here.

    // Configure interface objects here.
    if let locationDict = context as? Dictionary<String, AnyObject> {

        if let latitude = locationDict["Latitude"] as? Double {

            if let longitude = locationDict["Longitude"] as? Double {
                let location = CLLocation(latitude: latitude, longitude: longitude)

                let prettyLocation = String(format: "%.2f, %.2f", location.coordinate.
                latitude, location.coordinate.longitude)

                coordinatesLabel?.setText(prettyLocation)

                currentLocation = CLLocation(latitude: latitude, longitude: longitude)

                locationMap?.addAnnotation(location.coordinate, withPinColor:
                WKInterfaceMapPinColor.Red)
```

```
                let mapRegion = MKCoordinateRegionMake(location.coordinate,
                MKCoordinateSpanMake(0.1, 0.1))

                locationMap?.setRegion(mapRegion)

                geocodeLocation()

            }

        }

        if let timestamp = locationDict["Timestamp"] as? NSDate  {
            ...
        }

    }
}
```

Listing 8-23 provides the geocodeLocation() method, which performs the geocoding operation.

Listing 8-23. Geocoding (LocationInterfaceController.swift)

```
func geocodeLocation() {

    if currentLocation != nil {
        let geocoder = CLGeocoder()
        geocoder.reverseGeocodeLocation(currentLocation!, completionHandler: { (placemarks:
        [CLPlacemark]?, error: NSError?) -> Void in
            //sd
            if error == nil {
                if placemarks?.count > 0 {

                    let currentPlace = placemarks![0]
                    let placeString = "\(currentPlace.subThoroughfare!) \(currentPlace.
                    thoroughfare!)"

                    dispatch_async(dispatch_get_main_queue()) {
                        self.coordinatesLabel?.setText(placeString)
                    }

                    let zipCode = currentPlace.postalCode!
                    self.retrieveWeather(zipCode)

                }
            } else {
                print(error?.description)
            }
        })
    }

}
```

Once you have verified that the result contains a valid zip code, call the `retrieveWeather()` method to begin the network operation.

In the retrieveWeather() method, you need to create an `NSURLSession` object and call the `dataTaskWithURL(url!, completionHandler: { (responseData: NSData?, response: NSURLResponse?,error:NSError?) -> Void)` method to process the result. The input is an `NSURL` object and the output is a completion handler with response data and an error.

In looking at the Weather Underground API reference, you can determine that the "conditions" endpoint is the appropriate method to call to get the local weather for a location (`www.wunderground.com/weather/api/d/docs?d=data/conditions`). Weather Underground provides the following as an example for how to call the API:

```
http://api.wunderground.com/api/748504be0ff02aa3/conditions/q/CA/San_Francisco.json
```

In this example, the string after the /api/ represents the API key. Weather Underground uses CA/San_Francisco as the input for the location. However, you can safely change it to a zip code.

Use a formatted string to build your URL (uniform resource locator) for the data task, as shown in Listing 8-24:

***Listing 8-24.** Building the API URL String*

```
let apiKey = "YOUR_UNDERGROUND_KEY"

let urlString = "https://api.wunderground.com/api/\(apiKey)/conditions/q/\(zipCode).json"

let url = NSURL(string: urlString)
```

Listing 8-25 provides the initial implementation for the `retrieveWeather()` method. In this example, I used the `NSURLSession.sharedSession( )` singleton for the session, as there is no need to maintain multiple network sessions at once in the app. As has been the trend for the other applications in this book, checking to make sure error is nil indicates success. To execute a data task, you need to explicitly call the `resume()` method on it (remember, it is designed to work in a queue).

***Listing 8-25.** Initiating a URL Session (LocationInterfaceController.swift)*

```
func retrieveWeather(zipCode: String) {

    let apiKey = "YOUR_API_KEY"

    let urlString = "https://api.wunderground.com/api/\(apiKey)/conditions/q/\(zipCode).json"

    let url = NSURL(string: urlString)
    let session = NSURLSession.sharedSession()
    let urlTask = session.dataTaskWithURL(url!, completionHandler: { (responseData: NSData?,
    response: NSURLResponse?,error:NSError?) -> Void in
```

```
        if error == nil {

        } else {
            print(error?.description)
        }
    })
    urlTask.resume()
}
```

Handling a JSON Response

Having successfully completed the network operation, you need to perform one more step to handle the output from Weather Underground: you need to convert the JSON (JavaScript Object Notation) data in the response to a dictionary. Fortunately, Apple has chosen to also port the `NSJSONSerialization` class to watchOS, which will allow you to convert `NSData` objects to dictionaries. In Listing 8-26, I attempt to decode to a JSON dictionary. The `JSONObjectWithData()` method returns errors via exceptions, so remember to implement it in a `try-catch` block. This code will eventually go into the `ConfirmInterfaceController` class.

Listing 8-26. JSON Serialization

```
let urlTask = session.dataTaskWithURL(url!, completionHandler: { (responseData: NSData?,
response: NSURLResponse?,error:NSError?) -> Void in
            if error == nil {
                do {
                    let jsonDict = try NSJSONSerialization.JSONObjectWithData(responseData!,
                    options: NSJSONReadingOptions.AllowFragments)

                        }
                    }
                } catch {
                    print("error: invalid json data")
                }

            } else {
                print(error?.description)
            }
        })
```

Referring back to the API documentation for the “conditions” endpoint, the current temperature for a location is stored as the “temp_f” key-value pair, in the “current_observation” dictionary (see Listing 8-27).

Listing 8-27. API Response

```
{
  "response": {
    "version": "0.1",
    "termsofService": "http://www.wunderground.com/weather/api/d/terms.html",
    "features": {
      "conditions": 1
    }
  },
```

```
  "current_observation": {
..
        "temp_f" : 86.5
}
}
```

Listing 8-28 provides the final implementation for the `retrieveWeather()` method. To extract a key from a dictionary, in another dictionary, perform a series of consecutive optional unwrapping operations.

Listing 8-28. Completed Implementation for retrieveWeather() Method

```
func retrieveWeather(zipCode: String) {

    let apiKey = "YOUR_API_KEY"

    let urlString = "https://api.wunderground.com/api/\(apiKey)/conditions/q/\(zipCode).json"

    let url = NSURL(string: urlString)
    let session = NSURLSession.sharedSession()
    let urlTask = session.dataTaskWithURL(url!, completionHandler: { (responseData: NSData?,
    response: NSURLResponse?,error:NSError?) -> Void in
        if error == nil {
            do {
                let jsonDict = try NSJSONSerialization.JSONObjectWithData(responseData!,
                options: NSJSONReadingOptions.AllowFragments)

                if let resultsDict = jsonDict["current_observation"] as? Dictionary<String,
                AnyObject> {
                    if let tempF = resultsDict["temp_f"] as? Double {
                        self.weatherLabel?.setText("\(tempF) F")
                    }
                }
            } catch {
                print("error: invalid json data")
            }

        } else {
            print(error?.description)
        }
    })
    urlTask.resume()
}
```

Having completed the steps in this chapter, the CarFinder app should look like the screenshot in Figure 8-5, where the location list now shows human-readable addresses, the detail list now shows weather, and an alert will appear when the user's meter has expired.

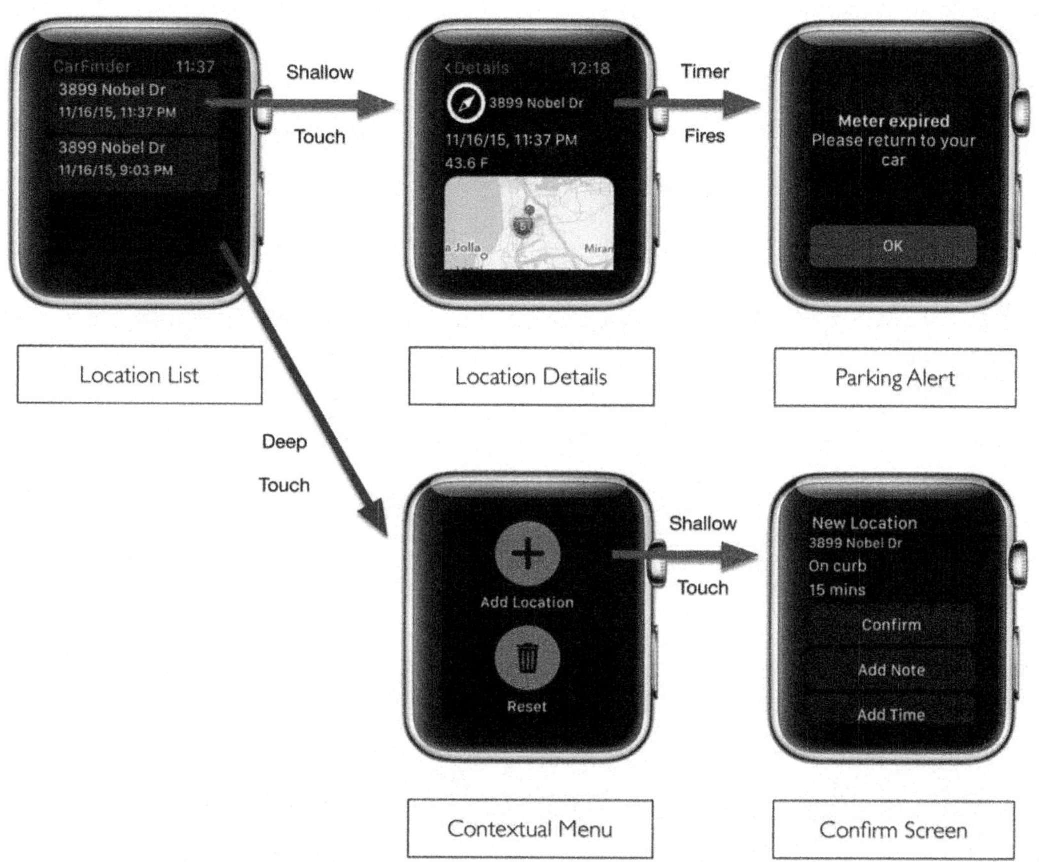

***Figure 8-5.** Updated user interface for CarFinder app*

Summary

In this chapter, you learned different ways to make a watchOS app independent, by allowing it to take advantage of the expanded set of frameworks based in watchOS 2. First, you learned how to create a permissions prompt and get a user's current location using `CoreLocation`. Next, you used this same general process to create a calendar reminder using `EventKit`. Finally, you learned how to make network calls to the Weather Underground API directly from the watch to show the weather at the user's current location. The Apple Watch can be an extremely powerful tool in the right hands and now you have some more ways of making a powerful tool when the user is nowhere next to his or her phone.

Chapter 9

Connecting to a Bluetooth LE Device

Manny de la Torriente

Thanks to its open standards, Bluetooth Low-Energy (LE), also known as BLE,has established itself as a leader for hardware manufacturers looking to create connected accessories for iOS. This chapter introduces Core Bluetooth, Apple's framework for Bluetooth-based communication, to send and receive messages from a Bluetooth LE device. Additionally, we will discuss Bluetooth best practices for battery life and a positive user experience.

Introduction to the Apple Bluetooth stack

Apple's Core Bluetooth is the representation of Bluetooth LE on iOS platforms. It's the framework that you will use to talk to accessories and host peripherals.

The framework is an abstraction of the Bluetooth LE protocol stack, and it hides many of the low-level details of the specification so you can focus on your application.

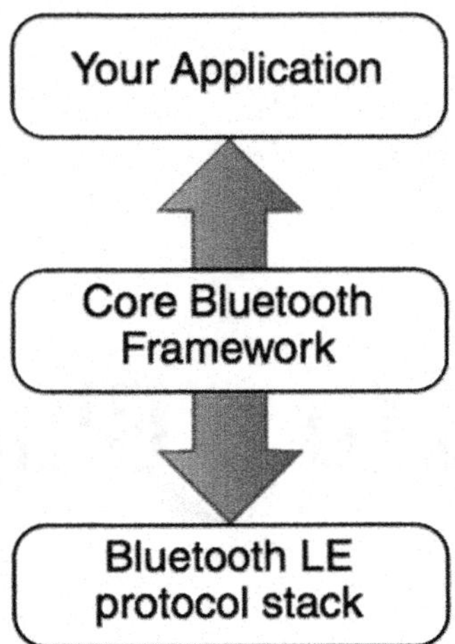

Figure 9-1. Core Bluetooth Technology Framework

The framework is built on the Bluetooth 4.0 Standard and provides all the classes you'll need to easily communicate with other Bluetooth LE devices.

Key Terms and Concepts

The framework adopts many key concepts and terminology from the specification.

Central

A device that supports the central role scans and listens for peripheral devices that are advertising information. A central role device is responsible for initiating and establishing a connection. We refer to a device operating in the central role as a central.

Peripheral

A device that supports the peripheral role transmits advertising packets, which describe what services the peripheral has to offer. A peripheral role device is responsible for accepting the establishment of connection. We refer to a device operating in the peripheral role as a peripheral.

Service

A service is a collection of data called characteristics that describes particular functions or features of a peripheral's services.

Characteristic

A characteristic is a value used in a service along with properties and descriptors that contain information that describes the value.

Discovery

Bluetooth devices use advertising and scanning either to be discovered or to discover nearby devices. Advertising peripherals broadcast advertising packets. A scanning central device will scan and listen and can use filters to prevent discovery of all nearby devices.

Core Bluetooth Objects

The Core Bluetooth framework is mapped to Bluetooth LE communication in a straightforward way.

Central Role Objects

A device that supports the central role uses the `CBCentralManager` object to scan for, discover, connect, and manage discovered peripherals. The peripheral is represented by a `CBPeripheral` object to handle services and characteristics. `CBService` and `CBCharacteristic` objects represent a peripheral's data. Figure 9-2 illustrates the peripheral's tree of services and characteristics.

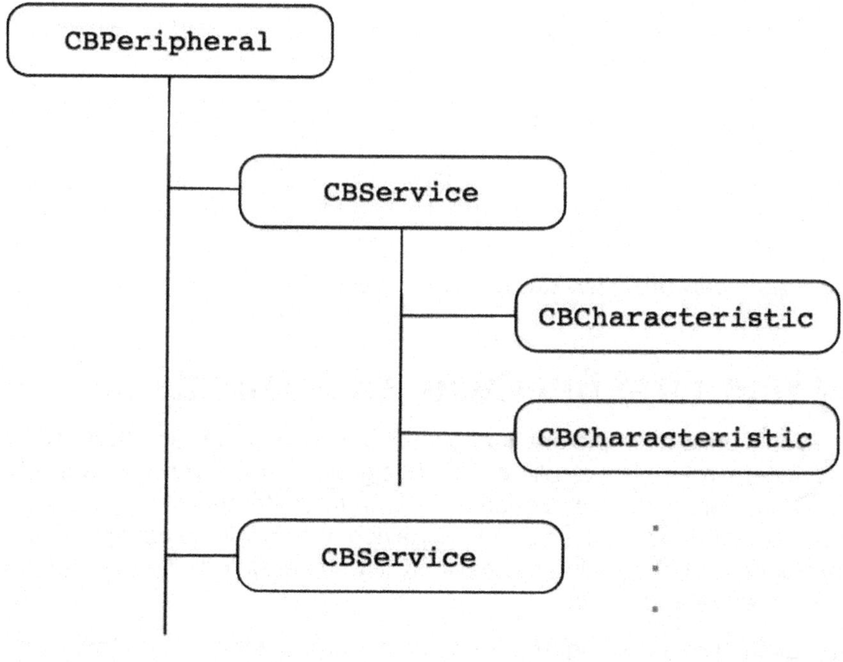

Figure 9-2. Peripheral's tree of services and characteristics

Peripheral Role Objects

A device that supports the peripheral role is represented by the CBPeripheralManager object to advertise services, manage published services, and respond to read/write requests from centrals. A CBCentral object represents a central. CBMutableService and CBMutableCharacteristic objects represent a peripheral's data when in this role. Figure 9-3 illustrates the peripheral's tree of services and characteristics.

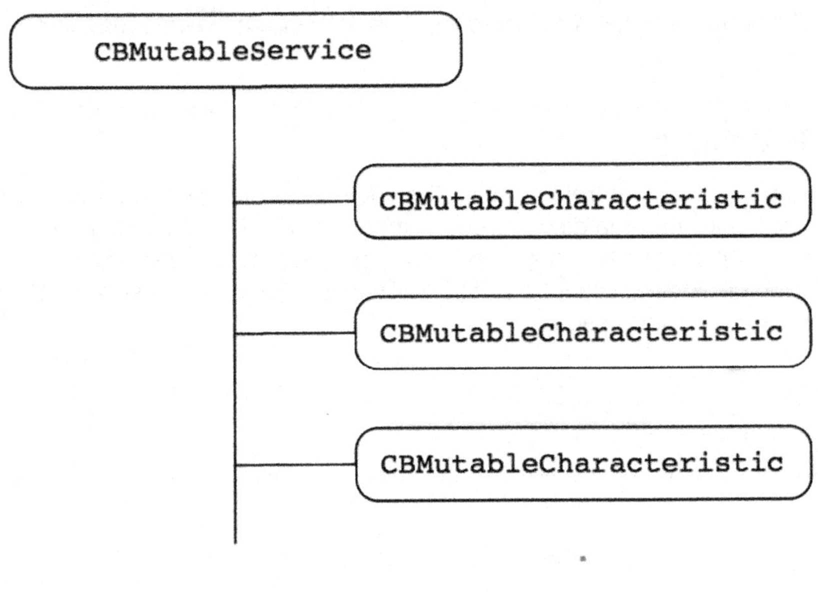

Figure 9-3. Peripheral's mutable tree of services and characteristics

Building Your First Bluetooth LE Application

In this section you'll build a simple application using an agile approach that will support both central and peripheral roles. The application is designed to run on two separate Bluetooth LE-capable iOS devices, with each device running in the different roles. The central role device will scan and connect to the peripheral device, which will be advertising a simple service. Once connected, the peripheral device will transfer data to the central device, which will then present that data to the user.

The feature requirements are straightforward and we present them in a story form. The main focus for the first part of this exercise will be on setting up the application to accommodate each mode using a simple user interface (UI) followed by a deep dive into Core Bluetooth.

When you complete this exercise, you should have a solid understanding of the central and peripheral roles and how they work using the Core Bluetooth framework, as well as several reusable modules that you can bring into your own projects.

Backlog

There are several features that are represented by stories and are labeled "must have." They are the focus in this section. The story labeled "nice to have" is left as an exercise for you do to later on if you wish. You can find the full implementation for this chapter in the Source Code/Download area of the Apress web site (`www.apress.com`).

Base Application and Home Scene

The following are "must have" features.

Story

As an iOS developer, I want an application that runs on a Bluetooth LE-capable device and provides access to two scenes, so I can run each scene in a different mode.

Acceptance Criteria

- The home scene provides a button labeled Central Role that, when pressed, transitions to new blank scene titled Central Role.
- The home scene provides a button labeled Peripheral Role that, when pressed, transitions to a new blank scene titled Peripheral Role.
- The home scene provides a single indicator that shows when Bluetooth is powered on or off.
- The application prohibits any transition if Bluetooth is not powered on, or the device doesn't support Bluetooth LE.
- The application displays an alert to the user if Bluetooth is not powered on, or the device doesn't support Bluetooth LE.
- Each scene provides a Back button in the navigation bar that transitions back to the home scene when pressed (see Figure 9-5).

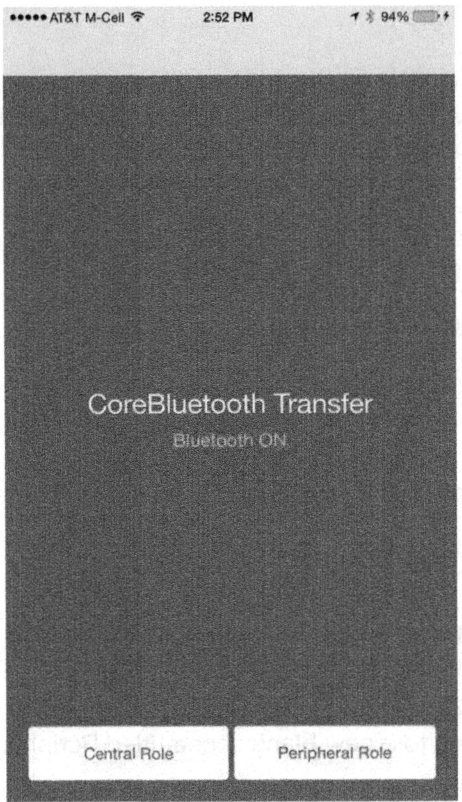

Figure 9-4. The home scene mock-up

Central Role Scene

Importance: must have.

Story

As an iOS developer, I want a scene that implements the central role, so I can scan for peripherals that I can connect to and retrieve data.

Acceptance Criteria

- The scene provides a Scan button that toggles device scanning on and off.
- The scene provides a view that will be populated with data transferred from a discovered peripheral device.
- The scene provides a progress indicator when scanning.
- The application can scan for peripherals.
- The application uses a filter for a specific service when scanning.

- The application can initiate a connection and connect to a discovered peripheral with the desired service.
- The application can request data.
- The application can receive data.
- The application disconnects from the peripheral when data transfer completes
- The application can present the data to the user.

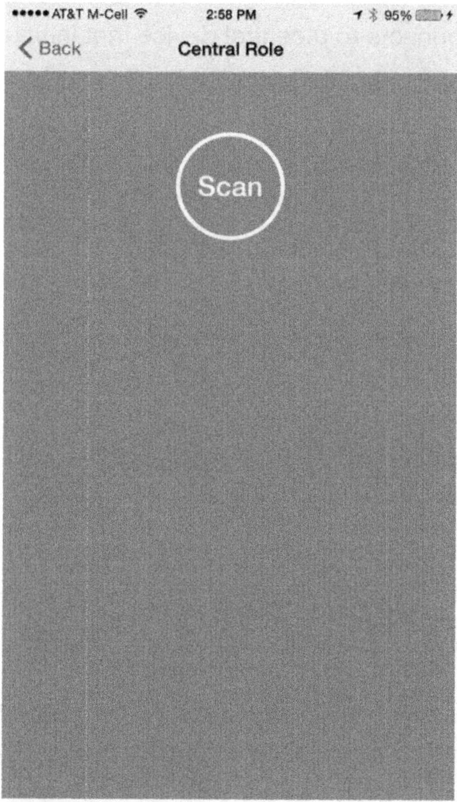

Figure 9-5. The central role scene mock-up

Peripheral Role Scene

The following are must have features"

Story

As an iOS developer, I want a scene that implements the peripheral role and advertises a service, so a central role device can connect and retrieve data.

Acceptance Criteria

- The scene provides a switch labeled "Advertise" that toggles advertising on and off.
- The scene provides a text view that contains preset text.
- The application sets up a simple transfer service.
- The application will broadcast advertising packets when advertising is enabled so that the application can be discovered.
- The application can stop broadcasting when disabled.
- The application connects to a central device that initiates a connection.
- The application sends data when it receives a request.

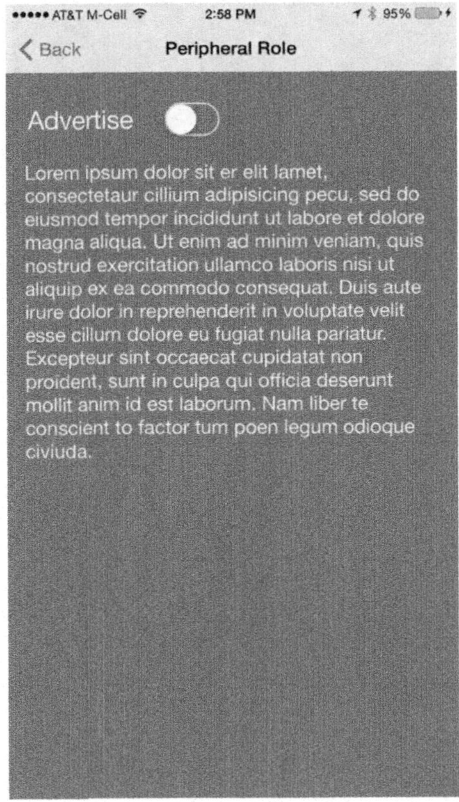

***Figure 9-6.** The peripheral role scene mock-up*

Editable Text

The following are "nice to have" features.

Story

As a Core Bluetooth transfer application user, I want an editable text view in the peripheral role scene (see Figure 9-7), so I can enter text that can be transferred to a central role device.

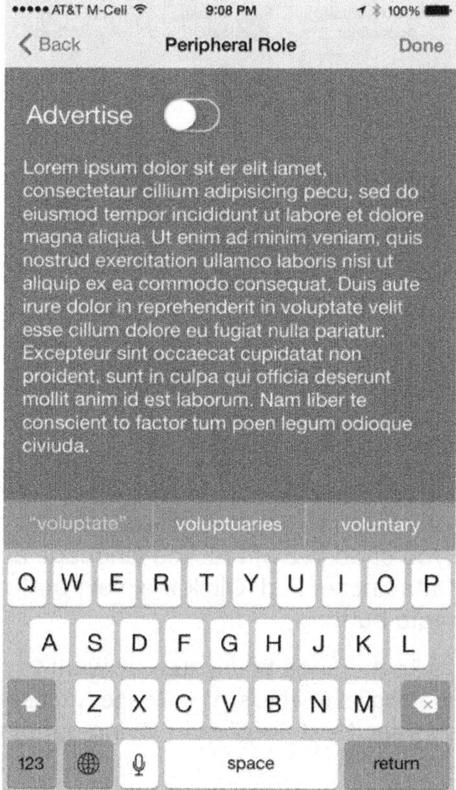

Figure 9-7. Editable text view

Acceptance Criteria

- The existing text view is editable and presents a keyboard when I tap inside the text view.
- The title bar presents a Done button to dismiss the keyboard when the user is done typing.
- The text that I type is the same text that is transferred to a connected central device.

Setting Up the Project

This application will use a single-view application project template (see Figure 9-8). To create a new single-view Swift application project, from Xcode select File ➤ New ➤ Project.

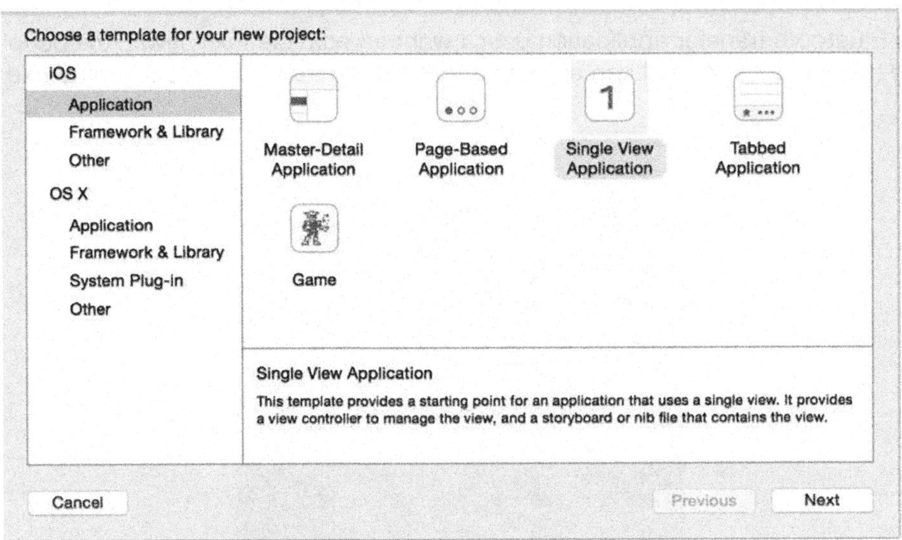

Figure 9-8. Creating a single-view application project

After clicking Next, you'll be prompted to enter a project name and select the language and the target device. Make sure you choose Swift for the language and Universal for the device. Leave the option User Core Data unchecked. Click the Next button, choose a location for your project, and click the Create button.

Once the project is created, to keep things tidy, you may want to move some of the files/folders you use less often (e.g., `AppDelegate.swift`, `Images.xcassets`, and `LaunchScreen.xib`) into the Supporting Files folder. Next you'll start laying out the UI.

Building the Interface

Now it's time to lay out the UI, so refer to the mock-ups in section "Backlog." Look at the subsection "Base Application and Home Scene Story." There you will see acceptance criteria that call for navigation controls to navigate back to the home scene. So, the first thing you need to add is a Navigation Controller. Open up the `Main.storyboard` and select the View Controller from either the storyboard or the Document Outline. Then, from the menu, select Editor ➤ Embed In ➤ Navigation Controller. Xcode will add a Navigation Controller to the storyboard and set as the Storyboard Entry Point, and add a relationship between the Navigation Controller and the existing View Controller. Your storyboard should look something like Figure 9-9.

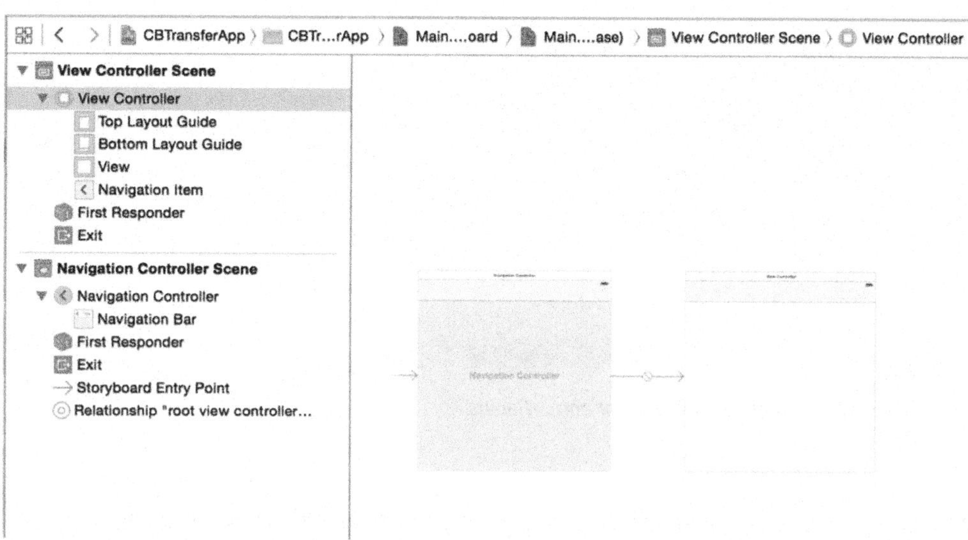

Figure 9-9. Adding a Navigation Controller

At this point, you should be able to build and run your app. If all went well you should see an empty white scene.

To change the color of the View Controller background to match the mock-up, select View in the View Controller tree, and show the attribute selector by clicking Attributes Inspector at the top of the Utilities panel. Then bring up the color picker by clicking Background control and selecting "Other..." In the color picker, choose Web Safe Colors and then find and select value 0066CC. Remember these steps because in future sections, you'll only be given the color values.

I'll assume you already know how to add controls to the scene, so I won't cover that here. Next you'll add two buttons, one labeled Central Role and the other labeled Peripheral Role. Set the button background color to white. Make the corners of each button rounded using User Defined Runtime Attributes. In the Utilities panel click the Identity inspector tab. In the User Defined Runtime Attributes section, click the Add button (+) in the lower left of the table. Double-click the Key Path field of the new attribute and change the value to `layer.cornerRadius`. Set the type to Number and the value to 4.

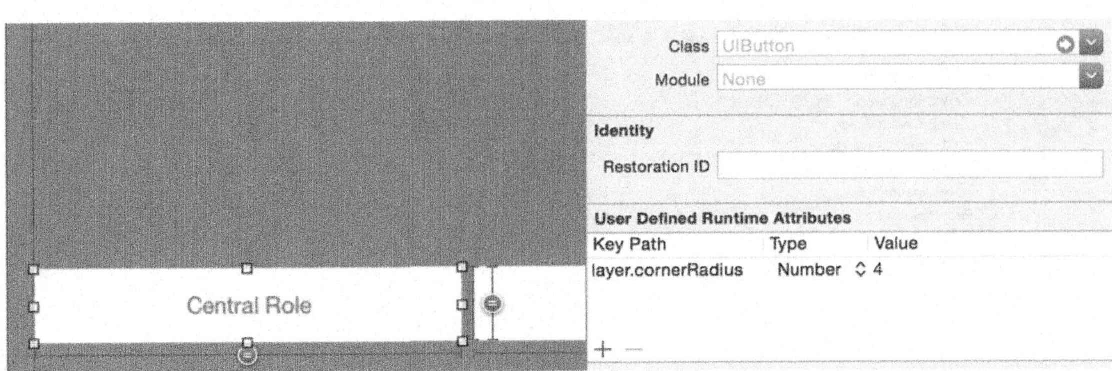

***Figure 9-10.** User-defined runtime attributes for cornerRadius*

> **Tip** Use user-defined runtime attributes to set an initial value for objects that do not have an Interface Builder inspector. The user-defined values are set when the storyboard is loaded.

Later in the chapter you'll learn how to use `IBInspectable` and `IBDesignable` attributes, which are new features in Xcode 6.

Now you need to add constraints for each button. See Figures 9-11 and 9-12 for constraint type and values for each button. There are a few ways to add constraints in Interface Builder. You can let Interface Builder add them for you; you could use the Pin and Align tools located at the bottom of the storyboard canvas or you can control-drag between views. To create a Leading Space constraint, control-click the Central Role button and drag to the left edge of the View Controller. When you release the mouse, a pop-up menu is displayed with a list of possible constraints. Choose Leading Space to Container Margin. When you drag vertically, Interface Builder will present options to set vertical spacing between the views and options to horizontally align the views. Likewise, when you drag horizontally, you'll be presented with options to set the horizontal spacing between the views and options to vertically align the view. Both gestures may include other options such as setting the view size.

Apply the constraints in Figure 9-11 to the Central Role button.

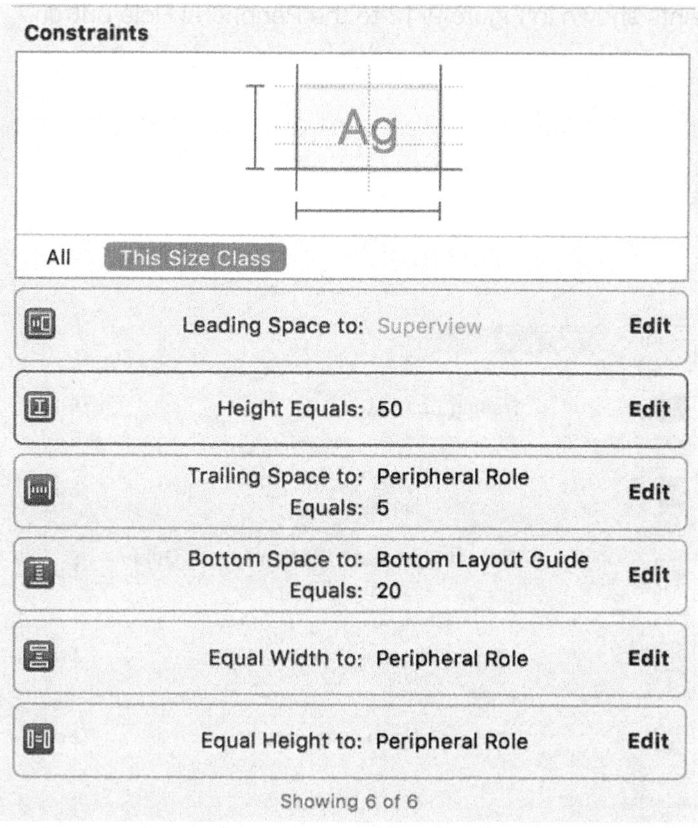

***Figure 9-11.** Constraints for Central Role button*

Now apply constraints shown in Figure 9-12 to the Peripheral Role button.

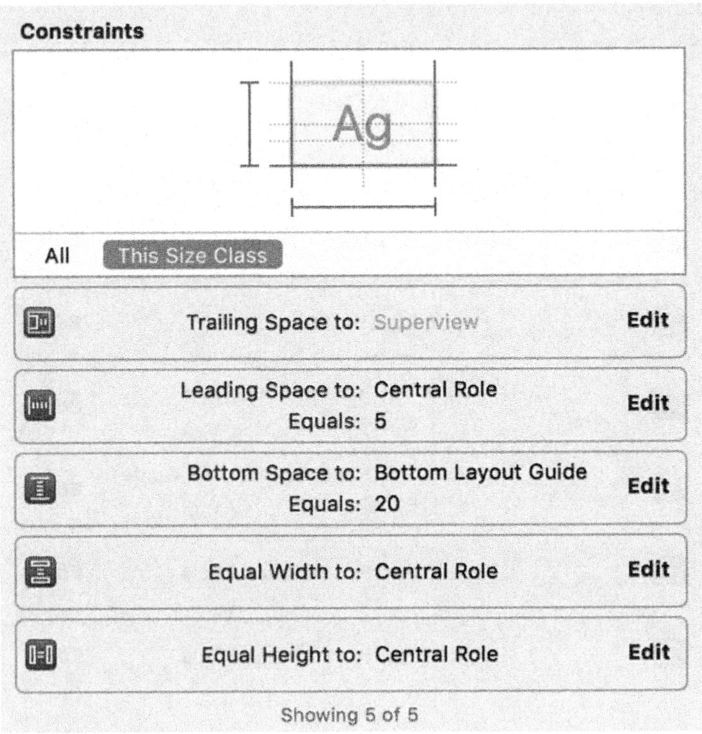

***Figure 9-12.** Constraints for Peripheral Role button*

Next you will add two scenes to the storyboard, one for central role and the other for peripheral role. Drag and drop a View Controller for each scene onto the storyboard and situate them so they look like Figure 9-13.

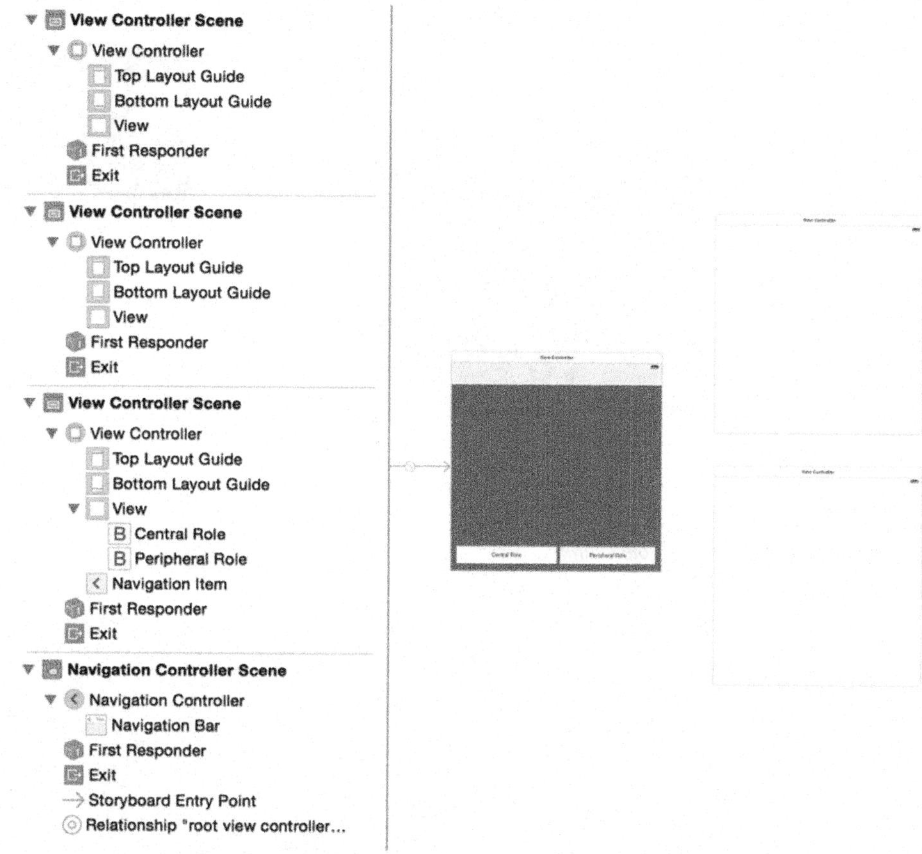

***Figure 9-13.** Add central and peripheral View Controllers*

To add a segue for the central role scene, select the Central Role button from the Document Outline on the left, then control-drag to the top View Controller on the right and release. Select *show* from the Action Segue pop-up. (See Figure 9-14.)

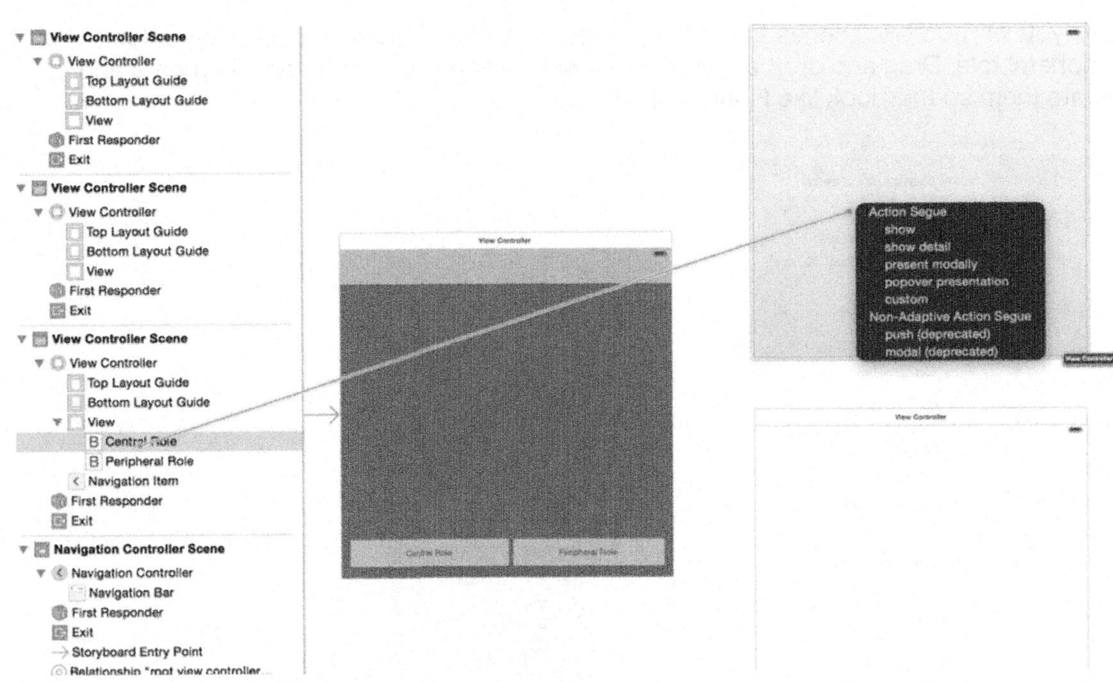

Figure 9-14. Adding a segue for central role scene

Repeat the same steps for the Peripheral Role button. Your layout should look similar to the one in Figure 9-15.

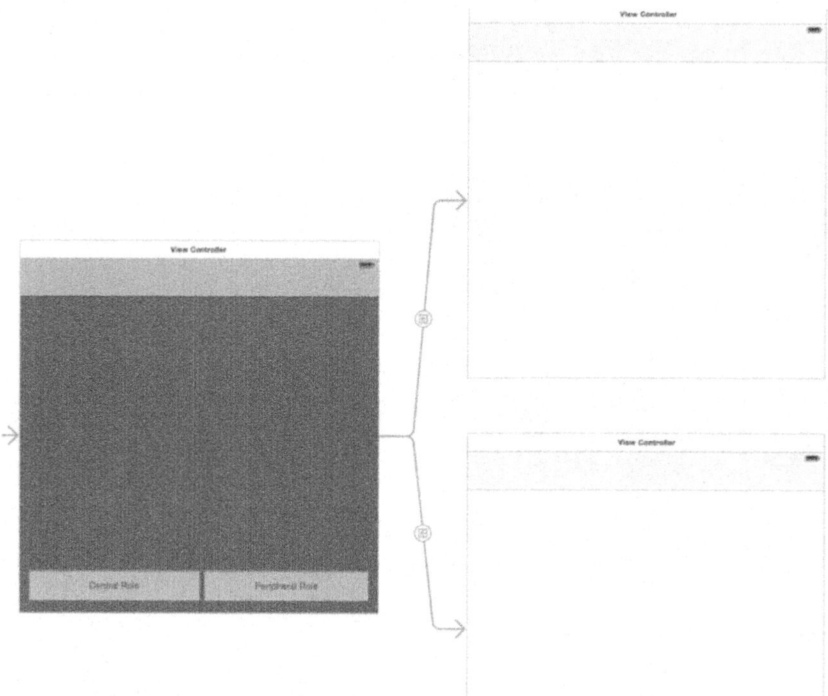

***Figure 9-15.** Segues for central and peripheral scenes*

Now set the title for each of the new View Controllers. Open up the Utilities panel and click the Attributes Inspector. Now select the top View Controller and set its title to Central Role from the View Controller section of the Attribute Inspector. Repeat these steps for the peripheral role View Controller.

Set the background colors for each of the views. The value for the central role view is FF6600, and for the peripheral role view, 009999.

Now build and run the app. Press each button and verify that you transition to the appropriate scene, that it has the proper title, and that you can navigate back to the home scene.

There is one more UI element that you need to add, and then it's time to jump in and start writing some code. Add a `UILabel` to the home scene and set the text to "Bluetooth Off" (see Figure 9-16) and the text color to FF0000. You can set up constraints so it stays centered in the view.

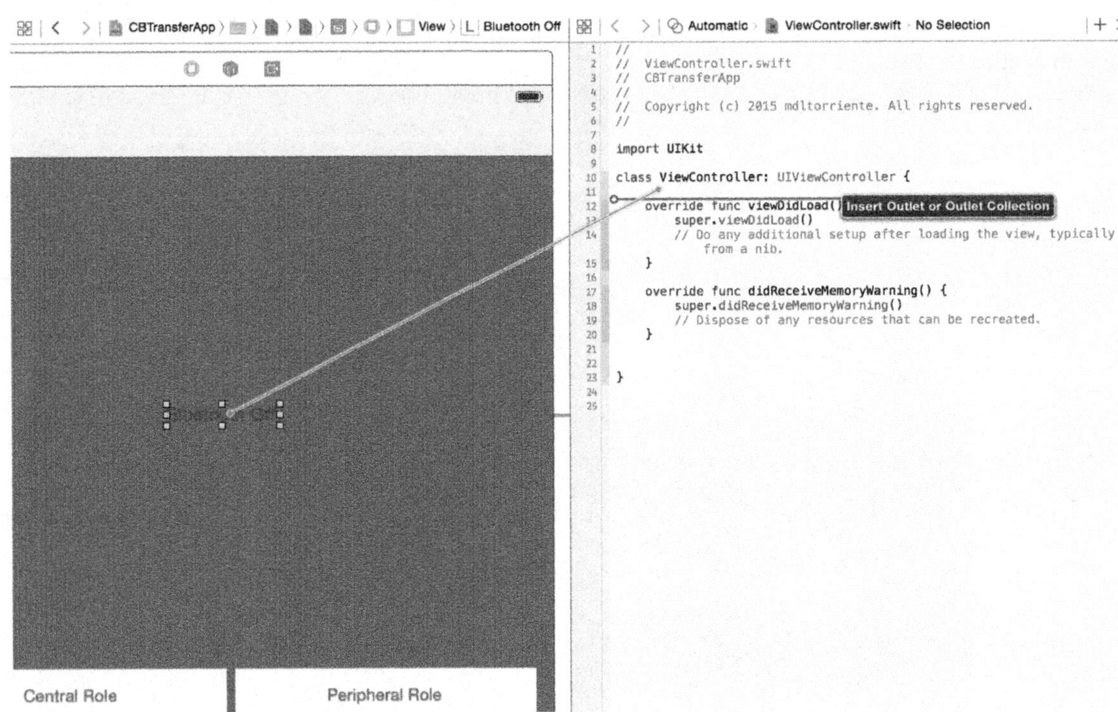

***Figure 9-16.** Connect Label to ViewController class*

Now you need to connect the label to a property of the `ViewController`. First, close the Utilities view on the right if it's open, and click the Assistant Editor. You should now see a split window in Xcode with the `Main.storyboard` on the left and the `ViewController.swift` file on the right (you could dismiss the Document Outline for even more room). Next, control-drag the Label from the storyboard, to the `ViewController` source and drop it inside your `ViewController` class.

In the pop-up, name the outlet `bluetoothStateLabel` and use the default options, then click the Connect button. Your `ViewController` class should now have an outlet defined.

```
@IBOutlet weak var bluetoothStateLabel: UILabel!
```

If you review the acceptance criteria, you'll see that we need to satisfy the requirement "The home scene provides a single indicator that shows when Bluetooth is either powered on or off." That means you now have to utilize the Core Bluetooth framework. In the next section, you'll learn how to start up a central manager and use it to determine the Bluetooth state.

Using a Central Manager

In this section, you'll learn how to start up a central manager and use it to determine if a device supports Bluetooth LE and is available to use on the central device.

The `CBCentralManager` object is a Core Bluetooth representation of a central role device. When a central manager is initialized, it calls the `centralManagerDidUpdateState` method of its delegate. This means you must adopt the delegate protocol and implement this required method.

Open the `MainViewController.swift` file and import the framework and add the `CBCentralManagerDelegate` protocol to your class declaration.

```
import CoreBluetooth

class ViewController: UIViewController, CBCentralManagerDelegate {
```

You'll see an error indicator, which says the `ViewController`, does not conform to protocol. That's because you need to implement the required delegate method.

```
func centralManagerDidUpdateState(central: CBCentralManager!) {

}
```

Now add a property for a `CBCentralManager` and initialize it in the `viewDidLoad` method.

```
var centralManager: CBCentralManager!

override func viewDidLoad() {
    super.viewDidLoad()
    centralManager = CBCentralManager(delegate: self, queue: nil)
}
```

The central manager is initialized with `self` as the delegate so the `ViewController` will receive any central role events. By specifying the queue as `nil`, the central manager dispatches central role events using the main queue. The central manager starts up after this call is made and begins dispatching events.

Listing 9-1 shows how to examine the central manager state in the `centralManagerDidUpdateState` callback when the state change event fires. Here is where you can update the text and text color of the `bluetoothStateLabel` property based on the central state.

Listing 9-1. Central State Change

```
func centralManagerDidUpdateState(central: CBCentralManager!) {
    switch (central.state) {
    case .PoweredOn:
        bluetoothStateLabel.text = "Bluetooth ON"
        bluetoothStateLabel.textColor = UIColor.greenColor()
        break
    case .PoweredOff:
        bluetoothStateLabel.text = "Bluetooth OFF"
        bluetoothStateLabel.textColor = UIColor.redColor()
        break
    default:
        break;
    }
}
```

The PoweredOn state indicates that the central device supports Bluetooth LE and the Bluetooth is on and available for use. The PoweredOff state indicates that Bluetooth is either turned off, or the device doesn't support Bluetooth LE.

Build and run the application. If your device has Bluetooth enabled, the indicator label should read "Bluetooth On" and its color should be green. Use the slide-up settings panel to turn Bluetooth off. The indicator label should now read "Bluetooth Off" and its color should be red.

Now that you can determine the Bluetooth state, you can use that information to satisfy the remaining acceptance criteria. Add the Bool property isBluetoothPoweredOn that will be used to reflect the Bluetooth state.

```
var isBluetoothPoweredOn: Bool = false
```

Set its value in the centralManagerDidUpdateState method accordingly.

You'll use this value to determine whether or not transition is allowed to the central or peripheral mode scenes. You set up two segues in the previous section to those scenes. In order to interact with the storyboard, you need to add identifiers for each segue. Create a new file named Const.swift and add a global constant for each.

```
let kCentralRoleSegue: String = "CentralRoleSegue"
let kPeripheralRoleSegue: String = "PeripheralRoleSegue"
```

Open Main.storyboard and select the segue for the central role scene. Open the Utilities panel and click the Attributes Inspector. You will see a section named Storyboard Segue with a field where you can enter an identifier (see Figure 9-17). Enter the string value you defined for the central role segue. This string is only used for locating the segue inside the storyboard.

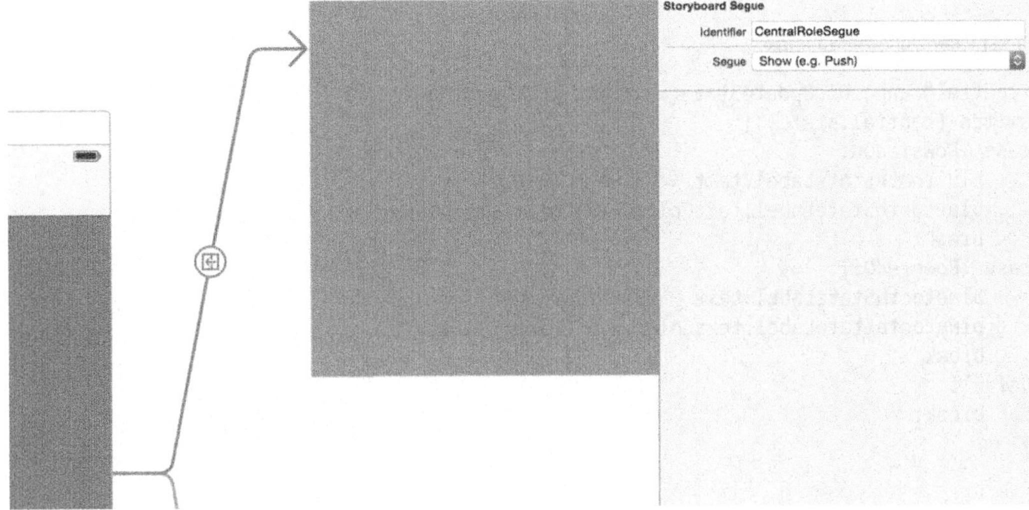

Figure 9-17. Adding segue identifiers

Repeat the foregoing steps for the peripheral role segue.

The UIViewController provides an override method which allows you to control whether a particular segue should be performed. Open ViewController.swift and add the method shouldPerformSegueWithIdentifier to the ViewController class (see Listing 9-2).

Listing 9-2. Override Method to Control Segue

```
override func shouldPerformSegueWithIdentifier(identifier: String?, sender: AnyObject?) ->
Bool {
    if identifier == kCentralRoleSegue || identifier == kPeripheralRoleSegue {
        if !isBluetoothPoweredOn {
            return false;
        }
    }
    return true
}
```

When you initiate a segue, this method will be called with the string value that identifies the triggered segue, and the object that initiated the segue. The return value for this method should be true if you want the segue to be executed; otherwise, return false.

In this method you're only interested in the identifier; the sender object is for informational purposes only and can be ignored here. Compare the identifier value with the constants you defined earlier. If you find a match, then check the Bluetooth state. If Bluetooth is powered on, you can allow the segue to execute by returning a value of true.

In the case where Bluetooth is powered off, you want to display an alert and provide an option to go to the Settings app where the Bluetooth setting can be changed. Add the method shown in Listing 9-3 to the ViewController class. Call this method from within the shouldPerformSegueWithIdentifier method.

```
if !isBluetoothPoweredOn {
        showAlertForSettings()
    return false;
}
```

Listing 9-3. Configure and Present an Alert

```
func showAlertForSettings() {
    let alertController = UIAlertController(title: "CBTransferApp", message: "Turn On
    Bluetooth to Connect to Peripherals", preferredStyle: .Alert)

    let cancelAction = UIAlertAction(title: "Settings", style: .Cancel) { (action) in
        let url = NSURL(string: UIApplicationOpenSettingsURLString)
        UIApplication.sharedApplication().openURL(url!)
    }
    alertController.addAction(cancelAction)

    let okAction = UIAlertAction(title: "OK", style: .Default) { (action) in
        // do nothing
    }
```

```
    alertController.addAction(okAction)

    presentViewController(alertController, animated: true, completion: nil)
}
```

This method configures a `UIAlertController` object to display an alert modally with a title, a message, and a style. Additionally, actions are associated with the controller. The cancel action is labeled Settings and is used to open the Settings app. The OK action is used to simply dismiss the alert.

Build and run the application. Turn Bluetooth off, and then press each button to verify that the alert is displayed and access to the other scenes is prohibited. Press the Settings button on the alert to make sure it opens the Settings app. At this point you've satisfied all the requirements for the first backlog item. In the next section, you'll move on to the next backlog item and implement the central role.

Connecting to a Bluetooth LE Device in Your App

In this section, you'll build the central role scene. You'll learn how to

- Scan for peripherals that advertise a specific service
- Connect to a peripheral and discover services
- Discover and subscribe to characteristics for a specific service
- Retrieve characteristic values
- Customize and animate a button

At this point, you have a running application that can detect whether or not Bluetooth is powered on and has the ability to transition to two different scenes.

Building the Interface

The UI for this scene has a single custom `UIButton` object and a read-only `UITextView` object. Refer to the mock-up in the section "Central Role Scene."

> **Tip** Use the Interface Builder Live Rendering feature in Xcode 6 to design and inspect a custom view. The custom view will render in Interface Builder and appear as it will in your application.

Start by adding a new Swift file to your project named `CustomButton.swift`, and declare the class `CustomButton` as a subclass of `UIButton` using the new `IBDesignable` attribute. Then add inspectable properties using `IBInspectable` for `cornerRadius`, `borderWidth`, and `borderColor` (see Listing 9-4).

Listing 9-4. The CustomButton class

```
import UIKit

@IBDesignable
class CustomButton: UIButton {

    @IBInspectable var cornerRadius: CGFloat = 0 {
        didSet {
            layer.cornerRadius = cornerRadius
            layer.masksToBounds = cornerRadius > 0
        }
    }

    @IBInspectable var borderWidth: CGFloat = 0 {
        didSet {
            layer.borderWidth = borderWidth
        }
    }

    @IBInspectable var borderColor: UIColor? {
        didSet {
            layer.borderColor = borderColor?.CGColor
        }
    }
}
```

When you add the `IBDesignable` attribute to the class declaration, Interface Builder will render your custom view. Your custom view will update automatically as you make changes by using the `IBInspectable` attribute to declare variables as inspectable properties.

Now open up the storyboard and add a `UIButton` to the central role scene. In the Utilities panel, click the Identities Inspector tab and change the class type from `UIButton` to `CustomButton` you just created. Now click the Attributes Inspector tab and set the button title to Scan. Notice that there's a section named Custom Button with a field for each of the inspectable properties you declared. Set the values for Corner Radius to 50, Border Width to 4, and Border Color to White Color. In the Button section, set the *Shows Touch on Highlight* to *checked* so when a user presses the button, there will be a white glow where the touch event occurred on the button (see Figure 9-18).

> **Tip** Set the corner radius to half the width of the view to give it a circular shape.

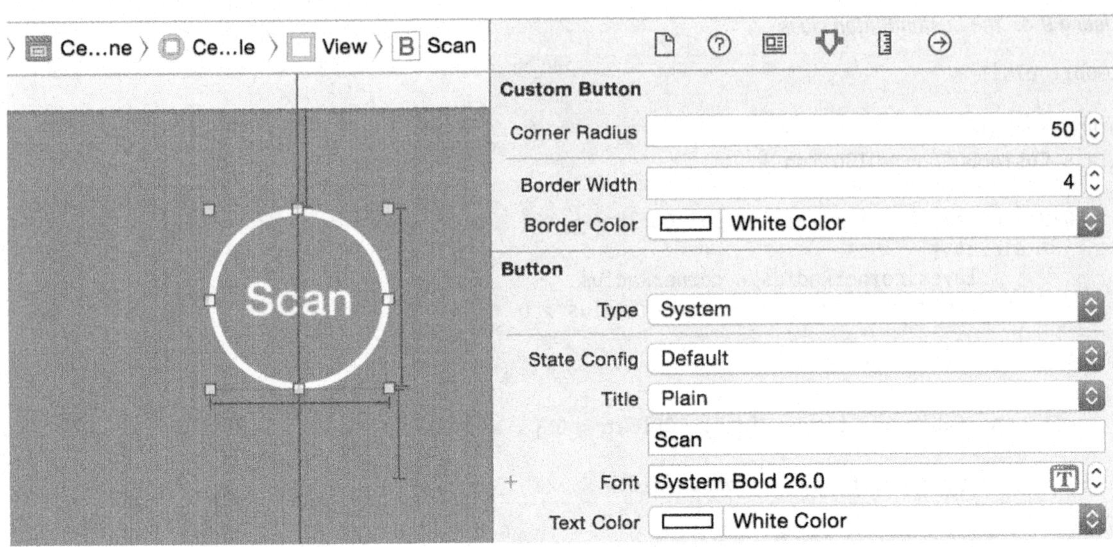

Figure 9-18. Setting button attributes

If you haven't added constraints, you won't see the constraint graphics. In that case you will only see layout handles. See Figure 9-19 as a guide to set up your constraints.

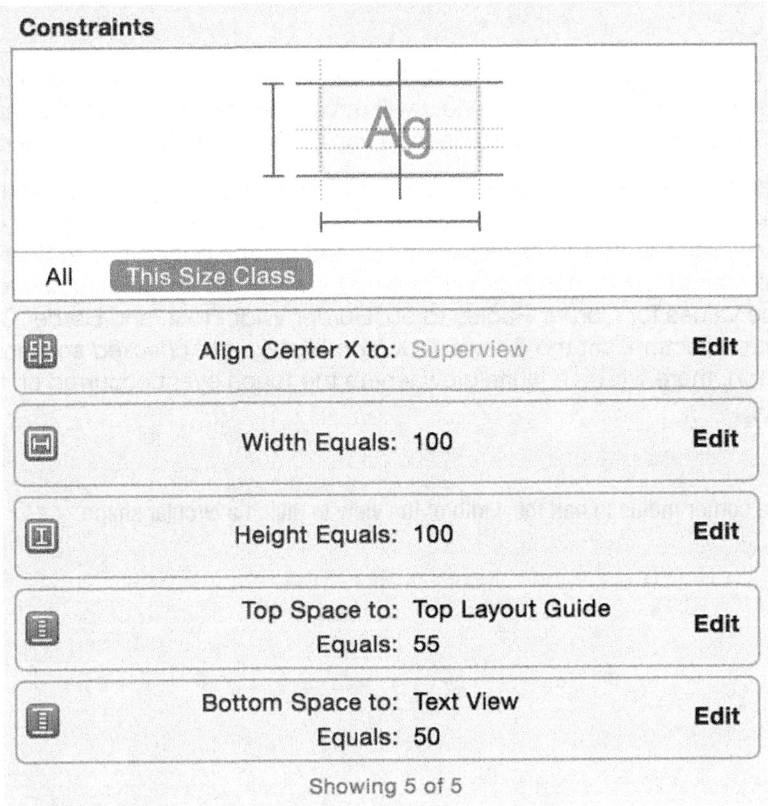

Figure 9-19. Scan button constraints

Now you need to add a UITextView object to the scene and position it so it looks similar to the illustration in Figure 9-20. Then in the Attributes Inspector, set the Text View text color to White Color and the background color to Clear Color. Set the Font to System 18.0.

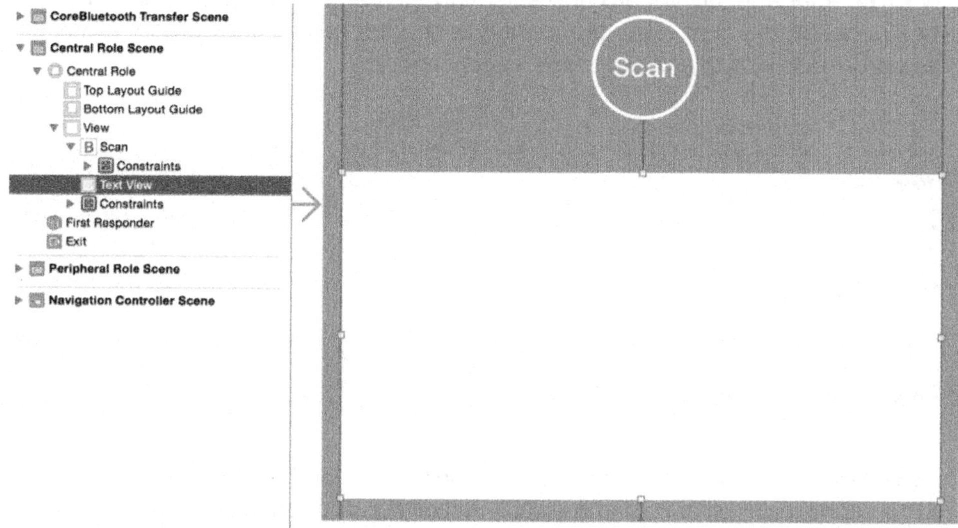

***Figure 9-20.** Setting attributes for UITextView*

Set the constraints for the text view to match the illustration in Figure 9-21.

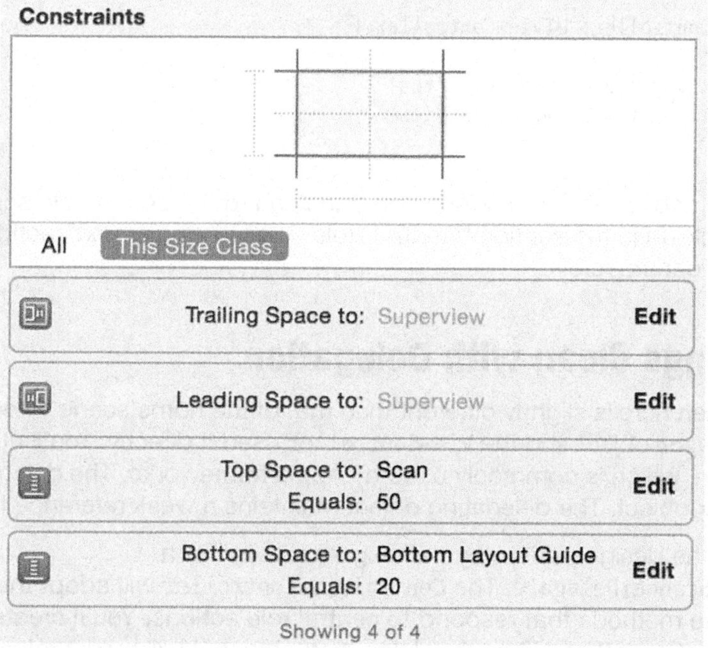

***Figure 9-21.** Constraint settings for UITextView*

For the last steps in building the UI, you need to connect the button and text view to a property of the View Controller. First, add a new Swift file to the project named `CentralViewController.swift` and declare the class `CentralViewController` as a subclass of `UIViewController`. Then assign the `CentralViewController` as the class for the central role identity by opening the storyboard and selecting the central role scene (see Figure 9-22). In the Utilities panel on the right, click the Identity Inspector tab. In the Custom Class section, use the class drop-down to select `CentralViewController`.

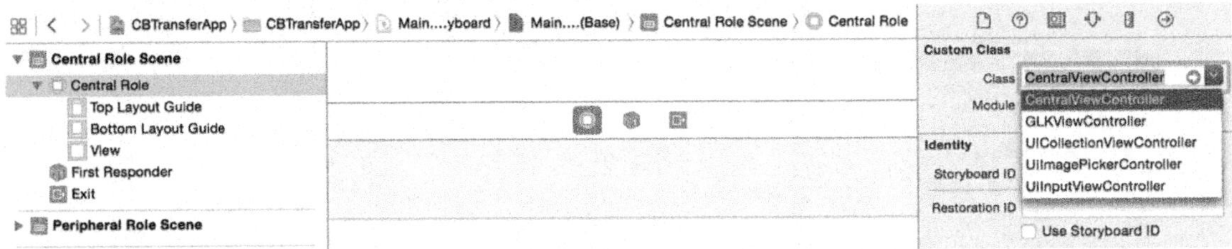

***Figure 9-22.** Assign central role identity*

Now using the Assistant Editor, control-drag and drop each of the UI controls inside the `CentralViewController` class. Name the `UIButton` connection `scanButton` and the `UITextView` to `textView`; use the default options. Your class should look like that shown in Listing 9-5.

***Listing 9-5.** The CentralViewController class declaration*

```
import UIKit

class CentralViewController: UIViewController {

    @IBOutlet weak var scanButton: UIButton!
    @IBOutlet weak var textView: UITextView!
}
```

At this point build and run the app. When you transition to the central role scene, it should resemble the mock-up in the section "Central Role Scene." In the next section, you'll start implementing the central role.

Keeping Things Clean with Delegation

The approach taken here is slightly different than that of the home scene where you created the `CBCentralManager` object and the `ViewController` used it directly. You'll utilize the Delegation pattern, which is commonly used by Apple frameworks. The delegate is typically a Custom Controller object. The delegating object maintains a weak reference to its delegate.

You'll implement the design pattern by defining a protocol for a `TransferServiceScannerDelegate`. The `CentralViewController` will adopt this protocol and implement the methods that respond to central role actions. You'll create a new class `TransferServiceScanner` that will be the delegating object. It will hold a reference to the

CentralViewController, which will act as the delegate. The TransferServiceScanner object will act as the delegate for the CBCentralManager and CBPeripheral objects. The sequence diagram in Figure 9-23 illustrates the interaction between the objects. ,

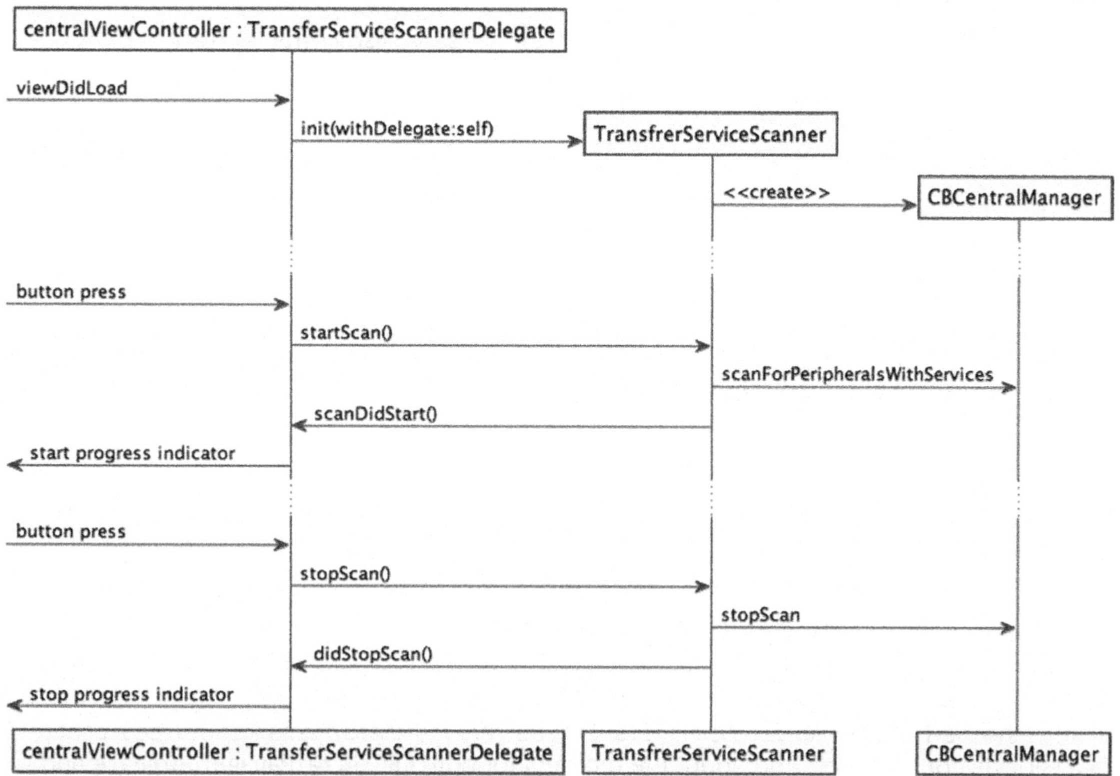

Figure 9-23. *Sequence diagram for TransferServiceScanner*

Create a new Swift file named TransferServiceScanner.swift and define a protocol for the TransferServiceScannerDelegate. The delegate will respond to scan start and stop actions, which will be used to start a scanning progress indicator. It will also respond to data transfer action that will be used to present data to the user (see Listing 9-6).

Listing 9-6. *TransferServiceScannerDelegate Protocol*

```
import CoreBluetooth

protocol TransferServiceScannerDelegate: NSObjectProtocol {
    func didStartScan()
    func didStopScan()
    func didTransferData(data: NSData?)
}
```

Now update the CentralViewController to adopt the TransferServiceScannerDelegate protocol and add stubs for the required delegate methods (see Listing 9-7). You'll complete the method implementation once we build out the TransferServiceScanner.

Listing 9-7. TransferServiceScannerDelegate Protocol Methods

```
class CentralViewController: UIViewController, TransferServiceScannerDelegate {

    // MARK: TransferServiceScannerDelegate methods

    func didStartScan() {

    }

    func didStopScan() {

    }

    func didTransferData(data: NSData?) {

    }
}
```

> **Tip** In Swift, the comment // MARK: is the equivalent to the Objective-C pre-processor directive #pragma mark. Use it to define areas in your source code.

Next, in the file TransferServiceScanner.swift, declare the class TransferServiceScanner as a subclass of NSObject, and adopt the protocol for both CBCentralManagerDelegate and CBPeripheralDelegate. Also you'll need to import Core Bluetooth. Then add properties for CBCentralManager, CBPeripheral, NSMutableData, and TransferServiceScannerDelegate.

Listing 9-8.

```
class TransferServiceScanner: NSObject, CBCentralManagerDelegate, CBPeripheralDelegate {

    var centralManager: CBCentralManager!
    var discoveredPeripheral: CBPeripheral?
    var data: NSMutableData = NSMutableData()

    weak var delegate: TransferServiceScannerDelegate?
}
```

You must make sure that you declare the delegate property *weak* to avoid a strong reference cycle. A strong reference cycle will prevent TransferServiceScannerDelegate from being deallocated, which will cause a memory leak in your application. Also, a weak reference is allowed to have *no value*, so it must be declared as having an optional type.

At the top of the class body, implement an initializer method that you will call when you create a new instance of TransferServiceScanner (see Listing 9-9). The primary role of an initializer is to ensure that a new instance of a type is set up properly before first use.

Listing 9-9. TransferServiceScanner Initializer Method

```
init(delegate: TransferServiceScannerDelegate?) {
    super.init()
    centralManager = CBCentralManager(delegate: self, queue: nil)
    self.delegate = delegate
},
```

The initializer starts by calling `super.init()`, which calls the initializer of `TransferServiceScanner` class's superclass, `NSObject`. Then the `centralManager` property is initialized with an instance of `CBCentralManager` and initialized with `self` as the delegate. Finally the `delegate` property is initialized with the `TransferServiceScannerDelegate` object that is passed as a parameter.

Next, you must implement the required protocol method `centralManagerDidUpdateState`. Add the code from Listing 9-10 to the `TransferServiceScanner` class. The implementation is similar to the one in section "Using a Central Manager," except in this case the state information is being output to the log window. Later in this section, you'll update this method.

Listing 9-10. The centralManagerDidUpdateState delegate method

```
func centralManagerDidUpdateState(central: CBCentralManager!) {

    switch (central.state) {
    case .PoweredOn:
        print("Central Manager powered on.")
        break

    case .PoweredOff:
        print("Central Manager powered off.")
        break;

    default:
        print("Central Manager changed state \(central.state)")
        break
    }
}
```

Build and run the application. You should see the log output "Central Manager powered on" when you transition to the central role scene.

Scanning for Peripherals

At this point, you are ready to start interacting with the central manager. Refer back to the section "Central Role Scene" and look at the requirements. The requirements call for the ability to toggle scanning on and off. In this section, you will provide support for that.

You will focus on the following requirements:

- The application can scan for peripherals
- The application uses a filter for a specific service when scanning
- The scene provides a Scan button that toggles device scanning on and off
- The scene provides a progress indicator when scanning

First you need to define a constant that will be used to uniquely identify the specific service that the scanner is interested in. In the file `Const.swift` add the following line:

```
let kTransferServiceUUID: String = "3C4F8654-E41B-4696-B5C6-13D06336F22E"
```

You will use this constant to initialize a `CBUUID` instance. The `CBUUID` object represents the 128-bit identifier. The advantages are that the class provides some factory methods for dealing with long UUIDs (universally unique identifiers), and the object also can be passed around instead of the string.

> **Note** If you want to provide your own UUID, you can open up a terminal window and type the command *uuidgen*. It will generate a UUID that you can then copy and paste.

Now you'll implement the method `startScan` (see Listing 9-11). The `CentralViewController` will call this method when the user taps the Scan button when the application is not scanning.

Listing 9-11. The `TransferServiceScanner` `startScan` Method

```
func startScan() {
    print("Start scan")
    let services = [CBUUID(string: kTransferServiceUUID)]
    let options = Dictionary(dictionaryLiteral:
    (CBCentralManagerScanOptionAllowDuplicatesKey, false))
    centralManager.scanForPeripheralsWithServices(services, options: options)
    delegate?.didStartScan()
}
```

In this method you create two local variables that will be passed to the `centralManager`. The `services` variable is an array of `CBUUID` objects that represent the services the app is scanning for. In this case it's an array with a single element. The `options` local variable is a dictionary specifying options to customize the scan. The key `CBCentralManagerScanOptionAllowDuplicatesKey` specifies whether or not the scan should run without duplicate filtering. The value assigned to that key is `false`. What this means is that notification should be sent each time the peripheral is discovered. If the value were set to `true`, then notification would only be sent once per discovery.

Next, the method `centralManager.scanForPeripheralsWithServices` is called which starts the scan for peripherals that are advertising services. And, finally, the delegate is notified that the scan did start by calling through `didStartScan`.

Next, you'll implement the method `stopScan` (Listing 9-12). The `CentralViewController` will call this method when the user taps the Scan button while the application is scanning. It will also be called when the central manager state changes to the powered off state.

Listing 9-12. The TransferServiceScanner stopScan Method

```
func stopScan() {
    print("Stop scan")
        centralManager.stopScan()
    delegate?.didStopScan()
}
```

This method tells the central manager to stop scanning and then notifies the delegate that scanning has stopped. Update the switch block in the `centralManagerDidUpdateState` method for the `PoweredOff` case, adding a call to `stopScan`.

Listing 9-13. The switch block in the centralManagerDidUpdateState method

```
switch (central.state) {
case .PoweredOn:
    print("Central Manager powered on.")
    break

case .PoweredOff:
    print("Central Manager powered off.")
    stopScan()
    break;

default:
    print("Central Manager changed state \(central.state)")
}
```

Handling User Input

To keep track of the scanning state, add a `Bool` property `isScanning` to the `CentralViewController` class and set its initial value to `false`.

```
var isScanning: Bool = false
```

Add an action method to handle the Scan button tap event. Open the storyboard and control-drag the Scan button into the `CentralViewController` class and name the method `toggleScanning` (see Listing 9-14). You'll use this method to start and stop the scanning based on the `isScanning` property value.

Listing 9-14. The toggleScanning method

```
@IBAction func toggleScanning() {
    if isScanning {
        scanner.stopScan()
    } else {
        scanner.startScan()
    }
}
```

The `CentralViewController` is a delegate for the `TransferServiceScanner`, so when scanning starts or stop, the View Controller will be notified through the delegate methods. Update the delegate methods to set up the scan state.

Listing 9-15. The didStartScan and didStopScan methods

```
func didStartScan() {
    if !isScanning {
        textView.text = "Scanning..."
        isScanning = true
    }
}

func didStopScan() {
    textView.text = ""
    isScanning = false
}
```

Build and run the application. Transition to the central role scene and then tap the Scan button. You should see the text "Scanning . . ." displayed in the text view. Tapping the Scan button a second time should clear the text.

Scan Progress

This simple text that is displayed could serve as an indicator for the scanning state, but it's static and it's boring. It's hardly a scanning progress indicator. Adding a simple rotation animation to the Scan button is quick and easy and will serve as an effective progress indicator for when scanning starts and stops.

You'll implement an extension to the `UIView` class that adds functionality to rotate the view using keyframe animation.

Open the `CentralViewController.swift` and above the class declaration add the code in Listing 9-16.

Listing 9-16. Adding an Extension to UIView to Apply Rotation to Any View

```
extension UIView {

    func rotate(fromValue: CGFloat, toValue: CGFloat, duration: CFTimeInterval = 1.0,
    completionDelegate: AnyObject? = nil) {

        let rotateAnimation = CABasicAnimation(keyPath: "transform.rotation")
        rotateAnimation.fromValue = fromValue
        rotateAnimation.toValue = toValue
        rotateAnimation.duration = duration

        if let delegate: AnyObject = completionDelegate {
            rotateAnimation.delegate = delegate
        }
        self.layer.addAnimation(rotateAnimation, forKey: nil)
    }
}
```

The parameters `fromValue` and `toValue` represent rotation and are specified in radians. The `duration` is specified in seconds.

The `CABasicAnimation` class provides single-keyframe animation for a layer property. It will allow you to interpolate between two values over time. It also allows you to set a delegate so you can receive notification when the animation completes by calling the delegate's `animationDidStop` method.

For this use case, rotating the Scan button 360 degrees would constitute one animation cycle. Each time an animation cycle completes the delegate is notified.

Override the `animationDidStop` method of the View Controller (see Listing 9-17). This method will evaluate the scan state and restart the animation if scanning is still in progress.

Listing 9-17. The CentralViewController animationDidStop Method

```
override func animationDidStop(anim: CAAnimation finished flag: Bool) {
    if isScanning == true {
        // if still scanning, restart the animation
        scanButton.rotate(0.0, toValue: CGFloat(M_PI * 2), completionDelegate: self)
    }
}
```

Now update the `didStartScan` method so it starts the rotation animation.

```
scanButton.rotate(0.0, toValue: CGFloat(M_PI * 2), duration: 1.0, completionDelegate: self)
```

When the scanning stops, the animation will end when the animation cycle completes. This guarantees that the Scan button will be in the correct orientation.

Build and run the application. Transition to the central role scene and tap the Scan button. You should see the Scan button spinning. The animation should stop when you tap the Scan button again.

Discover and Connect

While scanning, if a central manager discovers a peripheral that is advertising, it will notify its delegate by calling the `didDiscoverPeripheral` method (see Listing 9-18).

Listing 9-18. Initiating a Connection with a Discovered Peripheral in the TransferServiceScanner Class

```
func centralManager(central: CBCentralManager, didDiscoverPeripheral peripheral:
CBPeripheral, advertisementData: [String : AnyObject], RSSI: NSNumber) {
    print("didDiscoverPeripheral \(peripheral)")

    // reject if above reasonable range, or too low
    if (RSSI.integerValue > -15) || (RSSI.integerValue < -35) {
        print("not in range, RSSI is \(RSSI.integerValue)")
        return;
    }

    if (discoveredPeripheral != peripheral) {
        discoveredPeripheral = peripheral

        print("connecting to peripheral \(peripheral)")
        centralManager.connectPeripheral(peripheral, options: nil)
    }
}
```

Included in the parameters are the discovered peripheral, advertising data, and the signal strength. In this method you need to determine if the peripheral is within range. If so, then you can initiate a connection to it. You must, however, store a local copy of the peripheral; otherwise, Core Bluetooth will dispose of it.

Once you initiate a connection, the central manager will notify the delegate as to whether or not the connection was successful. There is a separate method for each case, `didConnectPeripheral` or `didFailToConnectPeripheral` (see Listings 9-19 and 9-20).

Listing 9-19. Connection to Peripheral Succeeded in the TransferServiceScanner Class

```
func centralManager(central: CBCentralManager!, didConnectPeripheral peripheral:
CBPeripheral!) {
    println("didConnectPeripheral")
    stopScan()
    data.length = 0
    peripheral.delegate = self
    peripheral.discoverServices([CBUUID(string: kTransferServiceUUID)])
}
```

Listing 9-20. Connection to Peripheral Failed in the TransferServiceScanner Class

```
func centralManager(central: CBCentralManager!, didFailToConnectPeripheral peripheral:
CBPeripheral!, error: NSError!) {
    println("didFailToConnectPeripheral")
}
```

If the connection is successful, scanning should stop to save power, and any data previously held should be released. In order to receive discovery notifications, you must assign the peripheral's delegate to `self`. Now you're ready to explore the specified services. In this case you are interested in a transfer service.

Explore Services and Characteristics

When a specified service is discovered, the peripheral will notify its delegate by calling the `didDiscoverServices` method with a reference to the peripheral that the services belong to, and an `NSError` object. You must evaluate the error to determine whether the discovery was successful.

Listing 9-21. Service Discovery Notification in the TransferServiceScanner Class

```
func peripheral(peripheral: CBPeripheral, didDiscoverServices error: NSError?) {
    print("didDiscoverServices")

    if (error != nil) {
        print("Encountered error: \(error!.localizedDescription)")
        return
    }

    // look for the characteristics we want
    for service in peripheral.services! {
        peripheral.discoverCharacteristics([CBUUID(string: kTransferCharacteristicUUID)],
        forService: service)
    }
}
```

If the service discovery is successful, you must iterate the services to find the characteristic of interest. In this case you want the `kTransferCharacteristicUUID`.

Add a definition for the transfer characteristic to the `Const.swift` file.

```
let kTransferCharacteristicUUID: String = "DEB07A07-463E-4A65-BABB-0DA17E4E517A"
```

Subscribe and Receive Data

When you discover a specified characteristic, the peripheral will notify its delegate by calling the `didDiscoverCharacteristicsForService` method with a reference to the peripheral that is providing the information, the service that the characteristic belongs to, and an `NSError` object. You must evaluate the error to determine whether the discovery was successful (see Listing 9-22).

Listing 9-22. Subscribe to a Characteristic in the TransferServiceScanner Class

```
func peripheral(peripheral: CBPeripheral, didDiscoverCharacteristicsForService service:
CBService, error: NSError?) {
    print("didDiscoverCharacteristicsForService")
```

```
    if (error != nil) {
        print("Encountered error: \(error!.localizedDescription)")
        return
    }

    // loop through and verify the characteristic is the correct one, then subscribe to it
    let cbuuid = CBUUID(string: kTransferCharacteristicUUID)
    for characteristic in service.characteristics! {
        print("characteristic.UUID is \(characteristic.UUID)")
        if characteristic.UUID == cbuuid {
            peripheral.setNotifyValue(true, forCharacteristic: characteristic)
        }
    }
}
```

If the characteristic discovery is successful, you must iterate the service characteristics to verify that the characteristic is the one you're interested in. You must subscribe to the characteristic by calling the peripherals `setNotifyValue` method. The first parameter is a Boolean which indicates whether or not you want to receive notifications for the specified characteristic. In this case you pass true, signaling to the peripheral that you want to receive the data it contains. Notification is sent each time a characteristics value changes.

The peripheral will now start sending data and notify its delegate by calling its `didUpdateValueForCharacteristic` method with a reference to the peripheral that is providing the information, the characteristic whose value is being retrieved, and an `NSError` object (see Listing 9-23).

***Listing 9-23.** Retrieve Characteristic Value in the TransferServiceScanner Class*

```
func peripheral(peripheral: CBPeripheral, didUpdateValueForCharacteristic characteristic:
CBCharacteristic, error: NSError?) {
    print("didUpdateValueForCharacteristic")

    if (error != nil) {
        print("Encountered error: \(error!.localizedDescription)")
        return
    }

    let stringFromData = NSString(data: characteristic.value!, encoding:
    NSUTF8StringEncoding)
    print("received \(stringFromData)")

    if stringFromData == "EOM" {
        // data transfer is complete, so notify delegate
        delegate?.didTransferData(data)

        // unsubscribe from characteristic
        peripheral.setNotifyValue(false, forCharacteristic: characteristic)
```

```
        // disconnect from peripheral
        centralManager.cancelPeripheralConnection(peripheral)
    }

    data.appendData(characteristic.value!)
}
```

Not all characteristics have readable values. Typically, you would determine whether the value is readable by examining its properties. For the purposes of this example, it's known that the characteristic value is of type String.

Here, the transfer service peripheral sends text from a text field in small amounts. The data is accumulated until you receive an end-of-message (EOM) string indicating that the data transfer is complete. At this point, you notify the `TransferServiceScannerDelegate` that the transfer is complete and pass the data. You then unsubscribe from the characteristic and disconnect.

Subscription Status

When you attempt to subscribe to a characteristic, the peripheral calls its delegate method `didUpdateNotificationStateForCharacteristic` with a reference to the peripheral that is providing the information, the characteristic for which notifications are to be configured, and an `NSError` object. You must evaluate the error to determine whether the discovery was successful. This method is also invoked when you unsubscribe (see Listing 9-24).

***Listing 9-24.** Subscription Status Notification in the TransferServiceScanner Class*

```
func peripheral(peripheral: CBPeripheral, didUpdateNotificationStateForCharacteristic
characteristic: CBCharacteristic, error: NSError?) {
    print("didUpdateNotificationStateForCharacteristic")

    if (error != nil) {
        print("Encountered error: \(error!.localizedDescription)")
        return
    }

    if characteristic.UUID != CBUUID(string: kTransferCharacteristicUUID) {
        return
    }

    if characteristic.isNotifying {
        print("notification started for \(characteristic)")
    } else {
        print("notification stopped for \(characteristic), disconnecting...")
        centralManager.cancelPeripheralConnection(peripheral)
    }
}
```

Here you are only interested in the transfer characteristic. In the case where you unsubscribe, notifications will stop and you can disconnect from the peripheral.

Peripheral Role

At this point, you have an application that implements the central role. In the following sections, you will implement the peripheral role. You'll learn how to

- Start up a peripheral manager
- Set up a service and characteristic for the peripheral
- Advertise the service
- Handle requests from a connected central device
- Send data to a subscribed central device

Building the Interface

The UI for this scene has a single `UISwitch` object and an editable `UITextView` object. Refer to the mock-up in the section "Peripheral Role Scene."

Start by adding a new Swift file to your project named `PeripheralViewController.swift` and declare the class `PeripheralViewController` as a subclass of `UIViewController`. Then assign the `PeripheralViewController` as the class for the peripheral role identity by opening the storyboard and selecting the peripheral role scene. In the Utilities panel on the right, click the Identity Inspector tab. In the Custom Class section, use the class drop-down to select `PeripheralViewController`.

Now open up the storyboard if not already open and add the following controls to peripheral role scene; then arrange them so they look similar to the illustration in Figure 9-24.

- `UILabel` titled Advertise
- `UISwitch`
- `UITextView`

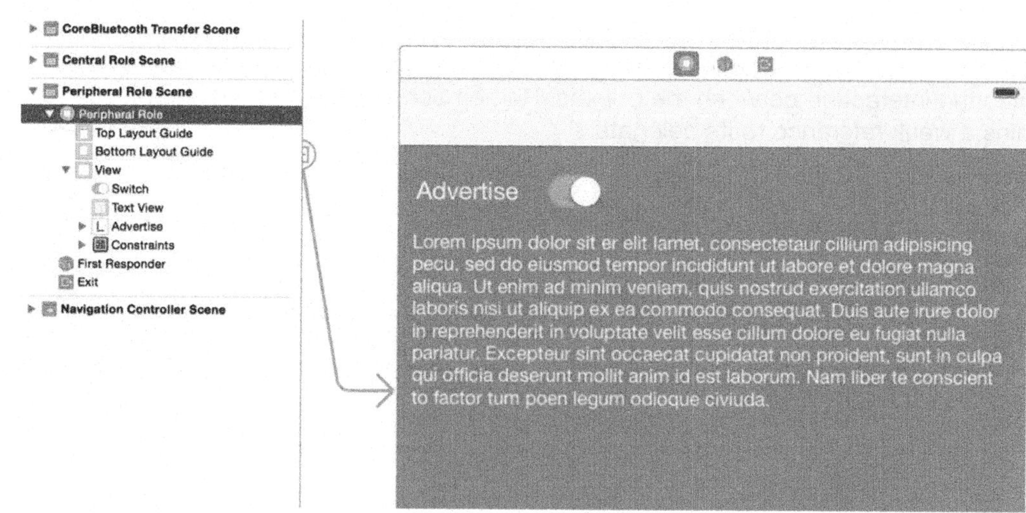

Figure 9-24. *Peripheral role scene*

Now control-drag and drop the `UISwitch` and the `UITextControl` inside the `PeripheralViewController` class. Leave the default text in the text view. Your `PeripheralViewController` class should look like the code in Listing 9-25.

Listing 9-25. *The PeripheralViewController class declaration*

```
import UIKit

class PeripheralViewController: UIViewController {

    @IBOutlet weak var advertiseSwitch: UISwitch!
    @IBOutlet weak var textView: UITextView!
}
```

Add an action method to handle the advertise switch event. Open the storyboard and control-drag the advertise switch into the `PeripheralViewController` class and name the method `advertiseSwitchDidChange`. You'll use this method to start and stop advertising.

```
@IBAction func advertiseSwitchDidChange() {
}
```

At this point build and run the app. When you transition to the peripheral role scene, it should resemble the mock-up in the section "Peripheral Role Scene." In the next section, you'll start implanting the peripheral role.

Delegate Setup

You'll use the Delegation pattern again and implement the design pattern by defining a protocol for a `TransferServiceDelegate`. The `PeripheralViewController` will adopt this protocol and implement the methods that respond to peripheral role actions. You'll create a new class `TransferService` that will be the delegating object. It will hold a reference to the

PeripheralViewController that will act as the delegate. The TransferService object will act as the delegate for the CBPeripheralManager object. The sequence diagram in Figure 9-25 illustrates the interaction between the objects. Remember that the delegating object maintains a weak reference to its delegate.

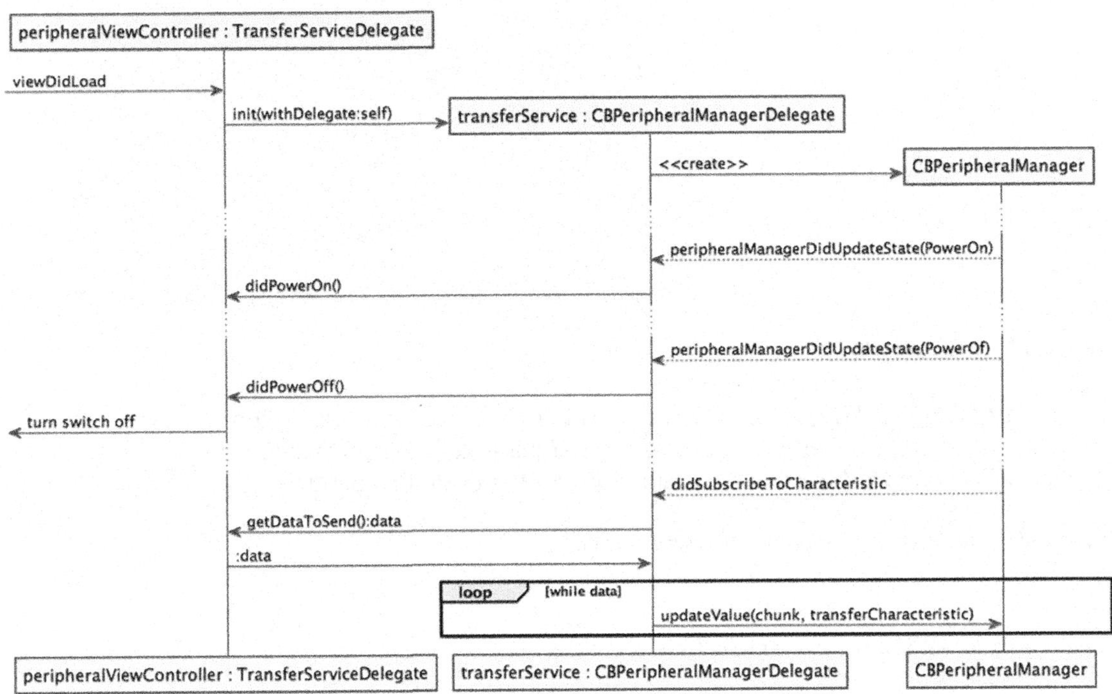

***Figure 9-25.** Sequence diagram for TransferService*

Create a new Swift file named TransferService.swift and define a protocol for the TransferServiceDelegate. The delegate will respond to power on/off events which will change the advertise switch state. It will also respond to a send data request that will be used to pass text data to the service.

***Listing 9-26.** TransferServiceDelegate Protocol*

```
protocol TransferServiceDelegate: NSObjectProtocol {
    func didPowerOn()
    func didPowerOff()
    func getDataToSend() -> NSData
}
```

Now update the PeripheralViewController to adopt the TransferServiceDelegate protocol (Listing 9-27) and add stubs for the required delegate methods. In the didPowerOff method, set the advertiseSwitch state to off. In the method getDataToSend return the textView object's text value.

Listing 9-27. TransferServiceDelegate Protocol Methods

```
class PeripheralViewController: UIViewController, TransferServiceDelegate {

    @IBOutlet weak var advertiseSwitch: UISwitch!
    @IBOutlet weak var textView: UITextView!

    // MARK: TransferServiceDelegate methods

    func didPowerOn() {

    }

    func didPowerOff() {
                advertiseSwitch.setOn(false, animated: true)
    }

    func getDataToSend() -> NSData {
        return textView.text.dataUsingEncoding(NSUTF8StringEncoding)!
    }
}
```

Next, in the file `TransferService.swift`, declare the class `TransferService` as a subclass of `NSObject` and adopt the protocol for `CBPeripheralManagerDelegate` (Listing 9-28) Also you'll need to import CoreBluetooth. Then add properties for `CBPeripheralManager`, `CBMutableCharacteristic`, `NSData`, an index counter, and `TransferServiceDelegate`.

Listing 9-28. The TransferService class declaration

```
class TransferService: NSObject, CBPeripheralManagerDelegate {

    var peripheralManager: CBPeripheralManager!
    var transferCharacteristic: CBMutableCharacteristic!
    var dataToSend: NSData?
        var sendDataIndex: Int?

        weak var delegate: TransferServiceDelegate?
}
```

Make sure that you declare the delegate property as *weak* to avoid a strong reference cycle.

Now implement an initializer method (see Listing 9-29) that will be called when you create a new instance of `TransferService`.

Listing 9-29. The TransferService Initializer Method

```
init(delegate: TransferServiceDelegate?) {
    super.init()
    peripheralManager = CBPeripheralManager(delegate: self, queue: nil)
    self.delegate = delegate
}
```

The initializer starts by calling `super.init()`, which calls the initializer of `TransferServiceScanner` class's superclass, `NSObject`. Then the `peripheralManager` property is initialized with an instance of `CBPeripheralManager` and initialized with `self` as the delegate. Finally the `delegate` property is initialized with the `TransferServiceDelegate` object that is passed as a parameter.

Next, you must implement the required protocol method `peripheralManagerDidUpdateState` (see Listing 9-30).

Listing 9-30. Required Protocol Method peripheralManagerDidUpdateState in the TransferService Class

```
func peripheralManagerDidUpdateState(peripheral: CBPeripheralManager!) {

    switch (peripheral.state) {
    case .PoweredOn:
        print("Peripheral Manager powered on.")
        setupServices()
        delegate?.didPowerOn()
        break

    case .PoweredOff:
        print("Peripheral Manager powered off.")
        teardownServices()
        delegate?.didPowerOff()
        break

    default:
        print("Peripheral Manager state changed: \(peripheral.state)")
        break
    }
}
```

In this method, you set up or tear down services and notify the delegate according to the state. In the next section you will implement both methods: `setupServices` and `teardownServices`.

Setting up a Service

The services and characteristics of a peripheral are identified by UUIDs. The Bluetooth Special Interest Group (SIG) has published a number of commonly used UUIDs. However, the transfer service doesn't use any of those predefined Bluetooth UUIDs. Earlier in this chapter, you defined UUIDs for the transfer service and characteristic in `Const.swift`.

Now implement the `setupServices` method that will be called when the peripheral manager's state changes to `PoweredOn`. Make the method private so that it's only accessible from within the `TransferService` class (see Listing 9-31).

Listing 9-31. Setting Up Services in the TransferServices Class

```
private func setupServices() {

    var cbuuidCharacteristic = CBUUID(string: kTransferCharacteristicUUID)

    transferCharacteristic = CBMutableCharacteristic(type: cbuuidCharacteristic,
    properties: CBCharacteristicProperties.Notify, value: nil, permissions:
    CBAttributePermissions.Readable)

    var cbuuidService = CBUUID(string: kTransferServiceUUID)

    var transferService = CBMutableService(type: cbuuidService, primary: true)
    transferService.characteristics = [transferCharacteristic]

    peripheralManager.addService(transferService)
}
```

In this method you create a mutable characteristic and set its property, value, and permissions. The property and permissions are set to readable. The value is set the value to `nil` because this will ensure that the value will be treated dynamically and is requested by the peripheral manager when it receives a read/write request. Otherwise the value is cached and treated as read-only.

Next, you create a mutable service and associate the mutable characteristic with it by setting the service's array of characteristics. Finally, publish the service by calling `addService` that adds the service to the peripheral's database. The service cannot be changed once this step is complete. Once the service is published, the peripheral calls the delegate method `didAddService`.

Now implement the `teardownServices` method that will be called when the peripheral manager's state changes to `PoweredOff` (see Listing 9-32).

Listing 9-32. Teardown Services in the TransferService Class

```
private func teardownServices() {
    peripheralManager.removeAllServices()
}
```

The only step in this method is to remove all published services from the peripheral's database.

Build and run the application. You should see the log output "Peripheral Manager powered on" when you transition to the peripheral role scene.

Advertising Services

Once services and characteristics have been published, you can start advertising one or more of them by calling the peripheral manager's `startAdvertising` method. Add the code in Listing 9-33 to the TransferService class.

Listing 9-33. Start Advertising in the TransferService Class

```
func startAdvertising() {
    print("Start advertising")

    var cbuuidService = CBUUID(string: kTransferServiceUUID)

    var services = [cbuuidService]

    var advertisingDict = Dictionary(dictionaryLiteral: (CBAdvertisementDataServiceUUIDsKey,
    services))

    peripheralManager.startAdvertising(advertisingDict)
}
```

You construct a dictionary with `CBAdvertisementDataServiceUUIDsKey` as the only key, with a value of an array of `CBUUID` objects that you want to advertise, then pass that dictionary as a parameter to the peripheral manager's `startAdvertising`. The peripheral manager will then call its delegate method `peripheralManagerDidStartAdvertising`. Once advertising begins, any remote central role device can discover and initiate a connection. To stop advertising, you call the peripheral manager's `stopAdvertising` method (see Listing 9-34).

Listing 9-34. Stop Advertising in the TransferService Class

```
func stopAdvertising() {
    print("Stop advertising")

    peripheralManager.stopAdvertising()
}
```

In the `PeripheralViewController` class, add a property to hold a TransferService object.

```
var transferService: TransferService!
```

Then initialize it in the `viewDidLoadMethod` as such:

```
transferService = TransferService(delegate: self)
```

Now update the method `advertiseSwitchDidChange` to start and stop advertising (see Listing 9-35).

Listing 9-35. Starting and Stopping Advertising in the PeripheralViewController Class

```
@IBAction func advertiseSwitchDidChange() {
    if advertiseSwitch.on {
        transferService.startAdvertising()
    } else {
        transferService.stopAdvertising()
    }
}
```

Sending Data

Once connected, a remote device will subscribe to one or more characteristic values. You are responsible for sending notifications to the subscribers when the value of any characteristic they are subscribed to changes. The peripheral manager will then call its delegate method `didSubscribeToCharacteristic`. From this method, you should start sending data (see Listing 9-36).

Listing 9-36. Sending Data in the TransferService Class

```
func peripheralManager(peripheral: CBPeripheralManager!, central: CBCentral!,
didSubscribeToCharacteristic characteristic: CBCharacteristic!) {
    print("didSubscribeToCharacteristic")

    dataToSend = delegate?.getDataToSend()
    sendDataIndex = 0
    sendData()
}
```

This method calls the `TransferServiceDelegate` method `getDataToSend` to retrieve the data to be sent to the remote device. It then initializes a data index counter and starts sending data (see Listing 9-37).

Listing 9-37. Sending Data to a Remote Central Device in the TransferService Class

```
private func sendData() {
    print("sendData")

    let MTU = 20

    struct eom { static var pending = false }

    func sendEOM() -> Bool {
        eom.pending = true
        let data =  ("EOM" as NSString).dataUsingEncoding(NSUTF8StringEncoding)
        print("sending \(data)")
        if peripheralManager.updateValue(data!, forCharacteristic: transferCharacteristic,
        onSubscribedCentrals: nil) {
            eom.pending = false;
        }
        return !eom.pending
    }

    if eom.pending {
        if sendEOM() { return }
    }

    if sendDataIndex >= dataToSend?.length {
        return
    }
```

```
    var didSend = true
    while didSend {
        var amountToSend = dataToSend!.length - sendDataIndex!
        print("amountToSend is \(amountToSend)")
        if (amountToSend > MTU) {
            amountToSend = MTU
        }
        let chunk = NSData(bytes: dataToSend!.bytes+sendDataIndex!, length: amountToSend)
        didSend = peripheralManager.updateValue(chunk, forCharacteristic:
        transferCharacteristic, onSubscribedCentrals: nil)
        if !didSend {
            return
        }
        print("didSend \(chunk)")

        sendDataIndex! += amountToSend
        if sendDataIndex >= dataToSend?.length {
            sendEOM()
            return
        }
    }
}
```

In this method, you send data in MTU-sized chunks until there is no more data to send, followed by an EOM indicator. The MTU (Maximum Transmission Unit) is defined at 20 bytes. For each chunk you call the peripheral manager's `updateValue` method, which will then forward the data to the connected central role device. The return value indicates whether the update was successfully sent or not. If the underlying queue was full, the method returns false. In that case the peripheral manager will call its delegate method `peripheralManagerIsReadyToUpdateSubscribers` when more space becomes available. You will implement that method to resend the data.

***Listing 9-38.** The peripheralManagerIsReadyToUpdateSubscribers method in the TransferService Class*

```
func peripheralManagerIsReadyToUpdateSubscribers(peripheral: CBPeripheralManager) {
    sendData()
}
```

Enabling Your App for Background Communication

System resources are limited on iOS devices, so by default many of the Core Bluetooth tasks are disabled while your app is in the background. In order for the application to support background mode, you can declare your app to support the Core Bluetooth background execution modes. This will enable your app to wake up from a suspended state and process Bluetooth-related events.

In the Project navigator right-click the `Info.plist` file and select Open As ➤ Source Code and add the `UIBackgroundMode` key, and set the keys value to an array containing the following strings:

- `bluetooth-central`: The app communicates with Bluetooth LE peripherals using the Core Bluetooth framework.
- `bluetooth-peripheral`: The app shares data using the Core Bluetooth framework.

```
<key>UIBackgroundModes</key>
<array>
    <string>bluetooth-central</string>
    <string>bluetooth-peripheral</string>
</array>
```

Bluetooth Best Practices

The Core Bluetooth framework gives you control over implementing most aspects of both the central and peripheral roles. This section provides guidance for using this control in responsible way.

Central Role Devices

- Only scan for devices when you need to. Once you discover a device you're interested in, stop scanning for other devices. This will help limit radio usage and power consumption.
- When exploring peripheral end-of-sentence services and characteristics, use a filter to look for and discover only the services and characteristics you need. Otherwise it can negatively affect your battery life.
- It's best to subscribe to a characteristic's value when possible especially if the value changes often. This will eliminate the need to poll.
- Cancel any subscriptions and disconnect from a device when you have all the data you need. This will help reduce your app's radio usage.

Peripheral Role Devices

- Advertise data only when you need to. Advertising peripheral data uses your device's radio, which affects your device's battery. Once a device is connected, stop advertising.
- Let the user decide when to advertise, since your app is unaware of nearby devices.
- Allow connected central role devices to subscribe to your characteristics. When you create a mutable characteristic, configure it to support subscriptions by setting the characteristics properties with the `CBCharacteristicsPropertyNotify` constant.

Summary

In this chapter, you learned some key terms and concepts related to the Bluetooth specification, and how Apple adopted these in its Core Bluetooth framework. You also learned how to use the Core Bluetooth framework to discover and connect to Bluetooth LE-compatible devices, as well how to send and receive data between devices. Apply this knowledge along with best practices to build your own high-quality Bluetooth LE application.

Chapter 10

Building Location Awareness with iBeacons

Manny de la Torriente

This chapter introduces iBeacon technology and will show you how to use the Core Location framework to interact with beacons. You'll learn how to establish a region around an object, determine when a region has been entered or exited, and estimate your proximity to a beacon. You'll also learn how to configure your iOS device to act as an iBeacon transmitter.

Introduction to iBeacons

Apple standardized the iBeacon technology, which introduces a class of low-cost transmitters that utilize Bluetooth Low Energy (LE). A device with iBeacon technology is used to establish a region that allows an iOS device to determine when it has entered or exited the region and to estimate its proximity to the transmitter. The Apple Store, for example, uses beacons to bring up its app on your phone when you enter the store.

iBeacon Advertisement

A device that is configured to be an iBeacon transmitter provides information via Bluetooth LE. The information contains a unique user ID (UUID) that is specific to a deployment use case and major and minor values, which provide identifying values for the iBeacon.

iBeacon Accuracy

When an iOS device detects an iBeacon's signal, it uses the RSSI (received signal strength indicator) to determine its proximity to the beacon. The signal strength increases as the receiver moves closer to the beacon.

The calibrated transmission power of a device is its known measured signal strength in RSSI at 1 meter. The distance provided by iOS is in meters and is an estimate based on the ratio of the beacon's signal strength over the transmission power.

Privacy

User authorization is required in order to use any location services on an iOS device, which means the user can choose to allow access. Applications that utilize iBeacon functionality will also appear in the Settings app.

Region Monitoring

An application can be notified when a user enters or exits a region that is defined by a beacon. A beacon region is an area defined by a device's proximity to a Bluetooth LE beacon, not geographical coordinates. In iOS, registered regions persist between launches of an app, so regions associated with an application are monitored at all times, even when the app is in a suspended state or not running.

Regions are a shared application resource, and the number of regions available system-wide is limited. Therefore, a single application is limited to 20 regions that can be monitored simultaneously.

Ranging

The process of determining the approximate proximity of one or more beacons to a device is known as *ranging*. Filters are applied to a distance estimate to determine an estimated proximity to a beacon. iOS defines four proximity states: unknown, immediate, near, and far (see Table 10-1).

***Table 10-1.** Proximity States*

Proximity State	Description
Unknown	Indicates that the proximity of a beacon can't be determined. Ranging may have started, or there are insufficient measurements to determine state.
Immediate	Indicates that a device is physically very close or directly held up to the beacon.
Near	Indicates that a device is approximately within 1 to 3 meters of a beacon. This state may not be reported if there are any obstructions between the device and the beacon.
Far	Indicates that a beacon is detected, but the signal strength is too low to determine a near or immediate state. When in this state, use the accuracy property to determine potential proximity to the beacon.

Core Location will report multiple beacons in an order that's based on a *best guess* of their proximity. This order may not be correct if there are any obstructions that affect signal strength. Also, some beacon devices may emit stronger signals than others, so a device that is physically further away than others may be reported first.

Building the iBeaconApp Application

In this section you'll build a simple dual-purpose application that demonstrates how to scan for specific nearby iBeacons and configure your Bluetooth LE-capable iOS device as an iBeacon transmitter. The app consists of three master scenes: a home scene, a Region Monitor scene, and an iBeacon scene. The home scene provides segues to the other scenes and an indicator label that reflects the current Bluetooth on/off state of the device. The Region Monitor scene supports two basic methods for interacting with beacons, region monitoring and ranging. The iBeacon scene allows you to configure your iOS device as an iBeacon transmitter. Figure 10-1 illustrates the storyboard view of the iBeaconApp.

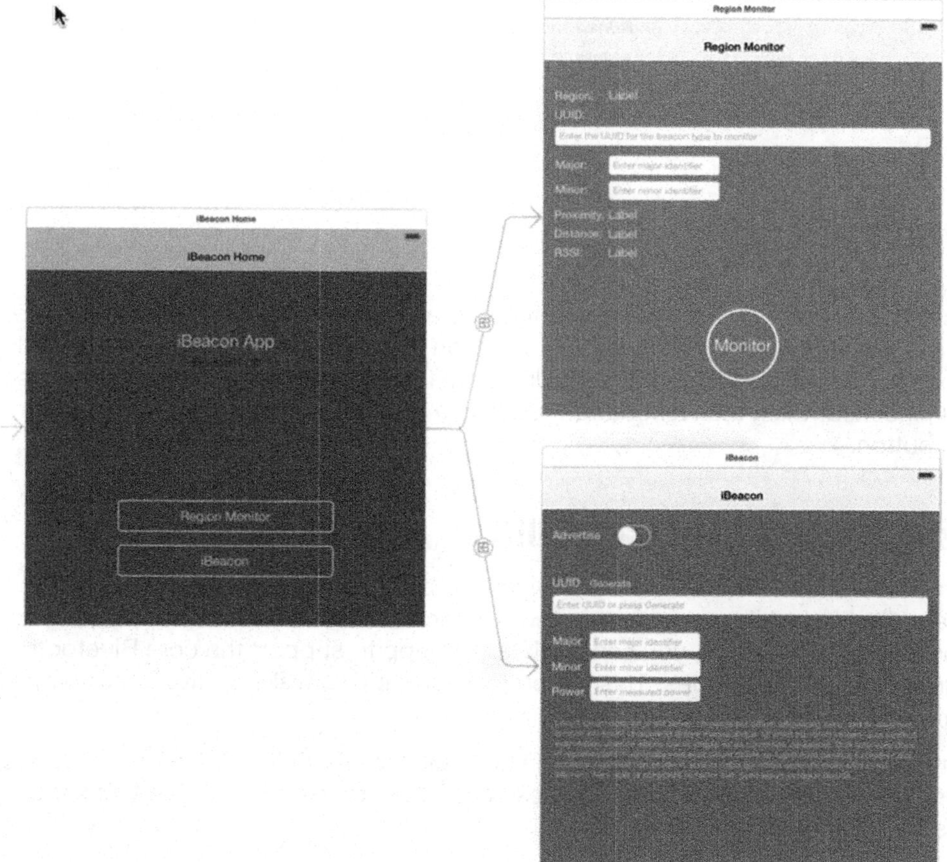

***Figure 10-1.** Storyboard view of iBeaconApp*

Creating the Project

This application will use a single-view application project template. To create a new single-view Swift application project, from Xcode file menu select File ➤ New ➤ Project and you'll be presented with the view shown in Figure 10-2.

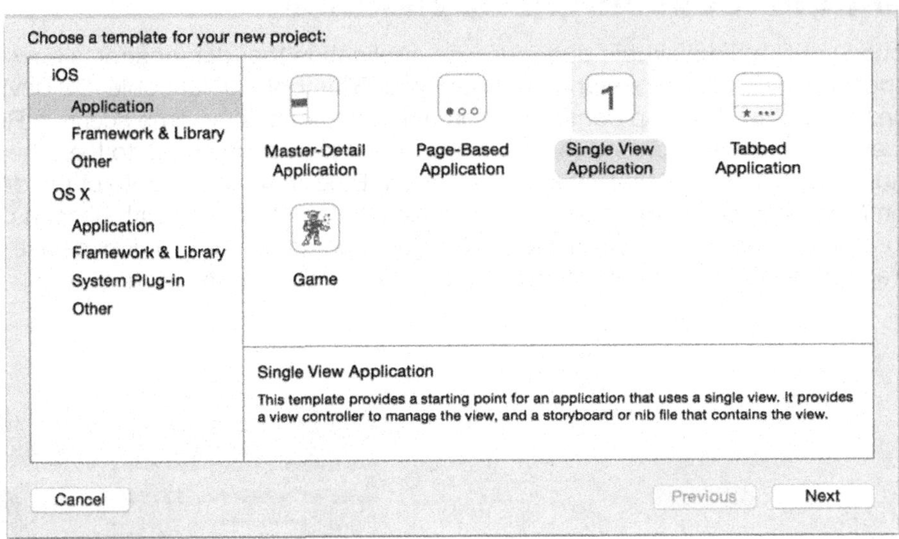

Figure 10-2. Creating a single-view application project

After selecting Next, you'll be prompted to enter a project name, select the language, and select the target device. You can name it iBeacon App or choose another name. Make sure you choose Swift for the language and Universal for the device. Leave the option User Core Data unchecked. Click the Next button, choose a location for your project, and click the Create button.

Setting Background Capabilities

System resources are limited on iOS devices, so by default many of the Core Bluetooth tasks are disabled while your app is in the background. In order for the application to support background mode, you can declare your app to support the core Bluetooth background execution modes. This will enable your app to wake up from a suspended state and process Bluetooth-related events.

From the main project in Xcode select the Capabilities tab. In the Background Modes section, turn the switch to ON, then check Location updates and Acts as a Bluetooth LE accessory (see Figure 10-3).

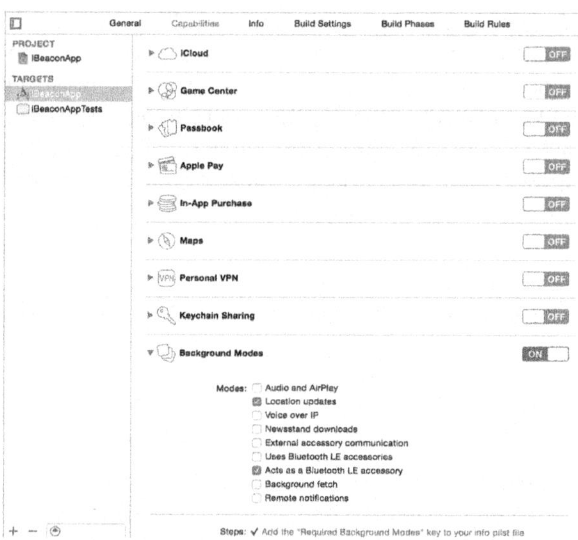

***Figure 10-3.** Setting background capabilities in Xcode*

Enabling the Background Modes option adds the `UIBackgroundModes` key and the corresponding background mode values to your app's `Info.plist` file. Table 10-2 lists the background modes you must specify so your iOS device can act as an iBeacon transmitter.

***Table 10-2.** Xcode Background Settings*

Xcode Background Mode	UIBackgroundMode Value	Description
Location updates	Location	The app keeps users informed of their location, even while it is running in the background.
Acts as a Bluetooth LE accessory	Bluetooth-peripheral	The app supports Bluetooth communication in peripheral mode through the Core Bluetooth framework. Note: using this mode requires user authorization.

Building the Home Scene

In this section you'll build out the home master scene. It's assumed that you're already familiar with the basics of building an application and using Interface Builder, so this section will briefly cover creating a project, how to add user interface (UI) elements, adding constraints, and how to connect interface behaviors to your code.

The scene is very basic. It will contain a label for the app title, a label that will be used as an indicator for the Bluetooth power status, and two custom buttons used to segue to the other scenes (see Figure 10-1).

The first thing you need to add is a navigation controller. Its primary job is to manage the presentation of your view controllers as well as providing a back button that makes it easy to return to the previous level. Open up the `Main.storyboard` and select the view controller from either the storyboard or the Document Outline. Then from the menu, select Editor ➤ Embed In ➤ Navigation Controller. Xcode will add a v controller to the storyboard, set it as the Storyboard Entry Point, and add a relationship between the navigation controller and the existing view controller. Your storyboard should look like the one in Figure 10-4.

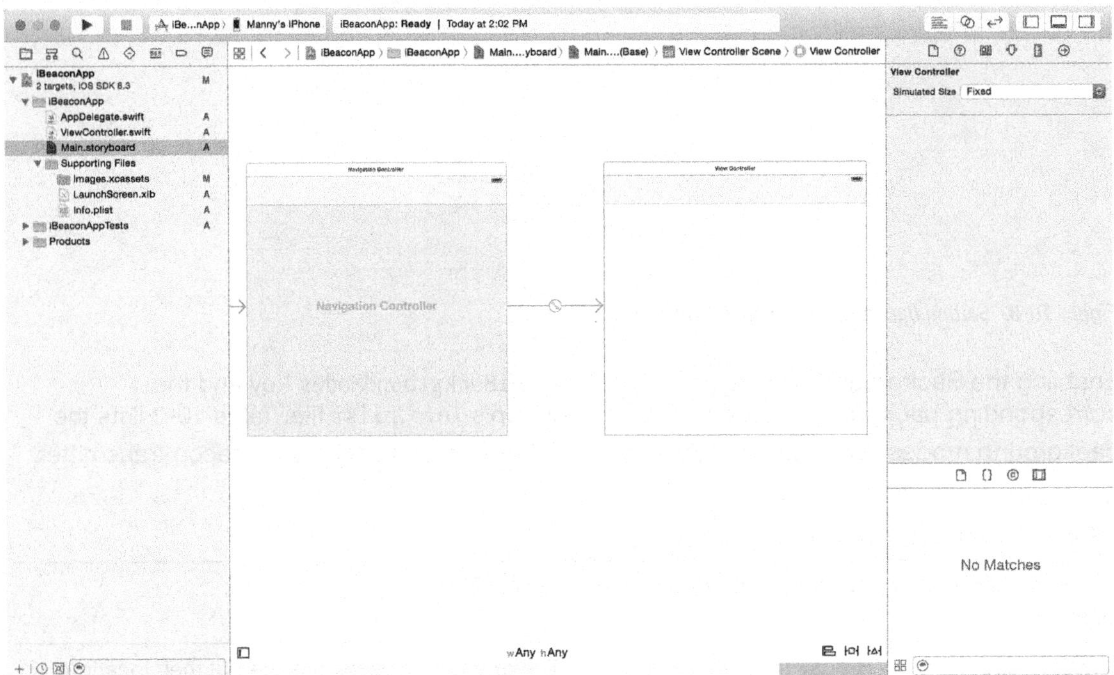

***Figure 10-4.** Adding a Navigation Controller*

At this point, you should be able to build and run your app. If all goes well you should see an empty white scene.

Setting Up UI Elements

On the storyboard, double-click the navigation bar of the view controller and set the title text of the navigation item to iBeacon Home. Now select the view inside view controller and then, from Attributes Inspector, change the color of the background to 0066CC.

For the application title, drag a `UILabel` from the Object library to the center of the storyboard. With the label selected, open the Utilities panel and use the Attributes Inspector to set the text to *iBeacon App* (or to the name you chose for the app). Set the font color to white, the font size to 26, and the text alignment to centered. With the label still selected, use the Align control and select Horizontal Center in Container to create an X alignment constraint. Control-drag upward from the label to the View and select Top Space to Top Layout Guide to create a Vertical Space constraint.

For the Bluetooth indicator, add another `UILabel` just below the title label and set the text to Bluetooth Off. Set the font color to FF0000, the font size to 17, and the text alignment to centered. Use the Align control and select Horizontal Center in Container to create an X alignment constraint. Control-drag upward from the label to the title label directly above and select Vertical Spacing.

Creating an Outlet Connection

Now connect an outlet from the label to the `ViewController` implementation. Using the *Document Outline*, control-click the *Bluetooth Off* label and drag a connection from the *New Referencing Outlet* well and drop it onto the controller source (see Figure 10-5).

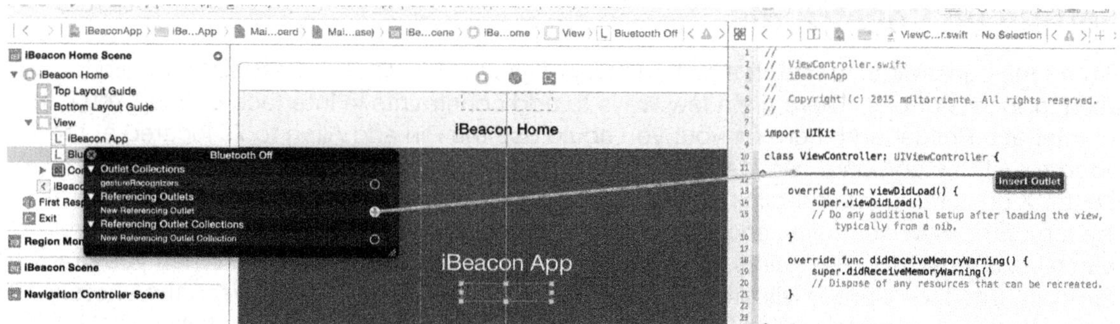

Figure 10-5. Connecting a new referencing outlet

In the pop-up, name the outlet `bluetoothStateLabel` and click the Connect button (see Figure 10-6).

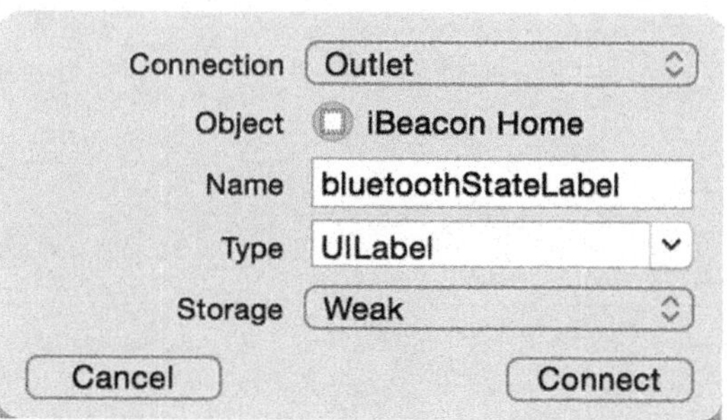

Figure 10-6. Naming the outlet connection

Your `ViewController` class should now have an `IBOutlet` defined.

```
@IBOutlet weak var bluetoothStateLabel: UILabel!
```

Later in this chapter, you'll utilize the Core Bluetooth framework and start up a central manager and use it to determine the Bluetooth state and set the indicator accordingly.

There are two custom buttons on the home screen that you will use to switch between different modes of operation. The steps that follow will guide you through the process of adding the first button, and then you can repeat those steps to add the second button.

Add a `UIButton` to the scene and place it below the Bluetooth indicator label. From the Attributes Inspector, set the button title to Region Monitor, set the font size to 20.0, and set the text color to white. In the Button section, set the Shows Touch on Highlight to *checked* so when a user presses the button, there will be a white glow where the touch event occurred on the button. Don't worry about the button size and borders; you'll fix that shortly.

Setting up Constraints

Set up the constraints to match those shown in Figure 10-7. These constraints should be used for both buttons. There are a few ways to add constraints in Interface Builder. You can let Interface Builder add them for you; you could use the Pin and Align tools located at the bottom on the storyboard canvas; or you can control-drag between views. To create an Align Center X constraint, control-click on the Region Monitor button and drag vertically toward the top of the view controller, and then release the mouse. A pop-up menu is displayed with a list of possible constraints. Choose Center Horizontally in Container. When you drag vertically, Interface Builder will present options to set vertical spacing between the views, and options to horizontally align the views. Likewise, when you drag horizontally, you'll be presented with options to set the horizontal spacing between the views and options to vertically align the view. Both gestures may include other options such as setting the view size.

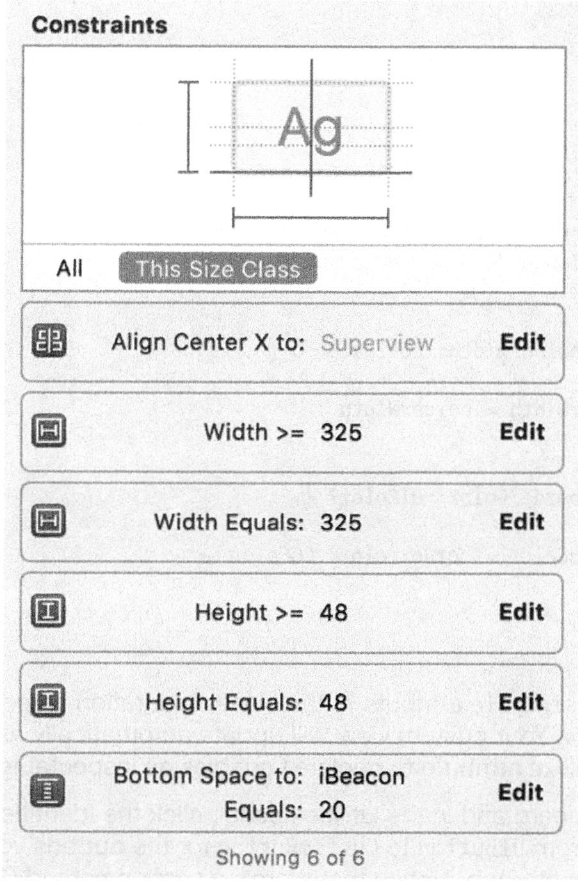

Figure 10-7. Setting up button constraints

Creating a Custom Button

You don't see the border around the buttons because there isn't a way to set all the required layer properties for the view from Interface Builder alone. This is where the new Xcode Live Rendering feature comes into play.

> **Tip** Use the Interface Builder Live Rendering feature in Xcode 6 to design and inspect a custom view. The custom view will render in Interface Builder and appear as it will in your application

Start by adding a new Swift file to your project named `CustomButton.swift`, and declare the class `CustomButton` a subclass of `UIButton` using the new `IBDesignable` attribute (Listing 10-1). Then add inspectable properties using `IBInspectable` for `cornerRadius`, `borderWidth`, and `borderColor`.

Listing 10-1. CustomButton Class

```
import UIKit

@IBDesignable
class CustomButton: UIButton {
    @IBInspectable var cornerRadius: CGFloat = 0 {
        didSet {
            layer.cornerRadius = cornerRadius
            layer.masksToBounds = cornerRadius > 0
        }
    }
    @IBInspectable var borderWidth: CGFloat = 0 {
        didSet {
            layer.borderWidth = borderWidth
        }
    }
    @IBInspectable var borderColor: UIColor? {
        didSet {
            layer.borderColor = borderColor?.CGColor
        }
    }
}
```

When you add the `IBDesignable` attribute to the class declaration, Interface Builder will render your custom view. Your custom view will update automatically as you make changes by using the `IBInspectable` attribute to declare variables as inspectable properties.

Now open up the storyboard and in the Utilities panel, click the Identities Inspector tab and change the class type from `UIButton` to `CustomButton` for the buttons you just created. Now click the Attributes Inspector tab. Notice that there's a section named Custom Button with a field for each of the inspectable properties you declared. Set the values for Corner Radius to 6; set the Border Width to 2; set the Border Color to White Color. Your buttons should now look similar to those in Figure 10-8.

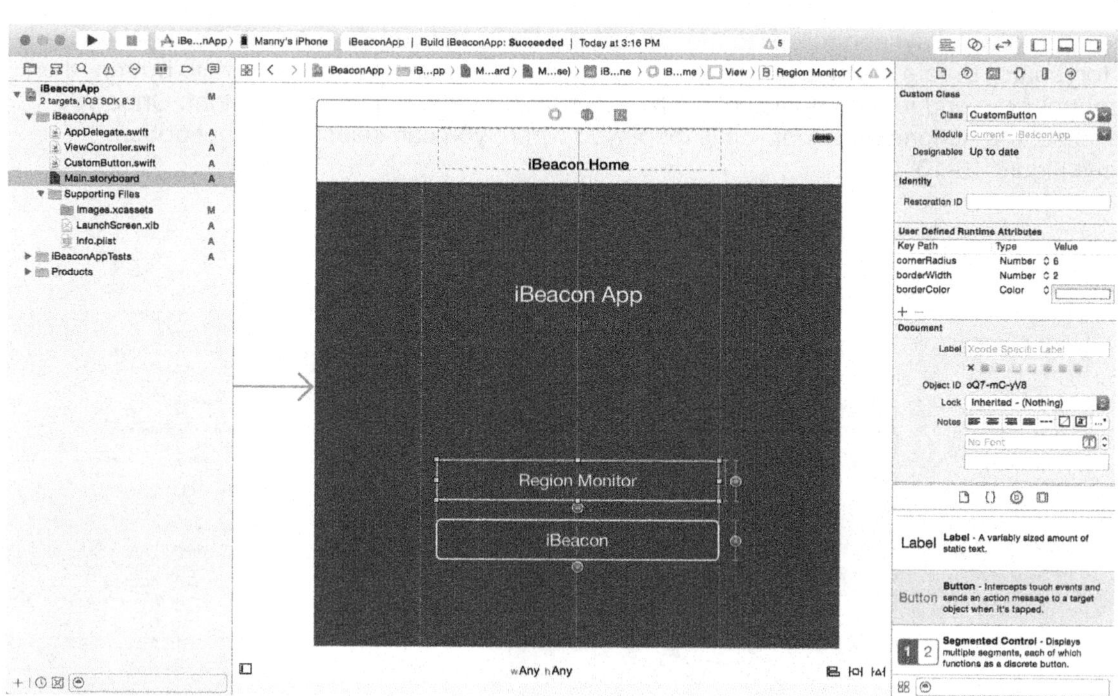

***Figure 10-8.** Configuring a CustomButton*

Build and run the app to make sure the constraints are set properly and your scene looks similar to the mock-up in Figure 10-1.

Next you'll be adding two new scenes to the storyboard, one for each button you've just added. Start by renaming the file `ViewController.swift` to `HomeViewController.swift` so it can be easily identified later on. Currently, Xcode doesn't support the Refactor feature with Swift, so you'll have to manually rename the class in the source file as well as in the storyboard. Select the view controller from the Identity Inspector, manually type it in or select HomeViewController from the pulldown (see Figure 10-9). You must do this in order to connect interface elements to your code.

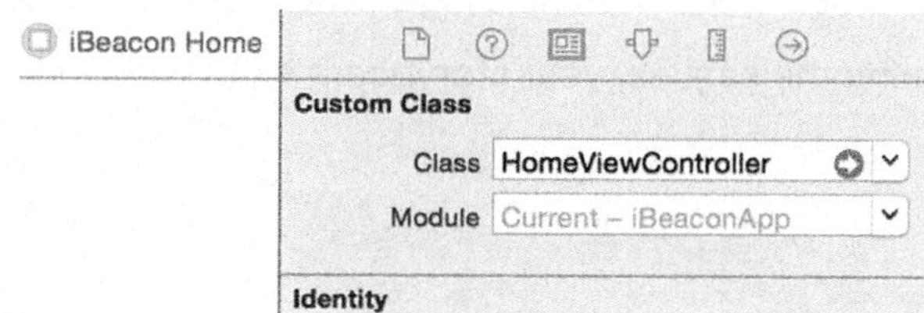

***Figure 10-9.** Assigning View Controller identity*

Now drag two view controllers to the right of the iBeacon Home view controller on the storyboard. Create a segue to each view controller by selecting the appropriate button, then control-drag and release on top of each view controller you placed on the right. Once you release, the Action Segue pop-up is displayed where you can select the *show* option (see Figure 10-10).

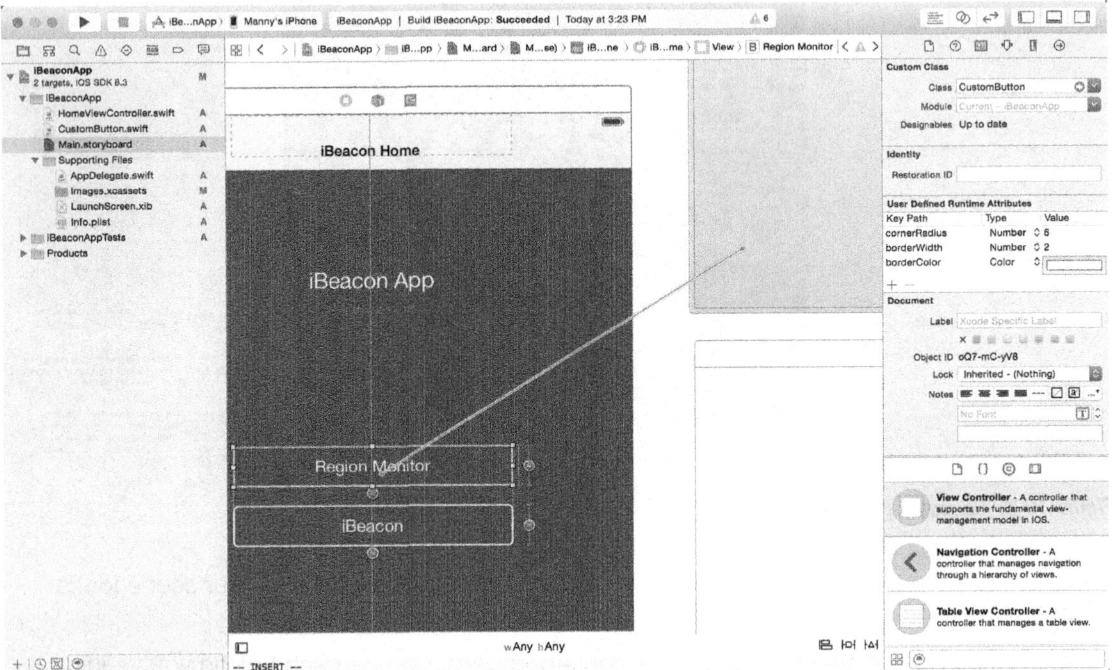

Figure 10-10. Creating a segue to a new scene

For each segue you've just created, select the connector on the storyboard, and then from the Attributes Inspector set the identifier. Use the names *RegionMonitorSegue* and *iBeaconSegue*

For each scene, drag a navigation item from the Object Library onto the navigation bar area. Set the names to match those in the buttons, Region Monitor and iBeacon.

When you're finish creating the segues, your storyboard should look similar to the one in Figure 10-11.

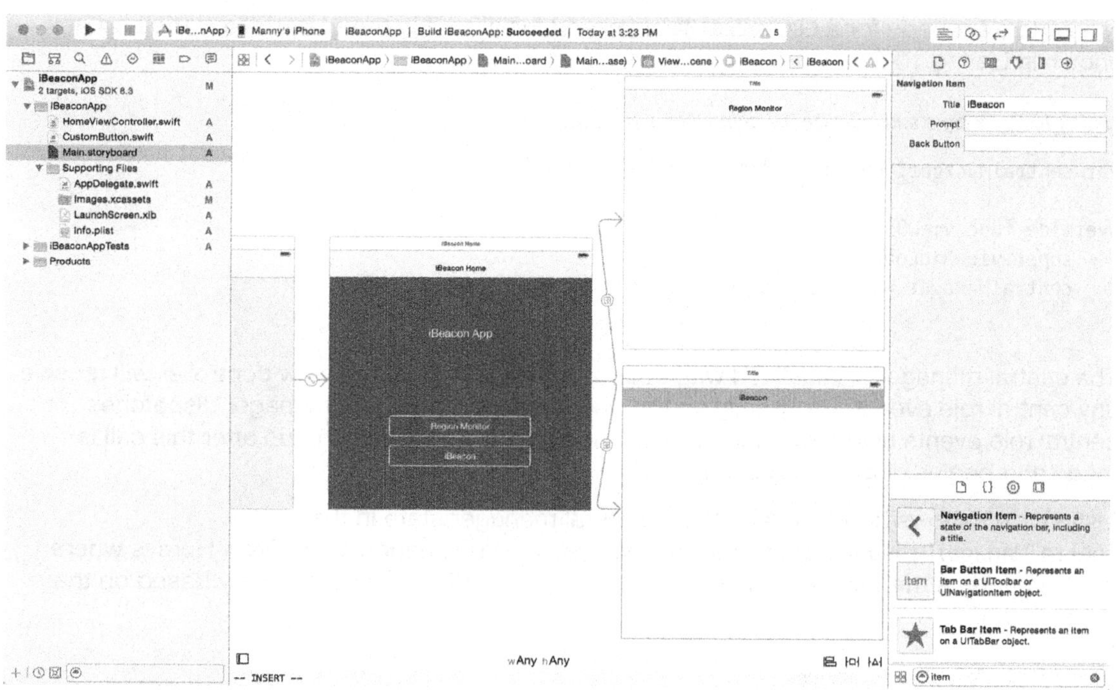

Figure 10-11. Home scene with segues

Build and run the application, tap the buttons, and verify that the segues and navigation controls are working as expected.

Detecting Bluetooth State

In this section, you'll learn how to start up a central manager and use it to determine if a device supports Bluetooth LE and is available to use on the central device.

The `CBCentralManager` object is a Core Bluetooth representation of a central role device. When you initialize a central manager, it calls the `centralManagerDidUpdateState` method of its delegate. This means you must adopt the delegate protocol and implement this required method.

Open the `HomeViewController.swift` file and import the framework and add the `CBCentralManagerDelegate` protocol to your class declaration.

```
import CoreBluetooth

class HomeViewController: UIViewController, CBCentralManagerDelegate {
```

You'll see an error indicator, which says that the HomeViewController does not conform to protocol. That's because you need to implement the required delegate method.

```
func centralManagerDidUpdateState(central: CBCentralManager) {

}
```

Now add a property for a CBCentralManager and initialize it in the viewDidLoad method as shown in Listing 10-2.

Listing 10-2. Declare and initialize the centralManager property

```
var centralManager: CBCentralManager!

override func viewDidLoad() {
    super.viewDidLoad()
    centralManager = CBCentralManager(delegate: self, queue: nil)
}
```

The central manager is initialized with self as the delegate so the view controller will receive any central role events. By specifying the queue as nil, the central manager dispatches central role events using the main queue. The central manager starts up after this call is made and begins dispatching events.

Listing 10-3 shows how to examine the central manager state in the centralManagerDidUpdateState callback when the state change event fires. Here is where you can update the text and text color of the bluetoothStateLabel property based on the central state.

Listing 10-3. Central State Change

```
func centralManagerDidUpdateState(central: CBCentralManager) {
    switch (central.state) {
    case .PoweredOn:
        isBluetoothPoweredOn = true
        bluetoothStateLabel.text = "Bluetooth ON"
        bluetoothStateLabel.textColor = UIColor.greenColor()
    case .PoweredOff:
        isBluetoothPoweredOn = false
        bluetoothStateLabel.text = "Bluetooth OFF"
        bluetoothStateLabel.textColor = UIColor.redColor()
    default:
        break
    }
}
```

As we discussed in Chapter 9, the PoweredOn state indicates that the central device supports Bluetooth LE and the Bluetooth is on and available for use. The PoweredOff state indicates that Bluetooth is either turned off or the device doesn't support Bluetooth LE.

Build and run the application. If your device has Bluetooth enabled, the indicator label should read "Bluetooth On" and its color should be green. Use the slide-up settings panel to turn Bluetooth off. The indicator label should now read "Bluetooth Off" and its color should be red.

Add a Boolean property `isBluetoothPoweredOn` near the top of the `HomeViewController` class that will be used to reflect the Bluetooth state.

```
var isBluetoothPoweredOn: Bool = false
```

Set its value in the `centralManagerDidUpdateState` method accordingly, as shown in Figure 10-3. You'll use this value to determine whether or not transition is allowed to any other scene.

The `UIViewController` provides an override method which allows you to control whether a particular segue should be performed. Open `HomeViewController.swift` and add the method `shouldPerformSegueWithIdentifier` to the `ViewController` class (see Listing 10-4).

Listing 10-4. Override Method to Control Segue

```
override func shouldPerformSegueWithIdentifier(identifier: String, sender: AnyObject?) -> Bool {
    if identifier == "RegionMonitorSegue" || identifier == "iBeaconSegue" || identifier ==
    "ConfigureSegue" {
        if !isBluetoothPoweredOn {
            showAlertForSettings()
            return false;
        }
    }
    return true
}
```

When a segue is initiated, this method will be called with the string value that identifies the triggered segue and the object that initiated the segue. The return value for this method should be true if you want the segue to be executed; otherwise, return false.

In this method you're only interested in the identifier; the sender object is for informational purposes and can be ignored here. Compare the identifier value with the constants you defined earlier. If you find a match, then check the Bluetooth state. If Bluetooth is powered on, you can allow the segue to execute by returning a value of true.

In the case in which Bluetooth is powered off, you want to display an alert and provide an option to go to the Settings app where the Bluetooth setting can be changed. Add the method shown in Listing 10-5 to the `ViewController` class. Call this method from within the `shouldPerformSegueWithIdentifier` method as shown in Listing 10-4.

Listing 10-5. Configure and Present an Alert

```
private func showAlertForSettings() {
    let alertController = UIAlertController(title: "iBeacon App", message: "Turn On
    Bluetooth!", preferredStyle: .Alert)

    let cancelAction = UIAlertAction(title: "Settings", style: .Cancel) { (action) in
        if let url = NSURL(string:UIApplicationOpenSettingsURLString) {
            UIApplication.sharedApplication().openURL(url)
        }
    }
```

```
    alertController.addAction(cancelAction)

    let okAction = UIAlertAction(title: "OK", style: .Default, handler: nil)
    alertController.addAction(okAction)

    self.presentViewController(alertController, animated: true, completion: nil)
}
```

This method configures a `UIAlertController` object to display an alert modally with a title, message, and a style. Additionally, actions are associated with the controller. The cancel action is labeled *Settings*, and is used to open the Settings app. The OK action is used to simply dismiss the alert.

Build and run the application. Turn Bluetooth off, then press each button to verify that the alert is displayed and access to the other scenes is prohibited. Press the Settings button on the alert to make sure it opens the Settings app.

Building the Region Monitor Scene

In this section, you'll build the master scene for the Region Monitor as shown in Figure 10-12. The Region Monitor will support two basic methods for interacting with beacons, region monitoring and ranging. The UI will utilize four labels to display the status during monitoring, and three input fields where the user can enter information to scan for a specific beacon type. There will be a single custom button used to toggle monitoring on and off.

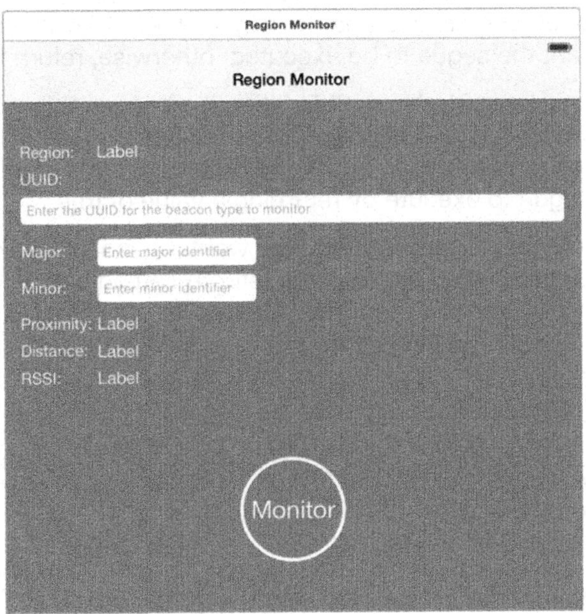

Figure 10-12. Region Monitor scene mock-up

Create a new Swift file named RegionMonitorViewController.swift and declare the class RegionMonitorViewController as a subclass of UIViewController. Then adopt the protocol for UITextFieldDelegate by adding the UITextFieldDelegate protocol declaration.

```
import UIKit
import CoreLocation

class RegionMonitorViewController: UIViewController, UITextFieldDelegate,
RegionMonitorDelegate {

}
```

Assign the RegionMonitorViewController as the class for the Region Monitor identity by opening the storyboard and selecting the Region Monitor scene. In the Utilities panel on the right, click the Identity Inspector tab. In the Custom Class section, use the class drop-down to select *RegionMonitorViewController*.

Set the background color to for the Region Monitor view to FF6600. Add a UIButton to the scene and place it so that it looks similar to Figure 10-12. Set the button title to Monitor, the text color to white, and the font size to 26.0. In the Utilities panel, click the Identities Inspector tab and change the class type from UIButton to CustomButton. Click the Size Inspector tab and set both the width and height to 110. Now click the Attributes Inspector tab. In the section named Custom Button set the values for Corner Radius to 55, Border Width to 4, and Border Color to White Color. In the Button section, set the Shows Touch on Highlight to checked so when a user presses the button, there will be a white glow where the touch event occurred on the button.

Next, add UILabel and UITextField objects to the scene such that it looks similar to the one in Figure 10-13. The yellow tags A, B, C, and D are labels that will be used to display status related to ranged beacons. The blue tags 1, 2, and 3 are text fields that are used as search criteria when monitoring beacons. The property names correspond to those in Table 10-3.

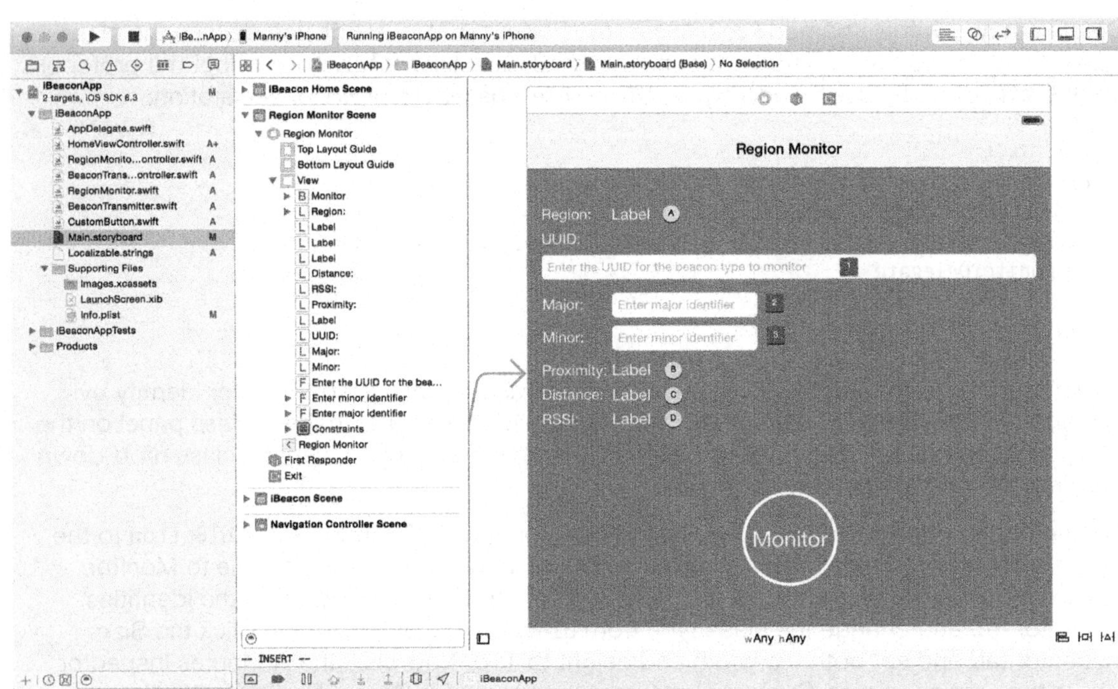

***Figure 10-13.** Region Monitor scene after label and text field placement*

***Table 10-3.** Region Monitoring Properties*

Tag	Property Name	Description
A	regionIdLabel	This is a `CLBeaconRegion` identifier: a user-defined unique identifier to associate with the returned region object. You use this identifier to differentiate regions within your application. This value must not be nil.
B	proximityLabel	This value corresponds to the `CLProximity` constants that represents the relative distance to the beacon: unknown, immediate, near, far.
C	distanceLabel	This value is the estimated distance in meters to a beacon. You can use this value to differentiate between beacons with the same proximity values. A negative value signifies that the accuracy could not be determined.
D	rssiLabel	This value represents the average received signal strength indicator. It's a measurement of the power present in a received radio signal in decibels.
1	uuidTextField	This is a unique identifier of the beacon being targeted; use this to identify your beacon. You typically generate only one UUID for your beacons. You can use the `uuidgen` command-line tool to generate this value.
2	majorTextField	The value identifying a group of beacons.
3	minorTextField	The value identifying a specific beacon within a group.

You should already be familiar enough with autolayout and constraints, so we won't cover that topic here. For each of the UITextField objects, you can add placeholder text that will be visible when a field is empty. The placeholder text is a hint to the user as to what information is expected to be input in each of the fields. From the Attributes Inspector, set the Capitalization field for the *uuidTextField* object to All Characters. For the majorTextField and the minorTextField objects, set the Keyboard Type to Number Pad.

Open the Main.storyboard file and select the Region Monitor scene. For each of the UI objects that you'll be interacting with programmatically, connect an outlet to the view controller by control-dragging and dropping them inside the view controller implementation and name each accordingly (see Listing 10-6).

***Listing 10-6.** The RegionMonitorViewController class declaration*

```
class RegionMonitorViewController: UIViewController, UITextFieldDelegate, RegionMonitorDelegate {

    let kUUIDKey = "monitor-proximityUUID"
    let kMajorIdKey = "monitor-transmit-majorId"
    let kMinorIdKey = "monitor-transmit-minorId"

    let uuidDefault = "2F234454-CF6D-4A0F-ADF2-F4911BA9FFA6"

    @IBOutlet weak var regionIdLabel: UILabel!
    @IBOutlet weak var uuidTextField: UITextField!
    @IBOutlet weak var majorTextField: UITextField!
    @IBOutlet weak var minorTextField: UITextField!
    @IBOutlet weak var proximityLabel: UILabel!
    @IBOutlet weak var distanceLabel: UILabel!
    @IBOutlet weak var rssiLabel: UILabel!
    @IBOutlet weak var monitorButton: UIButton!
}
```

The UITextField objects will be taking user input, so a keyboard will be presented. You'll want to know when the user starts and stops editing to perform certain actions. In order to handle messages sent as part of the text editing sequence, implement the delegate methods textFieldDidBeginEditing and textFieldDidEndEditing shown in Listing 10-7. When the text fields take focus, you want to present a Done button in the navigation bar so the user can dismiss the keyboard as needed. As a convenience, when the user leaves each field, the values the user entered are stored in the standard user defaults and used to initialize the text fields.

***Listing 10-7.** Implementing UITextField Delegate Methods*

```
// MARK: UITextFieldDelegate methods

func textFieldDidBeginEditing(textField: UITextField) {
    navigationItem.rightBarButtonItem = doneButton
}

func textFieldDidEndEditing(textField: UITextField) {

    let defaults = NSUserDefaults.standardUserDefaults()
```

```
    if textField == uuidTextField && !textField.text!.isEmpty {
        defaults.setObject(textField.text, forKey: kUUIDKey)
    }
    else if textField == majorTextField && !textField.text!.isEmpty {
        defaults.setObject(textField.text, forKey: kMajorIdKey)
    }
    else if textField == minorTextField && !textField.text!.isEmpty {
        defaults.setObject(textField.text, forKey: kMinorIdKey)
    }
}
```

Override the `viewDidLoad` method and set the text field delegates to `self`, otherwise you won't receive any notifications. The `doneButton` property is initialized only once and is used to set the `navigationItem.rightBarButtonItem` each time text field takes focus. Notice that in the last parameter to `UIBarButtonItem` initializer, the action is set to "dismissKeyboard" (see Listing 10-8). This corresponds to a method you define. The action is called automatically for you when the user taps the Done button.

***Listing 10-8.** Property Initialization in the RegionMonitorViewController Class*

```
override func viewDidLoad() {
    super.viewDidLoad()
    uuidTextField.delegate = self
    majorTextField.delegate = self
    minorTextField.delegate = self
    doneButton = UIBarButtonItem(title: "Done", style: UIBarButtonItemStyle.Done, target: self,
    action: "dismissKeyboard")
    initFromDefaultValues()
}

func dismissKeyboard() {
    uuidTextField.resignFirstResponder()
    majorTextField.resignFirstResponder()
    minorTextField.resignFirstResponder()
    navigationItem.rightBarButtonItem = nil
}
```

When initializing the text fields from user defaults, you can use the Optional Binding feature of Swift.

```
if let uuid = defaults.stringForKey(kUUIDKey) {
    uuidTextField.text = uuid
}
```

> **Tip** Use *optional binding* to find out whether an optional contains a value or not. It's a clean way to check for a value inside an optional and extract it in a single line of code (see Listing 10-9).

Listing 10-9. Initialization from User Defaults Using Optional Binding in the RegionMonitorViewController Class

```
private func initFromDefaultValues() {
    let defaults = NSUserDefaults.standardUserDefaults()
    if let uuid = defaults.stringForKey(kUUIDKey) {
        uuidTextField.text = uuid
    }
    if let major = defaults.stringForKey(kMajorIdKey) {
        majorTextField.text = major
    }
    if let minor = defaults.stringForKey(kMinorIdKey) {
        minorTextField.text = minor
    }
}
```

To make sure the user defaults are persisted, call the `NSUserDefaults.synchronize()` method when the app is about to go in the background or exit. Take note that this method is called periodically in the background so you shouldn't need to call it at any other time. Add the method from Listing 10-10 to the `RegionMonitorViewController` class.

Listing 10-10. Persisting Defaults When the Application Is About to Go in the Background

```
override func viewWillDisappear(animated: Bool) {
    NSUserDefaults.standardUserDefaults().synchronize()
}
```

The RegionMonitor Class

The `RegionMonitor` class manages all the interactions with `CLLocationManager`. At appropriate times, the Region Monitor will inform its delegate, the view controller, of events that it handled, or that it is about to handle.

Using the Delegation Pattern

For region monitoring, you'll utilize the Delegation pattern, which is commonly used by Apple frameworks. The delegate is typically a Custom Controller object that acts on behalf of another object.

You'll implement the pattern by defining a protocol for a `RegionMonitorDelegate`. The `RegionMonitorViewController` will adopt this protocol and implement the methods that respond to Location Monitoring actions. You'll create a new class `RegionMonitor` that will be the delegating object. It will hold a weak reference to the `RegionMonitorViewController` that will act as the delegate. The `RegionMonitor` object will act as the delegate for the `CLLocationManager` object. The example sequence diagram in Figure 10-14 illustrates the interaction between the objects.

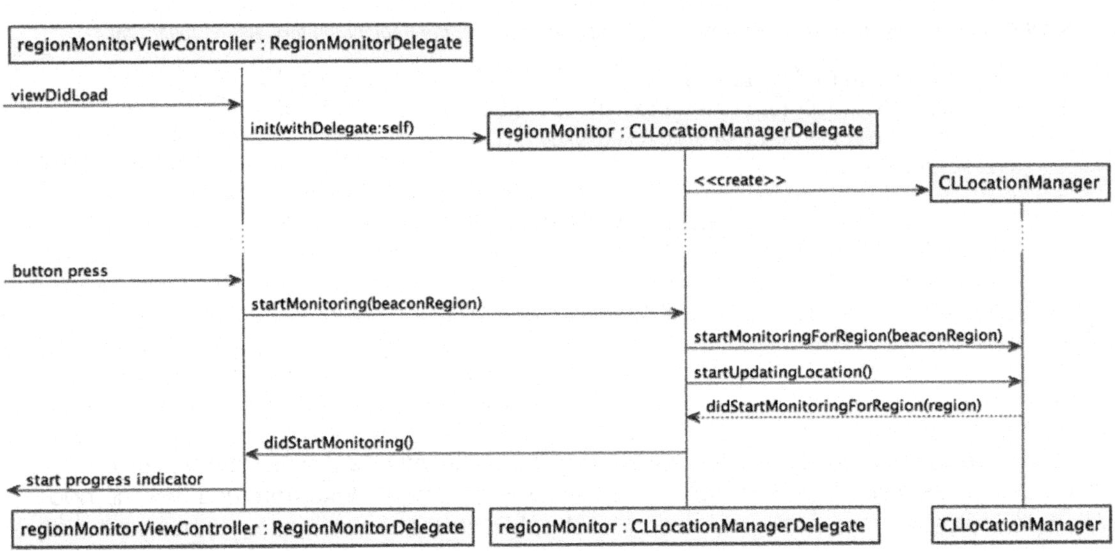

***Figure 10-14.** Sequence diagram—delegation pattern example*

Create a new Swift file named `RegionMonitor.swift` and define a protocol for `RegionMonitorDelegate` as shown in Listing 10-11.

***Listing 10-11.** Defining the RegionMonitorDelegate protocol*

```
protocol RegionMonitorDelegate: NSObjectProtocol {
    func onBackgroundLocationAccessDisabled()
    func didStartMonitoring()
    func didStopMonitoring()
    func didEnterRegion(region: CLRegion!)
    func didExitRegion(region: CLRegion!)
    func didRangeBeacon(beacon: CLBeacon!, region: CLRegion!)
    func onError(error: NSError)
}
```

Creating the RegionMonitor Class

Next, in the file `RegionMonitor.swift` below `RegionMonitorDelegate`, declare the class `RegionMonitor` as a subclass of `NSObject`, and adopt the protocol for `CLLocationManagerDelegate`. Also, you'll need to import CoreLocation. Then add properties (Listing 10-12) for `CLLocationManager`, `CLBeaconRegion`, `CLBeacon`, and `RegionMonitorDelegate`.

***Listing 10-12.** RegionMonitor Class Declaration*

```
class RegionMonitor: NSObject, CLLocationManagerDelegate {

    var locationManager: CLLocationManager!
    var beaconRegion: CLBeaconRegion?
```

```
    var rangedBeacon: CLBeacon! = CLBeacon()
    var pendingMonitorRequest: Bool = false

    weak var delegate: RegionMonitorDelegate?
}
```

You'll want to store a strong reference to the CLLocationManager, but you must make sure that you declare the delegate property for RegionMonitorDelegate as weak to avoid a strong reference cycle. A strong reference cycle will prevent RegionMonitorDelegate from being deallocated, which will cause a memory leak in your application. Also, a weak reference is allowed to have "no value," so it must be declared an optional type. We cover the property pendingMonitorRequest later in section **RegionMonitor Methods**.

Now implement an initializer method (Listing 10-13) that will be called when you create a new instance of RegionMonitor. The primary role of an initializer is to ensure that a new instance of a type is set up properly before first use.

***Listing 10-13.** RegionMonitor Initializer Method*

```
init(delegate: RegionMonitorDelegate) {
    super.init()
    self.delegate = delegate
    self.locationManager = CLLocationManager()
    self.locationManager!.delegate = self
}
```

The initializer starts by calling super.init(), which calls the initializer of RegionMonitor class's super class, NSObject. Then the locationManager property is initialized with an instance of CLLocationManager and then initializes self as its delegate. Finally, the delegate property is initialized with the RegionMonitorDelegate object that is passed as a parameter.

Delegate Methods

onBackgroundLocationAccessDisabled

The onBackgroundLocationAccessDisabled delegate method is called after RegionMonitor invokes CLLocationManager.authorizationStatus and receives a return value of Restricted, Denied, or AuthorizedWhenInUse. The delegate should respond to this notification by prompting the user to change his location access settings. Add the code shown in Listing 10-14 to the RegionMonitorViewController class.

***Listing 10-14.** Constructing a Location Access Settings Alert in the RegionMonitorViewController Class*

```
func onBackgroundLocationAccessDisabled() {
    let alertController = UIAlertController(
        title: NSLocalizedString("regmon.alert.title.location-access-disabled", comment: "foo"),
        message: NSLocalizedString("regmon.alert.message.location-access-disabled",
        comment: "foo"),
        preferredStyle: .Alert)
```

```
    alertController.addAction(UIAlertAction(title: "Cancel", style: .Cancel, handler: nil))

    alertController.addAction(
        UIAlertAction(title: "Settings", style: .Default) { (action) in
            if let url = NSURL(string:UIApplicationOpenSettingsURLString) {
                UIApplication.sharedApplication().openURL(url)
            }
        })
    self.presentViewController(alertController, animated: true, completion: nil)
}
```

> **Note** `NSLocalizedString` is used to pull string resources from a file. You can add a file to your project named `Localizable.strings` and define your strings there. The format is simple, one string per line: `"regmon.alert.title.location-access-disabled" = "Background Location Access is Disabled";`

The code from Listing 10-14 will present an alert prompting (Figure 10-15) the user to change the location access settings.

Background Location Access is Disabled

Please change the location access to "Always" in app setttings.

Cancel Settings

***Figure 10-15.** Prompt for location access settings change*

didStartMonitoring

The `didStartMonitoring` delegate method is called when `RegionMonitor` receives the notification `didStartMonitoringForRegion` from `CLLocationManager`. The delegate can respond to this notification by updating its state and displaying a progress indicator. Add the code shown in Listing 10-15 to the `RegionMonitorViewController` class.

***Listing 10-15.** Delegate Method didStartMonitoring in the RegionMonitorViewController Class*

```
func didStartMonitoring() {
    isMonitoring = true
    monitorButton.rotate(0.0, toValue: CGFloat(M_PI * 2), completionDelegate: self)
}
```

didStopMonitoring

The didStopMonitoring delegate method is called when the RegionMonitor.stopMonitoring method is called. The delegate can respond to this notification by updating its state. Add the code shown in Listing 10-16 to the RegionMonitorViewController class.

Listing 10-16. Delegate Method didStopMonitoring in the RegionMonitorViewController Class

```
func didStopMonitoring() {
    isMonitoring = false
}
```

didEnterRegion

The didEnterRegion delegate method is called when RegionMonitor receives the notification didEnterRegion from CLLocationManager. The CLRegion object is passed as a parameter and is provided to the delegate. The delegate can respond to this notification by providing feedback to the user. Add the code shown in Listing 10-17 to the RegionMonitorViewController class.

Listing 10-17. Delegate Method didEnterRegion in the RegionMonitorViewController Class

```
func didEnterRegion(region: CLRegion!) {

}
```

didExitRegion

The didExitRegion delegate method is called when RegionMonitor receives the notification didExitRegion from CLLocationManager. The CLRegion object is passed as a parameter and is provided to the delegate. The delegate can respond to this notification by providing feedback to the user. Add the code shown in Listing 10-18 to the RegionMonitorViewController class.

Listing 10-18. Delegate Method didExitRegion in the RegionMonitorViewController Class

```
func didExitRegion(region: CLRegion!) {

}
```

didRangeBeacon

The didRangeBeacon delegate method is called when RegionMonitor receives the notification didRangeBeacons from CLLocationManager. The RegionMonitor is passed an array of CLBeacon objects and determines which one is the closest. That CLBeacon object is provided to the delegate. The delegate can respond to this0 notification by providing feedback to the user. Add the code shown in Listing 10-19 to the RegionMonitorViewController class.

Listing 10-19. Delegate Method didRangeBeacon in the RegionMonitorViewController Class

```
func didRangeBeacon(beacon: CLBeacon!, region: CLRegion!) {
    regionIdLabel.text = region.identifier
    uuidTextField.text = beacon.proximityUUID.UUIDString
    majorTextField.text = "\(beacon.major)"
    minorTextField.text = "\(beacon.minor)"

    switch (beacon.proximity) {
    case CLProximity.Far:
        proximityLabel.text = "Far"
    case CLProximity.Near:
        proximityLabel.text = "Near"
    case CLProximity.Immediate:
        proximityLabel.text = "Immediate"
    case CLProximity.Unknown:
        proximityLabel.text = "unknown"
    }

    distanceLabel.text = distanceFormatter.stringFromMeters(beacon.accuracy)

    rssiLabel.text = "\(beacon.rssi)"
}
```

> **Caution** Formatters are expensive to create. It's recommended that you create an instance once and reuse that instance.

Add a property to the RegionMonitorViewController class.

```
let distanceFormatter = NSLengthFormatter()
```

Notice the distanceLabel text is set using a specialized formatter object NSLengthFormatter. The formatter provides property formatted, localized descriptions of linear distances.

onError

The onError delegate method is called when RegionMonitor encounters an error. An NSError object is provided to the delegate. The delegate can respond to this notification by handling the error and/or providing feedback to the user. This notification is currently ignored by this example app. Add the code shown in Listing 10-20 to the RegionMonitorViewController class.

Listing 10-20. Delegate Method onError in the RegionMonitorViewController Class

```
func onError(error: NSError) {

}
```

RegionMonitor Methods

There are only two public functions for the RegionMonitor class, startMonitoring and stopMonitoring. The view controller is responsible for configuring a beacon region and telling the Region Monitor when to start and stop monitoring.

startMonitoring

Upon entering, the property pendingMonitorRequest is set, signaling that a *start monitoring* request has been made. In the event that the request to start monitoring is deferred, this value will be used in a notification to determine whether startMonitoringForRegion should be called. Also, a strong reference to the beaconRegion is held so that it can be used by the delegate methods.

Before monitoring can actually start, authorization status must be taken into consideration. To get the authorization status for your application, you must call CLLocationManager.authorizationStatus. Only when the status AlwaysAuthorized is returned can monitoring for a beacon region start. We will cover the authorization sequence in detail in the section "Authorization and Requesting Permission." Add the code shown in Listing 10-21 to the RegionMonitor class.

Listing 10-21. RegionMonitor startMonitoring Method

```
func startMonitoring(beaconRegion: CLBeaconRegion?) {
    print("Start monitoring")
    pendingMonitorRequest = true
    self.beaconRegion = beaconRegion

    switch CLLocationManager.authorizationStatus() {
    case .NotDetermined:
        locationManager.requestAlwaysAuthorization()
    case .Restricted, .Denied, .AuthorizedWhenInUse:
        delegate?.onBackgroundLocationAccessDisabled()
    case .AuthorizedAlways:
        locationManager!.startMonitoringForRegion(beaconRegion!)
        pendingMonitorRequest = false
    }
}
```

stopMonitoring

In this method, location manager is told to stop ranging and monitoring beacons and to stop updating location. The delegate is also notified that monitoring has now stopped. Add the code in Listing 10-22 to the RegionMonitor class.

Listing 10-22. RegionMonitor stopMonitoring Method

```
func stopMonitoring() {
    print("Stop monitoring")
    pendingMonitorRequest = false
    locationManager.stopRangingBeaconsInRegion(beaconRegion!)
    locationManager.stopMonitoringForRegion(beaconRegion!)
    locationManager.stopUpdatingLocation()
    beaconRegion = nil
    delegate?.didStopMonitoring()
}
```

Authorization and Requesting Permission

In order to use location services, you must request authorization from the user to use those services.

> **Caution** You should request authorization at the point where you will use location services to perform a task. Requesting authorization may display an alert to the user. If it's not clear to the user that location services are about to be used for a useful purpose, the user may deny the request to use those services.

In the Region Monitor `startMonitoring` method, when `CLLocationManager.authorizationStatus()` is called and returns a value of `NotDetermined`, you need to call the `requestAlwaysAuthorization()` method. The user will then be presented with an alert requesting permission to use location services where he or she can choose to allow access as shown in Figure 10-16.

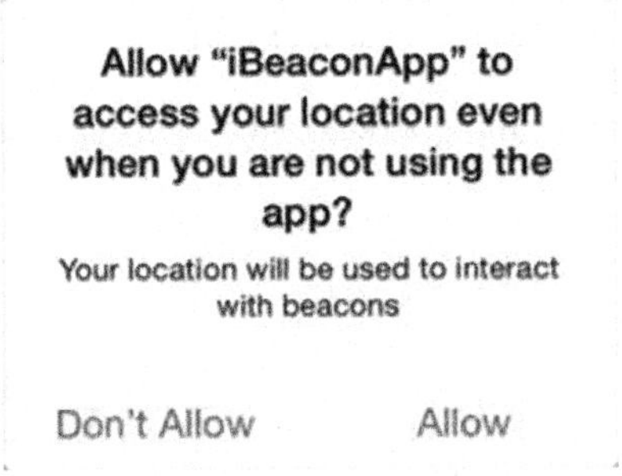

Figure 10-16. Request location services authorization prompt

If the user chooses Don't Allow from the alert shown in Figure 10-16 the next time he calls the `startMonitoring` method, the `CLLocationManager.authorizationStatus()` will return Denied, causing the Region Monitor to notify its delegate by calling the `onBackgroundLocationAccessDisabled` method (see Listing 10-21). The user will be presented with an alert to change the settings as shown in Figure 10-17.

Background Location Access is Disabled

Please change the location access to "Always" in app setttings.

Cancel Settings

***Figure 10-17.** Request settings change prompt*

If the user selects Settings, the app will transition to the `Settings.app` where the user can change permission settings for location services as shown in Figure 10-18.

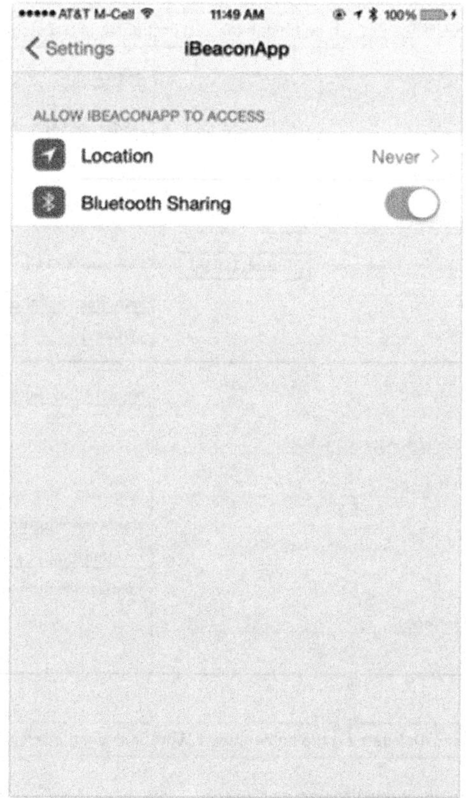

***Figure 10-18.** Location services settings for iBeaconApp in the Settings.app*

CLLocationManagerDelegate Methods

The `RegionMonitor` adopts the `CLLocationManagerDelegate` so that it can receive notifications from the location manager. The Region Monitor will need to respond to events such as a change in authorization state, when beacon region boundaries have been crossed and when one or more beacons have come into range. In this section you'll learn how to interact with the location manager and respond to these events through delegation.

The diagram shown in Figure 10-19 illustrates the interaction between the location manager and the Region Monitor, which is acting as the delegate. It shows the complete sequence for the "start monitoring" event which also includes authorization.

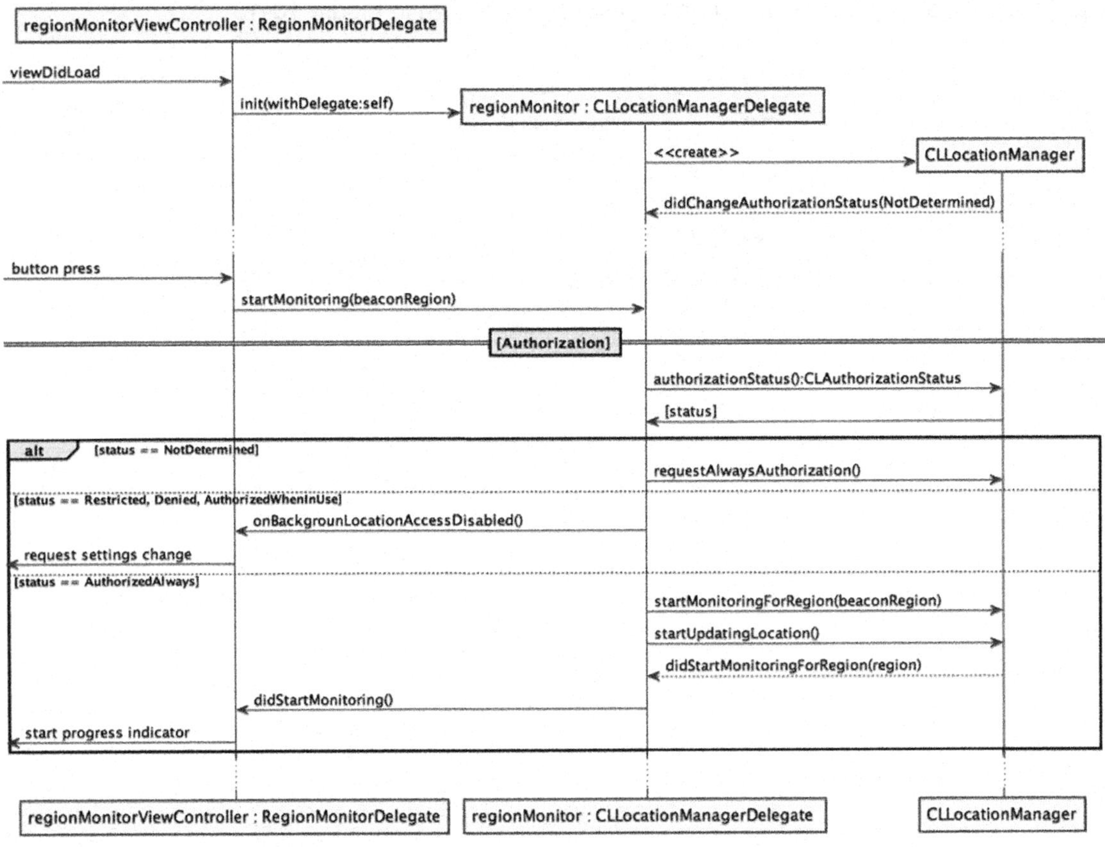

***Figure 10-19.** Sequence diagram for start monitoring sequence*

> **Note** Right after the location manager has been initialized, it will call its delegate method with a status value of `NotDetermined`.

The next sections cover each of the location manager delegate methods you'll be using in the iBeaconApp application.

Regions Are Shared Resources

Following are a few things you'll want to keep in mind when dealing with regions:

- Recall that regions are a shared resource; therefore, the manager object that gets passed in to the callback represents the location manager object reporting the event. This may not be the one you stored in the `locationManager` property.
- The region object passed as a parameter to delegate methods may not be the same object that was registered. When determining equality, use the region's identifier string.
- It's possible that multiple location managers share a delegate object. When this is the case, that delegate will receive a message multiple times.

didChangeAuthorizationStatus

The location manager calls this delegate method when the authorization status for the application has changed. Consider the use case where a user taps a button to start monitoring but has not yet granted the application permission to access location services. See the flow diagram in Figure 10-20.

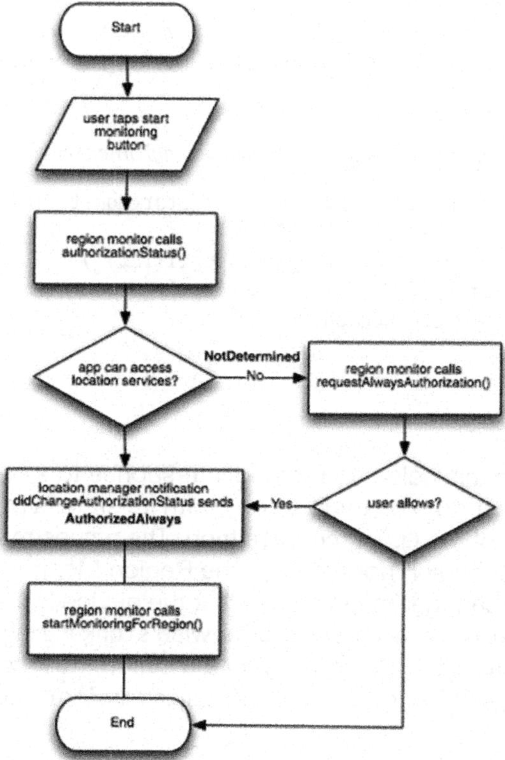

Figure 10-20. Flow diagram for the "start monitoring" event

The implementation in Listing 10-23 checks for the `AuthorizeWhenInUse` and `AuthorizeAlways` status. You can see that it's also testing the value of `pendingMonitorRequest`. If the call to `startMonitoringForRegion` was deferred, it can be called here.

Listing 10-23. CLLocationManager Delegate Method didChangeAuthorizationStatus

```
func locationManager(manager: CLLocationManager, didChangeAuthorizationStatus
status: CLAuthorizationStatus) {
    print("didChangeAuthorizationStatus \(status)")
    if status == .AuthorizedWhenInUse || status == .AuthorizedAlways {
        if pendingMonitorRequest {
            locationManager!.startMonitoringForRegion(beaconRegion!)
            pendingMonitorRequest = false
        }
        locationManager!.startUpdatingLocation()
    }
}
```

didStartMonitoringForRegion

The location manager calls this delegate method after `startMonitoringForRegion` has been called, and when a new region is being monitored (Listing 10-24). The Region Monitor notifies its delegate by calling `didStartMonitoring` so a progress indicator can be presented to the user at the right time. At this point, the Region Monitor can ask the location manager about the new region's state by calling `requestStateForRegion` with the new region object passed as a parameter.

Listing 10-24. CLLocationManager Delegate Method didStartMonitoringForRegion

```
func locationManager(manager: CLLocationManager, didStartMonitoringForRegion
region: CLRegion) {
    print("didStartMonitoringForRegion \(region.identifier)")
    delegate?.didStartMonitoring()
    locationManager.requestStateForRegion(region)
}
```

didDetermineState

The location manager calls this delegate method in response to a call to its `requestStateForRegion` method. The region along with its state is passed in as a parameter. The state contains a value of the `CLRegionState` type. The values reflect the relationship between the device and the region boundaries. The Region Monitor uses these values to determine which location manager method to call. If the device is inside the given region, then `startRangingBeaconsInRegion` is called; otherwise `stopRangingBeaconsInRegion` is called. The property `beaconRegion` that was set in the call to `startMonitoring` is passed in as a parameter. Add the code in Listing 10-25 to the `RegionMonitor` class.

Listing 10-25. CLLocationManager Delegate Method didDetermineState

```
func locationManager(manager: CLLocationManager, didDetermineState state: CLRegionState,
forRegion region: CLRegion) {
    print("didDetermineState")
    if state == CLRegionState.Inside {
        print(" - entered region \(region.identifier)")
        locationManager.startRangingBeaconsInRegion(beaconRegion!)
    } else {
        print(" - exited region \(region.identifier)")
        locationManager.stopRangingBeaconsInRegion(beaconRegion!)
    }
}
```

didEnterRegion

The location manager calls this delegate method when the user enters the specified region. The Region Monitor notifies its delegate by calling `didEnterRegion` and passes the `region` object containing information about the region that was entered. Add the code in Listing 10-26 to the `RegionMonitor` class.

Listing 10-26. CLLocationManager Delegate Method didEnterRegion

```
func locationManager(manager: CLLocationManager, didEnterRegion region: CLRegion) {
    print("didEnterRegion - \(region.identifier)")
    delegate?.didEnterRegion(region)
}
```

didExitRegion

The location manager calls this delegate method when the user exits the specified region. The Region Monitor notifies its delegate by calling `didExitRegion` and passes the `region` object containing information about the region that was exited. Add the code in Listing 10-27 to the `RegionMonitor` class.

Listing 10-27. CLLocationManager Delegate Method didExitRegion

```
func locationManager(manager: CLLocationManager, didExitRegion region: CLRegion) {
    print("didExitRegion - \(region.identifier)")
    delegate?.didExitRegion(region)
}
```

didRangeBeacons

The location manager calls this delegate method when one or more beacons become available in the specified region, or when a beacon goes out of range. This method is also called when the range of a beacon changes (i.e., getting closer or farther). The implementation here only notifies the Region Monitor's delegate with the closest beacon. Add the code in Listing 10-28 to the `RegionMonitor` class.

Listing 10-28. CLLocationManager Delegate Method didRangeBeacons

```
func locationManager(manager: CLLocationManager, didRangeBeacons beacons: [CLBeacon],
inRegion region: CLBeaconRegion) {
    print("didRangeBeacons - \(region.identifier)")

    if beacons.count > 0 {
        rangedBeacon = beacons[0]
        delegate?.didRangeBeacon(rangedBeacon, region: region)
    }
}
```

Error Handling

Several of the location manager delegate error reporting methods are optional, but it is recommended that you implement them in your applications. The iBeaconApp sample only dumps a message to the log.

monitoringDidFailForRegion

The location manager calls this delegate method when region monitoring has failed. It passes in the region for which the error occurred and an `NSError` describing the error. Implementation of this method is optional but recommended. Add the code in Listing 10-29 to the `RegionMonitor` class.

Listing 10-29. CLLocationManager Delegate Method monitoringDidFailForRegion

```
func locationManager(manager: CLLocationManager, monitoringDidFailForRegion region:
CLRegion?, withError error: NSError) {
    print("monitoringDidFailForRegion - \(error)")
}
```

rangingBeaconsDidFailForRegion

The location manager calls this delegate method when registering a beacon region failed. If you receive this message, check to make sure the region object itself is valid and contains valid data. Add the code in Listing 10-30 to the `RegionMonitor` class.

Listing 10-30. CLLocationManager Delegate Method rangingBeaconsDidFailForRegion

```
func locationManager(manager: CLLocationManager, rangingBeaconsDidFailForRegion region:
CLBeaconRegion, withError error: NSError) {
    print("rangingBeaconsDidFailForRegion \(error)")
}
```

didFailWithError

If the user denies your application's use of the location service, this method reports a `Denied` error. If you receive this error, you should stop the location service. Implementation of this method is optional but recommended. Add the code in Listing 10-31 to the `RegionMonitor` class.

Listing 10-31. CLLocationManager Delegate Method didFailWithError

```
func locationManager(manager: CLLocationManager, didFailWithError error: NSError) {
    print("didFailWithError \(error)")
    if (error.code == CLError.Denied.rawValue) {
        stopMonitoring()
    }
}
```

Configuring Region Monitoring

The view controller is responsible for handling user input starting the monitoring process, so that is where you'll configure your beacon regions.

The `CLBeaconRegion` is the key class for managing your beacons. It defines a region that you're interested in that is based on the beacon's proximity to a Bluetooth LE device. A beacon's identity is programmed directly into its hardware using tools provided by the manufacturer. In your application you use those values to identify one or more beacons. When a device comes into range with matching criteria, the region triggers a notification.

Using the RegionMonitor Class

Open the file `RegionMonitorViewConroller.swift` file, and in the `RegionMonitorViewController` class add a property to hold a `RegionMonitor` object.

```
var regionMonitor: RegionMonitor!
```

Then create an instance in the `viewDidLoad` method.

```
regionMonitor = RegionMonitor(delegate: self)
```

Beacon Identity

You specify a beacon's identity by using a combination of three properties.

- `proximityUUID`—this property holds a unique identifier for the beacons you want to target. This property is required.
- `major`—this property holds a value used to identify a group of beacons you want to target. This value is optional, and if not assigned, it will be ignored during the matching process.
- `minor`—this property holds a value used to identify a specific beacon within a group. This value is optional, and if not assigned, it will be ignored during the matching process.

Initializing a Beacon Region

Depending on how specific you want to be when receiving notifications, you can set up a region in one of three ways.

1. Target a beacon with a specific proximity ID. The beacon's major and minor values will be ignored.

```
beaconRegion = CLBeaconRegion(proximityUUID: uuid, identifier: "my.beacon")
```

2. Target a beacon with a specific proximity ID and major value. The beacon's minor value will be ignored.

```
beaconRegion = CLBeaconRegion(proximityUUID: uuid, major:
CLBeaconMajorValue(major), identifier: "my.beacon")
```

3. Target a beacon with a specific proximity ID, major value, and minor values. This would be used in a more complex environment.

```
beaconRegion = CLBeaconRegion(proximityUUID: uuid, major: CLBeaconMajorValue(major),
minor: CLBeaconMinorValue(minor), identifier: "my.beacon")
```

An additional user-defined unique identifier is associated with the beacon during initialization. You use this identifier to differentiate regions with your application. This value cannot be nil.

Initializing Beacon Notifications

There are three properties you will use to indicate the types of notifications you want to receive.

- `notifyEntryStateOnDisplay`—this property indicates whether beacon notifications should be sent while the device's display is on. When this value is `true`, beacon notifications are sent when the user turns on the display when the device is already inside a region. If your app isn't running, the system will launch your app in the background so the notification can be handled. The location manager's delegate method `didDetermineState` is called.
- `notifyOnEntry`—indicates that a notification should be sent upon entry to the region. The system will launch your app in the background to handle the notification. The location manager's delegate method `didEnterRegion` is called.
- `notifyOnExit`—indicates that a notification should be sent upon exit from the region.

Start and Stop Region Monitoring

To start and stop the region monitoring process, add the code in Listing 10-32 to the `RegionMonitorViewController` class.

***Listing 10-32.** Start and Stop Region Monitoring*

```
@IBAction func toggleMonitoring() {
    if isMonitoring {
        regionMonitor.stopMonitoring()
    } else {
        if uuidTextField.text!.isEmpty {
            showAlert("Please provide a valid UUID")
            return
        }

        regionIdLabel.text = ""
        proximityLabel.text = ""
        distanceLabel.text = ""
        rssiLabel.text = ""

        if let uuid = NSUUID(UUIDString: uuidTextField.text!) {
            let identifier = "my.beacon"

            var beaconRegion: CLBeaconRegion?

            if let major = Int(majorTextField.text!) {
                if let minor = Int(minorTextField.text!) {
                    beaconRegion = CLBeaconRegion(proximityUUID: uuid, major:
                    CLBeaconMajorValue(major), minor: CLBeaconMinorValue(minor),
                    identifier: identifier)
                } else {
                    beaconRegion = CLBeaconRegion(proximityUUID: uuid,
                    major: CLBeaconMajorValue(major), identifier: identifier)
                }
            } else {
                beaconRegion = CLBeaconRegion(proximityUUID: uuid, identifier: identifier)
            }

            // later, these values can be set from the UI
            beaconRegion!.notifyEntryStateOnDisplay = true
            beaconRegion!.notifyOnEntry = true
            beaconRegion!.notifyOnExit = true

            regionMonitor.startMonitoring(beaconRegion)
        } else {
            let alertController = UIAlertController(title:"iBeaconApp", message: "Please
            enter a valid UUID", preferredStyle: .Alert)
             alertController.addAction(UIAlertAction(title: "OK", style: .Default,
             handler: nil))
            self.presentViewController(alertController, animated: true, completion: nil)
        }
    }
}
```

Handling a Ranged Beacon

A beacon that was encountered during region monitoring is sent through delegate notifications using the CLBeacon class. The identity of the beacon corresponds to the information used when you initialized the beacon region.

> **Note** You don't create an instance of a CLBeacon class directly; this is done by the location manager.

The Region Monitor delegate method simply updates the appropriate fields.

Monitoring Progress Indicator

There's one last detail to cover, and that's a progress indicator. It's important that when a user interacts with the application, you provide some type of feedback for each action. When the user taps the Monitor button, you want to indicate that monitoring is in progress. You could use a static text field and toggle the text, but that's boring. Adding a simple rotation animation to the Monitor button is quick and easy and will serve as an effective progress indicator for when monitoring starts and stops.

Animating the Monitor Button

An extension will be used to apply an animation to the Monitor button. You use an extension to add functionality to an existing class for which you don't have the original source code. The extension will add a function to rotate a view object using keyframe animation.

At the top of the RegionMonitorViewController.swift file after the import statements, add the code from Listing 10-33.

Listing 10-33. Adding an Extension to the UIView Class

```
extension UIView {

    func rotate(fromValue: CGFloat, toValue: CGFloat, duration: CFTimeInterval = 1.0,
    completionDelegate: AnyObject? = nil) {

        let rotateAnimation = CABasicAnimation(keyPath: "transform.rotation")
        rotateAnimation.fromValue = fromValue
        rotateAnimation.toValue = toValue
        rotateAnimation.duration = duration

        if let delegate: AnyObject = completionDelegate {
            rotateAnimation.delegate = delegate
        }
        self.layer.addAnimation(rotateAnimation, forKey: nil)
    }
}
```

The parameters fromValue and toValue represent rotation and are specified in radians. The duration is specified in seconds. The CABasicAnimation class provides single-keyframe animation for a layer property. It will allow you to interpolate between two values over time. It also allows you to set a delegate so you can receive notification when the animation completes by calling the delegate's animationDidStop method.

For this use case, rotating the Scan button 360 degrees would constitute one animation cycle. Each time an animation cycle completes the delegate is notified.

Override the animationDidStop method of the view controller. This method will evaluate the scan state and restart the animation if scanning is still in progress. Add the code in Listing 10-34 to the RegionMonitorViewController class.

Listing 10-34. Override for the animationDidStop Method in the RegionMonitorViewController Class

```
override func animationDidStop(anim: CAAnimation, finished flag: Bool) {
    if isMonitoring == true {
        // if still scanning, restart the animation
        monitorButton.rotate(0.0, toValue: CGFloat(M_PI * 2), completionDelegate: self)
    }
}
```

The animations will be controlled from the delegate methods that you implemented earlier. The delegate method didStartMonitoring started the animation by calling the rotate method of the Monitor button.

```
monitorButton.rotate(0.0, toValue: CGFloat(M_PI * 2), duration: 1.0, completionDelegate: self)
```

The delegate method didStopMonitoring stopped the animation by simply setting the value of the property isMonitoring to false. Notice in the override method, the value of isMonitoring is checked; when set to false, the animation is not applied. The animation will end when the animation cycle completes. This guarantees that the Scan button will be in the correct orientation.

Build and run the application. Transition to the Region Monitor scene and tap the Monitor button. You should see the button spinning. The animation should stop when you tap the button again.

Building the iBeacon Scene

In this section, you'll build the master scene for the iBeacon (Figure 10-21). The iBeacon scene allows you to configure your iOS device as an iBeacon transmitter. The UI is similar to that of the Region Monitor. It will utilize a switch to turn the transmitter on and off; one button to autogenerate a UUID; four input fields to where the user can configure the device, and several labels for informational purposes; and one text view which will display help text for each input field.

This section will briefly cover the steps on how to build the UI for this scene. Many of the steps are a repeat of those found in the section "Building the Region Monitor Scene."

Create a new Swift file named BeaconTransmitterViewController.swift and declare the class BeaconTransmitterViewController a subclass of UIViewController. Then adopt the protocol for UITextFieldDelegate by adding the UITextFieldDelegate protocol declaration (Listing 10-35).

Listing 10-35. BeaconTransmitterViewController Class Declaration with Properties

```
import UIKit

class BeaconTransmitterViewController: UIViewController, UITextFieldDelegate {

    let kUUIDKey = "transmit-proximityUUID"
    let kMajorIdKey = "transmit-majorId"
    let kMinorIdKey = "transmit-minorId"
    let kPowerKey = "transmit-measuredPower"

    @IBOutlet weak var advertiseSwitch: UISwitch!
    @IBOutlet weak var generateUUIDButton: UIButton!
    @IBOutlet weak var uuidTextField: UITextField!
    @IBOutlet weak var majorTextField: UITextField!
    @IBOutlet weak var minorTextField: UITextField!
    @IBOutlet weak var powerTextField: UITextField!
    @IBOutlet weak var helpTextView: UITextView!

    var doneButton: UIBarButtonItem!
    var beaconTransmitter: BeaconTransmitter!
    var isBluetoothPowerOn: Bool = false

    let numberFormatter = NSNumberFormatter()
}
```

Assign the BeaconTransmitterViewController as the class for the Beacon Transmitter identity by opening the storyboard and selecting the iBeacon scene. In the Utilities panel on the right, click the Identity Inspector tab. In the Custom Class section, use the class drop-down to select *BeaconTransmitterViewController*.

Set the background color to for the iBeacon view to 009999. Add controls to the storyboard so that it looks like the mock-up shown in Figure 10-21.

- For the Advertise UISwitch add two connections: IBOutlet named advertiseSwitch and IBAction named toggleAdvertising.
- For the Generate UIButton add two connections: IBOutlet named generateUUIDButton and IBAction named generateUUID.
- For each UITextField add a single connection: IBOutlet named uuidTextField, IBOutlet named majorTextField, IBOutlet named minorTextField, and IBOutlet named powerTextField. Add placeholder text.
- For the UITextView add a single connection: IBOutlet named helpTextView.

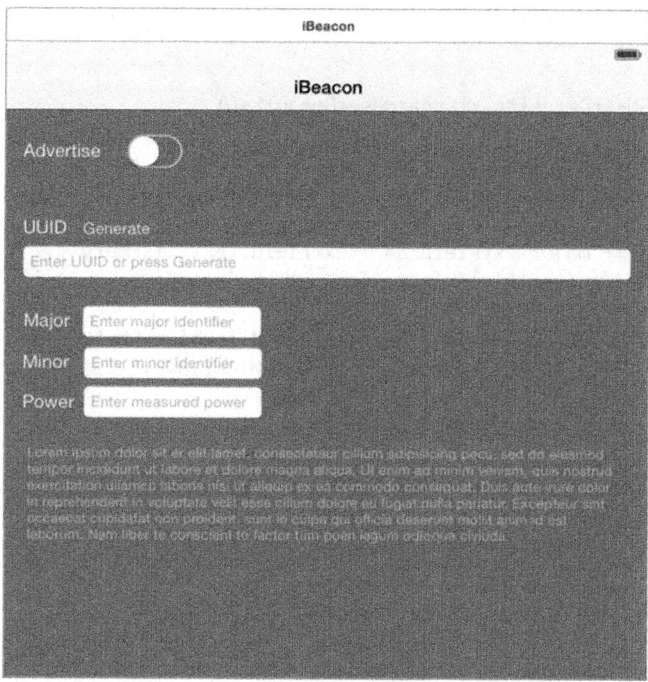

***Figure 10-21.** iBeacon scene mock-up*

Add constraints for each of the controls in the scene.

Implement the `UITextFieldDelegate` methods. Add the code in Listing 10-36 to the `BeaconTransmitterViewController` class.

***Listing 10-36.** UITextFieldDelegate Methods textFieldDidBeginEditing and textFieldDidEndEditing in the BeaconTransmittrViewController Class*

```
// MARK: UITextFieldDelegate methods

func textFieldDidBeginEditing(textField: UITextField) {
    navigationItem.rightBarButtonItem = doneButton
    advertiseSwitch.setOn(false, animated: true)

    if textField == uuidTextField {
        helpTextView.text = NSLocalizedString("transmit.help.proximityUUID", comment:"foo")
    }
    else if textField == majorTextField {
        helpTextView.text = NSLocalizedString("transmit.help.major", comment:"foo")
    }
    else if textField == minorTextField {
        helpTextView.text = NSLocalizedString("transmit.help.minor", comment:"foo")
    }
    else if textField == powerTextField {
        helpTextView.text = NSLocalizedString("transmit.help.measuredPower", comment:"foo")
    }
}
```

```
func textFieldDidEndEditing(textField: UITextField) {
    helpTextView.text = ""

    let defaults = NSUserDefaults.standardUserDefaults()

    if textField == uuidTextField && !textField.text!.isEmpty {
        defaults.setObject(textField.text, forKey: kUUIDKey)
    }
    else if textField == majorTextField && !textField.text!.isEmpty {
        defaults.setObject(textField.text, forKey: kMajorIdKey)
    }
    else if textField == minorTextField && !textField.text!.isEmpty {
        defaults.setObject(textField.text, forKey: kMinorIdKey)
    }
    else if textField == powerTextField && !textField.text!.isEmpty {
        // power values are typically negative
        let value = numberFormatter.numberFromString(powerTextField.text!)
        if (value?.intValue > 0) {
            powerTextField.text = numberFormatter.stringFromNumber(0 - value!.intValue)
        }
        defaults.setObject(textField.text, forKey: kPowerKey)
    }
}
```

The BeaconTransmitter Class

Just like the RegionMonitor class, the BeaconTransmitter class manages all the interactions with the CBPeripheralManager. The Delegation pattern will be used so the beacon transmitter can inform its delegate of events that it handled, or is about to handle.

Defining the BeaconTransmitterDelegate Protocol

You'll start by defining a protocol for a BeaconTransmitterDelegate. The BeaconTransmitterViewController will adopt this protocol and implement the methods that respond to CBPeripheralManager actions. You'll create a new class BeaconTransmitter that will be the delegating object. It will hold a weak reference to the BeaconTransmitterViewController that will act as the delegate. The BeaconTransmitter object will act as the delegate for the CBPeripheralManager object.

Create a new Swift file named BeaconTransmitter.swift and define a protocol for BeaconTransmitter. Add the code in Listing 10-37 to the BeaconTransmitterViewController class.

Listing 10-37. Defining the BeaconTransmitterDelegate Protocol

```
protocol BeaconTransmitterDelegate: NSObjectProtocol {
    func didPowerOn()
    func didPowerOff()
    func onError(error: NSError)
}
```

Delegate Methods

The BeaconTransmitter will use the methods in the `BeaconTransmitterDelegate` protocol to communicate back to its delegate to notify when a device's Bluetooth powers on or off, and to report any errors it may encounter.

didPowerOn

The `didPowerOn` delegate method is called after the `BeaconTransmitter` receives notification from the `CBPeripheralManager` method `peripheralManagerDidUpdateState` and peripheral manager's state accessor returns `PoweredOn`. The delegate should update its state to reflect that. Add the code in Listing 10-38 to the `BeaconTransmistterViewController` class.

Listing 10-38. The didPowerOn Method in BeaconTransmitterViewController Class

```
func didPowerOn() {
    isBluetoothPowerOn = true
}
```

didPowerOff

The `didPowerOn` delegate method is called after the `BeaconTransmitter` receives notification from the `CBPeripheralManager` method `peripheralManagerDidUpdateState` and peripheral manager's state accessor returns `PoweredOff`. The delegate should update its state to reflect that. Add the code in Listing 10-39 to the `BeaconTransmistterViewController` class.

Listing 10-39. The didPowerOn Method in BeaconTransmitterViewController Class

```
func didPowerOff() {
    isBluetoothPowerOn = false
}
```

onError

The `onError` delegate method is called when the `BeaconTransmitter` encounters an error. An `NSError` object is provided to the delegate. The delegate can respond to this notification by handling the error and/or providing feedback to the user. This method is currently not used by this example. Add the code in Listing 10-40 to the `BeaconTransmitterViewController` class.

Listing 10-40. Delegate Method onError in the BeaconTransmirtterViewController Class

```
func onError(error: NSError) {

}
```

Creating the iBeaconTransmitter Class

Next, in the file BeaconTransmitter.swift below BeaconTransmitterDelegate protocol, declare the class BeaconTransmitter a subclass of NSObject, and adopt the protocol for CBPeripheralManager. Also, you'll need to import CoreLocation and CoreBluetooth. Then add properties for CBPeripheralManager and BeaconTransmitterDelegate. Add the code in Listing 10-41 to the BeaconTransmitter class.

Listing 10-41. BeaconTransmitter Class Declaration

```
class BeaconTransmitter: NSObject, CBPeripheralManagerDelegate {

    var peripheralManager: CBPeripheralManager!

    weak var delegate: BeaconTransmitterDelegate?
}
```

Store a strong reference to the CBPeripheralManager, but you must make sure that you declare the delegate property for BeaconTransmitterDelegate as weak to avoid a strong reference cycle.

Now implement an initializer method that will be called when you create a new instance of BeaconTransmitter. The primary role of an initializer is to ensure that a new instance of a type is set up properly before first use. Add the code in Listing 10-42 to the BeaconTransmitter class.

Listing 10-42. BeaconTransmitter Initializer

```
init(delegate: BeaconTransmitterDelegate?) {
    super.init()
    peripheralManager = CBPeripheralManager(delegate: self, queue: nil)
    self.delegate = delegate
}
```

The initializer starts by calling super.init(), which calls the initializer of BeaconTransmitter class's super class, NSObject. Then the peripheralManager property is initialized with an instance of CBPeripheralManager, passing in self as delegate. Finally, the delegate property is initialized with the RegionMonitorDelegate object that is passed as a parameter.

BeaconTransmitter Methods

There are only two public functions for the BeaconTransmitter class, startAdvertising and stopAdvertising. The view controller is responsible for configuration and telling the beacon transmitter when to start and stop advertising.

startAdvertising

In this method, the peripheralManager is told to start advertising given a specific beacon region and transmit power value. Add the code in Listing 10-43 to the BeaconTransmitter class.

Listing 10-43. Start Advertising in the BeaconTransmitter Class

```
func startAdvertising(beaconRegion: CLBeaconRegion?, power:NSNumber?) {
    let data = NSDictionary(dictionary: (beaconRegion?.peripheralDataWithMeasuredPower
(power))!) as! [String: AnyObject]
    peripheralManager.startAdvertising(data)
}
```

stopAdvertising

In this method, the peripheralManager is told to stop advertising. Add the code in Listing 10-44 to the BeaconTransmitter class.

Listing 10-44. Stop Advertising in the BeaconTransmitter Class

```
func stopAdvertising() {
    peripheralManager.stopAdvertising()
}
```

Configure Your iOS Device as an iBeacon

The magic behind setting up your iOS device to act as an iBeacon transmitter is calling the peripheralDataWithMeasuredPower of the CLBeaconRegion class. The return value will be a dictionary that is encoded with the device's identifying information that can be used to advertise the device with the Core Bluetooth framework.

```
let data = NSDictionary(dictionary: (beaconRegion?.peripheralDataWithMeasuredPower(power))!)
as! [String: AnyObject]
peripheralManager.startAdvertising(data)
```

The peripheralDataWithMeasuredPower takes a single parameter representing the measured power. The measured power of a device is its known measured signal strength in RSSI at 1 meter. The distance provided by iOS is in meters and is an estimate based on the ratio of the beacon's signal strength over the transmission power.

The power values typically have a negative value.

Initialize a Beacon Region

As covered previously in the section "Configuring Region Monitoring," the view controller is responsible for handing user input and setting up the beacon region.

The first step is to specify the beacon identity. For easy setup of the UUID, there's a Generate button just above the UUID field. You created a connection for an IBAction named generateUUID. You can easily generate the UUID programmatically by creating an instance of NSUUID and getting its UUIDString property. Take that value and assign it to the uuidTextField text (see Listing 10-45). That's it.

Listing 10-45. Generating a Unique Identifier Programmatically in BeaconTransmitterViewController

```
@IBAction func generateUUID() {
    uuidTextField.text = NSUUID().UUIDString
}
```

For an explanation of the property values for major and minor, look back at the section "Initializing a Beacon Region." For a recap on setting up the notification properties, see the section "Initializing Beacon Notifications."

Start Advertising

Earlier you created a connection for an `IBAction` named `toggleAdvertising`. This, of course, is where you make the request to start and stop advertising. Listings 10-46 and Listing 10-47 show the complete implementation.

Listing 10-46. Start and Stop Advertising in the BeaconTransmitterViewController Class

```
@IBAction func toggleAdvertising() {
    if advertiseSwitch.on {
        dismissKeyboard()
        if !canBeginAdvertise() {
            advertiseSwitch.setOn(false, animated: true)
            return
        }
        let uuid = NSUUID(UUIDString: uuidTextField.text!)
        let identifier = "my.beacon"
        var beaconRegion: CLBeaconRegion?

        if let major = Int(majorTextField.text!) {
            if let minor = Int(minorTextField.text!) {
                beaconRegion = CLBeaconRegion(proximityUUID: uuid!, major:
                CLBeaconMajorValue(major), minor: CLBeaconMinorValue(minor),
                identifier: identifier)
            } else {
                beaconRegion = CLBeaconRegion(proximityUUID: uuid!, major:
                CLBeaconMajorValue(major), identifier: identifier)
            }
        } else {
            beaconRegion = CLBeaconRegion(proximityUUID: uuid!, identifier: identifier)
        }

        beaconRegion!.notifyEntryStateOnDisplay = true
        beaconRegion!.notifyOnEntry = true
        beaconRegion!.notifyOnExit = true

        let power = numberFormatter.numberFromString(powerTextField.text!)

        beaconTransmitter.startAdvertising(beaconRegion, power: power)
    } else {
        beaconTransmitter.stopAdvertising()
    }
}
```

Listing 10-47. Logic for Determining if Advertising Can Start in the BeaconTransmitterViewController Class

```
private func canBeginAdvertise() -> Bool {
    if !isBluetoothPowerOn {
        showAlert("You must have Bluetooth powered on to advertise!")
        return false
    }
    if uuidTextField.text!.isEmpty || majorTextField.text!.isEmpty
        || minorTextField.text!.isEmpty || powerTextField.text!.isEmpty {
            showAlert("You must complete all fields")
        return false
    }
    return true
}
```

Build and run the application and transition to the iBeacon scene. Test each of the fields to make sure they behave as you expect. Press the Generate button to make sure a UUID is generated.

Test the Application

At this time you should perform some basic testing of the functionality that was covered in this chapter.

If you already have an iBeacon device and you know the UUID, you can run the app and go into region monitoring mode. Enter the UUID and tap the Monitor button. You should see the fields populate as soon at the beacon is detected. Move closer to the beacon to see that the fields being reported make sense. Place your iOS device right next to the beacon. The proximity should be reported as immediate.

If you don't have an iBeacon but have a second iOS device, install and run the app on that device. Go into iBeacon mode and configure your device and then start advertising. Now, on your first device running in Region Monitor mode, enter the same UUID and then perform the same steps as previously.

Summary

In this chapter you learned how to use the CoreLocation framework to interact with beacon. You learned about region monitoring and how to scan for specific beacons and receive notification when entering or exiting an area defined by a beacon's proximity. You learned how to use your iPhone to act as an iBeacon transmitter.

Chapter 11

Home Automation Using HomeKit

Manny de la Torriente

Much like Apple sought to unify health data with HealthKit, HomeKit is Apple's entry into home automation. Apple created a unified communications protocol—HomeKit Accessory Protocol— for connected home manufactures. HomeKit is a common set of APIs (application programming interfaces) for applications that provides integration between iOS devices and accessories that support the HomeKit Accessory Protocol.

This chapter explains the key concepts behind the HomeKit framework (home, room, accessory, services) and how to easily build an app that can configure, monitor, and control home automation accessories, as well as integrate with Siri for voice commands. Additionally, you'll learn how to set up and use the HomeKit simulator to help develop and debug your application.

Introduction to HomeKit Concepts

HomeKit provides integration between iOS devices and accessories that support Apple's HomeKit Accessory Protocol. HomeKit allows an application to discover these accessories and add them to a cross-device home configuration database where the data can then be accessed and modified to suit the needs of the end user. The database is also available to Siri, which gives the user the capability of controlling the accessories with voice commands.

A home manager is represented by the `HMHomeManager` class, which manages a collection of homes. It is used to access HomeKit objects such as home, room, accessory, service, and other related objects from the HomeKit database.

A home is considered to be a single-dwelling home and is represented by the HMHome class. It provides access to a collection of automated accessories with which you can communicate and configure. Each home may optionally have one or more rooms. HomeKit will assign accessories to a default room if you have not configured any rooms. A room is represented by the HMRoom class. A zone is an arbitrary optional grouping of rooms that a user considers a single area; for example, upstairs or downstairs. Rooms can be added to one or more zones. A zone is represented by the HMZone class.

> **Note** your application should provide the means for users to create their own useful groupings and labels.

An accessory is a physical home automation device that is assigned to a room, such as a ceiling fan. An accessory is represented by the HMAccessory class, and can provide one or more services; for example, a ceiling fan has a service to turn the fan on and off, and another service that can change the speed of the fan. A service can be a user-controllable function provided by an accessory, like a light, or it can be an activity internal to a device, such as a firmware update. HomeKit is most concerned with user-controllable services. A service is represented by the HMService class.

Each service is described by a collection of characteristics; for example, if a light is on or off, or what the brightness value is set to. A characteristic is represented by the HMCharacteristic class and is described by an array of properties and metadata. Characteristics can be queried to discover their state, or they can be modified to affect an accessory's behavior.

HomeKit Delegation Methods

Like many other Apple frameworks, HomeKit uses the delegation pattern for the notification of events or changes in the application. An important note about HomeKit delegation is that when your application initiates a change, the delegate messages won't be sent to your app. Instead, they are sent to other apps that might be running on your iOS device that also support HomeKit. For example, you might purchase a thermostat that includes an app to control it. You would want to see any changes you make in your app reflected in the thermostat app or vice versa. Your app is expected to use completion handlers to reload data and update views. However, you still need to add code to both the completion handler and the associated delegate methods. Applications need to be in the foreground to receive delegate messages, as they are not batched while your app is in the background. When an app comes back to the foreground it will receive a homeManagerDidUpdateHomes message which signals your app to reload all its data.

Building a HomeKit Application

The application you'll create in this chapter will use grouped table views to present information. The app will provide a simple user interface (UI) for creating homes, browsing for and adding accessories, and controlling the accessories in a home, such as a ceiling fan with services for turning the fan off and on, as well as for changing the rotation speed and the rotation direction. When you're finished, your app should look similar to the one in Figure 11-1.

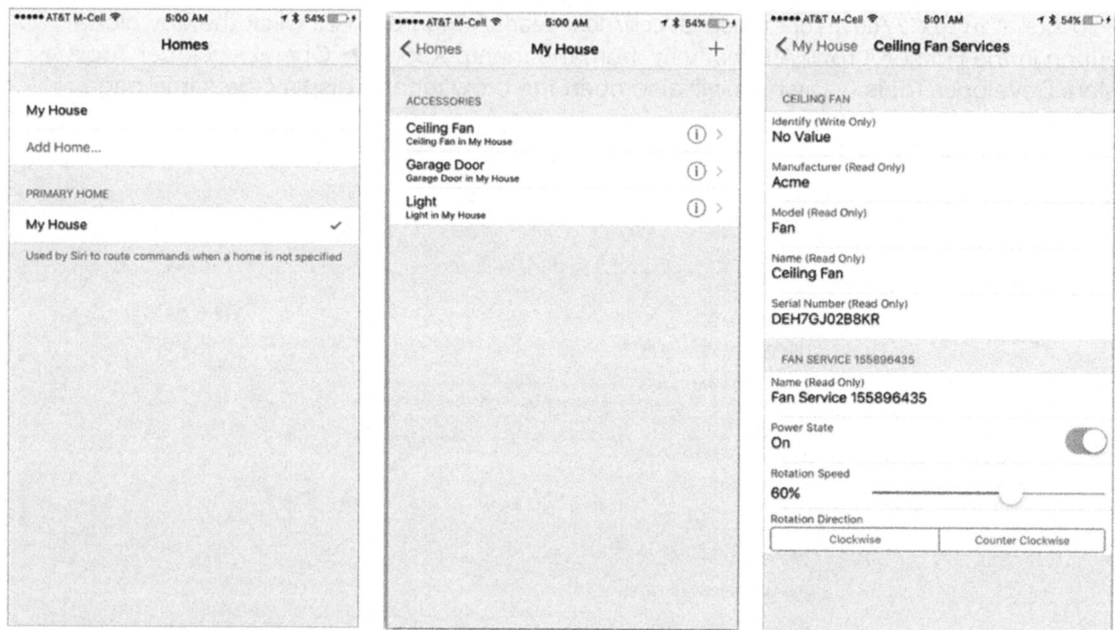

***Figure 11-1.** The HomeKit app*

Requirements

HomeKit is a service that is only available to applications that are distributed through the App Store, so you must have the ability to provision and code-sign your app. To do so, you'll need the following:

- Membership in the iOS developer program.
- Permission to create code signing and provisioning assets in the member center.

> **Note** To create your team provisioning profile, follow the steps in the online document App Distribution Quick Start which can be found in the iOS developer library.

HomeKit Accessory Simulator

Apple provides a HomeKit Accessory Simulator to help you develop your HomeKit apps. The simulator communicates with an iOS device the same way an actual HomeKit accessory would using the HomeKit Accessory Protocol (HAP) over Bluetooth Low Energy (LE) or Wi-Fi, so there's no need buy specific hardware to develop your app. With the simulator, you can create accessories with services and add characteristics to those services.

The simulator is not provided with Xcode, so you'll have to download it from the developer's web site at `https://developer.apple.com/downloads/` (Figure 11-2). Click the download button in the HomeKit row. Alternatively, from the menu, Xcode ➤ Open Developer Tools ➤ More Developer Tools . . ., which will also open the browser and display the same page.

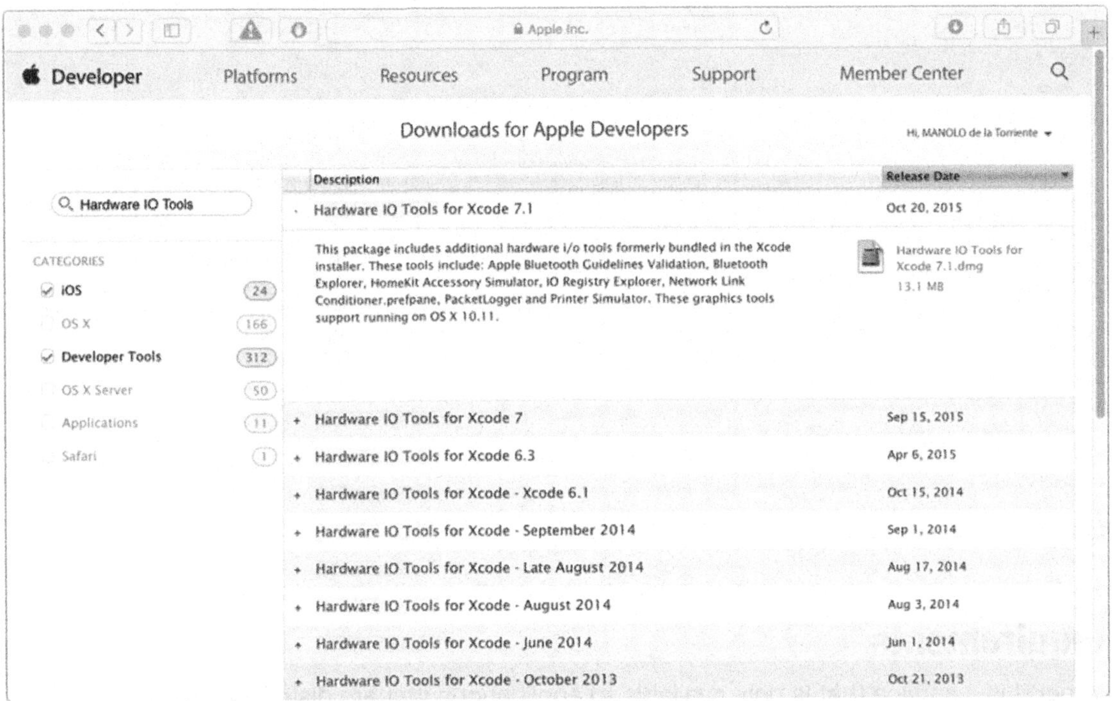

Figure 11-2. Downloads for Apple Developers web page

Search for Hardware IO Tools and select the download which is compatible with your version of Xcode. Once downloaded, double-click the `.dmg` file, and drag HomeKit Accessory Simulator to the /Applications folder. Later on in this chapter, you'll use the simulator to build and test your app.

Creating the Project

We will create an iOS single-view application Xcode project named HomeKitApp. Select Swift as the Language and use the defaults for Language and Devices (see Figure 11-3). You can use HomeKit-enabled accessories with your iPhone, iPad, and iPod touch.

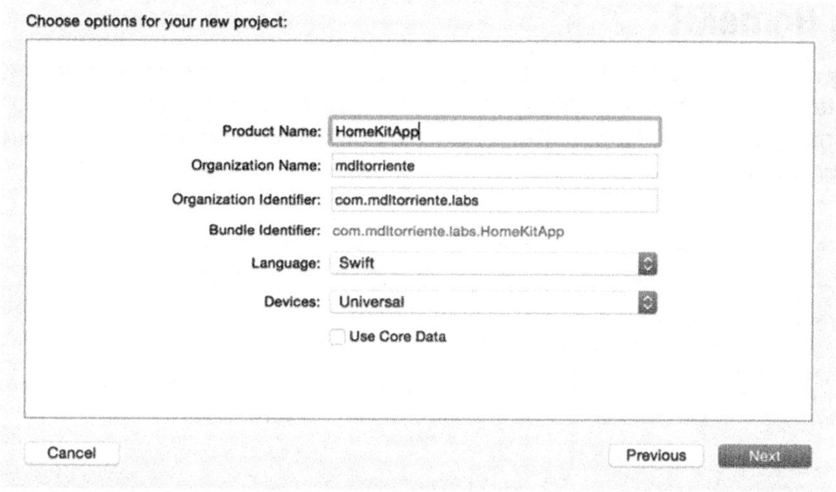

Figure 11-3. *Creating a new single-view Xcode project*

Choose the `HomeKitApp` target from the Targets list and click the General tab to view the General pane (Figure 11-4). In the lower portion of the Identity section, click the Team pop-up menu and select your profile.

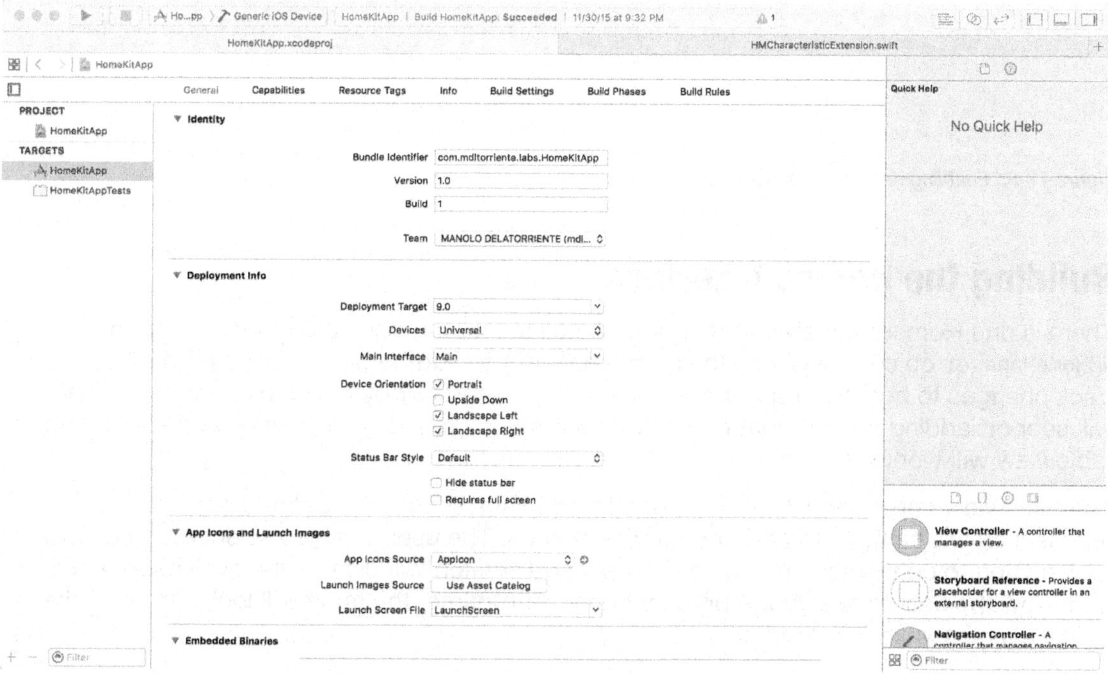

Figure 11-4. *Selecting the team profile*

Enabling HomeKit

HomeKit requires an explicit App ID which is created when you enable HomeKit. Click the Capabilities tab and locate the HomeKit row (see Figure 11-5). Click the switch to the ON position to enable HomeKit. Notice that a new file named `HomeKitApp.entitlements` was added to your project.

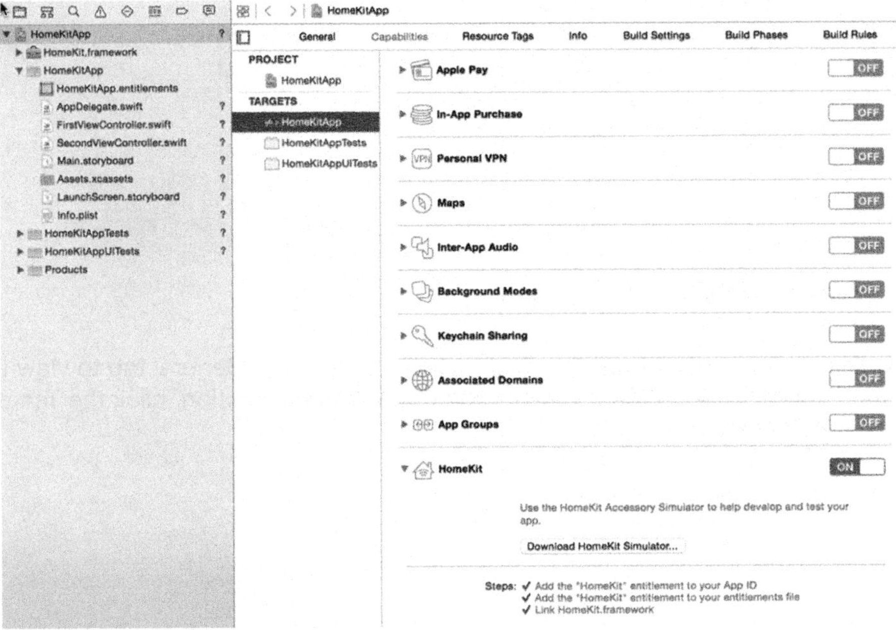

***Figure 11-5.** Enabling HomeKit in app services*

Building the Homes Interface

There is one HomeKit database per home. A collection of homes are managed by an `HMHomeManager` object. You'll use the home manager to add homes, retrieve a list of homes, track changes to homes, and remove homes. You'll start out by building an interface that will support adding one or more homes and the means to assign a primary home. A grouped table view will work well for this.

The table view controller will use sections to present a list of user-defined homes. The first section will be used to add and remove homes. The user can also select a home from that section to configure and control. The second section will display the available homes and allow the user to assign the primary home. At runtime, the table will look similar to the illustration shown in Figure 11-6.

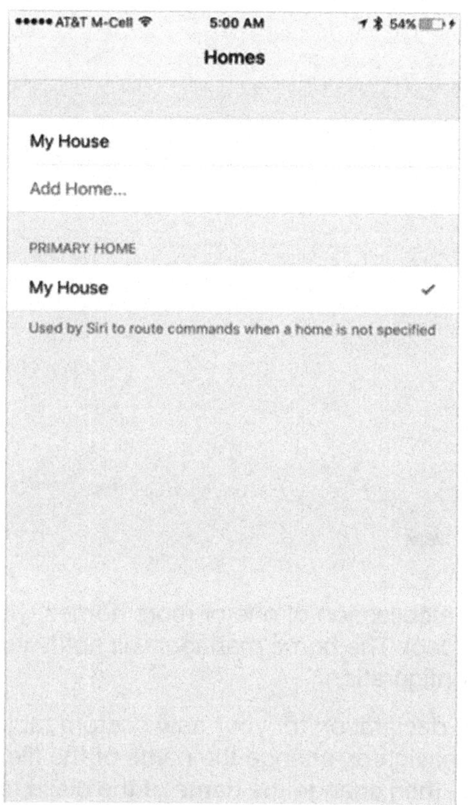

Figure 11-6. *The HomesViewController scene at runtime*

Open the storyboard, then delete the current view controller and replace it with a table view controller. Select the table view controller, then from the Attributes Inspector, set it as the initial view controller for the storyboard by setting the check box *Is initial view controller*. Embed the table view controller in a navigation controller by selecting the table view controller and then from Xcode menu choose Editor ➤ Embed In ➤ Navigation Controller. From the Documents Outline on the left, select the Table View object and change its style to *Grouped* in the Attributes Inspector. Set the title for the navigation item in the table view controller to *Homes*. Your storyboard should look similar to the one Figure 11-7.

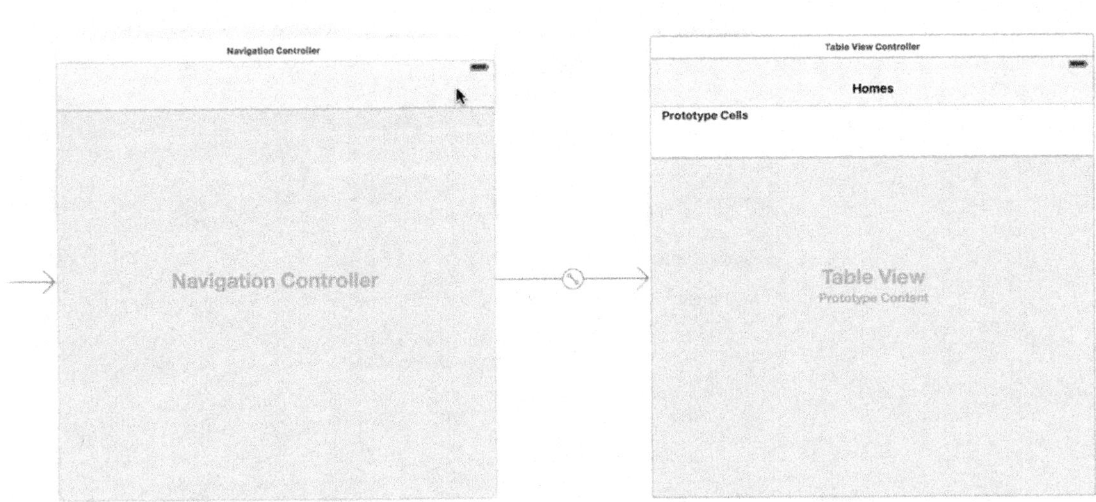

Figure 11-7. Main.storyboard initial view

In order to track changes to a collection of one or more homes, you'll need to implement the `HMHomeManagerDelegate` protocol. The home manager will notify its delegate when there are any changes to the home configuration.

Begin by changing the class declaration for your new custom table view controller (see Listing 11-1). From the navigator, change the name of the file `ViewController.swift` to `HomesViewController.swift`, then change the name of the class to `HomesViewController`, the parent class to `UITableViewController`, and add the protocol for `HMHomeManagerDelegate`.

Listing 11-1. The HomesViewController Class Declaration

```
class HomesViewController: UITableViewController, HMHomeManagerDelegate {
}
```

Then in the storyboard, set the Custom Class for the table view controller to `HomesViewController` in the Identity Inspector (Figure 11-8).

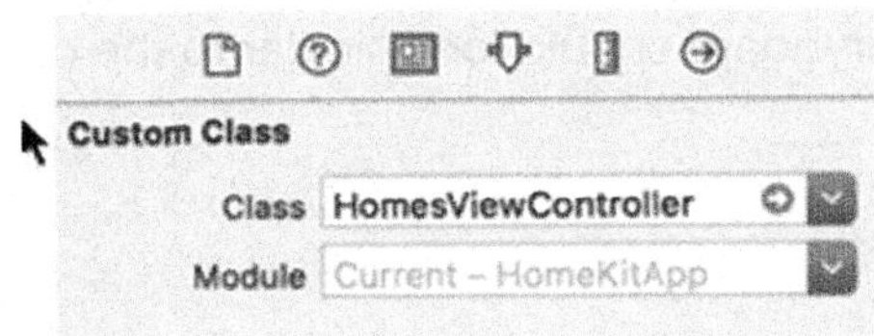

Figure 11-8. Setting custom class HomesViewController

Implementing the Home Manager Delegate Methods

The home manager communicates changes when homes are added, when they are removed, or when significant changes are made to the home configuration. These changes are communicated through the following delegate methods:

- `didAddHome`: Tells the delegate that the home manager added a home.
- `didRemoveHome`: Tells the delegate that the home manager updated its collection of homes.
- `homeManagerDidUpdateHomes`: Tells the delegate that the home manager updated its collection of homes.

Implement these methods in `HomesViewController` (see Listing 11-2). In the `homeManagerDidUpdateHomes` method call `tableView.reloadData()`.

Listing 11-2. Implementing HomeManagerDelegate Methods

```
class HomesViewController: UITableViewController, HMHomeManagerDelegate {

    // MARK: HMHomeManagerDelegate methods

    func homeManagerDidUpdateHomes(manager: HMHomeManager) {
        print("homeManagerDidUpdateHomes")
        tableView.reloadData()
    }

    func homeManager(manager: HMHomeManager, didAddHome home: HMHome) {
        print("didAddHome \(home.name)")
    }

    func homeManager(manager: HMHomeManager, didRemoveHome home: HMHome) {
        print("didRemoveHome \(home.name)")
    }
}
```

Instantiating the HMHomeManager

For the purposes of this application, you'll utilize the singleton pattern to provide a global point of access to an `HMHomeManager` object as well as the current selected `HMHome` object. Create a new file named `HomeStore.swift` and add the code from Listing 11-3.

Listing 11-3. The HomeStore Class Declaration

```
import HomeKit

class HomeStore: NSObject {

    static let sharedInstance = HomeStore()

    var homeManager: HMHomeManager = HMHomeManager()
    var home: HMHome?
}
```

Listing 11-4 updates the HomesViewController to define a computed property homeStore and then assign self as the home manager delegate.

Listing 11-4. Setting a Computed Property for homeStore

```
class HomesViewController: UITableViewController, HMHomeManagerDelegate {

    var homeStore: HomeStore {
        return HomeStore.sharedInstance
    }

    override func viewDidLoad() {
        super.viewDidLoad()
        homeStore.homeManager.delegate = self
    }
```

The HomesViewController will be responsible for setting the value of the HomeStore.home to reflect the current home, based on user input.

Setting Up the Table View

Open the storyboard and add four custom prototype cells to the Homes table view as shown in Figure 11-9.

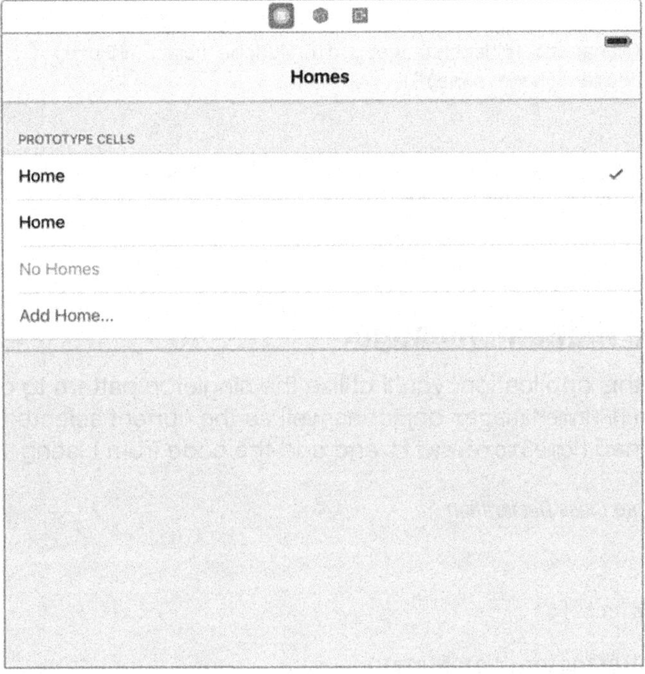

Figure 11-9. Custom prototype cells in the storyboard

At the top of the HomesViewController class body, add a structure named Identifiers and define a constant property for each of the prototype cells. The cells are listed in the same order as shown in Listing 11-5.

Listing 11-5. Reuse Identifiers for Custom Prototype Table View Cells

```
struct Identifiers {
    static let addHomeCell = "AddHomeCell"
    static let noHomesCell = "NoHomesCell"
    static let primaryHomeCell = "PrimaryHomeCell"
    static let homeCell = "HomeCell"
}
```

Now in the storyboard using the Attributes Inspector, assign each of the custom table view cells to the corresponding reuse identifier from the Identifiers struct. This is the same reuse identifier you will send to the table view in the dequeueReusableCellWithIdentifier message. Make sure you assign Checkmark in the Accessory pop-up window for the PrimaryHomeCell shown in Figure 11-10.

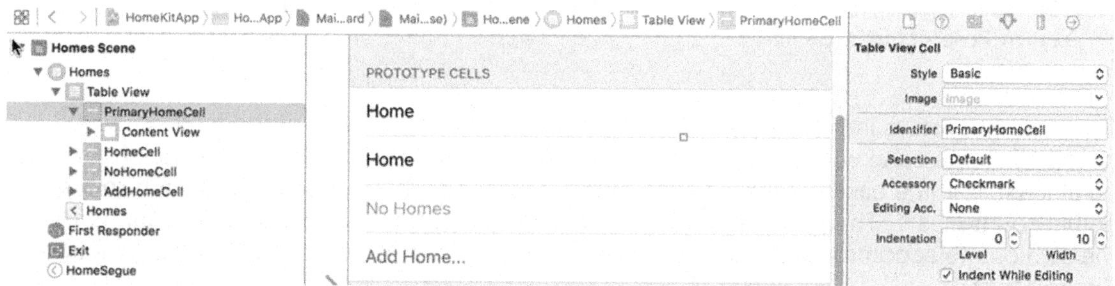

***Figure 11-10.** Assign a custom table view cell identifier*

Implementing UITableView Methods

At the top of the HomesViewController class body, add an enum named HomeSections with values for Homes and PrimaryHome. These values correspond to the IndexPath.section index number which is passed in as a parameter to table view delegate methods and will be used to identify a specified section of a UITableView object (Listing 11-6).

Listing 11-6. HomeSections Enum for Table View Sections

```
enum HomeSections: Int {
    case Homes = 0, PrimaryHome
    static let count = 2
}
```

To help determine which type of table row is associated with a table view section, use the helper method shown in Listing 11-7. The isHomesListEmpty method simply returns whether or not the homes count equals zero, and the isIndexPathAddHome method returns true if the specified row in the homes section is the last row.

Listing 11-7. Table View Helper Methods

```
// MARK: UITableView helpers

func isHomesListEmpty() -> Bool {
    return homeStore.homeManager.homes.count == 0
}

func isIndexPathAddHome(indexPath: NSIndexPath) -> Bool {
    return indexPath.section == HomeSections.Homes.rawValue
        && indexPath.row == homeStore.homeManager.homes.count
}
```

The value of the `HomeSections` count, which is currently defined at 2, determines the number of sections in the table view (see Listing 11-8).

Listing 11-8. The Number of Sections in the Table View

```
// MARK: UITableView methods

override func numberOfSectionsInTableView(tableView: UITableView) -> Int {
    return HomeSections.count
}
```

The number of rows in a section will be dependent on which section of the table view is specified. In the case where the section is `PrimaryHome`, the number of rows value should be at least 1. In the case where the section is `Homes`, the number should always return the actual count plus 1. This guarantees that there will always be at least one row in each of the sections to accommodate the AddHome . . . and No Homes cells (see Listing 11-9 and Figure 11-11).

Listing 11-9. The Number of Rows in a Given Section of a Table View

```
override func tableView(tableView: UITableView, numberOfRowsInSection section: Int) -> Int {

    let count = homeStore.homeManager.homes.count

    switch (section) {
    case HomeSections.PrimaryHome.rawValue:
        return max(count, 1)
    case HomeSections.Homes.rawValue:
        return count + 1
    default:
        break
    }

    return 0
}
```

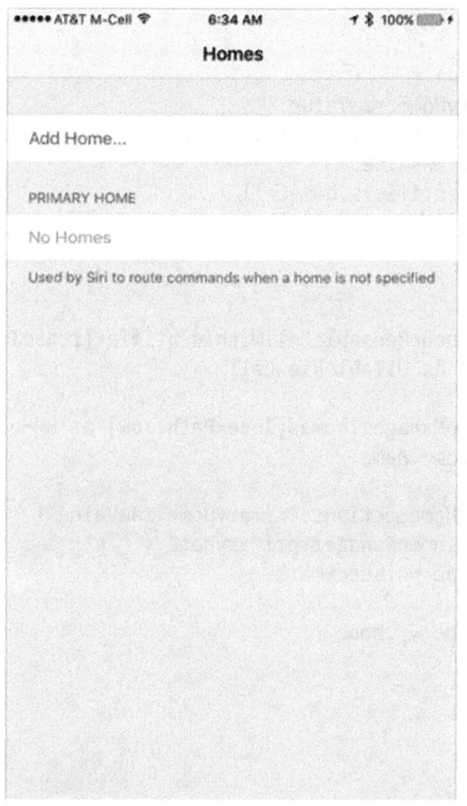

***Figure 11-11.** Initial empty state of homes view*

The delegate method cellForRowAtIndexPath returns a UITableViewCell object that corresponds to the specified row and section. In the case where the row/section corresponds to a row which contains a home defined by the user, the reuse identifier is set based on whether or not the home section is for the primary home. The cell object is then initialized with the home name and corresponding cell accessory type (see Listing 11-10).

***Listing 11-10.** Cell to Insert in a Particular Location of the Table View*

```
override func tableView(tableView: UITableView, cellForRowAtIndexPath indexPath:
NSIndexPath) -> UITableViewCell {

    if isIndexPathAddHome(indexPath) {
        return tableView.dequeueReusableCellWithIdentifier(Identifiers.addHomeCell,
        forIndexPath: indexPath)
    } else if isHomesListEmpty() {
        return tableView.dequeueReusableCellWithIdentifier(Identifiers.noHomesCell,
        forIndexPath: indexPath)
    }
```

```
    var reuseIdentifier: String?

    switch (indexPath.section) {
    case HomeSections.PrimaryHome.rawValue:
        reuseIdentifier = Identifiers.primaryHomeCell
    case HomeSections.Homes.rawValue:
        reuseIdentifier = Identifiers.homeCell
    default:
        break
    }

    let cell = tableView.dequeueReusableCellWithIdentifier(reuseIdentifier!,
    forIndexPath: indexPath) as UITableViewCell

    let home = homeStore.homeManager.homes[indexPath.row] as HMHome
    cell.textLabel?.text = home.name

    if indexPath.section == HomeSections.PrimaryHome.rawValue {
        if home == homeStore.homeManager.primaryHome {
            cell.accessoryType = .Checkmark
        } else {
            cell.accessoryType = .None
        }
    }

    return cell
}
```

Listing 11-11 indicates that the section for the primary home has a header and a footer.

Listing 11-11. Primary Home Section Header and Footer

```
override func tableView(tableView: UITableView, titleForHeaderInSection section: Int) ->
String? {
    if section == HomeSections.PrimaryHome.rawValue {
        return "Primary Home"
    }
    return nil
}

override func tableView(tableView: UITableView, titleForFooterInSection section: Int) ->
String? {
    if section == HomeSections.PrimaryHome.rawValue {
        return "Used by Siri to route commands when a home is not specified"
    }
    return nil
}
```

Adding a New Home to the Home Manager

When the user selects the table row labeled Add Home . . ., the onAddHomeTouched method is invoked from the didSelectRowAtIndexPath method and the user is presented with a simple UIAlertController prompting for a name. Once you enter a valid name, the home is added using the home manager method addHomeWithName (see Listing 11-12).

Listing 11-12. Adding a New Home to the Home Manager

```
self.homeStore.homeManager.addHomeWithName(homeName, completionHandler: { home, error in
    if error != nil {
        print("failed to add new home. \(error)")
    } else {
        print("added home \(home!.name)")
        self.tableView.reloadData()
    }
})
```

On success, the table view is refreshed, and the new home appears in the list. If the home is the first home, it's assigned as the primary home. You can find the complete method in Listing 11-13.

Listing 11-13. A UIAlertController Used to Add a New Home

```
private func onAddHomeTouched() {

    let controller = UIAlertController(title: "Add Home", message: "Enter a name for the
    home", preferredStyle: .Alert)

    controller.addTextFieldWithConfigurationHandler({ textField in
        textField.placeholder = "My House"
    })

    controller.addAction(UIAlertAction(title: "Cancel", style: .Cancel, handler: nil))

    controller.addAction(UIAlertAction(title: "Add Home", style: .Default) { action in
        let textFields = controller.textFields as [UITextField]!
        if let homeName = textFields[0].text {

            if homeName.isEmpty {
                let alert = UIAlertController(title: "Error", message: "Please enter a
                name", preferredStyle: .Alert)
               alert.addAction(UIAlertAction(title: "Dismiss", style: .Default, handler: nil))
                self.presentViewController(alert, animated: true, completion: nil)

            } else {
                self.homeStore.homeManager.addHomeWithName(homeName, completionHandler: {
                home, error in
```

```
                    if error != nil {
                        print("failed to add new home. \(error)")
                    } else {
                        print("added home \(home!.name)")
                        self.tableView.reloadData()
                    }
                })
            }
        }
    })
    presentViewController(controller, animated: true, completion: nil)
}
```

Setting the Primary Home

When the user selects a home listed in the Primary Home section, the home manager's `updatePrimaryHome` method is called (Listing 11-14). The completion handler reloads the table view if the call succeeded.

Listing 11-14. Setting the Primary Home

```
homeStore.homeManager.updatePrimaryHome(home, completionHandler: { error in
    if let error = error {
        UIAlertController.showErrorAlert(self, error: error)
    } else {
        let indexSet = NSIndexSet(index: HomeSections.PrimaryHome.rawValue)
        tableView.reloadSections(indexSet, withRowAnimation: .Automatic)
    }
})
```

Siri Integration

Siri recognizes home, room, zone, accessory, and characteristic names. Siri uses the primary home when the command does not specify a home name.

Setting the Current Home

When the user selects a home listed in the first section, the current home is set in the home store.

```
homeStore.home = homeStore.homeManager.homes[indexPath.row]
```

The view will then transition to a detailed view for the home where the user can configure or control its accessories.

Listing 11-15. Informing the Delegate About the New Row Selection

```
override func tableView(tableView: UITableView, didSelectRowAtIndexPath indexPath:
NSIndexPath) {

    if isIndexPathAddHome(indexPath) {
        tableView.deselectRowAtIndexPath(indexPath, animated: true)
        onAddHomeTouched()

    } else {
        homeStore.home = homeStore.homeManager.homes[indexPath.row]
        if HomeSections(rawValue: indexPath.section) == .PrimaryHome {
            let home = homeStore.homeManager.homes[indexPath.row]
            if home != homeStore.homeManager.primaryHome {
                homeStore.homeManager.updatePrimaryHome(home, completionHandler: { error in
                    if let error = error {
                        UIAlertController.showErrorAlert(self, error: error)
                    } else {
                        let indexSet = NSIndexSet(index: HomeSections.PrimaryHome.rawValue)
                        tableView.reloadSections(indexSet, withRowAnimation: .Automatic)
                    }
                })
            }
        }
    }
}
```

Removing an Existing Home

When you swipe a table row, it enters into editing mode. The table view invokes its `canEditRowAtIndexPath` method where the application can determine on a row-by-row basis to allow editing.

Listing 11-16. Verify That the Given Row Is Editable

```
override func tableView(tableView: UITableView, canEditRowAtIndexPath indexPath:
NSIndexPath) -> Bool {
    return !isIndexPathAddHome(indexPath)
        && !isHomesListEmpty()
        && indexPath.section == HomeSections.Homes.rawValue
}
```

If editing is allowed for a row, the row displays a Delete button. If the user taps the Delete button, the view controller receives a `commitEditingStyle` message from the table view. If the `editingStyle` is *Delete*, `removeHome` can be called on the home manager.

```
let home = homeStore.homeManager.homes[indexPath.row] as HMHome
homeStore.homeManager.removeHome(home, completionHandler: { error in
})
```

In the completion block, if there is no error, `tableView.deleteRowsAtIndexPaths` is called. See Listing 11-17 for the complete method.

Listing 11-17. Requesting Deletion

```
override func tableView(tableView: UITableView, commitEditingStyle editingStyle:
UITableViewCellEditingStyle, forRowAtIndexPath indexPath: NSIndexPath) {

    if (editingStyle == .Delete) {

        let home = homeStore.homeManager.homes[indexPath.row] as HMHome
        homeStore.homeManager.removeHome(home, completionHandler: { error in

            if error != nil {
                print("Error \(error)")
                return

            } else {
                tableView.beginUpdates()
                    let primaryIndexPath = NSIndexPath(forRow: indexPath.row,
                    inSection: HomeSections.PrimaryHome.rawValue)
                    if self.homeStore.homeManager.homes.count == 0 {
                        tableView.reloadRowsAtIndexPaths([primaryIndexPath],
                        withRowAnimation: UITableViewRowAnimation.Fade)
                    } else {
                        tableView.deleteRowsAtIndexPaths([primaryIndexPath],
                        withRowAnimation: .Automatic)
                    }
                   tableView.deleteRowsAtIndexPaths([indexPath], withRowAnimation: .Automatic)
                tableView.endUpdates()
            }
        })
    }
}
```

Security

When home manager has been called for the first time on a device, it will alert the user and ask for permission to access the user's accessory data.

Selecting "Don't Allow" (Figure 11-12) prevents HomeKit from providing information to your application, in which case the settings will have to be changed in the `Settings.app` in the Privacy/Homekit section.

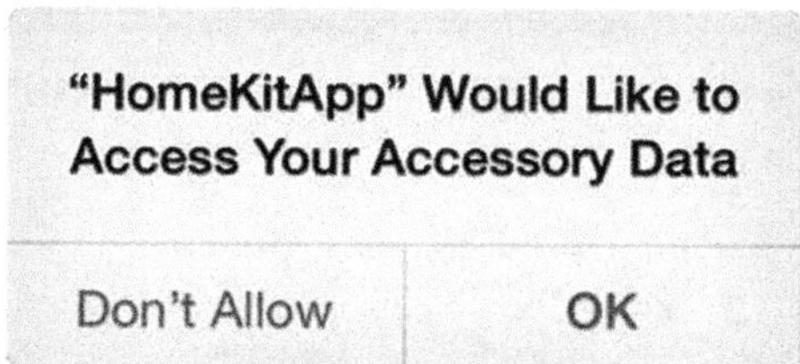

Figure 11-12. Don't Allow stops HomeKit from supplying data to your app

If the user is signed into an iCloud account on the device but hasn't enabled the iCloud keychain, HomeKit will prompt the user to turn on the iCloud keychain to allow access from the user's other devices.

Building the Home Interface

The Home scene will display all the accessories that are associated with the selected home. It will also provide the means to add discoverable accessories. For this scene, you will need a table view that uses a standard prototype cell and a navigation bar item to invoke an accessory browser.

The Home table scene will use a grouped table view to present a list of accessories for the selected home. The Add (+) navigation bar item will open an accessory browser. Selecting an accessory from the browser will add the accessory to the current home, then send a notification and return to the Home scene. The `HomeViewController` will handle the notification and refresh the view. When you select an accessory from the table, the scene will transition to the Services scene where accessories can be controlled.

At runtime, the table will look similar to the illustrations in Figure 11-13. The first view is empty; the second is populated with three accessories.

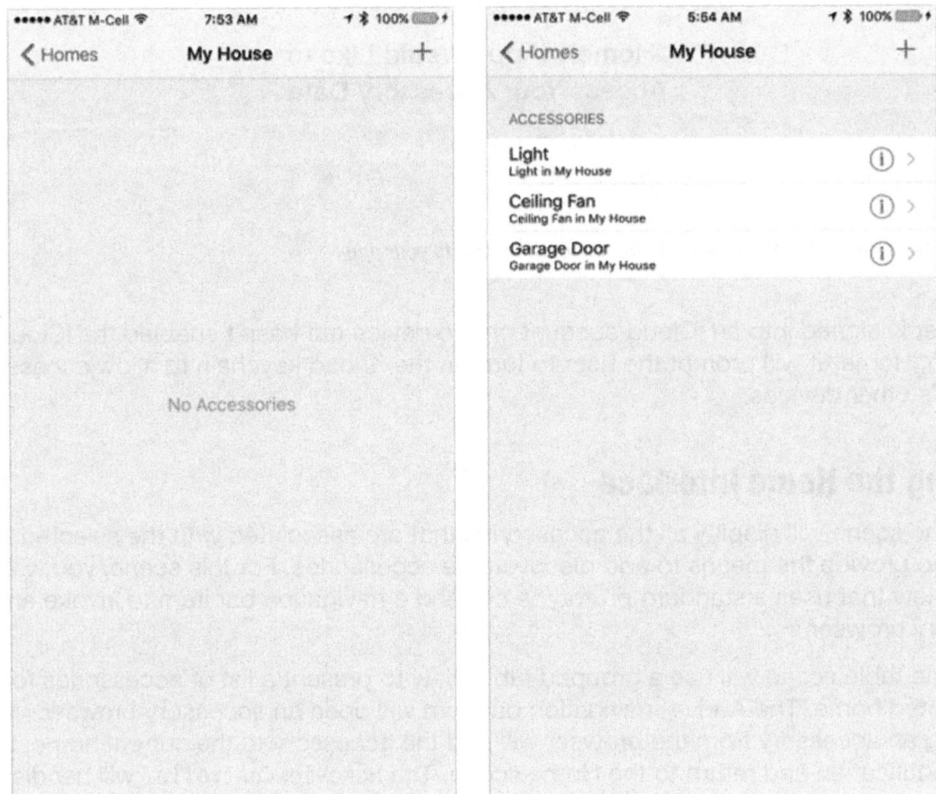

***Figure 11-13.** The Home scene with empty table, and populated with accessories*

Open the storyboard and add a new `UITableViewController` to the storyboard canvas.

Select the table view and in the Attributes Inspector, change the style to *Grouped*.

Select the table view cell (Figure 11-14) and in the Attributes Inspector, change its style to *Subtitle*; Identifier to *AccessoryCell*; Accessory type to *Detail Disclosure*.

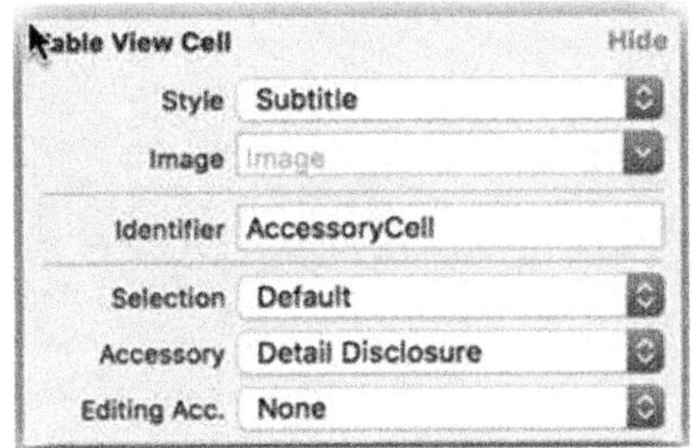

***Figure 11-14.** Setting up the table view cell*

Now add a segue from the `HomeCell` of the `HomesViewController` to the new table view controller you've just added (see Figure 11-15).

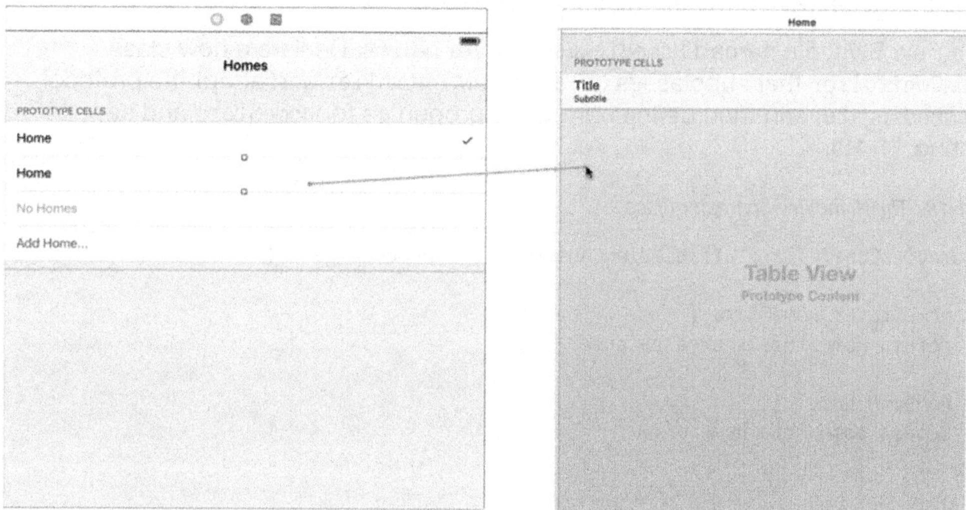

***Figure 11-15.** Adding a segue to the home view controller*

Notice a navigation bar was automatically added for you. Change the navigation bar title to *Home* (see Figure 11-16).

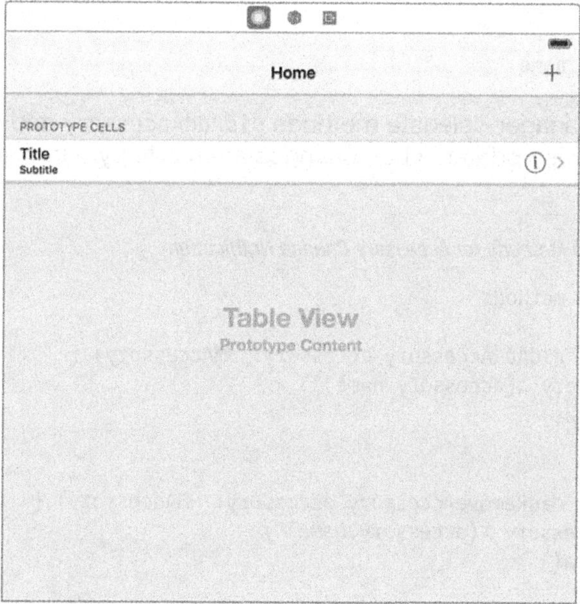

***Figure 11-16.** The home view controller interface*

Next, add a *Bar Button Item* to the navigation bar. From the Attributes Inspector in the *Bar Button Item* section, change the System Item *Add* so that a plus (+) symbol is displayed. This control will be used to invoke an *Accessory Browser*, which you'll build in the section "Building the Accessory Browser" (see Figure 11-26).

Create a new Swift file named HomeViewController.swift. Declare a new class HomeViewController that subclasses UITableViewController and adopt the protocol for HMHomeDelegate, and then define computed properties for homeStore and home (see Listing 11-18).

Listing 11-18. The HomeViewController Class

```
class HomeViewController: UITableViewController, HMHomeDelegate {

    var homeStore: HomeStore {
        return HomeStore.sharedInstance
    }
    var home: HMHome! {
        return homeStore.home
    }
}
```

In the storyboard set the custom class for the table view controller to HomeViewController in the Identity Inspector.

Assign self as the current home delegate, and set the view controller's title to the name of the current home in the viewDidLoad method after the line with super.viewDidLoad() (see Listing 11-4).

```
home?.delegate = self
title = homeStore.home!.name
```

Implement the home manager delegate methods didAddAccessory and didRemoveAccessory such that the table view is updated when changes are made by other HomeKit apps (see Listing 11-19).

Listing 11-19. Home Delegate Methods for Accessory Change Notification

```
// MARK: HMHomeDelegate methods

func home(home: HMHome, didAddAccessory accessory: HMAccessory) {
    print("didAddAccessory \(accessory.name)")
    tableView.reloadData()
}

func home(home: HMHome, didRemoveAccessory accessory: HMAccessory) {
    print("didRemoveAccessory \(accessory.name)")
    tableView.reloadData()
}
```

Signaling Changes within the Application

Remember, your app is expected to use completion handlers to reload data and update its views. A convenient method is the use of `NSNotificationCenter`.

In the `HomeStore` class, add a constant for `AddAccessoryNotification` at the top of the class body as shown in Listing 11-20.

Listing 11-20. Declaring a Constant as a Notification Identifier to Be Used with NSNotificationCenter

```
struct Notification {
    static let AddAccessoryNotification = "AddAccessoryNotification"
}
```

In the `viewDidLoad` method of the `HomeStore` class, add the following line shown in 11-21 to register an observer for the `AddAccessoryNotification`.

Listing 11-21. Registering an Observer to Receive Notifications When an Accessory Is Added

```
NSNotificationCenter.defaultCenter().addObserver(self,
    selector: "updateAccessories",
    name: HomeStore.Notification.AddAccessoryNotification, object: nil)
```

Add a new method shown in Listing 11-22, which will be used for the notification selector. This method will reload the data for the table view when the notification is received.

Listing 11-22. The Selector That's Invoked When the AddAccessoryNotification Is Posted

```
func updateAccessories() {
    print("updateAccessories selector called from NSNotificationCenter")
    tableView.reloadData()
}
```

Implementing More UITableView Methods

There will be two sections in the Home table view. The first section will be used as the "Accessories" section heading, and the second is for the accessories list (see Listing 11-23).

Listing 11-23. Determine the Number of Sections in the Table View

```
override func numberOfSectionsInTableView(tableView: UITableView) -> Int {

    if homeStore.home?.accessories.count == 0 {
        setBackgroundMessage("No Accessories")
    } else {
        setBackgroundMessage(nil)
    }
    return 2
}
```

A background message is also set in the `numberOfSectionsInTableView` method if the table is empty; otherwise no message is displayed (see Listing 11-24).

Listing 11-24. Method to Dynamically Set a Simple Background Message

```
private func setBackgroundMessage(message: String?) {
    if let message = message {
        let label = UILabel()
        label.text = message
        label.font = UIFont.preferredFontForTextStyle(UIFontTextStyleBody)
        label.textColor = UIColor.lightGrayColor()
        label.textAlignment = .Center
        label.sizeToFit()
        tableView.backgroundView = label
        tableView.separatorStyle = .None
    }
    else {
        tableView.backgroundView = nil
        tableView.separatorStyle = .SingleLine
    }
}
```

The number of rows in the first section of table view is 0, as only the section heading is displayed. The number of rows in the second section is determined by the number of accessories associated with the current home (see Listing 11-25).

Listing 11-25. Determine the Number of Rows for Each Section

```
override func tableView(tableView: UITableView, numberOfRowsInSection section: Int) -> Int {
    if section == 1 {
        return homeStore.home!.accessories.count
    }
    return 0
}
```

The data source for the table is a list of accessories that are assigned to the current home. Each row maps to an element in the accessories list. Accessories are added by the Accessory Browser (see Listing 11-26).

Listing 11-26. Setting up a Table Cell for an Accessory

```
override func tableView(tableView: UITableView, cellForRowAtIndexPath indexPath:
NSIndexPath) -> UITableViewCell {
    let accessory = homeStore.home!.accessories[indexPath.row];
    let reuseIdentifier = "AccessoryCell"

    let cell = tableView.dequeueReusableCellWithIdentifier(reuseIdentifier,
    forIndexPath: indexPath)
    cell.textLabel?.text = accessory.name

    let accessoryName = accessory.name
    let roomName = accessory.room!.name
    let inIdentifier = NSLocalizedString("%@ in %@", comment: "Accessory in Room")
    cell.detailTextLabel?.text = String(format: inIdentifier, accessoryName, roomName)
    return cell
}
```

Listing 11-27. Returning a Header for a Specified Section

```
override func tableView(tableView: UITableView, titleForHeaderInSection section: Int) ->
String? {
    if section == 0 {
        return homeStore.home?.accessories.count != 0 ? "Accessories" : ""
    }
    return nil
}
```

Removing an Accessory from a Home

When an accessory table row is swiped, the table enters into editing mode. The table view invokes its `canEditRowAtIndexPath` method where the application can determine on a row-by-row basis to allow editing. In this case, the accessories list row is always editable (see Listing 11-28).

Listing 11-28. Verify That the Given Row Is Editable

```
override func tableView(tableView: UITableView, canEditRowAtIndexPath indexPath:
NSIndexPath) -> Bool {
    if indexPath.section == 1 {
        return true
    }
    return false
}
```

If editing is allowed for a row, the row displays a Delete button. If the user taps the Delete button, the view controller receives a `commitEditingStyle` message from the table view (see Listing 11-29). If the `editingStyle` is *Delete*, then `removeAccessory` can be called on the current home. In the completion block, if there is no error, `tableView.deleteRowsAtIndexPaths` is called.

Listing 11-29. The UITableViewDelegate Method commitEditingStyle

```
override func tableView(tableView: UITableView, commitEditingStyle editingStyle:
UITableViewCellEditingStyle, forRowAtIndexPath indexPath: NSIndexPath) {

    if (editingStyle == .Delete) {

        let accessory = homeStore.home?.accessories[indexPath.row]
        homeStore.home?.removeAccessory(accessory!, completionHandler: { error in
            if error != nil {
                print("Error \(error)")
                UIAlertController.showErrorAlert(self, error: error!)

            } else {
                tableView.beginUpdates()
```

```
                let rowAnimation = self.homeStore.home?.accessories.count == 0 ?
                UITableViewRowAnimation.Fade : UITableViewRowAnimation.Automatic
              tableView.deleteRowsAtIndexPaths([indexPath], withRowAnimation: rowAnimation)
            tableView.endUpdates()
            tableView.reloadData()
          }
      })
    }
}
```

Using the HomeKit Accessory Simulator

The HomeKit Accessory Simulator is a developer tool that allows you to define accessories for which you don't have a physical accessory. You can create accessories and add services and characteristics to closely represent physical devices. For example, you can define a ceiling fan and then add services to turn power on and off and change the rotation speed and rotation direction. From your application, you can scan for and add the accessories you define in the simulator, and then control the services just as you would with a physical accessory. The simulator allows you to pair with a device, change values, and receive changed values. So when you flip a switch in your app you can see the result immediately in the simulator, and vice versa; if you change values in the simulator, it sends the changed values to your app.

You can start by creating a lamp accessory. Launch the simulator (`/Applications/HomeKit Accessory Simulator.app`) and then, located in the lower left corner of the app, click the Add button (+) and select New Accessory from the pop-up. When prompted, enter a name and manufacturer for accessory and leave the default for serial number as shown in Figure 11-17. Click the Finish button.

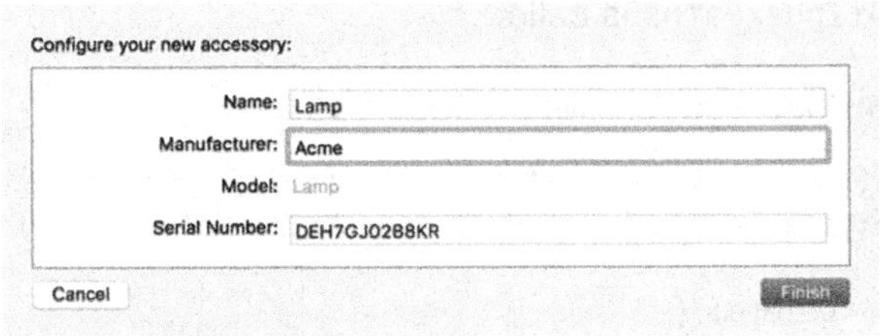

***Figure 11-17.** Configure new accessory options pop-up*

You should see a new accessory item in the left panel under IP Accessories, and the main view on the right where you can add services and characteristics (see Figure 11-18).

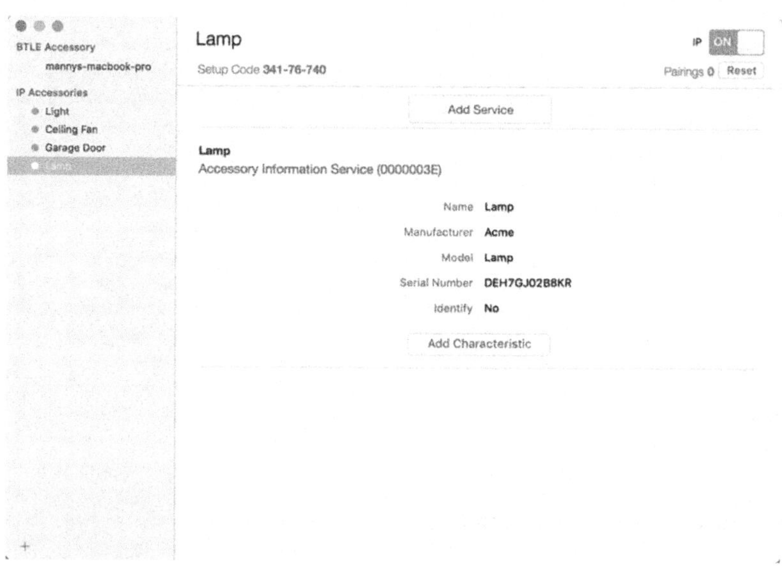

Figure 11-18. Accessory detail view

Your new lamp accessory needs a service with characteristics that you can control from your app. Select your accessory from the list on the left side of the window, and then click the Add Service button located in the upper portion of the main view. From the options pop-up, click the Service pull-down, select Lightbulb Service, and then click the Finish button (see Figure 11-19). The new service appears in the detail view.

Figure 11-19. Configure new service options pop-up

The simulator automatically creates a common characteristic for each service type, so for the lamp accessory you just created, an On characteristic was added for you (Figure 11-20). Some characteristics are mandatory, like the On power switch, but if you wanted to add an additional characteristic like a dimmer, for example, you would click the Add Characteristic button and add a Brightness characteristic from the Characteristic pull-down in the options pop-up.

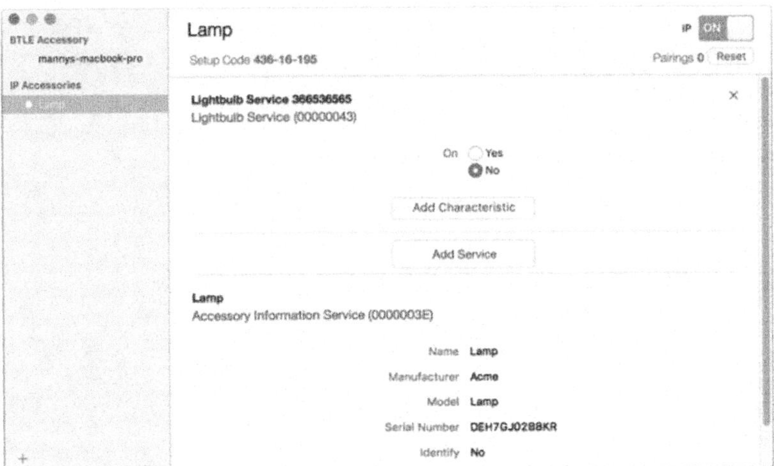

Figure 11-20. Accessory detail view with On characteristic

You now have an accessory that can be discovered and controlled from your app. Later in this chapter, you'll add support to browse for available accessories.

Pairing with a New Accessory

In your application when you attempt to add a new accessory, the system will present an Add HomeKit Accessory dialog that states that the accessory is not certified. This is allowed when using the HomeKit Accessory Simulator, so click the Add Anyway button (see Figure 11-21).

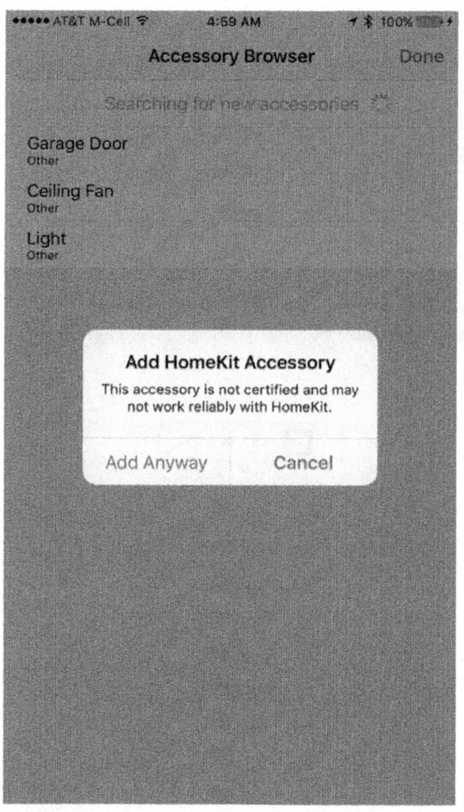

***Figure 11-21.** Add HomeKit accessory dialog*

The system will present a screen that asked you to provide a setup code for the accessory. Click the Enter code manually button located at the bottom of Figure 11-22.

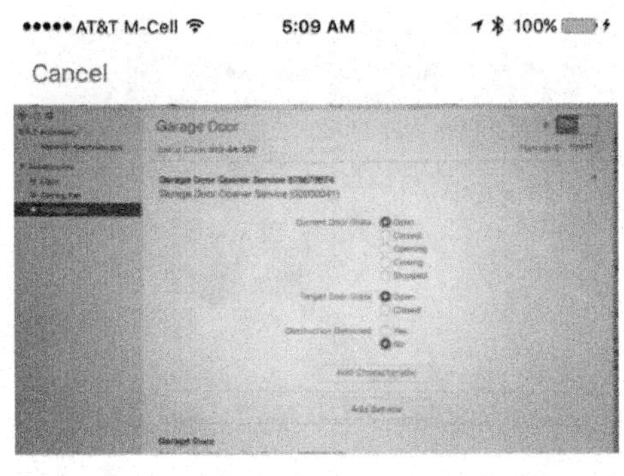

***Figure 11-22.** Add Accessory option screen*

Another screen is presented that allows you to enter an eight-digit code. Enter the setup code from the simulator's main view detail area below the accessory name (Figure 11-23).

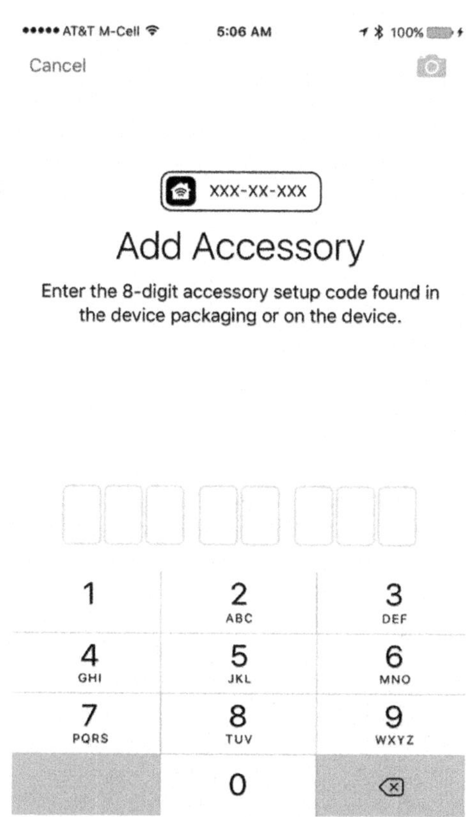

***Figure 11-23.** Add setup code entry screen*

The system displays a progress indicator while it processes the setup code. If you entered the wrong code (or selected cancel), you will be presented with a screen that allows you to enter the code again. If you entered the correct code, the system presents a screen that states that the accessory was added and is ready to use (Figure 11-24).

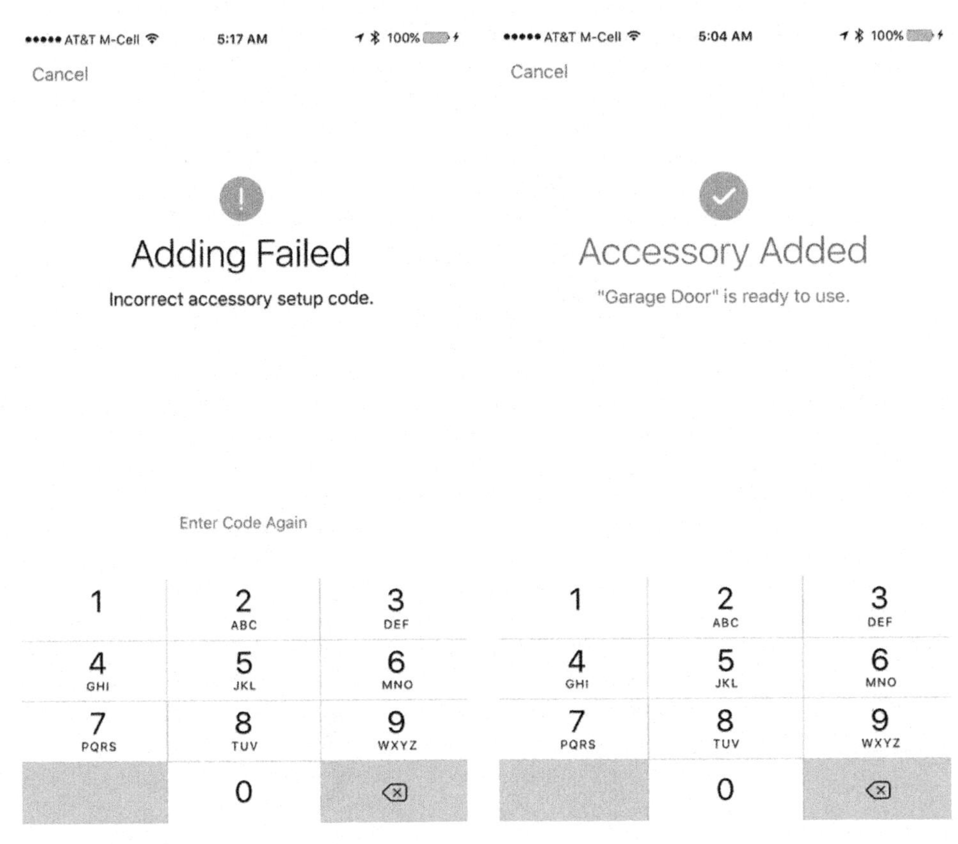

***Figure 11-24.** Setup code result screens*

Building the Accessory Browser

The accessory browser is used to scan for HomeKit-enabled accessories. The scene will use a grouped table view to present a list of HomeKit-enabled accessories that are not already associated with the selected home.

At runtime, the table will look similar to the illustration in Figure 11-25.

***Figure 11-25.** The Accessory Browser scene with available accessories*

Open the storyboard and drag a new navigation controller from the Object library onto the storyboard canvas. A new `UITableViewController` will automatically be added to the storyboard canvas.

Change the title of the table view navigation item to *Accessory Browser*.

Select the table view and in the Attributes Inspector and change the style to *Grouped*.

Select the table view cell and in the Attributes Inspector, change its style to *Subtitle* and Identifier to *AccessoryCell*.

Drag a *View* from the Object library and insert it above the table view cell.

Add a *Label* to the view you just added and set the text to *Searching for new accessories.*

Add an *Activity View Indicator* to the right of the label you just added. The Accessory Browser Scene in the Document outline should look similar to the one in Figure 11-26.

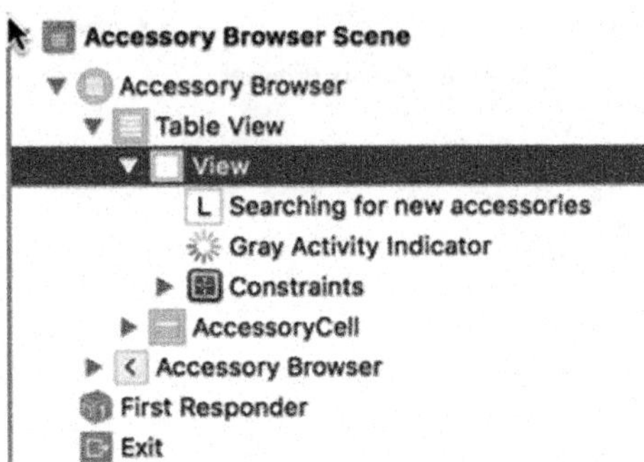

***Figure 11-26.** Accessory Browser Scene outline*

Add a *Bar Button Item* to the navigation bar. From the Attributes Inspector in the *Bar Button Item* section, change the System Item to *Done.* This control will be used to dismiss the *Accessory Browser*.

Your Accessory Browser scene should look similar to the illustration in Figure 11-27.

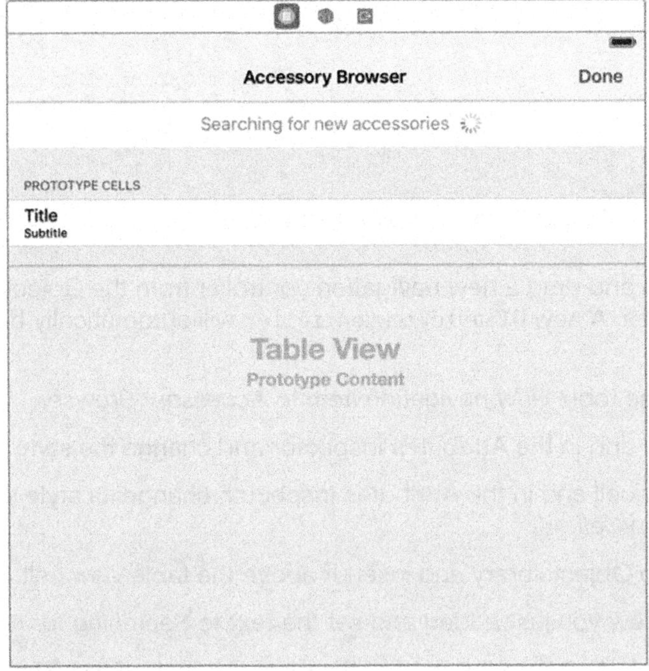

***Figure 11-27.** Complete Accessory Browser scene*

Create a new Swift file named AccessoryBrowser.swift. Declare a new class AccessoryBrowser that subclasses UITableViewController and adopts the protocol for HMAccessoryBrowserDelegate (see Listing 11-30). Add the properties accessoryBrowser, accessories, and selectedAccessory.

Listing 11-30. The AccessoryBrowser Class

```
class AccessoryBrowser: UITableViewController, HMAccessoryBrowserDelegate {

    let accessoryBrowser = HMAccessoryBrowser()
    var accessories = [HMAccessory]()
    var selectedAccessory: HMAccessory?
}
```

In the storyboard set the *Custom Class* for the table view controller to AccessoryBrowser in the Identity Inspector.

Assign self as the accessory browser delegate in the viewDidLoad method after the line with super.viewDidLoad().

```
accessoryBrowser.delegate = self
```

Implement the accessory browser delegate methods didFindNewAccessory and didRemoveNewAccessory such that the specified accessory is added or removed from the table view (see Listing 11-31). When adding a new accessory, check that it doesn't already exist.

Listing 11-31. Accessory Browser Delegate Methods

```
// MARK: HMAccessoryBrowserDelegate methods

func accessoryBrowser(browser: HMAccessoryBrowser, didFindNewAccessory accessory:
HMAccessory) {
    print("didFindNewAccessory \(accessory.name)")
    if !self.accessories.contains(accessory) {
        self.accessories.insert(accessory, atIndex: 0)
        let indexPath = NSIndexPath(forRow: 0, inSection: 0)
        tableView.insertRowsAtIndexPaths([indexPath], withRowAnimation: .Automatic)
    }
}

func accessoryBrowser(browser: HMAccessoryBrowser, didRemoveNewAccessory accessory:
HMAccessory) {
    print("didRemoveNewAccessory \(accessory.name)")
    if let index = accessories.indexOf(accessory) {
        let indexPath = NSIndexPath(forRow: index, inSection: 0)
        accessories.removeAtIndex(index)
        tableView.deleteRowsAtIndexPaths([indexPath], withRowAnimation: .Automatic)
    }
}
```

Scanning for Accessories

To start scanning for available accessories, call the accessory browser's startSearchingForNewAccessories method. In this example app, it's called from the viewDidLoad method of the view controller.

```
accessoryBrowser.startSearchingForNewAccessories()
```

To stop searching, call the accessory browser's stopSearchingForNewAccessories method. The example app calls this from the viewWillDisappear method of the view controller.

```
override func viewWillDisappear(animated: Bool) {
    accessoryBrowser.stopSearchingForNewAccessories()
}
```

Implementing UITableView Methods

The data source for the table is a list of accessories that are assigned to the current home. Each row maps to an element in the accessories list.

The number of rows is determined by the number of available accessories (Listing 11-32).

Listing 11-32. Determine Number of Rows

```
override func tableView(tableView: UITableView, numberOfRowsInSection section: Int) -> Int {
    return accessories.count
}
```

Listing 11-33. Setting Up a Table Cell for an Accessory

```
override func tableView(tableView: UITableView, cellForRowAtIndexPath indexPath:
NSIndexPath) -> UITableViewCell {
    let accessory = accessories[indexPath.row];
    let cell = tableView.dequeueReusableCellWithIdentifier("AccessoryCell",
    forIndexPath: indexPath)
    cell.textLabel?.text = accessory.name
    cell.detailTextLabel?.text = accessory.category.localizedDescription
    return cell
}
```

Reload the table data from the viewWillAppear method of the view controller of the AccessoryBrowser class as shown in Listing 11-34.

Listing 11-34. The viewWIllAppear Method of the AccessoryBrowser Class

```
override func viewWillAppear(animated: Bool) {
    super.viewWillAppear(animated)
    tableView.reloadData()
}
```

Adding a New Accessory to the Home

When the user selects an accessory from the list, the table view delegate method `didSelectRowAtIndexPath` is called. Assign the `selectedAccessory` to the corresponding element in the assessor's list.

```
selectedAccessory = accessories[indexPath.row]
```

To add the accessory to the current home, you call the home objects `addAccessory` method as shown in Listing 11-35, and pass in the `selectedAccessory` as the parameter. The completion block is executed after the request is processed. The value of `error` will be `nil` on success.

When the accessory has been successfully added to the home, post a notification so any registered observers can update their views (see Listing 11-35).

To assign the new accessory to a room, you call the home objects `assignAccessory` method and pass in the `selectedAccessory` along with the room to which the accessory will be assigned. The accessory must already have been added to the home. The room must already exist in the home. In this example, the default room for the home is being used. Later, you can extend the application and provide support to add new rooms (see Listing 11-35).

***Listing 11-35.** The didSelectRowAtIndexPath Delegate Method to Add a New Accessory to the Home and Assigning It to a Room*

```
override func tableView(tableView: UITableView, didSelectRowAtIndexPath indexPath:
NSIndexPath) {

    tableView.deselectRowAtIndexPath(indexPath, animated: true)

    selectedAccessory = accessories[indexPath.row]
    HomeStore.sharedInstance.home?.addAccessory(self.selectedAccessory!,
    completionHandler: { error in

        if (error != nil) {
            print("Error: \(error)")
            UIAlertController.showErrorAlert(self, error: error!)

        } else {
            NSNotificationCenter.defaultCenter().postNotificationName(HomeStore.
            Notification.AddAccessoryNotification, object: nil)
            HomeStore.sharedInstance.home?.assignAccessory(self.selectedAccessory!,
            toRoom: (HomeStore.sharedInstance.home?.roomForEntireHome())!,
            completionHandler: { error in
                if let error = error {
                    print("failed to assign accessory to room: \(error)")
                } else {
                    print("added \(self.selectedAccessory!.name) to room")
                }
            })
        }

    })
}
```

Dismissing the Accessory Browser

To dismiss the accessory browser and return to the Home scene, create an action connection (see Listing 11-36). Control-drag from the *Done* Button Bar Item control to the implementation file. In the Connection pop-up, set the name of the action to `done` and then click *Connect*. Add a call to `dismissViewControllerAnimated`.

Listing 11-36. Action Connection to Dismiss the Accessory Browser

```
@IBAction func done(sender: AnyObject) {
    dismissViewControllerAnimated(true, completion: nil)
}
```

Building the Services Interface

The Services scene will display all the services that are available for a specific accessory. Each service will be presented in its own section followed by a list of associated characteristics.

At runtime, the table will look similar to the illustration in Figure 11-28.

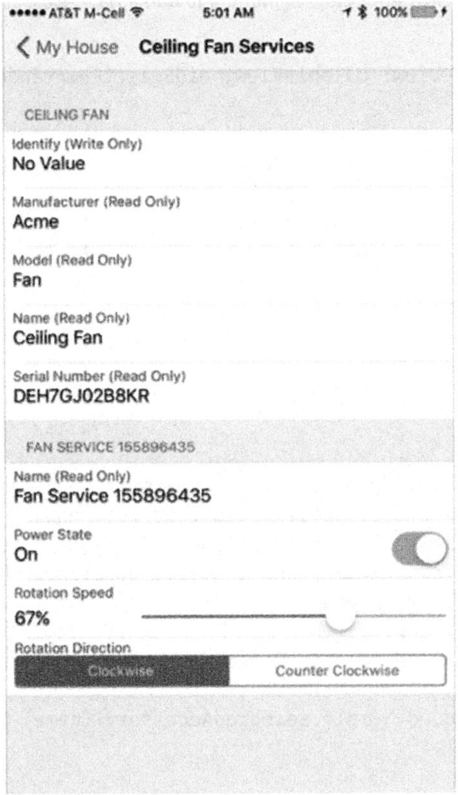

Figure 11-28. The available services

Open the storyboard and add a new `UITableViewController` to the storyboard canvas.

Select the table view and in the Attributes Inspector, change the style to *Grouped*.

Add two labels to the table view cell and position them on the left in Figure 11-29. From the Attributes Inspector, change the font for the top label to Footnote and the bottom label to Body.

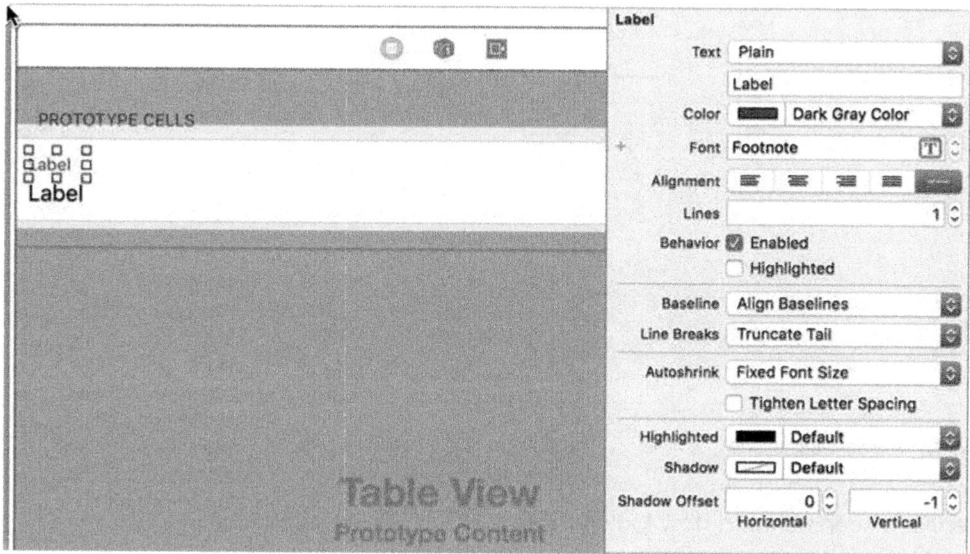

***Figure 11-29.** Setting up a predefined prototype table view cell*

Select the table view and, from the Attributes Inspector, change the number of prototype cells to four. You should see four identical cells.

Change the table view cell identifier for the first cell to *CharacteristicCell*.

Change the table view cell identifier for the second cell to *PowerStateCell*, and then add a `UISwitch` and position it on the right side.

Change the table view cell identifier for the third cell to *SliderCell*, and then add a `UISlider` and position it to the right.

Change the table view cell identifier for the fourth cell to *SegmentedCell*. Remove the second label and replace it with a `UISegmentedControl`, and then position it so that your result appears as in Figure 11-30.

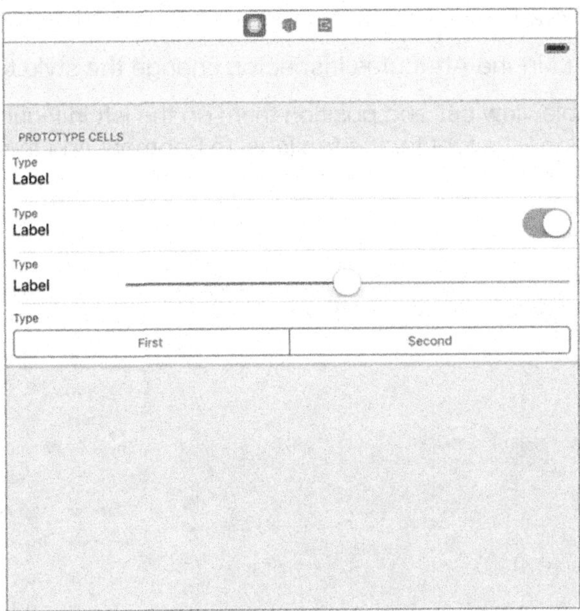

Figure 11-30. The Services scene

Your Services scene should now look similar to the illustration shown in Figure 11-30.

Create a new Swift file named `ServicesViewController.swift`. Declare a new class `ServicesViewController` that subclasses `IUTableViewController` and adopt the protocol for `HMAccessoryDelegate` as shown in Listing 11-37.

Listing 11-37. The ServicesViewController Class Declaration

```
class ServicesViewController: UITableViewController, HMAccessoryDelegate {
}
```

In the storyboard, set the custom class for the table view controller to `ServicesViewController` in the Identity Inspector.

Add a stored property called `services` and initialize it with a new, empty array of `HMService` values.

```
var services = [HMService]()
```

Add a stored property called `accessory` to hold a `HMAccessory` and define a property observer to set `self` as delegate (see Listing 11-38).

Listing 11-38. Stored Property for Accessory

```
var accessory: HMAccessory? {
    didSet {
        accessory?.delegate = self
    }
}
```

In the viewDidLoad method, set the view controller's title to the accessory's name.

```
title = "\(accessory!.name) Services"
```

Configuring Services

Recall that each service will be presented in its own section followed by a list of its characteristics. The first section will show information about the accessory, so you'll need to iterate through the services for the accessory, checking its type. Insert the service of type HMServiceTypeAccessoryInformation at the front of the array. Call the configureServices method shown in Listing 11-39 from the viewDidLoad method.

Listing 11-39. The configureServices Method

```
private func configureServices() {

    for service in accessory!.services as [HMService] {
        if service.serviceType == HMServiceTypeAccessoryInformation {
            services.insert(service, atIndex: 0)
        } else {
            services.append(service)
        }
    }
}
```

Receiving Value Change Notifications for Characteristics

To display the current state of a services characteristic, you'll want to receive notifications when the characteristic's value changes. You do this by calling the enableNotification method for a characteristic that supports notifications. You can check this by testing if the characteristics properties contain the constant HMCharacteristicPropertySupportsEventNotification. You want to selectively turn notifications on or off, so create a method called enableNotifications that takes a Boolean as a parameter (see Listing 11-40).

Listing 11-40. Enable or Disable Notifications for Characteristics in a Service

```
private func enableNotifications(enable: Bool) {
    for service in services {
        for characteristic in service.characteristics {
            if characteristic.properties.contains(HMCharacteristicPropertySupportsEvent
            Notification) {
                characteristic.enableNotification(enable, completionHandler: { error in
                    if let error = error {
                        print("Failed to enable notifications for \(characteristic):
                        \(error.localizedDescription)")
                    }
                })
            }
        }
    }
}
```

You'll want to call enableNotifications(true) to enable notifications from the viewDidLoad method after you've set up the services array and call enableNotifications(false) to disable notifications from the viewWillDisappear method.

Implementing UITableView Methods

The data source for the table view will be the services array, so the number of sections in the table is determined by the number of services, and the number of rows for each section is determined by the number of characteristics for each service (Listing 11-41).

Listing 11-41. Determine the Number of Sections and Rows for the Table View

```
override func numberOfSectionsInTableView(tableView: UITableView) -> Int {
    return services.count
}

override func tableView(tableView: UITableView, numberOfRowsInSection section: Int) -> Int {
    return services[section].characteristics.count
}

Set the title for the section to the service name.

override func tableView(tableView: UITableView, titleForHeaderInSection section: Int) -> String? {
    return services[section].name
}
```

The cell style presented for each row is determined by the properties and metadata of a characteristic. Character properties are represented by the following constants:

- HMCharacteristicPropertySupportsEventNotification: The characteristic supports notifications using the event connections established by the controller.
- HMCharacteristicPropertyReadable: The characteristic is readable.
- HMCharacteristicPropertyWritable: The characteristic is writable.

Characteristic metadata is information that further describes a characteristic's value. Character metadata is represented by the HMCharacteristicMetadata object. You query the metadata to find out information such as the data format, units, numeric value ranges, and manufacturer's descriptions.

In the delegate method cellForRowAtIndexPath, evaluate each characteristic to determine the cell style (see Listing 11-42).

Listing 11-42. Determining the Cell Style for a Characteristic

```
override func tableView(tableView: UITableView, cellForRowAtIndexPath indexPath:
NSIndexPath) -> UITableViewCell {

    var reuseIdentifier = Identifiers.CharacteristicCell

    let characteristic = services[indexPath.section].characteristics[indexPath.row]
```

```
    if characteristic.isReadOnly || characteristic.isWriteOnly {
        reuseIdentifier = Identifiers.CharacteristicCell
    } else if characteristic.isBoolean {
        reuseIdentifier = Identifiers.PowerStateCell
    } else if characteristic.hasValueDescriptions {
        reuseIdentifier = Identifiers.SegmentedCell
    } else if characteristic.isNumeric {
        reuseIdentifier = Identifiers.SliderCell
    }

    let cell = tableView.dequeueReusableCellWithIdentifier(reuseIdentifier,
    forIndexPath: indexPath)
    if let cell = cell as? CharacteristicCell {
        cell.characteristic = characteristic
    }

    return cell
}
```

At the top of the `ServicesViewController` class, define a structure named `Identifiers` with properties for each cell prototype in the table (see Listing 11-43).

Listing 11-43. A Structure Named Identifiers

```
struct Identifiers {
    static let CharacteristicCell = "CharacteristicCell"
    static let PowerStateCell = "PowerStateCell"
    static let SliderCell = "SliderCell"
    static let SegmentedCell = "SegmentedCell"
}
...
```

Create a new file named `HMCharacteristicExtension.swift` and declare a new extension for `HMCharacteristic`. The purpose of this extension is to provide stored properties and constants that can be used that help determine data formats, units, and such by inspecting a characters properties and metadata (see Listing 11-44).

Listing 11-44. HMCharacteristic Extension

```
import HomeKit

extension HMCharacteristic {

    private struct Const {
        static let numberFormatter = NSNumberFormatter()

        static let numericFormats = [
            HMCharacteristicMetadataFormatInt,
            HMCharacteristicMetadataFormatFloat,
            HMCharacteristicMetadataFormatUInt8,
```

```
            HMCharacteristicMetadataFormatUInt16,
            HMCharacteristicMetadataFormatUInt32,
            HMCharacteristicMetadataFormatUInt64
        ]
    }

    var isReadOnly: Bool {
        return !properties.contains(HMCharacteristicPropertyWritable)
            && properties.contains(HMCharacteristicPropertyReadable)
    }

    var isWriteOnly: Bool {
        return !properties.contains(HMCharacteristicPropertyReadable)
            && properties.contains(HMCharacteristicPropertyWritable)
    }

    var isBoolean: Bool {
        guard let metadata = metadata else { return false }
        return metadata.format == HMCharacteristicMetadataFormatBool
    }

    var isNumeric: Bool {
        guard let metadata = metadata else { return false }
        guard let format = metadata.format else { return false }
        return Const.numericFormats.contains(format)
    }

    var isFloatingPoint: Bool {
        guard let metadata = metadata else { return false }
        return metadata.format == HMCharacteristicMetadataFormatFloat
    }

    var isInteger: Bool {
        return self.isNumeric && !self.isFloatingPoint
    }

    var hasValueDescriptions: Bool {
        guard let number = self.value as? Int else { return false }
        return self.descriptionForNumber(number) != nil
    }

    var valueDescription: String {
        if let value = self.value {
            return descriptionForValue(value)
        }
        return ""
    }

    var unitDecoration: String {
        if let units = self.metadata?.units {
            switch units {
            case HMCharacteristicMetadataUnitsPercentage: return "%"
```

```
            case HMCharacteristicMetadataUnitsFahrenheit: return "°F"
            case HMCharacteristicMetadataUnitsCelsius: return "°C"
            case HMCharacteristicMetadataUnitsArcDegree: "°"
            default:
                break
            }
        }
        return ""
    }

    var valueCount: Int {
        guard let metadata = metadata, minimumValue = metadata.minimumValue as? Int else {
        return 0 }
        guard let maximumValue = metadata.maximumValue as? Int else { return 0 }
        var range = maximumValue - minimumValue
        if let stepValue = metadata.stepValue as? Double {
            range = Int(Double(range) / stepValue)
        }
        return range + 1
    }

    var allValues: [AnyObject]? {
        guard self.isInteger else { return nil }
        guard let metadata = metadata, stepValue = metadata.stepValue as? Double else {
        return nil }
        let choices = Array(0..<self.valueCount)
        return choices.map { choice in
            Int(Double(choice) * stepValue)
        }
    }

    func descriptionForValue(value: AnyObject) -> String {
        if self.isWriteOnly {
            return "Write-Only"

        } else if let metadata = self.metadata {
            if metadata.format == HMCharacteristicMetadataFormatBool {
                if let boolValue = value.boolValue {
                    return boolValue ? "On" : "Off"
                }
            }
        }

        if let intValue = value as? Int {
            if let desc = self.descriptionForNumber(intValue) {
                return desc
            }
            if let stepValue = self.metadata?.stepValue {
                Const.numberFormatter.minimumFractionDigits = Int(log10(1.0 / stepValue.
                doubleValue))
```

```
                if let string = Const.numberFormatter.stringFromNumber(intValue) {
                    return string + self.unitDecoration
                }
            }
        }

        return "\(value)"
    }

    func descriptionForNumber(number: Int) -> String? {
        switch self.characteristicType {
        case HMCharacteristicTypePowerState, HMCharacteristicTypeInputEvent,
        HMCharacteristicTypeOutputState:
            return Bool(number) ? "On" : "Off"

        case HMCharacteristicTypeObstructionDetected:
            return Bool(number) ? "Yes" : "No"

        case HMCharacteristicTypeTargetDoorState, HMCharacteristicTypeCurrentDoorState:
            if let state = HMCharacteristicValueDoorState(rawValue: number) {
                switch state {
                case .Open: return "Open"
                case .Opening: return "Opening"
                case .Closed: return "Closed"
                case .Closing: return "Closing"
                case .Stopped: return "Stopped"
                }
            }

        case HMCharacteristicTypePositionState:
            if let state = HMCharacteristicValuePositionState(rawValue: number) {
                switch state {
                case .Opening: return "Opening"
                case .Closing: return "Closing"
                case .Stopped: return "Stopped"
                }
            }

        case HMCharacteristicTypeRotationDirection:
            if let dir = HMCharacteristicValueRotationDirection(rawValue: number) {
                switch dir {
                case .Clockwise: return "Clockwise"
                case .CounterClockwise: return "Counter Clockwise"
                }
            }
        default:
            break
        }
        return nil
    }
}
```

Subclass UITableViewCell for Characteristics

Characteristic Information

Create a new file named CharacteristicCell.swift and declare a new class CharacteristicCell that subclasses UITableViewCell. This will act at the base class for all characteristic table view cells (see Listing 11-45).

Listing 11-45. Base Class for Characteristics

```
import HomeKit

class CharacteristicCell: UITableViewCell {

    @IBOutlet weak var typeLabel: UILabel!
    @IBOutlet weak var valueLabel: UILabel!

    var characteristic: HMCharacteristic! {
        didSet {
            var desc = characteristic.localizedDescription
            if characteristic.isReadOnly {
                desc = desc + " (Read Only)"
            } else if characteristic.isWriteOnly {
                desc = desc + " (Write Only)"
            }
            typeLabel.text = desc
            valueLabel?.text = "No Value"

            setValue(characteristic.value, notify: false)

            selectionStyle = characteristic.characteristicType ==
            HMCharacteristicTypeIdentify ? .Default : .None

            if characteristic.isWriteOnly {
                return
            }

            if reachable {
                characteristic.readValueWithCompletionHandler { error in
                    if let error = error {
                        print("Error reading value for \(self.characteristic): \(error)")
                    } else {
                        self.setValue(self.characteristic.value, notify: false)
                    }
                }
            }
        }
    }

    var value: AnyObject?
```

```
    var reachable: Bool {
        return (characteristic.service?.accessory?.reachable ?? false)
    }

    required init?(coder aDecoder: NSCoder) {
        super.init(coder: aDecoder)
    }

    func setValue(newValue: AnyObject?, notify: Bool) {
        self.value = newValue
        if let value = self.value {
            self.valueLabel?.text = self.characteristic.descriptionForValue(value)
        }

        if notify {
            self.characteristic.writeValue(self.value, completionHandler: { error in
                if let error = error {
                    print("Failed to write value for \(self.characteristic):
                    \(error.localizedDescription)")
                }
            })
        }
    }
}
```

Power State Control

Create a new file named PowerStateCell.swift and declare a new class PowerStateCell that subclasses CharacteristicCell. A UISwitch is used to toggle the value that represents a characteristics power state (see Listing 11-46).

Listing 11-46. Power State Control Table View Cell

```
import HomeKit

class PowerStateCell: CharacteristicCell {

    @IBOutlet weak var powerSwitch: UISwitch!

    @IBAction func switchValueChanged(sender: UISwitch) {
        setValue(powerSwitch.on, notify: true)
    }

    override var characteristic: HMCharacteristic! {
        didSet {
            powerSwitch.userInteractionEnabled = reachable
        }
    }
```

```
    override func setValue(newValue: AnyObject?, notify: Bool) {
        super.setValue(newValue, notify: notify)
        if let newValue = newValue as? Bool where !notify {
            powerSwitch.setOn(newValue, animated: true)
        }
    }
}
```

Slider Control

Create a new file named SliderCell.swift and declare a new class SliderCell that subclasses CharacteristicCell. A UISlider control is used to change a characteristic's numeric value (see Listing 11-47).

Listing 11-47. Slider Control Table View Cell

```
import HomeKit

class SliderCell: CharacteristicCell {

    @IBOutlet weak var slider: UISlider!

    @IBAction func sliderValueChanged(sender: UISlider) {
        let value = roundedValueForSliderValue(slider.value)
        setValue(value, notify: true)
    }

    override var characteristic: HMCharacteristic! {
        didSet {
            slider.userInteractionEnabled = reachable
        }

        willSet {
            slider.minimumValue = newValue.metadata?.minimumValue as? Float ?? 0.0
            slider.maximumValue = newValue.metadata?.maximumValue as? Float ?? 100.0
        }
    }

    override func setValue(newValue: AnyObject?, notify: Bool) {
        super.setValue(newValue, notify: notify)
        if let newValue = newValue as? NSNumber where !notify {
            slider.value = newValue.floatValue
        }
    }
```

```
    private func roundedValueForSliderValue(value: Float) -> Float {
        if let metadata = characteristic.metadata,
            stepValue = metadata.stepValue as? Float where stepValue > 0 {
                let newValue = roundf(value / stepValue)
                let stepped = newValue * stepValue
                return stepped
        }
        return value
    }
}
```

Segmented Control

Create a new file named SegmentedCell.swift and declare a new class SegmentedCell that subclasses CharacteristicCell. A UISegmentedControl is used to represent a range of values that represents descriptions.

Listing 11-48. Segmented Control Table View Cell

```
import HomeKit

class SegmentetCell: CharacteristicCell {

    @IBOutlet weak var segmentedControl: UISegmentedControl!

    @IBAction func segmentValueChanged(sender: UISegmentedControl) {
        let value = titleValues[segmentedControl.selectedSegmentIndex]
        setValue(value, notify: true)
    }

    var titleValues = [Int]() {
        didSet {
            segmentedControl.removeAllSegments()
            for index in 0..<titleValues.count {
                let value: AnyObject = titleValues[index]
                let title = self.characteristic.descriptionForValue(value)
                segmentedControl.insertSegmentWithTitle(title, atIndex: index, animated: false)
            }
        }
    }

    override var characteristic: HMCharacteristic! {
        didSet {
            segmentedControl.userInteractionEnabled = reachable

            if let values = self.characteristic.allValues as? [Int] {
                titleValues = values
            }
        }
    }
```

```
    override func setValue(newValue: AnyObject?, notify: Bool) {
        super.setValue(newValue, notify: notify)
        if !notify {
            if let intValue = value as? Int, index = titleValues.indexOf(intValue) {
                segmentedControl.selectedSegmentIndex = index
            }
        }
    }
}
```

Accessory Delegate Methods

When a characteristic value of an accessory changes, the accessory notifies its delegate through the `didUpdateValueForCharacteristic` method (see Listing 11-49). The *accessory* parameter represents the object for which the characteristic value has changed. The *service* parameter represents the service with a changed characteristic value. The characteristic parameter represents the characteristic whose value changed.

Listing 11-49. Delegate Method didUpdateValueForCharacteristic in the ServicesViewController Class

```
// MARK: HMAccessoryDelegate methods

func accessory(accessory: HMAccessory, service: HMService, didUpdateValueForCharacteristic
characteristic: HMCharacteristic) {
    if let index = service.characteristics.indexOf(characteristic) {
        let indexPath = NSIndexPath(forRow: index, inSection: 1)
        let cell = tableView.cellForRowAtIndexPath(indexPath) as! CharacteristicCell
        cell.setValue(characteristic.value, notify: false)
    }
}
```

Transitioning to the Services Scene

Add a segue to transition to the Services scene when the user selects an accessory from the table. Open the storyboard and control-drag from the Home scene table view cell to the services view controller. Set the segue identifier to *ServicesSegue*.

In the `HomeViewController` class, override the `prepareForSegue` method and set the `accessory` property of the `ServicesViewController` (see Listing 11-50).

Listing 11-50. Setting the Accessory for the Destination View Controller

```
override func prepareForSegue(segue: UIStoryboardSegue, sender: AnyObject?) {
    if segue.identifier == "ServicesSegue" {
        let controller = segue.destinationViewController as! ServicesViewController
        let indexPath = tableView.indexPathForSelectedRow;
        controller.accessory = homeStore.home!.accessories[(indexPath?.row)!];
    }
}
```

Running the Application

Build and run the application. Add a new home; you should see a new entry in the first table section. You should also see an entry with that home name in the Primary Home section with a check mark to the right side of the cell. Now add a second home; you should see a second entry in the first table section as well as in the second section. The first home added should still be marked as the Primary Home. Select the second home in the Primary Home section; the check mark should now appear to the right of the table cell indicating that the second home is now the Primary Home.

Adding Accessories

- Select a home from the first section; the app should transition to a view with the home name shown in the navigation bar and an empty table view. The background should show a label with the text No Accessories.
- Tap the (+) Add button in the navigation bar; the view should transition to the Accessory Browser. If you've added any accessories to the simulator, you should list them here.
- Select an accessory from the list; a pop-up should appear warning that the accessory is not certified and may not work reliably with HomeKit. This is normal when using the simulator.
- Select Add Anyway; you should be presented with a scene prompting you for an eight-digit accessory setup code.
- Tap the Enter code manually text at the bottom of the view; you should be presented with a scene that has a keypad where you can enter the eight-digit accessory setup code which can be found in the simulator app at the top of the main view.
- Enter the code; if you've entered the incorrect code, you should see the message Adding Failed. If you've entered the correct code then the message Accessory Added will appear briefly and the view should automatically transition back to the Accessory Browser. Notice that the accessory you selected is no longer listed in the table view.
- Tap the Done button in the navigation bar; you should now see the accessory listed in the home view.
- Select the accessory in the table view; you should transition to the Services scene. The accessory name should appear as the title in the navigation bar. You should see several table sections. The first section is informative only. It should show the same information as shown in the simulator. The second table section should be labeled with the service name. There will be one or more table cells, one for each characteristic, with a control that can be used to change the value or state of the characteristic. For example, if you see a Lightbulb service, there should be a switch available to turn the power on and off.

- Change the state of the characteristic; notice that the associated value in the simulator changes as well.
- Change the value from the simulator; notice the associated value in your app changes.

Experiment with the simulator by adding more accessories and then add the accessories to the homes you have in your app. Notice that you can't add an accessory to more than one home.

Summary

This chapter covered some of the basic concepts of HomeKit and how you can use the HomeKit framework in an application. It also covered the basics for using The HomeKit Accessory Simulator to help you develop and test your application.

There's so much more that can be done. The sample app only scratches the surface of what can be done using the HomeKit framework. It's up to you to extend the functionality to accommodate your needs.

Chapter 12

Building an App That Interacts with a Raspberry Pi

Gheorghe Chesler

In this chapter, we will write an app that communicates with a Raspberry Pi device on the local Wi-Fi network that allows us to flip the lights on and off on a custom module with LEDs. This might not seem like a significant accomplishment, but keep in mind that just as you can flip on and off some LED lights, you can control any other connected devices in a similar fashion.

About Your Raspberry Pi

Raspberry Pi is a miniaturized ARM computer that can run different operating systems. By default, this runs a variant of Debian Linux customized for this device, called Raspbian. On the Raspberry Pi 2 you can also install Ubuntu, RiscOS, and recently even a slimmed-down, custom version of Windows 10. Of course, we need to keep in mind that the CPU is not very powerful, and the Raspberry Pi device does not have a lot of memory: the B version has 512MB RAM, and the latest version (Pi 2) has 1GB of RAM, which happens to be the maximum memory supported by the ARM7 CPU. This is definitely not enough memory to do any fancy computing: as of this writing there is no easy way to install a popular browser. The chromium browser is supported, but Google Chrome is not yet available; even if it were, it is too big for the available system resources to do anything you are accustomed to on a regular computer.

What the Raspberry Pi loses in terms of computing power it makes up for with the very low power usage and the ability to connect smart devices and accessories like LED lights, relays, motors, cameras, and pressure, acceleration, and humidity sensors, to name just a few.

Another factor is the price: the regular Pi model B is available for about $30, and you can get most extension modules at really accessible prices from a lot of online and local retailers.

The Pi 2 Model B is based on a Broadcom BCM2836 SoC, which includes a Quad Core ARM7 900 MHz processor, 1GB of RAM, and 4 USB ports where you can plug in external devices. The Pi also has an Ethernet connector, a HDMI connector for the display, and an audio port. The older Pi model B+ uses a less powerful, single core Broadcom BCM2835 ARM11 700MHz processor and has only 512MB of RAM, while the very first model came only with 256MB of RAM.

To power the Raspberry Pi, you will need to connect it via a micro-USB to any wall charger or to a computer that provides enough power for the Pi and the connected devices. In most cases 1A would be sufficient, which is what the regular USB ports provide. In addition to power needs of the main board, you have to add the current consumed by your plug-in boards. The Pi does not include a built-in hard disk or solid-state drive, instead relying on a microSD card for booting and long-term storage.

The Raspberry Pi does not come with a real-time clock, so an OS must use a network time server, or ask the user for time information at boot time to get access to time and date info to enable + file time and date stamping. However, a real-time clock (such as the DS1307) with battery backup can be easily added via the I2C interface.

The Raspberry Pi also provides two onboard ribbon slots to connect a camera and a display. Most plastic cases that you would buy to host your Raspberry Pi provide holes for guiding these cables outside the enclosure.

To accommodate the scope of this chapter, we picked a very simple module that has a number of LEDs on a miniature board, along with the chip that controls them. The module is named "PiGlow" and is marketed by the company Pimoroni:

`https://shop.pimoroni.com/products/piglow`

In Figure 12-1, we can see our Raspberry Pi B+ with a PiGlow board attached.

Figure 12-1. Raspberry Pi B+ with a PiGlow board attached

If you have an older Raspberry Pi, you will still be able to do everything we do in this chapter; the only advantages to the new model are a faster processor and more memory. Some of the commands we will run are specific to the model of Raspberry Pi you own; inline comments will specify these differences.

Control Interfaces on your Raspberry Pi

Each embedded platform has one or more ways to access connected or native devices on the local hardware.

A very common one is GPIO (General Purpose Input Output). This allows you to flip on a light or a relay on or off, and for that purpose it is really great; but there is a limit to how many devices it can address (more or less limited by the number of pins available on the custom connector).

The I2C (Inter IC) interface gives you more flexibility in what you can do with individual devices, and of course it allows you to attach more devices.

The I2C bus was designed by Philips in the early 1980s to allow easy communication between components that reside on the same circuit board. For a complete reference on the I2C interface, see the following URL: `www.i2c-bus.org/i2c-bus/`.

I2C uses 7 bit addressing. The maximum number that can be expressed with 7 bits is 128, which means you can have more than 120 devices you can access via the same bus. I2C is also much simpler to implement in hardware—it requires only two connection lines, one for the clock and the other for the data.

Setting up your Raspberry Pi

The easiest way to get started with Raspberry Pi is to install the Raspbian operating system. The Raspberry Pi official web page has it available for download here: `www.raspberrypi.org/downloads/`.

To make things easy, use the NOOBS (New Out-Of-Box Software) zip file.

On the same page there are also installation instructions; after unpacking the downloaded zip file, you format a reasonably large micro-SD card (4GB or more) with the FAT file system, and copy the files on the card. Then, insert the card in your Raspberry Pi device and start it. When the device boots, it will prompt you with the choice of OS and language, and you can get it installed.

For the installation phase, you can use a HDMI monitor or a VGA monitor via a HDMI to VGA adapter; this will not be needed later on, because you can SSH (secure shell) into the device from another computer.

To SSH into the Raspberry Pi device from another computer you can use the following credentials:

```
user:     pi
password: raspberry
```

If you did not install the GUI (graphical user interface) by default, you can start the GUI at any time using the following command:

```
startx
```

To configure the device and ports you can use the Raspberry Pi configuration utility:

```
raspi-config
```

After you installed the OS, the first step is to bring the system up to date. For that, you can enter the following in your SSH window:

```
sudo apt-get update
sudo apt-get upgrade
```

To force a command to be executed with root privileges we use the sudo command in front of a regular command. This is necessary because the standard "pi" user does not have enough rights to modify system files or install applications.

The apt-get utility is the standard Debian package manager, which you might be familiar with if you are using Ubuntu. The first command fetches the list of the latest available packages, while the second one installs updates available for the currently installed system modules/packages.

Choosing the Scripting Language

On the Raspberry Pi, Python has become the de facto standard scripting language, because there are so many packages made available to control every device imaginable. This being said, you have to keep in mind that most of them will be Python 2, and some will be Python 3. The Python language has a split personality: the Python 2 is the older, more established version, with wider support. Python 3 is the new, "better" version that offers modern language constructs for object oriented design, but the support for it on platforms such as Raspberry Pi is limited, and the scripts and packages written for Python 3 will not work for Python 2.

At the same time, there is considerable support for Perl on embedded platforms; however, installing some of the Perl packages could be a daunting task that most novices would have a hard time completing.

Configuring I2C

You can find most of the instructions in this section at the following URL, where you can also find more tutorials on how to install other accessories and plug-ins for your Raspberry Pi:

```
https://learn.adafruit.com/adafruits-raspberry-pi-lesson-4-gpio-setup/configuring-i2c
```

I2C is a very commonly used standard designed to allow one chip to talk to another.

Since the Raspberry Pi can talk to I2C, we can connect it to a variety of I2C-capable chips and modules.

Following are some of the Adafruit projects that make use of I2C devices and modules:

- `http://learn.adafruit.com/mcp230xx-gpio-expander-on-the-raspberry-pi`
- `http://learn.adafruit.com/adafruit-16x2-character-lcd-plus-keypad-for-raspberry-pi`
- `http://learn.adafruit.com/adding-a-real-time-clock-to-raspberry-pi`
- `http://learn.adafruit.com/matrix-7-segment-led-backpack-with-the-raspberry-pi`
- `http://learn.adafruit.com/mcp4725-12-bit-dac-with-raspberry-pi`
- `http://learn.adafruit.com/adafruit-16-channel-servo-driver-with-raspberry-pi`
- `http://learn.adafruit.com/using-the-bmp085-with-raspberry-pi`

The I2C bus allows multiple devices to be connected to your Raspberry Pi--each with a unique address. The device address can often be set by changing jumper settings on the module. It is very useful to be able to see which devices are connected to your Pi as a way of making sure everything is working. To do this, it is worth running the following command in the Terminal to install the `i2c-tools` utility:

```
sudo apt-get install i2c-tools
```

To keep things simple, we will use Python for the application we write for the Raspberry Pi. To use Python with I2C tools, we need to install the python-smbus package:

```
sudo apt-get install python-smbus
```

If you plan to use Perl to build tools that control the I2C devices, you will need to install some extra packages that provide an interface to the I2C tools to Perl packages, as well as a basic framework that allows writing compact applications:

```
sudo apt-get install libi2c-dev build-essential libmoose-perl
sudo cpan Device::SMBus
```

Installing Kernel Support for I2C

Run the raspi-config as root and follow the prompts to install `i2c` support for the ARM core and Linux kernel:

```
sudo raspi-config
```

Select Advanced Options/I2C and enable the interface, and allow the I2C kernel module to be loaded by default. After you made the changes, you have to reboot the device; the modules should be loaded and available after reboot.

Verify that the `i2c` modules are available, by looking at the content of the following file:

```
cat /etc/modules
```

The file will have contents similar to the following example:

```
# /etc/modules: kernel modules to load at boot time.
#
# This file contains the names of kernel modules that should be loaded
# at boot time, one per line. Lines beginning with "#" are ignored.

i2c-bcm2708
i2c-dev
```

If after reboot, these modules do not exist in the `/etc/modules` file: you can edit the file with vi and append the two previously mentioned lines. You have to edit this file with root privileges:

```
sudo vi /etc/modules
```

Another easy way to do this is with the following one-liners:

```
sudo echo "i2c-bcm2708" >> /etc/modules
sudo echo "i2c-dev" >> /etc/modules
```

Depending on when you installed your OS and with what version, as well as on any other experiments you might have run with your Raspberry Pi, some of these modules could have landed in the modprobe blacklist. This is a file that disables certain modules, preventing them from loading at the start. To look at the file contents, see:

```
sudo cat /etc/modprobe.d/raspi-blacklist.conf
```

You can edit the file with vi, and comment out or delete the lines if they exist in that file as we did with the /etc/modules. Here too, you have to use root privileges to edit the file:

```
sudo vi /etc/modprobe.d/raspi-blacklist.conf
```

There is a fancier way to do just about the same thing with the following one-liner:

```
MPBL=/etc/modprobe.d/raspi-blacklist.conf; [ -f ${MPBL} ] && sudo perl -p -i -e
's:^(blacklist (spi|i2c)-bcm2708):#$1:g' ${MPBL}
```

This line does the following:

- Creates an environment variable named MPBL that contains the path to the file
- If the file exists, it uses Perl to find the lines that contain the two module names
- If the lines were found, it comments them out by prefixing them with a hash

While it might seem very fancy to run one-line commands that do stuff for you, it is much more convenient to do things the regular way, by editing a file in a normal text editor and seeing right away what you are doing.

After making the changes mentioned previously, you can restart your Raspberry Pi:

```
sudo reboot
```

Verify that I2C can be Accessed

After the device reboots, the first step is to check that the module is loaded.

```
sudo modprobe i2c-dev
```

If the module could not be loaded, this would return "`modprobe: FATAL: Module i2c-dev not found`", otherwise it will return no message.

If all is well, you should be able to test the I2C connectivity by running the following command:

```
i2cdetect -y 1
```

If you have an older Raspberry Pi (before model B), the command would be instead:

```
i2cdetect -y 0
```

The makers of Raspberry Pi changed that 0 to a 1 when the model B was released. An easy way to remember is that any module with 256MB of RAM uses 0; the others use 1.

In either case, the output of the command would be similar to the following:

```
     0  1  2  3  4  5  6  7  8  9  a  b  c  d  e  f
00:          -- -- -- -- -- -- -- -- -- -- -- -- --
10: -- -- -- -- -- -- -- -- -- -- -- -- -- -- -- --
20: -- -- -- -- -- -- -- -- -- -- -- -- -- -- -- --
30: -- -- -- -- -- -- -- -- -- -- -- -- -- -- -- --
40: -- -- -- -- -- -- -- -- -- -- -- -- -- -- -- --
50: -- -- -- -- -- -- -- -- -- -- -- -- -- -- -- --
60: -- -- -- -- -- -- -- -- -- -- -- -- -- -- -- --
70: -- -- -- -- -- -- -- --
```

If you already have I2C devices connected, they might appear in the table, pointing to the address of your devices.

One interesting fact: if you have the PiGlow module plugged in, it will not show up in the i2cdetect output, but it will still work just fine.

If you are running a recent Raspberry Pi (3.18 kernel or higher), you will also need to update the `/boot/config.txt` file. Edit the `/boot/config.txt` file and uncomment or add the following lines:

```
dtparam=i2c1=on
dtparam=i2c_arm=on
```

After you make these changes you need to reboot your device.

Configuring GPIO

The GPIO pins can be used as both digital outputs and digital inputs. As digital outputs, you can write programs that turn a particular pin HIGH or LOW. Setting it HIGH sets it to 3.3V; setting it LOW sets it to 0V.

To drive an LED from one of these pins, you need a 1kΩ resistor in series with the LED as the GPIO pins can only manage a small amount of power.

If you use a pin as a digital input, then you can connect switches and simple sensors to a pin and then be able to check whether it is open or closed (i.e., activated or not). The following are some Adafruit projects that use just GPIO:

```
http://learn.adafruit.com/raspberry-pi-e-mail-notifier-using-leds
http://learn.adafruit.com/playing-sounds-and-using-buttons-with-raspberry-pi
http://learn.adafruit.com/basic-resistor-sensor-reading-on-raspberry-pi
```

To program the GPIO ports in Python, we need to install a very useful Python 2 library called RPi.GPIO (Raspberry Pi General Purpose Input Output). This module gives us a simple to use Python library that will let us control the GPIO pins. The installation process for this is the same whether you are using Raspbian or Occidentalis. In actual fact, some versions of

Raspbian include this library, but these instructions will also have the effect of updating to the latest version, which is worth doing.

To install RPi.GPIO, you first need to install the Python Development toolkit that that RPi. GPIO requires. To do this, enter the following command into LXTerminal:

```
sudo apt-get install python-dev
```

Then, to install Rpi.GPIO itself, type:

```
sudo apt-get install python-rpi.gpio
```

Install PyGlow

To make the PyGlow module work with Python, we need to install the package that interacts with the I2C libraries and controls the device.

```
sudo pip install git+https://github.com/benleb/PyGlow.git
```

Now, you can create a small Python test script that would flash the lights blue for one second, red for two seconds, then green for 3 seconds (Listing 12-1).

Listing 12-1. Flashing the PiGlow LEDs

```
from PyGlow import PyGlow
   from time import sleep
   pyglow = PyGlow()
   pyglow.all(0)
   pyglow.color("blue", 100)
   sleep(1)
   pyglow.color("blue", 0)
   pyglow.color("red", 100)
   sleep(2)
   pyglow.color("red", 0)
   pyglow.color("green", 100)
   sleep(3)
   pyglow.color("green", 0)
```

Save the text in the Listing 12-1 in a file called `flash.py`, then run it in the SSH terminal:

```
python flash.py
```

This is all there is to it; simple, right?

Now imagine that the more complex control commands you will write will be nothing but encapsulated scripts such as the one in Listing 12-1, which takes control of a given interface and device and effects some changes.

Providing an API to Control your Device

So far, we have seen that we have the ability to interact with attached devices on our Raspberry Pi. What we want now is to be able to interact with the devices from an external source, such as our iOS device.

There are two parts to this: the server on the Raspberry Pi that provides the API to control the attached devices (PiGlow in our case) and an iOS application that makes requests to this API.

Since we started writing Python code, it feels only right to do the API server also in Python. There are many Python frameworks that can be used to build an API: we need to use one that is lightweight and easy to customize. A good choice here is Flask. You will find a considerable number of online tutorials to help you get started with Flask, and as frameworks for API development, you will find out how easy it is to get started.

Install Flask

This is a very simplified step-by-step tutorial to get started with Flask. We implement very basic features to allow us to control the device. Following this model you can add security, scale the service to support multiple commands, or do whatever your project requires.

Before anything, we use Pip to install Flask:

```
sudo pip install flask
```

This will install the Flask framework and the basic modules used by the framework. The installation process is deceptively simple; it installs just like any other package.

The Hello World Daemon

This is traditionally the first thing we would do to start experimenting with a new language.

Create a file named `hello-flask.py` with the contents shown in Listing 12-2. Normally you would configure a service to use port 80 since it is serving an HTTP response.

We use a higher number port for two reasons: to allow you to run a separate http server on port 80 if you need to, especially because ports smaller than 1024 can only be used by programs that run with root privileges. This is an older limitation for security reasons, and it makes sure that applications running on certain well-known ports should be run only by the system.

Listing 12-2. The "Hello World!" script n Python using Flask

```
from flask import Flask
app = Flask(__name__)

@app.route("/")
def hello():
    return "Hello World!"
```

```
if __name__ == "__main__":
    app.run(host='0.0.0.0', port=8080, debug=True)
```

When you start the daemon from the command line, it will tell us that it is running and show any incoming calls on the command line. Listing 12-3 is what we get when we start it the first time. You will notice that the browser is trying to also get the `favicon.ico` file, a file that we do not have, because the daemon that we build in this example is not configured to serve static files directly. The `favicon.ico` is the image that can customize how your web site icon shows up to the left of the URL in the browser, and it will only show up once, then the browser will cache the state and will not try to fetch it again.

Listing 12-3. ***Running our Flask program***

```
pi@raspberrypi:~$ python hello-flask.py
 * Running on http://0.0.0.0:8080/ (Press CTRL+C to quit)
 * Restarting with stat
10.0.1.25 - - [12/Oct/2015 05:26:18] "GET / HTTP/1.1" 200 -
10.0.1.25 - - [12/Oct/2015 05:26:18] "GET /favicon.ico HTTP/1.1" 404 -
```

The last two lines in Listing 12-3 are the result of loading the URL of the device, using the device IP (Internet Protocol) address:

```
http://10.0.1.128:8080/
```

In our example code we will not go to the length of setting up a discovery daemon or any fancy features, limiting ourselves to demonstrating functionality.

Building a Very Simple Listener Daemon

With our knowledge accumulated from this test program, it is time to integrate a call that executes the commands we put together in the previous example. What we want to build is a daemon that informs us of the system time and offers a service to execute a simple command. Since we already spent some time writing a bit of code in the previous example, we will integrate that code in our listener. You can see the results in Listing 12-4.

You will notice that we have all the imports at the top, combining the needs of all the code written in this script.

Listing 12-4. ***The Listener Daemon on Raspberry Pi, written in Python and Flask***

```
from flask import Flask
from PyGlow import PyGlow
from time import sleep
import datetime

app = Flask(__name__)

@app.route("/")
def hello():
    now = datetime.datetime.now()
    return now.strftime("%Y-%m-%d %H:%M")
```

```
@app.route("/blink")
def getData():
    pyglow = PyGlow()
    pyglow.all(0)
    pyglow.color("blue", 100)
    sleep(1)
    pyglow.color("blue", 0)
    pyglow.color("red", 100)
    sleep(2)
    pyglow.color("red", 0)
    pyglow.color("green", 100)
    sleep(3)
    pyglow.color("green", 0)
    return "OK"

@app.route("/blink/<color>")
def blinkColor(color):
    pyglow = PyGlow()
    pyglow.all(0)
    pyglow.color(color, 100)
    sleep(1)
    pyglow.color(color, 0)
    return "OK"

if __name__ == "__main__":
    app.run(host='0.0.0.0', port=8080, debug=True)
```

With this, we have our first very simple command handler daemon. Try now to bring up the base URL, and it will display the current date and time:

```
http://10.0.1.128:8080/
```

This Flask daemon is now taking a command to blink the lights on PiGlow, when somebody calls the /blink end point. When invoking the URL, you will see that our code is being executed and the LEDs will blink just as in our earlier example; then, when completed, the page will show "OK":

```
http://10.0.1.128:8080/blink
```

We also have a second service that allows us to blink a single color: for that, call the URLs:

```
http://10.0.1.128:8080/blink/green
http://10.0.1.128:8080/blink/red
```

The listener daemon shows the calls on the command line, as they are being made:

```
10.0.1.25 - - [12/Oct/2015 06:04:44] "GET /blink/green HTTP/1.1" 200 -
10.0.1.25 - - [12/Oct/2015 06:05:03] "GET /blink/red HTTP/1.1" 200 -
```

I am sure you will derive a lot of enjoyment from trying to add new commands and features.

Setting up an iOS Project for Our App

We begin by creating an empty, single-page project. This chapter aims to show how to communicate with the Raspberry Pi API through the I2C interface we just created, not how to build an UI interface around it, so our application will be minimalistic, exposing just a few UI elements to trigger actions on the Raspberry Pi. We will be using a similar approach to the code in Chapter 5, so this will be familiar ground if you read that chapter.

Using this demo application, you will be able to trigger commands that switch the lights on and off on the PiGlow board on your Raspberry Pi.

Allowing Outgoing HTTP Calls

You will run into this quite often: you rig your app to make an HTTP call and you see a stack trace like the following:

Application Transport Security has blocked a cleartext HTTP (http://) resource load since it is insecure. Temporary exceptions can be configured via your app's `Info.plist` *file.*

Going to the Apple docs, we read about Application Transport Security:

> *App Transport Security (ATS) lets an app add a declaration to its Info.plist file that specifies the domains with which it needs secure communication. ATS prevents accidental disclosure, provides secure default behavior, and is easy to adopt. You should adopt ATS as soon as possible, regardless of whether you're creating a new app or updating an existing one.*
>
> *If you're developing a new app, you should use HTTPS exclusively. If you have an existing app, you should use HTTPS as much as you can right now, and create a plan for migrating the rest of your app as soon as possible.*

To handle this issue, you need to create an entry for "Allow Arbitrary Loads" set to "true" in your `info.plist`, as shown in Figure 12-2. Xcode will autosuggest the name (App Transport Security Settings) the moment you start typing; it will also suggest the Dictionary type, and the first key-value pair (Allow Arbitrary Loads). You can see how this appears in the Figure 12-2.

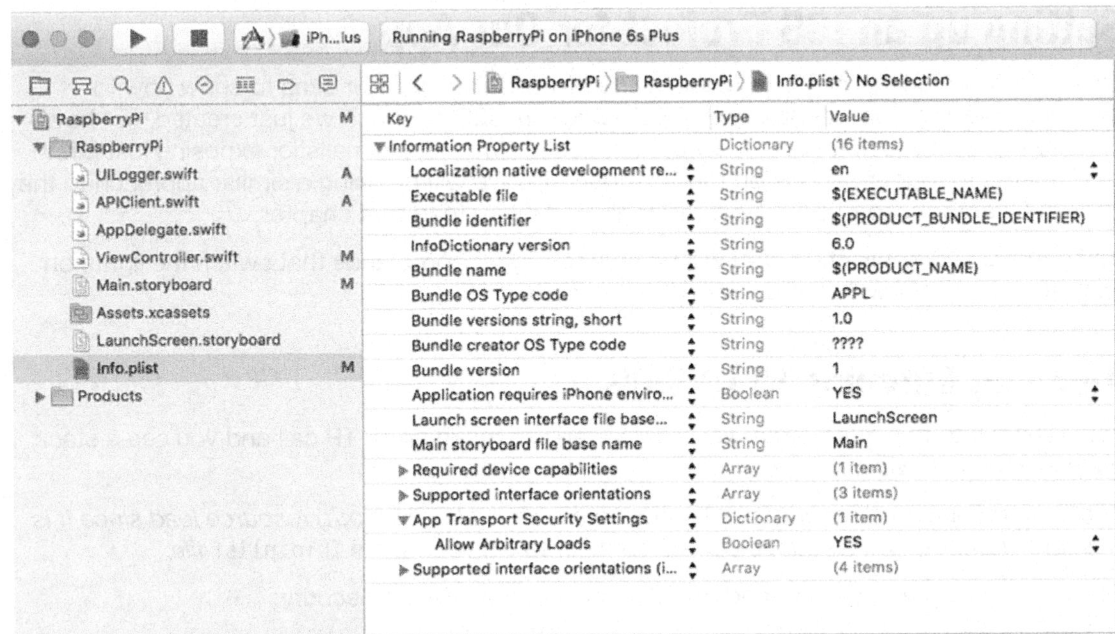

Figure 12-2. Setting the Allow Arbitrary Loads for the App Transport Security Settings

The View Controller

A basic View Controller for this chapter will only show a few buttons and a text area that we will use to display the communication with the API.

To initialize and to be able to use these buttons and fields, they have to be assigned macros that make them available/visible in the Interface Builder. We also define the variables used for the API and logger objects. Since these will be initialized at a later time, these variables need to be defined as optional (Listing 12-5).

Listing 12-5. The Header of the UIViewController Class

```
class ViewController: UIViewController {
    @IBOutlet var clearButton : UIButton!
    @IBOutlet var labelButton : UIButton!
    @IBOutlet var labelButton2 : UIButton!
    @IBOutlet var textArea : UITextView!
    var api: APIClient!
    var logger: UILogger!
```

In the `viewDidLoad()` function (Listing 12-6) we initialize the API object, as well as the log library that will output text to our textArea field. The content and functionality of these libraries will be explained as we go.

Listing 12-6. The viewDidLoad Override Function

```
override func viewDidLoad() {
    super.viewDidLoad()
    // Do any additional setup after loading the view, typically from a nib.
    api = APIClient(parent: self)
    logger = UILogger(out: textArea)
}
```

To assign an action to a button, we create a function that performs the action, and is also annotated with the proper macro to make it available in the Interface Builder. We will add a log statement to show the beginning of the request, and we can also change the title of the button, while it is pressed (Listing 12-7):

Listing 12-7. The clickButton Function

```
@IBAction func clickButton() {
    logger.logEvent("=== Blink All Lights ===")
    api.blinkAllLights()
    labelButton.setTitle("Request Sent", forState: UIControlState.Normal)
}
```

We can wire these button actions in the storyboard as shown in Figure 12-3.

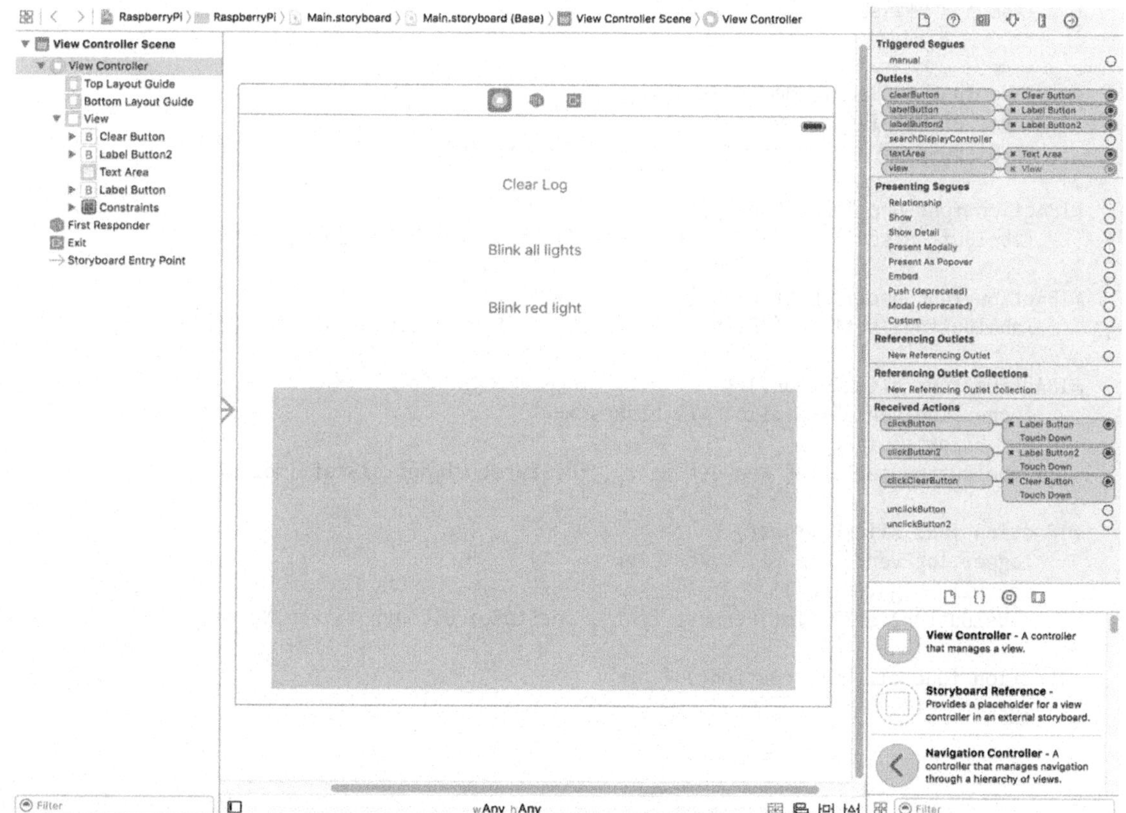

Figure 12-3. The storyboard

In Listing 12-8 we can see the entire `ViewController.swift` code that we will use to test the command sent to the Raspberry Pi API.

Listing 12-8. The Code for the ViewController.swift

```
import UIKit

class ViewController: UIViewController {
    @IBOutlet var clearButton : UIButton!
    @IBOutlet var labelButton : UIButton!
    @IBOutlet var labelButton2 : UIButton!
    @IBOutlet var textArea : UITextView!
    var api: APIClient!
    var logger: UILogger!

    required init?(coder aDecoder: NSCoder) {
        super.init(coder: aDecoder)
    }

    override func viewDidLoad() {
        super.viewDidLoad()
        // Do any additional setup after loading the view, typically from a nib.
        api = APIClient(parent: self)
        logger = UILogger(out: textArea)
    }

    override func didReceiveMemoryWarning() {
        super.didReceiveMemoryWarning()
        // Dispose of any resources that can be recreated.
    }
    @IBAction func unclickButton() {
        labelButton.setTitle("Blink All Lights", forState: UIControlState.Normal)
    }
    @IBAction func unclickButton2() {
        labelButton2.setTitle("Blink Red Light", forState: UIControlState.Normal)
    }
    @IBAction func clickButton() {
        logger.logEvent("=== Blink All Lights ===")
        api.blinkAllLights()
        labelButton.setTitle("Request Sent", forState: UIControlState.Normal)
    }
    @IBAction func clickButton2() {
        logger.logEvent("=== Blink Red Light ===")
        api.blinkLight("red")
        labelButton2.setTitle("Request Sent", forState: UIControlState.Normal)
    }
    @IBAction func clickClearButton() {
        logger.set()
    }
}
```

The Logger Library

The logger library was assigned a variable in the View Controller that will keep an instance of the logger around with the proper target assigned; in our case we use a text area field for the activity logging.

When the main thread updates an UI element, there is no need for special treatment. However, since the calls that write to this log are running in a child thread, we make sure that updates to an UI element will be dispatched as async (Listing 12-9).

Listing 12-9. Dispatching an async Event

```
func set(text: String?="") {
    dispatch_async(dispatch_get_main_queue()) {
        self.textArea!.text = text
    };
}
```

To keep things simple, we implement just a couple of functions that will allow us to track the API activity. These functions will interact with the textArea field we set up in the View Controller. Just as in the View Controller, the textArea field is declared optional, as it will be initialized in the `init()` function. You can see the entire code of the `UILogger.swift` file in Listing 12-10.

Listing 12-10. The UILogger Library

```
import Foundation
import UIKit

class UILogger {
    var textArea : UITextView!

    required init(out: UITextView) {
        dispatch_async(dispatch_get_main_queue()) {
            self.textArea = out
        };
        self.set()
    }

    func set(text: String?="") {
        dispatch_async(dispatch_get_main_queue()) {
            self.textArea!.text = text
        };
    }

    func logEvent(message: String) {
        dispatch_async(dispatch_get_main_queue()) {
            self.textArea!.text = self.textArea!.text.stringByAppendingString("=> " +
            message + "\n")
        };
    }
}
```

The API Client Library

Now we will create now the `APIClient.swift` library. This library is for the functions that make async requests to the API. The header of the class contains the URL and other variables needed for the API functionality.

Defining the Device URL

You can create a pop-up screen to enter this on the device, or you can write a discovery service using Bonjour to discover the device. To keep things simple, we hard-coded the IP address and the port of the device as a variable (Listing 12-11).

Listing 12-11. The Header of the APICLient Library

```
import Foundation
class APIClient {
    var apiVersion: String!
    var baseURL: String = "http://10.0.1.128:8080"
    var viewController: ViewController!

    required init (parent: ViewController!) {
        viewController = parent
    }
}
```

Creating a GET Handler

A generic function to perform a `GET` from a service looks like the code in Listing 12-12. This code is part of the APIClient class, which we saved as the `APIClient.swift` file.

Listing 12-12. Generic Function to Perform a GET

```
func getData (service: APIService, id: String!=nil, urlSuffix: NSArray!=nil, params:
[String:String]!=[:]) {
    let blockSelf = self
    let logger: UILogger = viewController.logger
    self.apiRequest(
        service,
        method: APIMethod.GET,
        id: id,
        urlSuffix: urlSuffix,
        inputData: params,
        callback: { (responseJson: NSDictionary!, responseError: NSError!) -> Void in
            if (responseError != nil) {
                logger.logEvent(responseError!.description)
                // Handle here the error response in some way
            }
```

```
            else {
                blockSelf.processGETData(service, id: id, urlSuffix: urlSuffix, params:
                params, responseJson: responseJson)
            }
    })
}
```

For the urlSuffix we use the NSArray data type that will hold all elements of the URL being accessed. Since we do not know what data we will send to the API, the NSArray type is ideal because by default it contains AnyObject elements. We also pass the urlSuffix to the `processGETData` function, so that we can make a decision about what to do with the response, given the service being called, the optional id of the item, and the urlSuffix. We also defined default values for urlSuffix and params to allow our functions to make calls without providing all nil parameters in tow.

The optional input params is a dictionary with strings for keys and values. This is the most convenient format, considering that `POST` is not any different from `GET` in the way the parameters are passed to the API.

The block passed to the `NSURLConnection.sendAsynchronousRequest` is a closure, which is why we need to assign the `blockSelf` variable that will be used to make calls in the context of the APIClient library.

The function is the actual handler of that response, which takes the generic form shown in Listing 12-13.

Listing 12-13. Implementing a GET Request Handler

```
func processGETData (service: APIService, id: String!, urlSuffix: NSArray!, params:
[String:String]!=[:], responseJson: NSDictionary!) {
    // do something with data here
}
```

Creating a POST Handler

Just like the `GET` request, the `POST` request can have the same structure seen in Listing 12-14. This, too, is part of the `APIClient` class (the `APIClient.swift` file).

Listing 12-14. Implementing a POST Request Handler

```
func postData (service: APIService, id: String!=nil, urlSuffix: NSArray!=nil,
params: [String:String]!=[:]) {
    let blockSelf = self
    let logger: UILogger = viewController.logger
    self.apiRequest(
        service,
        method: APIMethod.POST,
        id: id,
        urlSuffix: urlSuffix,
        inputData: params,
```

```
        callback: { (responseJson: NSDictionary!, responseError: NSError!) -> Void in
            if (responseError != nil) {
                logger.logEvent(responseError!.description)
                // Handle here the error response in some way
            }
            else {
                blockSelf.processPOSTData(service, id: id, urlSuffix: urlSuffix, params:
                params, responseJson: responseJson)
            }
    })
}

func processPOSTData (service: APIService, id: String!, urlSuffix: NSArray!, params:
[String:String]!=[:], responseJson: NSDictionary!) {
    // do something with data here
}
```

Of course, we can implement the request process in many different ways, but having a common handler for an API request type allows us to avoid callback hell.

Defining the verbs and services

We notice that the verb is not a string but an enum value: `APIMethod.GET`. This is an enum that we define in this library, to provide easy access to the verbs as strings, rather than using the strings directly. It also allows us to define which HTTP verbs are supported by the API client (Listing 12-15). This too, is part of the `APIClient` class (the `APIClient.swift` file).

Listing 12-15. The APIMethod Enum

```
enum APIMethod {
    case GET, POST
    func toString() -> String {
        var method: String!
        switch self {
        case .GET:
            method = "GET"
        case .POST:
            method = "POST"
        }
        return method
    }
}
```

We provide the `hasBody()` function as an example that could be useful in the apiRequest to properly format the request, so that `GET` and `DELETE` use the parameters as key-value pairs, while `PUT` and `POST` use it as JSON.

There is another enum we define in the APIClient library, that provides shortcuts to actual services via the `toString()` function. We saw this in the View Controller used as `APIService.GOOD_JSON`. We will extend this later to add other services and also provide a function to return the suffix we might want to use for some calls, but for now Listing 12-16 shows the basic format.

Listing 12-16. The APIService Enum

```
enum APIService {
    case BLINK
    func toString() -> String {
        var service: String!
        switch self {
        case .BLINK:
            service = "blink"
        }
        return service
    }
}
```

Adding an Extension to the String Type

We add in the same `APIClient.swift` file an extension to the string type to add a simple escaping method for the URL params we might want to pass to a call (Listing 12-17).

Listing 12-17. The Extension to the String Object

```
extension String {
    func escapeUrl() -> String {
        let source: NSString = NSString(string: self)
        let chars = "abcdefghijklmnopqrstuvwxyz"
        let okChars = chars + chars.uppercaseString + "0123456789.~_-"
        let customAllowedSet = NSCharacterSet(charactersInString: okChars)
        return source.stringByAddingPercentEncodingWithAllowedCharacters(customAllowedSet)!
    }
}
```

The apiRequest() Function

Next to be defined is the `apiRequest()` function (Listing 12-18). This function will make the actual API request, and that includes handling the eventual verification of the response data. The method signature is showing that the only required params are the service, the method, and the callback function. This is also part of the `APIClient` class.

Listing 12-18. The apiRequest Function

```
func apiRequest (
        service: APIService,
        method: APIMethod,
        id: String!,
        urlSuffix: NSArray!,
        inputData: [String:String]!,
        callback: (responseJson: NSDictionary!, responseError: NSError!) -> Void ) {
    // Code goes here
}
```

The services currently available are INFO and BLINK: the API overloads them with a variable list of params, so in essence your calls will need to provide the larger APIService, then provide via the urlSuffix, the URL path extension to point to the right resource. This will be explained in more detail later.

As to the content of the method, the following is what we need to do for an API request:

1. Compose the base URL of the service
2. Add the URL suffix if it was specified
3. Serialize and append to the URL the input params
4. Make the API request as an async call

In the code block passed to the async call, we also need to do the following:

1. De-serialize the JSON response, if JSON was found
2. Call the callback function

To **compose the base URL of the service** we use the code shown in Listing 12-19.

Listing 12-19. Composing the Base URL

```
var serviceURL = baseURL + "/"
if apiVersion != nil {
     serviceURL += apiVersion + "/"
}
serviceURL += service.toString()
if id != nil && !id.isEmpty {
     serviceURL += "/" + id
}
var request = NSMutableURLRequest()
request.HTTPMethod = method.toString()
```

In the same segment, we create the request object and assign it the request method. The serviceURL is still being composed, so it would be premature to assign it to the request at this point.

If this API would support a JSON request body for POST requests, we could use something like the code in Listing 12-20 to serialize the input data.

Listing 12-20. Serializing JSON Data

```
var error: NSError?
request.HTTPBody = NSJSONSerialization.dataWithJSONObject(inputData, options: nil, error:
&error)
if error != nil {
    callback(responseJson: nil, responseError: error)
    return
}
request.addValue("application/json", forHTTPHeaderField: "Content-Type")
```

To handle the composition of the URL, we create the `asURLString()` function. This function is located in the `APIClient` class and takes a dictionary of input params and creates a URL-encoded string, with the parameters sorted alphabetically (Listing 12-21).

Listing 12-21. The asURLString Function

```
func asURLString (inputData: [String:String]!=[:]) -> String {
    var params: [String] = []
    for (key, value) in inputData {
        params.append( [ key.escapeUrl(), value.escapeUrl()].joinWithSeparator("=" ))
    }
    params = params.sort{ $0 < $1 }
    return params.joinWithSeparator("&")
}
```

The URL suffix needs to be made part of the URL— - we have in the input an NSArray of strings or numbers that will be used to compose the suffix— - they will be all reduced to a simple string, appended to the base URL. You can find the following example (Listing 12-22) in the `postData()` function in the `APIClient` class:

Listing 12-22. Composing a URL

```
// The urlSuffix contains an array of strings that we use to compose the final URL
if urlSuffix?.count > 0 {
    serviceURL += "/" + urlSuffix.componentsJoinedByString("/")
}
```

Now we are ready to make the API request as an async call. Note how we created a local variable logger that points to the logging handler of the View Controller; this is necessary because inside the closure we don't have visibility to variables and functions from the current library or from the View Controller. The callback block for the async calls contains the basic code needed to handle the result data and call the callback function that we got when we invoked `apiRequest()`. Once again, when interpreting the response, an error can occur parsing the JSON data, which will be handled by the callback function.

To parse an API response into a JSON object, we use an NSDictionary object that will hold any combination of key-values. This is necessary since the API responses can contain any combination of numbers, strings, arrays, and dictionaries, and NSDictionary supports by default AnyObject types. The `NSJSONReadingOptions.MutableContainers` specifies that arrays and dictionaries be created as mutable objects. We can see this in Listing 12-23. This code is located in the `postData()` function in the `APIClient` class.

Listing 12-23. Parsing a JSON Response

```
var jsonResult: NSDictionary?
if urlResponse != nil {
     let rData: String = NSString(data: data!, encoding: NSUTF8StringEncoding)! as String
     if data != nil {
          do {
```

```
            try jsonResult = NSJSONSerialization.JSONObjectWithData(data!, options:
            NSJSONReadingOptions.MutableContainers) as? NSDictionary
        } catch {
// we expect an "OK" from the API, not JSON, so it's OK if we don't do anything here
        }
    }
```

When encountering an error case that we need to report, we can create our own error object. To do this in Swift, we use the following approach:

```
error = NSError(domain: "response", code: -1, userInfo: ["reason":"blank response"])
```

We added some logging for the response data, with an example on how to pretty-print JSON to the textarea used for logging. We do want to format the response in such a way that is easy to read, and pretty-printed JSON appears as one key-value per line, nicely indented. We can see the results in Listing 12-24. This code is located in the `postData()` function in the `APIClient` class.

Listing 12-24. Handling a REST Call

```
let logger: UILogger = viewController.logger
let session = NSURLSession.sharedSession()
let task = session.dataTaskWithRequest(request) { (data : NSData?, urlResponse :
NSURLResponse?, error: NSError?) -> Void in
    //the request returned with a response or possibly an error
    logger.logEvent("URL: " + serviceURL)
    var error: NSError?
    var jsonResult: NSDictionary?
    if urlResponse != nil {
        let rData: String = NSString(data: data!, encoding: NSUTF8StringEncoding)! as String
        if data != nil {
            do {
                try jsonResult = NSJSONSerialization.JSONObjectWithData(data!, options:
                NSJSONReadingOptions.MutableContainers) as? NSDictionary
            } catch {
                // we expect an "OK" from the API, not JSON, so it's OK if we don't do
                anything here
                // print("json error: \(error)")
            }
        }
        logger.logEvent("RESPONSE RAW: " + (rData.isEmpty ? "No Data" : rData) )
        print("RESPONSE RAW: \(rData)")
    }
    else {
        error = NSError(domain: "response", code: -1, userInfo: ["reason":"blank response"])
    }
    callback(responseJson: jsonResult, responseError: error)
}
task.resume()
```

Displaying pretty-formatted JSON can be useful in other places too, so we extracted the code in Listing 12-25 in the prettyJSON() function. This code is located in the postData() function in the APIClient class.

Listing 12-25. Displaying Pretty-Formatted JSON Responses

```
func prettyJSON (json: NSDictionary!) -> String! {
    var pretty: String!
    if json != nil && NSJSONSerialization.isValidJSONObject(json!) {
        if let data = try? NSJSONSerialization.dataWithJSONObject(json!, options:
        NSJSONWritingOptions.PrettyPrinted) {
            pretty = NSString(data: data, encoding: NSUTF8StringEncoding) as? String
        }
    }
    return pretty
}
```

Listing 12-26 shows the entire code we have so far for the APIClient library.

Listing 12-26. The APIClient.swift Library

```
import Foundation
class APIClient {
    var apiVersion: String!
    var baseURL: String = "http://10.0.1.128:8080"
    var viewController: ViewController!

    required init (parent: ViewController!) {
        viewController = parent
    }

    func blinkAllLights () {
        // GET /blink
        getData(APIService.BLINK)
    }

    func blinkLight(color: String) {
        // GET /blink/red
        getData(APIService.BLINK, id: color)
    }

    func postData (service: APIService, id: String!=nil, urlSuffix: NSArray!=nil, params:
    [String:String]!=[:]) {
        let blockSelf = self
        let logger: UILogger = viewController.logger
        self.apiRequest(
            service,
            method: APIMethod.POST,
            id: id,
            urlSuffix: urlSuffix,
            inputData: params,
```

```
            callback: { (responseJson: NSDictionary!, responseError: NSError!) -> Void in
                if (responseError != nil) {
                    logger.logEvent(responseError!.description)
                    // Handle here the error response in some way
                }
                else {
                    blockSelf.processPOSTData(service, id: id, urlSuffix: urlSuffix, params:
                    params, responseJson: responseJson)
                }
        })
    }

    func processPOSTData (service: APIService, id: String!, urlSuffix: NSArray!, params:
    [String:String]!=[:], responseJson: NSDictionary!) {
        // do something with data here
    }

    func getData (service: APIService, id: String!=nil, urlSuffix: NSArray!=nil, params:
    [String:String]!=[:]) {
        let blockSelf = self
        let logger: UILogger = viewController.logger
        self.apiRequest(
            service,
            method: APIMethod.GET,
            id: id,
            urlSuffix: urlSuffix,
            inputData: params,
            callback: { (responseJson: NSDictionary!, responseError: NSError!) -> Void in
                if (responseError != nil) {
                    logger.logEvent(responseError!.description)
                    // Handle here the error response in some way
                }
                else {
                    blockSelf.processGETData(service, id: id, urlSuffix: urlSuffix, params:
                    params, responseJson: responseJson)
                }
        })
    }

    func processGETData (service: APIService, id: String!, urlSuffix: NSArray!, params:
    [String:String]!=[:], responseJson: NSDictionary!) {
        // do something with data here
    }

    func apiRequest (
        service: APIService,
        method: APIMethod,
        id: String!,
        urlSuffix: NSArray!,
        inputData: [String:String]!,
        callback: (responseJson: NSDictionary!, responseError: NSError!) -> Void ) {
```

```
// Compose the base URL
var serviceURL = baseURL + "/"
if apiVersion != nil {
    serviceURL += apiVersion + "/"
}
serviceURL += service.toString()

if id != nil && !id.isEmpty {
    serviceURL += "/" + id
}
let request = NSMutableURLRequest()
request.HTTPMethod = method.toString()
// The urlSuffix contains an array of strings that we use to compose the final URL
if urlSuffix?.count > 0 {
    serviceURL += "/" + urlSuffix.componentsJoinedByString("/")
}
request.addValue("application/json", forHTTPHeaderField: "Accept")

request.URL = NSURL(string: serviceURL)

if !inputData.isEmpty {
    serviceURL += "?" + asURLString(inputData)
    request.URL = NSURL(string: serviceURL)
}
//now make the request
let logger: UILogger = viewController.logger
let session = NSURLSession.sharedSession()
let task = session.dataTaskWithRequest(request) { (data : NSData?, urlResponse :
NSURLResponse?, error: NSError?) -> Void in
    //the request returned with a response or possibly an error
    logger.logEvent("URL: " + serviceURL)
    var error: NSError?
    var jsonResult: NSDictionary?
    if urlResponse != nil {
        let rData: String = NSString(data: data!, encoding:
        NSUTF8StringEncoding)! as String
        if data != nil {
            do {
                try jsonResult = NSJSONSerialization.JSONObjectWithData(data!,
                options: NSJSONReadingOptions.MutableContainers) as?
                NSDictionary
            } catch {
                // we expect an "OK" from the API, not JSON, so it's OK if we
                don't do anything here
                // print("json error: \(error)")
            }
        }
        logger.logEvent("RESPONSE RAW: " + (rData.isEmpty ? "No Data" : rData) )
        print("RESPONSE RAW: \(rData)")
    }
```

```
            else {
                error = NSError(domain: "response", code: -1, userInfo: ["reason":"blank
                response"])
            }
            callback(responseJson: jsonResult, responseError: error)
        }
        task.resume()
    }

    func asURLString (inputData: [String:String]!=[:]) -> String {
        var params: [String] = []
        for (key, value) in inputData {
            params.append( [ key.escapeUrl(), value.escapeUrl()].joinWithSeparator("=" ))
        }
        params = params.sort{ $0 < $1 }
        return params.joinWithSeparator("&")
    }


    func prettyJSON (json: NSDictionary!) -> String! {
        var pretty: String!
        if json != nil && NSJSONSerialization.isValidJSONObject(json!) {
            if let data = try? NSJSONSerialization.dataWithJSONObject(json!, options:
            NSJSONWritingOptions.PrettyPrinted) {
                pretty = NSString(data: data, encoding: NSUTF8StringEncoding) as? String
            }
        }
        return pretty
    }

}

extension String {
    func escapeUrl() -> String {
        let source: NSString = NSString(string: self)
        let chars = "abcdefghijklmnopqrstuvwxyz"
        let okChars = chars + chars.uppercaseString + "0123456789.~_-"
        let customAllowedSet = NSCharacterSet(charactersInString: okChars)
        return source.stringByAddingPercentEncodingWithAllowedCharacters(customAllowedSet)!
    }
}

enum APIService {
    case BLINK
    func toString() -> String {
        var service: String!
        switch self {
        case .BLINK:
            service = "blink"
        }
        return service
    }
}
```

```
enum APIMethod {
    case GET, POST
    func toString() -> String {
        var method: String!
        switch self {
        case .GET:
            method = "GET"
        case .POST:
            method = "POST"
        }
        return method
    }
}
```

You should now be able to send commands to the device, and you will see the results in the text area as shown in Figure 12-4.

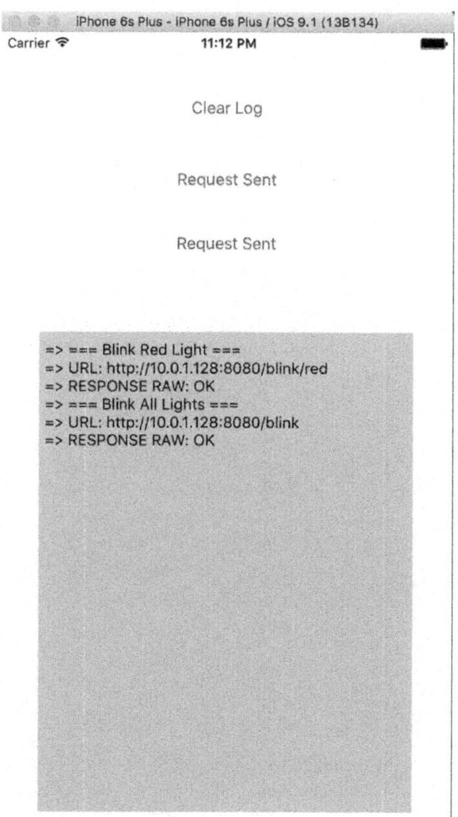

Figure 12-4. *The request/response view of the application*

Summary

In this chapter, you learned to set up a basic script that interacts with resources on a Raspberry Pi, the service necessary to run a listener that takes remote commands, and how to write a very basic iOS application that makes an HTTP request to interact with the device via the very simple API you created.

Chapter 13

Using Keychain Services to Secure Data

Gheorghe Chesler

Although the iPhone boasts the lowest rate of security issues for a major computing platform, many developers only take advantage of a handful of these features. In this chapter, we will introduce Keychain Services, Apple's security framework for encrypting notes, passwords, and SSL (Secure Socket Layer) certificates at the system level.

At the core of modern encryption systems is the concept of public-key cryptography. Also known as "asymmetric" encryption, this mechanism allows the use of distinct keys for encryption, as opposed to decryption where you can use the public key only to encrypt and verify signatures, and you can use the private key only to decrypt content encrypted with the public key. The keys are generated using a very large random number to provide entropy, as seen in Figure 13-1.

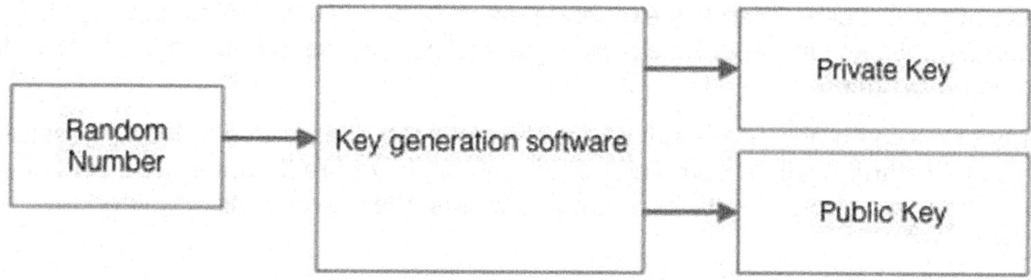

***Figure 13-1.** Generating the pair of private/public keys*

This mechanism is used by the SSL encryption in the browser (the Transport Layer Security), S/MIME, and well-known encryption platforms like GPG and PGP. The well-known RSA cryptosystem uses both key distribution and secrecy (Diffie-Hellman key exchange) to secure data transfer.

If you have ever generated a secure key on a Linux box or even in a Windows program like GnuPG or TrueCrypt, you probably noticed that generating the random number takes a bit of time, and that it is using some random data from the environment, like asking you to move the mouse around for a while. This ensures that the random number does not depend on any factors that can be replicated at any time by somebody else. One of the common flaws of some systems is that they rely on weak entropy to base their random number generation, and therefore the randomness is somewhat predictable and in some cases reproducible.

When two parties want to communicate securely, they each send data that they encrypted with the public key of the other party. A well-known analogy is the one of Alice and Bob exchanging messages as shown in Figure 13-2.

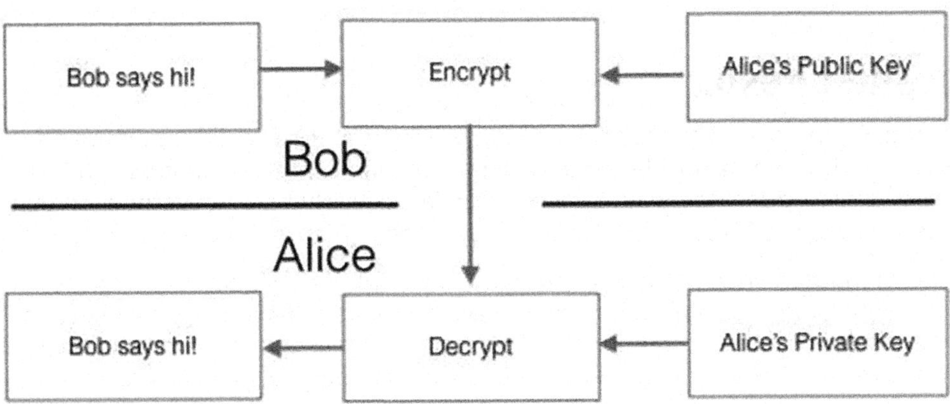

Figure 13-2. Bob and Alice exchanging messages

In the case of the Diffie-Hellman key exchange, each party uses its private key and the counterpart's public key to generate a shared secret that can be then used to encrypt data as a symmetric cypher.

The beauty of the math behind the private/public key properties is that it allows generation of the same key starting with a combination of a public key from the other user and one's own private key, so that no private key changes hands. We can see this depicted in Figure 13-3.

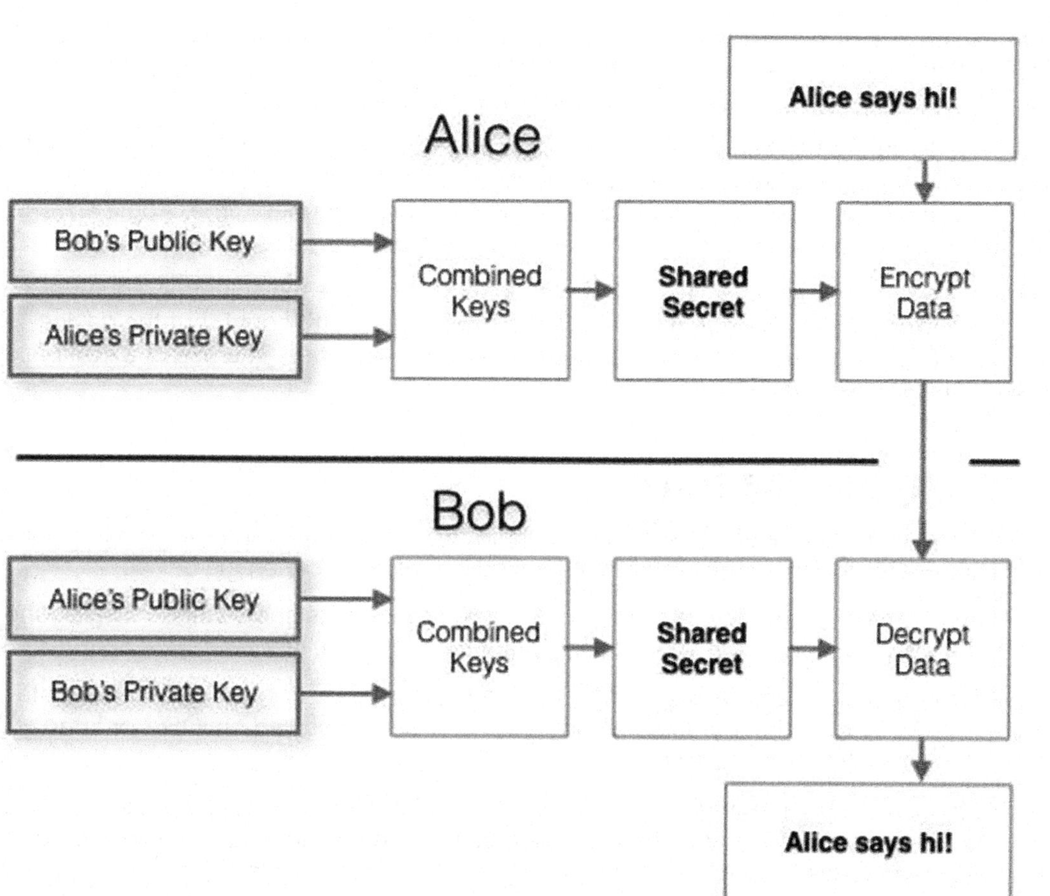

Figure 13-3. The Diffie-Hellman key exchange mechanism

Hardware Security on iOS Devices

Since the person who can access the private key is able to access the encrypted data, Apple does not provide the ability to access that key. On current iOS devices there is a crypto chip named the "Secure Enclave." This chip is completely isolated from the device CPU and its memory and can be used only for the crypto operations. Each crypto chip is programmed with a unique 256-bit key for each device, and the firmware of the crypto chip is secured with a signing key known only to Apple.

That way Apple should not be able to decrypt your password, since it does not know the UID (user identification number). It is not known whether Apple has the ability to extract the UID from a crypto chip. According to Apple, the "Secure Enclave" crypto chip maintains its security even if the device is jailbroken.

The crypto chip does not store any of your passwords but instead provides a way to encrypt and decrypt any content and hide the encryption keys from the outside world.

When you enter a password in the device, the Apple Key Derivation function combines the password with the UID then applies a slow derivation function (PBKDF2-AES), and the iteration count is chosen so that it takes about 80ms on the particular device.

If one were to attempt to hack the device password, that attempt would have to run on the device itself, since only the device knows the UID. The number of combinations required to crack a large enough password would take a considerable amount of time: Apple advertises that time to be more than five years for a random six-character password.

A device is considerably better secured if you configure it to erase itself after a number of invalid password retries. Note that retries with a thumbprint don't count, but the device will stop accepting a thumbprint-based log-in after a few bad tries. The use of a complex password is also recommended.

Securing the File Data

In addition to the hardware encryption features built into iOS devices, Apple uses a technology called Data Protection to further protect data stored in flash memory on the device.

Data Protection allows the device to respond to common events such as incoming phone calls, but it also enables a high level of encryption for user data.

Key system apps, such as Messages, Mail, Calendar, Contacts, Photos, and Health data values, use Data Protection by default, and third-party apps installed on iOS 7 or later receive this protection automatically.

Data Protection is implemented by constructing and managing a hierarchy of keys, and it builds on the hardware encryption technologies built into each iOS device. Data Protection is controlled on a per-file basis by assigning each file to a class; accessibility is determined by whether the class keys have been unlocked.

Every time a file on the data partition is created, Data Protection creates a new 256-bit key (the "per-file" key) and gives it to the hardware AES engine, which uses the key to encrypt the file as it is written to flash memory using AES CBC mode. The initialization vector (IV) is calculated with the block offset into the file, encrypted with the SHA-1 hash of the per-file key.

The per-file key is wrapped with one of several class keys, depending on the circumstances under which the file should be accessible. Like all other wrappings, this is performed using NIST AES key wrapping, per RFC 3394. The wrapped per-file key is stored in the file's metadata.

When a file is opened, its metadata is decrypted with the file system key, revealing the wrapped per-file key and a notation on which class protects it. The per-file key is unwrapped with the class key, then supplied to the hardware AES engine, which decrypts the file as it is read from flash memory.

The metadata of all files in the file system is encrypted with a random key, which is created when iOS is first installed or when a user wipes the device data. The file system key is stored in Effaceable Storage.

Since it's stored on the device, this key is not used to maintain the confidentiality of data; instead, it's designed to be quickly erased on demand (by the user, with the "Erase all content and settings" option, or by a user or administrator issuing a remote wipe command from a mobile device management (MDM) server, Exchange ActiveSync, or iCloud). Erasing the key in this manner renders all files cryptographically inaccessible.

The content of a file is encrypted with a per-file key, which is wrapped with a class key and stored in a file's metadata, which is in turn encrypted with the file system key. The class key is protected with the hardware UID and, for some classes, the user's passcode. This hierarchy provides both flexibility and performance. For example, changing a file's class only requires rewrapping its per-file key, and a change of passcode just rewraps the class key. Figure 13-4 visualizes this process.

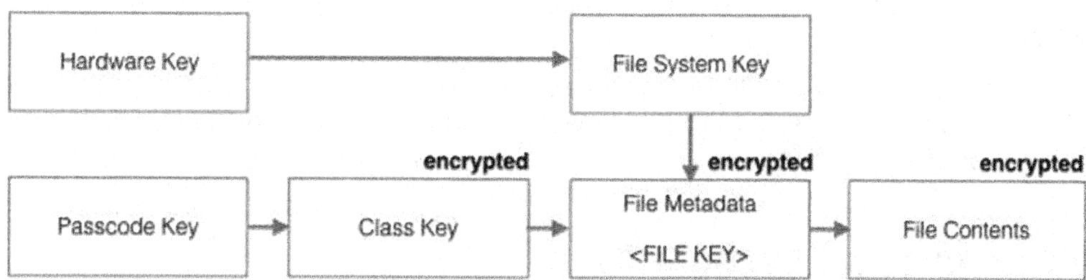

***Figure 13-4.** Overview of Apple key derivation and encryption (iOS Security Guide)*

The Apple Keychain

The Apple Keychain is Apple's platform "vault" for your application's sensitive data. Available on every device in the Apple landscape, the Apple Keychain allows applications to store different bits of information in a secure way, which can be retrieved next time the application starts. This allows for a certain level of security from attempts to access private bits of information by accessing the application as it is stored on the device.

Naturally, once secured data is accessed by the application, the data is still vulnerable to device memory snoop attacks, but at least the application and its stored data that you back up from your device, does not store the very sensitive bits in a vulnerable format. This is not as much an issue, because accessing the device memory does require direct access to the device from a trusted computer.

You might have noticed that every time you connect it to another PC or Mac, your iOS device already sends you an alert asking whether you trust that device—this is considered a reasonable first line of defense. Furthermore, when backing up a device, sensitive data like the keychain does not get backed up.

Even when you back up the device in secure mode, you have the ability to save the entry in your keychain with the `ThisDeviceOnly` option that ensures that your data is saved only on the current device, and that way it does not get backed up.

One aspect of the keychain implementation on iOS devices is that whatever you store in it is locked to that device or its backup. On an OSX device (Macbook, Mac Pro, or iMac), the keychain is stored under the user's `~/Library/Keychains/` path, and the files there can be copied to a different Mac and imported in its keychain, if you know the password to the keychains.

The keychain from an iOS device can only be backed up when you back up the iOS device in encrypted mode, so it is fairly inaccessible to the normal user.

To save and access data in the keychain, Apple provides the Apple Keychain Services API to any application.

The Apple Keychain Services

Apple Keychain Services is an API that allows applications to store key-value pairs in encrypted format on your iOS device. An app can save sensitive bits of data in the keychain, such as passwords, tokens, and keys. The keychain items can be shared between apps from the same developer.

The actual storage is a single SQLite database, accessed by a system daemon: this daemon queries for entries that correspond to the "keychain-access-group" of the app and the "application-identifier" entitlement.

Components of a Keychain Item

Along with the access group, each keychain item contains administrative metadata (such as "created" and "last updated" timestamps).

It also contains SHA-1 hashes of the attributes used to query for the item (such as the account and server name) to allow look-up without decrypting each item. And, finally, it contains the encryption data, which includes the following:

- Version number
- Access control list (ACL) data
- The value indicating which protection class the item is in
- A per-item key wrapped with the protection class key
- The dictionary of attributes describing the item (as passed to `SecItemAdd`), encoded as a binary plist and encrypted with the per-item key

For more detailed information, the iOS security guide is found at `www.apple.com/business/docs/iOS_Security_Guide.pdf`.

Implementing Keychain Services for Storing Passwords

You can store a user name and password, or other credentials that you use to access a resource, after you successfully authenticate to the resource. That way, when you reload your application, you can retrieve those credentials from the keychain, instead of from the less secure local storage. If the application is restored from an unencrypted backup to a different device, it will not have the entry in the keychain to go back to, so your credentials are safe.

In the following example we will store a string that could be a password or a token. We use the `SecItemAdd()` function available in the Security framework to save data for a given key. Looking at the function signature in the Keychain Services Reference, we see the following:

```
func SecItemAdd(_ attributes: CFDictionary!, _ result: UnsafeMutablePointer<Unmanaged
<AnyObject>?>) -> OSStatus
```

The attributes parameter is a dictionary that describes the data to be inserted and the security class of the item to be inserted, as well as a variety of optional parameters that describe the return type for the result.

To add multiple items to a keychain at once, use the `kSecUseItemList` key with an array of items as its value. This is only supported for non-password items.

Listing 13-1 provides an example of the code needed to insert a password in the keychain.

***Listing 13-1.** Inserting a Password in the Keychain*

```
let key = "password"
let value = "my Password"
if let data = value.dataUsingEncoding(NSUTF8StringEncoding) {
  let query = [
      (kSecClass as String) : kSecClassGenericPassword,
      (kSecAttrAccount as String) : key,
      (kSecValueData as String) : value
  ]
  SecItemAdd(query as CFDictionaryRef, nil)
}
```

In our example, we assume that the key did not exist before. In a practical implementation, we would want to delete an existing key before inserting it with a given value. We can express this a bit more cleanly by using a `NSMutableDictionary` object that allows us to pass the keys and values as lists (Listing 13-2).

***Listing 13-2.** Inserting Keys and Values as Lists*

```
let key = "password"
let value = "my Password"
if let data = value.dataUsingEncoding(NSUTF8StringEncoding) {

  let query = NSMutableDictionary(
      objects: [ kSecClassGenericPassword, key, value ],
      forKeys: [ kSecClass, kSecAttrAccount, kSecValueData ]
  ) as CFDictionaryRef
  SecItemAdd(query, nil)
}
```

We see in the examples in Listing 13-2 that the value string was converted to a `NSData` object, which is necessary since the value could be unicode.

Retrieving Data from Keychain Services

To read from the keychain services, we use the function `SecItemCopyMatching()`, which returns one or more keychain items that match a search query, or copies attributes of specific keychain items.

The function signature is as follows:

```
func SecItemCopyMatching(query: CFDictionary!, _ result:UnsafeMutablePointer<Unmanaged
<AnyObject>?>) -> OSStatus{...}
```

The `OSStatus` return value is a result code. See Keychain Services Result Codes in the Security Framework Reference for more detail on these codes. This is buried in the documentation and you can get to it selecting the path `Security Framework Reference / Keychain Services Reference / Search Results Constants`.

By default, this function returns only the first match found. To obtain more than one matching item at a time, specify the search key `kSecMatchLimit` with a value greater than 1. The result will be an object of type `CFArrayRef` containing up to that number of matching items.

To retrieve any data for the given key, we need to pass to the `result` a reference to an object that will be populated by the function. Just as for the insert operation, the `query` is a dictionary that specifies the attribute name, its type, and a couple of parameters that enable the data return and the number of items to retrieve.

Obviously, the response is optional, as the key could not exist, and there is a chance that the operation will fail so we also need to check for the call return code that takes the value `noErr` when the operation succeeded (Listing 13-3).

Listing 13-3. Checking for the Call Return Codes

```
let key = "password"
var password : String!;
var response: Unmanaged<AnyObject>?

let query = NSMutableDictionary(
    objects: [ kSecClassGenericPassword, key, kCFBooleanTrue, kSecMatchLimitOne ],
    forKeys: [ kSecClass, kSecAttrAccount, kSecReturnData, kSecMatchLimit ]
) as CFDictionaryRef

let status = SecItemCopyMatching(query, &response)

if status == noErr && response != nil {
    if let data = response!.takeRetainedValue() as? NSData {
             password = NSString(data: data, encoding: NSUTF8StringEncoding)
       }
}
```

In this example, we read and assign a simple string to the `password` variable. As mentioned before, for data types other than passwords we can store multiple values.

Invalidating Keychain Service Records

To delete individual items, we use the `SecItemDelete` function. This function has the following signature:

```
func SecItemDelete(query: CFDictionary!) -> OSStatus
```

The query is a dictionary containing an item class specification and optional attributes for controlling the search. As always, for details on the currently defined search attributes you should consult the Security Framework Reference, as the API might change with future versions of Swift or iOS.

Just as for the other calls, the `OSStatus` return value is a result code.

Let's see how deleting a password would look (Listing 13-4).

Listing 13-4. Deleting a Password from the Keychain

```
let key = "password"

let query = NSMutableDictionary(
    objects: [ kSecClassGenericPassword, key ],
    forKeys: [ kSecClass, kSecAttrAccount ]
) as CFDictionaryRef

let status = SecItemDelete(query)
if status == noErr {
    print("password deleted")
}
```

If we want to delete all passwords, we can use the same function call, this time with no value for the `kSecAttrAccount`. This will have the effect of deleting all items of the class `kSecClassGenericPassword` (Listing 13-5).

Listing 13-5. Deleting All Passwords from the Keychain

```
let query = NSMutableDictionary(
    objects: [ kSecClassGenericPassword ],
    forKeys: [ kSecClass ]
) as CFDictionaryRef

let status = SecItemDelete(query)

if status == noErr {
    print("all passwords deleted")
}
```

Of course, this could be compressed as

```
if SecItemDelete([(kSecClass as String) : kSecClassGenericPassword]) == noErr {
    print("all passwords deleted")
}
```

Setting Up an Application to Test Keychain Services

We will use a one-page application just as we did for the Fitbit application, and we will reuse some elements, particularly the `UILogger.swift`. To handle the Keychain API calls, we set up a class named `Keychain`, which will be described in detail later.

To be able to use Keychain Services, we need to link the binary with the `Security.framework` library, just as in Figure 13-5.

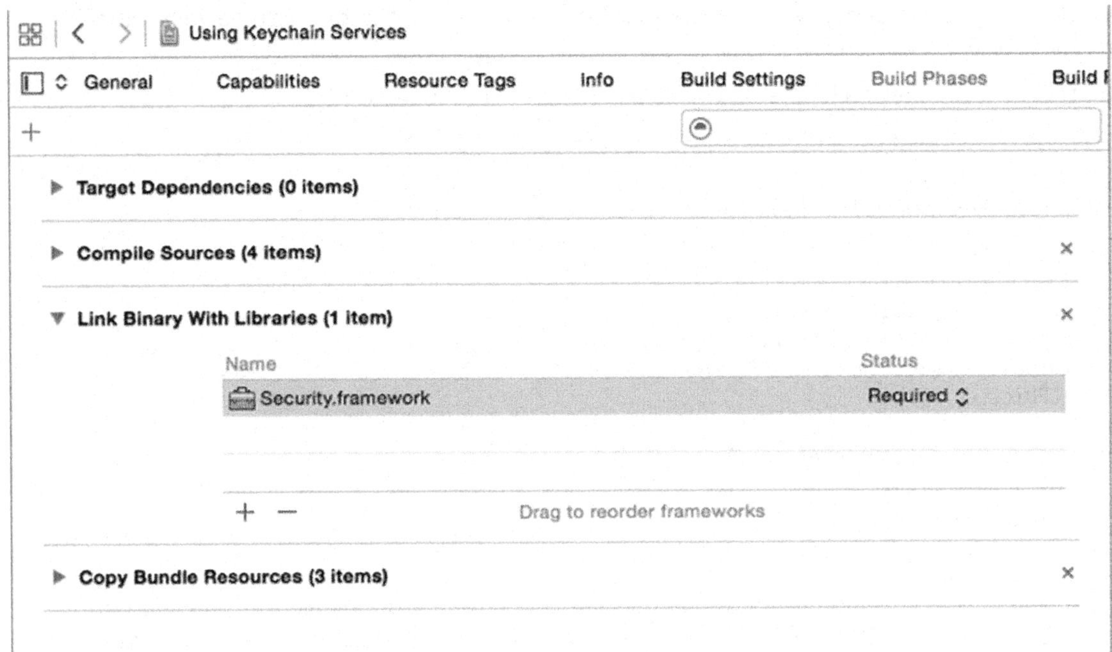

Figure 13-5. Linking the app with the Security Framework

The View Controller

The view controller code is very simple. We created a text input field where one can enter the string to be saved to the keychain. In this example we save to the keychain a field named "token." To make things more interesting, if no value was provided, we populate it with the current date/time: this will help with debugging and verifying that the application reads correctly from the keychain after it was restarted (Listing 13-6).

Listing 13-6. The ViewController.swift file

```
import UIKit

class ViewController: UIViewController {
    @IBOutlet var clearButton : UIButton!
    @IBOutlet var clearKeychainButton : UIButton!
    @IBOutlet var saveButton : UIButton!
    @IBOutlet var readButton : UIButton!
```

```
    @IBOutlet var textArea : UITextView!
    @IBOutlet var textField : UITextField!
    var logger: UILogger!

    override func viewDidLoad() {
        super.viewDidLoad()
        // Do any additional setup after loading the view, typically from a nib.
        logger = UILogger(out: textArea)
    }

    override func didReceiveMemoryWarning() {
        super.didReceiveMemoryWarning()
        // Dispose of any resources that can be recreated.
    }

    @IBAction func saveToKeychain() {
        var value = textField.text!;
        if value.isEmpty {
            let dateFormatter:NSDateFormatter = NSDateFormatter()
            dateFormatter.dateFormat = "yyyy-MM-dd HH:mm:ss"
            value = dateFormatter.stringFromDate(NSDate())
        }

        logger.logEvent("Save to keychain: \(value)")
        Keychain.set("token", value: value)
    }

    @IBAction func readFromKeychain() {
        // the response is an Optional<NSData> so it needs to be unwrapped
        if let value = Keychain.get("token") {
            logger.logEvent("Read from keychain: \(value)")
        }
        else {
            logger.logEvent("No value found in the keychain")
        }
    }
    @IBAction func clickClearButton() {
        logger.clear()
    }
    @IBAction func clickClearKeychainButton() {
        Keychain.clear()
        logger.logEvent("The keychain data has been cleared")
    }
}
```

We can see that we created a `textArea` for the inline logging of the activity and a `textField` that will be used to input the inserted value, as well as a few buttons. Figure 13-6 shows a detail view of the `Main.storyboard` that shows how the buttons and fields are wired.

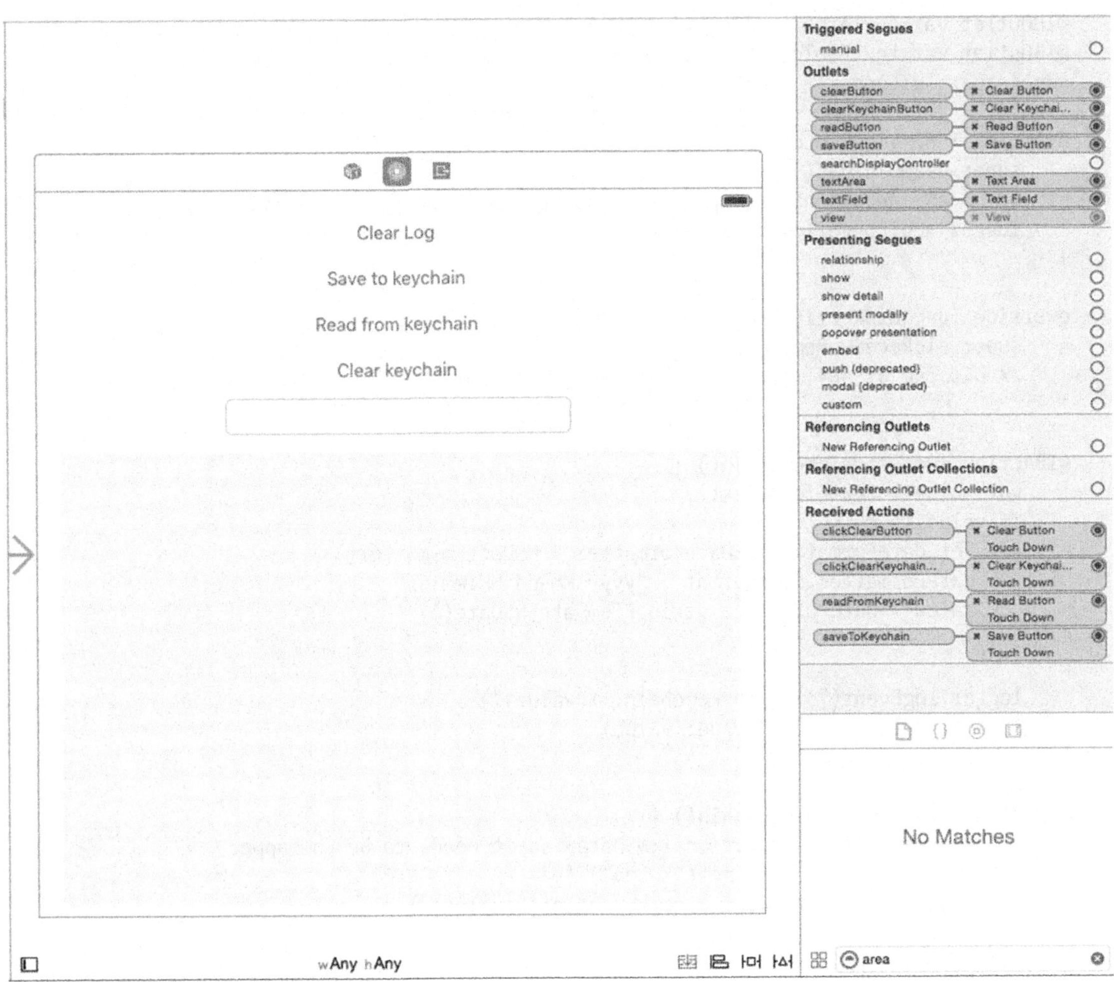

Figure 13-6. The application storyboard

The Keychain Class

We create a few private class methods to encapsulate the query constructors. We will save them as the `Keychain.swift` file.

For the create/update query, we take a key name and the value to be inserted, as shown in Listing 13-7. We have to convert the values to String before assigning them to the dictionary—this used to work without the need of an explicit conversion in earlier versions of Swift.

Listing 13-7. The updateQuery() Function

```
private class func updateQuery(key: String, value: NSData) -> CFDictionaryRef {
    return NSMutableDictionary(
        objects: [ kSecClassGenericPassword, key, value ],
        forKeys: [ String(kSecClass), String(kSecAttrAccount), String(kSecValueData) ]
    )
}
```

The deleteQuery looks very similar to the updateQuery, but it takes only a key String (Listing 13-8).

Listing 13-8. The deleteQuery() Function

```
private class func deleteQuery(key: String) -> CFDictionaryRef {
    return NSMutableDictionary(
        objects: [ kSecClassGenericPassword, key ],
        forKeys: [ String(kSecClass), String(kSecAttrAccount) ]
    )
}
```

The set function uses the two queries previously mentioned to first delete an existing key and then add the key with the new value (Listing 13-9).

Listing 13-9. The set() Function

```
public class func set(key: String, value: String) -> Bool {
    if let data = value.dataUsingEncoding(NSUTF8StringEncoding) {
        SecItemDelete(deleteQuery(key))
        return SecItemAdd(updateQuery(key, value: data), nil) == noErr
    }
    return false
}
```

To read existing entries, we use the functions shown in Listing 13-10. The get() is rather simple, since it relies on the getData() to do the heavy lifting, and it only returns a NSString object. For the getData() we need to do a fancy dance to extract the status and the response.

Listing 13-10. The get() and getData() Functions in the Keychain.swift File

```
public class func get(key: String) -> NSString? {
    let query = searchQuery(key)
    if let data = getData(query) {
        return NSString(data: data, encoding: NSUTF8StringEncoding)
    }
    return nil
}

public class func getData(query: CFDictionaryRef) -> NSData? {
    var response: AnyObject?
    let status = withUnsafeMutablePointer(&response) {
        SecItemCopyMatching(query, UnsafeMutablePointer($0))
    }
    return status == noErr && response != nil
        ? response as! NSData?
        : nil
}
```

We observe that the response comes (eventually) as NSData and has to be converted back to a String. The getData() function can be used on its own to fetch a value given a well-formatted query (not necessarily password type). It returns an NSData object that can be converted to any given data type we expect to read back from the keychain.

Listing 13-11 shows the code for the entire Keychain class. We leave as an exercise for the user to create a setData() function that would handle a variety of item types. Keep in mind that you have to use the same value for kSecClass when deleting the entries before inserting them.

Listing 13-11. The Keychain.swift File

```
import Foundation
import Security

public class Keychain {
    public class func set(key: String, value: String) -> Bool {
        if let data = value.dataUsingEncoding(NSUTF8StringEncoding) {
            SecItemDelete(deleteQuery(key))
            return SecItemAdd(updateQuery(key, value: data), nil) == noErr
        }
        return false
    }

    public class func get(key: String) -> NSString? {
        let query = searchQuery(key)
        if let data = getData(query) {
            return NSString(data: data, encoding: NSUTF8StringEncoding)
        }
        return nil
    }

    public class func getData(query: CFDictionaryRef) -> NSData? {
        var response: AnyObject?
        let status = withUnsafeMutablePointer(&response) {
            SecItemCopyMatching(query, UnsafeMutablePointer($0))
        }
        return status == noErr && response != nil
            ? response as! NSData?
            : nil
    }

    public class func delete(key: String) -> Bool {
        return SecItemDelete( deleteQuery(key) ) == noErr
    }

    public class func clear() -> Bool {
        if SecItemDelete([(kSecClass as String) : kSecClassGenericPassword]) == noErr {
            print("all passwords deleted")
        }
        return SecItemDelete( clearQuery() ) == noErr
    }
```

```
    private class func updateQuery(key: String, value: NSData) -> CFDictionaryRef {
        return NSMutableDictionary(
            objects: [ kSecClassGenericPassword, key, value ],
            forKeys: [ String(kSecClass), String(kSecAttrAccount), String(kSecValueData) ]
        )
    }
    private class func deleteQuery(key: String) -> CFDictionaryRef {
        return NSMutableDictionary(
            objects: [ kSecClassGenericPassword, key ],
            forKeys: [ String(kSecClass), String(kSecAttrAccount) ]
        )
    }
    private class func searchQuery(key: String) -> CFDictionaryRef {
        return NSMutableDictionary(
            objects: [ kSecClassGenericPassword, key, kCFBooleanTrue, kSecMatchLimitOne ],
            forKeys: [ String(kSecClass), String(kSecAttrAccount), String(kSecReturnData),
            String(kSecMatchLimit) ]
        )
    }
    private class func clearQuery() -> CFDictionaryRef {
        return [ (kSecClass as String) : kSecClassGenericPassword ]
    }

}
```

Running the Demo Application

There is no magic to this application: it simply saves some password-type values and retrieves them from the keychain, with the output shown in Figure 13-7.

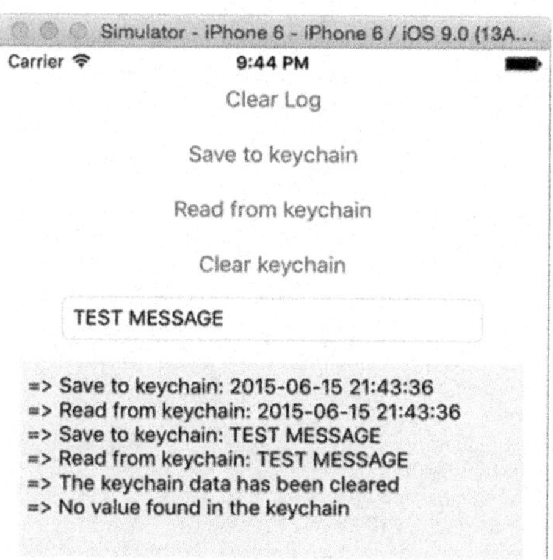

***Figure 13-7.** Application output*

Summary

In this chapter, you learned some of the basics of key encryption, some of the particulars of Apple's implementation of Keychain Services, and finally how to enable your app to interact with the Keychain Services.

Chapter 14

Using Touch ID for Local Authentication

Manny de la Torriente

Ever-increasing rates of phone theft and identity fraud have pushed second-factor authentication from a desired feature to a necessity. Touch ID allows developers to use the iPhone's built-in fingerprint sensor without any of the heavy lifting of pattern recognition or low-level encryption. In this chapter, readers will learn about the framework and how to add fingerprint identification to their apps.

Introduction to Touch ID

Touch ID is a fingerprint sensing system that makes secure access to an iOS device fast and easy. In this chapter you'll learn how to integrate and use the `LocalAuthentication` framework to request authentication from users using Touch ID. The `LocalAuthentication` class allows you to invoke Touch ID verification without involving the keychain.

Touch ID is an easy-to-use mechanism and is very secure. All Touch ID operations are handled inside Secure Enclave. The Secure Enclave is a coprocessor within the Apple A7 or later A-series processor, and it is responsible for processing fingerprint data from the Touch ID sensor. An application cannot access data associated with an enrolled fingerprint (or the kernel); it is only notified once a user has successfully authenticated (see diagram in Figure 14-1).

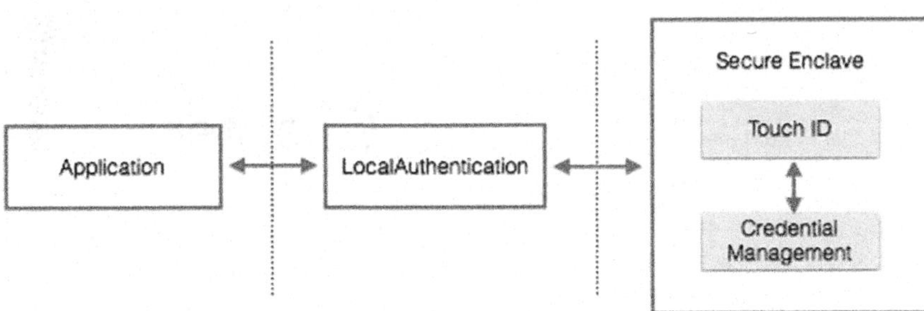

Figure 14-1. Architecture

`LocalAuthentication` security differs from that of keychain. In the keychain case, the trust is between the operating system and Secure Enclave. In the `LocalAuthentication` case, the trust is between the application and the operating system. No secrets will be stored in the case of `LocalAuthentication` as there is no direct access to Secure Enclave—only knowledge of any authentication results.

LocalAuthentication Use Cases

`LocalAuthentication` can be used as a generic policy evaluation mechanism to do the following:

- Verify that a user is enrolled so you can unlock certain features of an application.
- Enables parental control to be sure that the device owner is present.
- Provide first-factor authentication, without passcode backup.

The sample app you'll write in this chapter requires a device that supports Touch ID. The iPhone 5s and newer, iPad Air 2, and iPad Mini 3 all support Touch ID.

Building a Touch ID Application

The sample application you'll build will demonstrate a simple use case, which is to authenticate a user utilizing Touch ID without keychain. The app will consist of a single scene with a grouped table view similar to the illustration in Figure 14-2. The table view will have a single row that will be used to initiate an authentication flow when selected. Below the table view will be a text view that will serve as a window for log output.

Figure 14-2. *The TouchIDApp main scene*

If at some point you decide to support additional use case examples, you can simply add a new row for each use case.

The Touch ID prompt is a standard iOS user interface (UI), which can include a custom prompt message that you define. Also provided by the system is an Enter Passcode option as a fallback, as shown in Figure 14-3. The fallback case is detailed in the section "Creating the Project."

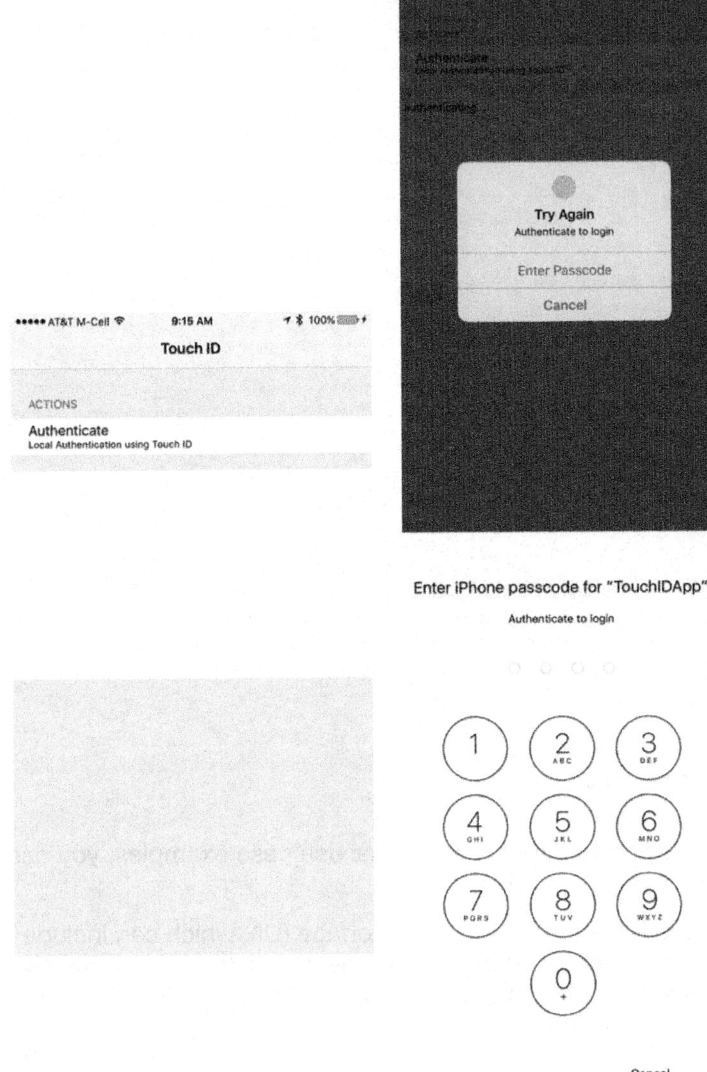

***Figure 14-3.** Standard system UI for Touch ID and passcode input*

Creating the Project

We are going to create an iOS single-view application Xcode project named TouchIDApp, select Swift as the Language, and use the defaults for Language and Devices.

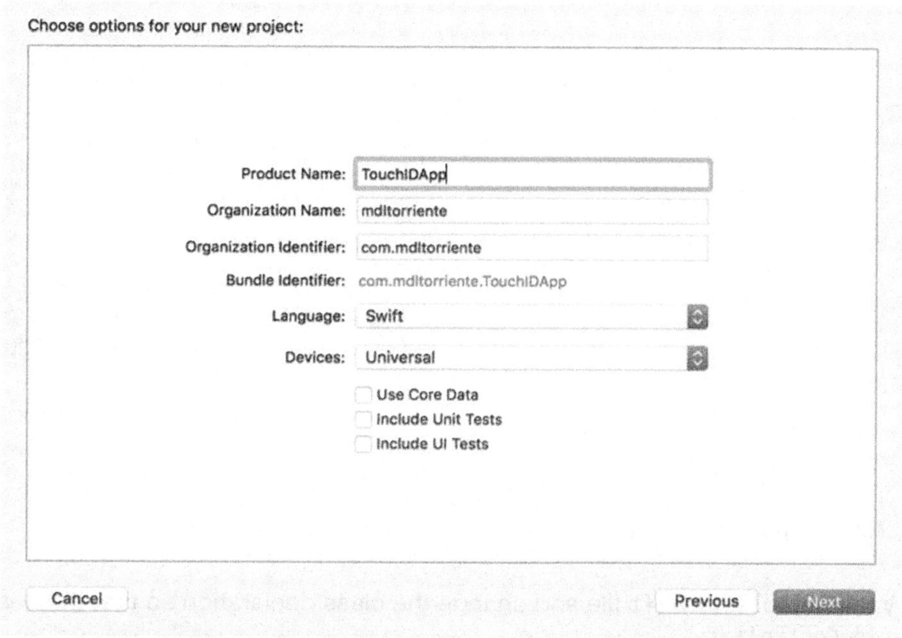

Figure 14-4. Creating a new single-view Xcode project

Building the Interface

Open the storyboard, then delete the current view controller and replace it with a table view controller. Select Table View Controller, and then from the Attributes Inspector, set it as the initial view controller for the storyboard by setting the check box for Is Initial View Controller as shown on the right in Figure 14-5.

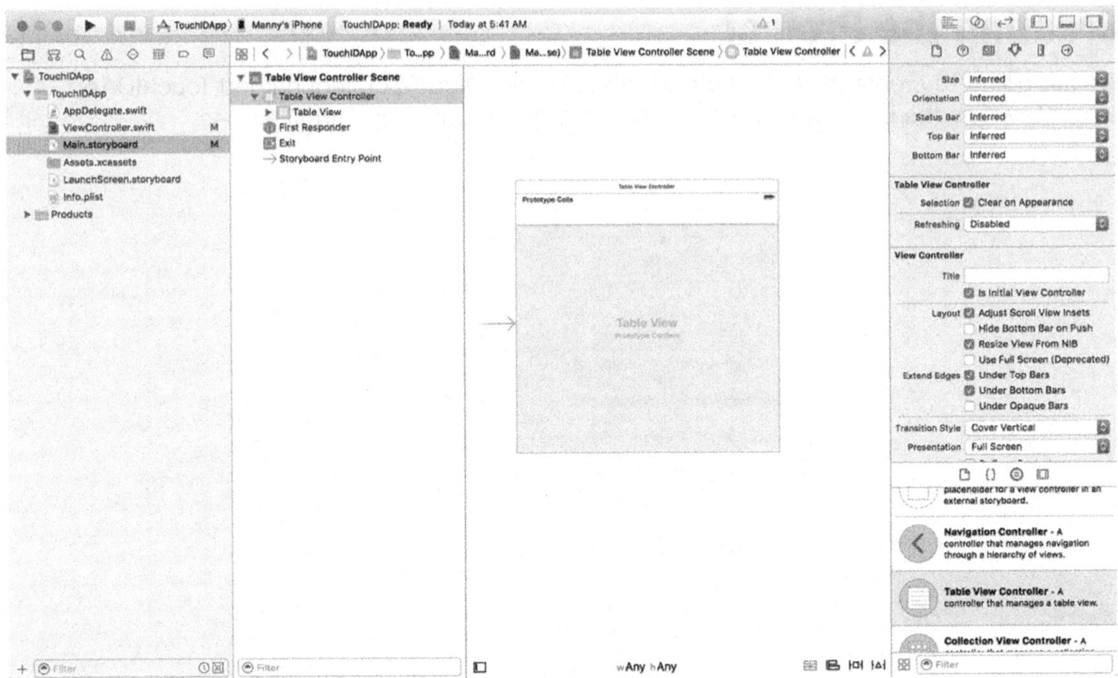

Figure 14-5. Main storyboard initial view

Open the `ViewController.swift` file and change the class declaration so that the base class is `UITableViewController`.

```
class ViewController: UITableViewController {
}
```

Open the storyboard and from the Identity inspector in the *Custom Class* section, set the *class* to `ViewController` as shown in Figure 14-6.

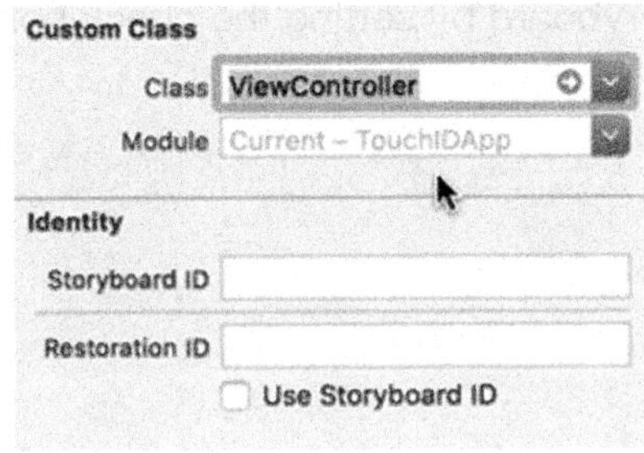

Figure 14-6. Setting the custom class

> **Note** If `ViewController` is not visible in the drop-down, build the project and it will appear.

Now select the table view cell, and then from the Attributes Inspector, change the table view cell style to *Subtitle*. Also set the reuse *Identifier* to `AuthenticateCell` as shown in Figure 14-7.

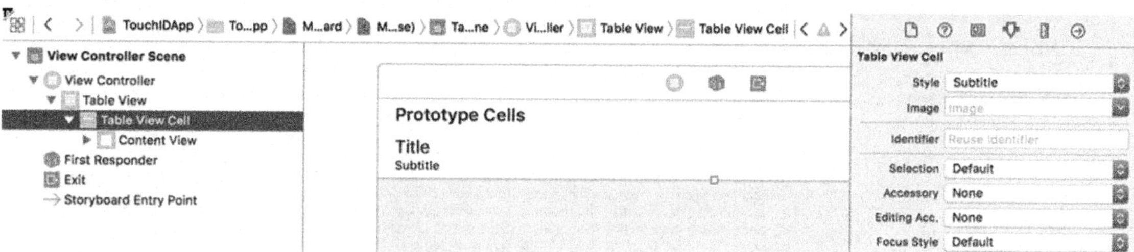

***Figure 14-7.** Setting the table view cell style*

Embed the table view controller in a navigation controller by selecting the table view controller, and then from the Xcode menu choose *Editor ➤ Embed In ➤ Navigation Controller*. From the Documents Outline on the left, select the Table View object and change its style to *Grouped* in the Attributes Inspector. Set the title for the Navigation Item in the table view controller to *Touch ID*. Your storyboard should look similar to the one in Figure 14-8.

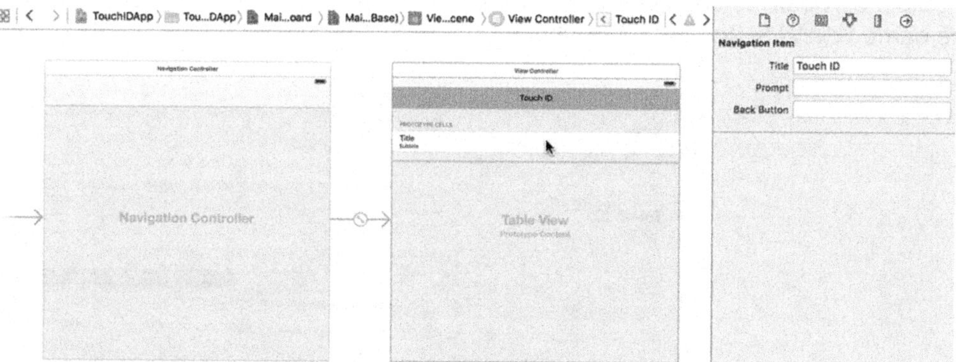

***Figure 14-8.** Embed the table view controller in a navigation controller*

Add a text view below the table view cell and adjust the height so it's similar to Figure 14-9. The text view will be used as a window to display log output.

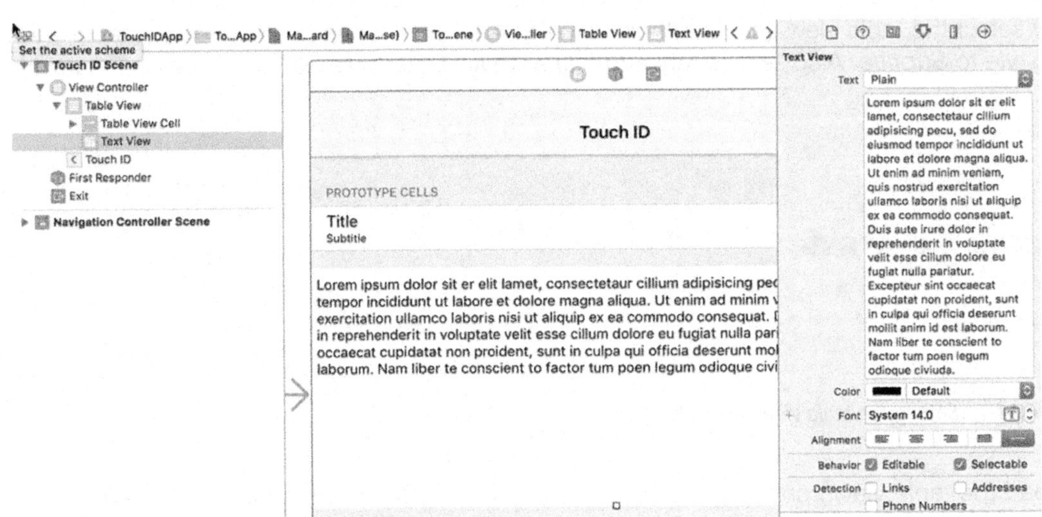

Figure 14-9. Adding a text view for log output

Use the Assistant editor such that you have a split view with the storyboard on one side and the `ViewController.swift` file in the other, as in Figure 14-10. Control-drag from the text view on the storyboard to the view controller file to create an outlet. In the pop-up window type the name `textView` and click *Connect*.

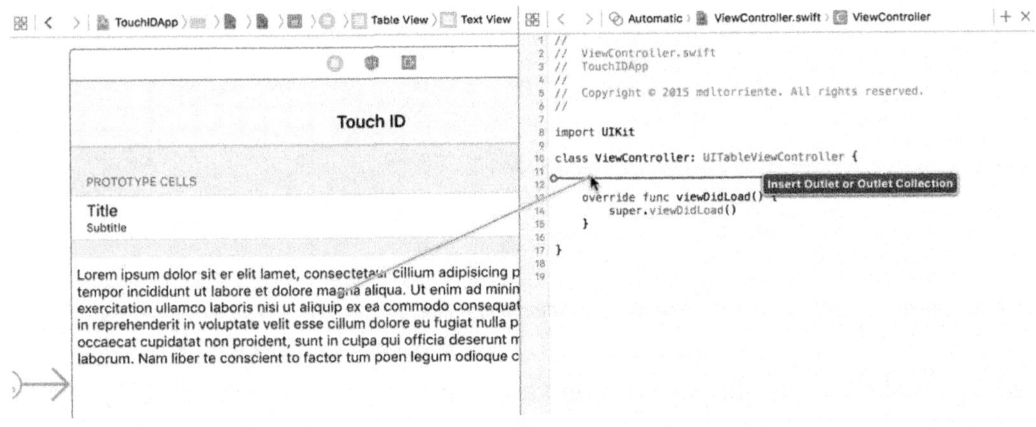

Figure 14-10. Creating an outlet

In the `viewDidLoad` method, initialize the text view text to an empty string (see Listing 14-1).

Listing 14-1. The viewDidLoad Method in the ViewController Class

```
override func viewDidLoad() {
    super.viewDidLoad()
    textView.text = ""
}
```

Implementing the UITableView Methods

Because this sample only has a single section that contains a single row, you won't need an actual data source. So the numberOfSectionsInTableView method should always return a value of 1. The table view method numberOfRowsInSection should also return a value of 1 as shown in Listing 14-2.

Listing 14-2. Setting Up the Number of Table View Sections and Rows

```
override func numberOfSectionsInTableView(tableView: UITableView) -> Int {
    return 1
}

override func tableView(tableView: UITableView, numberOfRowsInSection section: Int) -> Int {
    return 1
}
```

When the table view object asks for the title of a section, because there is only a single section, you return a string containing "Actions" to represent the section header as in Listing 14-3.

Listing 14-3. Setting Up the Section Header

```
override func tableView(tableView: UITableView, titleForHeaderInSection section: Int) ->
String? {
    return "Actions"
}
```

When the table view object asks for a cell to insert in a particular row, return a reusable table view cell object for the cell you set up in the storyboard with the reuse identifier AuthenticateCell. Set the cell's text label text to *Authenticate* and its detailed text label text to *Local Authentication using Touch ID* (see Listing 14-4).

Listing 14-4. Setting Up the Authentication Table View Cell

```
override func tableView(tableView: UITableView, cellForRowAtIndexPath indexPath:
NSIndexPath) -> UITableViewCell {
    let cell = tableView.dequeueReusableCellWithIdentifier("AuthenticateCell",
    forIndexPath: indexPath)
    cell.textLabel?.text = "Authenticate"
    cell.detailTextLabel?.text = "Local Authentication using Touch ID"
    return cell
}
```

When you select a table view row, the table view object informs its delegate about the new row selection. Here is where the authentication workflow is initiated. Call the table view deselectRowAtIndexPath method, which will ensure that the table view row is deselected after any operation completes (see Listing 14-5). Then call the authenticate method which you will implement in an upcoming section.

Listing 14-5. Setting Up the Actions When a Table View Row Is Selected

```
override func tableView(tableView: UITableView, didSelectRowAtIndexPath indexPath:
NSIndexPath) {
    tableView.deselectRowAtIndexPath(indexPath, animated: true)
    authenticate()
}
```

Integrating Touch ID for Fingerprint Authentication

In the file `ViewController.swift`, import the `LocalAuthentication` framework; place it just below the `UIKit` import statement as shown in Listing 14-6.

Listing 14-6. The authenticate Method in the ViewController Class

```
import UIKit
import LocalAuthentication
```

Evaluating Authentication Policies

Authentication contexts are used to evaluate the authentication capabilities of an iOS device on which the application is run. An iOS device may or may not have a fingerprint scanner, or Touch ID may have been disabled by actions such as too many failed attempts to authenticate. Using a context to preflight an authentication policy allows an application to determine if it's possible for authentication to succeed; for example, requesting the user authentication using personal information such as Touch ID. An authentication context is represented by the `LAContext` object.

Touch ID Authentication without Keychain

Touch ID without keychain is done in two steps.

The first step is to preflight an authentication policy to see if it's possible for Touch ID authentication to succeed on the device. This is accomplished by calling the `canEvaluatePolicy` method of a local authentication context object. The authentication policy being evaluated is `DeviceOwnerAuthenticationWithBiometrics`, which is device owner authentication using a biometric method (Touch ID). The `DeviceOwnerAuthenticationWithBiometrics` is a property of the `LAPolicy` class.

If the `canEvaluatePolicy` conditions aren't met, then the guard statement shown in Listing 14-7 is used to transfer program control out of scope.

Listing 14-7. A Guard Statement to Evaluate Whether or Not Authentication Can Proceed

```
let context = LAContext()
var error: NSError?

guard context.canEvaluatePolicy(.DeviceOwnerAuthenticationWithBiometrics, error: &error) else {
    printMessage("canEvaluatePolicy failed: \(error!.localizedDescription)")
    return
}
```

If conditions are met and Touch ID is available, the second step is to obtain authorization from the user. This is accomplished by calling the `evaluatePolicy` method of a local authentication context object. The authentication policy being evaluated is `DeviceOwnerAuthentication`. The call must include a string with a short concise description of the reason for requesting authentication. The `localizedReason` parameter is required, so an empty string or `nil` value is not accepted. Notice that the error parameter is passed by value. See the code in Listing 14-8.

> **Note** The `canEvaluatePolicy` method must not be called in the response block of `evaluatePolicy` because doing so could lead to a deadlock.

Listing 14-8 shows the complete `authenticate` method. Place this code at the bottom of the `ViewController` class.

***Listing 14-8.** The authenticate Method Using Touch ID*

```
func authenticate() {
    printMessage("authenticating...")

    let context = LAContext()
    var error: NSError?

    guard context.canEvaluatePolicy(.DeviceOwnerAuthenticationWithBiometrics, error: &error)
    else {
        printMessage("canEvaluatePolicy failed: \(error!.localizedDescription)")
        return
    }

    // Touch ID is available

    let reason = "Authenticate to login"
    context.evaluatePolicy(.DeviceOwnerAuthentication, localizedReason: reason, reply: {
    (success, error) -> Void in

        if success {
            self.printMessage("Authentication success!")
        } else {
            if let error = error {
                self.printMessage("Error: \(error.localizedDescription)")
            }
        }
    })
}
```

The response block from `evaluatePolicy` is executed when policy evaluation finishes. This block is evaluated on a private queue internal to the framework in an unspecified threading context. If you intend to access any of the UI components from within the response, then be sure to access them in the main thread. The example in Listing 14-9 demonstrates how the printMessage convenience method updates a text view in the main thread. Add the code from Listing 14-9 to the end of the ViewController class.

Listing 14-9. Ensure a Text View Is Updated in the Main Thread

```
func printMessage(message: String) {
    dispatch_async(dispatch_get_main_queue()) { () -> Void in
        self.textView.text = self.textView.text.stringByAppendingString(message + "\n")
        self.textView.scrollRangeToVisible(NSMakeRange(self.textView.text.characters.
        count-1, 0))
    }
}
```

The dispatch_async method submits a block for asynchronous execution on the main queue and returns immediately. The dispatch_get_main_queue method returns the serial dispatch queue associated with the application's main thread.

User-Defined Fallback for Authentication

In the case where the biometric authentication fails, the *Try Again* prompt will present an *Enter* ***Password*** button. Tapping the *Enter Password* button will cause the response block to cancel the operation and return an error that indicates that a user defined fallback is expected. Table 14-1 shows the possible errors.

Table 14-1. LAContext Error Codes

Error Code	Description
AuthenticationFailed	Authentication was not successful because the user failed to provide valid credentials.
UserCancel	Authentication was canceled by the user—for example, the user tapped Cancel in the dialog.
UserFallback	Authentication was canceled because the user tapped the fallback button (Enter Password).
SystemCancel	Authentication was canceled by system—for example, if another application came to foreground while the authentication dialog was up.
PasscodeNotSet	Authentication could not start because the passcode is not set on the device.
TouchIDNotAvailable	Authentication could not start because Touch ID is not available on the device.
TouchIDNotEnrolled	Authentication could not start because Touch ID has no enrolled fingers.

Run the Application

Build and run the application. You'll have to use a physical iOS device because the simulator doesn't support Touch ID.

- Tap the `Authenticate` cell. If the device supports Touch ID, and Touch ID has been enabled and configured by the user, a touch request prompt will be presented.
- Authenticate with a registered fingerprint. An Authentication Success message should be output to the text view log window.
- Authenticate with an unregistered fingerprint. You should be prompted to Try Again, and an Enter Passcode option should be present.
- Enter a valid passcode. An Authentication Success message should be output to the text view log window.

Things to Remember

- Only foreground applications can use Touch ID.
- Policy evaluation may fail.
  - The device may not support it.
  - The device supports it, but it could be in a lockout state or some other configuration setting preventing its use.
- Your application should provide its own fallback password entry mechanism in the event policy evaluation fails.

Summary

In this chapter you built a sample app that demonstrates how `LocalAuthentication` can be used as a generic policy evaluation mechanism. You learned how to integrate and use `LocalAuthentication` to start Touch ID authentication and how to avoid a deadlock situation. You learned about how using different policy evaluation affects the workflow in the case where biometric authentication fails.

You also reviewed how to call into the main thread in a response block from an unspecified threading context.

Chapter 15

Using Apple Pay to Accept Payments

Gheorghe Chesler

In the short time since its introduction, Apple Pay has driven Near-Field Communication (NFC) payments with unprecedented momentum. Apple now takes this a step further by allowing developers to use Apple Pay to accept payments for physical goods in their apps, a feature which has been successfully adopted by Uber and Starbucks. This chapter introduces readers to Apple Pay by demonstrating how to integrate the framework for in-app payments, as well as discussing traditional challenges in implementing payment systems.

Apple Pay vs. Alternative Payment Systems

In a normal e-commerce transaction that was initiated from a web site, there are multiple ways to wrap up a payment. The following are some examples:

One-stop-shop: The back-end software on the shopping cart server processes an order submit form and connects synchronously with the merchant gateway where it submits the payment. The pass or fail of the transaction is received and delivered back over the same connection to the browser. This is typical usage for shops using established merchant gateways like Authorize.Net, Worldpay, Stripe, and many others.

Offline card processing: The shopping cart back-end captures the credit card information, stores it securely, and then uses that information to process an order asynchronously. High-volume sites (e.g., Amazon) prefer this method. These sites cannot afford to have synchronous transactions that take too long, and that block the server resources until the payment is processed. This method is also used when your order is not ready to ship right away, and you can only charge the card when the goods have shipped. You might have noticed that Amazon splits your order in smaller suborders that can be shipped separately, and you are billed separately as they ship. This is also very convenient when you expect that parts of the order could be canceled due to delays in availability, and you don't want to deal with the fallback of doing partial refunds on tax and shipping costs.

Delegate to the merchant pay interface: Smaller shops with less trust/visibility or those that don't want to deal with the hassles of managing a merchant account use a payment broker like PayPal, which offers a feature called IPN (Instant Payment Notification). Instead of taking the credit card number, the back end only validates the input and then redirects the user to PayPal. The customer has the confidence of a large and trusted entity to perform a transaction that can be disputed if necessary. Once the user decides whether to complete the transaction, PayPal gives the user the ability to go back to the shop site, while completing the final part of the transaction by sending a callback to the web site with a predefined set of parameters. The shop will then know to show the customer the order invoice for the completed order.

Taking payments through a mobile device app using one of the methods shown previously, requires you to do the same kind of wiring as is done for a server. You can still choose to process a payment by collecting the user credit card information (number, expiration date, pin) and sending it to the merchant gateway along with the user mailing, billing, and shipping address (for those gateways that require that level of information). This requires you to either enter the credit card information in a form field or use a card reader to scan that information and then place an order.

Naturally, the systems that collect this user information have an issue of liability: just as with back-end applications; we don't know with certainty that the agent/application/API that handles the data for this process is secure and does not "call home" to the developer with the credit card number of the user. At the same time, the credit card information goes over the wire, increasing the risk of a third party (man-in-the-middle) snooping around your sensitive data.

In a mobile app that allows you to pay for a good or service, there has to be a way to avoid handling the credit card information directly. This is where Apple Pay comes in.

Apple introduced the in-app purchase to allow application developers to take in payments for virtual goods like extended functionality or premium content for an app. This is wrapped up using your Apple account, which is why you see those charges on your iTunes bill.

For other software or hardware goods, and especially for the case when your shop already uses a merchant gateway, Apple Pay allows your app to use the information stored in your Apple Wallet to submit a payment, without actually exposing this information to the application itself.

You can use Touch ID within your app to authorize payments, releasing tokenized credit and debit card payment credentials that are securely stored on your iOS device (iPhone, iPad). Users can also save their billing and shipping information in the Wallet app, and that information can then be relayed to the merchant gateway to process your payment.

Apple Pay Prerequisites

The Apple Pay Programming Guide provides details on how to use the PassKit framework to integrate Apple Pay. The In-App Purchase Programming Guide (found in the iOS developer library) provides details on how to use the StoreKit framework to integrate in-app purchases.

You can find the Apple Pay Programming Guide at `https://developer.apple.com/library/ios/ApplePay_Guide/`.

In addition to implementing Apple Pay with the PassKit framework, you must

- Set up an account with a payment processor or gateway
- Register a merchant identifier via Certificates, Identifiers & Profiles
- Submit a Certificate Signing Request (CSR) to obtain Public and Private keys that will be used to encrypt and decrypt Payment Tokens
- Include an Apple Pay entitlement in your app

If you don't already have an account with a payment processor/gateway, you can find a list at `https://developer.apple.com/apple-pay`.

Depending on what your app is offering for sale, you might not be able to use Apple Pay. Apple Pay is only available to businesses offering physical goods or services for use outside their iOS app. If the goods or services are used in the app itself, then you must still use Apple for your in-app payments.

In addition, the payment provider might not support all processors: for example, Authorize.Net only supports processors that support the Visa token service and the tokenization solutions developed by MasterCard and American Express. For example, at the time of this writing, Authorize.Net supported:

- Chase Payment Tech
- Global Payments
- TSYS
- First Data (should be supported late 2015)

For Authorize.Net you can see what processor is assigned to your merchant account on the payment provider account page (account / merchant profile / payment methods). If your processor is not supported, you will not be able to configure and use Apple Pay.

An extract from the Authorize.Net documentation shows this in detail:

`http://developer.authorize.net/api/reference/features/apple_pay.html`

"The Apple Pay solution uses payment network tokenization. You can sign up for this solution only if your payment processor supports tokenization. If your processor does not support payment network tokenization or if Authorize.Net does not support your payment processor's tokenization interface, you will not be able to sign up for this payment solution."

Using Apple Pay to accept payments

Payment Providers

The first thought you might have is to provide your own server-side solution to receive payments from your app, decrypt payment tokens, and interface with the payment provider. Handling credit and debit card payments can be complicated, and unless you already have the expertise and systems in place, it could turn into a complex project that has its own issues of security and maintenance.

Most payment gateways offer for that purpose a Software Development Kit (SDK) that aims to be the most reliable way to support Apple Pay in your app. You can find a list of payment providers that support Apple Pay with their SDKs at `https://developer.apple.com/apple-pay/`.

Using one of these SDKs is highly recommended. Contact your payment provider for more information. Most providers that offer Apple Pay support make SDKs available for common programming languages; this means that you might get just Objective-C support and not Swift support. This is expected, since Swift is still rather new and merchant gateways don't usually provide code for fast-moving targets such as Swift. Fortunately, you can easily embed Objective-C code in your Swift app, if there is an Objective-C SDK available.

The basic elements required to process an Apple Pay transaction are as follows:

- Present the Apple Pay button
- Present the payment sheet
- Allow the user to authorize the transaction with Touch ID
- Finalize the transaction using the payment token

The Apple Pay button

To allow the user to pay with Apple Pay, the following requirements have to be met:

- The device needs to provide a secure element that is in charge of the request encryption
- The user has to have registered on the device payment modes that you as a vendor support

To be able to identify these requirements, we have to use the APIs from PassKit. The same APIs give you the ability to present the user a "Buy with Apple Pay" button.

Should the device not be set up for Apple Pay, you can present instead a "Set up Apple Pay" button. Finally, if there is no available payment method that would work with Apple Pay, you can decide not to show the Apple Pay button at all.

The Payment Sheet

Once the user has added items to the shopping cart and selects the Apple Pay button; you have to create a payment request, and use the PassKit API to show to the user a summary of the order.

Your app provides the information that will be displayed on the payment sheet, where the user can see the order total and select a shipping address with a valid zip code. You can calculate the correct shipping charges based on the zip code from the shipping address.

To minimize confusion, only ask for information that is strictly necessary to process the order. The user is at all times in control and can change the billing and shipping information, so the tax and shipping charges will be recalculated as necessary. The user can also enter on the payment sheet a different e-mail address or phone number for the order confirmation.

The proper flow is to show the payment sheet immediately after the user selects Apple Pay as the payment method, without any pop-ups or intermediary screens.

The data (updated) on the payment sheet is submitted when the user confirms it using Touch ID.

The Payment Token

When the user authorizes the transaction with Touch ID, PassKit returns a payment token to your app.

The payment token contains all the information necessary to complete a payment transaction. This includes the amount charged for the order, the account number specific to the device, and a cryptogram that can be used only once.

This data is encrypted with the merchant's public key and can only be decrypted with the merchant's private key by either the merchant or the payment processor, on behalf of the merchant, via the SDK.

Your app must make it clear when it acts as an intermediary party, in particular when the app decrypts the payment token and passes it to the merchant over the wire to process the payment with its specific processor.

Figure 15-1 illustrates a typical payment flow. Your app will first check if the device is compatible with and set up for Apple Pay. If Apple Pay is physically supported (the device has a secure element), your app will show the "Set up Apple Pay" and offer the user the ability to set up a payment method that can be used with Apple Pay.

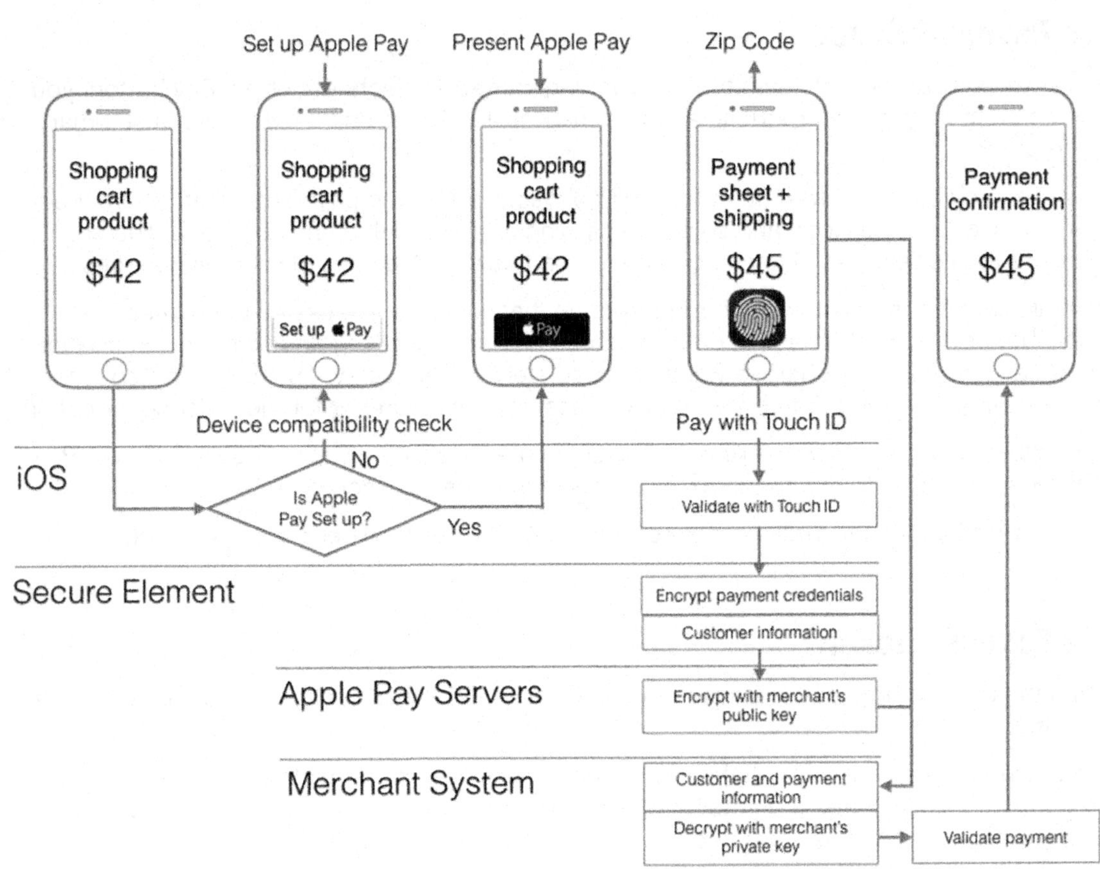

***Figure 15-1.** Typical payment workflow*

If all conditions are met, your app will display the Apple Pay button. The order is not finalized yet, as the user still should have the ability to change his billing and shipping information. This happens in the next step, after the user taps Apple Pay and it displays the payment.

Once the user finalizes the order information, they can use Touch ID to submit the order. For the payment to be authorized, the order information relevant to finalizing the financial transaction has to be packaged and sent to the payment processor. For that, the app uses the PassKit API to get a payment token from the secure element.

With all this gathered information, your app calls the appropriate APIs in the payment processor SDK, and attempts to finalize the payment. Of course, that means there is still a chance that things are not going to go as planned, and the payment processor will reject the payment (card invalid, expired, fraud attempt, etc.).

If the transaction was successful, your app can then display the order confirmation and set in motion the process of delivery of the order payload, which can be shipping, e-delivery, plug-in installation, feature activation—whatever is the nature of the product purchased.

Taking a closer look at the final part of the transaction, before the payment request is sent to the merchant system, we can see the role of the payment authorization view controller in this process. We are at the point where the order amount is known, and that includes all taxes and shipping costs. The user has used Touch ID to authorize the payment.

Apple Pay sends the payment request to the secure element, a specialized chip on your device. The secure element adds the payment data to the customer information and encrypts it in form of a payment token.

The secure element sends the prepared payment token to the Apple's payment servers, where the token is encrypted yet again, this time with your merchant identifier certificate. Other than encrypting the content, the Apple servers do not store or alter the payment information in any way.

The re-encrypted token is returned to your app for processing. This is convenient, as you never need to package the merchant identifier in your app, so nobody can snoop in your memory and extract that information from your app.

To accept payments, Apple provides the `PKPaymentAuthorizationViewController` class. This class allows us to create a prompt for the user to authorize a payment request. After the user authorizes the payment request for the transaction, the delegate is called with a payment token used to authorize payment for the transaction.

Figure 15-2 shows this interaction.

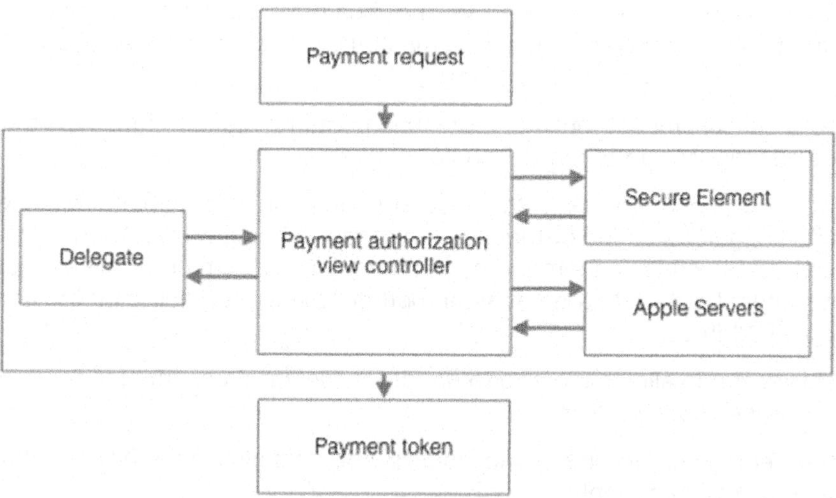

Figure 15-2. *The payment authorization view controller*

Your app can now use the SDK offered by the merchant system to wrap up the last leg of the process. If you have an existing payment infrastructure, you can send the encrypted payment token to your servers, where it can be decrypted and the payment can be processed.

Transaction Types Supported by the Payment Processor

For a payment processor SDK to be able to support Apple Pay, it has to be able to handle a specific set of e-commerce transactions that give an app the ability to cover all scenarios of a transaction:

- Authorization
- Capture
- Partial shipment
- Recurring billing
- Order refund
- Transaction chargeback

Authorization: This scenario allows the app to put a hold on a specific amount on the customer's account and reserve the funds needed to cover the total amount of the order. This is usually done when the processing of the order is greatly simplified if the processor can work with the confidence that the funds could be retrieved when the order is finalized.

Take, for example, the case of e-delivery of content that needs to be processed before delivery, like watermarking a PDF or preparing personalized content. If the app can verify that the payment method chosen is valid and the account has the funds needed to cover the order amount, it can trigger the content processing, while the user is waiting. Some of this processing could fail for a variety of reasons, and thus the order could not be completed. In this case no funds have changed hands, and the authorization can be released, along with showing the proper error message to the user.

Capture: After a successful authorization, or when no authorization of funds is needed, Capture is actually triggering the funds transfer right away.

Capture can fail in one of many ways: the payment can be invalid, expired, or lacking funds; the card can be flagged as stolen or the location of the transaction can trigger a stolen card alert; and so on. These checks are made by the merchant system or by the entities used by the merchant system to validate the payment method, the signed name on the card, or the billing or shipping address.

Recurring: This scenario allows the app to handle repeating payments for services, by setting up a recurring payment plan.

Refund: If an order is returned or a service is disputed, this allows the app to return the money to the customer's account.

Chargeback: This is provided to give the app the ability to handle fraudulent or disputed transactions.

Example: using Authorize.Net as the Payment Processor

When using Authorize.Net as your payment processor, there are two ways to process an Apple Pay transaction.

The API method: The merchant server receives the order request from the app and passes it along to Authorize.Net. You would use the API method when you need to extract and centralize the payment data on your server before sending the request to Authorize.Net. Your server will then format the transaction as an XML or NVP request to the AIM API. The encrypted transaction data is base64 encoded and contains a format descriptor. Authorize.Net processes the request and sends the response back to your server. Your server then replies to your app with the order confirmation data or with the error it received from Authorize.Net.

The SDK method: The Authorize.Net SDK handles signing the transaction and the interaction with Authorize.Net. You have to read the Authorize.Net SDK Developer Reference to see the steps required to wire this in the application:

```
http://www.authorize.net/content/dam/authorize/documents/ApplePay_sdk.pdf
```

For the time being, Authorize.Net only offers an Objective-C SDK. This is true for most other payment processors (Stripe is in the same boat), as Swift is a new language that still shows changes in syntax and API methods from version to version, and it would be a hassle for Authorize.Net to maintain code in a moving target.

The SDK only supports the first two types of transactions: Authorization and Capture and Authorization Only. For all other subsequent transactions (Capture, Refund, Void) your app will have to use the regular payment APIs. Note that if you use Authorization Only, you still need to complete the capture to receive the funds from the transaction.

The reason the subsequent transactions are not directly supported by the SDK is that they are not relevant to the main process of Apple Pay.

Also important to mention is that testing your code using the sandboxed Authorize.Net environment should be done connected to the Apple developer system and not to the Apple production systems.

In Figure 15-3 we can see the two methods compared.

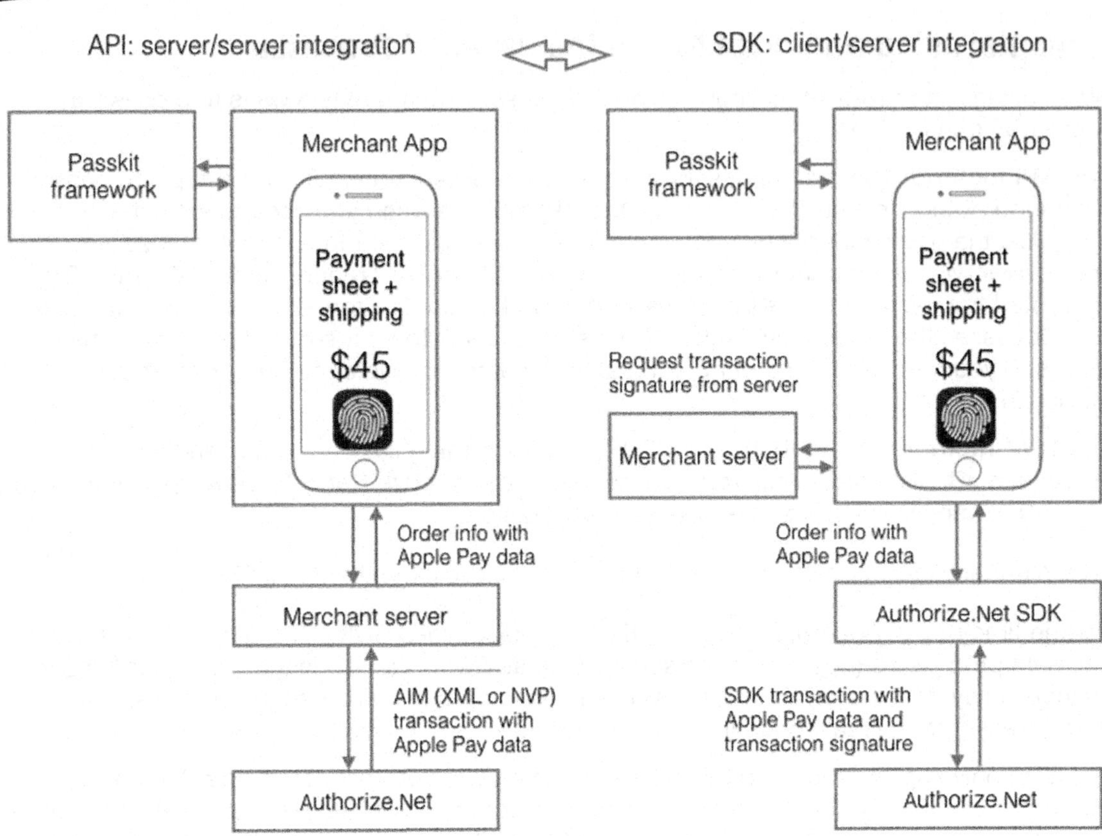

Figure 15-3. *API vs. SDK for Authorize.Net transactions*

Configuring your Environment for Apple Pay

In the section "Apple Pay Prerequisites," we showed the steps required to configure Apple Pay.

- Set up an account with a payment processor or gateway
- Register a merchant identifier
- Submit a certificate signing request
- Include an Apple Pay entitlement in your app

Let's take a closer look at what needs to be done, once you know which payment processor you will use.

To set up the merchant identifier and the certificate signing request go to the Member Center on your account page in the Apple Developer site and open the "Certificates, Identifiers & Profiles" as shown in Figure 15-4.

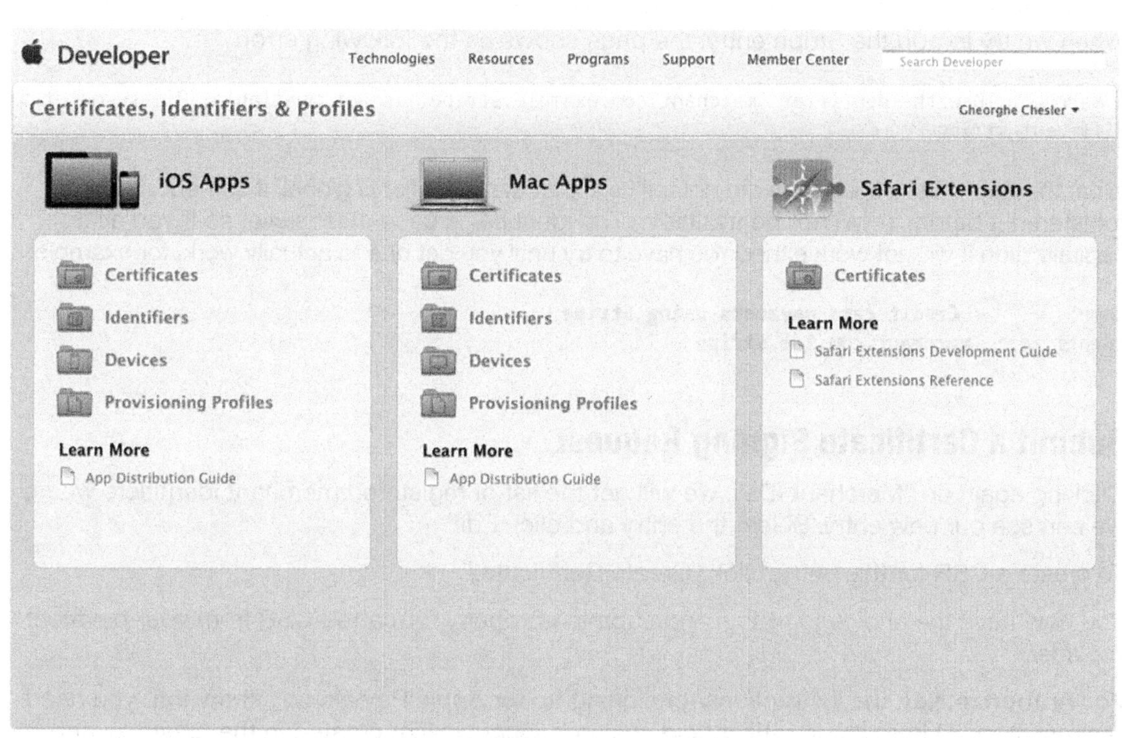

Figure 15-4. Setting up Certificates, Identifiers & Profiles

Register a Merchant Identifier

Select Identifiers, then Merchant IDs. Use the "+" in the upper right corner to create a new entry. Enter a descriptive name for your merchant account (e.g., "Credit card payments"), and a unique identifier in the requested format: the identifier starts with "merchant" then follows a dot-separated format (e.g., `merchant.com.example.authorizenet`).

The form will ask you to confirm your configuration and then will allow you to create the entry. When working with a payment provider, you will need to provide them the merchant identifier to complete your certificate generation.

Our sample entry shows the following:

```
Name: Credit card payments using Authorize.Net
Identifier: merchant.com.example.authorizenet
```

Let's say we also want to support Stripe in our app, or we create a second app that supports Stripe, so we try to add another merchant identifier:

```
Name:        Credit card payments using Stripe
Identifier:  merchant.com.example.stripe
```

When we try to add the Stripe entry, the page shows us the following error:

```
A Merchant ID with Identifier 'merchant.com.example.stripe' is not available. Please enter a different string.
```

What the Apple Developer page did not tell us is that this identifier is global. If somebody else registered it before, it will not be available. The identifier is case-insensitive, so if you alter capitalization it will not work either. You have to try until you get one to actually work, for example:

```
Name:        Credit card payments using Stripe
Identifier:  merchant.com.iot.stripe
```

Submit a Certificate Signing Request

Clicking again on “Merchant IDs”, we will get the list of registered merchant identifiers where we can see our new entry. Select the entry and click Edit.

To create a CSR for this entry, click “Create Certificate.”

You now have the choice to obtain and submit a properly formatted CSR from your payment provider.

For Authorize.Net: the instructions for signing up for Apple Pay already show that you need the merchant ID from the Identifier field, which is what we just created in the previous step.

You can login to the merchant interface on your Authorize.Net account, click Account in the main toolbar, and then select Digital Payment Solutions from the left menu. You can now click the “Sign Up” in the Apple Pay section. You will need the merchant ID you generated on the Apple member page.

To generate a CSR file, click Apple Pay on the left menu, enter your merchant ID in the Apple Merchant ID field, and click the “Generate Apple CSR” button.

For Stripe: go to the account Apple Pay section:

```
https://dashboard.stripe.com/account/apple_pay
```

This section will not appear by default in your account view, if you never set up Stripe with Apple Pay before, so following the link will enable that option in the account view. Click “Create a new certificate”, which should download a CSR file named `stripe.certSigningRequest`.

Adding the Merchant CSR to your Apple Account

With the obtained CSR file, you can now go back to the Apple Developer Center, “Certificates, Identifiers & Profiles” page:

```
https://developer.apple.com/account/ios/identifiers/merchant/merchantList.action
```

In the iOS Merchant ID Settings page, click “Create Certificate” and follow the instructions to submit the CSR that you created on the Merchant page.

If you see a warning in Keychain Access that the certificate was signed by an unknown authority or that it has an invalid issuer, make sure you have the WWDR intermediate certificates—G2 and the Apple Root CA—G2 installed in your keychain. You can download them fromapple.com/certificateauthority.

Once the CSR was uploaded to the Apple page, a new certificate will be generated and offered for download. You can now download the certificate file (the file is apple_pay.cer).

For Stripe, go back to the Stripe guided menu and upload the certificate. When all is completed, it will appear as in Figure 15-5.

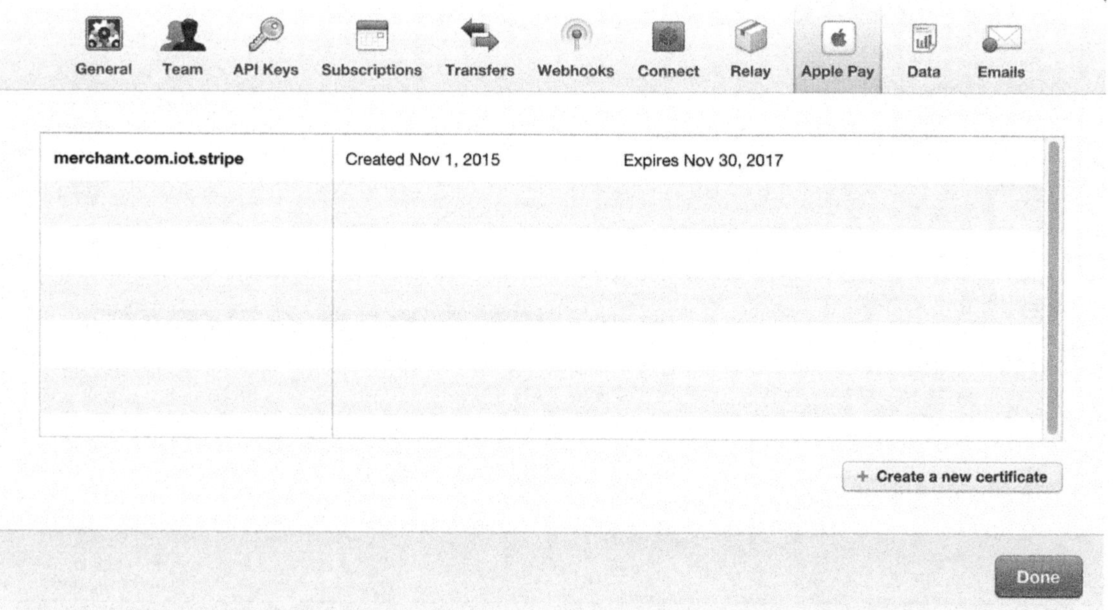

***Figure 15-5.** Apple Pay certificate created on Stripe*

Include an Apple Pay Entitlement in your app

To enable Apple Pay for your app in Xcode, open the Capabilities pane. Select the switch in the Apple Pay row, and then select the merchant IDs you want the app to use. Figure 15-6 illustrates this process.

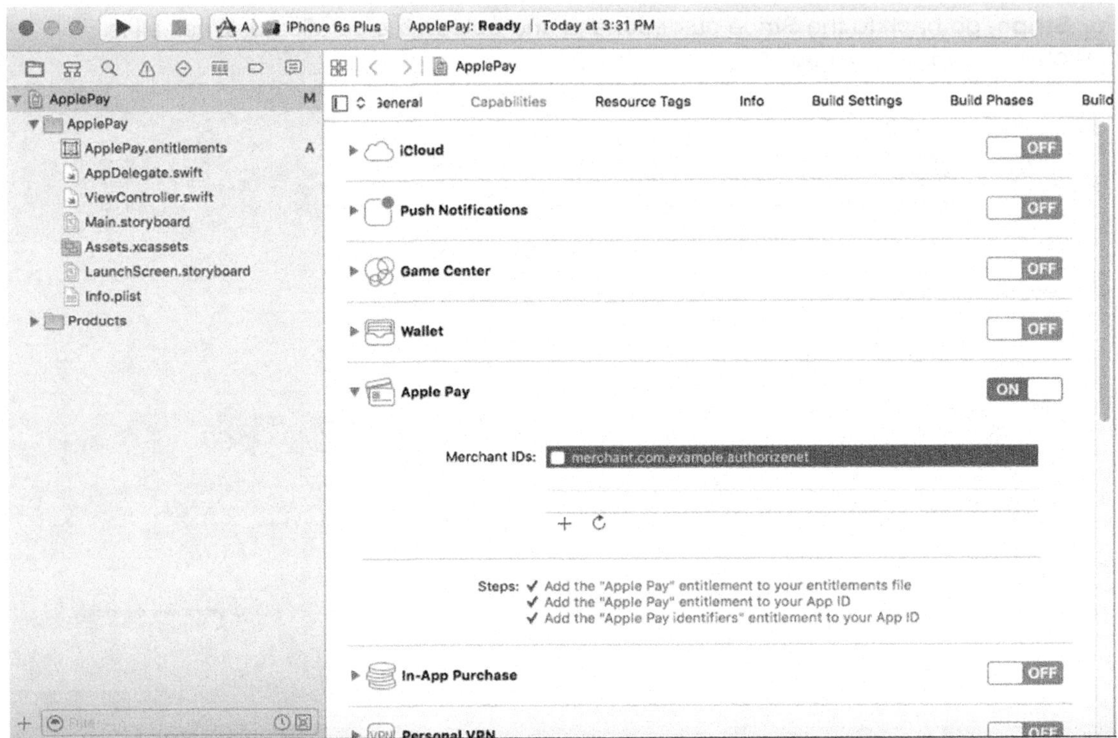

Figure 15-6. Enabling Apple Pay support in the app

Install Prerequisites for Working with a Payment Processor SDK

As mentioned earlier, you would be hard pressed to find a payment processor that supports Swift natively. Until that happens, you will have to embed the Objective-C version of the SDK in your code.

Install the Payment Processor SDK

You can install the SDK manually into your project, which is bit more work; the easiest way is to install a dependency manager that will allow us to install the SDK on our Mac, such as Cocoapods or Carthage.

The easiest way is to use Cocoapods.

```
sudo gem install cocoapods
pod init ApplePay.xcodeproj
```

The first command is run with root privileges to install Cocoapods, then as the regular user, the second command will create a file called Podfile. Use a text editor or vim to edit the Podfile file and add Authorize.Net support.

```
target 'ApplePay' do
pod 'authorizenet-sdk'
end
```

If you are configuring for Stripe support, the target will look like

```
target 'ApplePay' do
pod Stripe'
end
```

Now you can install the SDK in your project by typing "pod install" in your terminal window (Listing 15-1):

Listing 15-1. Installing the Payment Processor SDK in Your Project

```
$ pod install
Creating shallow clone of spec repo `master` from `https://github.com/CocoaPods/Specs.git`
Updating local specs repositories
Analyzing dependencies
Downloading dependencies
Installing authorizenet-sdk (1.9.3)
Generating Pods project
Integrating client project

[!] Please close any current Xcode sessions and use `ApplePay.xcworkspace` for this project
from now on.
Sending stats
Pod installation complete! There is 1 dependency from the Podfile and 1 total pod installed.
```

Follow the suggestion of the installer: close your Xcode project and open instead the `ApplePay.xcworkspace` project.

Verify now that support for Objective-C embedding is enabled: in your project settings, go to the "Build Settings" tab, and make sure -ObjC is present under "Other Linker Flags." You can see this in the project in Figure 15-7.

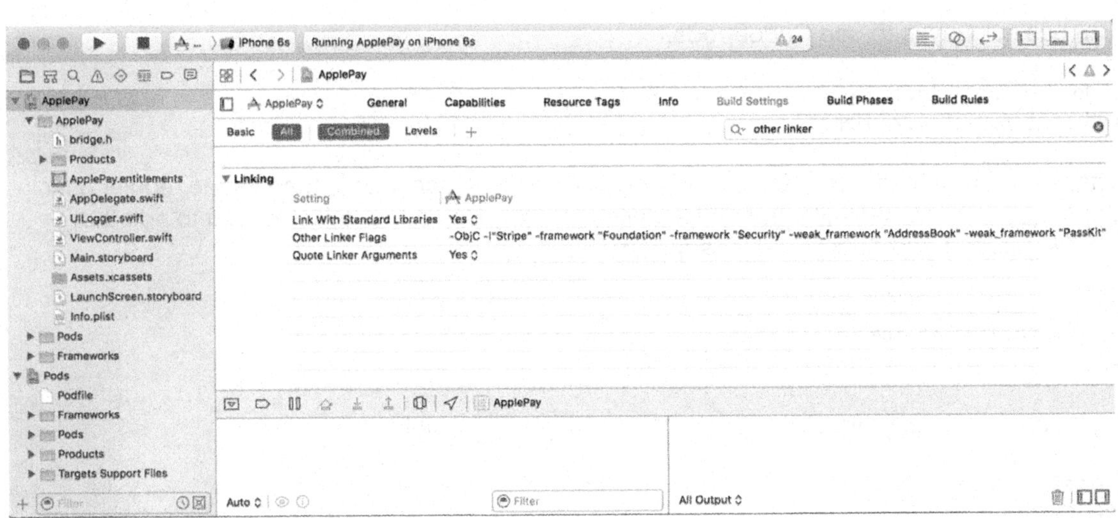

Figure 15-7. The project after installing the SDK

For Stripe you also need to add the string `STRIPE_ENABLE_APPLEPAY` to the preprocessor macros in the build settings of your project, as shown in Figure 15-8. The entry needs to be added to both debug and release entries in the preprocessor macros.

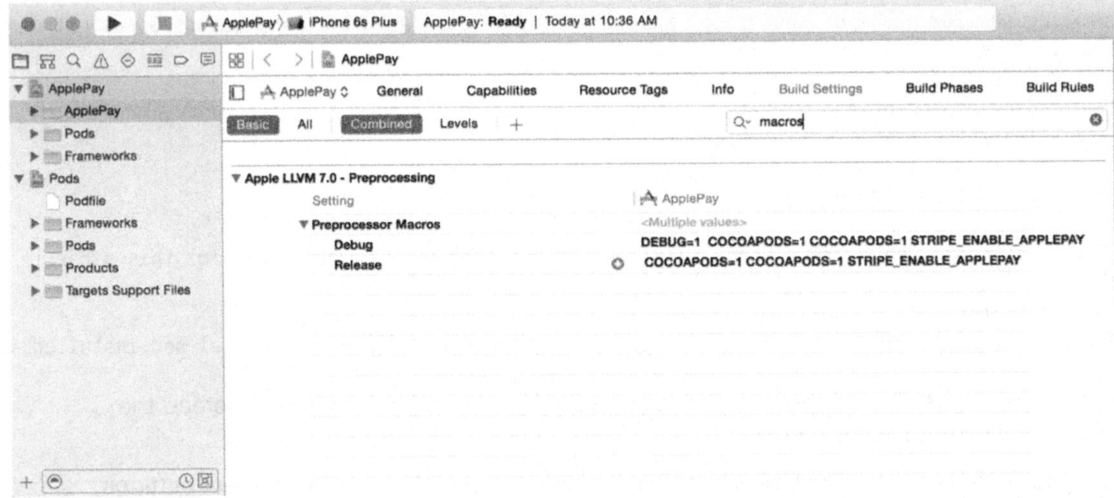

Figure 15-8. Adding a Preprocessor Macro entry for Stripe

The Objective-C to Swift Bridging Header

To be able to use the SDK in our Swift code, we need to create a bridging header that allows us to use Objective-C code from within our Swift code. As mentioned before, most payment processors offer SDKs in Objective-C, and it will be a while until they will start offering a Swift version. This will be true of most SDKs you will embed in an app, so writing bridging headers will be a popular pastime of the Swift warrior.

In the Xcode menu, click File ➤ New ➤ File ➤ iOS ➤ Source ➤ Header File, then click “Next”; name the file “bridge” and click Create. You can see this in Figure 15-9.

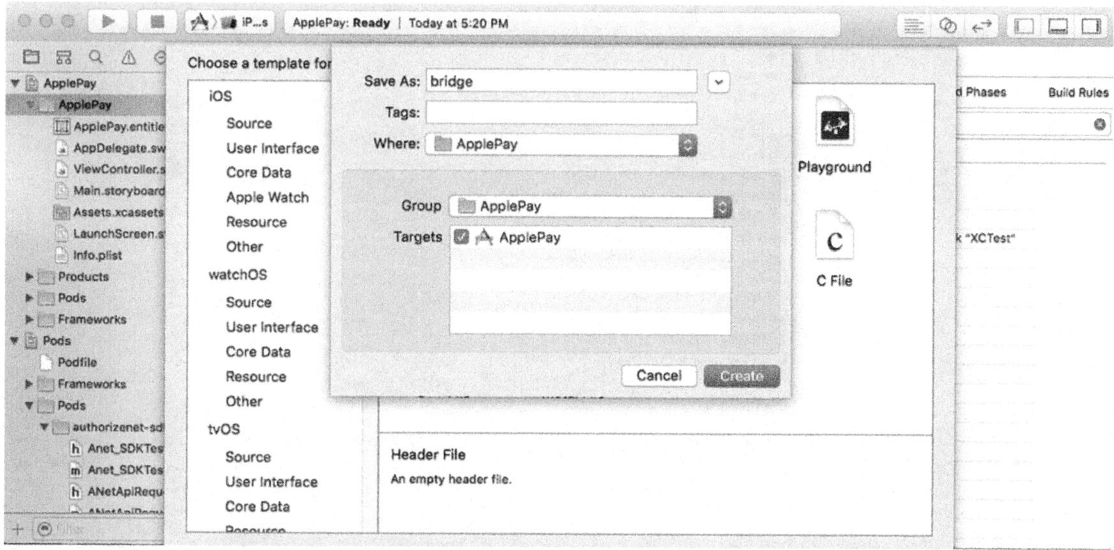

Figure 15-9. Creating the header file

In the `bridge.h` type the following import statement at the top of the file (Authorize.Net):

```
#import <authorizenet-sdk/AuthNet.h>
```

If you are configuring your app to use Stripe as a payment processor, you will use instead

```
#import <Stripe/Stripe.h>
```

Select the Project folder and navigate to Build Settings, search for “Swift Compiler.”Verify that the “Install Objective-C Compatibility Header” is set to “Yes.” Edit the Objective-C generated interface header name entries for Debug and Release and set their value to the `bridge.h`, the header file.

The Main Storyboard

For a simple storyboard we only define the field where we can specify the order amount, the Pay button, and a text area that will be used by our logger library to show the ongoing activity. Figure 15-10 illustrates.

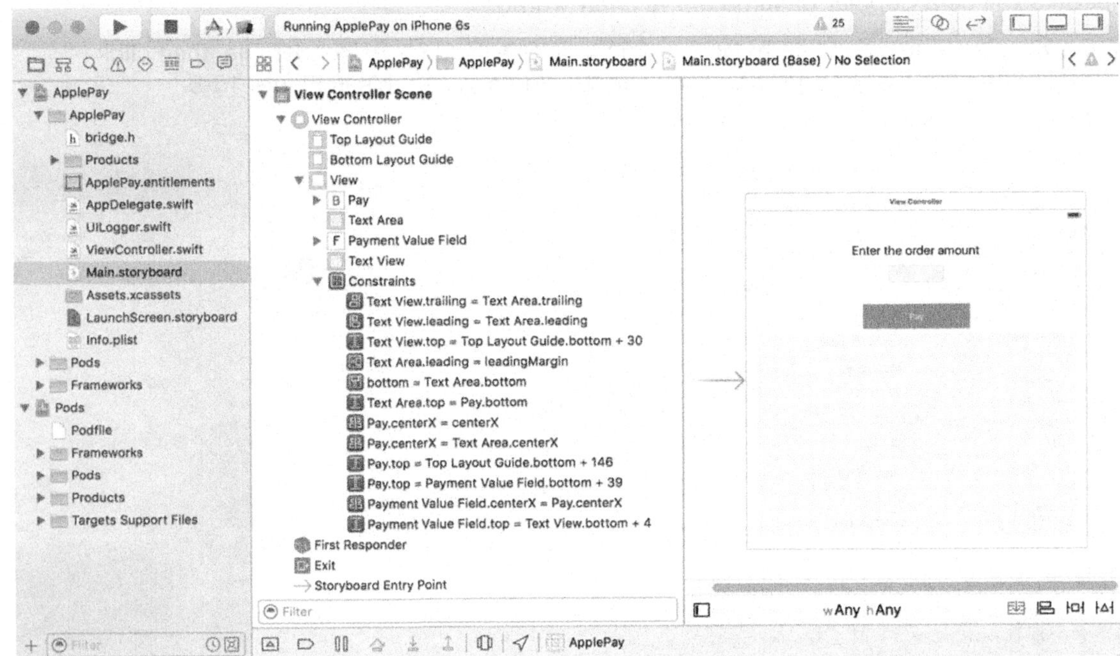

Figure 15-10. The main storyboard

The logger library

The logger library was assigned a variable in the view controller that will keep an instance of the logger around with the proper target assigned —in our case we use a text area field for the activity logging.

We will use the same logger library as in Chapter 12. The logger library has just a couple of functions that will allow us to track the API activity. These functions will interact with the textArea field we set up in the view controller. Just as in the view controller, the textArea field is declared optional, as it will be initialized in the `init()` function. Listing 15-2 shows the entire code of the `UILogger.swift` file.

Listing 15-2. The UILogger Library

```
import Foundation
import UIKit

class UILogger {
    var textArea : UITextView!

    required init(out: UITextView) {
        dispatch_async(dispatch_get_main_queue()) {
            self.textArea = out
        };
        self.set()
    }

    func set(text: String?="") {
        dispatch_async(dispatch_get_main_queue()) {
            self.textArea!.text = text
        };
    }

    func logEvent(message: String) {
        dispatch_async(dispatch_get_main_queue()) {
           self.textArea!.text = self.textArea!.text.stringByAppendingString("=> " + message + "\n")
        };
    }
}
```

We can see the view controller scene with the minimum set of requirements wired in Figure 15-11. We see the mappings for paymentValueField and textArea, as well as the payWithApplePay button wiring to the default action.

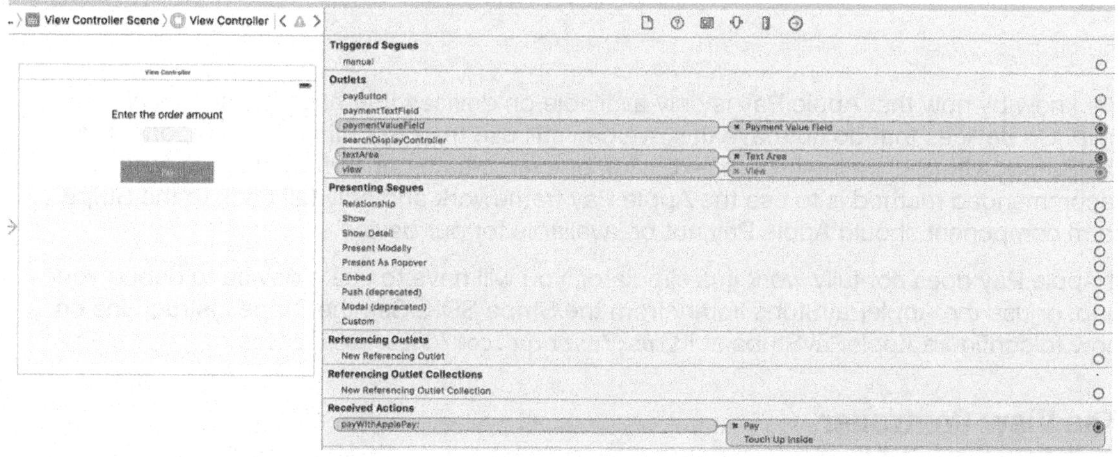

***Figure 15-11.** The view controller scene*

Implementing Apple Pay payments with Stripe

To keep things simple, we will continue implementing an example with Stripe—all other payment processors will have different ways of approaching this, given that some might have an SDK, and the SDK is usually in Objective-C. Further down the road when the payment processors warm up to a stable version of Swift, they might even offer a pure Swift implementation of their SDK.

Your application needs to be able to communicate with your Stripe account and use the publishable key that was generated when you created your account. You generated two sets of keys: a test key and a live key. For now, we will set up the test key and initialize the SDK instance in the `AppDelegate.swift` file `didFinishLaunchingWithOptions()` function. This will make sure this value will be set for the lifecycle of the app. Listing 15-3 shows the relevant code from `AppDelegate.swift`.

Listing 15-3. Setting the Stripe Public Key

```
import UIKit
import Stripe

@UIApplicationMain
class AppDelegate: UIResponder, UIApplicationDelegate {

let StripePublishableKey = "pk_test_i65Y88AqZG908xvGwFIJYkSE"
var window: UIWindow?

func application(application: UIApplication, didFinishLaunchingWithOptions launchOptions:
[NSObject: AnyObject]?) ->Bool {
// Override point for customization after application launch.
Stripe.setDefaultPublishableKey(StripePublishableKey)
returntrue
    }
...
}
```

We know by now that Apple Pay is only available on devices that have the secure element chip. On devices that do not have this, we can still use the pre-build form component from the Stripe SDK (STPPaymentCardTextField), or even create our own credit card form. The recommended method is to use the Apple Pay framework and only fall back to the Stripe form component should Apple Pay not be available for our device.

If Apple Pay does not fully work in a simulator, you will have to use a device to debug your app, or use the ApplePayStubs library from the Stripe SDK. See the Stripe instructions on how to configure ApplePayStubs at `https://stripe.com/docs/mobile/ios`.

The View Controller

This is a very simple application that uses only one view for everything, so our view controller will have to be a delegate for both PassKit and the Stripe SDK. When you implement multiple views, you will have to assign the correct delegate to your views.

The class shows the delegate assignments as mentioned earlier. Then we defined the payment networks that we decide to support in our apps. This is sometimes a requirement for certain merchants that can only use Visa/MC but do not want to use Amex because of the higher rates, or whatever other reason.

The pay button is assigned to the payButton variable that needs to be of UIButton type. The textArea field is used by our logger library. The paymentValueField is a simple text field we created to allow us to change the amount being charged for the order.

The paymentTextField is of STPPaymentCardTextField type. This field, as well as the functions prefixed with "payment," is used by the Stripe SDK.

We can see the header of the view controller in Listing 15-4:

Listing 15-4. The ViewController.swift Header

```
import UIKit
import PassKit
import Stripe

class ViewController: UIViewController, STPPaymentCardTextFieldDelegate,
PKPaymentAuthorizationViewControllerDelegate {
let SupportedPaymentNetworks = [PKPaymentNetworkVisa, PKPaymentNetworkMasterCard,
PKPaymentNetworkAmex]
let ApplePayMerchantID = "merchant.com.iot.stripe"
@IBOutletvar payButton: UIButton?
@IBOutletvar textArea: UITextView!
@IBOutletvar paymentTextField: STPPaymentCardTextField?
@IBOutletvar paymentValueField: UITextField!
var logger: UILogger!
  ...
}
```

There is a bit of work we need to do in the viewDidLoad() function, to initialize our logger and the paymentTextField, as well as enable or disable the pay button depending on the app having the ability to use the specified payment networks. Listing 15-5 shows the code for the viewDidLoad() function from the ViewController.swift.

Listing 15-5. The viewDidLoad() Function

```
overridefunc viewDidLoad() {
super.viewDidLoad()
// Do any additional setup after loading the view, typically from a nib.
logger = UILogger(out: textArea)

paymentTextField = STPPaymentCardTextField()
paymentTextField?.center = view.center
view.addSubview(paymentTextField!)
paymentTextField?.delegate = self
payButton?.enabled = PKPaymentAuthorizationViewController.canMakePaymentsUsingNetworks
(SupportedPaymentNetworks)
    }
```

The pay button can also be enabled/disabled when the payment user changes the information. Once the user gets the Apple Pay pop-up, he can switch the card to a different card, select a different shipping address, and so on. Some of these changes might invalidate our ability to pay with Apple Pay and our restrictive list of payment networks, which is why we need to update the pay button. Listing 15-6 shows the code for the `paymentCardTextFieldDidChange()` function, which is located in the `ViewController.swift` file.

Listing 15-6. The paymentCardTextFieldDidChange() Function

```
func paymentCardTextFieldDidChange(textField: STPPaymentCardTextField) {
payButton?.enabled = textField.valid
    }
```

Finally, we need another helper method that would handle how the view controller for the pop-up is dismissed once the payment cycle is completed. You can see this in Listing 15-7.

Listing 15-7. The paymentAuthorizationViewControllerDidFinish() Function

```
func paymentAuthorizationViewControllerDidFinish(controller:
PKPaymentAuthorizationViewController) {
        controller.dismissViewControllerAnimated(true, completion: nil)
    }
```

We saw in the view controller scene that the pay button's "Touch Up Inside" action was wired to the function `payWithApplePay()`. To keep things simple, we only log the error condition when the amount was not a valid number. If the amount is valid, we call the `applePay()` function. Listing 15-8 shows the code for the `payWithApplePay()` function in the `ViewController.swift` file.

Listing 15-8. The payWithApplePay() Function

```
@IBActionfunc payWithApplePay(sender: UIButton) {
iflet total = Double(paymentValueField.text!) {
logger.logEvent("Pay with Apple Pay the amount: \(total)")
self.applePay(total);
        }
else {
logger.logEvent("No valid amount specified")
        }
    }
```

The `applePay()` method prepares a request using the shopping cart item that we conveniently created here with the label "New Charge". The request is assigned the ApplePayMerchantID that we set up previously and the SupportedPaymentNetworks that define which cards we accept. The request also is set to work for US transactions effected in US dollars.

Once the request is prepared, we test with the `canSubmitPaymentRequest()` function from the Stripe SDK. This will fail if Apple Pay is not available, or a default credit card was not set up. We can choose in case of error to default to Stripe's PaymentKit Form. We leave this part of implementation to you, concentrating instead on completing the Apple Pay transaction, when we can. Listing 15-9 shows the code for the `applePay()` function.

Listing 15-9. The applePay() Function

```
func applePay(price: Double) {
let item = PKPaymentSummaryItem(label: "New Charge", amount: NSDecimalNumber(double: price))
let request = PKPaymentRequest()
        request.merchantIdentifier = ApplePayMerchantID
        request.supportedNetworks = SupportedPaymentNetworks
        request.merchantCapabilities = .Capability3DS
        request.countryCode = "US"
        request.currencyCode = "USD"
        request.paymentSummaryItems = [item]
ifStripe.canSubmitPaymentRequest(request) {
logger.logEvent("Paying with Apple Pay and Stripe")
// Apple Pay is available and the user created a valid credit card record
let applePayController = PKPaymentAuthorizationViewController(paymentRequest: request)
            applePayController.delegate = self
presentViewController(applePayController, animated: true, completion: nil)
        } else {
logger.logEvent("Cannot submit Apple Pay payments")
//default to Stripe's PaymentKit Form
        }
    }
```

The PKPaymentAuthorizationViewController will call the `paymentAuthorizationViewController()` function in our code, which was created to comply with the SDK's interface. This method creates a token with the payment information; you can now send this token to your server, to be able to charge the card. Listing 15-10 shows the code for the `paymentAuthorizationViewController()` located in the `ViewController.swift` file.

Listing 15-10. The paymentAuthorizationViewController() Function

```
func paymentAuthorizationViewController(
        controller:                         PKPaymentAuthorizationViewController,
        didAuthorizePayment payment: PKPayment,
        completion:                         (PKPaymentAuthorizationStatus) ->Void) {
let this = self
Stripe.createTokenWithPayment(payment) { token, error in
iflet token = token {
                    this.logger.logEvent("Got a valid token: \(token)")
//handle token to create charge in backend

                    completion(.Success)
                } else {
                    this.logger.logEvent("Did not get a valid token")
                    completion(.Failure)
                }
            }
    }
```

Testing our app

Let's give our app a first try. Bring up the simulator, and enter a valid amount, then click the Pay button. You will see an output similar to the one in Figure 15-12. Now the user can change the card being used. There is no shipping or billing information, because we did not configure any of that information yet, so the most basic thing is the ability to change the card. The simulator has three demo cards set up, a VISA, a MasterCard, and an Amex card. The simulator will naturally not show Touch ID, but will show "Pay with Passcode" instead.

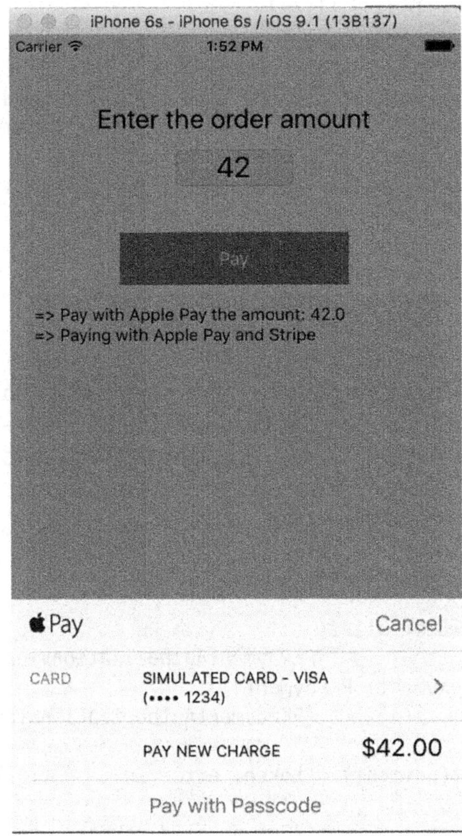

Figure 15-12. First test of the app

To verify that we get a valid token, we can set a breakpoint in the view controller and walk through, as shown in Figure 15-13.

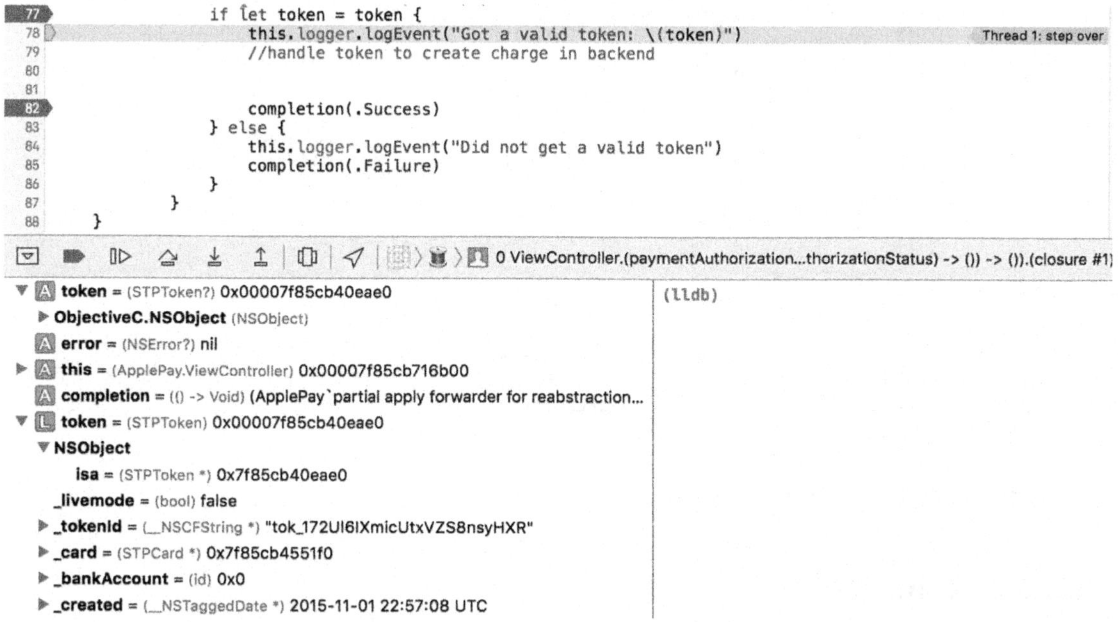

***Figure 15-13.** Debugging a Stripe payment*

If the transaction was successful, once the transaction reached completion (`.Success`), the pop-up window will show a confirmation screen for a couple of seconds, then go back to our app. Figure 15-14 shows the confirmation screen.

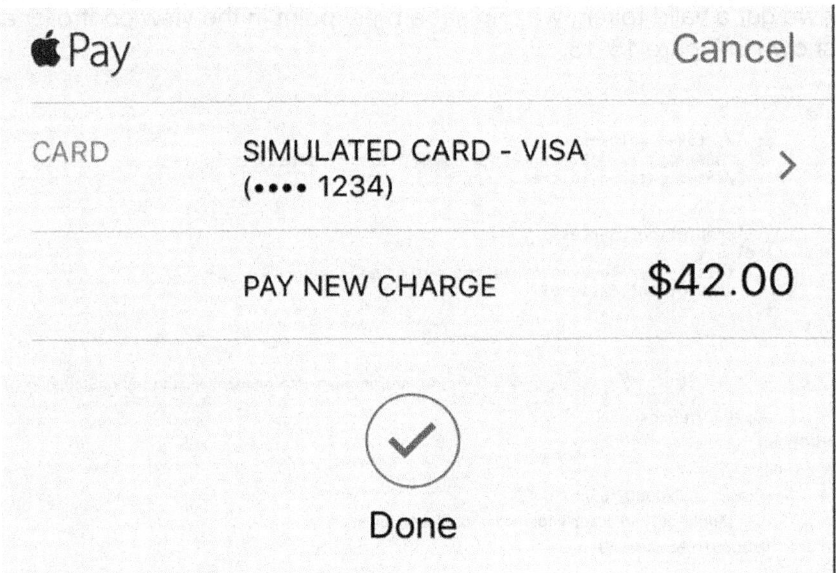

Figure 15-14. The Apple Pay confirmation screen

Processing the charge

To charge the card, you have to build a server-side application that takes the generated payment token and submits a charge request to Stripe. This is necessary since you will be using your Stripe secret key to finalize the payment, and it would not be wise to expose that in your application code. Furthermore, your payment workflow needs to centralize all placed orders, to allow accounting to manage the orders submitted from mobile devices.

Every payment processor has a decent amount of sample code available along with server-side SDKs that simplify your development. For Stripe, the tutorials for charging a card are located at `https://stripe.com/docs/tutorials/charges`.

The View Controller code

Our application is essentially contained in the `ViewController.swift` file. Listing 15-11 shows the full code for this file.

Listing 15-11. The ViewController.swift File

```
import UIKit
import PassKit
import Stripe

class ViewController: UIViewController, STPPaymentCardTextFieldDelegate,
PKPaymentAuthorizationViewControllerDelegate {
let SupportedPaymentNetworks = [PKPaymentNetworkVisa, PKPaymentNetworkMasterCard,
PKPaymentNetworkAmex]
```

```
let ApplePayMerchantID = "merchant.com.iot.stripe"
@IBOutletvar payButton: UIButton?
@IBOutletvar textArea: UITextView!
@IBOutletvar paymentTextField: STPPaymentCardTextField?
@IBOutletvar paymentValueField: UITextField!
var logger: UILogger!

overridefunc viewDidLoad() {
super.viewDidLoad()
// Do any additional setup after loading the view, typically from a nib.
logger = UILogger(out: textArea)

paymentTextField = STPPaymentCardTextField()
paymentTextField?.center = view.center
view.addSubview(paymentTextField!)
paymentTextField?.delegate = self
payButton?.enabled = PKPaymentAuthorizationViewController.canMakePaymentsUsingNetworks
(SupportedPaymentNetworks)
    }

func paymentCardTextFieldDidChange(textField: STPPaymentCardTextField) {
payButton?.enabled = textField.valid
    }

func paymentAuthorizationViewControllerDidFinish(controller:
PKPaymentAuthorizationViewController) {
        controller.dismissViewControllerAnimated(true, completion: nil)
    }

overridefunc didReceiveMemoryWarning() {
super.didReceiveMemoryWarning()
// Dispose of any resources that can be recreated.
    }

@IBActionfunc payWithApplePay(sender: UIButton) {
logger.set()
iflet total = Double(paymentValueField.text!) {
logger.logEvent("Pay with Apple Pay the amount: \(total)")
self.applePay(total);
        }
else {
logger.logEvent("No valid amount specified")
        }
    }
func applePay(price: Double) {
let item = PKPaymentSummaryItem(label: "New Charge", amount: NSDecimalNumber(double: price))
let request = PKPaymentRequest()
        request.merchantIdentifier = ApplePayMerchantID
        request.supportedNetworks = SupportedPaymentNetworks
        request.merchantCapabilities = .Capability3DS
        request.countryCode = "US"
```

```
        request.currencyCode = "USD"
        request.paymentSummaryItems = [item]
ifStripe.canSubmitPaymentRequest(request) {
logger.logEvent("Paying with Apple Pay and Stripe")
// Apple Pay is available and the user created a valid credit card record
let applePayController = PKPaymentAuthorizationViewController(paymentRequest: request)
            applePayController.delegate = self
presentViewController(applePayController, animated: true, completion: nil)
        } else {
logger.logEvent("Cannot submit Apple Pay payments")
//default to Stripe's PaymentKit Form
        }
    }

func paymentAuthorizationViewController(
        controller:                   PKPaymentAuthorizationViewController,
        didAuthorizePayment payment: PKPayment,
        completion:                   (PKPaymentAuthorizationStatus) ->Void) {
let this = self
Stripe.createTokenWithPayment(payment) { token, error in
iflet token = token {
                    this.logger.logEvent("Got a valid token: \(token)")
//handle token to create charge in backend
                    completion(.Success)
                } else {
                    this.logger.logEvent("Did not get a valid token")
                    completion(.Failure)
                }
            }
    }
}
```

Summary

In this chapter we looked at the rather complex landscape of Apple Pay. You learned how to set up your developer account to be able to use Apple Pay, and then how to set up a certificate to work with a payment processor. After this, you set up a very basic application that shows how these pieces fit together. You will still need to create your back-end application that will process the payment, schedule repeat payments, or process refunds.

Index

A

Advertising Services, 289–290
API client library
    APIClient.swift, 139–140, 146–150
    API request, 141–142, 145
    APIService, 141
    error object, 144
    extractRateLimits(), 145
    GET, 138
    NSDictionary, 144
    NSURLConnection.
        sendAsynchronousRequest, 139
    OAuth signature, 143–144
    POST request, 139, 142
    prettyJSON() function, 145
    pretty-printed JSON, 144
    URLString() function, 143
    URL suffix, 138, 143
API method, 465
apiRequest function, 417
AppDelegate.swift, 476
Apple Pay
    Apple Pay button, 460
    applePay() Function, 479
    Authorize.Net account, 468
    Certificates, Identifiers & Profil, 467
    Certificate Signing Request, 468
    charge processing, 482
    confirmation screen, 482
    CSR file, 468
    logger library, 474–475
    main storyboard, 474
    Merchant Identifier, 467–468
    payment authorization
        view controller, 463
    Payment Processor, SDK, 470–472
    Payment Providers, 460
    Payment Sheet, 461
    Payment Token, 461–463
    prerequisites, 459
    Stripe guided menu, 469
    Stripe payment, 481
    Swift Bridging Header, 473
    transaction types, 464–466
    View Controller, 476–477
    View Controller code, 482–483
    vs. alternative payment
        systems, 457–458
Apple Pay Programming Guide, 459
Apple's Core Bluetooth, 247–248
asURLString function, 419
authorizationStatus() method, 25

B

BeaconTransmitterDelegate Protocol
    application testing, 341
    beacon region initializing, 339
    BeaconTransmitter methods
        startAdvertising, 338
        stopAdvertising, 339
    BeaconTransmitterView
        Controller class, 336
    didPowerOff method, 337
    didPowerOn method, 337
    iBeaconTransmitter Class, 338
    iOS device configuration, 339
    onError method, 337
    Start Advertising, 340
Bluetooth Low-Energy (BLE)
    Backlog, 251, 256
    central manager, 264–268
    central role identity, 248, 272
    CentralViewController
        class declaration, 272

Bluetooth Low-Energy (BLE) (*cont.*)
characteristic discovery, 248, 282
constraints
central role button, 259, 261, 263
peripheral role, 260–261
Core Technology Framework, 248
CustomButton class, 269
Delegation pattern, 272–275
Navigation Controller, 257
peripheral role, 248
Scan button constraints, 270
scanning, peripherals, 276
Sending Data,
TransferService Class, 291
service, 248
Service Discovery
Notification, 281
Setting button attributes, 270
Subscription Status, 283–284
system resources, 292
TransferServiceScanner Class, 280–283
single UISwitch object, 284
for UITextView, 271
user-defined runtime attributes, 258
ViewController clas, 264
Bluetooth Special Interest
Group (SIG), 288–289

C

CarFinder WatchKit app, 170, 190
CentralViewController
animationDidStop Method, 279
Chase Payment Tech, 459
CLLocationManagerDelegate methods
Beacon region initializing, 330
CLBeacon class, 332
CLBeaconRegion, 329
didChangeAuthorizationStatus, 325
didDetermineState, 326
didEnterRegion, 327
didExitRegion, 327
didRangeBeacons, 327
didStartMonitoringForRegion, 326
error handling
didFailWithError, 329
monitoringDidFailForRegion, 328
rangingBeaconsDidFailForRegion, 328
major property, 329
minor property, 329
Monitor button animation, 332
notifyEntryStateOnDisplay property, 330
notifyOnEntry property, 330
notifyOnExit property, 330
progress indicator, 332
proximityUUID property, 329
RegionMonitor Class, 329
start and stop region monitoring, 331
start monitoring event,
sequence diagram, 324
configureRows() method, 206
Constructor method, 45
Core Bluetooth objects
Base Application
and Home Scene, 251–252
Central Role Devices, 293
Central Role Objects, 249
Central Role Scene, 252–253
devices, peripheral role, 293
Editable Text, 255
peripheral role, 250, 253–254
peripheral's mutable tree of
services and characteristics, 250
Peripheral's tree of services and
characteristics, 249
single-view application project, 256
CoreLocation, 226
CLLocationManager
Delegate protocol, 228
definition, 226
initialization, 228
NSTimer class
alert controller, 236–237
ConfirmDelegate Protocol, 235
incrementTime() method, 234
initialization, 236
modified storyboard, 234
playHaptic(_:), 238
properties, 233
Total Time Updates, 235
permissions requests, 228–229
presentConfirmController, 227
requestLocation() method, 227
reverseGeocodeLocation, 231
awakeFromContext() method, 230
ConfirmDelegate Protocol, 231

human-readable string, 229
saveLocation() Delegate method, 231
Table View, 232
updated table, 233
Weather Underground
adding label, 239–240
API response, 243
Data Task type, 239
geocoding, 241–242
JSON serialization, 243
location list, 244–245
retrieveWeather() method, 242, 244
URL Session, 242–243
URL string, 242
weather look-up, 240–241
Core Motion
access motion hardware
CreateWorkoutView Controller class, 100
iOS's motion-sensing framework, 100
M-series motion coprocessor, 100
pedometer, 100
request user permission, 100
Swift streamlines, 100
saving data
converting activity type, 114
CreateWorkoutView Controller class, 110, 113
CreateWorkoutView Controller.swift, 111–113
HKQuantitySample, 111
sampleArray, 115
saving HKWorkout, 114
WorkoutTableView Controller class, 111
Step Count
CMPedometer object, 103
CreateWorkoutView Controller.swift, 104
detecting activity type, 108
detecting live updates, 106
invalidate() method, 106
startWorkout() method, 104
stopWorkout() method, 104
updateTime() method, 105

D

DataManager class, 26
Delegation pattern, 285
Detail interface controller
auto-layout, 194
automatic resizing, 194
CarFinder, 198
Default behavior, 192
LocationInterface Controller class, 195–196
multiple groups, interface controller, 191
push segue, 197
table selection segue handler, 197
user interface, 195
Device capabilities, 79
didDiscoverCharacteristics ForService method, 281
didDiscoverPeripheral method, 280
didDiscoverServices method, 281

E

ErrorType protocol, 53

F

Fitbit API
account data, 120
communication, 120
defintion, 119
iOS project
API client library (*see* API client library)
bridging header, 135
Crypto.swift, 135
escapeUrl() function, 134
hmac() function, 133
logger library, 133
new crypto header file, 134
OAuth library(*see* OAuth liarary)
sha1() function, 133
testing, 157
view controller, 130
JSON format, 120
PUT operation, 121

Fitbit API (*cont.*)
- request process
  - assemble, 159
  - body weight logging, 166
  - curl, 160
  - getBloodPressure() function, 165
  - nonexhaustive list, 163
  - OAuth versions, 167
  - processGETData() callback function, 164
  - retrieve user profile, 161
  - ViewController.swift, 163
- RESTful API
  - API call rate limits (*see* Fitbit API call rate limits)
  - async calls, 128
  - callbacks, 128
  - DELETE option, 121
  - GET request, 121
  - implementation, 122
  - OAuth1.0a authentication model, 125
  - OAuth implementation, 126
  - POST action, 121
  - PUT, 121
  - return format, 121
  - setting up, 123

Fitbit API call rate limits
- client rate limit, 127
- Client+Viewer rate limit, 127
- hitting rate limit, 128
- response headers, 127

Flask installation
- hello world daemon, 406–407
- listener daemon, 407–408

Force Touch
- Connection Inspector, 205–206
- contextual menu, 202
- Detail View Controller, 207–209
- interface controller, 202–203
- InterfaceController.swift, 205
- location list, 206
- menu item, 204
- requestLocation()/resetLocations() method, 205
- simulation, 209–210
- tab bar/bar button item, 204

Format specifier, 46

G

General Purpose Input Output (GPIO), 399
Global Payments, 459

H

Handling user input, BLE
- Extension to UIView to Apply Rotation, 279
- Scan button tap event, 277
- toggleScanning method, 278

HealthKit
- definition, 59
- prompting user
  - capability, 83
  - HKHealthStore class, 85
  - HKQuantityType objects, 87
  - permission view, 86
  - requestAuthorizationToShareTypes() method, 86
  - UIAlertController, 84
  - viewDidLoad() method, 83
  - WorkoutTableViewController.swift, 85, 87
- retrieving data
  - getWorkouts(), 88–89, 91
  - HKSampleQuery and HKObserverQuery, 88
  - HKSampleQuery object, 91
  - reloadData() method, 90
  - Table View Controller, 90
  - workoutArray, 90
- RunTracker app, 60
- setting up
  - adding labels, 69
  - app registration, 81
  - capabilities, 82
  - cell and a detail view controller, 79
  - changing button's background color, 73
  - changing label attributes, 70
  - changing text color, 72
  - click Touch Up, 75
  - CreateWorkoutViewController, 68, 82
  - default capabilities, 80
  - device capabilities, 79
  - dragging bar buttons, 76
  - "Embed In" feature, 65

handler method, 78
Main storyboard, 62, 64
master-detail fashion, 64
navigation controller, 66
prepareForSegue() method, 78
referencing outlets, 71
setting constraints, 74
setting device target, 62
Single View Application template, 61
UIBarButtonItem, 77
UITableViewController subclass, 67
view controller's parent class, 68
table view
background updates, 95
Extensions.swift, 94
NSDateFormatter class, 93
numberOfSections
InTableView() method, 92
switch() statement, 93
WorkoutTableViewController, 92
WorkoutTableViewController.swift, 95
hello-flask.py file, 406
HomeKit
accessory simulator, 346
acessory removal
canEditRowAtIndexPath method, 367
Delete button, 367
editable row verification, 367
HomeKit Accessory Simulator, 368
New Accessory pairing, 370
UITableViewDelegate Method
commitEditingStyle, 367
custom class setting, 350
delegation methods, 344
explicit App ID, 348
HMAccessory class, 344
HMCharacteristic class, 344
HMHomeManager class, 343
HMHomeManager
Delegate protocol, 350
HMHomeManager object, 348
HMService class, 344
HMZone class, 344
HomeKit app, 345
HomeKitApp.entitlements file, 348
Home Manager delegate methods
didAddHome, 351
didRemoveHome, 351
homeManagerDidUpdateHomes, 351
implementation, 351
Table View setup, 352
UITableView methods, 353
Home Manager Home
Manager delegate methods, 351
HomesViewController
Class Declaration, 350
HomesViewController scene, 349
initial view controller, 349
Main.storyboard initial view, 350
New Home addition
Accessory Browser, 364
Accessory Change Notification, 364
addHomeWithName method, 357
Add (+) navigation bar item, 361
Bar Button Item, 364
current home delegate, 364
Current Home setup, 358
empty table, 362
Existing Home deletion, 359
HomeViewController, 361, 364
home view controller interface, 363
navigation bar, 363
NSNotificationCenter, 365
onAddHomeTouched method, 357
populated with accessories, 362
Primary Home setup, 358
security, 360
segue addition, 363
Siri Integration, 358
table view cell setup, 362
UIAlertController, 357
UITableViewController, 362
UITableView methods, 365
requirements, 345
single-view Xcode project, 347
table view controller, 348–349
team profile selection, 347

I, J

I2C configuration
access verification, 403–404
Adafruit projects, 401
device address, 401
python-smbus package, 402
standard design, 401
support, ARM core and kernel, 402–403

iBeacon
accuracy, 295
advertisement, 295
background settings, 299
Bluetooth state, 307
home scene, 297
Action Segue pop-up, 306
button constraints, 303
Custom Button, 304
navigation controller, 300
outlet connection, 301
UI elements, 300
View Controller identity, 305
iBeacon scene, 297
background color, 334
BeaconTransmitter Class, 336
BeaconTransmitterDelegate Protocol (*see* BeaconTransmitter Delegate Protocol)
BeaconTransmitterView Controller Class Declaration, 334
UIButton, 334
UISwitch, 334
UITextField, 334
UITextFieldDelegate methods, 335
UITextView, 334
privacy, 296
ranging, 296
region monitoring, 296
Region Monitor scene, 297
authorization and requesting permission, 322
background color, 311
CLLocationManager Delegate methods (*see* CLLocation ManagerDelegate methods)
Delegation pattern, 315
didEnterRegion method, 319
didExitRegion method, 319
didRangeBeacon method, 319
didStartMonitoring method, 318
didStopMonitoring method, 319
font size, 311
label and text field placement, 312
onBackgroundLocation AccessDisabled method, 317
onError method, 320
Optional Binding feature, 314–315
placeholder text, 313
properties, 312
RegionMonitor class, 315–316
RegionMonitor methods (*see* RegionMonitor methods)
RegionMonitorView Controller class, 314–315
RegionMonitorViewController class declaration, 313
RegionMonitorView Controller.swift, 311
text color, 311
UITextField Delegate Methods, 313
single-view application, 298
storyboard view, 297
Interface controller
Attributes Inspector, 212
awakeWithContext() method, 213–215
ConfirmInterfaceController, 211
definition, 214
delegation
Context Dictionary, 217
delegate property, 216
implementation, 216
location saving, 216
message-passing scheme, 215
protocols, 215
handler methods, 212–213
layout setting, 210–211
text input modal
confirm() method, 219
expanded user interface, 222
message receiving, 221
modified protocol declaration, 219
notification processing, 221–222
presentTextInputController WithSuggestions, 218
sendMessage() method, 220
Siri text-to-speech recognition, 217–218
updateApplication Context() method, 219
user's location, 214
Internet of Things
CoreLocation and MapKit frameworks, 5, 7

GPS hardware, 5
location permission
accuracy, mapping service, 22
adaptive strategy, 22
class variables, 25
CLLocationManager class, 25
Maps capability, 23
new key-value pair, 24
polling, 25–26
user access, 26
mock-up, CarFinder application, 1–2
programming language, 4–5
tab bar, iOS music application, 2–3
Tabbed Application template, 3–4
user interface (UI)
controller (*see* View controller)
default storyboard, 7–8
map view controller
(*see* Map view controller)
user's location
data source, map view, 30
table view controller, 28
viewDidAppear() method, 30
iOS app
WatchConnectivity, 188–189
WatchKit extension, 189

K

Keychain Services
Alice and Bob
exchanging messages, 428
application output, 441
components, 432
Data Protection, 430–431
data retrieval, 434
device memory snoop attacks, 431
Diffie-Hellman key
exchange mechanism, 428–429
encryption platforms, 428
hardware security, 429–430
invalidation, 435
keychain-access-group, 432
password storage, 432–433
private/public keys, 427
Security.framework library, 436
view controller code
class methods, 438
deleteQuery() function, 439
get() and getData() function, 439–440
Keychain.swift file, 440–441
set() function, 439
updateQuery() function, 439
ViewController.swift file, 436–438

L

Logger library
APIClientSwift library
APIMethod Enum, 416
apiRequest() function, 417–418
APIService Enum, 417
entire code, 425
GET handler, 414–415
hasBody()function, 416
header, 414
postData() function, 421
POST request handler, 415–416
String Object extension, 417
async Event dispatch, 413
UI element, 413
UILogger.swift file, 413

M

Map view controller
auto-layout, 19
MapKit framework, 21
MKMapView class, 18
pinning constraints, 20
Resolve Auto Layout
Issues menu, 20
second tab, 19
storyboard connection, 21–22
Merchant pay interface, 458
Message-passing
dot-syntax, 44
multiple parameters, 44
Smalltalk syntax, 44

N

NSArray class, 47

O

OAuth 1.0a, 125, 167
OAuth 2.0, 167
OAuth library
  creation, 154
  OAuth1a.swift file, 151
  OAuth1a.swift, 155
  signRequest(), 152
Objective-C. Swift
Offline card processing, 457

P, Q

paymentAuthorizationView
    Controller() Function, 479
paymentCardTextFieldDid
    Change() function, 478
PeripheralViewController
    class declaration, 285
postData() function, 419
Protocol Method peripheralManager
    DidUpdateState, 288

R

Raspberry Pi
  accessible prices, 398
  API, device control
    (*see* Flask installation)
  chromium browser, 397
  control interfaces, 399
  Ethernet connector, 398
  iOS project setup
    HTTP calls, 409
    logger library (*see* Logger library)
    View Controller (*see* View Controller)
  low power usage, 397
  microSD card, booting and storage, 398
  PiGlow board, 398
  Raspbian, 397
  real-time clock, 398
  setup
    apt-get utility, 400
    configuration utility, 400
    downloading website, 400
    GPIO configuration, 404
    GUI, 400
    I2C. I2C configuration
    installation phase, 400
    PyGlow module, 405
    Python language, 401
RegionMonitor methods
  startMonitoring, 321
  stopMonitoring, 321
reloadData() method, 29
Remote Central Device, 291–292
RunTracker app. *See* Core Motion

S

SDK method, 465
Secure Enclave, 443
sharedInstance property, 27
shouldPerformSegue
    WithIdentifier method, 267
Simple object access protocol (SOAP), 120
String class, 35
Swift
  API documentation, 35
  Apple platform, 34
  auto-completion results,
    NSMutableString, 55–56
  classes and methods, 56
  Cocoa Touch tutorials, 34
  design, 34
  dot-syntax alone, 34
  file selection, 54–55
  object-oriented programming
    casting, 50
    class declaration, 41
    class keyword, 42
    collections, 47–49
    compilation errors, 42
    h and .m files, 42
    message-passing (*see*
      Message-passing)
    method signature, 43
    NSMutableString class, 46
    NSString class, 46
    object instantiation, 45
    protocols, 42–43
    strings formatting, 46–47
  project creation, 54
  specific language feature
    nil keyword, 50
    optional-chaining operation, 51–52

optional concept, 51
try-catch blocks, 52–53
syntax
calling methods (Hello World), 35
compound data types, 37
conditional logic, 38
enumerated type, 39–40
loops, 40–41
variables, 36–37
switch statement, 39

T, U

tableView(_\:cellForRow AtIndexPath\:) method, 29
Touch ID
architecture, 444
Assistant editor, 450
custom class setting, 448
definition, 443
Enter Passcode option, 445
fingerprint authentication
authenticate Method, 452
passcode, 455
policies evaluation, 452
registered fingerprint, 455
unregistered fingerprint, 455
user-defined fallback, 454
without keychain, 452
Initial View Controller, 447
LocalAuthentication, 443–444
main scene, 445
Main storyboard initial view, 448
Secure Enclave, 443
single-view Xcode project creation, 447
Standard system UI, 446
table view cell style, 449
table view controller, 449
text view addition, 450
UITableView methods, 451
viewDidLoad Method, 450
Transaction
API vs. SDK f, 466
authorization, 464
capture, 464
chargeback, 464
recurring, 464
refund, 464
TransferService class declaration, 287
TransferServiceDelegate method, 291
TransferServiceDelegate Protocol, 286
TransferService Initializer Method, 287
TransferServiceScanner startScan Method, 276
TransferServiceScanner stopScan Method, 277

V

View controller
clickButton function, 411
communication display, API, 410
storyboard, button actions, 411
table
connection, 12
Connections Inspector, 16
FirstViewController class, 12
navigation bar, 15
pop-up menu, 11
radio button, 16
selection, 8–9
selector connection, 17
storyboard, 9–11
Stub, addLocation Function, 15
template selection, 18
UIViewController Class, 410
variables, 410
ViewController.swift code, 412
viewDidLoad Override Function, 411

W, X, Y, Z

WatchConnectivity, application contexts, 189–190
watchOS
application, 176
CarFinder project, 175
Cocoa Touch Frameworks, 171
hierarchy, 178
Interface Builder's Attributes Inspector, 180
interface controller, 177–178, 185
Interface.storyboard file, 175

watchOS (*cont.*)
  iOS programming terminology, 179
  LocationRowController table row controller, 182–184
  LocationTable property, 185–187
  Switching group layout to vertical, 180
  vs. iOS Apps, 170–172
  WatchKit application, 173
  WatchKit target, 174
  WatchKit user interface elements, 184
  Xcode menu, 172
Web services description language (WSDL), 120

Get the eBook for only $5!

Why limit yourself?

Now you can take the weightless companion with you wherever you go and access your content on your PC, phone, tablet, or reader.

Since you've purchased this print book, we're happy to offer you the eBook in all 3 formats for just $5.

Convenient and fully searchable, the PDF version enables you to easily find and copy code—or perform examples by quickly toggling between instructions and applications. The MOBI format is ideal for your Kindle, while the ePUB can be utilized on a variety of mobile devices.

To learn more, go to www.apress.com/companion or contact support@apress.com.

Get the eBook for only $5!

Why limit yourself?

CPSIA information can be obtained
at www.ICGtesting.com
Printed in the USA
LVOW05s1832070217
523494LV00005B/248/P